A RECORD OF MEETINGS

P. D. Ouspensky was born in Moscow in 1878. His first book, *The Fourth Dimension* (1909), offered a contribution to mathematical theory; it was *Tertium Organum* (1912) and *A New Model of the Universe* (1914) that revealed his stature as a thinker and his deep preoccupation with the problems of man's existence. His meeting with Gurdjieff in 1915 marked a turning point in Ouspensky's life. From this time his interest centred on the practical study of methods for the development of consciousness in man, as expounded in *In Search of the Miraculous*, *The Psychology of Man's Possible Evolution* (both published after his death in 1947) and *The Fourth Way* (1957). These methods are also discussed in *A Further Record*. *Strange Life of Ivan Osokin*, published in 1947, the year of his death, was Ouspensky's only novel, though he also wrote two short stories, *Talks with a Devil*. Many of his books are published by Arkana, including *Letters from Russia 1919* and *Conscience: The Search for Truth*, a collection of essays.

P. D. Ouspensky died in England in 1947.

A record of some of the meetings held by

P. D. OUSPENSKY

between 1930 and 1947

NOT FOR RESALE

ARKANA
PENGUIN BOOKS

ARKANA

Published by the Penguin Group
Penguin Books Ltd, 27 Wrights Lane, London w8 5tz, England
Penguin Books USA Inc., 375 Hudson Street, New York, New York 10014, USA
Penguin Books Australia Ltd, Ringwood, Victoria, Australia
Penguin Books Canada Ltd, 10 Alcorn Avenue, Toronto, Ontario, Canada m4v 3b2
Penguin Books (NZ) Ltd, 182–190 Wairau Road, Auckland 10, New Zealand
Penguin Books Ltd, Registered Offices: Harmondsworth, Middlesex, England

First published in South Africa, in a limited edition of twenty copies,
by the Stourton Press, Cape Town, 1951
Published in Penguin Books 1992
1 3 5 7 9 10 8 6 4 2

Printed in England by Clays Ltd, St Ives plc
Set in 10/12 pt Monophoto Garamond

Summary of contents

Being inactive with attention—Life long enough for real things—Meaningless words and phrases disparaged—Right effort only from long and repeated trial—Effort must be made by oneself without help—Illusion of believing in 'I'

March 12th 1947 (COLET GARDENS) (611)

System did not help—Begin with impermanent aim—Ask simple questions; Only they must be real—Living in the present—One cannot begin without knowing something—No belief in change—First step is to know oneself—The questions do not refer to Mr. O.—To begin is not easy—No new knowledge; Old knowledge—Standard of values as a beginning—Can only reply to simple, ordinary, normal questions

May 7th 1947 (COLET GARDENS) (628)

Questions must have more meaning—Discussion must come first but from a point where one can begin; Several points rejected or encouraged—Fear—Necessary to have aim and to try something

May 21st 1947 (COLET GARDENS) (633)

'Necessary to start from that "to remember"'—Memory; Remembering; Self-remembering—Questioners must ask something that means something to them—Questioners are bringing more material—Find what is missing

June 18th 1947 (COLET GARDENS) (638)

Rules no longer exist; Question is what you want—More material needed—Remembering; Self-remembering—Think more definitely what one wants—Put all material together—Words mean nothing … Find what you want—One has right to everything—Necessity and difficulties of finding what one wants and how to begin—Necessary to be able to say clearly what you want; What direction; Try to remember it: this moment: that moment

Thursday. December 18th 1930.

When Mr. O. came in, after answering a few questions, he said that if we had any questions on what he had said last time, we must ask them then, as he would not come back to the subject again; we would have other things to talk about later. During the meeting he would go over what he had said.

After a certain number more questions, he said that when speaking of 'I', it was necessary to realize that, in Special Doctrine, 'I' could be spoken of in five ways, on five different levels.

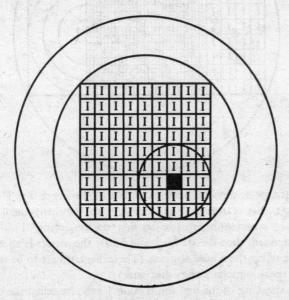

Man, in his ordinary state, is a multiplicity of 'I's. This is the first meaning. On the diagram this is indicated by the square of 'I's. When he decides to start work, an observing 'I' appears. This is shown shaded in on the diagram. This is the second meaning. The next meaning, indicated by the smallest circle, is where deputy-steward appears who has control over a number of 'I's. The fourth meaning, indicated by the middle circle, is where steward appears; he has control over all 'I's. The fifth meaning is that of master. He is drawn as a big circle outside, as he has time-body; he knows the past and also the future, although there must be degrees of this.

It was interesting to connect this diagram with that of the 'carriage', 'horse', 'driver' and 'master'.

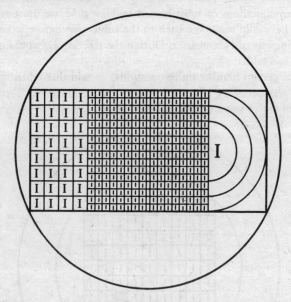

In the carriage or physical body are certain of the larger 'I's. The horse and driver, that is in feeling and thought, are the many small 'I's. In the square representing master is, first the observing 'I', then the deputy-steward, then the steward, and finally the master is shown as a circle encircling the whole diagram. (These diagrams are to be regarded as, so to speak, supplementary diagrams.)

When speaking of the division 'I' and 'Jones', he called the division 'Jones' false personality. This phrase was for convenience when talking, and avoided having to say either 'Ouspensky', 'Smith', 'Jones', etc. It must not be confused with the division 'essence' and 'personality'. The divisions which he spoke about last time must be kept separate. For instance the idea of 'rolls' must not be connected with that of 'I's. Rolls were connected with the idea of centres, which were regarded as consisting of rolls. 'I's, on the other hand, were connected with the idea of consciousness, of the four states of consciousness—sleep state, waking state, state of self-remembering, and objective state. It was the continuous change of 'I's which made up our ordinary waking state. The idea of 'rolls' and the idea of 'I's were two quite different aspects of man. They were as different as gas and electric light.

There were some questions about essence. Mr. O. said that we must remember all that we had heard about essence. Essence was what we were born with—capacities and incapacities. It was also connected with type. Essence was also connected with physical body. From the point of view of work, all we had was personality. At the very beginning magnetic centre would bring the observing 'I' into being. This 'I' was also a personality, which would have to educate the rest of personality and essence.

There was a question as to what would happen if master came while personality was in its ordinary state. Mr. O. said that master could not come. Even if he could, he would not be recognized by personality. There were two theories about master. One was that he exists already but can make no use of personality as it is. The other theory is that master has to grow.

He spoke also about exercises again. If a person older in the work suggests to one that one should try practising certain exercises, then any questions about them or about experiences connected with them we must ask that person, who must be able to answer us. What he said last time was for those people who had not had these exercises suggested to them by such a person.

Miss G. asked a question in which she said something about choosing certain 'I's in herself. Mr. O. answered that, to start with, we could not choose certain 'I's in ourselves; this would be 'doing'. By working, however, something will grow. This 'choosing of "I"s' or not, both the difficulty and the time necessary, are very much underestimated. With the pilgrim, after only a few months' work, the prayer becomes emotional.* In these exercises of repetition, the first stage is

* The reference is to a Russian book, since translated into English with the title *The Way of a Pilgrim* (Philip Allan. 1930). In *A New Model of the Universe*, Mr. O. wrote: ' "The Narrations of a Pilgrim" cannot serve as a manual for the practical study of "mental

to be able to read, while repeating the phrase or prayer to oneself. The next stage in difficulty is to be able to continue repeating it to oneself while other people are talking. The third is to be able to listen to music and still continue the repetition in oneself; and lastly the most difficult is to be able to continue the inner repetition while talking oneself.

To attain anything objective by this method, it is necessary to be of a certain type. As far as we were concerned, its danger lay in imagination. It is very liable to increase imagination, to make us imagine that we are gaining definite results from it. It also tends to make one feel satisfaction with oneself. These exercises, however, could be useful if taken solely from the point of view of observation—they could help one to observe oneself. Here imagination could not come in.

Our line of work lay more in work on attitude, rather than in these kinds of exercises, except in so far as they could help us in our observations of ourselves.

*　　*　　*

prayer", because the description of the method of study contains a certain probably intentional incorrectness, namely, far too great an ease and rapidity in the pilgrim's study of "mental prayer".'

Thursday. August 20th 1931.

MR. O. I have received a certain number of questions and I can answer them now, but perhaps if you have some more now you can try to formulate them.

Say what you like. [Pause.]

Well? [Short pause.]

Well, some time ago I told you that work has to be organized on new principles. Several people last week asked me what I meant and what were the new principles to which we have come now. I will give you one example of the most important point which has to be different. One of the first and most important factors in changing oneself is the division of oneself. Right division—'I' and 'Ouspensky'. If this division is not made, if one forgets it and continues to think of himself in the usual way, or if one continues to use 'I' and 'himself' but in the wrong way, work stops. If one does not keep this division and the right kind of division, work stops. The first line of work can only go on the basis of this division. No other lines are open if this division is forgotten, but it must be right division. It happens often that people make wrong division. What they like in themselves they call 'I', what they dislike or what is weak or unimportant, this they call Ouspensky, Petroff, Ivanoff, or anything else. If they divide in this way it is quite wrong. I have met several people who were in these groups in the beginning and they still think they are working. For example X ... sky—'I' and 'X ... sky'. 'I'—the part which he described as 'keeping him alive', and the rest 'X ... sky'. This is wrong division. It changes nothing and he remains as he was. This separation is the most necessary and important principle. Up to now it was advised and recommended, but now it is obligatory, at least in some things—speaking about the work, speaking about people in the work and speaking about me, one must remember oneself. If one does not do this, it will be against the work and will be dealt with accordingly. You remember long ago I told you this principle that the group is responsible for one and one for the group.

As to how it will be, this refers to further details, but this will be the first new principle that will come. [Pause.]

Now you may ask what you want in relation to this, and if you have nothing to say, I will pass to other questions. [Pause.]

It is necessary to remember all important principles in the work. In speaking about people in the work it is necessary to remember all rules—and in speaking of me also it is necessary to remember rules. In fact in all cases it is better to say that it is necessary to remember all principles and all rules.

MR. W. When you say that it is obligatory, do you mean in the sense of rules?

MR. O. Yes, absolutely, that will be general responsibility.

MRS. M. But that would be almost 'doing'.

MR. O. No, this is only remembering, 'not-doing'—not doing what is wrong.

MISS G. Are these two separate things or the same thing—making the right division between 'I' and 'Miss G.' and in taking. . . .

MR. O. You make right division to-day and forget it tomorrow—this is not enough. You must make right division and keep it in your memory.

MR. W. Must one tell a person when they are breaking this rule?

MR. O. One must not wait. In this case one must not wait until one is asked—this is necessary in the next stage of the work, which we should have come to long ago. It is useless to talk without it. There are many other things but this is the first.

MISS G. Would it not be possible to remember oneself when speaking about the work, people or you and yet not make the right division?

MR. O. No, this gives wrong result because one will remember imaginary things which do not exist or simply one's picture of oneself.

MISS H. How is it possible to have all the rules in one's mind at once?

MR. O. It is not necessary. At one moment you must remember one or two or at the maximum three. It is not necessary to remember what you do not require at the present moment. If you speak to someone about someone else, you must only remember not to discuss anyone who is not present; that is only one rule. It is ridiculous to remember that you must not attract attention to yourself or some other rule at that moment. [Pause.]

Well?

MISS G. When you say someone still goes on using the wrong division but still uses the same language. . . .

MR. O. This wrong division is simply lying, lying to oneself which is worse than anything as it will immediately be seen because the moment when one meets with the smallest difficulty it will show itself by inner arguing and wrong understanding—if one uses wrong division. It will not be reliable; at the moment of need it will fail. You see I did not specify it as a special rule—but 'not arguing' is not only a rule but a principle which means that you must remember yourself. Supposing someone tells you something and you think it is wrong; you have to try to find what is right, and if you make some effort you will see at once what is right. This is what always happens—someone says something and immediately you begin arguing and you cannot see what is right. [Pause.]

Why do only two people talk?

MR. J. When some other member of the group says something which I think is wrong and I try to see what is right, is this. . . .

MR. O. Partly, but speak of what I said.

With other people also you must not argue, you must try and see what is right. [Pause.]

Then there is another interesting result of self-remembering in the right way and unfortunately absence of right self-remembering makes many misunderstandings. When I say something people always take it in the wrong way. People never wait; they take one sentence and this cannot equally refer to all. Maybe it does refer to one, to another it may only refer a quarter, to another three times; maybe to some person it does not even refer at all. But the wrong people always take it to themselves and ask questions about it and the right people do not ask any questions at all. But if one can take it in the right way and with full gravity, then one will see what is right. So there are many ways by which I can see who remembers himself—I mean again in the right way.

MRS. E. I feel guilty about speaking of people who are not there. It was explained once that one must not derive pleasure from negative criticism of other people.

MR. O. And you took only the words and said to yourself that nothing is wrong because you do not have negative criticism.

MRS. E. Then some rules ought to be taken quite literally?

MR. O. Yes, and again _not_, because if you are afraid to break this rule by mentioning a name, it will be very funny.

MISS G. What is the principle behind not talking about other people?

MR. O. Not talking. It is the most mechanical thing—talking about other people. This is what all life is based on. Most people do nothing else but talk about other people and in this work it is useful to try to do something different. There are other lines but this is already sufficient. In speaking, writing, thinking (as thinking is the same thing) about the work, people or me, one must ask oneself: who is speaking? who is writing? who is thinking? Then after a little time one will begin to hear who is speaking, etc., and after all this time you should all know these voices. You see it is of no use going on without this as we turn in a circle and come back to the same spot. There can be no movement and unless this is taken seriously we shall never get out of the circle.

MRS. H. Is it for this reason that you brought about the re-organization of the work?

MR. O. This is the first thing—there are many others. You did not hear what I said to begin with. I am answering all questions as to what will be different, but I said that this is the first thing which must be different. For some time in these three cases when one begins to say something, one must ask oneself: who is speaking? And if he can be sure that it is 'he', then he can speak.

MRS. M. Is there not so little 'I' in most of us that we would never speak at all?

MR. O. No, in these three cases—speaking of the work, of people, and of me, you must already be able to use 'I'. If you want to speak and it is Mrs. M. who speaks, it is quite useless. You must already begin to mistrust 'Mrs. M.' If after all these years you do not begin to mistrust her, then I can give no advice because this is the first step.

MRS. A. If we could do this, we should save a lot of energy.

MR. O. This will be your own profit if you save energy.

MR. W. You say that this is one of the things that will be altered. Will this increase our rate of progress in the work?

MR. O. This we shall see when the time comes.

MR. W. But one is allowed to hope.

MR. O. Nothing can be guaranteed. One must know that one is doing it for oneself and not for reward.

8

MR. W. For oneself?

MR. O. Yes, but you wish the reward to be guaranteed. The idea is important for yourself and of itself it is sufficiently interesting without any question of reward. I wonder you do not speak more of this idea of separation for there must be many sides which are not clear. There are many things involved and connected with this, and many methods how to do this.

MRS. K. I feel that it would be very difficult to speak to my new people. . . .

MR. O. Leave them alone, we do not speak about them.

MR. W. The first subject you mentioned about the way we speak of people, the work and yourself, there was nothing about principles and rules in speaking of new people. Did you mean. . . .

MR. O. Speaking of new people—just the same thing; it means self-remembering—principles, rules, everything.

MRS. E. What is the test that this rule is being observed? When this is obligatory, how is one to know. . . .

MR. O. I will know. I have just told you several results and how I shall see whether this is kept.

MR. W. Are group meetings here sufficient to give this material?

MR. O. Meeting people was never prohibited. People can meet when they like.

MR. W. It seems that more is necessary. [Long pause.]

MR. H. If I can remember myself when these three subjects come up, it would be the greatest possible help. . . .

MR. O. What do you wish to ask me?

MR. H. I am not asking a question.

MR. O. Try to keep to questions.

MRS. N. How can one know when one refrains from breaking a rule through fear of being reported or whether it is 'I'. . . .

MR. O. I cannot hear. Repeat what you said.

MRS. N. To refrain from breaking a rule for fear of being reported.

MR. O. I do not get your second word. What was it?

MRS. N. [hesitating] I do not know.

[Miss D. repeats 'refraining from fear of being reported'.]

MR. O. I did not speak of 'refraining'.

[Mrs. N. again tries to formulate question.]

MR. O. This is an old story—this fear of being reported—and is all nonsense. If it is necessary to speak, it is another thing. It all comes to the same thing: who speaks? Not what you speak, but 'who' speaks! All this fear of being reported—'you' will not think about it; 'you' will not mind. 'Mrs. N.' will mind, not 'you'.

MRS. P. Are there any general methods?

MR. O. What are general methods?

MRS. P. Methods that all can use, or must one find one's own method for reminding oneself?

MR. O. This is not a question. I cannot answer, I would have to make a theory. You must formulate more definitely. [Long pause.]

I advise you to think, because we have not very long now.

MRS. J. Is saying what is unnecessary one of the tests that is used in remembering oneself?

MR. O. That depends on what is unnecessary. There are degrees even of unnecessary talking.

MR. M. I feel it would be hard to know in speaking to someone in the work whether they are remembering themselves.

MR. O. Well, you can ask him and if you don't agree, then you can ask a third person.

MRS. H. Is it my duty to remind the person I am speaking to that he must remember himself?

MR. O. Yes certainly, if you see he does not remember himself—and if you remember yourself. [Short pause.]

There are several other questions but they are much lighter and I advise you not to miss this point, because this opportunity may not come again. For instance, 'not arguing', and 'being serious', all this is connected with what we have been speaking about.

MRS. M. How does one become serious if one does not think one is serious enough? [She continues along this line but could not be followed.]

MR. O. There are fifteen questions here. How can one become serious if one is not serious? This is not a question. How to keep silence if one is talking? Stop talking! How to stand if one sits? Get up! How to be in another room if one is in this one? Go into the other room!

MRS. M. Some of one may want to be serious?

MR. O. Question is wrong. I am trying to explain and you continue to ask. If I try to explain and at the same time you try to ask, this is not being serious. I tried about four times and each time you interrupt. So my explanation is mixed with your own thoughts and we have already lost the beginning.

MRS. M. Can I put it another way?

MR. O. How can you put it another way? You asked your question, I explained to you, I answered you but you did not wait until I answered. What is the use of explaining what you said when you speak before I have answered. You could wait.

MRS. M. I thought you had finished.

MR. O. How could you say this? I was speaking—you could wait, and I was trying to answer your question. Again you speak and again I answer. 'How to be serious if one is not serious'! This is wrong formulation because it means nothing at all. To try to be serious, first you must understand what it means, first ask yourself: 'Do I know what it means to be serious?' If you don't know, that would be a question. Then you can try to find what is connected with that, what is disconnected, what happens when you are serious and when you are not. If you just throw out such a question you use words without meaning; with such words we shall not move one inch from the spot. For instance, 'to be serious' means listening, not arguing, trying to understand. There is nothing difficult in this—this is what means 'to be serious'. [Short pause.]

Think about arguing, this is a very good example. I can guarantee that in ninety-nine cases out of a hundred in examples which you may find in yourselves, you will always find excuses for yourselves. Start with this.

MISS M. Does this go in line with the sacrificing of our decision?

MR. O. No, this has nothing to do with it.

MISS H. If we remember ourselves we should not argue with other members of the group.

MR. O. I did not say with other members of the group.

MISS H. Only with you?

MR. O. I did not say that. I said all cases of arguing, first of all with yourself. Why of the comprehensible make the incomprehensible, instead of the simple make the difficult and instead of the complete make the incomplete?

MR. W. Is it possible to think at all without arguing?

MR. O. This is too formatory. You add 'at all', and this changes it. In everything there are extremes and I speak of the centre of gravity. Better if someone finds an example of his own arguing because I mean a special kind of arguing. Certainly intellectual centre works by means of comparison and comparison is a special kind of arguing—quite a different thing.

MRS. H. [Unrecorded.]

MR. O. Talk based on unserious attitude.

MRS. H. That seems to relate to Mrs. H.

MR. O. Certainly, I explained how to remember yourself—all this is only different sides of the same thing.

MRS. H. Is the purpose of this. . . .

MR. O. Purposes were explained over ten years.

MISS M. I do not understand what you mean by arguing with oneself?

MR. O. Try to catch yourself, then you will understand.

MR. W. I know I have often argued about certain rules, about the sensibleness of such rules as not using Christian names—whether it was a good thing or not.

MR. O. Yes, instead of trying to understand the meaning, you discussed as to whether it was necessary in general.

MISS G. Is analysing something the same as arguing?

MR. O. Analysing what?

MISS G. An idea.

MR. O. Which idea? What do you mean by analysing? I have never used this word. For analysis it is necessary to know laws. If you analyse a fact in relation to laws, it is analysis; otherwise it is no good.

MRS. P. What is the origin and source of this difficulty in dividing oneself?

MR. O. The origin is 'you' and 'Mrs. P.' 'Mrs. P.' thinks she knows better than 'you' do; she thinks she is more important and wishes 'you' to do as she wants.

MRS. P. The origin would be the same for everyone?

MR. O. Yes, certainly.

MR. M. One of the difficulties is that 'M.' knows better than 'I'. In certain situations. . . .

MR. O. 'M.' knows nothing.

MR. M. But he thinks he does.

MR. O. You have to obey? There is something incomprehensible in this. If you think he knows best, simply study him and this will bring him to the right understanding. The first condition is that you must believe nothing. If you believe something, then you must believe it and there is nothing more to say. The first condition is to believe nothing. What is the use of creating permanent 'I' while you continue to believe 'Mr. M.'?

MR. M. But you must believe something in this world.

MR. O. I never said that. You must believe nothing. Besides, what does it mean 'in this world'?

MRS. S. We have to believe that we can make this division?

MR. O. As a matter of fact, if you want to know, we cannot make this division. 'I' is created by desire to be and to know and the rest is all nonsense. So really we cannot divide. We must believe nothing or we cannot come to that. If we say we believe this, this and this, that will be knowledge, we may admit that there must be something there, but we don't know in any practical way how it looks, its colour, form, etc. We can say it is growing out of my desire to know and the rest is out of imagination. This is the right attitude.

MR. M. This is what I call 'believing'.

MR. O. This is the system. If you did not believe this, it would be contradiction. Every thought, every serious attitude will give proof that there is nothing reliable, nothing that you can promise, nothing that is firm, so what is the doubt? It is too self-evident.

MR. W. I am having an inner argument now about what is inner arguing. There are two sides. If one immediately begins to argue. . . .

MR. O. No, too complicated an example again. It is necessary to understand what is the centre of gravity. Try to find the right side—if you start from the negative side you will never understand. I can give you examples but that would mean my bringing in things I don't wish to speak of. Perhaps I may, but it would be better if you found them for yourselves. Perhaps we may have example.

MR. W. I want to give an example of what is arguing. There are two sides—one, that it is obviously no use to argue and the other side, the danger that if one immediately looks on the positive side, this may lead to self-deception.

MR. O. It is not looking for the positive side, it is looking for examples.

MR. W. But if one does not argue. . . .

MR. O. First it is necessary to establish what is arguing—very often we start with second step, 'Is arguing always wrong?' You often do this, and you come to the conclusion that it is sometimes necessary. First it is necessary to find concrete examples.

MR. H. I find I argue if I do not really listen.

MR. O. Certainly, this is always connected. Sometimes if you stop you will see what was meant. Most cases of argument which I mean, presuppose that you have not heard or understood, and you argue against your own imagination.

MR. M. You mean that is why we argue?

MR. O. I did not say 'why' but 'what'.

MR. M. But you said earlier 'why'.

MR. O. No, I said 'what'!

MR. M. But yes, really you did earlier on. . . .

MR. O. [interrupting and looking at W.] This is your example—a good example. [Laughter.]

MR. H. I find it takes longer than one thinks for the centre of gravity to be heard. Arguing goes so quickly that it is difficult to get the centre of gravity.

MR. O. Quite right, but do you wish to ask something?

MR. H. It is necessary to wait. . . .

MR. O. It means to be serious, not to speak before one understands what has been said to you.

MRS. E. I argue if I think that a little right enters in. Could this be Mrs. E. who argues because she thinks she is right?

MR. O. I think that this is a little outside the question.

MRS. P. If we really could make inner stop, would we find that we could understand a great deal more?

MR. O. Why introduce new words? In every condition it is necessary to use as few words as possible. I did not use the words 'inner stop'; the word 'stop' was used only in connection with exercises.

MR. W. I wish it were possible to give examples of the kind of arguing you mean. I do not think I have grasped it yet.

MR. O. You heard M.?

MR. W. Yes, he said something while you spoke, but I did not see where the arguing came in.

MR. O. You never can see when there is so much talk.

MRS. J. I argue against the words and not against the meaning of the words.

MR. O. This is unimportant.

MRS. H. I can give Mr. W. a good example.

MR. O. Enough about that for the moment. There may be other questions.

MISS G. May I ask one more question about arguing?

MR. O. I have just said it was enough—you did not hear?

MISS M. In reference to what you said to Mrs. S. . . .

MR. O. Try to say something of your own and new. I am trying to stop associations.

MISS M. It was connected with what. . . .

MR. O. I don't want connections, I want your own. Otherwise we can speak for a week and get nothing. [Pause.]

I have read some terrible accounts of meetings when one person spoke, a second answers a phrase out of this, a third answers one word out of the second phrase, and the fourth answers a word out of the third phrase, and it goes like this. It is necessary to learn to stop associations. It cannot go on for ever, there are other things. [Long pause.]

Mrs. K. and Mrs. J., will you repeat your questions?

MRS. J. As I understand it, one of the principles of esotericism is that the teaching must be passed from one conscious being to another. Man No. 6 gets it from man No. 7, 5 from 6 and so on. And after the general principles of the work are received it is necessary to keep the line unbroken. I ask this because it seems as if the line was broken when you left G.

MR. O. Who asked this question?

MRS. K. First Mrs. M. and then Mrs. J.

MR. O. Is there anything else?

MRS. K. No, I think this is all.

MR. O. You mix things up in a very wrong way—facts and principles. One thing—that No. 6 learns from No. 7 etc.—this is right from one point of view. But do you know people 6 or 7? So why ask about them? This is general principle. But the question is why you cannot learn from 5, 6 or 7. So you mixed something, which explains one principle, with quite a different thing. What has all this to do with G. and me? I was working with G. until I saw a difference in him. This has nothing to do with esotericism. When I found that I could not work with him any longer I left him. That is all. This was all explained. You can only judge by the knowledge of a person and not by his being. The idea is that one can have only such a teacher as one deserves. But only so long as he is teacher. If he ceases to be teacher—well—then why talk about it? I went to G. in 1916, but in 1918 I found that I could not continue to work with him.

In 1922 again I started to work with him, and again I came to the conclusion that it was impossible to continue, and in 1924 you remember that I spoke to you about this and said: 'I may be wrong but I had to part with him'. . . .

MRS. J. [interrupting] That is all. . . .

MR. O. What do you mean? Why do you ask such questions? And then interrupt? Why these philosophical questions? I can never understand them. I always explained that you may meet with a teacher but never meet with a principle.

MRS. J. But the work is carried on with certain principles? One wants to relate principles to facts.

MR. O. Please relate them.

MRS. J. It does not seem to correspond. I know that you said this about No. 6 man learning from 7, etc.

MR. O. But why don't you listen? I said that you learn from a man who knows more than you. How can you know what man No. 7 is like? He wears no special uniform! Practical! Practical! I met G.— How can I know what number man he is? I know only one thing; that he knows more than I of certain principles. He changed all these principles and I parted from him. Why introduce the idea of man No. 4, 5 and 6 which have nothing to do with that. [Not taken down further.]

MISS G. I find it very difficult to see the value of these principles which cannot be translated into fact.

MR. O. Can anyone explain?

MR. W. I should have thought that all principles are facts, only on different scales.

MR. O. Yes! But in this particular case it would be necessary for Miss G. to distinguish between man No. 4, 5 and 6.

MISS G. No, I did not mean this.

MR. O. Then why speak in this way?

MISS G. Because I hear principles spoken of in this system.

MR. O. We cannot change level of being. Man can change only by his knowledge. Suppose you meet someone who says he is man No. 7, how can you distinguish? So why speak of this apart from principles? There are rings round Saturn. Because you cannot see them, it does not mean that they do not exist. In reality, if all this exists as we think it does, then certainly it must be an uninterrupted line. If ideas really do come from esoteric sources, then certainly there must be a line. But where is the question? As I said before, [I] can guarantee nothing, but

I know these ideas cannot be found in books. Ideas are proofs in themselves, not words. [Long pause.]

Well?

MRS. H. Earlier in the evening you said that we must remember ourselves in speaking of the work and the people. . . .

MR. O. And to me.

MRS. H. And you said that this was the most important point but there would be many other things.

MR. O. Well?

MRS. H. What are the other things? [Laughter.]

MR. O. I have said many other things.

MISS H. What can help to increase the desire to divide oneself? Can one do anything by oneself or must it be done with the help of others? [Short pause.]

MR. O. There are three questions here. Very often such questions are asked and, when I say what should be done, people immediately begin to argue, and not only argue but become negative. ([to Miss H.] This does not refer specially to you. I speak generally.) This is really why help cannot be given, and why, after so many years, I have to put it as a rule, as a definite demand; otherwise, if it were just to show people what to do, it would be simple and we should have come to things in a much simpler way. It is not always easy to explain chief feature. Sometimes it is seen clearly, but sometimes it is more hidden and difficult to see, and then one has only to think generally of false personality. But there was not a single case where I showed chief feature when people did not start violent arguing. [Short pause.]

This question of Miss H.'s is asked very often, but it is impossible to answer, because it immediately creates wrong atmosphere.

MRS. S. Then this rule about remembering oneself in speaking of the work, to people and to you includes also reporting?

MR. O. Certainly.

MRS. S. That is a kind of talking?

MR. O. Certainly. [Pause.]

What is the difference between reports and not reports? I do not understand. It is the same thing.

MRS. S. I wanted to know if you included it in 'talking', in speaking of the work, etc.—if one must remember oneself.

MR. O. It means one must start with this. It is desirable to remember oneself when one does anything, but most important is what I have said already in reference to speaking of the work, of people, and of me. [Pause.]

MRS. E. I should like to ask something about a rule. I had a conversation yesterday with Mrs. P. . . .

MR. O. This is not important. [Pause.]

Words and questions have definite weight. You have heard that this principle or rule which I explained includes questions—at least at the meetings—that must be of a certain weight. In ordinary life we have quite a different standard for weighing questions. We always think that MY questions are important. But here we must have a different standard, and our questions must have a certain weight.

MR. M. Was it because of the system that you left G.?

MR. O. What do you mean by this? In a sense, yes.

MR. M. Then you must have believed something.

MR. O. There is no question of belief; it is a question of fact. I saw. I saw that things had changed. You have been thinking of this question of belief for the last forty minutes, and you have added it on to the question of myself and G., with which it has no connection. This means that you have heard nothing of what I have been saying since. [to Mr. W.] Here is the example you wanted of arguing. [to Mr. M.] You say 'Was it in the system that I left G.?'

[M. denied that this was what he said, and Mr. O. made him write down what he said and what Mr. O. said on a sheet of paper. The two phrases were: 'Was it because of the system that you left G.?' and 'Was it in the system that I left G.?' Mr. O. read them out and said they were exactly the same. Mr. M. did not agree. Mr. W. and Mrs. M. tried to explain that they are not entirely the same. The discussion continued on the meaning of the words. Mr. O. explained that he was speaking a foreign language and had tried to repeat what Mr. M. had said. The two phrases meant exactly the same. Mr. M. and Mrs. M. did not agree. . . . etc., etc.]

*　　*　　*

Wednesday. January 16th 1935.

Ray of Creation. It is necessary to look at the Ray of Creation from many different sides. Only when the idea of it is understood will it be possible to sort things out. Idea of the Ray of Creation uses no new facts; it only disposes of them differently. (Disposition and enunciation. The solution of many mathematical problems depends on a right disposition of a problem. It must be put in a certain form, then—enunciation—one can think of a possible solution.) The difficulty may be only about the Absolute, but beginning with all worlds there can be no doubt about the facts.

Ray of Creation gives possibility to study principle of relativity and principle of scale. Ray of Creation must be understood as an instrument for new thinking. Old thinking is No. 1—chiefly imitation; No. 2—emotional, based on likes and dislikes; No. 3—logical thinking which cannot be applied to bigger things. Thinking No. 4 is the beginning of a thinking which, little by little, disposes of all contradictions. Ray of Creation is a method which disposes of contradictions. In ordinary life one idea always contradicts another. There are always two theories about everything. Examples: has universe appeared or is it created? is it created according to plan, or is it a chaos with organized islands? are events predestined or accidental? On logical level one accepts one theory in one sense, another theory in another sense, but one cannot say which is true. All are true, but only in a certain sense. Human mind cannot invent anything absolutely false—there is always some semblance of truth in everything it invents. Example: inventing a new animal. All these theories: will—mechanicalness; predestination—accident; evolution—creation by will, they are all right, each in its own place. Ray of Creation shows where and how each of them is right.

Influences. One must find analogies in ordinary life. In ordinary conditions there is a great quantity of bigger and smaller influences; sometimes one is more free, at others less free.

Principle of scale. What is nearer to us is studied on a larger scale; what is further from us is studied on a smaller scale.

Principle of relativity. Definition in a psychological sense: <u>law according to which every phase of experience is influenced by all phases of it</u>. So every phase of existence of earth is influenced by all the previous experience in the Ray of Creation.

Man lives under a great many laws: physical, physiological, biological, laws created by man, etc. until we come to laws of personal life and, finally, to imaginary 'I' which is the most important law that governs our life and makes us live in the non-existing seventh dimension. A great many forces act on one at any given moment. Now people are chiefly controlled by imagination. We imagine ourselves different from what we are and that creates illusions. But there are necessary laws. We are limited to certain food and certain air, a certain temperature, etc. We are so conditioned by influences that we have very little possibility of freedom. It is necessary to change our inner attitude.

Law of Three. No event can happen without the concurrence of three forces. Three orders of triads:

$$1\text{-}2\text{-}3 \quad 2\text{-}1\text{-}3 \quad 3\text{-}1\text{-}2$$
$$1\text{-}3\text{-}2 \quad 2\text{-}3\text{-}1 \quad 3\text{-}2\text{-}1$$

Building and burning a house. Triads beginning with third force we cannot distinguish.

Life phenomena, birth, death, etc. mostly go by the first triad. Certain phenomena in our organism go by the second triad. We must understand that things may be of very different kind and origin: like building and burning—it is not the same action. At present we can study only two triads. Sometimes, without knowing, we can use the third triad. When we come to such a state as to use it knowingly, we will be able to 'do'.

Q. Is being under fewer influences better?

MR. O. Or worse. Energy, will, understanding, consciousness can be created only by effort.

One can see laws by taking man, animal, plant and mineral. Man is more free. At present it is only imaginary freedom, but he can acquire real freedom.

Law of Seven. All events are created by triads. But the succession of events is governed by a certain law. In speaking of the Law of Three, we spoke about the origin of events; now we will speak about how they develop one from another. We take the world as world of vibrations. Vibrations are supposed to go regularly, either increasing or decreasing. Law of Seven says that it is not so. All vibrations develop, slow down, again develop, again slow down. It was found that between, say, a thousand and two thousand vibrations there are two intervals when vibrations slow down. This law was put into a formula. Later this formula of uneven increase of vibrations was used for musical scale.

Everything in the world happens according to this scheme. Deviation of line of development [diagram]. This is what happens to all our activity when we do not know this law and do not know how to use it.

Later you will see that there are many octaves in our machine. We come to the conclusion that we do not use all our forces. Why? At a certain point of the octave there is an interval where forces do not pass. If we want to be conscious, we must find this place and make a special effort. As a result, inner activity, instead of slowing down, will go on even stronger. Then we must find a second place. If we give two shocks to our organism, we begin to develop. The first shock is self-remembering.

The Ray of Creation can be regarded as a descending octave. Interval do-si is filled by the Will of the Absolute. Interval fa-mi: nature has provided here an instrument which gives the additional shock between planets and earth. Without this shock certain vibrations will not pass below planets, they will be reflected by earth. Organic life on earth is a sensitive film which helps to receive certain influences. All organic life on earth plays a certain cosmic rôle and has a cosmic purpose. Organic life is attached to its place. Man, being so small, is less attached, is more free and can escape. If he does not escape, while he lives he is food for the earth, and when he dies he is food for the moon. Moon feeds on organic life; when it disintegrates moon sucks in all that is important for it. In this way moon grows.

Organic life is arranged on hard principles: it eats itself. And moon eats all. In this way, Ray of Creation shows how everything is interconnected—everything exists, not for itself but for several different purposes. There are many other sides to organic life.

Organic life starts in sun (octave, sun - moon).

Mi of the second octave enters into mi (earth). We can see how organic life enters into earth and plays an important part in the structure of the surface of the earth.

Moon takes from organic life something that makes life-energy: some electric, magnetic, chemical energy, a kind of radiant energy that is called the soul of things.

*　　*　　*

Wednesday. January 9th 1935. Thursday. January 10th 1935. Saturday. January 19th 1935.

Questions about staircase.

Questions about whether a man can work by himself, and if not, why?

Questions about the possibility of further study, about future plans and the possibility of continuing.

Summary of Mr. O.'s answer. Taking the last question first: this depends chiefly on people. It would be worth continuing if this is what people want. Necessity to try to understand and decide whether this is what people really want, or whether they want something else. Necessity to understand the fundamental principles of the system.

Plan. Until now only psychological side was spoken of. This must continue. But some questions asked need, to answer them, a bigger view. They cannot be answered on purely psychological grounds, for they depend on the surroundings of man. Many things cannot be understood without understanding man's place in the world.

Question: Why man cannot study alone?

Summary of Mr. O.'s answer. There are many reasons. The first reason: one must learn from somebody who knows. A school is necessary. One must find where to learn and one man cannot find a teacher who will spend time on him alone. Second: one cannot work without other people. Only working with other people can one fulfil certain demands connected with the study. One of them is putting someone else in one's place. Third reason: study of system needs discussion, exchange of observations. Discussion helps understanding. One can discuss what one heard only with those who heard it themselves. We have to learn a new language. No language can be learnt without practice. This is another reason why one cannot work alone.

So one has to work in connection with certain people, a group. Working in a group one has to obey certain rules and regulations. Even a preliminary attempt of a school cannot exist without rules. Who wants to study, must keep these rules and give time to the study of rules. These rules are not arbitrary. By keeping them we study the organization of schools. First rule: a man must agree not to talk about things he hears here outside these groups. This rule has many sides. The first reason for it is that it involves a struggle against the habit of talking and helps self-remembering. Second reason is that it is very good for studying oneself. It is necessary to learn to talk to people who are in this work and not to talk to people outside.

Questions about staircase and putting someone in one's place.

Summary of Mr. O.'s answer. Questions show that nobody thought rightly about this condition. People don't realize they cannot 'do' and 'doing' is not demanded from them. Who arranged these lectures and why? They are arranged by people who want to put others in their place. They cannot do it themselves, they can only do it through Mr. O.

Study of system begins with study of language. The word 'man'. The word 'knowledge'. Seven categories of knowledge. All we know is knowledge 1, 2, 3. Influences a and b. Influences b contain certain amount of knowledge higher than knowledge 3, but it is mixed up with knowledge 1, 2, 3. We want to study knowledge No. 4.

From the point of view of the system word 'to know' is used rightly if it means to know all. In knowledge 1, 2, 3 anything is accepted as knowledge: to know one side of something is already knowledge. In the system knowledge of one side is ignorance. Knowledge of all is possible with the use of two principles: principle of relativity and principle of scale. Principle of relativity has been explained in the 'New Model'. Everything has meaning only in certain conditions. In different conditions it loses its meaning. A chair in interplanetary space or in high mountains. In relation to ourselves this principle must be understood that we must study things to which we have relation and which have relation to us. The principle of scale means to study things nearer to us on a larger scale and things further from us on a smaller scale.

Book of aphorisms. 'To know means to know all. In order to know all one must know very little. But in order to know this "little" one must know pretty much.' So we have to start with 'pretty much' with the idea of coming to this very little which is necessary for the knowledge of all.

The word 'world'. What it means? In ordinary thinking people will answer differently. We have to come to a certain understanding about this word and be able to speak with a certain precision about it. World nearest to us is earth. All planets of Solar System make a world by themselves in which earth lives. Next world—Solar System, sun. Next—Milky Way. Next—other agglomerations of stars, similar to our Milky Way. Next—the Absolute. This diagram shows our position. Living on earth we at the same time live in all these worlds and are under the influences of all these worlds.

Law of Three Forces. No event can take place without three forces meeting at a certain place. When we begin to observe things, we see two forces. Sometimes we see the presence of the third either in the form of result, or as something accidental, or as something the action of which we cannot explain. Example: certain processes in chemistry that cannot take place without the presence of a third substance which plays no part in this process, but without the presence of which nothing happens. In our state of being we are third force blind. We have to study something we cannot see.

Absolute is a state of things where everything is one, so the three forces are also one. By their own decision and free will they meet at a certain place and create worlds. In this created world forces are already divided and although they start consciously, their point of meeting is already accidental. Worlds created by them are more mechanical and the three forces in them start mechanically and meet mechanically.

Ray of Creation. Number of order of laws. Will of the Absolute does not go beyond World 3. We live on earth under 48 orders of mechanical laws. This scheme contradicts the ordinary idea of creation of the world. Moon is the youngest and sun is the oldest in our Solar System. Moon is the growing end of the branch. In time it will become like earth and earth become like sun.

We live in a bad place of the universe—near the North Pole.

Three forces are called active, passive and neutralizing, or positive, negative and neutralizing. They are all active, although perhaps not equally at a given moment. Forces are constantly changing from one to another and all variety of phenomena we observe depends on this.

Moon also plays an important part in our life, or rather the life of organic life on earth. Organic life is like a sensitive film on which moon acts as an electro-magnet. In conditions of ordinary life we can be more free or less free. When one understands that, one will understand that one can become more free by not identifying, not considering, etc. Now we are like marionettes moved by wires. If wires are cut, marionettes simply collapse. So wires cannot be cut at once. It is necessary to learn to move first. At present all our movements depend on the moon. We cannot move one step without the energy of the moon. Moon is like a weight on a clock. If the weight is cut, all movement stops. All our mechanicalness depends on the moon.

* * *

Thursday. January 24th 1935.

It is a pity that there are so many questions people write to me instead of asking them at the meeting. It is better to remember all the questions one might have during the week and then ask them here. The most important are people's own questions which come when ideas of the system meet with ordinary ideas of life. Technical questions are not so important.

*　　*　　*

In connection with the Ray of Creation, I will speak now more about the matter from which the universe is made. In the system, matter is regarded from the point of view of which force works through it. If active force works through it, it is called carbon; if passive force works through it, it is called oxygen; if neutralizing force works through it, it is called nitrogen; if it is taken without relation to any force, it is called hydrogen. It is necessary to remember that every matter, every element or compound, can be called hydrogen. We shall speak separately about forces (first, second and third) and matters (carbon, oxygen, nitrogen and hydrogen). It is necessary to remember that every kind of matter (wood, iron, etc.) can be carbon, oxygen, etc.

Now we take the Ray of Creation as three octaves or radiations: Absolute - sun; sun - earth; earth - moon. [See diagram p. 28.]

Each note shows a certain layer of matter. As it goes down the scale it becomes denser and denser. The lightest matter is on the level of do. The quickest vibrations are also on the level of do, then they become slower and slower.

First triad. do　c　1 1 1)
si　o　2 3 2) h6
la　n　3 2 3)

Forces stand in relation: 1-2-3 and work in carbon, oxygen and nitrogen. But nitrogen, by density, is between carbon and oxygen, so that when the triangle begins to form we must put them in the order 1-3-2. When matters stand in this order, event happens. The total will be

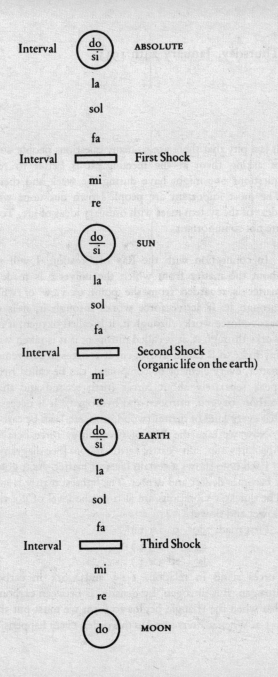

Interval	do / si	ABSOLUTE
	la	
	sol	
	fa	
Interval		First Shock
	mi	
	re	
	do / si	SUN
	la	
	sol	
	fa	
Interval		Second Shock (organic life on the earth)
	mi	
	re	
	do / si	EARTH
	la	
	sol	
	fa	
Interval		Third Shock
	mi	
	re	
	do	MOON

Note											Note	
do	C	1	1	1							do	
si	O	2	3	2	H6						si	H6
la	N	3	2	3		C	2	2	2		la	
sol						O	4	6	4	H12	sol	H12
fa	C	4	4	4		N	6	4	6		fa	
—	O	8	12	8	H24						—	H24
mi	N	12	8	12		C	8	8	8		mi	
re						O	16	24	16	H48	re	H48
do	C	16	16	16		N	24	16	24		do	
si	O	32	48	32	H96						si	H96
la	N	48	32	48		C	32	32	32		la	
sol						O	64	96	64	H192	sol	H192
fa	C	64	64	64		N	96	64	96		fa	
—	O	128	192	128	H384						—	H384
mi	N	192	128	192		C	128	128	128		mi	
re						O	256	384	256	H768	re	H768
do	C	256	256	256		N	384	256	384		do	
si	O	512	768	512	H1536						si	H1536
la	N	768	512	768		C	512	512	512		la	
sol						O	1024	1536	1024	H3072	sol	H3072
fa	C	1024	1024	1024		N	1536	1024	1536		fa	
—	O	2048	3072	2048	H6144						—	H6144
mi	N	3072	2048	3072		C	2048	2048	2048		mi	
re						O	4096	6144	4096	H12288	re	H12288
do						N	6144	4096	6144		do	

Table 1

Table 2

Notes		
do		
si	H6	H1
la		
sol	H12	H6
fa		
—	H24	H12
mi		
re	H48	H24
do		
si	H96	H48
la		
sol	H192	H96
fa		
—	H384	H192
mi		
re	H768	H384
do		
si	H1536	H768
la		
sol	H3072	H1536
fa		
—	H6144	H3072
mi		
re	H12288	H6144
do		

Table 2

Table 3

Notes			
do			
si	H6	H1	
la			
sol	H12	H6	H1
fa			
—	H24	H12	H6
mi			
re	H48	H24	H12
do			
si	H96	H48	H24
la			
sol	H192	H96	H48
fa			
—	H384	H192	H96
mi			
re	H768	H384	H192
do			
si	H1536	H768	H384
la			
sol	H3072	H1536	H768
fa			
—	H6144	H3072	H1536
mi			
re	H12288	H6144	H3072
do			

Table 3

H6. From the first triad there comes the second triad. Second triad comes out from neutralizing force which becomes active. So they must again stand in the order 1-2-3. This change of place of matters in the triad is what produces action.

These hydrogens represent all layers of matter in relation to human machine. The scale is larger than in ordinary chemistry, and many different matters enter into one hydrogen.

This third scale will serve us for the study of human machine. Human machine must be regarded as a three-storied chemical factory which receives raw materials and transforms them into finer matters. In the state of man Nos. 1, 2 and 3 the factory works uneconomically and spends on itself all that it produces. Out of the raw material it receives in twenty-four hours it produces different fuel for its different engines. But in another twenty-four hours everything it produces is spent.

The factory receives three kinds of raw material: food (including water), air and impressions. Impressions are also matter, or energy. With every, the smallest, impression, a certain amount of energy enters into us. From the combination of all three foods the factory produces all that is necessary for its work and development. But as it is at present, everything is spent and nothing remains for development. If, however, by certain training and method certain economy is exercised, certain matters are stored in the factory. When a sufficient quantity of these matters accumulates, other processes begin which mean development. For this, first, economy is necessary, and, second, increase of production. With certain efforts at the right moment it is possible to increase production. But effort must be permanent.

The study of three octaves in the human organism. We have to do with three intervals. Nature has provided a shock for only one interval, but not for the other two. For the other two we have to produce the necessary shock by our own efforts.

Necessary to understand the meaning of these hydrogens—what they are. Food is H768. A great variety of matters comes under H768. And yet, in reality, the range of matters that can serve as food for man is very limited. H384 is water, liquids. H192 is air that man breathes. H96 is many things. For instance it is arterial blood, or very hot air, or very rarefied air, etc. H48, H24, H12 and H6 are all impressions. But

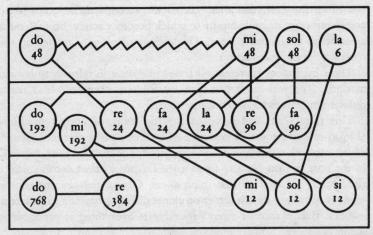

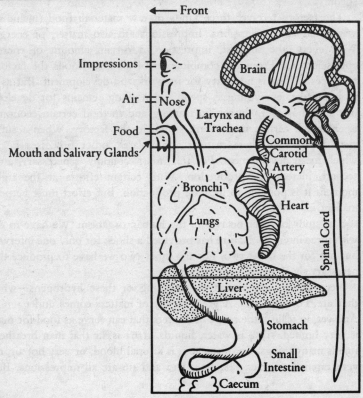

← Front

Impressions

Air — Nose

Food

Mouth and Salivary Glands

Brain

Larynx and Trachea

Common Carotid Artery

Heart

Bronchi

Lungs

Spinal Cord

Liver

Stomach

Small Intestine

Caecum

impressions above H48 are not a rule but an exception. Man 1, 2, 3 has impressions 48, and even does not make very much of these as you shall see. [See diagram p. 32.]

Impressions enter as do 48 and stop, because at this place there is no corresponding carbon 12. Carbon 12 can be brought here only by a special effort. If we know this moment and can make this effort it brings carbon 12 to this place and the octave can develop further. At the same time it touches mi 48 of the air octave and allows it to develop further by providing the necessary shock. Without this effort only an infinitesimal amount of the third food (do 48) passes further. It is enough for life but not enough for development. So we can say that do 48 does not develop further.

The second shock brings the three octaves to si 12, mi 12 and sol 12. Si 12 and mi 12 cannot develop further. Sol 12 develops into la 6, but it is a very small la because it comes from air. But mi and si which are very powerful, stop here. A special effort is needed to transform them into fa 6 and do 6. The nature of these efforts we began to study from the first day. The first is self-remembering and self-observation. The second is struggle with negative emotions.

This is our inner alchemy, the transmutation of base metals into precious metals. But all this alchemy is inside us, not outside.

Up to fa 96 and re 96 the diagram can be followed physiologically. Ordinary physiology shows even more details than this diagram. [See diagram p. 32.]

Food coming into the mouth meets with saliva, then in the stomach with gastric juices, then in the intestines with intestinal juices. Then it is absorbed into venous blood, is carried into the liver, passes through the heart into the lungs, is oxidized there and becomes arterial blood H96.

Study of hydrogens and their relation to one another also helps to understand centres and their different speeds. Intellectual centre works with H48, moving centre with H24, emotional centre should work with H12. But it never receives the right fuel and never works as it should. If we could make it work faster, it would mean a great difference in perceptions, etc.

So up to 96 we can follow the process and describe it in detail. Further than 96 we cannot follow the process physiologically. After 96 we can study the Table of Nutrition only psychologically. Psychologically we can establish the difference between 48 and 24, 24 and 12. But this needs observation. When we can distinguish the difference between certain perceptions and feelings we shall be able to understand which hydrogen is working.

Our aim is to come back to psychology again, but with better material and better weapons, so as to be able to establish the position of each phenomenon in relation to other phenomena.

* * *

Q. Why do you employ terms carbon, oxygen, nitrogen and hydrogen?
MR. O. You must try to understand it yourself. They are not used in the ordinary meaning, but very near it. These names are not accidental. Try to think what is the real reason for employing them.

Q. Is it connected with the four elements?
MR. O. It is the same thing. Personally I think that earth is H; fire is C; air is N, and water is O. But this is my personal interpretation.

Q. Where do you get the energy necessary for the special effort needed for the first shock?
MR. O. Impressions 48 are colourless impressions. If you make the effort to be conscious, by this effort you can bring carbon 12 to the necessary place. C12 can produce a certain emotional state and a certain state of consciousness. This moment of consciousness transforms colourless impressions into colourful impressions. We have enough energy for this effort if only we limit ourselves a little—limit our fantasy, the expression of negative emotions, etc.

Q. Do impressions vary in colourfulness and intensity?
MR. O. Impressions vary depending on how conscious they are. Impressions 24 are emotional to a certain extent. Impressions 12 are very emotional. Revelation of St. John is written with H6. Impressions vary depending on the element of emotion and element of consciousness in them. We spend all our energy in negative emotions, and this prevents us from having emotional impressions. It is all very simple, constructed according to very simple principles. If we could control two or three small things in ourselves all would be different. The question is how to control them? We are accustomed to let things happen. Control means effort at every step.

* * *

Thursday. February 28th 1935.

MR. O. I want you to think about three lines of work. These lectures, as they were proposed, are finished. I gave you all the words necessary, and I have explained the position of this system in relation to other systems. I told you about the four ways. In the three ways one begins with the most difficult: one has to give everything up and start a completely new life. In the Fourth Way one can go on continuing almost exactly what one did before. This system has all the features and peculiarities of the Fourth Way. But schools are very different, depending on people who study in them. There are schools for man No. 6, schools for man No. 5, schools for man No. 4 and schools for people who study how to become No. 4. All schools have particular features:

1. They are always connected with a certain objective work. For instance, schools were behind the building of Gothic cathedrals. For a certain reason this building of Gothic cathedrals was their objective, visible aim. Whether people see it or not, such an aim always exists.

2. School-work can be successful only if one works on three lines: first, personal work; second, work with people; third, work for the benefit of the school, work for a certain definite purpose, whether one knows this purpose or not.

So far you worked on the first line. Now time has come to try and also work on the second line. The third line comes later. You must think how to pass to work on the second line and later to approach the third. Without this, work will bring no result. You must think how to remain connected with some kind of work. Lectures are finished as they are.

MR. H. Do you mean discussion?

MR. O. Discussion by itself will not help much.

MR. C. What besides?

MR. O. You must think about it. You need instruction, showing the way. You cannot find the way by yourselves. This is the position of a human being: no one can find the way by himself. . . . In this way you can enter into the second way. You must think that these groups have been going on for some time. There were people before you. You can get instruction not only from me, but also from people who were before you. Their experience is very important for you. You must learn how to use their experience, how to make them speak.

Then we have organized a house. At present you cannot profit much by it, for it is so fully occupied. Occasionally—yes. But at present seventy or eighty people come there regularly, and sometimes as many as sixty people at one time. The house is already beginning to burst.

Experience shows that in order to get what is possible from these ideas certain organization is necessary—groups where people not only talk, but can work together: in the house, or the garden, or other work can be started. When they begin to work together they begin to see features they did not see when things were discussed. This is not obligatory. There may be different things for different people. People can always find what will suit them without unnecessary sacrifices. Sacrifices are not expected.

Until now people looked after you. Now you have to look after yourselves. Think how to keep connection. Later you will have to look not only after yourselves, but also after new people. Thus you will enter into the third line.

You can begin in this now. Every organization must have certain rules. One rule there was that you should not talk to people outside. I did not insist at first on this rule, because experience shows that nobody obeys it. People only realize the necessity of this rule when their talk turns against them.

Until now there was this rule. Now I change it. Now I say: try to speak, try to interest your friends, tell them about lectures, bring them here. It will be an interesting experience what your friends will tell you about yourselves and the ideas.

This rule was to help you not to lie. The study of lying is very important. One has to struggle with lying.

Now you must try to speak the truth, not to lie. You have full permission to speak, on condition that you tell your impressions here. At the same time you will in this way prepare people who may come— or not. People are mostly very impatient, they make their conclusions and decisions after too short a time.

MR. R. May one use this system to understand other systems? For instance, Upanishads?

MR. O. Not yet. You must know more. Particularly this refers to older systems, that do not belong to our time. Division into four ways belongs to our times. A thousand years ago there were no such divisions. If you study the system sufficiently long you will be able to understand their language.

MR. R. Am I lying when I say I understand Buddhism better through this system?

MR. O. I am very glad to hear that. Self-understanding certainly helps to understand many things.

[Mr. O. said that he may have to go away for a week or two, and in that case we will have chapters on octaves, the Food Diagram and Hydrogen Table to read. If he is here next week, we shall continue this conversation.]

MR. P. If you are not here, we shall have diagrams?

MR. O. Yes, and to-day talk and see how you can look after yourselves.

*   *   *

Thursday. March 7th 1935.

[Written questions read and answered.]
[Notes of previous Thursday meeting read.]

MR. O. First of all because it is better for your memory, in addition to what I said about talking to your friends, you must try to limit all you say to them by the first lecture that you heard. In the first lecture—you can ask later, Madame K. is not here to-night, but she can give you programme—not programme, but she can show you how it was written in short form—that will help you to orientate—you cannot keep it but you can read it and return. So if you speak to anybody you cannot speak of last lecture but you can start with first, and don't go even to second until you get a result and you bring result here and we talk about it, and then perhaps in some cases we can add something to first lecture, but even first lecture has enough material to realize whether people want to hear it or study it or not.

Secondly, there were two questions last time which I wanted to answer—after I left—one question was how to continue lectures—some people said they realize that lectures are necessary, and I think somebody said they would like to hear it all from the beginning. That is quite right, that is the best thing possible; if I could start again from the beginning it would be very useful and very profitable, but we cannot go on for ever repeating and repeating although there are means to get to hear lectures second time. If you work enough on yourself, and study in second line of work, and find enough people who are interested and want to come to these lectures, if you bring these people, if I have time, if it is possible to arrange, if there are good circumstances connected with that, then you will hear lectures again from the beginning which will not be given to you but to the people whom you bring; in that way you will have possibility to listen again to the same things, but you will hear them differently as other people who brought you heard again what they heard years before.

Second thing, there was question, and I don't want to make a mystery about it, I want to give you the way how to think about it, and that is how to understand objective work in relation to this—I don't like the word 'school' because it sounds too big in relation to this thing, but objective work in connection with my work is kind of investigation which I began long before I met with this system, and this work I am continuing, and later when you know all that I can give you in relation to this system, you will see if you are interested in my object and would like to work with me in my object; in any case you lose nothing, you get useful knowledge and you can do what you like with it, but if you are interested in my investigation maybe you will continue to work with me. This is objective aim by which I define it in general way, but later we can come to more exact definition of that.

There is another thing I want to say; last time when you discussed things you mixed up two things: what it was necessary to think about second line, work in groups, exchange of observations, interchange of opinions and things like that, and organization of the whole thing. These ideas must be separated. In relation to groups you can do nothing by yourself—that will be arranged and it will be settled which day, and to which group, who will look after that—all that refers to your connection with older people—all that will be arranged, but what you have to think about is general organization—until now people have looked after you and arranged these lectures, now you have to try to begin, you cannot do it, but you must try to think about yourself, how to organize it, how to continue it, and later, as I said, you will look after other people. This is part of the general plan of school-work: in the beginning people are looked after, then they look after themselves and then they look after other people.

* * *

Q. How can I find out that type of work which would be most useful for me to. . . .

MR. O. Only by trying.

Q. Is it possible to get copies of all lectures?

MR. O. Unfortunately, no. Generally they are burned very soon after, but later we shall have other notes which we shall be able to read.

Q. What work are we supposed to do in our own group?

MR. O. The very principle of group organization is that one has to sacrifice his decision and accept things as they are arranged, because whether people see it or not, they will choose what they like, because all our life we choose what we like and avoid what we dislike, and in organization of groups sometimes exactly what you dislike is good, not in an unpleasant form, but sometimes we cannot choose ourselves quite right. It will be seen, many things can be adjusted and corrected, but first principle of group organization is that group doesn't organize itself, group is organized from centre so to say, not from outside. This is most anti-democratic work!

Q. Can we ask older people to organize it or have we to do it all ourselves? I mean in trying to find out what to do, can we talk to the people who brought us in to help us?

MR. O. Yes, you can talk and ask them, and they will tell you in what position things are, what is possible and what is not, but don't expect that things move at once. As a matter of fact next week I shall not be in London but there will be Wednesday and Thursday meetings and you can talk with older people and little groups will be formed, not at once, but this is beginning.

Q. Can we ask anybody, or must we ask each time before we bring somebody?

MR. O. You can try, then it will be seen with whom it is useful for you to speak and who can better answer your questions.

Q. I don't quite understand what Mr. O. means by general organization. Does it mean that what is important for us is to plan our own affairs so that we have time to devote to the work?

MR. O. It is difficult to say in general; just wait until next week and perhaps it will be easier and things will begin to settle themselves.

No, I didn't mean that. I think almost everybody, with the exception of very extreme cases, can give sufficient time to take certain part in the work without actually changing his work. In extreme cases it is necessary to speak in details and speak about each case separately.

Q. Does he mean experimenting with different kinds of work and finding out which is suitable for us?

MR. O. There are not so many things to experiment, and more or less it is possible to see what one must try first and if one doesn't like it or if it is not successful there may be more kinds, but we cannot have great varieties of different kinds of work.

Q. If we find anybody suitable to bring, who are we to inform about it?

MR. O. Write to me with more or less possible details about this person, and then I will speak with you as to when next group starts.

Q. Are we to only ask people who appear to be suitable to us or are we to ask people who appear to be unsuitable as well?

MR. O. Rather dangerous experiment! You will find it is dangerous even with people who look suitable.

Q. Is it a good thing to introduce people to 'The New Model of the Universe' before we tell them that there is a system?

MR. O. Yes, generally speaking it is useful, only again there are different people. Some people could like 'New Model' and find something there and find nothing in this—I already heard several reports like that.

Q. I can think of one or two people who, if I said there was something behind it, would read it.

MR. O. You must not speak about 'something behind'—perhaps there is nothing behind.

Q. If we hear that the lectures are starting again may we attend even if we haven't been able to bring anybody?

MR. O. Very difficult, because we are limited by space and time in all that we do in this world—sometimes, but I cannot promise anything.

Q. I don't understand, if we cannot do anything by ourselves, how can we start organizing things by ourselves?

MR. O. Yes, that is rather difficult.

First of all it is necessary to understand that it is necessary to talk and think—we always think we can start with 'doing'. This is one of our chief mistakes, and 'doing', even when it is possible in a small way, it is always lost, as it is necessary to have a plan and only then try to do something even when it is possible.

Q. If people hear that there are lectures and do want to come, should we give any idea that it is possible that there will be lectures within the next three months?

MR. O. I cannot say just now, it may be sooner or later, I cannot say just now. Partly it depends on the quantity of people; if certain numbers are ready, or more or less ready or wishing to come, then we can start earlier, but if there are only a few people we have to wait until there will be more. Experience shows that it is difficult, almost impossible to begin with large group, also it is useless to begin with too small group. For instance, we have here now about seventy people—it is absolutely useless to begin with seventy, or it will be ordinary lecture to them, they will come and listen and remember nothing. From the very beginning it is necessary to start with conversation, and very many of them will soon dislike it and find that this is not what they want—much better than they should continue without understanding. It is not the idea of these lectures to make people learn more words, they know quite enough words and more words will not give anything, quite opposite, they must learn to have less words and that cannot be made by just ordinary lecture. People have too many words; it is one of the misfortunes about them that they have too many words.

Q. If people meet and you are not here, aren't they likely to get into too many words?

MR. O. Little by little they lose this habit and find that too many words are not necessary at all, and that the fewer words they use the easier it is to understand.

Q. But some people don't know what to do if they are not talking.

MR. O. But here we have definite object, we have observation, group work and organization, and each of these aims gives material for discussion.

Q. Should one report to anybody about one's observations?

MR. O. Yes, very good, but that will be done in small groups; it will be necessary, and one of the most important things.

Q. How do we start looking after ourselves if we are not told what to do?

MR. O. Again, 'doing'—I said you must think about it. Suppose small group and they come to conclusion that they want to hear lectures, and if you bring new people I can provide these lectures, but if you don't bring new people I wait, but if you talk to people you ... [?] ... This is example.

Q. Would one form of the work be for some people to live together and do daily work?

MR. O. Yes, but in order to live together it is necessary to have house, so it does not start with the idea of living together, it starts with a house, and again it is not right if people think themselves about it because they will choose things wrongly, because if they decide to live together it will end in their quarrelling with one another.

Q. It is not possible for most of us to give up our lives and do that sort of thing.

MR. O. No. I said that if they come to this point of view they must look at practical side. I am perfectly sure in most cases, with the exception of quite extreme cases, everybody can continue to do and live as one is accustomed, because this is a thing that does not need special time. Everything one does can become work, there is nothing that one does in ordinary way that cannot become work if one tries to remember oneself, tries not to identify, tries to understand that everything happens, and so on; it is not necessary to change circumstances, quite opposite—to change circumstances is even worse, particularly in the beginning; later it may be useful but not in the beginning.

Q. What do you mean by general organization as opposed to being put in groups?

MR. O. I think it is quite clear what I said, that every kind of work needs certain plan and certain organization. A certain number of people have to take part in some kind of work—suppose ordinary school—you must know who will do this and who will do that, all that will be arranged.

Q. I think you spoke about organization that you could do for yourself as opposed to what will be arranged.

MR. O. No. I said you must think—you will think about one thing and think about another thing—'doing' comes much later, first it is necessary to have plan.

Q. I cannot make out why we should try to do it, because if we are all mechanical third man, why do we try to do anything? If we have a school what is the object—can we do anything?

MR. O. If there was no possibility then there would be no talk—but there is possibility, that is the difference, you know; this is the point where this system differs from other existing systems, because existing systems say, 'Do this' or 'Do that' or 'Not do', but in this system we know that it is impossible to do, everything happens, but we know that there are possibilities, no definite power to do or not to do, but possibility to develop this power, so I never denied possibility, but I said we have not full power. Possibility can be developed in certain circumstances, certain conditions, but to come closer to the subject, two things can develop, knowledge and being. First our knowledge must change, we must change our points of view, we must see things as they really are not as we imagine them to be, and at the same time we must work on our being; it begins by trying to remember ourselves because this is the first feature of our being which we find, that we don't remember ourselves. If we find we do not remember ourselves, from this point begins possibility of change of being and so on, but it is necessary to distinguish between having something and having the possibility to have something; this is the difference.

Q. Did you mean when you said that everything in life can be a possibility to work. . . .

MR. O. I meant (talking without extremes) ordinary occupation—every ordinary occupation in life can become work. If one tries not to identify, and remember oneself, little by little, it does not mean that one can do it at once—and observe oneself—whatever one does it becomes work.

Q. Can one supplement one's knowledge through reading contemporary psychology—Freudism for instance?

MR. O. I don't think so, it is not psychology, it is study of abnormal sex which is applied to everybody which might be quite unnecessary. I told you once how I regard modern psychology. If you take the nineties of last century, psychology of that time was an interesting science in a sense, but rather dull because it has no practical application, but there were some interesting theories and facts, I mean up to the nineties, and then after that this psychology was really finished, it is transformed into what is called different schools, different kinds of psychoanalysis, behaviourism, and one is called [?] God knows why, and different kinds of statistics all based on wrong assumptions; and the other side of psychology, which was more philosophical, went in other directions and began to study psychology of religions, Eastern thought and so on, and again in some cases produced good results and in some cases identified with weak lines of thought, so I don't know really what could be called scientific psychology, they all contradict one another, one denies consciousness and says it is not necessary, and another recognizes consciousness and speaks about it without knowing what it means, and so on.

Q. When you use the word being do you mean conscience?

MR. O. No, I mean everything—this table has a being. It is combination of all features or qualities of my being or table's being; it is simply certain level—if you remember man in the Table of Hydrogens, if we find mean hydrogen of this table and mean hydrogen of man, then we can say, for instance, which place in the Table of Hydrogens man occupies and which place table occupies; that will be level of being on a large scale, but as man we are all on the same level from that point of view; at the same time, by studying ourselves individually, we establish our own level of being. We realize that we are like this and we are like that, and we have imagination about this and that, and that defines our being—it means plurality, not unity. In relation to all of us it means we are not one, we are many, we cannot 'do', we are asleep, we don't remember ourselves; these are features of our state of being. Even if we want to we cannot awake because we have so many favourite dreams that immediately these favourite dreams put us to sleep again, even if we awake for a second, and it is very hard work and needs very many efforts to begin to awake. This is our present level of being; we are not collected, we always lose ourselves in everything, that means we are identified with everything.

Q. What is the practical application of this system?

MR. O. For instance, a possibility to establish our state of consciousness and possibility by self-remembering to increase our consciousness—that immediately becomes practical; that is what first struck me when I began to study it, that this is particularly important and particularly interesting (because Eastern systems miss this point) that we are not conscious and secondly that we can become conscious.

There were interesting plays and interesting books, but they were very specialized like [?] or they went under name of philosophy, and generally written in such difficult language that they remained unknown to general public. I thought in the nineteenth century the best psychologist was [?]—very few people know of him.

Q. Can this system as a practical application be used by doing things better, or making things better?

MR. O. How can you do better if you cannot make at all? No, we cannot start with that, it is not the first step, it is very far, the only thing we can do is to become more conscious.

Q. I must find another word because I do make things which I call 'doing'—cannot I do it better?

MR. O. No, neither better nor worse, nor for long time. When your state of consciousness begins to change, when you become more conscious than ordinary. . . .

Q. Somebody asked a question after you left last time as to whether you thought we could build cathedrals.

MR. O. It means very much study, because people who came to school—suppose there are schools which were connected with building cathedrals, people came to study these things, they came to study geometry and mathematics that were used for building, they did not build, maybe they had to work thirty years before they took some active part in the building of cathedrals, so if you take this example of objective work it means preparation. The same process of acquiring knowledge shows the aim or shows its object. By studying the system one studies the aim of the system itself, it is the same process; this is where the difficulty comes—we think it is two different processes, we think understanding of the system is one thing and studying the object is another thing, but it is the same thing.

Q. You said we must change our knowledge in order to see things as they really are; do you consider [?] truth [?] reality?

MR. O. No, no, I mean in a much limited way; we cannot come in this state of consciousness to things as they are, but we can take some layers of lying. Things are surrounded by lying, we can take one, two or three skins away—we can come nearer to real things. . . .

People can spend their lives studying systems and existing words and never come to real things—three-quarters or nine-tenths of our ordinary knowledge doesn't exist really, it exists only in imagination. For instance, there was question about psychoanalysis—I compare that with Mediaeval Demonology—it was elaborate system of all classes of demons with their names, and it was definitely calculated that for every man there are 27 millions of demons or something, in any case, that explained fully why man is powerless before demons, and each of these 27 millions they were classified and had definite names and so on; it was very interesting and exactly like modern psychoanalysis, only they speak of complexes and the other spoke of demons.

Q. Must a science be necessarily wrong if it deals with symbols?

MR. O. There were many interesting philosophical systems and they gave preparation for possible esoteric knowledge if we are able to get it. Man can think not necessarily wrongly, he can often find more or less rightly.

Q. Does starting on the second line of work depend to a certain extent on progress on the first line?

MR. O. Absolutely, because how can one work on second line if one does not work on the first line; there is absolutely no chance. If one knows more about oneself, if one tries to observe oneself, tries to struggle with habits and lying, then one has chance to work on second line. This is the beginning of the whole thing; we are machines, and we must see where we can change something, because in every machine of every kind there is always point where it is possible to begin. I forget whether it was in this group or not, but there was a question, 'Is there anything permanent in us?' There are two things, buffers and weaknesses which are sometimes called features, really weaknesses; everyone has one, two or three particular weaknesses, and everybody has certain buffers belonging to him; he consists of buffers, but some are particularly important, they enter into all his decisions and all his understandings and so on. This is all that is permanent in us, and this is lucky for us that there is nothing more permanent because these things can be changed. Buffers are artificial, they are not organic, they are acquired chiefly by imitation; children begin to imitate grown-up people and they create buffers, and some are created by education without knowing, and features, weaknesses, can be found out sometimes, and if one knows his feature, and if one begins to keep it in mind and to remember it, then he may find certain moment when he can act not from feature. Features are very interesting, these weaknesses, because sometimes they have simple forms like laziness, but in some cases they take such well-disguised forms that there are no ordinary words to describe them; they have to be described by some kind of diagram or drawings or things like that. We can some time speak, but that will be in smaller group when it will be easier to speak about features, but these are the only permanent things in us, and this is our luck, because if there was something else permanent it would be impossible to change.

Q. How can we trust our own judgment about features?

MR. O. You cannot, you have to be told, and then you will not believe it, you will say—anything, but not that! Even if you accept it and don't argue you will not see the importance of it, because you see features are very funny things in that way—everybody has many features, but everybody has two or three particularly important because they enter into every decision, every definition, every subjectively important thing—everything passes through it, all perceptions and all reactions, but very difficult to realize what this means, because you are so accustomed to it that you don't notice, even if it is drawn on the blackboard. I always remember a man. . . . [Example of fool as feature.]

Q. If feature is so important we must get at it somehow.

MR. O. Yes, but you must be prepared, otherwise it will be like little dog—you will hold him. You must realize that you need something, and if it comes at the right time it might help.

Q. Can we not find it by observation?

MR. O. Very great improbability, we are too much in them, we don't have enough perspective. But real work, serious work, begins only from feature. It doesn't mean that it is absolutely necessary; in many cases features cannot be defined, it will be such complicated definition that it has no practical value. In that case it is quite sufficient to take general division 'I and Ouspensky', only it is necessary to understand what is 'I' and what is 'Ouspensky', what is lying and what is himself. Even if you admit this possibility of division you will put what you like and what you dislike—if you like it you will say it is 'I' and if you dislike it you will say it is not. It is long work, it cannot be found at once; there must be some indications which you can find, for instance, if you formulated your aim in connection with this work—if you say 'I want to be free'—that is very good definition, but what is necessary? It is necessary to have results and understand that you are not free first of all. If you understand to what extent you are not free, and if you formulate your desire to be free, you will then see in yourself which part of yourself wants to be free and which part doesn't want to be free; this is the beginning.

Q. Chief feature, if you get rid of it, what takes its place?

MR. O. That depends on the feature; in most cases it simply disappears, it is not necessary at all—suppose my watch is going wrong, suppose it is always slow—etc., etc.

Q. Must the chief feature be necessarily bad?

MR. O. It is chief weakness; unfortunately we cannot think that our chief feature would be chief power because we have no powers.

Q. How can it be weakness if there is no not-weakness?

MR. O. It means mechanicalness, we are mechanical in all things, but in this particular thing we are particularly mechanical and particularly blind, that is why it is chief weakness; other things which are not weakness we can see. When you begin to divide yourself you will see that this is mechanical, this is like and this is dislike. We can see it around us, it may be some kind of psychological twist which produces this effect like watch that is going slow, but it is not mechanical necessity for this watch to go slow.

Q. If there is no not-weakness, how can you compare?

MR. O. I don't understand, but suppose there is weakness we can observe, it manifests, but if it disappears manifestation disappears; suppose one has bad habit, then if habit disappears manifestation disappears.

Q. What would you call weakness—by ethical standards?

MR. O. No, thing in which you are most mechanical; certainly if you cannot see where you are absolutely helpless, you are most asleep, most blind, because you know there are degrees in everything, and all qualities or manifestations in us, they all have different degrees; if there were no degrees in ourselves it would be very difficult to study. We can study ourselves only because everything in us exists in different degrees. Even feature is not always the same; it is almost the same because it is mechanical, but sometimes it is more definitely expressed, sometimes in very rare cases it is shown very little, only in that way it can be found. But this is difficult about feature; take mechanicalness, yes you are mechanical but in some cases, sometimes we are more mechanical, sometimes less mechanical; if we are ill, for instance, we become at once more mechanical, we cannot resist external world and things of external world even as we can resist ordinarily.

Q. Desire to be free is certainly not a weakness.

MR. O. It may be desire, and desire. Suppose one realizes that one wishes to get rid of weakness, at the same time one doesn't wish to learn methods how to get rid of weakness, one thinks he can do it himself, that will be second weakness to help one weakness, then there will be no result.

Q. But if one makes constant effort?

MR. O. Again that will belong to other side of you, what I call 'You'. It doesn't mean that it is power or force, it is merely combination of certain desires, desires to get rid of something. If you realize that something is wrong, and you formulate desire to get rid of it, then if you keep mind sufficiently long on that then it becomes certain plan of action, and if this line of action is sufficiently prolonged it can attain results, only it is necessary again to add that several different lines of action are necessary to attain result, not one—we have to work at the same time on this and on this and on that; if we work on one line it is impossible to go anywhere.

* * *

Thursday. July 4th 1935.

MR. P. Question about which has more practical value—physical work or intellectual work?

MR. O. Why use the word 'practical'? Value is value. All value is practical. Quite right—efforts may be stronger in relation to ideas than to physical work. But why put one against the other? At one time one is necessary, at another time—another. Work on points of view is most important work.

MR. L. Question about the rôle of destiny in development.

MR. O. Destiny is another word for fate. We can take fate only in relation to physical state, to health, etc. In relation to attainment fate has nothing to do. Cause and effect begins it. But cause and effect is when the result depends on one's own action, but unpremeditated action. In work one must try to use will, as much as we have it. If one has one inch of will and uses it, then one will have two inches, then three, and so on. This is how it works.

MRS. C. Question about how to get rid of laws.

MR. O. Try. It is necessary to know, to understand little by little, the nature of laws from which one can become free. Then it is necessary to try to get free from one law, then from another. This is the practical way to study them.

Question about what to get rid of.

MR. O. You can get rid from identifying, negative emotions, imagination. . . .

MRS. C. Does identifying come under laws?

MR. O. You want a stamp. I speak about principles.

Question about what philosophical, theoretical and practical mean.

MR. O. Try to formulate the question more concretely, otherwise it will be a question about words. As I first heard about it, I was told that schools of knowledge coming from higher mind are divided into three classes. Opposite to the ordinary meaning of these words, practical schools were the highest, then theoretical, and last—philosophical schools. But ordinarily a man understands by practical such things as gardening, making boots, etc. By theoretical he understands mathematics, geology, etc. And by philosophical he understands what he wants—philosophy. But here philosophical schools are preparatory schools.

The same words are applied to the division of inner circles, in themselves. Esoteric circle is said to be practical; mesoteric, theoretical; and exoteric, philosophical. But from our point of view they are all practical.

MISS C. I have observed in myself a constant desire to be comfortable. Is it general for everybody to feel this?

MR. O. This is one of the very important features of our life. To this desire we sacrifice everything. We are ready to give up everything to go by the line of least resistance. Sometimes this desire becomes so strong that one can be comfortable and nothing else. Even if something is not comfortable, one tries to arrange it so that it should be comfortable.

MRS. C. Where does this desire come from?

MR. O. This needs observation.

MRS. C. Is there any way to get rid of it in relation to the system?

MR. O. What to do, is a different question. We must come from a different side to it. It is a very big thing. Every effort is important, so every effort must be discussed specially—not all efforts together. Sleep is the most comfortable thing. To try to awake is very uncomfortable. Later, when we partly awaken, we will feel how uncomfortable it is to sleep, when anything may happen any moment. But it is necessary to come to that state.

MR. H. I think it was said that there is a connection between Law of Three and Law of Seven; and one example was given—man as a three-storied factory.

MR. O. No, three-storied factory has nothing to do with Law of Three. The connection between Law of Three and Law of Seven is very important, but at present you have to study them separately. You cannot see the connection.

MR. H. Is it Law of Seven that makes efforts die out? I put my watch on another wrist, on purpose, but a few days later I forgot to do it.

MR. O. Law of Seven is not guilty in that. At present it is only philosophical for us, slightly theoretical. It is everywhere; that is why we cannot see it. And we cannot change its course.

MRS. C. Can you take it as an exercise watching the speed of centres?

MR. O. No, I said—no exercises. Certainly to verify speed of centres is useful. Also perhaps sometimes one can create special conditions for observation. But usually one must take what each day gives.

MR. K. If I try not to identify with one 'I', so, having no permanent 'I', I identify with another.

MR. O. When we speak of man out of the work, we say that he has no 'I'. If man starts to study, this already means a certain state. He has magnetic centre. Magnetic centre is the beginning of 'I'. He has already no right to say he has no 'I'. Man in the street has no 'I'. In the study he certainly cannot say that he has a complete and permanent 'I', but he must already have a line of action. This must mean an 'I'. It is not yet fully conscious, but it grows. This is the difference between knowledge and being. 'I' belongs to being.

MRS. C. Are different states of consciousness different scales? Objective consciousness seems to belong to a philosophical idea?

MR. O. Quite the reverse. It is very practical. But if you mean for us, then, certainly objective consciousness is a philosophical idea. At the same time the study of descriptions of glimpses of this state are possible. If one studies these descriptions and tries to find similarities, it can become theoretical.

MISS C. Are efforts to self-remember practical?

MR. O. May be practical, may be theoretical and may be philosophical.

MRS. C. In writing down lists of philosophical, theoretical and practical things one becomes convinced that they are almost indissoluble.

MR. O. Some things can be taken in all three ways, some things only in two ways or one.

MR. L. Is there any connection between these three ideas and reality?

MR. O. What do you mean by reality? If we have an experience, then it has reality; reality as opposed to imagination.

MR. R. Is it possible to create something in oneself to survive after death?

MR. O. We cannot say. We can suppose only. Theoretically we can speak about it, but not from the point of view of this system. This system does not speak about it. But we have nothing to lose—so we can risk. In this state we cannot be sure; we don't know what happens after death. There are different theories: one theory that man disintegrates, another theory (spiritualistic) that there are spirits. Theosophists think that man can reincarnate. Christians have the idea of reward and punishment. Hindoos have the idea of transmigration, also as reward or punishment, etc. Every religion in every country has a theory. And all are right. From the ordinary point of view it sounds strange how contradictory ideas can all be right. But human mind cannot invent any theory of life after death without there being some truth in it. It will be either a distortion of esoteric ideas or simply an invention. In both cases they carry a certain amount of truth in them. People think about this question since the creation of the world and still they did not come to any conclusion. Evidently there is some obstacle that prevents them from knowing about it. I think it is length of ideas. Our ideas are too short. Perhaps if we were able to use higher centres, which have longer ideas, we could know. But as we are, we cannot.

MRS. C. Can you say that essence survives?

MR. O. It will be another theory.

MR. B. Does the state of being fix the boundary between theory and knowledge?

MR. O. Leave that.

MRS. W. It seems to me that in studying the machine one discovers that one is inefficient even as a machine. Machine is faulty. Is it possible to improve oneself as a machine?

MR. O. Not only possible, but it is all there. Only wrong work of the machine and wrong habits keep us on this level. We should be self-conscious. We live below our legitimate level. We could live on the ground floor and we live in the basement. If we were self-conscious all our activities would be different. Self-consciousness means work of higher emotional centre. It has enormous possibilities and can have glimpses of the work of higher mental centre. When it comes to objective consciousness and command of higher mental centre—it is a different state. But we should be self-conscious and have command of emotions. In the conditions we live we are not self-conscious.

MRS. C. Does a child come into the world with a capacity of self-consciousness?

MR. O. Yes, with the possibility. Our lack of self-consciousness is simply an accident of birth. We are born among sleeping people. A child is only an embryo, not developed. But by the time he is developed, he loses his chance of development. When one grows up among sleeping people one can become awake only by effort.

MR. L. If a child is put on an island without seeing people, would he be awake?

MR. O. This is a theoretical example. It is like another theoretical example: if a child is cut off from all impressions he will not be able to make a single movement. This is theoretically right, but in practice it cannot be verified. If a child is born among people who are awake, he will be awake. But there is no possibility to verify this.

MRS. W. A child often shows a certain alertness, at a certain age.

MR. O. If a child is put among people who are awake, he would not fall asleep. But at which age in these conditions he is more awake, it is impossible to say. Generally at the age of seven or eight there appears in him imaginary personality or imaginary 'I'.

MR. R. You say that man in the street has no aim. But when you get older you don't fly about so much, you become interested in one thing.

MR. O. This is one-sided. There are many other sides in one's being and knowledge that this line does not touch at all. Some people can, even in life, develop a certain oneness, but these are exceptions. If one becomes, as you say, interested in one thing, only one group of 'I's develops interest. Others don't know about it; only a very small minority is concerned. In this case simply a small number of 'I's improve. So there are two questions here: the question of minority and majority and, second, the fact that if a line appears, it does not touch many other things, it occupies only a small part of being; the whole being never enters.

MISS C. Are any negative emotions natural?

MR. O. What does natural mean? Start with those that are not. Don't justify them.

MISS N. If I cannot experience positive emotions, should I try to crush all the emotions I feel?

MR. O. No, they are not all negative, but they can become negative. There is no emotion about which we can be sure. Positive emotions may sometimes be experienced even in ordinary conditions. But as a principle—no. We have no time for them. We are too occupied with negative emotions. We have no energy for positive emotions, it is all spent on negative.

MR. L. Is the fact that man has been deprived of self-consciousness the result of accident or cause and effect?

MR. O. Of all. It is useless to think about it. It is a fact. We don't know why it happened, and if we knew it would not help.

MR. R. About laws that we can be free of. Why call them laws and not bad habits?

MR. O. Habits are smaller divisions. Laws govern us, control us, direct us. Habits are not laws.

MRS. C. You mean we must be subject to these laws on earth? They are the condition of our remaining on earth?

MR. O. We cannot fall under them or not fall under them. They don't ask us. We are chained.

MR. R. But we can get free?

MR. O. We can, on conditions.

MR. H. Any personal attainment is result of effort against fate?

MR. O. Fate may be favourable or not. It is necessary to know what one's fate is. But it cannot liberate us. Ways enter here. The four ways are ways to liberate us from laws. But each way has its own characteristic. In the three traditional ways, the first step is the most difficult. In the Fourth Way man remains in the same conditions and he must change in these conditions. These conditions are the best for him, because they are the most difficult.

MR. P. Positive emotions require a lot of energy?

MR. O. They require fuel. The same energy we have could be good for positive emotions, but we spend it on negative emotions. The word energy must be understood as fuel. We produce a little of higher hydrogens 6 and 12 which positive emotions need. But we spend it.

MRS. W. By denying expression of negative emotions one stores up energy?

MR. O. Not so much. A certain amount is certainly saved. But it is more for observation. It does not really mean economy.

MISS O. Surely you score a point if you don't express negative emotions?

MR. O. Certainly. We learn about them more.

MR. B. Would not a higher state of consciousness burn up a lot of energy so that you are left like a flat tyre?

MR. O. Yes, but first you learn methods to increase energy. It increases out of all proportion. But we never can spend so much energy on effort as we spend on explosions.

MR. L. Is energy spent on physical exercise wasted?

MR. O. It depends on exercise. One can kill oneself or increase energy. Also one can do physical exercise very differently if one observes oneself and remembers oneself.

MR. L. I am more fit after it.

MR. O. It depends on exercise.

Q. Is muscular tension a form of identifying?

MR. O. No, no need to call it identifying. It is a special thing and must have special work against it. Generally physical work helps. If one does a little physical work, one feels less tense. There are other means, but the simplest thing is physical work.

MISS C. I observe myself saying the same thing in exactly the same words in the same circumstances, and I cannot stop myself. Is this the last stage of identification?

MR. O. Why last? First and last. It is a very unpleasant realization, when we observe it. We decide not to say it, and cannot stop.

MISS C. What does it mean when we cannot stop?

MR. O. Machine.

MRS. C. Can one see the change of being in oneself? I can see change of knowledge, but I cannot see change of being.

MR. O. Acquiring of knowledge one can see in others. Change of being one can see only in oneself. Certain things come—I will not say which comes first. But you must have already some material to observe.

Q. Is it a good thing to follow a plan during the day?

MR. O. All efforts are good. The question is will you do them? But first it is necessary to study. It is necessary to become quite clear about identifying, imagination, idle talk, negative emotions, etc. It is necessary to be severe with oneself, not to make excuses.

Q. Why is it that we cannot keep the knowledge and resourcefulness that we are able to reach in moments of emergency?

MR. O. I cannot say why. Only it is a very interesting fact. You see that at certain moments you have powers, knowledge and resourcefulness greater than at others. It shows that we can have more than we ordinarily have. But the study of why is only possible when we change our situation and have more powers.

MRS. C. What one does in emergency may not necessarily be from the point of view of the system a right action. How can one be sure the action is the right one?

MR. O. I don't know.

MR. L. In a different state of emotion one seems to be in a different world. Is this imagination?

MR. O. It means that in emotional state emotions make you pass from one state to another. One can rarely observe degrees in our state.

MR. H. Mr. O. said that we live below normal. Does it mean that 1, 2, 3 man should be No. 4?

MR. O. Man should be No. 5, not 4, No. 5 is nearer to normality than 1, 2, 3. No. 4 means school. No. 5 is a certain crystallization already. I don't mean full No. 5, but beginning of No. 5 is normal. But in our conditions we can only come to it through being first No. 4. No. 4 is necessity for us. Without being No. 4 we cannot be No. 6. If we were normal we would be No. 5, and afterwards we would have to be No. 4 in order to become No. 6. But if we were normal we could be No. 5 without school.

MR. H. The characteristics of No. 4 are chiefly desire to awake?

MR. B. If all people are born with the possibility of awakening, is there nothing in later life that would kill that possibility? No matter what conditions one lives in, how long have you still this possibility?

MR. O. Some people have this possibility, some not. In some people it dies, they walk and talk—mostly talk—dead.

Try to prepare more questions during the week.

* * *

Wednesday. August 21st 1935.

MISS P. Is the cosmos connected like a tree, ever interchanging and independent, if one had another dimensional sense to realize it?

MR. O. We don't use the word cosmos in singular for the whole universe. The whole thing is not a cosmos; there are seven cosmoses. Certainly it is all connected. Even in the Ray of Creation you can see that.

MISS P. Can ordinary things disappear into the fourth dimension, as this would explain the tricks of mediums who have not merely sleight of hand?

MR. O. Are there such tricks that are not sleight of hand? It is unproven.

MISS P. Is it possible for some people to be much more conscious and generally adjusted to reality when they are in love?

MR. O. Maybe. Every kind of emotional state sometimes makes one more conscious. But it is not reliable. Our emotions are connected with identifying. Every emotion can become negative any time.

MISS P. Is taking a helpful and practical interest in people in one's employment a right kind of considering, or a waste of energy like a political activity?

MR. O. Generally it would be difficult to determine. . . .

MR. L. When making efforts to self-remember it seems that the moment becomes fuller in some way than in ordinary state. Is this due to imagination?

MR. O. In most cases. What means fuller? Efforts to self-remember must begin with efforts to realize that we don't remember ourselves. It must be a true realization, not just a general idea.

MR. L. I have noticed that when I feel inclined to work in a lazy way, in spite of myself I sometimes make myself work properly. Is this due to conflicting 'I's?

MR. O. It is impossible to say. It is for you to decide. It is matter for observation.

MR. L. I notice that I am often irritable, although before I thought myself good-tempered. Was this part of imaginary 'I'?

MR. O. Quite probably.

MISS T. If we don't exist for protocosmos how can it exist for us, except in theory?

MR. O. Why not? Many things exist for us and we don't exist for them. Existence is a complex relative term.

MISS T. If I am worrying about anything when I go to bed, I find it is the accelerated beat of my heart which prevents me from sleeping. Is this the result of the emotional centre trying to direct the instinctive centre?

MR. O. It may be. I think it is difficult to explain only in one way. There may be different causes. Observation is necessary.

MISS M. Must all negative emotions be completely lost before we can obtain consciousness?

MR. O. It is impossible to answer about future. It would be fortune-telling.

MISS M. When I am trying to think along some definite line (for instance, making a plan), I find that either my thought becomes automatic or even tails off into day-dreaming. If I try to remember myself, I forget about the plan, and soon find myself in other day-dreams without having even completed the plan in an automatic way.

MR. O. Which plan? About what? You observe one particular case and give it a general meaning.

MISS M. Is it wrong in this case to use such aids as writing things down, or is there any better way of overcoming this difficulty?

MR. O. Any method that will help.

MRS. S. Is each cosmos three-dimensional?

MR. O. For itself. As you are for yourself. I mean your body.

MISS M. Has each cosmos consciousness?

MR. O. We don't know. Intelligence—yes. We use consciousness in a special sense only. In the ordinary sense, consciousness means intelligence. Each cosmos is to a certain extent analogous to another, but not quite. Three cosmoses next to one another give a sufficient idea. One cosmos taken by itself may differ very seriously from another; they may have very little in common, although they may be side by side. All cosmoses are living beings, they all receive impressions, they all breathe, they all have a certain period of sleep and waking and they all have a period of life.

I wish to remind you what I said last time. I said that you have probably heard the expressions macrocosmos and microcosmos—universe and man. This is only a fragment of the ancient teaching that regards seven cosmoses ending with man—protocosmos, megalocosmos, macrocosmos, deuterocosmos, mesocosmos, tritocosmos, microcosmos. About names we will speak later. The strange thing is that between the first, the second and the third, there are different names. Taking them from the top, they correspond to the Ray of Creation. Protocosmos—Absolute. Megalocosmos—all worlds. Macrocosmos—all suns. Deuterocosmos—Solar System. Mesocosmos—all planets. Tritocosmos—organic life. Microcosmos—man. But the relations of cosmoses to each other are different to the Ray of Creation. In cosmoses there is always the same relation of one to another—as zero to infinity. It is the same as the geometrical relation of a point to a line, a line to a plane, a plane to a cube. It means that each time one dimension is added. The idea of infinity must be much readjusted. It does not mean mathematical infinity, although mathematical infinity is only a symbol and means a limit of possible calculation. Physically this limit comes much sooner.

MR. L. What names can you give to dimensions in tritocosmos? You have added one for it. Yet you say each cosmos has three. How many of them are new? I don't see.

MR. O. We have also four dimensions. The fourth is our life. But we don't take ourselves in this way. We take ourselves as section. In the same way each planet has an orbit. We don't take the orbit. Dimensions are not always the same, they pass into one another.

MISS T. Does a cosmos die? Then what renews it?

MR. O. Why this presupposed idea of renewing? In one phrase we cannot speak about renewal before we see that it is limited. We speak only about one life of each cosmos. We must try to be exact. In our state we have no possibility to know more than about one life. We must try to use only such words that can be verified by analogy.

MR. J. What means dying?

MR. O. It disappears, like a fly that is dead.

MR. D. What would tritocosmos sleeping mean?

MR. O. Each cosmos has a period of sleep and waking.

MR. D. When does it sleep?

MR. O. Our thought is not long enough to know that. We can only take an analogy on a smaller scale. Or else we can either believe or disbelieve—both would be a wrong method. So only analogy is possible.

MR. C. By microcosmos do you mean mankind or individual man?

MR. O. Individual man.

MR. C. And what is mankind?

MR. O. It depends on which scale you take it. Many divisions are possible between organic life and man.

MR. C. Are animals a cosmos?

MR. O. Yes, but not so complete. Every living being is a cosmos.

Lower, after microcosmos, comes a cell (a large cell). Next comes a smaller, ultra-microscopic, cell. In bacteriology there are examples of cells that differ from one another like zero to infinity. The difference between them is almost the same as that between man and a cell. Next (only approximately) comes a molecule—fourth microcosmos. Next (fifth microcosmos) comes the electron. They are all in the same relation to one another as zero to infinity.

MR. P. Do periods of time differ? Would life of tritocosmos be out of all knowing for us?

MR. O. Yes, only we start not with the period of life, but with breath. The cosmic measure of time is breath. Our breath is three seconds. Our time is calculated by this period of breath. Breath of organic life is twenty-four hours. It corresponds to the period of sleep and waking of the individuals of organic life. Almost all beings commensurable with man have this period of sleep and waking. Beings asleep and awake make the breath of organic life. Chemical absorption and extrusion are different. . . . If we divide twenty-four hours by three seconds, we have a figure roughly of 30,000. It is a very interesting figure. I mentioned it earlier in relation to centres. Here again we meet with 30,000. 30,000 breaths make up twenty-four hours. If we multiply it by 30,000, we have 80 years—the large average of life. If we divide three seconds by 30,000, we have 1/10,000th part of a second—the quickest eye perception. In each case the coefficient is 30,000. The same repeats in every cosmos. [See diagram p. 62.]

A long life of man is the quickest eye impression for the sun. So the sun cannot really see us individually.

This table gives us an idea of the universe, particularly of continuation of life in different cosmoses.

	electron	molecule	small cells	large cells	micro-cosmos (man)	trito-cosmos	meso-cosmos	deutero-cosmos	macro-cosmos	ayo-cosmos	proto-cosmos
impression					1/10 000 second	3 seconds	24 hours	80 years	3 million years	90 milliard years	3.10^{15} years
breath				1/10 000 second	3 seconds	24 hours	80 years	3 million years	90 milliard years	3.10^{15} years	9.10^{19} years
day and night			1/10 000 second	3 seconds	24 hours	80 years	3 million years	90 milliard years	3.10^{15} years	9.10^{19} years	3.10^{23} years
life	1/300 000 000 second	1/10 000 second	3 seconds	24 hours	80 years	3 million years	90 milliard years	3.10^{15} years	9.10^{19} years	3.10^{23} years	9.10^{28} years

3.10^{15} years (number of 16 figures) 9.10^{19} years (number of 20 figures)
3.10^{23} years (number of 24 figures) 9.10^{28} years (number of 29 figures)

MR. C. What do you mean by organic life? Has it not been going on for longer than two and a quarter million years?

MR. O. How do you know? And who knows? It is only guesses what science says.

MR. L. You say that cosmoses die. If a thing has once existed, can it cease to be?

MR. O. Men also live and die.

MR. L. But there is another level of existence?

MR. O. How do you know? We can take only what we can prove and see.

MR. L. But there is a physical law that matter is indestructible.

MR. O. Man is not matter. You cannot judge a picture by the material.

MR. L. Can material be destroyed?

MR. O. I speak about man. Material is like a river, always running. But if a man dies, something disappears. Instead of philosophizing accept the simple fact and go further. Our possible development goes from known to known, not from unknown to unknown.

MR. C. Is it more possible for us to see the cosmos above than the cosmos below?

MR. O. No, we can see much below too.

MR. H. How is it that the ray ends in moon and here it ends in man?

MR. O. We start here with man. We are interested in man. Man is taken as a cosmos. He is a cosmos in the sense that he lives in all cosmic laws. Moon here enters into mesocosmos.

MRS. A. I want to understand about intelligence of cosmoses. Where does it come from?

MR. O. Where does ours come from? You are a cosmos.

MRS. A. I don't know where it comes from. But it is so limited.

MR. O. Everything is limited.

Cosmoses are from a certain point of view analogous, that is, it is possible to take them as analogous. They have the same function, they are three-dimensional for themselves, they are alive, etc. In the Ray of Creation we take things from an absolutely different standpoint, we study them differently. We cannot see all on one scale, from one point of view. These diagrams open our eyes very considerably, but we must not ask too much of them.

MRS. A. Man's intelligence is faulty. Is the intelligence of the cosmoses above also faulty?

MR. O. I don't know. I have the right to take them as analogous to me.

MR. D. Why?

MR. O. Why not?

MR. L. You spoke of three lines of ideas: practical, theoretical and philosophical. You said that for esoteric man theoretical ideas become practical. Can ideas such as these ever become practical?

MR. O. If you are in esoteric circle. But you must be there. You cannot speak philosophically about practical things. If you understand the structure of this system, you will see that all limitations of ours are taken into consideration. Yet our knowledge can increase and increase. Only the idea of scale is taken into consideration. . . . The Ray of Creation is for something different, the division into cosmoses is for something different. Every construction of this kind is for one certain purpose. Try to find analogies: why is universe divided differently? Take man: how differently he can be divided. He can be divided into four parts: body, soul, essence and personality, and there is the anatomical division. Obviously we cannot mix them. It is just the same here.

MISS T. Is each centre a cosmos?

MR. O. No. Also each centre is not just one organ. It occupies the whole body.

MISS T. I asked because their time is different.

MR. O. Each centre connects man with a different cosmos by its speed of reaction. That is another thing. It is necessary first to understand the rules and then speak about exceptions.

MR. L. In space all cosmoses are inside one another?

MR. O. What is space? You ask as though it is understood.

MR. L. Is there a geological theory that puts the period of life of organic life at that? Has the system some evidence as to this period?

MR. O. No. It gives certain principles that can give a new view even of facts considered to be known. Apart from that—the length of geological periods is very unstable. There are so many different theories.

MR. C. You say each cosmos is three-dimensional. Do they have length, breadth and height, or something quite different? What is fourth dimension to us could be one of the three to them?

MR. O. No, it is just the same. What is fourth dimension to us is our life. All the fourth dimensions of microcosmos make tritocosmos, etc.

MR. J. Is mesocosmos all planets?

MR. O. All, and even one. It is not important. It is details.

There are some analogies that can be found in scientific theories, and very interesting ones in Indian writings—calculations of solar years, etc. One can find very interesting correspondences. For instance, in one place in Indian writings it says: Brahma inhales and exhales the universe. It is interesting that in this table, breath of Brahma corresponds to life of macrocosmos. Also, in another place, life of Brahma corresponds to life of sun (fifteen figures). Here Brahma is taken as sun.

It would be very interesting to apply to this table Minkovsky's formula. This formula means the speed of light multiplied by a certain period of time and multiplied by square root minus one (imaginary quantity) which transfers it from one denomination to another. By this formula life of an electron corresponds to 30 centimetres. That means that light passes 30 centimetres during the life of one electron. During the life of the next cosmos it passes 10 kilometres. This gives a definite visual picture of what the difference of time means.

I will give you a very interesting method of thinking about time. Think how time would be transformed looking on from another cosmos—phenomena of sound, rain, seasons, etc. You will see then how relative everything is. Things are such because of the rate of our perception. It also explains the idea of relativity—that everything exists only in certain conditions. In different conditions it changes.

MISS N. How can we observe this?

MR. O. We can only calculate like a physical problem.

MR. L. According to that, reality is a purely relative idea?

MR. O. Reality is a very complicated idea—more complicated than we think. We think one aspect of reality is real. But each one aspect is relative. But a combination of all aspects must be real.

The teaching on cosmoses is very important. The system says that science and philosophy only begin at that point. It gives the possibility of finding uniting principles, to see relations, connections.

MISS C. Each cosmos feeds on the one above?

MR. O. I did not say anything about feed.

MR. L. Are all physical phenomena connected together?

MR. O. Which? Forget words 'all', 'everything'. We have no right to use them. You must specify. Phenomena are different.

MR. L. Phenomena which pass within range of our experience. Are they connected?

MR. O. Maybe. We cannot take them as one thing. They are different. If you want to speak about a certain kind of phenomena, then speak; but not about all. You forget the characteristic thing about human life, that we are surrounded by the seventh dimension—by non-existing things. You don't know even the principle of how to divide existing from non-existing, and you speak about 'all phenomena'. And how to divide? By finding in oneself what is real and what is not real. When one is able to see it in oneself and to divide them, then one will be able to do it in everything else.

* * *

Thursday. September 19th 1935.

[Some questions were read and answered.]

MR. O. You may believe me or not, but if we go on in this way we need at least three hundred years to achieve some results. It is useless to continue in this way. Lectures began last September. I asked you to bring more questions to see if it is worth continuing. And I see that it is not worth while. So it will be the last meeting. Those who want to continue can write to me and explain why they should continue and why I should lose my time to continue.

Theoretical study of the system is impossible. It must be practical. And this means work on emotions and on will. Without this it is impossible. Influences C, if not taken in the right way, become influences B. This means that the system becomes ordinary philosophy. I advise you to think about it and to write to me. For some people it may be necessary still to continue in this way, but for others it is necessary to do something about it, not only to listen and talk. This refers to those who began last September or later. With those who began earlier I will speak separately.

Life is not long enough for changing being if one works like we do everything else in life. Something can be attained only if one uses a kind of perfected method. The first condition is understanding. All the rest is proportionate to understanding. There must also be efforts in connection with emotions and will. One must be able to go against oneself, to give up one's will. I mentioned it before, but nobody noticed it or thought what it means to give up will, and how one can do it and when.

MR. H. You mean going against what one likes?

MR. O. This is too general. First you must ask yourself—what is will? We have no will. So how to give up what we don't have? It means, first, that you never agree that you have no will. You only agree in words. Secondly—we don't always have will but only at times. Will means a strong desire. If there is no strong desire—there is nothing to give up, there is no will. Another moment we have a strong desire that is against work, and if we stop it, it means we give up will. It is not every moment that we can give up will, but only at special moments. And what does it mean 'against work'? It means against rules and principles of the work, or against something you are personally told to do or not to do. There are general and personal conditions. There are certain general rules and principles. Afterwards, when one is supposed to have understood the fundamental things, people may have separate conditions.

MR. C. Much more effort is needed on the psychological side?

MR. O. It is all psychological.

MR. L. Is it against school if one tries to study other systems?

MR. O. It depends what systems. Mathematics is harmless, study of astrology is stupid.

MR. L. Systems that increase our knowledge?

MR. O. If you run after two hares, you lose both.

MR. H. Why have you given up your time to us?

MR. O. The question is about you, not about me.

MR. B. Is laziness—work against system?

MR. O. Laziness may have different manifestations. I did not mean that.

MRS. W. Should one ask for further personal directions?

MR. O. Yes, but if one asks, one must obey. One is not obliged to do anything if one does not ask. But if one asks, one must obey. So before asking one must think twice.

MR. J. If one is prepared to obey, will you give directions?

MR. O. If opportunity offers. It must be a moment when you have will.

MR. J. The moment of asking is will?

MR. O. No, it may be curiosity. There must be a definite desire to do something that affects work or other people. Usually we have bad will. We very seldom have good will. If you have good will, I don't speak about it; I simply say, go on, continue, learn.

There are many things mixed here. You don't know how to think about it. On one side you realize you are machines, but the next moment you want to act according to your own opinion. Then at this moment you must be able to stop, not to do what you want. But not at moments when you have no intention of doing anything. You must be able to stop if it goes against rules, or principles, or against what you are told. It often happens that people go on studying and miss these moments. They think they work when nothing happens. And when such moments come, they miss them. We cannot work equally always. At one moment passive study, theories are sufficient. At another moment it is necessary to oppose your movement, to stop.

MR. R. What causes these moments?

MR. O. Desire. Resultant of desires is will. If one strong desire conquers, it gives direction to desires.

MR. R. It comes unexpectedly?

MR. O. Sometimes one can foresee that a man is reaching something.

I speak of such desire that may have connection with work. One has to work on three lines. If one works on the second or third line, his desires may affect other people.

MISS S. How can one work, except at self-observation?

MR. O. This is study. When your moment comes, you will see. If you don't understand now, leave it, talk with other people. Perhaps your moment has not come yet.

MISS M. Has obeying something to do with breaking up of personality?

MR. O. Sometimes, in serious cases. No orders will be given you that are not connected with work. Your personality has its own opinions. If you find it necessary to go against that, it will be work against personality.

*　　*　　*

[Written questions.]

MR. D. Is the reason why it takes so much longer to obtain results in following objective ways that one is under the Law of Accident, whereas in any of the four ways one is under the direction of conscious influences?

MR. O. The question answers itself. One is under the Law of Accident in everything. Everything happens in life, and even in relation to this work. Look at your life and see if you come to the realization of necessity of a school.

MR. D. If knowledge is material, I don't see how even the smallest amount of it can be communicated through a book, for example the New Testament. Surely something material must always be communicated directly by a human being?

MR. O. We speak about knowledge contained in influences C. In books it is only influences B. But you can always make B out of C, only you cannot get C out of B. This partly answers also Mr. L.'s question.

MR. D. In the Fourth Way is greater use made of the third triad than in the other ways?

MR. O. Who can measure?

MR. D. Are the catastrophic triads operating at the present moment due to moon's influence?

MR. O. What is a catastrophic triad? Everything is due to moon's influence. Catastrophes are produced by a combination of moon's and planets' influences.

MR. H. Mr. O. spoke once of there being an aim which concerns us all. Will he speak again about this?

MR. O. Which aim? In the sense of school? Or humanity?

MR. H. Where is it best to direct one's attention when any effort at self-remembering is too difficult?

MR. O. Maybe effort at self-remembering is difficult, but realization that we cannot remember ourselves cannot be difficult. If one is sincere for a moment, one realizes that it is so.

MR. H. Is trying to self-remember the most direct approach to the development of being?

MR. O. Yes, but not only alone. It must be in connection with other things.

MR. M. Is concentration a state in which one applies oneself to a piece of work and is also physically aware of one's surroundings; and identification a condition in which one is completely at the mercy of the thing which is engaging one's attention?

MR. O. I did not use the word concentration. Concentration presupposes control. As we cannot control anything, it is impossible for us. There are books written about necessity of concentration. But how to concentrate? We cannot keep our mind under control for two minutes.

MR. M. If you are doing some work. . . .

MR. O. Then the thing makes you concentrate. It is mechanical. It is not you that concentrate. It is like attention. Attention can be drawn and kept, or can one direct it? These are different facts. You must learn to see facts, see whether we can do it or not.

MR. M. Can I in my present state observe the interval in an octave of work?

MR. O. You may occasionally find intervals in your own work.

MISS S. Self-observation seems to weaken one's self-control. Is this imagination or just seeing clearly?

MR. O. Pure imagination. How can it weaken control if you have no self-control? It can only strengthen it, if it is the right self-observation.

MISS C. Does the magnetic centre develop with the development of being?

MR. O. No. Magnetic centre has nothing to do with work in groups. And being can develop even in life.

MISS C. When I go to a play I find that for some time after I have left the theatre I have an unsettled feeling, and find it difficult to talk to people. Is this identification?

MR. O. I don't know.

MR. R. What is the soul?

MR. O. In what sense? It is a theoretical question.

MR. R. Is a nation a cosmos?

MR. O. No, simply a white spot.

MR. R. Why is it that when people are in a crowd their emotions are intensified?

MR. O. Not necessarily. Sometimes, particularly with moving people No. 1 it is so, because their chief feature is imitation. But only with men No. 1. As the majority are No. 1, it may be so.

MR. S. Can one perceive buffers at our present level of consciousness?

MR. O. Yes, in other people, not in ourselves.

MR. S. If we raise our level of being will it be possible to change our chief feature?

MR. O. Probably, perhaps even get rid of it altogether.

MR. S. Why did you stress the intervals in Dr. Fludd's diagrams of octaves.

MR. O. Because in many other descriptions of octaves they don't mention intervals. Octaves are mentioned by other philosophers, but they don't mention intervals as something important.

MISS R. With regard to the fact that each cosmos is three-dimensional and stands in relation of zero to infinity to the one above, does it mean that what appears as space phenomena for one appears as time phenomena for the one above it?

MR. O. Possible, but I can say no further.

MISS R. If the different centres work at different speeds has each centre a different sense of time?

MR. O. Certainly quite different. There is a certain correspondence, because they all live together in the same body. That is why some people have an extraordinary capacity to know time. Instinctive centre knows it. If they are connected, then intellectual centre also knows time.

MISS R. Would time for an individual conscious in higher emotional centre synchronize with time as it appears in mesocosmos?

MR. O. It is too theoretical. We don't know. What we count by the movement of the sun is our own calculation, not that of mesocosmos.

MR. C. I find that imagination is often associated with muscular tension. Could Mr. O. say more of the special exercises to help one to relax?

MR. O. Before exercises are possible, use all the simple methods. The best method is hard physical work.

MRS. L. How can one choose the right impressions?

MR. O. What do you mean? How can one choose impressions?

MRS. L. The only way I know how to produce deep enough shocks is to continue to turn the shock over in my mind.

MR. O. It is impossible to say without an example. In some cases maybe.

MRS. L. One must give up. Does it mean change of attitude, or is it effort?

MR. O. May be effort, or change of attitude, or many other things.

MR. R. A few times a year a line of action becomes particularly clear to me. That which seemed very difficult then becomes very simple and is backed up by enthusiasm. I know by experience that if I put off following this line at once, the opportunity will not show itself again for a long time, if ever. Those well marked lines of action sometimes come as a result of effort, but quite often from no cause that I can discover. What is the reason of this, and how can these moments be made to come more often and last longer? I have been subject to these moments all my life and have come to think it useless to take any serious action without what would be ordinarily called inspiration.

MR. O. I cannot say without knowing in what direction, in relation to what. As a matter of fact it is quite right. There are periods in ordinary conditions when nothing happens, and then there come cross-roads. All life consists of streets and cross-roads. Even the turning in cross-roads may become more systematic if one has a centre of gravity. Then one thing continues to be important and one always turns in one direction. But inspiration has nothing to do with it. It is simply realization of a moment when you can do something.

MRS. R. Mr. O. told us of five states of real sleep and left it to us to find the corresponding states in waking sleep. Are they these: deep sleep corresponds to the usual state of ordinary man; deep sleep aware of having dreams but unable to remember them corresponds to the state of man when beginning to be interested in this system; sleep with dreams remembered corresponds to state of man when he has tried to work on himself; light sleep, dreams known in sleep to be dreams, corresponds to man able to recognize his own identifications; light sleep with dreams controlled corresponds to man able to self-remember.

MR. O. You began too high. There are many states below ordinary man. People who are ill, or too identified, or hypnotized by formatory ideas are more machines than ordinary man. Ordinary man is already a very high state, because from this state it is possible to move. All these religious and theosophical teachers are really below normal. They hypnotize themselves by words. When people speak of doing, it corresponds to changing the names of the days of the week. All our power is only over words. Change names of the days of the week is the maximum people can do. Normal man is a man who understands that it is all nonsense. He is on a higher level. Usually people are below normal: they are lunatics, tramps or sincere scoundrels. Lunatics have many variations. Only from the level of ordinary man does possibility begin.

MR. J. By what means can one quicken the change of being?

MR. O. By understanding only. The more one understands, the more one can do and have results from the same effort.

MR. J. You said that knowledge is material. Doesn't it mean that it should be used in a practical way?

MR. O. Quite right. But how? If you say it must be _understood_ in a practical way—yes. But act you cannot.

MR. J. Most of one's struggle for existence seems to belong to imaginary things. It takes such a lot of one's time that little is left for the study of real things. What is one to do?

MR. O. One can give the time that remains free. Or one may struggle too much.

MRS. H. Doesn't a real change of attitude through this work bring about a certain degree of change of being?

MR. O. Change of attitude does not bring about change of being by itself. But valuation is necessary. Nothing can be achieved without it.

MRS. H. Is it possible to learn something of essence from memories of childhood?

MR. O. You can if you have a good memory and can find things that change and that don't.

MRS. H. How can we learn more about the underlayer of thought that is going on all the time. Does it stop in our moments of self-remembering?

MR. O. By observation only. It may stop and it may not.

MISS R. I don't understand what consciousness is. It seems to be something apart from the cosmoses.

MR. O. Take it in yourself—you can know degrees in yourself. If you know that, you know what consciousness is.

MISS R. Is man's body from life to death his existence in the cosmos of organic life?

MR. O. Quite right.

MISS R. Is it possible for one centre to sleep when another is awake? For instance, can one consciously put moving centre to sleep?

MR. O. One must be conscious for that. But it often happens that one centre is asleep and another awake. For instance, instinctive centre, or moving, is awake, and intellectual asleep.

MISS R. What is the significance of the fact that the rotation of the earth corresponds in time with the breathing of organic life?

MR. O. The question is to find the answer.

MISS R. Can man ever become conscious on a scale higher than that of the sun cosmos? If not how can he ever know all?

MR. O. Let him become conscious on his own scale first.

MISS R. If a man can be conscious on the scale of a different cosmos surely the matter in him connected with these impressions must exist in that cosmos?

MR. O. Quite possible. I cannot answer for the situation in other cosmoses.

MR. S. I seem able to interrupt day-dreams with increasing frequency. But the interruption is only momentary and others take their place. Is any progress effected by the mere act of interrupting day-dreams?

MR. O. For observation only, not for actual stopping. To stop them many other things are necessary.

MR. S. In shooting I notice I am most successful in hitting birds when I have had a certain amount of alcohol. Am I right in supposing that the effect of alcohol is to correct in some way the wrong work of intellectual centre?

MR. O. I heard this many times. But it is an unreliable method. It is very difficult to calculate the right amount of alcohol necessary.

MR. S. Is the anxiety about catching a train, when there is no reason for it, due to employing centres wrongly?

MR. O. It is impossible to say. It is necessary to know associations connected with it.

MR. L. Does being depend entirely on state of consciousness?

MR. O. No. Do you mean is being determined by state of consciousness? Then yes. But other things also enter into being. Generally being is determined not by one feature, but by all together. On one level of being one is many, one is asleep, etc. On next level all these things change.

MR. L. How can one start to approach the accumulator of knowledge?

MR. O. By learning, if one has a chance.

MR. L. What differentiation does the system make between material and matter?

MR. O. Matter, as it is taken in physics, is not enough. Materiality goes further than that.

MR. L. What relationship is there between being and existence?

MR. O. We use the word being. Existence is used in the sense of process, but being—in the sense of determining the level.

MR. L. Have things in themselves a different existence from that which we infer them to have by our sense perceptions?

MR. O. It depends which things. You cannot take all things as similar. They are all different.

MR. L. Does time impose conditions that make it favourable or unfavourable to make attempts at 'doing'?

MR. O. What means time? For whom? How?

MR. L. There is time to sow and time to reap. . . .

MR. O. If it is in this sense, you refer to school-work. You cannot speak of school-work. Although certainly everything has its own time.

MR. L. Is correct proportion the result of a rightly completed octave?

MR. O. It is impossible to say.

MRS. W. You spoke of the dangers of using one centre for another. But is it not useful to try to apply each centre to a given problem, to try to get an intellectual grasp of it and to carry out action with emotion? One seems to go further with a plan if it is not only thought out, but carried out quickly when one has an emotion of enthusiasm.

MR. O. I did not speak from that point of view. We have no control. One centre works for another, but we cannot use them.

MRS. W. Is response to our environment a matter of being? One may travel to the ends of the earth and gain very little from the experience, if one goes as a tourist with everything done for one. But effort in travel and finding things for oneself do seem to enrich a personality.

MR. O. It depends on taste.

MRS. W. If an octave is broken is it simply lost or can it be resumed and carried on? Could you apply the law of octaves to a friendship and its interruption through some outside circumstance?

MR. O. It is more or less theoretical. It needs a long discussion.

MRS. W. I find that I often want to ask a question about something I have read or heard, and do not ask because it is not my own thought or experience. Does it show imitation or is it simply mental laziness?

MR. O. It would be quite good if you ask.

MR. P. I want to know all truth that it is good for me to know in the present state of my being. How can I discover if it is a lie?

MR. O. Almost for everything you know you have methods for verifying. But first you must know what you can know and what you cannot. That helps verifying. If you start with that you will soon hear lies without thinking even. Lies have a different sound, particularly lies about things we cannot know.

Q. I have found that the habit of smoking is much more difficult to break than the habit of reading papers. Is this because reading papers is only part of a larger habit of reading for entertainment, and smoking is more in instinctive centre?

MR. O. It is a personal observation—too insufficient to compare the two.

MR. S. Does responsibility for one's actions depend upon the level of one's being?

MR. O. Responsibility depends on many things. Personality can create responsibility. If one asks something, if one says one wants to work, one creates a responsibility. And being may not have yet reached the right level. Then personality must answer.

MR. S. Is it possible to know what one wants without imagination?

MR. O. Imagination won't help, it will only make the problem more difficult.

MR. S. Does right effort to change being depend on knowing clearly what one wants?

MR. O. You must know what you want.

MISS O. Is the purpose of the creation of man that a mere handful should attain to a higher state?

MR. O. I don't know.

MISS O. Would you explain how energy is gained by remembering impressions?

MR. O. Not by remembering, but by drawing attention to. Impression is doubled, intensified by observation.

MR. T. What organic changes have taken place in individual men and humanity during the last four hundred years from the point of view of the system? And what organic changes are taking place at this moment? I ask these questions because I want to know why work is necessary at all?

MR. O. I cannot answer from the point of view of the last four hundred years. You can find details in an encyclopaedia. About the necessity for work you must decide only for yourself and know only for you.

MR. T. How does it happen that ideas of the system get distorted? I see how they become distorted in other people and I am certain it is the same with me. Yet how can I avoid my mistakes?

MR. O. By not talking about things you don't understand.

MR. T. What is the meaning of organization? What is to be organized?

MR. O. It has many meanings. We may talk about it later. It is useful to speak about organization with those who will continue.

MR. T. I regard myself subjectively as the whole world for myself and I know that it is wrong. But is a machine objectively a world in itself?

MR. O. [Not recorded.]

MR. B. Mr. O. spoke of knowledge as material, and that there are accumulators of knowledge analogous to accumulators of energy in human machine, also that there is a main accumulator of knowledge and that a contact could be established with it. How can we work to find this main accumulator? Is it something within ourselves? Or is it something outside ourselves for which we must search? Does this refer to schools?

MR. O. You can work to come into contact with it just by learning what you can learn. It refers to both, to oneself and to schools.

MISS H. I have been making many unsuccessful efforts to deal with unpleasant circumstances, and the problem has been solved by an escape from these circumstances. Is it imagination that makes one feel that this is no solution and the same problem will come up again?

MR. O. It is possible.

MISS H. I was told that essence can be developed through a reform of personality. Is it right to suppose that a person with a highly developed personality would find it more difficult?

MR. O. Yes and no. Not so much depends on the weight of personality as on its state, whether it is educated, badly educated or uneducated. It may be in the power of imaginary 'I' and then it is wrong.

MISS M. You said, in speaking about will, that first it would be the will of other people, and later our own. How shall we come under the will of other people?

MR. O. When you come into contact with the second and third line of work you necessarily come into contact with will of others. . . .

*   *   *

Wednesday. October 2nd 1935.

MR. B. When I try to stop negative emotions something crops up in myself which says: If I stop expressing these emotions I shall be more comfortable. When I started out to try it was in order to save energy. What is the cause of this and what can I do about it?

MR. O. Cause of what?

MR. B. Cause of change of attitude?

MR. O. Where is change of attitude?

MISS C. Why is it that when I am doing something, such as walking, I have the feeling of watching myself?

MR. O. That is what you should do.

MRS. M. I constantly find myself playing a rôle, against my conscious wishes and efforts. Will you help me to understand what part of me does this and how to check it?

MR. O. It is necessary first to know all your rôles. When you know them all, then we can speak about it.

MRS. M. How can I give up my will?

MR. O. It is necessary first to find what you call your will. Then we can discuss it.

MRS. H. When one self-remembers does one stop the whole machine for that moment, and should not one be able to do something for the machine then, that one cannot do when it is going at its usual speed?

MR. O. Self-remembering is an <u>additional</u> function. It is really a state but it begins as function. Only it is <u>additional</u>.

MRS. H. I don't understand the difference between personality and false personality. Is false personality a large imaginary 'I'?

MR. O. It is imaginary 'I'.

MRS. S. The desire to succeed in whatever one undertakes must be good, because without it one makes no effort to attain one's aim. Yet the stronger the desire to succeed is, the more intense are the negative emotions of anger and disappointment when one fails. Is it possible to get rid of these unpleasant emotions and still retain in the same degree the desire to succeed?

MR. O. The question is who desires to succeed. I cannot answer in general.

MRS. S. Does the system teach that unless a man is self-conscious it is impossible for him to receive help from God?

MR. O. This is a religious question; I cannot answer it.

MR. H. Is it best for those who want to work in groups to ask your help or the help of other people who have been longer in the work?

MR. O. It depends in what.

MRS. W. If knowledge is material is thought also material? Is the word spiritual used at all in the system?

MR. O. Only to explain that it must not be used.

MRS. W. Will you tell us something about obedience and sacrifice of will required in addition to keeping rules?

MR. O. I will speak about that.

MRS. W. In trying to overcome the faults I can recognize in myself I find that I can see them more clearly but cannot affect them. Can we help each other in group work when individual effort seems to have no effect?

MR. O. In organized work, yes, but not by individual enterprise.

MISS C. Is there any particular effort one can make to try and conquer mood—if you try to do something and don't want to do it?

MR. O. There can be no general answer. Things are different.

MISS S. Is there anything else one can do except self-observation to further the understanding of the system?

MR. O. Yes, one must understand what and why one is doing. The more one understands, the more one can get.

*   *   *

Thursday. October 24th 1935.

MR. R. Is there not a very thin border-line between what Mr. O. calls 'understanding' in this system and faith?

MR. O. Faith on our level is only superstition. On another level faith may be a kind of higher knowledge; but this we cannot have. There may be a belief in something higher, and this may be the beginning of real faith.

MRS. A. About this question of faith—I thought that faith had been rather eliminated. I cannot remember any demands being made on our faith.

MR. O. Yes, I have said one must not simply believe what one is told. One must try to understand.

MR. N. Are all emotions acquired? Or are they all latent in us when we are born and then develop as occasion demands?

MR. O. To some extent emotions are born.

MISS V. If something that we hear here seems absolutely understandable and true without any need to think about it, is it that we are for that moment conscious? Because afterwards I forget what I understood and how I understood it—it is only words. That also happens with certain emotions—afterwards I can only remember them from outside, intellectually. Does that mean they were positive?

MR. O. Conscious or not conscious does not enter here. Without examples it is impossible to say. It may be that you understood with both intellect and emotions and then afterwards emotions disappear and the picture changes. Of one thing you can be sure, that if you once understood something it will return if you continue to work.

Q. Is there anything in this system which will help one of the students who is passing through some kind of trouble? You cannot just tell people that it would be an interesting opportunity to study their emotions!

MR. O. It depends on the trouble you speak about. In many cases knowing ourselves better will help. Most of our troubles are due to our own weaknesses, and if we know ourselves better this may change our attitude.

MR. M. Mr. O. has used the expression—'all organic life'. Is it suggested that there are other forms of life?

MR. O. There is no such term as <u>all</u> organic life.

MRS. H. It was said that all forms of organic life feed on each other. What feeds on man?

MR. O. Gnats and mosquitoes and bacteria feed on man.

MISS C. What kind of effort will help us to create more understanding, or do all efforts help?

MR. O. You must start from facts. It cannot be answered in general.

MRS. R. I find that inertia is my greatest opponent in the struggle to find myself—to become aware. How can I best overcome this powerful handicap? The inertia is mental as well as physical and almost paralyses my great desire to progress.

MR. O. What do you mean by inertia? It is just a descriptive term. Inertia works in everybody, and neither helps nor hinders in itself. You must continue to observe and try to see more concretely.

MRS. B. If at the moment I see mechanicalness and go against it with the right effort, I sometimes see and understand something. What happens that gives that understanding?

MR. O. It is a matter for observation. <u>You</u> must yourself answer this question. You will get an answer only if you observe facts and see the conditions, internal and external, which accompany understanding and which accompany lack of understanding.

MR. M. Among religious people there is a widely-held belief in the existence of a human soul. Does the system contain any concept which approximates to the idea of soul?

MR. O. The idea of soul as a separate organism controlling the physical body cannot be said to be based on anything. The nearest approach to the idea of soul as it was understood up to the seventeenth century is what is called essence. The term soul is used in the system, but in the sense of life principle only. Essence, personality and soul in the system, taken together, correspond to what used to be called soul. But soul was supposed to have a separate existence from the body, and we don't suppose a separate existence of these three from the body.

MRS. W. Can fate in no circumstances affect the things that happen to us, but only the things we are born with?

MR. O. Many things can happen because of fate, only in most cases they don't happen. Really the action of fate is only a possibility.

MISS C. Do you think that people must have some belief to carry them through their lives, or can the present feeling of futility go on indefinitely?

MR. O. What people do you mean?

MISS C. Any people.

MR. O. You cannot speak about 'any people'. You can speak about people out of school or in school. And according to that the answer will be different.

MISS C. Out of school, can one live without any belief at all?

MR. O. Most people believe in something. It is human nature to believe in something. In what, depends on education, surroundings, the period in which they live, reading, etc.

MISS C. When people rush about all the time they don't seem to have time to believe in anything. Can it go on through life?

MR. O. People are asleep and dream that they are awake. So they never want to awake and they never see how they pass their lives. People cannot become conscious unconsciously.

MISS C. But can you go on indefinitely if you don't believe in something higher?

MR. O. People can believe in higher, but quite impossible, things.

MR. R. When Mr. O. said that although different religions give quite different teachings they could all be true, did he mean that there is no such thing as absolute truth?

MR. O. I did not speak about all religious ideas, but only about all the existing ideas about future life. They are all true, with the exception, perhaps, of quite mad ideas. Human mind cannot invent a wrong idea, only each of them is true only in one case, another in another case, etc. They are all true, but not fully. Truth about future life is such a complicated truth that we can know it only in objective state of consciousness. I spoke about that even in the first lecture. In objective consciousness we can know truth about anything, perhaps it needs effort, but still we can. In self-consciousness we can know truth about ourselves. In our state of consciousness truth is relative. In the state of sleep we have no relation to truth at all.

MR. R. Is absolute truth only possible with objective consciousness? If Mr. O. would tell us more about truth we would understand better what he means by lying.

MR. O. Truth exists without us, but we can <u>know</u> truth only in objective state of consciousness. Not absolute truth, but simply—truth (truth does not need qualifications). In our state we cannot know truth with the exception of very simple things, and even then we make mistakes. It would be very good if we were in a state of objective consciousness, for then I would show you all the examples of truth. But in our state we must start with lying. We cannot study truth. But we can study lying.

MR. R. Can a man be said to be lying if he tells or teaches that which is true for him to those for whom it is not true? If so, all is lying that is not absolute truth?

MR. O. It is a little complicated. The question is—does he know what he teaches or does he simply imagine things. It is possible to verify this. Many people teach about things they cannot know. There are things we can know and things we cannot know. If people in the same state of consciousness as ourselves speak about things they cannot know, then obviously they lie.

MRS. R. If I felt sure, as Mr. O. does, that there is higher consciousness, and that this system comes from that source—then I could understand the desire to work on levels 2 and 3 and also the possibility of some form of permanent life. But being told so does not make me <u>know</u>.

MR. O. Even in your present state you can find in yourself very different levels of consciousness. If you see them, you can see the possibility of still higher states. This can be understood without any necessity to verify the third and fourth states of consciousness.

MRS. R. Is the knowledge of higher consciousness, and the certainty that this system could only come from such a source, attained by what we find in ourselves, by self-remembering and by no other means?

MR. O. Yes, this is the central figure. But the conviction that the ideas of the system come from a higher source can be attained in another way. If you cannot find these ideas in science, they must come from a different source. But the foundation of all is to find different states of consciousness.

MRS. S. Can Mr. O. tell us something about humour? Is humour a point of contact of two ideas that are usually very far apart, and which centres does it affect?

MR. O. Humour, sense of the comic, begins in the intellectual centre. In our state it is one of the higher faculties, but it does not go further. In higher centres there is no laughter.

MRS. S. How can we have an aim until we are more conscious? Must not our only aim at present be to become more conscious?

MR. O. Yes, but you don't speak with yourself in these terms. The direction must be taken from the very beginning but the definition of aim can change.

MISS C. Does lack of interest in current events, newspapers and suchlike, come from a deep state of sleep, or is its boredom a negative emotion? Could you define it?

MR. O. I cannot define it, it is just words. Lack of interest in those things can be lack of understanding or it can be understanding. Between the two there is a great difference. So how can I say what is the cause of your lack of interest? As a matter of fact it is very useful to be interested in things. If one is indifferent to one thing and to another, one will, after a time, be indifferent to everything. But only observation can show you the cause of your indifference.

MISS L. When I am shy or hurt I find that my emotional centre interferes with my moving and instinctive centres. How can I help to overcome this?

MR. O. Just observe and try not to identify. It is necessary to speak further about it. Maybe it is connected with feature.

MISS H. Is all visualization imagination? When I observe myself I find that I have to continually check my imagination from useless mental pictures because I seem to use it for nothing else.

MR. O. Imagination is what you cannot control. . . .

MRS. N. When is imagination constructive? Is it the same thing as visualization? Useless imagination and useful visualization appear to be very near together.

MR. O. We can only distinguish whether it is under control or not. Imagination is not under control. But without examples I can say nothing.

MISS H. I have noticed that when I am strung up or nervous this affects moving centre, even though I am going to use intellectual centre. I get these attacks of nerves apparently without any real cause, or identification with any particular thing, and trying to control them only makes things worse. Does this mean that emotional centre is not working properly, and if so, how can I try to correct this?

MR. O. In relation to observations you cannot use the word 'centre'. Centre is a theoretical principle. You cannot observe centres. Observations must be described in ordinary words.

MR. C. Does inner octave mean that between two notes of the major octave there is a whole octave different in quality and dimension of waves? Is there a causal relation between the two—the completion of the inner octave conditioning the passage from one note to the other in the major one—or is the relation one of simultaneity?

MR. O. We must wait till we come to this. Inner octaves play a very important part, but it is necessary to take the whole picture of inner octaves, for there is not one layer but many layers. Inside inner octaves there are still other inner octaves.

MISS R. This idea of separation has given me a feeling of great freedom. The sense of being unidentified with the whole machine, and viewing it objectively.

MR. O. It may be right and it may be imagination. What can you put against the machine? It is necessary to continue and not be satisfied. . . .

MISS R. In talking about separation Mr. O. said it was necessary to know if we had the right feeling. How can one know this?

MR. O. Examples are necessary.

MISS R. I understood that in our present state we were incapable of consciousness. Yet Mr. O. said that to accomplish anything in life work, it is done consciously.

MR. O. Relatively consciously. Consciousness is relative term. And I never said that. We have only glimpses of self-consciousness and no objective consciousness at all. But consciousness is measured by time. All depends how long consciousness remains. There are many things about which, in order to understand them, it is necessary to understand that they are measured by time.

MISS R. I do not know any of the new members personally, and I have not spoken to or discussed anything with them. Are we to form groups among ourselves?

MR. O. Groups will be organized soon, when we have material for them. Then you must meet and talk on definite questions.

*　　*　　*

I spoke about modern scientific ideas coming nearer to the ideas of the system. For some people it may be strange why we speak about the origin of worlds. But people cannot help thinking about it in one or another way, and it is better to have right ideas about it than quite wrong ideas. It is interesting that although modern psychology recedes

86

further and further from the ideas of the system, physics comes nearer. Many things in the article that you will hear are wrong and not valuable, so you must be careful how you take it. It cannot all be taken as pure money. Some things are right and some are wrong.

[Article on expanding universe read.]

It is largely a private opinion of the author. Also he uses terms which by themselves are blind-alleys, such as attraction and repulsion. But what is interesting is that it is almost the same as the origin of worlds in this system. The whole explodes and each subsequent unit explodes and produces smaller and smaller worlds. Also this idea of finite but limitless universe—it existed thousands of years ago in teachings similar to this system. [See diagram below.]

Here we have the whole Ray of Creation—the Absolute, then all worlds (all galaxies together); all suns (all solar systems); our solar system, earth and moon. Here you have everything in exactly the same right relationship, only in the system we take only one ray of creation

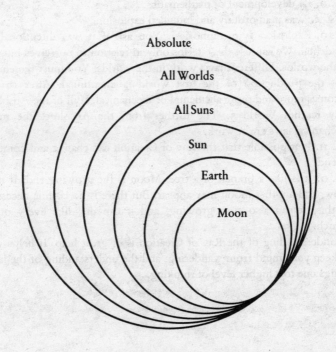

(our ray). We take only the Absolute as a whole, and then only one of each worlds.

MR. N. I don't understand the difference between bounded and unlimited universe.

MR. O. Better to say finite, yet unlimited. Limited is when you know the limit. The idea of finite universe is necessary. In the system this was accepted long ago. Even the time of the Absolute is known. And if the life of the Absolute is limited, then its extension in space is also limited. Take this as an idea. In mathematical sense even infinity means simply limit of possible calculation. But physically infinity comes much nearer to us. Two things compared by size may be mathematically calculable and yet one is infinity in relation to another. But that is not important. What is interesting is the correspondence between scientific ideas and the ideas of the system. Forty years ago it was much more difficult to fit the ideas of physics into the system than it is now. Not all is right, but lately physics has made tremendous steps forward.

MR. R. How could modern science come into line with the system?

MR. O. By development of mathematics. . . .

MRS. A. Was it an orderly and intended explosion?

MR. O. Explosion is metaphorical. You ask if it was intentional or accidental. We can use these terms only in relation to ourselves but not to the worlds. Different laws work in the worlds. You must remember that the production of the first world is intentional. After that it becomes more and more accidental or mechanical. Will of the Absolute only reaches World 3. The further from the Absolute, the more mechanical laws are at work.

MR. H. Is it possible that the Ray of Creation can change and come to an end?

MR. O. It is like a branch of a tree. Moon is the growing end. It may grow, and another moon may appear. But there is no cosmic necessity in this, it can also stop growing, and it can die, like every other branch.

Understanding of the Ray of Creation is of great help. It helps you to keep your mind from wandering, and the understanding of the laws brings one to a higher level of thinking.

*　　*　　*

Tuesday. October 29th 1935.

MR. O. It is a great pity that we cannot arrange larger meetings. It would be more interesting for you to hear people talk in new groups, because some very important things become forgotten; people use words, such as separation, without meaning, etc. But at present it cannot be arranged.

MR. W. Is the difficulty to find a room big enough?

MR. O. Yes. This size is useful to begin with. The difficulty is that we don't need a big room for permanent use, for every week. New groups must be small. But at present, in the second year, it would certainly be useful sometimes to meet in a larger place. But there are different sides to it. One question is: what shall we call ourselves? The difficulty is not only that we have not a large place, but other things as well. About fifty people is the right number for most talks. Only sometimes it is useful to have people together in a larger place.

* * *

MISS W. Is there a difference between attention being drawn and being identified?

MR. O. Difference of degree. If your attention is attracted, the next step may be identification.

MRS. M. I am very unclear how far we can use only words of the system?

MR. O. Words used in the system are a help. They must be used when it is necessary.

I cannot understand why there is a kind of tension produced by attempts to think in a new way. The ideas of the system must produce thinking, and instead of that they seem to stop thinking. Naturally one should be able to think with the help of these ideas easier. Ordinarily one line contradicts another. Here there must be no contradictions.

MRS. M. Things I hear in the system seem to illuminate some experiences I had before. Is it useful to give these things when talking to people? For instance, when we came to accumulators, I understood certain things. Are these things of value to tell?

MR. O. I don't know. Many things cannot be defined from the point of view of principles. One or another answer depends on the conversation.

MR. W. There are certain ideas about which you have not talked for a long time, for instance about barriers.

MR. O. That refers to group work. We can talk about them in small groups when a definite example can be given, otherwise it becomes theoretical. What do you wish to know about them?

MR. W. I understood it so little at the time that even the idea of them has almost gone. Are they certain definite steps?

MR. O. No. First this idea must be divided into two. Barriers may arise even out of general rules and tasks. But they arise more often out of individual tasks. Many people made barriers for themselves out of general tasks and could not pass over them by refusing to apply something in practice.

MR. W. The idea is that one gets stuck between two barriers?

MR. O. This is said simply to accentuate certain kinds of danger if people don't want to go over a barrier. But I don't remember a single case of that. Evidently this refers to harder conditions and quicker development, a quicker movement.

MRS. N. Is it characteristic of the Fourth Way that will is developed from self-will and wilfulness?

MR. O. Words, words. . . .

MR. W. Another term you used to use for which I am not sure whether I have invented a meaning. You used to speak about right and left hand. To me it means not to let W. pat himself on the back.

MR. O. It has many meanings and it may be applied to many things. Only in your example there is no secrecy about that, and this refers to secrecy, to the necessity of a certain concealment even from oneself.

Many things are forgotten because we forget the starting point. Things become dull, you have no questions. But the moment we connect with the beginning, we see why and where we are going, what we want to get. Then we realize what we got from the system and that we cannot expect more because of our own fault. We must always remember the starting point, remember that it is connected not simply with words, but with search for the miraculous. All this system would have no meaning if there is no search for the miraculous.

I will tell you a funny thing. Mrs. R. said at last meeting that she was interested in the first line, but not in the second and the third. As you will not hear my answer, I will tell you how I will answer it. The second line must be excluded; people themselves can do nothing themselves. Arrangements come from me and then people either work on second line or do not. But the difference between the first and the third line is this: people who like to slide down must also like to carry the sledge back (Russian proverb). It they like to slide down but don't like to carry the sledge back, then they like the first line but not the third.

We will have much work with the new house; it may begin in December. There will be much work for anyone who wants to do it. . . . Don't forget this example about the sledge.

*   *   *

Thursday. March 19th 1936.

MISS C. In answer to the question: why is conscious evil an impossibility—evil, that is to say, human evil, seems to be completely unnecessary. It is the result of unnecessary mechanical functions, such as unpleasant emotions. Does not the very presence of consciousness eliminate the possibility of purely mechanical actions? Is not evil the lack of consciousness where consciousness should be? Just as lies are a lack of truth?

MR. O. Yes, you can put it like that, only I think there are too many words to explain a simple thing. Evil can only be mechanical. In ordinary life there can only be a subjective idea of evil. Or, further, one can say that on the way to one's aim evil can only pass through mechanicalness.

MISS T. Would it be correct to say that evil cannot exist in a conscious state because complete understanding and evil cannot exist together?

MR. O. [Not recorded.]

MRS. M. Is it right to say that in the state of consciousness there is no identification? That without identification there are no negative emotions?

MR. O. Psychologically you can say that, because you can verify it. Everyone can find it for himself if he tries to manifest negative emotions consciously. He will see he cannot.

MR. N. Would it be true to say that evil is either a negative emotion or the result of one, and therefore cannot exist in a conscious state?

MR. O. That is narrowing the question and giving it a special meaning. It may be, only it is only one form. Illness is evil, but it is not a negative emotion. Illness is mechanicalness.

MRS. N. Does something once memorized remain with us always? If so, is our inability to recall it at all the result of wrong working of centres?

MR. O. It may disappear; there are many different degrees. It may be forgotten and then brought up again by special methods, or it may disappear altogether.

MISS V. For someone in the system does sin consist in not making an effort to remember oneself when one realizes that the effort is necessary and possible?

MR. O. No, better not to introduce unnecessary words. This word belongs to the religious way.

MISS C. I have tried to think why evil cannot be conscious, but I find I do not really understand what is meant by evil. If good and bad are merely relative, how can we know that what seems to us evil is evil in reality? Should we regard as evil simply that which is bad for our aim?

MR. O. You tried to think. It is the wrong way, you cannot find it by thinking, but only by experimenting. Yes, you can say that evil is what is bad for our aim and nothing more. Even that is already a big step from the ordinary idea of evil based on belief or on imitation. You already decide yourself what is evil for you. Actions that definitely go against aim can only be mechanical; many of them interrupt your advance towards your aim. You can only understand evil in relation to yourself; then, when you have understood it, you can understand it in relation to a group of people, a larger group of people, a still larger, and so on.

MISS C. I do not understand how war could ever be good, since it always seems to be the expression of negative emotions and entails maiming and killing people. Perhaps it is only because I can see only a part, and not the whole, and attach too much importance to suffering. Are there any historical examples of wars that were good? If so, how were they good?

MR. O. It is a very difficult question. It is necessary to speak very much, speak about history, about what was the aim of a particular historical period, about whether a war made the existence of schools possible or created situations which made it more difficult for schools to exist. Before I could answer we must agree about the terms we use, then it would be possible to go through times of history and see which wars were better and which were worse, and then perhaps go further. There are political situations that are more favourable for schools and others that are less favourable. Suppose a war creates a better situation, then it is useful. There are many other ways to approach this subject, only we must first speak about many principles. I want you to ask such questions, only I must first know what you know about different periods of history, how you regard, for instance, the nineteenth century, etc.

MR. L. What is evil?

MR. O. What is against awakening, against our becoming one, etc.

MR. L. Is the aim of consciousness to be in complete control of the machine, and is evil the outcome of negative emotions and identification and all that is mechanical and could not exist for conscious man?

MR. O. That is in general. In yourself you find features and tendencies that stand against consciousness, that help resistance. That is evil in oneself. You will see that evil can be manifested only mechanically. A long time is necessary to understand that fully. You may be mistaken, you may take for evil what is not evil, or take something mechanical for conscious.

Referring to a previous question—why it is difficult to speak about historical processes is that people generally mistake two things. First, in history there are events behind which there is a conscious intention that they regard as mechanical, and, second, there are quite mechanical events that are regarded as conscious. That is why we must agree about terms first.

MR. L. Is the temptation of Christ by Satan an analogy of the fact that there can be no conscious evil?

MR. O. No, we cannot take examples from the New Testament. It must be a subject of a special study, for there are too many meanings in what is said in the New Testament. Although, if you like, we may speak about it, only we must agree how to take Satan. If we take him as the spirit of this world—then it is the temptation of mechanical-ness.

MR. L. What is the feeling of remorse which comes from having committed an action which one feels certain in oneself is wrong? Is it conscience?

MR. O. No, conscience is different, stronger, more all-embracing. But even if one remembers the remorses it may be useful. Only it is necessary to know on what the remorse is based.

MRS. R. As to why there can be no conscious evil, is it because conscious man can have no negative emotions such as hate, jealousy, revenge, greed, etc.?

MR. O. Not because of that. You must take it practically, not philosophically. Try to do what you consider evil consciously, and you will see that you cannot.

MISS H. How can I help the part of me that is interested in the system to develop and the other parts to get weaker, so that they don't

94

interfere with the very small part that is for system and that is at the moment smothered by all these other parts?

MR. O. All the study, all you do, all this has the same aim. Everything that reminds you about the work, that gives a possibility of effort, is useful. It does not refer to you personally, but I have observed that people ask me the same question, but when the chance comes and they are told to do something, or not to do something, they go against it, for the very best of reasons. So they miss their opportunity, time passes and later they may see they have missed their opportunity, but it can no longer be replaced by anything. That is self-will.

MISS H. I can see that there is one 'I' which gets very negative and is directly opposed to the system, but when I try to analyse what it is precisely, I cannot explain to myself what it is all about. Sometimes there is no reason at all, and sometimes there are reasons. Sometimes I feel that it is a mistake and that I have got involved in something much bigger than I can ever understand and that I cannot do the smallest thing about it by myself. I cannot even get out of it by myself.

MR. O. Get out of it you can—if you let this 'I' grow, it will get you out. But valuation will grow and then it can be put against this 'I'. You will be able to say for yourself: 'I got this and I got that'. . . .

MISS M. Evil arises from mechanicalness. A conscious person could not act through negative emotion nor be conscious when identified. Also he would not be subject to the Law of Accident.

MR. O. This is narrowing the question. You must not think about conscious man, but only about yourself. You must ask yourself: Can evil be conscious in me? Everything else is philosophy.

MISS M. Some time ago Mr. O. said that we should have to give up wilfulness and submit to the will of other people in all except some very private matters. Does this refer to the so-called decisions which we are always taking, for example, where to go for our holidays? If not, to what things does it refer?

MR. O. This is quite a wrong formulation. These things, when people are told to do something or not to do something, come only after people have been some time in the work. They must deserve it first. And it does not mean that it happens always, but only sometimes. Then, when people are told to do or not to do something, they often say: 'What nonsense, why can't I decide for myself?'—And sometimes it is even said in connection with holidays. One man said once to me that he wanted to go to Italy on a holiday. I looked at him and said: 'You are not ashamed to go to Italy?' And probably even to this day he does not understand what I meant. He was a particular type of man—all his life consisted in passing from one holiday to another. He did not even attempt to understand, so I let it go.

MISS M. It seems that when one is doing things like washing-up, dusting, lighting fires or even walking, which are purely automatic, one should find opportunities for observation. I find, however, that I tend to day-dream even more than usual. Could you give us some advice as to how to do this kind of work for self-observation?

MR. O. Effort is necessary, doing things in an inconvenient way—that will remind you.

MISS M. I try to set myself small tasks such as not to talk about things which are not necessary to keep secret. The best thing that seems to happen is that I remember to do the task, but I do not observe myself or remember myself. Is there any way in which these tasks may become more profitable?

MR. O. It is the same thing—you must find what will remind you.

MISS R. As there can be no good or evil excepting in relation to aim it seems strange to me that good and evil seem to mean something for me in spite of the fact that I cannot exactly formulate my aim.

MR. O. This is philosophy. We are not satisfied with philosophy, we must have facts. On our level, for us, there is good and bad. Evil can pass only through involuntary actions, it cannot come through voluntary actions.

MISS P. Is the 'Song of Solomon' a poetical work of man No. 5 or 6?

MR. O. You must ask his contemporaries.

MRS. M. Is there conscious evil on the cosmic scale?

MR. O. Before asking this question it is necessary to think what evil on a cosmic scale means. Our possibility of thinking about it is so abstract that we cannot think about what it would be. We cannot speak about evil beyond our own life.

MRS. M. Is what we call evil on our own level due to the mechanical working of the formatory apparatus?

MR. O. This is limiting the question.

MRS. M. Can we be told what witchcraft is in the light of this system?

MR. O. What do you know about witchcraft? Most of it was imagination, or it may be the remains of magical knowledge. Usually it is simply hypnotism, occasionally it is the working of higher centres. So which do you mean and what do you know about it?

MISS W. I have observed that when I have an emotional feeling for something, sometimes I have a strong desire to say how much I feel, and then I begin to realize that there is much less emotion there, and that it is as if I am trying to make up for it by words. Is this wrong working of centres, or is it using wrong triad?

MR. O. That is guessing. It is necessary to observe more, perhaps observation will give you an understanding of where it comes from.

MISS W. Is it because evil is due to mechanicalness that there can be no conscious evil?

MR. O. Certainly.

MRS. L. Mr. O. said that energy could be wasted during sleep. What is the right attitude of mind before going to sleep to get the greatest benefit from sleep? I often think, before going to sleep, about what I must do the next day, and this probably leads to waste of energy.

MR. O. It is impossible to say. I think any kind of emotional worry can continue during sleep.

MRS. L. Mr. O. said that it might be possible to alter the past. Does this refer to recurrence, and if so, would it be of any use to try to impress the mistake one wanted to alter on one's mind in this present life, in the hope of remembering not to make the same mistake next time it came around?

MR. O. I prefer to answer this later. Now we have not enough material. I want to publish a novel I wrote long ago that has a connection with this question. I will tell you the beginning: A young man has made a mess of his life. He came to a magician and asked him to help him to go back and live his life all over again. The magician said that it would not help, but the young man said that if he remembered his old mistakes he would not do them again. So the magician sent him back.

MRS. L. Is the reason why consciousness can never do evil that the only real evil is that which obstructs the development of consciousness, and consciousness could not obstruct itself?

MR. O. You try to understand <u>why</u>, but I tell you that before that you must see that it <u>is</u> so—then you may see why. Try to do evil consciously and see whether you can do it. That is why it is dangerous to write down things. Six months later you may àsk me: why did I advise you to do evil consciously? It would seem like black magic.

MRS. A. There can be no conscious evil because human beings are never conscious, so therefore not even capable of conscious evil.

MR. O. That is not the reason. Even if we were conscious we could not do evil consciously, because evil cannot be conscious. Evil needs mechanicalness, just as some other actions need consciousness.

MRS. A. I understood Mr. O. to say there was very little conscious evil in the world, and what there was was in a very low and vulgar category. So there is a little. What is that little? Where does it come from?

MR. O. There is not a drop of conscious evil. Evil that exists is always mechanical on our level and in our conditions. Evil is always mechanical, but mechanicalness is not all evil.

MRS. A. If evil is human, and does not go beyond man, is there nothing in the symbolical story of Lucifer? And is everything on the cosmic plane harmonious?

MR. O. This is too far, perhaps later we may come to that. The cosmic plane has many planes. In the Ray of Creation in World 1 everything happens according to the Will of the Absolute, everything is premeditated and must be harmonious. Inside this world are created worlds 3. We will take one of them. World 3 is under the direct guidance of the Absolute, so again nothing wrong can happen there. In World 6 something is already mechanical. Mechanicalness begins in World 6, then it grows the lower you go; the three manifestations that are not mechanical become less and less, and more and more begins to depend on mechanicalness. So on the cosmic scale there are many planes.

MRS. A. As we arrive on earth with essence, is it not possible that the people who act well, even though unconsciously, must have worked on essence and personality in a previous existence?

MR. O. Leave out the word 'previous'. If one can do both good and evil equally unconsciously, good has no value. The whole thing is to have control.

MRS. A. I am afraid I have not yet extracted the essence from the Brahmin story. What was lacking in the Brahmin? I seem to know quite a number of people, even quite good people, who have this quality of being impossible to help. Is this being asleep? Lack of consciousness? What is it?

MR. O. The Brahmin story has nothing to do with essence. As to what it is it is impossible to say in general—it is different in different cases.

MRS. A. What is relativity of being?

MR. O. What is relativity? Ray of Creation is relativity.

MISS C. In the school language do the words sensation and emotion have the same meaning?

MR. O. Sensation—in the right sense of the word—is physical. But this word has also another meaning, which I think I used in describing parts of centres—in the sense of sensationalism.

MR. P. Can we say that evil is unconscious because it always calls itself something else? Crimes are always committed for the sake of some cause. And anger calls itself a sense of injustice.

MR. O. Too much interpretation—but it is very near the truth that evil is unconsciousness.

MISS C. From the point of view of our aim is not mechanicalness evil when it takes the place of what should be conscious?

MR. O. Certainly, but apart from that, conscience has a feeling of evil apart from all explanations and interpretations. Only it is asleep, so we cannot rely on it.

MISS V. Should we escape from evil if we could escape from the Law of Accident?

MR. O. Accident and mechanicalness are very near relations. If you escape from one you escape from the other.

MISS C. Is all evil caused by the wrong working of centres?

MR. O. No, it is a little too much to expect from wrong work of centres.

MR. S. Is trying to think in new categories another way in which we imitate conscious thought?

MR. O. Yes, only better replace the word 'imitate' by some other word.

MR. D. Mr. O. said that war is sometimes justified, because only by means of war, in some circumstances, could anything be settled. What is meant by 'circumstances'?

MR. O. Without speaking much about political questions and history it is difficult to answer. We may come to that, but it is better to leave it at present.

MISS H. I don't understand what thinking in new categories means. How can we start to do this?

MR. O. It is very difficult to explain without a practical example.

MR. C. When Mr. O. said that no conscious action could be evil, did he mean evil in the ordinary sense, or from the point of view of the system?

MR. O. In the ordinary sense, only a little justified, explained. We take not the purely conventional evil, but such things as we have the right to call evil, that have some substance. Our evil is worse than the ordinary evil, it is condensed, distilled.

MR. C. What is evil from the point of view of the system?

MR. O. What keeps us mechanical. Sleep is evil. Why? Because everything may happen in sleep.

MR. C. Mr. O. said that not all mechanical actions are evil. Are only those evil that are based on negative emotions, or that have the effect of increasing mechanicalness and negative reactions in other people?

MR. O. Yes, maybe, but it is necessary to say more. We cannot enumerate all of them. It is sufficient to establish the principle—anything that produces evil must be mechanical.

MR. C. Is there no higher consciousness that comes to people not in a school? There is the example of Jacob Boehme. I don't think there is any hint that he was in a school. He was only a simple shoemaker.

MR. O. How do you know he was not in a school? There is no proof that he was not. Yes, consciousness may come without a school, just as one can find money in the street. But one cannot live on that.

MR. C. After one has come into contact with a school, does it depend on one's essence or personality whether one will obtain higher consciousness?

MR. O. It depends on work, on effort—both on essence and personality.

MRS. W. Is it possible for one to possess a single aim before one is in possession of a permanent 'I'?

MR. O. Yes, certainly.

* * *

Tuesday. April 16th 1936.

MRS. W. Question about personality and essence, and being.

MR. O. Being does not enter into this division into personality and essence. Knowledge and being are two sides when we speak about the possibility of development. It is one pair of opposites, personality and essence are another pair of opposites on a different scale.

MRS. W. Personality is what we are working on now?

MR. O. Personality is acquired, essence is our own, what we are born with, what cannot be separated from us. They are mixed, we cannot distinguish the one from the other now. But it is useful to remember this division as a theoretical fact.

MISS M. A question about personality and imaginary 'I'.

MR. O. They have nothing in common, no connection. We don't know our personality as one thing. Imaginary 'I' we call 'I'. Personality is a theoretical term. I cannot explain the difference between two things that are not opposed to one another, that are 'from different operas'.

MRS. L. How to become conscious?

MR. O. All we talk about now has the aim to explain how to become conscious and how to create consciousness. It cannot be done without school-work.

MR. L. Was masonry a school?

MR. O. Which masonry? What do you know about it?

MR. L. That it came down through centuries.

MR. O. Do you know it? Are you sure? It is an imaginary thing, does not exist and never existed. In the eighteenth century certain things existed that could play the part of preliminary school. We have historical evidence of that. In France chiefly, and in Russia there existed half-esoteric movements, but they are dead now.

MISS H. I want to know whether you could remember yourself by being aware of the mechanism of the body.

MR. O. Very good, keep attention on the physical body. It does not matter where you begin. You have to observe all centres. Generally speaking, if you mean instinctive centre, you cannot do it. Movements—yes. We must observe three centres and compare them.

MISS P. Is not memory greatly overrated sometimes? If you remember too clearly, you cannot make fresh decisions because you are influenced by memory of former wrong decisions.

MR. O. I don't understand the case and the question. Try to formulate better. Give a concrete example.

MR. O. [to Mr. L.] You asked about masonry—a word, whether it is a way by itself. But what does this word mean? It is not defined. What do you really know about it and what do you mean?

MR. L. It is not a thing one can speak about. Any experiences I might have had I cannot speak about.

MR. O. Why?

MR. L. Others have not shared them. I thought your knowledge would have made you know about it.

MR. O. When I explained about four ways I said that there are three traditional ways, ways of Fakir, Monk and Yogi, which all refer to different types or categories. Fakir is exaggerated No. 1 with predominance of moving-instinctive centre. Monk is exaggerated 2 with emotional centre developed and others under-developed. Yogi is exaggerated No. 3. The division of ways is not artificial, it is natural and corresponding to facts. If that was all, there would be nothing for us. We are too over-educated for these ways. But there is a fourth way. It differs from the other three first of all by the fact that in the three ways the first step is the most difficult. One has to give up everything. In the Fourth Way there is no difficulty in the first step, all work is inner, there is no external giving up of things. You asked whether there is a fifth way. I say, many, but they are monkey ways.

MR. L. You said there are many fourth ways.

MR. O. I said probably.

MISS C. Does the way of Fakir lead to the same end as the way of the Monk?

MR. O. Yes, to almost the same, but not quite. In the way of Fakir, Fakirs buy children and make a child imitate them. Or people see a man sitting in a temple and imitate him. Some of them become so struck by this that they remain and do not return home. Fakirs create unity and will by conquering physical pain. They create physical will. It is a very important thing to create such a will and it cannot be done without achieving unity, fusion of 'I's. If a Fakir does not go mad, he is afterwards taken to a school of Yogis, and by a certain way consciousness is created. He has will, so in five months he can get what for others would take five years. Hatha Yoga is for such people.

Way of Monk. This is a way for emotional people. They work on emotions and create in themselves a higher level of work in emotional centre, and a particular capacity connected with emotions. Bhakti Yoga is for them.

Way of Yogi. That means Raja Yoga and Jnana Yoga. If a Yogi attains consciousness, he has to study two other Yogas. Experience of one is not sufficient, but three together give results.

But you very seldom meet a pure Monk or a pure Yogi. As a matter of fact the ways are mixed. In one school there are Yogi practices and Monk practices. They are combined. By practice it is known that one way is not sufficient.

You asked whether there are many schools of the Fourth Way. Logically there must be. But we don't know. Schools are not determined by addresses, but by methods. Part of work here is the study of school methods, otherwise you will never understand what you study; it will remain theoretical.

There was a question here: how to become conscious? First it is necessary to realize that we have no consciousness. Possibility to acquire it is exactly proportionate to the realization that we have not got it. It must be not only a firm conviction, but an actual realization. When we begin to feel its absence, the possibility to be conscious will become more and more active. This is the only way. We don't know what it means to be conscious. But we don't know fully our state either, because we live in illusions. If we were free from illusions, a strong impulse to get out of this state and to change would become possible. One cannot fully describe what this change means, and better not try. Imagination works and deceives us. Better study the present state. . . . We can lose nothing, we have nothing to lose.

MRS. W. One seems to lose more and more every day.

MR. O. Actually one loses only imagination.

MRS. W. One finds oneself repeating certain actions over and over again. It would be a good thing to break through.

MR. O. To 'do'. We cannot. First it is necessary to remember yourself, otherwise you will not see the moment when it is necessary to 'do'.

You cannot begin with 'doing'. Even struggle with habits is useful only as material for observation. Habits are in four centres. If you conquer a habit in one centre, others do not know it. A man decides to change his thinking. But he is accustomed to sit in a certain way. He assumes his customary posture—and thinks in the old way. He did not think of another centre, and yet he is in the power of three other centres.

MRS. W. You give attention to one centre only?

MR. O. Yes, you cannot control all four.

MRS. W. I fell into other ways easily visiting friends, but at home I got back to my old ways again.

MR. R. It is possible for people to get very depressed when they find they have no consciousness or 'I'. A man lives in a fool's paradise, happy and healthy. Otherwise you go mad.

MR. O. Madness is a physical illness, it cannot be changed by psychological methods. . . . One must know what one wants—to sleep or to awake. If it is to sleep—better not touch this man. The first thing is to decide.

MR. R. When you are aware you are asleep, you awake?

MR. O. For a moment only.

MR. R. But then you take steps to become conscious?

MR. O. Certainly, if it happens during this moment, one must realize it and adapt some mechanical practice to awake him.

MR. R. If we throw away imagination, we must get some reality in return.

MR. O. Unfortunately no one cares to compensate us. Only we ourselves care.

MR. P. Is it interconnection of habits that makes it difficult to find negative attitudes? That is, attitudes with which negative emotions are connected?

MR. O. Many negative emotions are connected with positive attitudes. If we had more negative attitudes we would have less negative emotions.

MISS P. How?

MR. O. Attitude is intellectual. Realizing that all people are asleep, for instance, helps to have less negative emotions.

MISS P. Attitude connected with emotions is connected with triads?

MR. O. Leave triads.

MR. L. If one is pleased or dissatisfied with daily work, does it mean one is identified?

MR. O. Better observe; maybe identified, maybe not. You are not one—who is displeased?

MRS. W. Identification is not clear to me. If I read a book and am absorbed, is this identification?

MR. O. It can be defined only by direct observation. Try to find a good example that leaves no doubt. Description and definition will not help. Same description can refer to identification or simply absorption. No negative emotions can exist without identification.

MISS S. How to observe the intellectual centre?

MR. O. It has many different compartments. From one one looks at another. Each centre is divided into three parts. From one part we can observe another.

MISS S. Is there a concrete advantage in becoming more conscious and less mechanical?

MR. O. You must decide for yourself. Find reasons for it. First understand what it means to be more conscious and less mechanical. Then decide. Only then it has real weight. If I answer, it will only be my opinion. There are things that one must decide for oneself, only then they have real meaning and show real understanding.

MR. L. Through which centre does conscience work? I did something and felt uncomfortable. . . .

MR. O. It depends what you did. Could be simply mechanical habit, good or bad, to break which is uncomfortable. This is mostly based on mechanical habits of thinking given by education—rules of conduct or moral rules. Conscience we never experience in most cases. It is a very unpleasant feeling. We have too many buffers. Buffers are partitions between our emotional attitudes. Conscience means that you see a hundred things at the same time; partitions disappear and you see all inner contradictions at the same time. It is very unpleasant.

MRS. W. Sometimes we voluntarily put ourselves in some compartments?

MR. O. Not voluntarily. It happens. The general principle of life is to avoid unpleasant sensations, realizations, etc. We run away from it. In this way we create inner buffers. If you see contradictions one after another, they do not appear contradictory.

MRS. L. Does one ever attain to that state of conscience?

MR. O. Yes, if one attains consciousness. They are different manifestations of the same thing. It is a long process. It is lucky it is long, otherwise it would be very difficult for us.

Question about triads.

MR. O. . . . With certain time and observation we can begin to distinguish triads beginning with neutralizing force. This is really work beyond our possibilities. In the fourth state of consciousness we can always see what truth is and how to approach it. In the third state we can know more than we do now.

MR. N. So these triads have no practical value?

MR. O. The greatest value, if we could use them. Man is asleep. They would be of greatest value if he was awake. We are half asleep, not fully. And there are degrees even in this state. We know too little, but even now we can easily see the use of a wrong triad. We can say: 'In this way we cannot do it.' But we cannot do it in any other way. We begin something and get negative results. How to get positive results, we have got to learn.

MR. C. How to recognize triads?

MR. O. Examples are given. Try to find analogies. You know too little to think easily and freely of this. You are only starting.

MR. C. When you are in a negative state, is it second triad?

MR. O. You think negative state means negative force? It has nothing to do with it. Active, passive and neutralizing are only names.

MR. C. When one is day-dreaming, can one say it is the destructive triad at work?

MR. O. Find analogy. Then we can speak about it. Again you begin from the wrong end. You must begin with facts, if you find them. Then it is possible to talk.

MR. N. Can one carry out an action with right centre but wrong triad?

MR. O. Yes. It produces a wrong result, different to what one wishes, but one persuades oneself that it is the right result.

MR. H. You want results. How does one activate oneself?

MR. O. . . . This is a different thing.

MR. M. Is the third triad necessary to get over an interval?

MR. O. We have an example in the Food Diagram. This is all we know in this case. There can be no law. It is a matter for observation.

MR. R. Is there any difference between ascending and descending octave in this sense?

MR. O. It is the same octave. Depends from which end you take it.

*　　*　　*

There was a question about schools. It is very necessary that we understand one another in this. People in the world are divided into seven categories according to their state. People 1, 2, 3 are divided according to the centre which predominates in them. These three categories are on the same level. All people are born 1, 2, 3 and die 1, 2, 3. They cannot become 4 without school-work, school organization, or certain cycle of ideas, or systems which come from people of higher level. Man No. 5 has self-consciousness, man No. 6 has objective consciousness, man No. 7 cannot lose those things. Schools can be of very different levels. There may be schools for No. 6 to become No. 7, for No. 5 to become No. 6, etc. Or for 1, 2 and 3 who want to become 4. There cannot be a school without direct, or indirect, guidance. A man 1, 2, 3, if he wants to organize a school for men 1, 2, 3; it will not be recognized as school. It will only be an individual attempt.

* * *

[Diagram of circles of humanity: esoteric, mesoteric, exoteric and outer circle. Four gates. No. 4 is already near the gate. Men 1, 2, 3 live happily without any gates.]

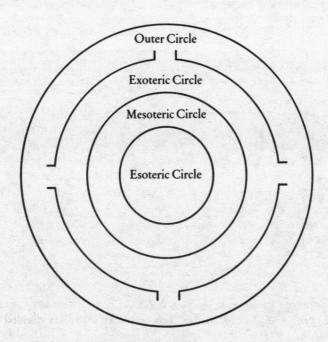

* * *

MR. D. A question about art.

MR. O. All the art we know is art 1, 2 and 3. Art 4 is a very great exception connected with school. Example—Gothic art. . . . There is a certain evidence that certain ideas came to Europe in the nineteenth century, through certain schools. Facts I know in connection with this are not generally known. . . .

* * *

Thursday. April 23rd 1936.

MR. O. About questions on three forces and triads—you must understand where the idea of triads came from. It came from old Indian philosophy—the teaching of Gunas. Guna is a force. Three Gunas are three forces. It is said in this teaching that there are seven combinations of Gunas—one incomprehensible and six comprehensible to our mind. But they are comprehensible only if they are explained well and are taken in connection with other things.

I will try to connect it with the Ray of Creation. The Absolute is World 1. The three forces in it make one. By his own will and consciousness the Absolute creates worlds. It is all intentional there, there is nothing accidental in World 3. But in World 6 mechanicalness enters.

Absolute	①	do
		connected by Will of Absolute
All Worlds	③	si
All Suns	⑥	la
Sun	⑫	sol
All Planets	㉔	fa
Organic Life	▭	
Earth	㊽	mi
Moon	96	re
Absolute	▽	do

We will represent the Absolute by a big triangle. Each Guna in it occupies each place, and this is incomprehensible to us. World 3 consists of three triangles, World 6 of six triangles, etc. The order in which Gunas enter the triad determines the kind of triad it is.

In World 3 there is nothing mechanical. In World 6 there are three triads of World 3 and three of its own, etc. Now we come to study not only the triads under which earth exists, but under which we exist. Suppose we take 96 as organic life and man as the next cosmos—192. 192 is the number of laws under which man exists. 189 of them come from different worlds, and three are created by man himself. Many interesting deductions can be made from this diagram.

MISS H. Can we understand which are the three laws of man?

MR. O. Yes, we can. If we take World 6, we see that there are six laws, three from the world above, and three of its own. So we can say that the laws belonging to World 6 are half of the laws under which it exists. Now take World 12. Three laws of its own make one half, equal to the other nine laws which make the other half; and so on, until we come to man. In man there are 192 laws. Three laws of man's own make a half. 96 will be half of the remaining laws, 48 a quarter, etc. You will see from this that very little comes to man from higher worlds; the finer the forces, the less of them comes to man. Then you can ask: how do these influences reach us? We can come to that by the Table of Hydrogens. H3 and H6 come from higher worlds; then come H12, H24, etc. We know that influences come through centres. Higher mental centre works with H6. This means that influence 6 can only reach us through higher mental centre (it is necessary to put 3 and 6 together, and 48 and 96 together, because hydrogens do not quite correspond to influences). In this way we can understand very much if we think about it in the right way. [See diagram p. 111.]

I will begin from the last hydrogen by the third scale, H3072. We see that H48 is almost touching sun, 24 is sun. So now we can see where influences come from and that we can have higher influences only if we have control of centres. Otherwise we are unable to receive them. Now remember about influences A, B, C. If we are entirely under influences A, influences B cannot reach us and we can only go lower and lower, because all influences have intelligence and can influence us. All depends to which influences we are open—to higher or to lower.

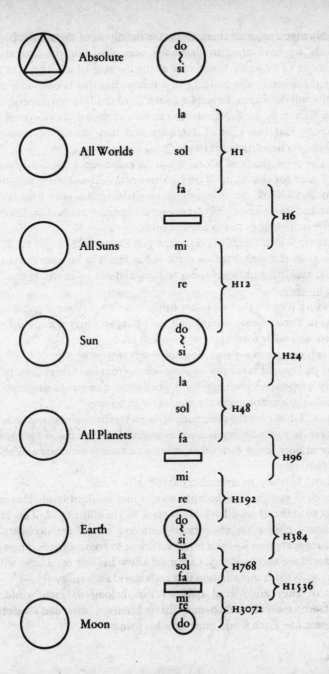

Absolute	do
	si
All Worlds	la
	sol	H1
	fa
		H6
All Suns	mi
		H12
	re
Sun	do
	si	H24
	la
	sol	H48
All Planets	fa
		H96
	mi
	re	H192
Earth	do
	si	H384
	la
	sol	H768
	fa
	mi	H1536
Moon	re	H3072
	do

Now you must all think about the definition of the six triads. Three triads we have tried to define by examples. For the first triad an example of violent actions, such as the burning of a house, was given; for the second—the building of a house. But this is only an example, not a full definition. Examples of the third triad, in our experience, we can find only in conscious work, not identified work, or in some activity that has a peculiar quality and that cannot be imitated by others, such as artistic creation.

The three triads of World 6 can be called mechanicalness, accident and time (or death). In World 3 there is no time. Time enters only in World 6. Many things we think inevitable come only gradually and manifest themselves differently in different worlds. Conditions are different in higher and in lower worlds.

MISS D. Which three laws does man make himself?

MR. O. Not makes, but they come out in him. For instance: mechanicalness, accident and time belong to him, and not to anything else. They are <u>his own</u>.

MISS D. Why do they represent half?

MR. O. Because they occupy half the place, and may occupy the whole even, and other forces may not work at all.

Q. Is it correct to say that mechanicalness is wrong?

MR. O. I would say that all wrong comes from mechanicalness, particularly where consciousness could work instead of mechanicalness. Then mechanicalness becomes the conductor of wrong.

MR. P. I don't see the difference between mechanicalness and accident.

MR. O. If you take one line—it is mechanicalness. But if two lines, or several lines, cross each other, when you cannot see cause and effect— it is accident.

MR. H. Is trying to remember oneself third triad?

MR. O. If you do it in the right way, it may be third triad. This is why it is so difficult—we have no control of the third triad. This is why ordinary efforts are insufficient—different efforts are necessary. But self-remembering by itself is not sufficient to control triads; knowledge and will are also necessary. One must know and one must have will.

MR. N. What is this addition that each world adds to laws?

MR. O. They are special qualities that belong to each world. For instance, individual man must have his own, that don't belong to organic life. Each world must have his own.

MR. N. But there are still mechanicalness, accident and time?

MR. O. They modify in each different world, they have different manifestations.

MR. N. How do you arrive to 192?

MR. O. In cosmoses we took man as microcosmos. If we take earth as one unit—48, then organic life as 96, man will be 192. These figures cannot be taken as exact, they only show the principle. If we take exact figures, the difference will be much bigger.

MISS M. What does it mean that hydrogens correspond to worlds?

MR. O. Because each comes from some world. For instance, air is 192. It only exists very near to earth. Higher it will be 96—very rarefied. Then there are many other things—the same air, if it is very hot, is 96.

MISS H. If we can escape from mechanicalness and accident, can we also escape from time?

MR. O. Time has many forms. Probably we can. It is a complicated question.

MR. C. In the World 6 the laws that come from above remain the same?

MR. O. They cannot remain the same, they are already mixed with others. But they also pass to World 12, both in pure and in mixed form, but always diminishing in intensity and quantity.

*   *   *

MR. O. Now we'd better try to speak about sincerity. Stupid sincerity means mechanical sincerity. It does not mean that one decided to be sincere, but simply that one cannot help it. If one is cleverly sincere, one first asks: can people understand it? Is it worth telling them? etc. There is nothing dishonest in it, it is simply control.

What is interesting is that there are many other, lower hydrogens that can affect man. If man is not under higher influences, he falls under lower influences and can live even under influence 1536 or 3072.

MR. C. What does it mean to fall under a lower influence?

MR. O. Influences come to men through centres. What do influences A, B and C mean? You can find that out. But there are lower influences than A. A is only normal. There are lower influences, like illness—it is a very low influence. And there are many others.

MISS P. Could one eat wrong hydrogens?

MR. O. Only very small mistakes are possible here. We are so well made that we can only make very small mistakes, or we will die.

MRS. M. Is negative emotion a bad influence?

MR. O. It is both influence and reaction. Every influence that comes must produce a suitable reaction. Negative emotion is a very low reaction. If our reactions stay on a very low level, what we receive also stays on a very low level.

MISS P. Where do they come from? From the moon?

MR. O. Yes. It is interesting that there are many things on the moon that are natural there and that cannot exist in a natural state on earth—things like liquid air, for instance, or other highly concentrated acids. On earth we can only produce them artificially, but on the moon they are natural.

MR. D. Moon can influence us only through lower centres?

MR. O. Influence of moon is very large. Psychologically it is better to cut oneself off from it, but its physical influence is necessary. It is like weight on a clock.

MRS. M. Is this why people are mad at full moon?

MR. O. It may not be influence of the moon. It cannot be accused directly. Moon is always there, whether it is full or not.

Q. How can lower hydrogens affect us?

MR. O. All hydrogens have intelligence. If we lower ourselves to their level they affect us.

MR. N. Has organic life a triad of its own?

MR. O. Yes.

MR. C. What is the difference between laws and hydrogens? What are these laws? You said these figures represent certain laws and they are not the same as hydrogens?

MR. O. Each level represents a certain hydrogen. You must understand that hydrogens work through centres. Higher mental centre works with H6, higher emotional centre with H12, etc. Starting from that you can collect material to compare and to think.

MISS M. Is a hydrogen vibration?

MR. O. No, matter. The higher the matter, the more vibrations in it.

MR. H. Can we see the effect of moon psychologically? Would it be mechanical thinking?

MR. O. Much worse than that.

MISS V. Does moon affect all centres?

MR. O. Through negative emotions.

MR. C. Is it when one centre works for another?

MR. O. It means the general weakening of the whole machine and creating difficulties.

MR. N. This implies a low influence?

MR. O. This wrong activity immediately stops receptivity to higher influences, and that in turn produces more wrong activity.

MR. N. Which comes first?

MR. O. This is matter for observation. It generally begins with our being asleep or negative when we should be awake. It is we that start. So we cannot accuse moon.

MR. N. Does organic life receive influences from earth? Is it why it is 96 although its position is above?

MR. O. This is simply a diagram. Organic life should really be put round the earth.

MR. L. Can man change his place in the universe by the influence of higher worlds?

MR. O. How can he? He will always remain on earth. What do you mean?

MR. L. Can he become free?

MR. O. Yes, he can become free from certain influences and be under other influences more, but he will still remain on earth.

MISS M. Does it mean that organic life is more intelligent than man? Is it higher?

MR. O. It is a different cosmos, not analogous. Your definition is wrong.

MISS T. I did not understand the difference between organic life and man.

MR. O. Individual man and the whole of organic life taken together are different cosmoses.

MISS T. What does it mean that mechanicalness enters in World 6?

MR. O. Things begin to happen. Above there is only will.

MR. H. Does all mechanicalness begin with the first force?

MR. O. It can begin with any. Which is second force is also very important. All these sweeping definitions are always wrong. We can only give examples, not definitions.

MR. L. In what lies the difference of effort to self-remember? You said it must be different.

MR. O. You must find it by observation.

Q. You said moon affects us physically and psychologically?

MR. O. The physical influence is different. When moon begins to affect our mind and emotions, then it is wrong.

Q. By physical influence do you mean it controls our moving centre?

MR. O. No, it is bigger than that.

MISS C. Does it control war?

MR. O. No, I speak of individual man.

MISS V. How can we know when moon controls our mind?

MR. O. It cannot happen by itself. It must be prepared by our own actions and emotions. There are many things necessary to prepare it.

MRS. A. So it is not like the tide?

MR. O. That is physical and normal. Moon is a big electromagnet, so it must affect things like tide. But when the influence becomes psychological, then it is wrong. It happens only when man is cut off from higher influences. But nothing can cut him off higher influences except he himself.

MR. H. Is giving way to negative emotions putting oneself under the moon?

MR. O. It is not so quick. The influence of the moon is very bad and rare. You cannot be bad for very long, not more than three hours at a time.

MRS. A. Why is man placed in the Ray in such a difficult position?

MR. O. He is in a difficult position, but there are also helps. He is like a marionette pulled by different strings. But he can develop something in himself, help some strings, then cut off others.

MRS. A. It is a terribly difficult situation.

MR. O. Man can help that, but not at once.

MRS. A. Do these difficulties serve any useful purpose?

MR. O. Difficulties are not created for man. Man is very small. He only thinks that everything is created for him.

MR. P. When hydrogens are transmitted from higher worlds to lower, are they made lower?

MR. O. No, they can be transmitted in a pure form. The question is: can you receive them? They can only be received by certain parts of centres and a certain activity.

MR. P. Can you receive them and then debase them?

MR. O. If one part of you receives high influences and another part low influences, that may create an explosion.

MR. O. [to Mrs. A.] You are right, our position is difficult. But it only looks so difficult when it is explained. There is a book of aphorisms that has never been published, and probably never will be. One of these aphorisms says: 'In order to know all, one must know very little. But in order to know that little, one must know pretty much.'

MRS. H. What takes the place of organic life in other worlds?

MR. O. We don't know. We can guess that there may be some other forms of organic life, but it will remain only a guess.

MISS P. Are there lots more earths?

MR. O. It does not concern us. We must think of what has a practical meaning for us, what can help us. If there are ten million other earths it will not help us if we live on this earth and are asleep on it. The difference between this system and the scientific method is that they study both what is necessary and not necessary. Here a definite selection is made and all that is not necessary is thrown out.

* * *

Monday. December 7th 1936. [About ten pages missing.]

MR. O. We must now speak about man's place in the world and, if we have time, also about schools.

MRS. S. What does it mean to give up self-will? Does it mean to give up the determination to awaken?

MR. O. Did you understand what I meant by self-will? It is always connected with self-opinions, a man always thinks he knows something. Then he comes to a school and realizes that he knows nothing. That is why preparation is necessary for school. One is usually full of self-opinions and self-will. Self-will is like a child saying: 'I know myself, I will myself.' Self-will has many features. One is told not to do something and at once one wants to do it; one is told that something is wrong and at once one says: 'No, I know better.' A man who comes to a school must be ready to accept the teaching and the discipline of the school, he must be free to accept it, or else he will get nothing. He cannot acquire Will unless he gives up self-will, just as he cannot acquire knowledge unless he gives up self-opinions.

There are in the system certain principles about knowledge. One of them is: <u>to know means to know all. To know a part cannot mean to know</u>. Knowledge begins with a general understanding of the whole and then with finding a place for each separate thing.

In school one cannot begin with knowledge of all. So one begins with fragments. First one studies fragments relating to the psychological side, then fragments relating to man's place in the world, etc. After several fragments have been studied, one is told to try and connect them together. If one is successful, one will have in this way the whole picture. And then one may be able to find the right place for each separate thing. There is no other way. One cannot learn the system from books.

As a matter of fact I have written down and described how we met the system and studied it. But I realized what a different impression it all produces on readers as compared to us who actually were there. A reader will never be able to find the right centre of gravity, so this book would be like any other book. This is why there are no text books on the system. Things can be written only for those who have studied. There are several books like that. The New Testament is one of them. There are also such books on old philosophies; they are really only short headings, there is no real exposition in them.

MISS W. You said it is easy to lose a school. How?

MR. O. One comes with the desire to know, one wants to learn. Then, when one begins, one gets dissatisfied, one says: 'This is not the knowledge I want, I want it this way and I am told it in another way.' So, instead of learning, one finds contradictions.

MR. D. Does one get in school answers to problems of life, to everyday facts?

MR. O. Some are simpler to explain, others are more difficult.

MR. D. Then why cannot the answer be written on paper? For instance, the answer to the question: is the League of Nations any use?

MR. O. This is an imaginary thing and the school tries to deal with reality. Partly in connection with your question—one of the strangest experiments I had was when I realized that many ideas, words, lines of thought did not exist at all, meant absolutely nothing. When one is awake a little, one may realize this. Many words are simply empty words. The League of Nations is one of them. So one cannot come with a definite demand to have the League of Nations explained.

MRS. S. I don't understand about heredity—I thought that certain physical things, like glands, affect one's nature?

MR. O. In a small way they may, but only to a small extent.

MR. Q. Are men 1, 2 and 3 incapable to apprehend reality at all?

MR. O. In simple things.

MR. Q. Then they have to exercise faith until they reach the stage of No. 4?

MR. O. No, not faith. But one can start from simple realities; tables and chairs, and then verify every new idea. Certainly, at first, one must accept certain hypotheses, but one has to try and verify them gradually. Faith belongs only to religious way.

MR. Q. You mean to test realities we don't know by those we know?

MR. O. Certainly.

* * *

MR. O. We shall speak now of man's place in the universe. In ordinary language and ordinary understandings it is difficult to connect many things. If I say, for instance, that many things look unpleasant because we live in a very bad place of the universe, it would sound strange because we take universe as uniform, with no better or worse places. But if we compare our place in the universe with the North Pole, we will realize that it is a bad place and that circumstances are difficult there. Earth is very near the North Pole, very near to the end of the universe. This is also an unknown idea for us—that there is an end. The moon is the end. Let us take the earth—it is part of the planetary system, one of the planets.

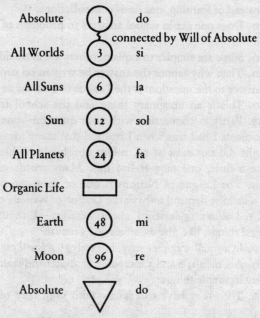

Absolute	1	do
		connected by Will of Absolute
All Worlds	3	si
All Suns	6	la
Sun	12	sol
All Planets	24	fa
Organic Life		
Earth	48	mi
Moon	96	re
Absolute		do

So we say that first it belongs to the planetary world. The planetary world belongs to the Solar System. The Solar System belongs to our galaxy. This galaxy is one of other, similar or unsimilar, galaxies. Astronomically we cannot go further. Then moon is in the sphere of influence of the earth.

We call this the Ray of Creation. It includes only the universe to which we belong. We take only our galaxy, from this we take our sun, etc. The last is moon, it is the end for us. Earth is very near the end of our ray.

This shows the beginning of a view of the universe on the basis of which we study ourselves and the universe. Planets are important for us only as a totality.

There were questions about the aim of man's existence. Man, and even mankind, does not exist separately, but only as part of the whole of organic life. Organic life is like a sensitive film round the earth that transfers influences from the sun and the planets to the earth and the moon, and from the earth and the moon to planets and to the sun. If there were no organic life, they could not communicate so well. So it is like a radio station.

Individual man is a highly specialized cell in it which has the possibility of further development. But this development depends on his own efforts and understanding. It enters into the cosmic purpose that a certain number of men develop. But not all, otherwise this would contradict another cosmic purpose. Evidently humanity must be on earth and must lead this life and suffer. But a certain number of men can escape and develop. This also enters into the cosmic purpose.

MR. D. Does earth have existence by itself? Has it parts, centres?

MR. O. There cannot be an exact analogy. All we can say is that certainly earth is a living being. There is nothing dead in nature. Only some men are dead.

MR. E. Is there consciousness in matter?

MR. O. There is intelligence, only intelligence can have different degrees. Intelligence in things is measured by their adaptability. For instance, a tree that is alive has better adaptability than a piece of wood.

MISS W. How is organic life a sensitive film?

MR. O. It covers the earth and serves a definite cosmic purpose; it receives certain vibrations and sends out certain vibrations.

MRS. S. Why do sun, planets and moon want to communicate?

MR. O. It is all one thing. Only for us things look separate; in reality they are all linked together, like one arm is connected with the other; it is like circulation of blood in the organism. The Ray of Creation can be regarded as a growing branch of which the moon is the end. Moon is the youngest. In time it will become like the earth. Sun is the oldest. Moon is not fully born yet.

MR. D. Has matter feeling?

MR. O. Yours is a wrong formulation. But it can be better organized or less well organized. Feeling is connected with the degree and form of organization.

MISS C. Where do planets come in?

MR. O. They are taken all together.

MISS C. Isn't earth one of them?

MR. O. Yes, but we are on earth, so we take earth separately.

MR. E. Does power of adaptability apply as a measure of man's intelligence?

MR. O. As regards man it is more complicated. But it begins with this.

Q. Is there a mind and purpose behind all this?

MR. O. Yes. We will speak about it later. The purpose of a branch is growing. This is why communication is necessary, like circulation of juices is necessary in a branch.

MRS. W. Why don't men develop naturally?

MR. O. If you understand what it means to develop, you will see that man can develop only by his own efforts. Will cannot develop mechanically, consciousness cannot develop unconsciously. It cannot grow out of nothing. One has to pay for everything. In this way we again come to schools and the question why one must be prepared for school. One must realize one's position and one must be prepared to pay. The more one is prepared to pay, the more one acquires. Nothing can be given.

Now we come to the question of compassion. If one has something and wants to give it, one cannot. The nature of the thing he wants to give is such that people must pay for it. He cannot make them take it. There is no other way—they must want it very much, and be prepared to pay for it. Only then can it become their own. Otherwise it is lost.

MISS N. If sympathy is just going to be lost you might as well stay in your little shell?

MR. O. Not necessarily. Only give it to those who are prepared to receive it.

MISS N. It is not good to make an effort to be sympathetic?

MR. O. It is good, but you must know when.

MR. W. Surely we need faith about the universe. We cannot verify what you said.

MR. O. There is nothing new here. It is only a different angle, and quite a normal angle. There is nothing that contradicts ordinary views. When things contradict ordinary views, I draw special attention to it. For instance, about moon being the youngest. It is a hypothesis, not a fact. There are many theories in science about such things, but not a single fact.

MR. D. Could such facts as these be established by people in schools? Could not we take them as established facts?

MR. O. They are established. But we are given it as material for study. We are not obliged to believe it. This scheme is given in order to study man's place in the universe.

MR. W. Will you explain a bit more the purpose of organic life?

MR. O. It exists for the purposes of planets, the sun, the earth and the moon. If there were no organic life, certain vibrations would not be able to pass. Organic life serves a definite mechanical purpose.

MR. S. What is the purpose of awakened man?

MR. O. It must be a subjective, a personal, purpose—it must be taken so. Man must not comfort himself that he can serve a cosmic purpose.

MR. Q. How to distinguish between will and self-will?

MR. O. By studying actual facts.

MR. E. You say we have no genuine emotions. If we analyse all compassionate feelings, is there no danger of inhibiting them?

MR. O. There is no such danger. If one tries to eliminate imagination, there is no danger to eliminate real feeling, for it cannot be eliminated if it is real—it will only become stronger. But it must be connected with study.

MISS B. Has a school only one teacher?

MR. O. It depends on the school.

MISS B. Is there a large class?

MR. O. That refers to details of inner organization.

MRS. S. If awakening is purely subjective, has school cosmic significance?

MR. O. We cannot ascribe to ourselves cosmic significance. We are too small. But do you remember what I said about prison? One man cannot escape, but perhaps twenty people can. Fifty people again cannot—it will be noticed. And those who want to escape cannot do so without the help of those who escaped before them. This is school. It cannot exist without others who were before.

MRS. S. It implies that school works against the general scheme?

MR. O. Absolutely—against Nature, against God.

MRS. S. Does man No. 7 disappear from earth?

MR. O. We don't know about man No. 7. He does not transmit the same vibrations.

MR. H. What is the nature of vibrations he transmits? Are they measurable vibrations?

MR. O. I think, finer vibrations. There are many things in that. For instance, moon has an effect on organic life. All movements on earth are controlled by moon. Moon is like a weight on a clock. Also moon is fed by organic life. Everything alive is controlled by moon, but when [a man] dies, a certain thing goes to the moon. Organic life is fed by earth and it feeds the moon. That is the nature of vibrations organic life transmits.

MRS. S. Is the influence of the moon constant, or does it vary?

MR. O. It is constant.

MR. D. Is astrology an exact science?

MR. O. It is mostly charlatanism. But there is something in it. If essence is sufficiently free, it is to a certain extent controlled by planetary influences. At the same time, events in the life of the masses, such as wars, revolutions etc. are controlled by planetary influences.

MR. H. Is man predestined if he is to rise to a higher type?

MR. O. It is difficult to take it so and to establish it. We must take it that each has the same possibilities. Maybe one has more possibilities than another, but we cannot establish that.

This is only the beginning of the study of the universe, a study of a new view of it, or rather of the view of higher mind. For if we don't admit that these ideas come from higher mind, they have no meaning, although they are interesting even from the ordinary point of view.

MR. D. Does the system believe in reincarnation?

MR. O. Now we must take man from birth to death. All the laws can be studied in one life. In this elementary study there is no need to bring reincarnation. And what do you mean by reincarnation? There are several possibilities—reincarnation in the future, in the past and in parallel time. There are many theories.

MRS. S. Must one break self-will oneself, or have it broken?

MR. O. One must do it oneself, and one must have it sufficiently broken to be in a school. One must be sufficiently free to accept things without fight. One cannot keep all old views and opinions and acquire new ones. One must be sufficiently free to give up the old, at least for a time. One must be able to understand the necessity of discipline. Will cannot be created until one accepts a certain discipline. Otherwise one may come very near a school and not be able to take anything.

There are many degrees of schools. Schools that begin on the ordinary level of life are very elementary. In them there are necessarily certain rules and conditions. If one forgets them, or makes exceptions for oneself, one cannot really consider oneself in a school. A school can be described as a certain number of people accepting certain rules. These rules cannot be enumerated. They are given gradually. A few are given, and then to those who remember them more are given gradually.

MR. E. Can one be disciplined to school life without being disciplined to ordinary conventions?

MR. O. School discipline is based on understanding—it is quite different.

MR. M. In a way then school is quite subjective?

MR. O. Quite objective. Rules have an objective meaning. Before anything else they are help to self-remembering.

MRS. S. Isn't there a danger of taking discipline as escape from responsibility?

MR. O. Then one would fail.

* * *

Monday. September 13th 1937.

[Questions read.]
[Questions read.]

MR. O. There are many questions on different subjects, but some I will answer later when we come to these subjects. Now I will speak about the Society and about what you call expansion.

The organization of the Society became necessary for several reasons, and some of these reasons you also feel in your questions, but you do not know how things must be organized. You see, even if we continue in the same way as we are working now we will have more and more people. Now we have about three hundred people; in a year or two we will have perhaps six hundred. But already now, in the present conditions, it becomes impossible to follow everybody's individual work and to really help people. Before, when there were less people, I knew them all personally, and knew what everybody was doing. But when the number of people passes a certain limit this becomes impossible, and it is not possible to help people enough without a special organization. Organization means division into groups. Suppose we are three hundred and I divide people into ten groups of thirty people each, and each group has one person who will look after this group, collect questions, bring me the questions, etc. From time to time I visit each group. In this way each person will be able to receive help in their personal difficulties and answers to their questions.

But even such a small organization (ten groups) needs a different place. So first of all it is necessary to have a house with a certain number of rooms where these groups can meet, because, if they meet in different places, in private houses—it is not the same thing. Apart from rooms for groups to meet we need one big room, about two or three times larger than this one, for it will save a lot of time for me if, instead of repeating the same thing three or four times at smaller groups (like this one), everybody could hear it at once. So we need a house with one big room and a certain number of smaller rooms.

This is connected with the idea of Society. Also a name is necessary.

On the technical side the formation of the Society is finished. At a certain moment it is necessary to register it, and then we will have a Society. But work with groups can start and go on only when we have an adequate place. Running or buying a house needs money, and at present, with the means we have, we can only exist as we are. We are short of money and cannot spend much—we can only just move, nothing more. So it is necessary to have more money.

I have decided to make one experiment. I have certain books that I want to publish: one novel, a new edition of *Tertium Organum*, maybe some lectures. But that will take time, it is impossible to say how much time this work will take, but when these books are published, I think that will give enough money. Besides, in three years' time, we shall have the *New Model* in our hands (until then it is in the hands of the publishers, and it is not satisfactory). In many places it cannot be found and it is too little known. It would be useful to publish a cheap edition of it, and then it may sell very well. In Russia I published all my books myself and had quite a good income from them. It is a question of a cheap edition.

The novel is connected with the idea of Eternal Recurrence. Some of you may have read it. It needs time to prepare it for publication. First I must go through the Russian text (for it was written and published in Russian long ago), and then through the translation, and work on the translation takes a great deal of time. Then these lectures must be rewritten, and may be published. Then I have for a long time wanted to bring *Tertium Organum* up to date, to connect it with the *New Model*—at present some of the terminology is different, and so on.

All this I can do only if I have more time. So you must not expect me to give so much time to these lectures. I will come when I can, from time to time, but not to every meeting.

How you will be organized you will hear. You will have probably four or five groups a week, maybe five, if we have a new one. But I will not come every day, so you must be able to go on and do your own work and the work you can do for other people, and for the school, and you must try to understand why this is necessary.

If books are published and are successful, all our problems will be solved. It will take a year, maybe two years, I cannot tell. So this is the situation at present.

As regards separate questions, I cannot answer questions about personal work now, but think about what I said and go on on these lines. You must remember that our aim is to create a school, and the Society is a necessary step towards this aim. And the Society cannot be organized without your help. Your help in this case is that you must give me more time. Now try to talk about it.

MRS. R. So there won't be a new group?

MR. O. This is another question. We may have a new group but, in the present conditions, there will not be much profit from it, for very few will be able to come to it. If we have sixty new people, only about ten more can come.

MR. E. Have we already been given the main body of the theory or of what is useful to us?

MR. O. Practically, this can be formulated very shortly: one must realize one is asleep and try to awake. That is all it is.

You see, first try to understand what I said. Even in the present situation work cannot go on successfully if we don't organize groups, and this needs place. So it cannot be done now. Groups can be given different tasks, different problems, even in some cases exercises (although in general I am against exercises). When groups are organized, special work can be introduced.

MR. P. Cannot groups meet at private houses?

MR. O. It is rather difficult to organize it seriously in private houses. One or two groups could perhaps meet, but it is a question of ten groups, and it must not be accidental—it must be regular and needs regular conditions.

MRS. R. Are private groups not to go on?

MR. O. I do not call that groups when you meet just to talk, exchange views, opinions. It does no harm, but it cannot give much results. It gives, maybe, some results: you get to know one another better, exchange observations, but this is not 'groups', about which I spoke.

MR. C. You want us to think about organization of the Society?

MR. O. No, I want you to think about giving me more free time. Now I took the organization of the Society in my own hands.

MR. P. Should not we also think about money?

MR. O. Yes, this is useful. But books should be published in any case. They will bring people. I have not published anything for a long time. And the *New Model* got into wrong hands; it is not known enough.

MR. P. I don't know how much people realize that money is needed.

MR. O. This is a subject for conversation, certainly. It must be realized. We already have this work here—this work must go on. What people do now is just enough for the present conditions, but it does not give the possibility of expansion.

MRS. J. So we can have no more till there is more money?

MR. O. That is it. You have to be patient. We cannot do very much now in the present conditions. Organization is necessary. But you can get much more when work is better organized. I have tried several times to explain that psychological work, self-study, self-observation needs organization. Otherwise, everybody would be able to work by himself.

MRS. J. Can you tell us what best to do when you are not there?

MR. O. No, you must tell me, not I tell you. I have said my part, I have been speaking of nothing else. How can I repeat it better? There are rules, for instance, there are principles. It is necessary to remember everything that was said.

MISS B. What did you mean by giving more time?

MR. O. You must be able to work without me; not quite without me, but require less of my time.

MR. H. Can we have lectures read again?

MR. O. Yes, when there will be something to read, you will have it. But everything that was written before must be re-written. Not in the sense that it was wrong, but it must be made easier to read and better connected. Certainly as soon as something is ready you will have it to read.

MR. S. In the meantime will these groups go on?

MR. O. Yes, but you cannot expect me to come every time. First of all everybody must be able to work for himself and by himself; remembering rules and everything that was said. Everything that was said was useful, there was nothing useless, only it is necessary to remember it, revive it and keep it. Then one must try to help other people.

MRS. R. Can we have the first lectures again?

MR. O. Yes, when they are re-written, and also there will be some more to read. This is part of our work: many things that I have written are not quite finished and must be finished now. All must be brought to such a state that, when necessary, they could be published.

MISS M. Will the person in charge of groups answer our questions?

MR. O. It depends on the question. Some questions perhaps.

MISS M. Will they bring them to you?

MR. O. Maybe. Much depends on the question.

MR. E. Will group leaders change or be the same person?

MR. O. This is a detail, I cannot answer that.

MRS. J. What is best for us to do?

MR. O. If you work on yourself you will know what to do. If you observe yourself seriously and ask yourself why you observe yourself, you will know. After some time things will begin to be better organized.

MR. S. In order to save your time we must make greater efforts to get in contact with older people who are in direct contact with you?

MR. O. Yes, certainly this is useful.

MRS. M. To know people better one must do practical work together, not only talk. Can Lyne be made bigger?

MR. O. Lyne cannot be touched at present, it must work as it is now; it cannot grow now in the sense of a bigger place. Now the order of the day is the Society and a house in London. When this is organized then perhaps we can think of how we can make Lyne grow.

MR. P. Isn't it to the advantage of all to have a new house in London?

MR. O. Certainly. In any case then we can start groups. Although I said in a year or two, it may be much quicker. I do not want to organize a search for a house yet, but everyone must know what we need—some kind of big studio or room, or hall, big enough for two hundred people, and then several rooms for groups.

MR. B. There is no question of groups now?

MR. O. Where will they meet? In the street?

MISS B. What is the difference between groups you speak of and now?

MR. O. These are not groups, these are lectures. Groups should be, first of all, much smaller, maximum thirty people, better less. And sometimes (I do not say necessarily always), a group must be selected in a special way. It wants a variety of types. If all people are of the same type, then it will not work. Then special tasks are given, one to one group, another to another.

MRS. S. You said just now it is important to get into closer contact with older people. How? By trying to meet them?

MR. O. I did not say that, somebody else said it. And I don't know how. But certainly from them you can learn—if they know. There is an Arab proverb, 'Learn from him who knows.'

MR. C. [A question about new members.]

MR. O. At present we cannot do much. Probably we will have one new group, but at present the situation is rather funny because we cannot manage even with people we have now. There are only five evenings and they are all occupied, when everybody is back in London. So if we have one new group all people will not be able to meet every week.

MR. C. Then it is not important to get new people now?

MR. O. It may be very important. I can only speak about results. It depends whom you bring, whether the person is prepared or not prepared, whether they can be useful in one or another way, either now or later. It is necessary to try. But, as I said, this is not a question of the present moment. We must have a better organization. We may have even two new groups, that is, one soon and one about Christmas. But every new person means some older person must give place to him. We are already full.

[Mr. O. left the room.]

* * *

[Questions read out when Mr. O. came back.]

MR. B. Is it useless to try and remember by reading? I find it helpful to look at notes sometimes.

MR. O. Maybe useful sometimes but you cannot rely on that, because it will become formatory.

MISS M. What is the difference between this class and groups?

MR. O. Groups will be smaller, it will be easier to answer personal questions. Also it will be possible to give definite tasks to groups, to study one particular subject, to make observations of one particular kind—many things that cannot be given to a larger group.

MRS. J. Is it observations of oneself that one should bring to a meeting?

MR. O. I cannot answer that. Everything that one finds that is new is useful.

MR. P. I think it is asking too much of Mr. O. that the development of the Society should depend on profits derived from the sale of his books. It is more up to us than up to him to provide funds for the expansion, since the Society is for our benefit.

MR. O. Just the same, if we can do something this way with books it will be very good. I think sooner or later, if we do it in the right way, we will have quite a good income from publishing. But it cannot be done at once, it needs time.

MR. P. I think it should be the responsibility of the people to find means.

MR. O. Both. But that I have already said. We have talked about it for a long time, we have talked about the Society and I saw nothing practical that came out of this, no practical conclusions. So I saw one practical thing—to publish these books. If we could do something besides that, so much the better.

MRS. A. We must all be on the wrong tack—we are always turned back in our suggestions, because we are not there. I feel we are all willing to do anything if we only knew what it was. I am waiting for something I can get hold of.

MR. O. I do not give definite tasks in a concrete form—the groups are too big. But I want you to understand the necessity of organization and the needs of organization. The technical part of the Society is almost ready. But it is no use beginning to talk about the Society before we have a house where it can meet. So at present it is the question of a house and that depends on how much money we have. That is why I think that if I can publish two or three books, that will give us the possibility to start. I only say what I can do.

MR. K. I think we must provide more material at meetings from our observations to see a meeting through without Mr. O. being there.

MR. O. Yes, but it cannot be done only at meetings. It is necessary to work during the week. And how and what, that is impossible to say in general. In groups, when there are groups, it would be possible to say, but here it would take too much time. That is why groups are necessary.

MRS. S. I don't see how these things, such as keeping rules, are going to give Mr. O. more time.

MR. O. No, keeping rules will not give me more time by itself. That was said in answer to another question: how to work. It is good to have rules, even small rules are very useful in the work—if you do not remember it you miss the opportunity to work. There are many rules you can learn from other people, people who have heard them, people it was explained to. Sometimes quite a small rule produces an enormous quantity of friction and difficulty. Rules are not made for comfort, they are specially made to make you uncomfortable. There is always a great temptation to forget them, to say they are not for me but for other people, etc.

MISS W. I feel that we don't remember enough how many ideas we have been given—we expect something new from Mr. O. every time he comes.

MR. O. Quite true. And the deduction from this is that it is necessary to remember what you already know. Certainly reading lectures again will be very useful in this respect, but I want to re-write them first.

MR. E. It seems many of the questions could be solved by working on attention.

MR. O. Quite right. But I am always against concentrating on one formulation. It is necessary to remember many things and then one thing helps another.

Next week I may come or not, I do not know yet. I do not know yet when I will start this work I spoke about. Anyway, next week will be the same, but later perhaps we may begin to change something. Think about all I have said and perhaps some questions will come, perhaps you will have some ideas to offer.

Possibly in a week or two we may already have something to read either in connection with the Society, or in connection with the lectures. For instance, I began to write a small lecture on transformism and psycho-transformism, because right understanding of these words will help very much to understand what this work is and to explain it to other people.

*   *   *

Monday. October 4th 1937.

MISS S. Is it correct to think men 1, 2 and 3 can only be in school at the moment when they are making real endeavours to wake up, and possibly during self-remembering?

MR. O. I don't quite understand this connection with time. It does not mean if they remember themselves they are in a school, and if they don't remember themselves they are not in a school. School is not mystical, it has a real meaning. People think usually that the only question is to find a school, and preferably to find a school with two, three or more degrees. They don't understand that the chief thing is preparation.

MRS. A. When it is said that only a school of two degrees can be considered reliable, in what sense is the word 'reliable' used?

MR. O. I did not say it exactly like that.

MRS. A. Something very interesting was read to us last Monday about the future belonging to emotional centre. Could we have this further explained?

MR. O. Yes, certainly, if there is a concrete question. As it is a very important question we will speak about it later.

MR. R. In order to have a permanent centre of gravity, must one be continually aware that one is asleep?

MR. O. No, one cannot put it like that, in a formatory way.

MR. R. Can it be said that if one of the twelve disciples had had a permanent centre of gravity, he would not have deserted Jesus on the night of his arrest?

MR. O. We cannot take the Gospel story and discuss it as historical facts.

MR. R. Can we know whether St. Paul was man No. 4 or man No. 5? He clearly seems to have had a permanent centre of gravity, but there are indications in the Epistles that he may not have achieved permanent unity. Could a man with permanent 'I' indulge in boasting—even jealousy—as in the Second Letter to the Corinthians?

MR. O. About St. Paul it is necessary to speak separately. I don't think he was a school man.

MR. R. Is man No. 4 no longer troubled by negative emotion?

MR. O. It is too much to expect.

MR. R. Were the Gospels produced in schools of the Fourth Way?

MR. O. We don't know. You must understand that some things we can know, and some things we obviously don't know.

MR. R. Is it useful to study theosophical ideas of the different types represented by the twelve signs of the Zodiac?

MR. O. You mean the astrological idea? I don't think you can get anything from that. Their description is always identical, only the characteristics are put in a different order.

MR. P. Mr. O. said that the question of expansion was not entirely a question of growth, but a question of scale. I take it that the question of growth would just mean more numbers, but if it is a question of scale, that might mean that, in order to raise the general level of understanding among people in the system, it was necessary to take some definite steps. Or it might mean that it is impossible to take this definite step unless the general understanding is higher than it is now. For myself, I don't feel personally particularly fitted—and this may apply to others who come on Mondays—to do anything but learn from those who know more than we do.

MR. O. There are several things mixed here. Scale is a simple thing. Every kind of work can go on, on one or another scale.

MR. R. I want to understand more about the principle of school work—particularly about the principle of payment and especially in relation to myself. I feel I am always making mistakes in this connection, and I want to get more emotional understanding of this.

MR. O. It is impossible to answer this definitely. I only mentioned about paying in relation to people who can never come near the work. In connection with people who are not in the work we cannot speak about payment, but only about potential payment. People who have enough curiosity, enough realization of their position, those people may potentially pay. But if you meet just people in society who have not got that, why speak to them? And then, the first payment is, of course, to take the trouble to study and understand the things people hear.

MR. R. Are the rules that regulate contact with people meant to be for the study of external considering?

MR. O. Maybe in some cases.

MR. S. It seems to me the change from the work we have been doing up to now to group-work is very fundamental indeed. What are the requirements before group-work can be formed? I feel that groups are essential in order to keep work up to a level that can produce any results at all. The present level of work seems rarely able to produce results. And I connect this with what Mr. O. said about pressure.

MR. O. I cannot understand what you want to know about requirements. I have already said that it is a question of space and time before anything else.

MISS W. In order not to think formatorily, must one always be self-remembering? So often my thinking is spoiled by a sense of 'I'.

MR. O. You cannot be expected to be always self-remembering when you are thinking. Thinking is a mechanical, or rather a more mechanical, process. Self-remembering is a state. You cannot get it before you get it. But when you have a moment of self-remembering you can make certain decisions, and those decisions can keep you from very wrong thinking.

MRS. S. I don't understand what is meant by: 'when one self-remembers there is no sense of "I"'. It seems to me the only time I can approach to self-remembering is when I can say 'I'.

MR. O. Who said that?

MRS. S. We have been told to give up self-will to the will of another. Keeping rules is doing this. But is there any other way in which we do this at present?

MR. O. This is not quite right. You were never told to *do*, but to understand the necessity of that at certain moments. You must understand that keeping self-will cannot get you anywhere. About the meaning of rules we will talk later.

MR. R. Mr. O. said something quite new when he spoke of two levels of school. How can we, as individuals, think about this? I can only understand this as a necessary enlargement of the organization, and new methods of increasing pressure of work, in which each of us could take part. I wonder if there are other ways of understanding this.

MR. O. No, this is not new at all. If you remember something that was read in *Fragments*—there were references to that. And what makes the possibility of what you call 'two levels'? Only the work of individual members, their state of being. Nothing else can do that. Level of school, condition of school depend only on that. Organization can help, but it cannot, by itself, change the level of people's being, and, therefore, cannot produce two levels.

MR. P. By scale does Mr. O. mean an increase in the number of activities in the system, for example, the formation of groups for people who so far have only attended these lectures; and, in addition to this, other and new activities for people who are more advanced?

MR. O. I meant that every work must achieve its right scale in order to go on successfully.

MISS W. Can we make use of schools before we know our aim quite clearly, or can schools help us to find our aim?

MR. O. If you have no aim, no school can help.

MR. P. Is the idea of expansion also connected with the idea of the necessity of putting someone in your place?

MR. O. Yes, you may put it so, only it is really much simpler. Every work must, sooner or later, come to its possible limits. Then it becomes necessary to change something. It is then a kind of crossroads. But we are still far from it.

MRS. N. There is one thing that I don't see clearly. I have always looked upon all the lines of work from my own point of view, and the idea of Mrs. N. getting a chance of furthering her own work. But the idea that, from the group's point of view, it is also necessary to have individuals—this idea is new to me, rather like looking at the thing from the other end of the telescope.

MR. O. I don't understand the question.

* * *

[Answers to previous week's questions.]

MR. P. Does this organization contain two levels of the kind Mr. O. spoke of?

MR. O. We must begin not with this organization, but with any organization. Any organization of this kind, with certain ideas and a certain system may be on different levels. The level depends on the being of the people who enter into it. No external conditions can determine the level.

MISS W. If there are two levels in the school, would the lower know of the existence of the higher one?

MR. O. They may know, or they may not. Again it depends on the level of being of those who want to know.

MISS H. Mr. O. emphasized very much lately the idea of the work being on a bigger scale; has this anything to do with the question of two levels? I have rather wondered what this idea of scale implied?

MR. O. I have already answered this. Scale in this connection only means size. Every kind of work may be on different scale. It must have a certain scale, otherwise it will not be a success.

MR. P. I understood Mr. O. to say in relation to the rule of not talking about ideas, that ideas are not to be talked or written about without acknowledgment, otherwise it was stealing.

MR. O. This referred really more to writing, but certainly it also refers to talking.

MR. P. It seems to be very difficult to get rid of ideas one has got. They seem to crop up when you are discussing ordinary ideas in the ordinary way, and it is difficult to express an opinion because it may be coloured by ideas of the system.

MR. O. First of all it depends with whom you are talking. And certainly they must not crop up by themselves. If it continues to happen there is no profit in such a talk. Any colouring by ideas of the system is certainly bad, because in this way you lose distinction between ordinary ideas and ideas of the system. You must learn to separate them, to know which ideas belong to the system and which do not. This is why I always argue against the idea of 'separation' without mentioning separation of what from what. People use this expression meaning separation of 'I' and 'Ouspensky', or else separation of essence from personality. But at first this expression was used in this sense: separating ideas of the system from ideas not of the system. Some years ago I spoke without dividing them and then gave people the task of separating ideas belonging to the New Doctrine (as we called it) from others. Then in the *New Model* I was very careful not to introduce any ideas of the system. There are only three, and they are specially marked. If you mix ideas, your valuation of the system will suffer.

MR. B. From the point of view of the school, is the spreading of school ideas and school language among other people important? Would the passage of school ideas and language into general currency be of any help from the point of view of the school?

MR. O. Ideas cannot be spread in the right form. It is important to understand this. It would be very good if it could be done, but it cannot be done. Words will remain, but ideas themselves will be different. If it were enough just to spread them, why should all these talks be necessary, why is school necessary? The language will spread by itself, maybe in our lifetime, maybe later. But the ideas will enter into general currency in a wrong form. There will be no distinction between 'doing' and 'happening'. Ideas will be different, only words will remain.

MRS. A. Are all discussions on philosophical subjects undesirable?

MR. O. It depends with whom.

MR. P. If a subject crops up in conversation and you feel something about it, you are apt to say what you feel, and that is very likely to be coloured with system ideas. The alternative is to act almost consciously and to say something you don't mean at all, which is very difficult. In practice one is always carried away, identified.

MR. O. I don't see why it is necessary to say something. Why not say nothing? But it is quite right that in practice people are carried away. Our aim, however, is that it should not happen.

MRS. C. Did Mr. O. say what our position would be when he publishes *Fragments*?

MR. O. Then you will be able to write anything you like about what is written in them.

MRS. C. He is publishing the book soon, isn't he?

MR. O. Oh no, don't worry.

MRS. N. Mr. O. said that the breaking of rules would be sufficient to destroy the possibility of work altogether, and I noticed that in this connection he mentioned only two, the rule of not talking and the rule of not having any association with people of the earlier group. Can one take these as the two major rules, or are there others?

MR. O. You speak of two rules, and someone else heard three rules, but as a matter of fact I spoke about <u>rules</u> and then gave some examples. In connection with this, some people ask for lists of rules; others are satisfied with headings. This is the most formatory method of learning rules. You cannot make a catalogue of them. There is only one method of learning rules and this other method explains two things: how to learn rules and how to think in a new way. Take one rule and try to understand it and study it: what it means, why there is this rule, etc. Then you will see ramifications of this rule. You will see that it touches certain other things and creates at least one other rule. Then try to understand this other rule, its purpose, etc., and in trying to do this you will come to a third rule. In this way you come back in the end to the first rule. In this way you can remember rules, but in trying to learn them in the ordinary way, you will always forget them.

Then, I never said anything about 'earlier group'. I said people must not talk to those who left the work. Then I spoke about the rule made in 1924 after I broke relationship with G. I see that even now it immediately produces questions that cannot be answered. This shows why I said that people must not talk about the reasons of my separation from G. among themselves. About 'major' rules—all rules are major, they are all the same.

MR. C. I think when questions were asked about rules we were referred to those who introduced us into the work.

MR. O. Quite right. It is their business to supply you with all the material to study rules, but not with a catalogue.

MR. P. Would it be possible to be reminded of what all the rules are?

MR. O. It will not help. Understanding is necessary, otherwise it immediately becomes formatory.

MISS G. Did Mr. O. not say that if people spoke about the work, that was stealing; and he said that the people must pay for these ideas?

MR. O. When I spoke of 'stealing' I meant more in writing than in talking. But even in talking one must say where these ideas come from. About payment—I meant potential payment, and that becomes possible only if people know where the ideas come from. Payment is necessary not for us, but before anything else for those people. Without paying they will not get anything. It is magical, not simple. If you want someone to get something, he must pay for it.

MRS. E. Don't you think we fail to connect rules with the system as a whole? We are inclined to take it in an arbitrary way, that we must not talk, etc., whereas if one takes them as a means of understanding the system one can perhaps look upon them differently. These ideas demand a much higher level of understanding than we are capable of, and perhaps rules are a link between ourselves as we are now and a higher level of understanding which is demanded of us if we are to understand these ideas?

MR. O. Quite right. Rules are connected with the idea of conduct. When we become No. 5 our conduct will be perfect in relation to what we are now. But we are not No. 5, so we must have rules. If we remember rules, understand and follow them, our conduct will be connected and leading in a definite direction; not erratic like conduct of men 1, 2 and 3.

MR. C. It is difficult to see whether one's ideas are coloured by the ideas of the system or not. One must be conscious practically all the time in order to see whether we are using system ideas or not.

MR. O. No, it must be done. But first of all ideas must not be mixed in your own thinking. If they are not separated in your thinking, they will not be separated in your conversation. You must start with right thinking about them.

MRS. A. I wonder if there are rules some of us never heard. Somebody told me a rule I never heard before—that we must not recognize one another in a theatre.

MR. O. There is no rule like that. But it sometimes happens that if you meet somebody who is with friends who are not in the system, it becomes necessary to introduce you to those friends. And then someone may have heard something and, during the conversation, may ask questions about lectures, or something like that. So sometimes it is better not to come near another person in the work in a theatre or another public place.

MR. B. Mr. O. spoke some time ago about two categories of schools: one that only gave out knowledge, and another that was connected with change of being. I wonder if it is connected with what he said to-day?

MR. O. It is a wrong quotation. I did not say it like that. It was said in connection with a special conversation: I said <u>responsibility</u> of people in connection with school is different depending as to whether the person who conducts the school gives knowledge or ascribes to himself certain powers. In the two cases responsibility and necessity of a certain understanding become different.

MRS. N. Such understanding as I got of rules I got really by breaking them. This made me very careless, and I thought of them from my own point of view. It was a shock to me to see that breaking them concerns the school. I can see it to a certain extent in the two rules Mr. O. gave us to-night.

MR. O. This 'two' is wrong. It was explained when rules were first mentioned that it cannot be otherwise. And I always gave examples how the breaking of a small rule stops work of school or of groups. Study by breaking rules is dangerous, and may have unexpected results.

MISS H. Is it a real rule that no one is to take notes at meetings? Some people who have been two years in the work said that everybody always takes notes and they have not been stopped.

MR. O. All people have heard this rule, only they don't want to follow it. If people take notes, they will never understand what they hear. The aim of this rule is to help understanding. If they don't want to follow it, I will not enforce it—it helps selection.

MR. S. Is one way of getting hold of a rule to see the result of one's action? Then the rule would tighten of its own accord.

MR. O. It cannot be done. Suppose you give a rule to children that they are not to cut their finger. If they say they want to, and cut off the finger, it will not grow again.

* * *

MR. T. I find that struggling with negative emotions is always unpremeditated with me. If I plan to do it beforehand, I don't do it. Yet I cannot give up the idea that planning is right in this connection. Which is right?

MR. O. I don't quite understand. Your idea is that you struggle when they appear. But in reality you can only struggle with them by thinking about them in the right way. Then after a time they may diminish. If you don't think about them, or if you think about them in the wrong way, they will grow. You can stop negative emotions only by right attitude to them: this will affect them in the long run. This is the only one real way.

MISS M. Speaking of the triad 3-2-1, Mr. O. said 3 did not represent direct effort, but some sort of indirect 'sly' effort. I have tried to understand this. Could it be connected with the alarms one tries to give oneself?

MR. O. No, this is a special question. Alarms are mechanical.

MRS. C. Has anyone remarked on the great help it has been to have what Mr. O. said about self-remembering? He said that in trying to self-remember we were never to use the word 'I', because it puts one in a wrong personality. This has been a great help to me.

MR. O. And which word did I say to use instead?

MRS. C. I thought to substitute 'you' for 'I'?

MR. O. No, I meant when anybody uses the word 'I' in the sense of the whole. This is what I meant when I said you must not use the word 'I'. Every moment we must know it is only a little part of us. It is not the word that is important, but the realization that you are never 'all', never the whole.

MRS. A. I understood Mr. O. to say that he would give us some notes about conduct. Could we hear about this? About the importance of our thoughts in relation to conduct?

MR. O. This I have answered.

MRS. S. Is there any way by which we can remember more clearly what we have understood when we were in a better state?

MR. O. It is a very important thing, but I don't know of a special method. These moments must be connected. Look backwards, try to compare. This is particularly important in relation to some definite question. You may understand something that you did not understand half an hour ago. But perhaps before there have been moments when you also understood something in this connection. Try to remember them and connect them.

MISS W. Mr. O. said that as a rule he did not like exercises. May we hear more why he does not like them?

MR. O. The ordinary idea of exercises is useless—mechanical. Mechanical help plays a very small part in this system. There are certain exercises, however, like the 'stop' exercise, which are used in this system, but they need special supervision.

MR. C. If, when one is making attempts at self-remembering instead of using the word 'I', one is trying to recognize which personality is uppermost at the time—is that right? It is the only method I know.

MR. O. It is right because it includes the realization that one is not one. In that sense it is right.

MRS. C. Last week someone asked how these meetings could become more real, more useful: I notice that they are not what they might be, but I do not see how they could be made better.

MR. O. They are what they are because you are not what you might be. There is a certain definite principle in the work—time is counted. For every person certain demands are made in the first month. Next months demands grow. If a person does not meet these demands, the bill becomes very big in the end. If a person considers he has the right to be on the level of the first month after he has been some years in the work, he cannot pay his bill. Payment means first of all being able to meet demands. If you are behind your time, if you cannot meet the demands, then nothing can be done, and for you things will look below level, because you are below level.

MR. B. How many types are there? And are there only definite types or intermediate ones?

MR. O. Study of types is impossible on our level. Full appreciation of types needs a different level.

MR. B. Are we to understand types in relation to what is said about them in the *New Model*?

MR. O. I use sometimes the word 'types' in the sense of types of personality. But types of essence are beyond us at present.

MR. H. Is it possible sometimes to borrow energy or understanding? Sometimes I feel, after a meeting, I go away with more energy. Energy does not seem entirely to depend on our own efforts.

MR. O. Quite right, but you have to pay for it sooner or later. And payment increases.

MRS. S. I understand that we may meet people from the Tuesday and Wednesday groups. May we repeat to them what is said at Monday meetings?

MR. O. At present, yes.

MRS. C. If, after a time of special effort, you feel tired, would another effort get you into another accumulator?

MR. O. It may, or it may not.

MISS W. You said if one makes decisions at moments of self-remembering about thinking . . .

MR. O. About anything.

MISS W. . . . . will it affect one for a short time or for long?

MR. O. It depends how deep self-remembering was. If self-remembering was imaginary, decision will also be imaginary. But real moment of consciousness means a moment of will.

MRS. S. I was very frightened going in an aeroplane because I thought we were going to crash. Then I thought, if one were ill, is there anything one can do in moments before death?

MR. O. You describe just work of imagination. You were frightened in the aeroplane—that is natural. But why think afterwards what would happen if you are ill, etc.? This is just imagination going on and on. What one could do is another thing—one must not increase Law of Accident, without necessity. This is a principle, because every increase of Law of Accident increases imagination.

MRS. C. You mean it is no good thinking soberly what one would do?

MR. O. Did I say that? You take a side thought and attach importance to it.

MR. P. Can there be wrong effort at self-remembering?

MR. O. You mean unsuccessful?

MR. P. No, I meant based on wrong understanding of the idea of it.

MR. O. That would mean unsuccessful, because it would bring no result.

MR. R. About stealing ideas. I thought of Priestley's play. . . .

MR. O. I am so accustomed to people stealing my ideas, from the age of ten. But about ideas of the system we must be careful, we must not give people system ideas. Our interest is to keep the ideas for school, not to make them public.

MR. C. Is there anything one can do that is wrong, if it helps?

MR. O. It depends on results. Later it may be interesting to speak of wrong methods, simply in order to know which results they can, and which they cannot, produce. For example, in some Eastern schools they use hypnotism for self-remembering. They hypnotize you and put into you the idea of a different personality or individuality. Then when you wake up you have to get out of it. Some people do, and then they begin to remember themselves. Sometimes this needs a year. But self-remembering does not become stronger because of that.

MRS. N. Are efforts to work and understand a form of payment?

MR. O. It creates the possibility of payment, but it is not payment in itself. Payment must be useful not only to you, but to someone else—to the school. But if you are not useful to yourself, you cannot be useful to the school either.

MR. P. Can enough energy for self-remembering be made only by self-remembering?

MR. O. We have enough. We must struggle with causes of waste of emotional energy.

MR. P. Can this process of struggling against a negative emotion be accomplished inside twenty-four hours?

MR. O. No, you cannot put it so. This waste depends chiefly on slow-eating negative emotions, such as suspicion, etc. They can take an enormous amount of energy.

MR. P. So you have to struggle for a week against it before you conquer it?

MR. O. At least six months.

MR. P. Nobody struggles consistently.

MR. O. They conquer you, but you struggle with them in your mind. Negative emotions have been developing for years, so at least you must spend an equal number of months to conquer them, or maybe more.

MRS. C. Do they make it so difficult for us to get more emotional life?

MR. O. Certainly.

MR. P. So a moment of self-remembering is the reward one can expect only after a long process of saving energy?

MR. O. I said we have enough energy. But suppose you are right and we don't have enough—then we can increase energy only in this way. But really it is not a question of energy but of lack of understanding of our position.

MRS. H. Really if we fully realized that we cannot remember ourselves, we would automatically remember ourselves?

MR. O. Nothing happens automatically in the work. I always say that we are not afraid enough and not curious enough. We don't realize that anything may happen to sleeping people. We don't realize the necessity of discipline—of rules. We think we can 'do' because we think of ourselves as men No. 7.

* * *

Monday. October 18th 1937.

MR. O. Try to think what you want to ask, but try to concentrate on the question of what is important and what is not important. It is important to learn to distinguish these things.

Causes of unsuccess in the work lie in the insufficient understanding of the importance of things. For instance, you don't think sufficiently; you do not give yourself sufficient account of the relation of work to life: what position work occupies in relation to life; how it stands in relation to life, etc. There are many questions like that. I don't say you can answer them, but you can think about it; see it from one angle and another angle. Unless you think in this way things will not be in their right perspective for you; you won't understand the work in the right way. And I don't notice these questions among the questions you ask.

Then, we must think about the house now. We have found one interesting house, and during this or next week we will have a special meeting to discuss this matter. We must see whether we can take this house or not. It is a long lease that is for sale, and also there will be some repairs. If we manage to take it, work will develop in London. If we find we cannot do it now, we may continue to look for houses. But all the houses I have seen show how difficult it is to find what we need. This house has a big hall that will easily hold all the people we have now together. It has got a stage and chairs for two hundred and fifty people now, but it can hold much more; I think easily about four hundred.

This house cannot be seen now by everybody, because there are some people living there who know us. But if anybody wants to see it and writes to me, it may be possible to arrange.

All the continuation and development of work depends on the understanding of the position of the work in life, of its relation to life. The work is a very small thing, and enormous things belong to life. I don't mean by this wars and revolutions, etc. I mean things which belong to everyday life. We live in very funny times.

MRS. J. Isn't it a fact that very little of these ideas goes much further than life things?

MR. O. For whom? For us, yes. If we don't try to comfort ourselves and understand their value ... but to think so generally is just to comfort oneself.

Sometimes people ask what to read. I have often said that it is useful to read newspapers, if you know how to read them. Here is, for instance, an article about a site lying side by side with Lyne.

[Reading.]

This is life. It is very significant. And living among these things you ask me how to distinguish between what is important and what is not important.

As I said, if you want to understand what is more important and what is less important, you will find an enormous amount of material if you ask yourselves what life means and what position work occupies in life. You will see that it occupies no position at all, that it need not exist at all from the point of view of life.

At the same time, it is the most important thing for those who understand it. So we must make the work go on, and not expect any help from life. We must go against life, do everything ourselves.

Now we can talk about the house or about anything you like.

MR. C. Are we to raise a large sum of money for the house?

MR. O. Yes, it cannot be got without. Certainly it is not as good as Lyne. Lyne is a freehold, so any improvements we do at Lyne will remain and increase its value. Here it is a long lease and the value of the house will diminish every year.

MR. S. Could it be fully used immediately?

MR. O. Only at the end of March. And then some time will be taken up by repairs and alterations—so it could not be used until summer. But this is unavoidable.

MR. S. Are there any possible activities by which the whole of it could be used?

MR. O. That refers to the time after buying the house. We may not need the whole house at once. We need the top of the house.

[Plan of the house put on the blackboard.]

MR. N. How long is the lease?

MR. O. Thirty-nine years. The ground floor has two rooms bigger than this, or the same, and also others. Then there is a separate story between the ground and the first floors which also has many rooms that may be used for groups. Also there is a big basement. We may not need it now. We could shut up part of the house in the beginning.

Q. Would Lyne be kept on as well?

MR. O. Certainly. Lyne is necessary for people who can come there, and also in one or two years Lyne will be self-supporting and will not need any particular help.

MRS. P. Is there any idea of the sum required?

MR. O. I don't know yet. Those who wish to come to the special meeting, not from curiosity, because they think they can help in one or another way, should give their names to Mme. K.

MRS. S. Isn't there a usual yearly rent, as well as lease?

MR. O. Yes, but the rent is comparatively small.

MRS. N. Is it fairly central?

MR. O. It is central for us, it is in this part of London.

MR. P. Isn't it very important not to lose this opportunity of getting this house? If we do not get it, it seems very difficult to find another. It might delay the expansion for a very long time if we do not get it.

MR. O. It is almost impossible to find a suitable house. It is quite right what you say. If we cannot take this house we will be obliged to take another, quite near here, on a short lease. But that will not give the same possibilities.

MRS. S. Apart from the financial side, what rests with us in the question?

MR. O. At the present moment the first thing is to decide the financial side.

MR. P. Does the house become the official headquarters of the Society at once? If we got the house, would it be a question of starting the Society at once?

MR. O. Quite right. Then it will be useful in many ways.

MRS. J. It seems a great deal hangs on the question of importance. The organization and house must go together. This is the most suitable house. Mr. O. said we must try to understand what this means, and what it is necessary for us to do. How can we better prepare for this organization?

MR. O. You cannot bring the question of importance and not importance of things here. It does not enter into the question of the house—it is too obvious.

MR. C. Can we have an idea of what qualifications are needed in order to help? Obviously financial help is important, but are there others?

MR. O. Yes, there are many ways to help the work.

Just now we must concentrate partly on the general idea of the relative importance of things and the relation of work to life. This is one idea. And, quite concretely, on this house. That is another thing.

MR. W. It seems to me the financial question must come first.

MR. O. Quite right.

MRS. P. The sum spread over several people would not be so much.

MRS. J. How much was the premium?

MR. O. The owners at present ask £6,000. I cannot tell the details yet. But we must have not only that; we must have money for alterations and repairs. For instance, there is no central heating there. Then we must have, separately, money to run it for at least three years. Because in three years' time we may find new means. But we must be prepared for three years.

MR. S. So about £10,000 is needed almost immediately?

MR. O. Yes, about that, I think.

*   *   *

Thursday. October 28th 1937.

[Descriptions of the moral side of the system read out.]

MR. O. Many things that were read refer to the system but not to the moral ideas; others refer to moral ideas, but not to the system. The system is limited and definite; it cannot be everything; it can only be what it is; it can only serve the purpose for which it is created: not <u>any</u> purpose.

What is morality? Understanding of laws of conduct? It is not sufficient. If we say, like a savage, or like our friends the bolsheviks say, 'If you steal from me it is bad, but if I steal from you it is good', it is not morality; it is merely savage conduct. Because morality begins when one has a feeling of good and bad in relation to one's own actions, and is capable of sacrificing what is bad, not doing what a man considers to be bad, and doing what he considers to be good.

What is good? And what is bad? Generally, at this first stage, man takes moral principles from religious, philosophical or scientific ideas, or simply adopts conventional taboos. He believes that some things are good and some things are bad. But this is subjective morality, because what is good in one country is bad in another. For instance, I have given before the example of blood revenge. In some countries it is considered the most immoral thing to refuse blood revenge. So it is all relative and subjective. All that can be said about ordinary morality is that it has no foundation and no basis. Some people say the destruction of life is definitely bad. But why is it better to kill a pig than a man? And why, in one case, a man can kill, and in another not? All that is known about ordinary morality is full of contradictions.

The aim of the system is to bring man to conscience. Conscience is a certain quality that is in every normal man. It is really a different expression of the same quality as consciousness. Only consciousness works more on the intellectual side, and conscience more on the moral side: it helps to realize what is good and what is bad in one's own conduct. How does conscience work? By uniting emotions. We can experience on the same day a great many contradictory emotions, pleasant or unpleasant, on the same subject, either one after another, or even simultaneously. And we do not notice it because of absence of conscience. Buffers prevent one 'I' or one personality from seeing another. But in a state of conscience a man cannot help seeing all these contradictions. If in the morning he said one thing, in the afternoon another, in the evening yet another: he will remember it. But in life he will not remember it, or he will insist that he does not know what is good and what is bad.

The way to conscience is through destroying buffers. And buffers can be destroyed through self-remembering, not identifying, etc.

The idea of conscience and the idea of buffers needs long study. But what can be understood from the beginning, if we want to speak about the moral side, is that a man must have a sense of good and bad. If he has not—nothing can be done. He must start with a certain moral sense, a sense of right and wrong, in order to get more. He must understand, first, the relativity of ordinary morality, and, second, he must realize the necessity of objective right and wrong. When he realizes the necessity of objective, permanent right and wrong, then he will look at things from the point of view of the system.

The system begins with the possibility of objective state of consciousness, and, therefore, of objective truth. The system says that in a state of objective consciousness man can know objective truth.

In our ordinary understanding objective truth refers more to the intellectual side of life. A man can say that he wants to know it also on religious side, moral side, aesthetic side, etc. The system explains that man 1, 2, 3, 4, 5, 6 and 7 are all in a different position. There is religion No. 1, No. 2, No. 3, No. 4, etc. And there is morality No. 1, 2, 3, 4, 5, etc. It does not mean that it is wrong, but that one cannot be explained by the other. Christ, if we take him, should be man No. 8. He did not preach inquisition. But if his teaching is distorted by men 1, 2 and 3 to use for criminal purposes, this cannot be attributed to Christ.

Coming back again to morality—a man must, first, have a moral sense. Second, he must be sufficiently sceptical in relation to ordinary morality and ordinary moral principles. He must understand that there is nothing general, nothing permanent in them, that they change according to conventions, place and period. And, third, he must understand the necessity of objective morality. If he understands these three things, then he will find a basis for distinguishing what is right and what is wrong in relation to each separate thing, and will distinguish what is criminal and what is not. Because there are definite standards, if one starts rightly. The whole thing is to start from the right point of view. If one starts from a wrong point of view, one will not find anything.

All this needs a long talk and we will continue this conversation. But now try to connect all I have said with what you have heard before.

Next Thursday you will begin the reading of *Fragments* where I describe how I met the system, the first years of work, and the system itself.

* * *

MR. B. How can we trust our own sense of right and wrong?

MR. O. You cannot trust or mistrust. It is there. So that is not the question. You can only hesitate and be in doubt in relation to the object. Certainly, without knowledge, without development, without consciousness you cannot say definitely whether it is right or wrong; but you may be on the way to it.

* * *

MR. O. Before we go on with questions I want to say why I made this rule for new people about interest in criminal politics, and explain what I call criminal politics. Certainly it is easy to say, like Mr. G—n said, 'I don't know anything about bolsheviks.' Unfortunately I know. The fact is that when power got into the hands of this party, which was a very small and despised party, all evolution stopped. In the last twenty years Russia has produced not a single book, not a single picture. If there are people who write or paint there, they are people who have been doing it before the revolution. And I saw what happened. I saw what an enormous progress Russia had made in the twenty years preceding the revolution—it was quite a different country; literature, art, everything was developing rapidly. And now all this has stopped. At the same time there are plenty of words and promises. On the economic side: the rich are destroyed, but the poor are much worse off than before. They are slaves. So everybody is in a worse position than before, except government spies.

I see that certain things I said last time were misunderstood. For instance, about persuasion. What I said was that a political party, within its own country, cannot use machine guns to persuade people to accept their views. There exist certain elementary standards: people who use force to make other people accept their own formatory ideas are criminals.

Also, I see that some people took it as though I defended war. There is nothing worse than war. But one must make a distinction between those who are responsible for war and simple participation in war. A soldier taking part in a war is not a criminal.

In relation to the bolsheviks: what particularly makes them criminals is spying, lies and pretence. They pretend that they have cultural aims. Actually it is all simply paid propaganda.

MR. M. I don't understand when you say that some people are responsible for war. How can a machine be responsible?

MR. O. You cannot introduce philosophical ideas into a practical conversation. For instance, when war broke out I was in India, in Colombo, so I had nothing to do with war. But certainly prime ministers, kings, journalists can—from the ordinary point of view—be called responsible for the war. There is a difference: people who take upon themselves the managing of states are responsible. At the same time they are not conscious, so they are not responsible. But in the ordinary sense they are responsible, and a man who is taken as a soldier is not.

MR. F. How would you classify non-criminal politics?

MR. O. Politics going according to certain standards or rules of the country. If politicians take bribes, for instance, this also is criminal. If they use violence, it is criminal; particularly if the views they want to enforce are utopian, invented, and have no relation to reality.

MISS F. Is morality a permanent thing or changing?

MR. O. Morality is always different, but moral sense is permanent. If people have not got moral sense, it is no use to speak to them. If they have, they will understand that morality is relative. If they understand this, and understand at the same time the possibility of objective consciousness and objective truth, then they will understand the possibility of objective morality.

MISS R. A man can refuse to take part in war if he realizes it is wrong?

MR. O. Then he will be shot.

MISS R. Surely, if he is drawn into the war, he is taking the same responsibility as a prime minister?

MR. O. No, he is taking no responsibility. It is necessary to distinguish between things. An individual man cannot change things, therefore he is not responsible. If we speak like that we make it impossible for us to understand anything. Or if we bring philosophical reasons in and say that both an individual soldier and a prime minister are machines.

MR. D. How to distinguish between a prime minister and an ordinary man?

MR. O. Ask them, who is who. If people take official posts they become responsible.

MISS H. You said conscience is unity of emotions. Can you explain it more?

MR. O. It is capacity to see all emotions at the same time. You have many opposite emotions and many opposite truths and you never see the contradictions. You must start by observing how one feeling contradicts another. If you have not observed this, you cannot see what I mean. You have many contradictory opinions, views, feelings. One moment you like something, another moment you hate it, etc. But you don't notice it. You cannot separate them.

MR. A. They are separated by different moments of time?

MR. O. They may be at the same time.

MR. T. If you apply a standard, it is whether a particular thing helps or hinders consciousness?

MR. O. The standard must be in connection with the system. Without a system (I don't mean only this system, but you must have a system) you cannot judge. You may have a feeling of right and wrong, but you won't <u>know</u>. So you must be guided by a system.

MR. D. Do you make a distinction between criminal and very bad?

MR. O. It is difficult to speak about words.

MISS F. I cannot see a state when you see everything all at once.

MR. O. You cannot. We cannot have conscience, just as we cannot have consciousness. But the more we become conscious, the more often moments will come when we will begin to feel conscience. But at present conscience is theoretical for us, we cannot experiment with it.

MISS M. Is there anything in Christian religion incompatible with this system?

MR. O. Christ taught on the level of man No. 8. So what can we know about Christian religion? It is a question of levels.

MISS M. I mean the accepted view.

MR. O. There is no accepted view. People always argue about the interpretation of Christian teaching. How many wars, how many arguments there were about some one small thing!

In the same way, I think it is a good idea that the cause of Russian revolution was an argument in the seventeenth century that arose in the Russian Church. Some people said you must cross yourself with two fingers, and some said with three. As a result it created two sects, and destroyed the possibility of the existence of middle class in Russia. And absence of middle class was the cause of the revolution.

If you take the original New Testament it is incomprehensible for us. We don't know its real meaning. We only know words and different interpretations of them. We must come to facts, to where we really are.

MRS. B. Can you say more about the objective right and wrong in connection with the system?

MR. O. If we make a general idea of it, it would be useless, because it would be too thin. I gave an example: mechanicalness and consciousness. There are many other examples.

MRS. B. I realize that ordinary morality does not exist, but I cannot find anything else.

MR. O. You must realize that it does not exist, that it is contradictory.

MRS. B. But if I can find nothing else?

MR. O. If you realize this, from this point you can begin. You cannot find it in one day. It needs development of consciousness and conscience. The way to the understanding of objective morality is through the development of conscience.

MR. A. Does self-remembering help?

MR. O. This is the way.

MR. A. But it is different?

MR. O. Certainly. Self-remembering is only an attempt, only the first step towards consciousness. But eventually it leads to it.

MR. M. Can the teaching of esoteric schools be wrong?

MR. O. What do you know about esoteric schools? If you knew several, you could compare. Generally, the teaching of esoteric schools does not reach us directly, but only by passing through the minds of ordinary people. And again there are different degrees of schools. But in comparison with, say an ordinary academy, certainly there is less chance of mistakes if a teaching comes from higher minds. But it comes to us through so many translations and interpretations of unconscious people that there can be no guarantee that it is not distorted.

Q. What is the nature of buffers?

MR. O. It is difficult to describe. When you learn to observe buffers you will know their nature. But I can give some examples. Sometimes buffers are very deep convictions through which man cannot see in himself. For instance, I knew a man who was convinced that he is never late. He was actually always late, but because of this conviction he could never see it, and was genuinely astonished if it was pointed out to him that he was late.

* * *

Monday. November 8th 1937.

MRS. C. Isn't the moral side of the system discrimination between good and evil?

MR. O. Quite. But what do you wish to say by it?

MRS. C. It can only be got from the sense of freedom. . . .

MR. O. From what?

MRS. C. From my own helplessness.

MR. O. What is there moral about it? You begin to speak about one thing and then speak of another which has no relation with the first. Where is morality here? You continue to speak without trying to understand. You cannot just pass from one thing to another.

MRS. W. Morality deals with human relationships?

MR. O. With conduct.

MRS. W. It seems that elimination of negative emotions. . . .

MR. O. You began to speak about morality, so keep to it.

MR. C. Is morality obedience to cosmic laws?

MR. O. Too big.

MR. C. To law of cause and effect?

MR. O. We are under it whether we want it or not.

This word 'morality', 'moral side' was not used, and so you never thought of it. And yet there is a very definite moral side of the system, which it is possible to separate. It does not mean that everything is included in the moral side: it is necessary to find out where it begins.

Morality is connected with the feeling of right and wrong. But the feeling of right and wrong is one thing, and the definition, the contents, is quite another. Two people may have a very strong feeling of right and wrong, but what is right for one will be wrong for the other. Feeling does not presuppose definition. A man may have the feeling of right and wrong, and wrong ideas about it.

In the system objective consciousness is described as a state in which we can know truth. If in objective state of consciousness we can know the truth, so we can also know about right and wrong. Consequently, the same way which leads to objective consciousness leads also to the understanding of right and wrong. As we have not got objective consciousness, we consider everything that helps us to develop consciousness as right and good, and everything that hinders it as wrong and bad. This is a good definition, only it is too far from life. There are many things about which we can find no visible indications as to whether they help or hinder. So it is necessary to look for other principles. And other principles we can find only when we think about concrete cases of conduct. In the system one can find many sufficient indications which show how to look at one or another thing.

The aim of the system is to find objective truth. We, as we are, may have a very strong feeling, and yet be mistaken about the contents of right and wrong.

MRS. H. Is the moral side of the system the struggle between 'yes' and 'no'?

MR. O. Yes, the struggle between 'yes' and 'no' may lead in this direction; it may lead to a better understanding of right and wrong, but it is not a fact by itself.

MR. W. Do you mean we must think of how we affect other people?

MR. O. No, we must think in which way we can come to a better understanding of right and wrong. For instance, several questions have been asked about the rule of warning new people. In one of the psychological lectures I gave an example about how to judge a political situation from the point of view of the system. Civilization can be measured by the amount of personal freedom. A certain minimum of personal freedom is necessary for the existence of a school. If personal freedom disappears, one can, therefore, say that it is a wrong state of country. This is the moral side of political situation. Fascism and bolshevism are both based on impressing their ideas on others by force, and the result actually is domination by a small party at the expense of the whole population of a country. For instance, in Russia peasants and workmen, in whose name the revolution was made, are now in a much worse position than before, and suffer much more than they did before the revolution. It is all words and lies, and the country only suffers.

From this point of view all political activities destroying personal freedom are criminal. Work needs personal freedom. From this point of view bolshevism and fascism have equally criminal methods, aims and results. Why? Because our aim is to find an objective definition of right and wrong and to understand it. And although we have not come to a full understanding, we can, maybe, begin to understand a little.

I have spoken before about different triads. I said that different activities depend on different triads. One kind of activity means one kind of triad, another kind of activity means another kind of triad. Art requires a certain triad, criminal activity means quite a different triad, etc. In art one must be able to use a certain particular triad or else it will not be art. In another case, if you use a certain particular triad of another kind your work is bound to be criminal.

Take two simple examples in order to try and understand this. In order to build a house, at every moment effort is needed, every single brick must be put into place by effort; no triad passes from one to another without effort. At last the house is built and furnished. Then, if you want to burn it, you just strike a match and burn it. From the ordinary point of view people do not understand that the two activities are totally different. In the second case one triad passes to another without any effort. This kind of triad needs only a very small initial effort.

Neither the one nor the other triad can make a picture. This means that in order to paint a good picture one must be able to use a different triad; something else is needed.

When we understand this, we shall understand what crime means. Crime needs a definite triad, and this triad will always produce crime.

There is a very limited number of fundamental triads—six triads (the seventh is incomprehensible for us). These six triads create all the phenomena of our life. If you take phenomena given in diagrams, I said that we can study octaves in them. And occasionally we can also see octaves in phenomena of human activity. The same applies to triads. There are only six types of triads:

$$1-2-3 \qquad 1-3-2$$
$$2-1-3 \qquad 2-3-1$$
$$3-2-1 \qquad 3-1-2$$

Triads can be divided according to the force by which they begin, and they can also be divided according to the force by which they end. Take the triads that end with 2. It means that the result is lower than the beginning. Something happens—either disaster, catastrophe or degeneration. These two triads show descending octaves. It does not mean that all descending octaves are necessarily of this kind; but that is sufficient for the moment. So there are four ascending octaves and two descending octaves. If you take this in relation to human activity, it is enough. If we take the same thing on a larger scale, we shall have three descending and three ascending octaves. So you see, not only the force in the beginning is important, but also the last. In this way, for practical purposes, triads can be judged by the beginning and the end. It is all very very far, but it shows the way to objective understanding of right and wrong.

MRS. W. What is the difference between 2-1-3 and 2-3-1?

MR. O. If we take the Food Table: the first do 768 comes in as 2. It meets with carbon which is 1, and results in nitrogen 384, which is 3. This is the triad 2-1-3. All the triads in the Food Diagram go in this order with the exception of one: do 48 comes in as 2, but there is no carbon 1. So you must first bring 3, and 2 and 3 together to make 1. Or rather, you must bring 3 first and then 3 brings 1. Self-remembering is 3, and it will bring the necessary carbon. In other triads carbon is arranged by nature, but in this case there is no carbon, it can only be brought by self-remembering. This is triad 2-3-1.

MR. F. Does the criminal triad end with 2?

MR. O. Yes, it is 3-1-2. But this triad has many legitimate functions also.

MRS. W. Does 3 always mean something higher than 1 and 2?

MR. O. No. 2 is the lowest always, but sometimes 1 is higher and sometimes 3. Normally 1 is the highest, although sometimes 3 is more important.

MR. R. Can one say that one particular triad causes friendship?

MR. O. Probably yes, sometimes. If you find examples, you may be able to connect it with one particular triad. It depends how it starts, etc.

MR. L. Is it right to say that in the triad 2-3-1, 1 is created by self-remembering and appears as a new element?

MR. O. Yes, it is not there, but why lay emphasis on 'creating'?

MRS. W. Why in the Ray of Creation does 1-2-3 have to change?

MR. O. I have explained all this. It has to do with forces and hydrogens. If you supplant forces by hydrogens, you will see.

MRS. C. What is the obstacle to making effort to self-remember?

MR. O. This is material for observation. How can I define all the obstacles?

MRS. C. Often I feel I am just beginning, but I cannot go on.

MR. O. You must find yourself the obstacle.

MR. R. What did you mean when you said that on a higher scale there are three descending octaves?

MR. O. Because in the Ray of Creation, expansion and differentiation cannot be put as ascending.

MRS. H. Learning how to use triad 2-3-1 is the only chance we have of escaping mechanicalness?

MR. O. Better think before asking for final definitions. Try to find more examples. Your question was wrongly put. You can say that this is the only triad that cannot go on mechanically; all the others can. Even if they require effort, it is mechanical effort. This triad is the only one that needs full attention.

MR. F. Are the different effects produced by the triad 3-1-2 due to different scale?

MR. O. In different cases, in different octaves, it can produce different effects. In human activity it is criminal, in nature it need not be.

MRS. W. How does 3-2-1 go mechanically?

MR. O. It can go unconsciously.

MISS P. Is there a better or worse mechanicalness?

MR. O. Ask in relation to facts.

MISS P. Is mechanicalness that needs effort better than mechanicalness that goes on by itself?

MR. O. This is not a sufficient definition. Some things must be mechanical, others need attention, intention, consciousness. Certainly if these become mechanical it will be a worse kind of mechanicalness. But some things happen even better by themselves. Mechanicalness by itself is not wrong, it is not an accusation. Some things must be mechanical, for instance, physiological processes.

MISS P. I was thinking of mass psychology.

MR. O. It does not exist. I gave you a better example.

MRS. W. 3-2-1 is creative work?

MR. O. Yes, and many other things. Nothing is exclusive. There are also other interpretations.

MRS. H. After World 6, where these triads start, it becomes mechanical.

How does one accept that in our world there is one triad that needs full attention? How does one distinguish it?

MR. O. There is such a big difference between our world and World 6! Even organic life does not belong to this scale—it is a different octave. If we say that organic life is 192, it is only approximate, to show its place. And if we take man as 384, how many triads would it be? Try to calculate.

MRS. W. When you say that things in nature may be triad 3-1-2, do you mean such things as earthquakes?

MR. O. No.

MR. C. Which triad is repetition such as reproduction on the same level?

MR. O. 1-2-3.

MISS P. Has morality something to do with obligations to others?

MR. O. It is difficult to speak about words. It is necessary to establish what you mean by obligation. Certainly in certain cases it can have connection with it. But if I put the question like this: what is first demanded of morality? Suppose I have a strong sense of right and wrong and the contents are wrong? Then the first aim becomes to find the contents, to find what is right and what is wrong. As we are now, we are at the very first step of approaching the understanding of what is right and wrong, and you already want the answer.

MISS P. Can that sense of obligation that one has be mechanical?

MR. O. Certainly it can. Everything can be mechanical.

MRS. H. Is psycho-transformism the work of a triad?

MR. O. Yes, it must be the work of a particular triad. But it is a complicated process; it works by triad 2-1-3 and 2-3-1. You can see that intervals in the ascending octave work by 2-3-1 and notes by 2-1-3. Triad 2-3-1 belongs to the ascending octave. Triad 2-3-1 works in the intervals, filling the places that cannot be passed.

MR. F. Can you approach the study of types through triads?

MR. O. No, in our state of consciousness and with the centres we use we can only know some principles. We can know that types exist, and nothing more. This is one of the things that belongs to the future. The only way of studying types for us is by direct observation. In this way, little by little, you can classify people you know personally. You can have glimpses of the idea. If your classification is right, it can serve as a starting point to the study of types, but no more than that.

MR. P. If there are no real differences between nationalities. . . .

MR. O. I have never noticed. I think people of the same nationality, class and education can be more different than people, similar inside, but belonging to different race, class and part of the world.

MR. P. In that case how is love of one's country to be explained?

MR. O. In some moments of history it is simply a realization of mutual interest, which may be more or less intelligent. It is difficult to explain how it appears and disappears. Sometimes it has a protective quality that leads to preservation; sometimes an aggressive quality that leads to destruction. Or sometimes the disappearance of this quality leads to destruction.

* * *

You will hear when the next meeting is to be. It is a question of room. The necessity to have a new house has become very great now. We have one house in view and, if we decide to take it, it will be possible for all people to meet at once. And for you it will be very interesting to meet at the same time with people of other groups. But it will not happen till spring or summer.

* * *

Thursday. January 6th 1938. (Warwick Gardens.)

MR. R. Is it desirable to self-remember when resting?

MR. O. What is desirable is to remember oneself when it is most difficult.

MR. A. Is self-remembering connected with 'I am that I am'?

MR. O. No, it has nothing to do with it. This is a philosophic idea. It is like the idea included in the Ray of Creation. The Absolute, in other words, can be called 'I' or 'Ego'—nothing to do with imaginary human 'I's. Also it is connected with another idea, that only God has the right to call himself 'I'—and we call ourselves 'I'.

Q. What did you mean when you said we must try to remember ourselves when it is most difficult?

MR. O. You know you must not do something. One part of you wants to do it. Then remember yourself and stop it. Self-remembering has an element of Will in it. If it were just dreaming 'I am, I am, I am' it would not be anything. You must give certain time simply to studying what remembering means and what not remembering means and what effects these have. Then you can invent many different ways to remember yourselves. But actually self-remembering is not intellectual, abstract—how can I put it?—it is moments of will. It is not thought; it is action. It means control. Otherwise what is the use of remembering yourself if it does not increase control? You can only control yourself in moments of self-remembering. Mechanical control—by training, education and so on—is not control: when one is taught to behave in a certain way in certain circumstances.

MR. H. For a long time I have been trying to observe the working of triads. When I try to remember what has been said, I can make no connection in my mind. I simply cannot see it.

MR. O. Leave triads. Try to think in this way. Human action may be different. We know difference in matter. We know there is metal, or wood, or cloth; that they are different. But action for us is always the same action. Our mind is so made (by education, associative reasoning, habit) that we do not understand, do not distinguish different action. Try to understand that there are a certain number of different actions in the same way as there are different matters, minerals, organic matter, living organic matter, and so on. Try to find parallels. For instance, one action is necessary to build a house; another action to burn a house. To burn a house is quite different, much easier. Try to think how much easier to burn. If you think about it, you will see the difference, that it is different action. Then neither the action which builds a house, nor the action which burns a house will paint a picture: quite different action is necessary. At the same time, action by which you paint a picture is not necessary to build a house. Much simpler effort is required than this. Only a few people can paint a picture. Everybody can take part in building a house. The same effort which is necessary for building a house will not be enough to invent, say, a new kind of electric bell. And action by which you can invent the electric bell will not make a picture—a bad picture perhaps, copy, but not a good picture. If somebody steals this picture from your house, this will be a different kind of action. There are six kinds really, but the sixth distinction is more difficult. Take these five: building, destruction, creation, invention, crime. And try to find analogies. This will bring you to the understanding of different triads. Begin with human actions, not with yourselves.

Q. How can one develop judgment of the difference between actions?

MR. O. One cannot at once. It is a long process. Think about these five kinds and try to find what is similar to this action and similar to another, and then you will have categories. You cannot be sure. You must compare, make mistakes, then find mistakes and so on. It is a new way of thinking.

Triads come later. Trying to remember which triad is which makes you lose the meaning. You will do better to leave triads. Different kinds of action mean different triads, but which kind you can leave for now. Only you must understand the meaning of different actions.

Q. Is it actions themselves, regardless of motive?

MR. O. Yes, the actions themselves are different, but you cannot say it exactly like that. They are connected with motive, only not in the way we think. You must understand that a certain kind of result can only be obtained by the corresponding action. At the same time, motive also determines action. But if you use the best possible motive and the wrong action you get wrong result.

MR. A. Has it to do with the quality of action?

MR. O. Yes, but that depends how we understand 'quality'. If we regard quality as a kind of law, as we do where matter is concerned . . . metal will sink, wood will float. Same thing in relation to action. Man thinks every kind of action is the same, or depends on what he wants it to be like, or that he has a certain amount of energy and can turn it this way or that way. He has different kinds of energy—one for building a house, another for burning a house. Some lack one kind and have another; some people have more of this kind and less of the other; or have both, and so on.

MR. A. What kinds of energy? Psychic, physical, etc.?

MR. O. No, different division altogether, no parallel at all.

MRS. N. Is it a different triad if you do a thing well or do it badly?

MR. O. You try to do something and use the wrong triad—no result. The triad may be too good and the action will have no result.

Think about different kinds of action. After you will see different kinds of energy, different triads. This is not necessary at the beginning.

MR. R. If we are deficient in a certain kind of energy, can we create more of it?

MR. O. Some. There is the energy we want for our work. We can create that.

MISS F. The different kinds of action, are they connected with different levels of consciousness?

MR. O. Certain kinds of energy, certain kinds of action are connected with certain being.

MR. T. Are all the kinds of energy necessary?

MR. O. Difficult to answer. We cannot speak about them from that point of view—necessity or not necessity.

MRS. D. Can one tell from the result of an action whether energy used was the right energy?

MR. O. Sometimes.

MRS. D. Must every action fall into one or other of these categories?

MR. O. No action can escape. No triad, no action.

MR. A. I find it very easy to think subjectively when apparently self-remembering. I mean, I think I am self-remembering and that is as far as it goes. Can one be sure that self-remembering ever comes?

MR. O. That is day-dreaming, simply. Yes, certainly. One can have glimpses. They may be short, but as I have said, they can come in ordinary life. When it happens by itself. You find this by memory and observation and then perhaps when you have this particular feeling or taste, you can never be mistaken about it. One realizes it from degrees of it.

Subjective thinking, that is another thing. As I said, self-remembering is action, not thinking. It is doing.

MRS. L. Is it possible, by work, to exclude from oneself the possibility of criminal action and destructive action?

MR. O. Difficult to put it like that. There are many hidden forms.

MR. T. I think it has been said that every action has in it the seed of another, the next action?

MR. O. Yes, quite right.

MR. T. If the action which built a house were completed, would it contain the seed of the life to be lived in the house?

MR. O. Do not expect too much. One is sufficient. We are under the Law of Accident. People build a house with one idea and something happens and it is different. People build a church, then bolshevism begins and they make it an Anti-Religious Museum.

MISS M. Is the practice of meditation self-remembering?

MR. O. What do you mean by it? Where do you get it?

MISS M. I mean the meditation that is advocated, for instance, in Indian books.

MR. O. They say meditation, then second word they say school: they say one must work under a teacher. We read and remember one thing and forget another—think we can study meditation or meditate by ourselves. If you can self-remember you can meditate; if not, you cannot. Self-remembering means control of thoughts, different state. Meditation is action of developed mind, and we ascribe it to ourselves. There are many things like that. It would be very good if we could do it. Self-remembering is the way towards these. It does not mean instead of using this way you can begin from the end. You have to begin from the beginning like in everything else. What does 'meditation' mean? Thinking about this system. Trying to connect ideas and reconstruct the system. This is meditation, not simply thinking about one word, or one idea.

MR. H. Is it the laws under which man lives which prevent us from doing what we know we ought to do?

MR. O. There are many laws. Certainly from another point of view everything can be called laws. But better to say that it is <u>avoiding</u> laws that makes us like that. Man is afraid to see himself. That is not a law. If it were there would be no chance for him. He can decide at a given moment to be brave and see what he is. This is not a law.

MR. F. You said the kind of energy used for self-remembering could be increased at will. How can it be done?

MR. O. By trying to remember yourself and by observation. Your impressions bring energy. If you look and do not see, you lose energy, but if you observe and see, that means you acquire more energy.

MRS. L. Can one suddenly change the energy of anger into something else? One has tremendous energy, but doesn't know how to use it.

MR. O. By not identifying. One has tremendous energy and it works by itself and makes one act in a certain way. Why? What is the connecting link? Identification is the link. Stop identification and you will have it at your disposal. How can you do this? Not at once. It needs practice. Practice at easier moments. When emotion is very strong, one cannot. It is necessary to know more, to be prepared. If you know how not to identify in the right moments, you will have great energy at your disposal. What you will do with this is another thing. You may lose it again on something quite useless. But it takes practice. You cannot learn to swim if you fall into the sea during a storm. You must learn in calm water. Then perhaps, if you fall in, you will be able to swim.

MR. A. Are we to understand that self-remembering means awareness. . . .

MR. O. There again, not only awareness. It means also a certain capacity to act in a certain way, to do what you want. You see, in our logical thinking, logical knowledge, we divide consciousness from will. Consciousness means will. In Russian, for instance, will is the same word as freedom. In the languages with Latin roots, they take the meaning away, give it another meaning. The word consciousness means a combination of all knowledge, as if you have all your knowledge before you at the same time. But consciousness also means will, and will means freedom.

MISS M. Does the word shock in connection with the diagrams mean the same thing as shocks in ordinary life?

MR. O. Shocks can come from ordinary life. But sometimes they must be very carefully given. Only the right kind of shock will help in those particular octaves, otherwise they will branch off. If you have a certain line of action and want to continue straight, then only the right shock will help.

MISS M. Where does it come from?

MR. O. If it is your action it must come from you. It is necessary to know the moment and remember to give shocks.

MR. A. Will you give a practical example?

MR. O. Practical examples are in the Food Diagram. You must find analogous things in your own actions. You will remember that the first shock is provided by nature, where air comes in. But at the second interval, no shock is provided by nature and shock must be provided by self-remembering. Also at the third interval, no shock is provided and it must be provided in exactly the way we have been speaking about. Transformation of negative emotions into positive, produced by non-identification.

MR. R. Are opportunities for the use of will always present if you can find them?

MR. O. Where there is friction. That depends on whether you want it, depends on your decision, your state and your position. If one builds a house, for instance, every moment one has to overcome laziness, inertia, wanting to stop. If one goes into the shade and sleeps, there is nothing to overcome. If you work at anything you have always to overcome your desire to stop work.

MR. R. Are there two kinds of shocks, conscious and accidental?

MR. O. Accidental does not count. Things happen. People find money in the street, but cannot rely upon it! When we speak about this 'giving shocks', we speak about conscious shocks. Or things can be arranged in a certain way to produce shocks. For instance, three lines of work—one line gives shocks to another line. A certain arrangement is created to give shocks.

Q. Would not death be a shock to the people who knew they were likely to go on?

MR. O. You mean the idea of Eternal Recurrence? That is theory. Why is Eternal Recurrence theory? Because you can do nothing about it; if it is so we cannot change it. There is only one thing we can change. We can try to awake and hope we remain awake. If we have to come back, we cannot stop it. We are in a train, the train is going somewhere.

We can pass differently the time in the train—do something useful or spend the time quite uselessly.

MISS L. Can we see false personality without help?

MR. O. There is nothing against it theoretically, only I never saw such a case and nobody else I know saw such a case. Even with help, people will not see it. You can show a man a mirror, an actual, real mirror, and he will say 'this is not me', 'this is an artificial mirror, not a real mirror, not a reflection of me'. What can we do?

MRS. N. Does the realization of mechanicalness give one choice in one's actions or must one wait for will?

MR. O. I would say it gives choice. Realization of one's state and so on gives choice. If one does not realize it, one has no choice. At the same time it is wrong to think when realization comes it brings already the possibility and power. One can know and not be able to do anything. It is the most difficult and most unpleasant situation—one of the possible results of wrong development. If one begins to see things and is unable to do anything. That is why in some cases it is better to do nothing if one is not ready to go to the end. Otherwise one remains between two chairs.

Well, think about the six kinds of action.

Q. What is the sixth kind?

MR. O. There is no secret, but I am not sure of the formulation. If you find something that does not fit into any of the five kinds, then you will find it.

Q. If I want to build a house, I have some sort of an idea how to set about it, but I don't feel the same way about self-remembering. How can I go about it?

MR. O. You can come to the understanding of self-remembering in many different ways. For instance, when I first heard about it, I remember it was very strange. The idea struck me as an enormous idea. I had been studying psychology for many years and realized that in all the psychology I had studied, this idea was not known. It struck me how wrongly we think, that we had missed the biggest fact; the fact that we did not remember and could remember is the biggest fact in all psychology—the possibility of consciousness a tremendous idea.

Or other people I know realized they were never masters of themselves; if one decides in sleep, without consciousness, to do a thing, then it is not one's own action, it just happens. Other people were interested like this. It is necessary to begin with this idea, to see its applications and connections. First necessary to understand it as an idea.

*　　*　　*

Thursday. January 13th 1938. (Warwick Gardens.)

MISS D. I have trained myself to be a very light sleeper and as a consequence my mind has become rather watchful and lucid—does this lessen the energy that our bodies are supposed to store up in sleep?

MR. O. Your own observation will show. You lose in sleep energy which you must accumulate for waking times.

MISS M. Will Mr. O. explain how or why self-remembering causes a division of personality?

MR. O. It does not cause division. If I mentioned the word, I said a sensation similar to division, if you imagine personality as one. It means one personality observes another personality.

MR. L. I have observed that negative emotions start in the intellectual function as thoughts. Is this correct?

MR. O. It may be. They may start with thinking or in many different ways. This is why you can correct, can contradict many negative emotions if you create right thinking. Not at once, but in time it may stop them.

MR. L. What is the emotional state of a man who has rid himself of negative emotion?

MR. O. That is a matter for observation.

MR. L. I seem to have found that impressions take on a deeper and more lasting meaning when I feel a kind of emotional understanding—is this a correct observation?

MR. O. It is possible, yes.

MR. L. Are animals and plants given the possibility of progress like man, but in a greater time?

MR. O. I do not know.

MR. L. What is meant by the statement 'man is a complete cosmos'?

MR. O. All laws which work in cosmos work in man.

MRS. G. I have been many times recently to the National Gallery and have noticed that there are two distinct types of religious art. One where the expressions show contemplation and peace and yet the features are sometimes almost ugly. The other type shows ugliness both in feature and expression and also gives me the impression of pain and suffering. Can this be objective and subjective art? If so, how can I find out the meaning of objective art?

MR. O. I am sorry, but you will not find objective art in the National Gallery. It is all subjective.

MRS. S. I find I am getting a bad setback with regard to negative emotions. There seems a much bigger force there which is almost frightening at times, and if I can refrain from expressing it, the results are extreme irritation and subsequent vulnerability to all outside things. It feels as though the force is turned inward and dissipates the little being I may have gained. Rightly understood should it not help growth? Must we find the way ourselves or can you help?

MR. O. It is not a question of understanding. There are two questions in what you say. First, negative emotion seems to grow. Simply you did not notice it before. Secondly, if you keep expression shut up you feel irritable. This means you identify. You try to keep identification and destroy expression. Necessary to begin to destroy identification.

MR. A. Is a moral action—as defined by the system such an action is without hope of reward—a sixth type of action? Is helping others a sixth kind of action?

MR. O. No, it does not enter into the sixth. There are six types of action. Moral action we can understand in this way: it must be <u>conscious</u>. Only then can it be called moral. Unconscious action cannot be called moral. It may happen good. It may happen bad.

MR. A. In what type of action comes driving a car? Or tennis or golf, for instance?

MR. O. No, wrong approach. You cannot approach it in this way.

MR. A. From the point of view of the Table of Hydrogens, is it of any value not to eat meat or fish? Dead meat comes under 'remains of organic life'—a very dense matter. Is it of value not to introduce dense matter into your body?

MR. O. But nobody eats dead meat, so far as I know! This does not enter into it. Animal cells, vegetable cells, equally in 768. In any case, if one comes to the necessity of vegetarianism, one must come from another side, not from this side. Otherwise it would be simply superstition.

MR. F. When emotional centre works, it often gives a taste of opposites—splendour and misery, delight and sadness, bitter and sweet.

If part of this were negative, it would taste so; but the whole, both opposites together, seems to form a unity with a positive taste.

What is the explanation of this double experience? Is it the contrast of suddenly becoming more awake than before? Or is it in fact a form of negative emotion, which the positive cannot overcome?

MR. O. You make a mistake about positive. It is not positive. It is simply pleasure and pain, not the opposition of positive and negative. In such as we are, there is one thing to remember. Every pleasant emotion can become negative the next moment. So even extreme pleasure reminds one of pain. Your observation only proves that statement.

MR. F. You spoke at the last lecture of a triad being 'too good' for some purpose possibly. Is this in reference to the triads using different energies—do some use finer energies than others?

MR. O. No, it means simply wrong triad. Suppose you use, without knowing, a certain triad which can produce some special kind of result, it would not be good for your purpose.

MR. F. Is the inferiority of the factory-hand as a type, compared with the craftsmen of former times, able to be expressed in terms of the type of triad, and therefore of energy demanded by two different forms of employment? For example, controlling a machine, compared with designing and making a chair.

MR. O. It can be. One can do only one thing and another can do this and that.

MR. F. Do certain parts of centres work chiefly or exclusively with certain triads?

MR. O. No, that is wrong. You must not try to invent things, but follow the lines that are shown. Analogies connected with centres and parts of centres are wrong.

MR. D. I find it extremely difficult to classify events according to the categories mentioned by Mr. O. If one understood, which I do not, the exact significance of each category, would it be possible to diagnose, in advance, circumstances likely to lead to certain events?

MR. O. Yes, it is very difficult. It takes years to do that. But it is possible. There are certain categories, and you must try to find what is analogous. If you find analogies, then little by little your knowledge will increase. Choose what does fit, not what does not fit. Not just take an accidental idea—say 'does it fit or not?' It is long, long work, quite new way of thinking.

MR. D. The classification of an event, after it has happened, appears to me, with my imperfect understanding, to be more of academic interest than of practical value. Will Mr. O. please explain this point further?

MR. O. Everything repeats. If you classify after it happens, you may know it next time before it happens.

MISS S. How can I stop myself being identified with the troubles of a person I am very fond of?

MR. O. There are many different ways. For instance, you can think how if you are not identified you will better understand the nature of the trouble and can perhaps help in some way. This is one way.

MISS S. Is it possible to use the energy of sex centre for the work?

MR. O. Yes, but not in a direct way. By struggle with negative emotions, indirectly, you use exactly this energy. Negative emotions are based on sex energy wrongly used.

MISS S. Is designing things, clothes or houses, for instance, the same form of activity as the inventing of the electric bell?

MR. O. Probably.

MRS. S. Is not the power of the athletic genius akin to that of the great painter, in that it is something one is born with rather than acquires? And is that why artists seldom have any athletic ability, while athletes seldom have artistic capacity?

MR. O. Quite different results. Simply they are two quite different things. No connection.

MRS. S. We have been told that things happen to us. We don't make them happen. But do not people induce certain circumstances? There is the original and adventurous man who always leads a dangerous life, and the stay-at-home who sinks by his own desire into a deep groove.

MR. O. But in both cases the things happen. It does not mean that one controls or another controls. This is very easy to verify. If you try to do something against the way things happen, then you will see whether you can do it or not.

MRS. D. Is destructive energy used accidentally? For instance, if I burn down a house by accident?

MR. O. How many houses have you burnt until now? If you burn many, then it can begin to happen by itself. I think the first time there must be some intention.

MRS. D. Can criminal energy be used accidentally, or must the motive behind be criminal?

MR. O. We cannot go into details about one kind. Energy is the same. But if it is accidental, it is not criminal.

MRS. D. Can an action be the result of both destructive and criminal energies, or are these energies quite separate?

MR. O. They are different, but can work together or can work separately.

MRS. D. Are the results of creative energy seen only in objective works of art?

MR. O. In different kinds of creative art. It depends what is created.

MRS. D. Do artists, musicians, writers, architects, etc. who produce only mediocre works, use the building energy?

MR. O. No. But that I do not know. I cannot go into detail. We must have standards for each kind, and speak about standards.

MRS. D. Do men Nos. 1, 2 and 3 possess the creative energy, and if they do possess it, can they know how to use it?

MR. O. No, they cannot know that in the ordinary way. This means school. In the ordinary way people do not know, but they can feel it emotionally.

MRS. D. Are men Nos. 1, 2 and 3 capable of distinguishing the six forms of energy in themselves?

MR. O. I do not know. I do not think so without explanation. Emotionally, maybe they can distinguish one or two kinds, but not more. Even that means an approximation to higher emotion or higher part of emotional centre very well developed.

MRS. D. Can men 1, 2 and 3 learn how to use the different energies?

MR. O. They must learn to understand them first. Then they can learn to use. We cannot speak about further degree before we understand the first degree.

MRS. D. Would the same energy be used for inventing a high explosive or a poison gas as was used for inventing the telephone?

MR. O. I do not know. Necessary to try.

MRS. D. We were told that a certain triad was used to transform dense matters into lighter matters. What energy is this?

MR. O. It will come later, when we speak about the manifestations of the same six energies in different spheres of activity, so to say, in a different way.

MRS. D. Does each action require a quite separate energy, or do energies overlap?

MR. O. May be mixed.

MR. S. I can see very little difference between the activities of painting a picture and that of invention. There appear so many similar actions in both activities that I find it very difficult to formulate the undoubted difference that I do feel. Can Mr. O. give me some line to think on?

MR. O. At the same time they are essentially different. It is necessary to understand that. One thing is that invention, scientific discovery, can be made by one centre. Another kind of activity needs all centres. In any case one centre cannot do it, or it will be invention.

MR. S. Need the activities connected with the burning of the house necessarily be destructive?

MR. O. Yes, that is what it is. This energy cannot build anything, cannot create anything. Every building needs constant effort between one triad and another. In this activity, one triad comes from another automatically after the first start. You will understand that this is very different. To build a house, every brick must be put in place with a certain effort. In burning a house there is only one effort—striking the match. House. cannot be built like that, by itself. They are two quite different kinds of energy, two quite different activities.

MISS K. Are the actions of catching a train, typing a poem (as distinct from composing it), in the same category as that of building a house?

MR. O. That is not the way to think about it.

MRS. S. Are not athletics and the use of sex centre both examples of the same triad, the same kind of action as burning the house, although neither is destructive?

MR. O. Again it is wrong way of thinking.

MR. C. Is reading a book like stealing a picture or like building a house?

MR. O. No. Not the way to think about it.

MR. H. How can one best work on considering?

MR. O. One must try not to consider. But before that one must observe and have enough observation, enough understanding to be prepared for it. Like with all manifestations of negative emotion one must think right when it is quiet. One must not justify, excuse, find reasons, explain. One must be sincere with oneself and know it can only be weakening. If one thinks right for a sufficiently long time it will disappear. Not at once, but little by little.

MRS. F. Should one try to direct energy? Suppose one has saved a little by checking the expression of negative emotion and one knows one lacks most the energy to build a house or to burn a house, should one try to direct it to one's need? Or does it go there of itself, automatically, as the resistance in the body goes to where the illness or the weakness lies? [End of written questions.]

* * *

MISS N. To which centre does the feeling of humour belong? Is laughter always mechanical?

MR. O. Yes. I cannot make myself laugh. It is mechanical. That means something produces it.

Many things can be said about it. On our level it is very useful capacity, but you must understand there is no humour, no sense of the comic in higher centres. It ceases to be useful. But on our level, in certain conditions, it is useful. All its functions are filled in another way in higher centres.

* * *

I want to speak again about the question of meat and fish. Behind this question is theosophical superstition. All kinds of superstitions are wrong from the point of view of the system, because they are not based on anything. For instance, they say that matters like these bring some kind of rough emanations with them. There is not the slightest evidence of that. So it is very dangerous to come to this question from the superstitious point of view.

MR. A. It is not exactly that, the idea I had at the back of my mind when I asked the question. We are purely mechanical and thoughts and feeling are conditioned by the state of our body, digestion. If we have in our bodies finer matters. . . .

MR. O. But these are not finer matters. They are the same. On which scale? That is what it is. You cannot say on which scale it is wrong. From the Hydrogens' point of view you can say yes. For the juices, it is easier to break up vegetable cells than animal cells. But you cannot say so from a moral or religious point of view.

There is no material to speak about it from. There is no evidence that one is better than another. It is just a question of taste. I personally like vegetables, you may like meat. There is no difference. We must not create wrong associations. I agree that vegetable food is better, but you must explain it in another way—easier to digest, that is all.

We must not invent fantastic explanations. Everything that is right can be explained without fantastic explanations.

MISS F. In these six kinds of action what is important to try and think about? Is it the sort of energy used?

MR. O. First the chief principle that actions are different just as matters are different. Our ordinary mind does not realize it. We understand that matter is different. For instance, we have just been discussing food—what is better, vegetables or meat. Or we do not eat wood. We know what can serve as food, what kind of matter. In relation to action we do not realize that they are different. From the moment we begin to think, grows and grows the idea that action is the same. It is necessary first to understand that actions are different and more varied, perhaps, even than matters. Later you will understand how the six categories branch. At present, first principles. It is necessary to understand first principles.

MISS F. Is it in the sort of energy used? Where does the difference lie?

MR. O. In different triads. For instance, you can say that some triads need constant efforts, some go by themselves after first shock. This is a first principle. If you understand even that, it already gives you material to think about.

MR. D. When we carry out a certain action, should we try to think how that particular action compares with these?

MR. O. We should think by emotional understanding of our action, does it correspond to our aim. This is how we can think. Then partly by mind, partly emotionally, we can realize that the way we are going can or cannot lead to the desired aim. That we can feel sometimes. Then we can either stop it or try to do something in another way.

For instance, you are speaking with somebody, trying to persuade this person of something in which you think you are right and they are wrong. The more you argue, the more he is convinced he is right. Stop, and suddenly you see this person understands you. This happens very often. The more you argue, the more difficult it is for him to understand. Or even pretend to agree with him, and in that way you may make him understand what you want. This is only an example, but you can find many examples. You started wrong. Arguing is one way to persuade, agreeing is another.

Q. I suppose in a case like that we should be capable of knowing whether to argue or agree?

MR. O. I meant if you do not identify you will see. What prevents us from seeing is generally identifying. Arguing is a very good subject for observation. It happens very often.

MR. C. When you say look for analogies to these five different kinds of energy, what exactly do you mean?

MR. O. It is not so simple. Occasionally you may find them. Observe or think about something and compare and you may say, 'Ah! that fits into this or this into that.' You may be right or you may make a mistake. If you just take some action and begin to think 'Where does this fit?' you will most probably be wrong. There may be differences in scale and many differences besides.

It is a question of the way of approach. Maybe later we will be able to explain even this thing by different triads. At present I can say only one thing—that some approaches are right, some are wrong. This is very clear in mathematics. Certain problems can be solved only in a certain way.

MR. A. Could I be reminded of the examples given last time with regard to the analysis of actions? Is this a comprehensive category of classes into which all actions fall?

MR. O. I think yes. I did not give all, but we do not want more because the sixth does not happen in ordinary life.

MISS L. To which category do conations belong? Doing something in order that something else shall ensue. For example, giving up something in order to save money for a purpose.

MR. O. That is a little complicated. I will think about it.

MRS. P. Are there six categories because there are six combinations of forces?

MR. O. Yes, quite right. But again you must understand there are combinations of the six. We speak only about the original six combinations.

MRS. N. Is the type of action in any way affected by the result? If you were going to burn a house and the match went out, for instance?

MR. O. Then it would be nothing.

MRS. P. Inside an action there seem to be hundreds of small actions. How can one say where an action begins? Is this connected with the intention?

MR. O. No. It is necessary to understand the principle of action, so to say. There is nothing more inside.

MISS R. Are all actions on the same level?

MR. O. What do you mean by level?

MISS R. I was thinking of the difference between so-called menial actions and, say, art.

MR. O. You mean cooking, writing poetry and so on? All on the same level. It depends on the level of the man.

Well, try to think about it and next time I will bring some material which we will be able to read about it.

* * *

Monday. January 17th 1938.

MR. O. In two questions triads were mentioned. What do you really remember about them? You see, I want to put it in the simplest form, because if people come and ask you, I want to know how much you remember and what you will say. First, do you remember how the idea of triads starts? It is said that every action, every manifestation is the result of the conjunction of three forces: positive, negative and neutralizing. This is the first idea that was explained in the system and at the time when we first spoke of it in St. Petersburg when we first learned it, I realized that this idea is the same as the idea of triads in Indian philosophy. In Sankhya philosophy you find the idea of three Gunas and it is explained there that they are three forces and their combination produces all the phenomena in the world. In Sankhya philosophy it is put like that: three Gunas have seven combinations, one combination incomprehensible for our mind and six combinations comprehensible for our mind. This is the principle, this is the idea. And if we connect this possibility of seven combinations with the Ray of Creation, we will get something out of it. But of this we will speak later. First we must begin with the general idea, and you must understand how you can start to study it. You can start to study it from two sides, and the first of these is from the point of view of human actions, because, although we don't understand it, there is the same, or even a bigger, difference between human actions, as between different objects. You know that this ash-tray is different from a pineapple, you will not mix them. But we don't understand that one action and another action are as different as two different objects. And this is what we must understand in relation to our actions, and we must try to find categories of actions. There are six different categories of actions—try to see them, without even knowing which is which, which represents which triad or which is using which triad. When you understand the difference between these six categories, then we will be able to speak further.

The other way of approaching this subject is from the side of the Ray of Creation. We can put it like that:

1	1-2-3	1-2-3	1-2-3		
3	1-2-3	2-1-3	3-2-1		
6	1-2-3	2-1-3	3-2-1	2-3-1	1-3-2	3-1-2
12					
24					
48					
96					

The incomprehensible triad belongs to World 1. In this triad each force occupies each place. World 3 consists of three triads, and World 6 consists of six triads.

Try to remember what you know about these worlds from the Ray of Creation. We know that World 3 is under the Will of the Absolute, so the three triads of World 3 are controlled by the Absolute, but the control of the Absolute ends at World 3. In World 6 enters mechanicalness. Mechanicalness means limitations, so we can call the second three triads in World 6: Mechanicalness, Space and Time. The first three triads we can call: Intelligence (or Mind), Consciousness and Will. But this is all on a very big scale, not comparable with our ordinary scale. This is all we can say, without trying to invent, approaching it from above. Then we can start on our own level with trying to find differences in human activity.

MRS. P. Can you give an example of one of human activities?

MR. O. I gave the examples of building a house and burning a house. These are two different kinds of human activity. At present don't try to connect them with definite triads, only try to understand the difference of activities. And then try to find other analogies, before you try to decide which activity belongs to which triad.

An example of one activity is building a house. Try to understand this activity, try to see all that is necessary for building a house—effort, labour at every step.

Then another triad, another activity is burning a house—destruction, the use of destructive force. These two triads must be studied together because they contradict one another.

Then, in human activity, art, for instance, means the use of a special capacity. Efforts at self-remembering, non-identifying also enter into the same triad.

And another triad may be called invention, discovery, adaptation, craft.

If you think about these four triads, they will give you material. Try to see why these four kinds of activity are different, and how they are different.

There are two more triads, which you can leave at present. I can give you the names of these two triads so that you don't mix them with others. One of them is represented by crime, for instance. Crime is very interesting; it is a special activity and has its own special triad, different from all other triads. And the sixth triad can be called 'magic'. It happens very seldom in life, and if it does happen, it happens in a wrong form. By the wrong form I don't mean 'black magic', but something quite different.

All human actions either belong to these six categories or are combinations of these six categories.

MR. B. I don't see the distinction between craft and building a house?

MR. O. In one case only energy, only effort is necessary, and in the other something more is needed, some knowledge or capacity—man invents something. One can build a house just by physical effort, nothing more.

MR. F. Did you put efforts at self-remembering with art?

MR. O. Yes, it is the same triad. Simple, blind effort, like in physical work, will not help in self-remembering. Neither will effort in the sense of invention, adaptation, help.

MRS. S. I don't understand about combinations of triads.

MR. O. Why? If there are six triads, many combinations are possible. Six triads give 144 combinations, by 3. But it does not mean that you must begin with figures. Try to understand the meaning.

MR. C. Does the sixth triad come about accidentally or by human effort?

MR. O. If we speak about human actions we take more intentional actions. If we speak about things that happen it would be a different division, a different calculation. We know that everything happens, but at the same time in our mind we divide things that happen from intentional actions. Now we speak about intentional actions.

MISS C. What kind of things do you mean by destroying a house? Is it symbolical?

MR. O. Well, burning it. It is not a symbolical expression. We speak about facts.

MR. R. I tried to understand the connection of space and time triads with mechanicalness.

MR. O. Mechanicalness means chance, Law of Accident. Law of Accident means limitations. Space and time are limitations.

MR. M. Does the crime triad refer to all crime?

MR. O. What do you mean? Crime is an objective idea. Some crimes may not be crimes at all, but only called crimes. But if it really is crime, all crimes are a manifestation of one particular triad—a very clever triad, a very easy triad. It needs a special capacity.

MR. P. When you spoke about magic, did you mean. . . ?

MR. O. I only mentioned it to give you the possibility of not mixing with others. Suppose you decide to build a house, but instead of carrying bricks you just make passes, and the house is built.

MR. C. Would that be necessarily wrong?

MR. O. No, there is nothing wrong. But it would be wrong if bricks climbed to the top and then fell on you.

MISS H. The activity of making armaments, would it come under invention or destruction?

MR. O. Invention enters here, ordinary labour, a little crime maybe—it makes a very good combination.

Now this should be an interesting work; it will cover a long time, will go on for years. Try to find analogies, try to find into which category one or another action can fit when you observe them. Certainly it is difficult, because it is difficult to find the right scale on which to look. Later we will divide these six categories like that: we will study the six categories in cosmic manifestations, in the working of the human machine and then in human actions. But at present we will begin only with human actions.

* * *

Thursday. January 20th 1938. (Warwick Gardens.)

[Written questions read.]

MISS M. Is the expression of negative emotion the same type of action as burning a house?

MR. O. No, these are quite different ideas.

MISS M. Is the action required for self-remembering the same as that required for painting a picture?

MR. O. Read on.

MISS S. When one is cooking a meal, one puts the food in the oven and the heat cooks it without further action on the part of the cooker. Is this the same sort of energy as that used in burning down a house?

MR. O. It will burn your dinner if you use same energy!

MR. A. In the action of painting a picture, I observe three actions: (1) building a house (2) painting a picture (3) invention. Is this correct and can that be further explained?

MR. O. It depends on the picture.

MR. L. Are the activities of different qualities, as for example, building a house a higher activity than burning a house?

MR. O. Higher from which point of view?

MR. L. I think it was an expression you used yourself.

MR. O. In some connection, probably; not just like that. Higher or lower, what does it mean, like that? They are simply different. Apple and pear are different, but which is higher? We cannot speak about what is higher in relation to nothing.

MR. L. Is stealing a picture the highest activity?

MR. O. Same answer.

MR. L. In that case, what is the attribute of stealing which makes it so high an activity?

MR. A. In self-observation, I discover myself very often, automatically, silently dividing my footsteps into series of five, or trying to form groups of five visually, scanning whatever is before me.

a. What group of activities does this wasted effort fall in? Burning, I suppose?

b. Has this strange habit any significance at all?

c. How can it be cured?

MR. O. The first, we do not know. We must establish that it is wrong or harmful. Why cure something that may have positive meaning or no meaning at all? Necessary to begin with what it is. There are many different kinds of automatic activities. It is necessary to take a particular case and see why it is wrong, if it is. It may have no meaning.

MRS. F. Have the various 'I's centres? From personal observations it seems they have quite different sorts of negative emotions, different ways and times of day-dreaming, imagining and identifying: have they also rudimentary centres?

MR. O. How can 'I's have centres? Each centre and part of centre is populated by certain 'I's.

MRS. D. Was the experiment of prohibition in America an example of the results being exactly the opposite of the aim?

MR. O. All political activities are examples of this. They never come to their advertised aim, always to the opposite aim.

MISS F. I find that I have got no result from my work in the form of questions. I go carefully over the same ground (self-observation on negative emotions, etc.), but get no fresh questions. Does this mean that I only imagine I am working?

MR. O. No, you cannot say just like that. Necessary to go deeper. Maybe you are avoiding just one necessary effort. If one avoids one effort, a special, individual kind; often all other work will give no result until one attempts to do something with this particular effort.

MISS F. I find that I can't _do_ anything until it has already happened. When trying to reason with myself about negative emotions, or trying to force myself to stop some argument going on in my mind, I can get no results. But on one or two occasions I have suddenly found myself having the right attitude without any effort. Is this the result of my previous effort or just an accident?

MR. O. Most probably.

MR. F. In the Food Diagram, what is the significance of breathing as a series of shocks?

MR. O. I do not understand.

MR. F. What is the significance other than that of the formation of carbon dioxide through the burning process? Is there a mental significance; is it a way of keeping the brain alive? You once said the body would die immediately without impressions.

MR. O. We must take this separately. Certainly physical impressions are also important.

MR. F. Can the shocks of breathing be used as a basis of, or a mechanical aid to, self-remembering?

MR. O. No, it won't do.

MISS M. In studying the system, what effect has motive over the accomplishment of one's aim? If, for instance, one wanted to study for a motive that was not the right one, would one make the same progress? It is so difficult to disentangle one's motives and be sure of the true one. How can one do this?

MR. O. You see, we have a rather different idea about motive from the ordinary one. From the ordinary point of view, people believe in motives. They think if somebody started with a certain motive he will continue with the same motive. They believe they can remember motives. We know they cannot. So we do not attach so much importance to them. One can start with one motive; five minutes later we have another and then another. <u>Consciousness</u> of motive or aim, this is very important. If you are conscious of why you are doing something, it will give ten times quicker, ten times bigger results. The motive may be forgotten next moment.

MR. J. From my observations of myself endeavouring to self-remember, I find that as long as I am looking in one direction with more or less fixed gaze, and seeing myself as well, I can remain awake, but as soon as I move about and look around, seeing different objects, the changing scenery causes me to change with it, and I become identified with one of the objects. Is there any sort of example of what to practise to help me while I am walking about?

MR. O. Quite. But as we are never still, we must learn to remember ourselves in movement, not only sitting still. Practise in the most difficult circumstances.

MR. J. Also if someone suddenly addresses me and I turn around, a person answers for me before I have the chance of readjusting myself to the new situation, and I wake up that person who answered, not the one who was working a moment before. I am beginning to know some of these personalities, but is there any way of checking them lying for me, because they invariably do?

MR. O. First, necessary to know them. We cannot start checking until we know them.

MR. S. There are some people who appear to have a much greater facility for playing ball games than others. They have what some people call a good eye. Can Mr. O. explain this?

MR. O. There are many different kinds of moving centres, with different kind of memory. There is not a single man similar to another man. One can do one thing better; another, another. There are thousands of impressions, so combinations are always different. I remember I spoke several times about different kinds of men—1, 2 and 3 and so on. One remembers one kind of impression better, one another kind.

MISS M. What is the energy we use up when asleep at night? Is it similar to that used up by our imagination in the day-time?

MR. O. Yes, if you like. It does not matter really. It is the same energy. We do not use different energy asleep or awake, only in sleep we cannot lose so much energy; though in half-sleep one can lose very much energy.

*　*　*

[Questions read out which had been asked before Mr. O. came.]

MRS. S. I don't know yet quite about laziness. Is it negative emotion or a group of 'I's? If the latter, should one try to struggle against it or not? I remember something Mr. O. said, in one of the very early lectures, I think, about not struggling against 'I's.

MR. O. It is neither. It is for some people three-quarters of their life or more. Sometimes it is very important. Sometimes it is what [is] called chief feature. It is very often feature. All the rest depends on laziness and serves laziness. Only again there are different kinds of laziness; it is necessary to find them. By observing yourself and observing other people. There are very busy people, always doing something, and their mind may be lazy. That happens more often than anything else. Laziness is not only the desire to sit and do nothing.

MISS R. Is there any special significance about its being a picture, in the 'stealing a picture' example of activity?

MR. O. I cannot even answer that. You must remember. I talked about burning a house, building a house, painting a picture, then stealing a picture. The word came quite, quite accidentally. Now you ask me what size is the picture, what is the frame—is the picture sold, I don't know what!

MR. T. Are permanent centre of gravity and consciousness and will in the Causal Body on two different scales?

MR. O. I do not understand. How does that come into it? Causal Body, that does not refer to us—we do not have Causal Body, that is certain. So what can we learn in that way?

MR. T. It was connected with aim. I feel that these ultimate things we are told about, we must get them clear. . . .

MR. O. Do not think about the things which do not concern us. Try to understand the next step.

MRS. S. Should it be possible to love a person without identifying?

MR. O. Only without identifying is it possible. With identifying, it is identifying, only that.

MISS S. The question was once asked about making a plan. I think Mr. O. said it was no good unless one made oneself a part of the plan. Did he mean that when making a plan one must make it so that one can keep it, remembering one's limitations?

MR. O. Plan for what? That is the first question. Second, can one make a plan—does one know enough? Third, can one remember a plan? These three questions change the whole thing. First they must be answered, then one can speak about it.

MRS. P. I waste a great deal of time and energy in making decisions of no importance: whether to catch this train or that, for instance. What is the best way to deal with this?

MR. O. There are many ways out of it, you know, but I cannot say in general. The general answer is <u>to be serious</u>. That is all that can be said in a general way. Then the next question that comes up is what does to be serious mean? That we may discuss later.

MISS R. I cannot see what class of action gardening and agriculture belong to. There are such long periods when nothing is done, as in the winter.

MR. O. If nothing is done, then there is no action—how can we speak about it?

MR. C. May I have a practical analogy with stealing a picture?

MR. O. Stealing something else. That is just the same. Why picture? Stealing a house—that is much better than stealing a picture! Then picture can be sold.

MR. B. It was said that the six actions corresponded to the six ways of combining the forces and then that there was a seventh which was incomprehensible?

MR. O. Yes, each combination of the three forces shows one of the possible actions.

MR. H. Does a man with greater knowledge have a responsibility towards those who have less? If so, what kind of responsibility? I mean a man who has esoteric knowledge.

MR. O. Esoteric knowledge, that means school and a man who comes from school or who is in school. Responsibility is towards school. When a man acquires school knowledge, he acquires responsibility. There may be many conditions you do not know. Certain knowledge may be given only on certain conditions and so on. How can we discuss it in general?

MISS R. Last week, Mr. O. said all actions were on the same level. I find that hard to accept in the case, say, of the craftsman and the factory worker.

MR. O. But in relation to what did I say that? And what was the question?

MISS R. It was my question about menial work and poetry. You said one was not higher than the other, that it depended on a man's being.

MR. O. What does 'higher' mean? It means nothing by itself like that. There is not enough material to speak about it. Better wait a little. Perhaps to-day or next time we may speak about it and I will try to show you how to approach this question.

[Questions from Thursday before, which were asked after Mr. O. left.]

MRS. P. I still don't understand where an action starts. If a house is half-built, is it an action, or only if it is fulfilled?

MR. O. All building action consists of a series of the same actions—effort, effort, effort every time—nothing happens by itself. That is the typical form of action for building a house.

MRS. S. The same action could be in quite a different category according to how it is done, couldn't it? For instance, reading a book, which may entail effort or be a waste of time!

MR. O. Reading a book is not an action in that sense. There are very many different forms of reading a book, aims of reading a book, ways of reading a book.

MR. F. Mr. O. once said painting a picture was done by the intellectual part of emotional centre. How does this coincide with his statement this evening that it cannot be done by one centre alone?

MR. O. It depends again on what picture. I did not say every picture. But the thing is that intellectual parts of centres do not work by themselves, separately, or only very seldom. Action of intellectual part of emotional centre necessarily will use material of other centres.

MR. A. Was the suggestion seriously made that we should analyse all our actions and put them into these categories—and do it all day long?

MR. O. All! All day long! Again these absolutes. I did not say <u>all</u> actions and I did not say <u>all day long</u>. First we have no power of analysis of such strength. If we could do this, we would know many things in a very short time. But if we find one action in a month which we can put in a definite category, even that would be good. You must understand our forces and capacities are always taken into consideration. We do not know how to analyse, how to qualify and we cannot do it all the time.

MR. A. Are all actions during the day painting or stealing or burning? Are there no actions that we, as automatons, can do which are outside these categories?

MR. O. These are only the fundamental categories. Then there are the combinations. For instance, take it simply arithmetically. There are six fundamental combinations: these give 144 different combinations. We will speak much later about these combinations.

MISS M. Are we at the moment to disregard the motive of an action?

MR. O. Not always. Why should we, if we know? If we can know, it may help to understand or it may not help us. Again this will enter into something we shall speak about either to-day or some other time. The meaning of different forces in a certain position. We will discuss the meaning of first force in the first place; of first force in the second place; of the first force in the third place; then of the second force in the first place; in the second place, in the third place; of the third force in the first place, second place, third place. That discussion may show you the approach to this question about motive.

MRS. D. You read that a country is fighting war in order to have peace. Isn't this an example of wrong triad?

MR. O. This is just ordinary political lying. It cannot be put in any category.

MR. H. In what category does the effort to self-remember fall?

MR. O. In a very definite category. But that is in connection with many other things. We must just leave that for the moment.

MR. A. Does every one of our incidental actions in the course of the day fall into one of the five main categories?

MR. O. That was answered before.

MRS. S. Can there be anything analogous to the triads for building up strength of being? Would negative emotion be the burning, self-remembering creative art, and so on?

MR. O. Yes, but that is a little different. We must try to understand them in one kind of activities, then we can look for them in another.

MR. F. Are certain 'I's better than others for a certain type of action?

MR. O. They exist only for a certain type of action. You cannot say one is better than another. One can do one thing, one another.

MR. A. I think negative emotions can be used as fuel for desirable objectives: for instance, letting one's feelings run away with one when reproving someone younger than oneself. I don't mean losing temper, but allowing oneself to become annoyed. I have observed this after adopting the attitude several times.

MR. O. That is one of our greatest illusions, to think we can control. Simply lack of observation. Try to observe again. You cannot control; always it will run away with you.

[End of written questions.]

* * *

MR. O. Well, try and talk about something else. This is very good but you must not try to think only about that. We cannot hurry with this question of different actions. You see, really it is beyond our possibilities to understand at present, but if we go slowly, we may get something out of it.

MISS F. I did not understand your answer to my question which was read out just now. I said I could get no results, but sometimes. . . .

MR. O. I said it might be the result of your previous attempts. You try many times and it looks as if you had no results. Then suddenly you have results without any apparent effort. That is the result of previous efforts.

MISS S. Could you say some more about my question? I meant was it a good thing to try to plan your day. . . .

MR. O. I said it was first necessary to know 'plan for what?' If you try to plan you may mix different scales. Can you be sure your plan will be to scale? Necessary to make ordinary plan. Necessary to learn how to do it. Like if you have to make the plan of your house; you have to learn about scale. Otherwise you make your plan and one room may be bigger than the whole house. And this is a more complicated kind of plan. It is not two-dimensional. You have to take many things into consideration.

MISS M. You said when we realized we did not remember ourselves we were nearest to self-remembering. I see now that I do not remember myself, but it goes no further.

MR. O. Go deeper. Nothing more is necessary. Realize more and more, deeper and deeper, that neither you nor other people remember, that nobody remembers himself. That will bring you to it better than anything else. Our difficulty is chiefly dependent on the lack of realization that we do not remember ourselves. If we realized more often that we do not remember ourselves and that other people do not, that nobody remembers himself, then we would begin, just by that.

MRS. D. Can you explain what you meant when you said about being serious?

MR. O. What do you think? Necessary to think about it, perhaps ask questions, talk about it, then when we have enough material, perhaps we will be able to discuss it.

MR. A. Is it wrong to try to observe a triad in an action?

MR. O. How can you? You cannot see it like this. It is just the same to try to see bacteria without a microscope. You must get a microscope. If you know action, if you can see it, then you can observe it.

MRS. N. In the *New Model*, I think you said there is a fifth dimension made entirely of possibilities. If so, in our state are there other possibilities? It seems that whatever we are we cannot do anything different. I cannot see whether the possibilities exist for us or not.

MR. O. Necessary to try. But I think we will leave these things for a time. We will come to the same problems in another way. This is very general and philosophical, this talk about possibilities and I do not think it is worth spending time over it. At present we must try to study how things happen. The mechanism. How they can happen in one way and in another way. When we know this mechanism, then perhaps we can ask ourselves what real possibilities we have.

MR. R. Can one alter one's chief feature?

MR. O. First necessary to know it. If you know it, much will depend on the quality of your knowing. If you know it well, then it is possible to change it.

MR. F. You say that intellectual parts of centres tend to work together. Would painting a picture be apt to associate them? Does invention separate them?

MR. O. No, leave this painting a picture. We have had enough of it. Speak in different words. Already wrong associations enter. Our formatory centre takes everything too literally and immediately begins to put its own associations and we cannot think right. It spoils the whole thing.

MISS F. You spoke about more than one sort of laziness and said a person who was active physically might be lazy mentally. What type of mental laziness were you referring to?

MR. O. You must observe if you do not know what I mean. Find a mental laziness in yourself and in other people, then you will know what I mean.

MRS. D. Is discovery the same as invention?

MR. O. More or less. But certainly there are differences. We have to put them in the same category more or less.

There is a particular quality about discovery and invention. It may have all the qualities of real discovery and yet may be false, without ceasing to be discovery.

MRS. S. I find a sort of passiveness in myself which makes me go on doing what I am doing. Is that a force or a personality?

MR. O. Difficult to say in general. It depends what is aim. You cannot find anything about it until you try to do something differently. We have tendencies to do habitual actions in the same way. Whether it is difficult to change, we can find only by trying to act in a different way. Necessary to experiment. Sometimes people find it is very easy; they never tried. Sometimes impossible. Without trying you cannot tell.

MISS M. About invention. There seem to be two entirely different ways of doing a thing. Writing a book, for instance. For one person it means endless research and effort, and another will tell you he knows it all before he begins to write, that it is dictated to him, he only has to write it down.

MR. O. Do not believe it! It never happens. If there are absolutes, this is one. And this is not even invention. If you like, it is—commercial invention.

MISS S. Is it of value always to try to do things in a different way?

MR. O. Always! Try to do it for half an hour even.

MR. A. What is the fundamental connection between self-consciousness in the system sense of the word and the other kind—lack of control, lack of dignity. . . .

MR. O. The second is only an English slang expression. It does not exist in any other language. It simply means a kind of embarrassment. It has nothing to do with consciousness, self-consciousness—just a word.

MISS M. You said once that there were planetary influences against evolution. What are these planetary influences?

MR. O. We live under many, many different influences. You remember when we spoke about the Ray of Creation. . . . And certainly all these tendencies, influences try to keep the present state of things, things as they are. Many of these influences have the aim of keeping things in a certain state, in a certain balance. The development of man is a break, it changes the balance, does not enter into the scheme of things on this plane. We do not understand that. Otherwise it would be mechanical, his development—a natural process. But it does not happen as a natural process. That is why it is so difficult.

MR. F. When you talk of influences, do you mean actual streams of matter?

MR. O. Everything is material. But the word material has more meanings than we think now, if we speak about planets, influences and things. Everything is material, only there are different kinds of materiality.

MRS. N. I asked what it would be if I started to build a house and ended up by burning it. What I meant was if I start one kind of action and it ends as quite a different action. Is the action the effort or the result?

MR. O. It may be many things. Suppose even you start in the right way and with right triad. Then suppose you did not make enough effort and the house is not finished. It may be simply that you stop your building and so nothing happens. Or that you started to build a house and at that time you started to think about something else and began to do something quite different. Instead of house you make a picture of a house, or even mental picture of a house, which happens very often. And even it may be wrong mental picture of house—one side one style, another another, quite different. That is what we usually do.

MR. L. How is one to think about the different parts of activities?

MR. O. First understand principles. Principle that actions can be as different as things, as objects. We know that objects can be different. About action we are simply not accustomed to think in that way. Many mistakes we make depend on that. But this is only the beginning. From time to time we will come back to this and each time you will see you understand more. But now only one thing, the enormous difference of actions between themselves. There is no place in our mind for this difference. We never heard about it, never thought about it. This is what it is necessary to get—a little understanding of this new idea.

MR. L. Does this come as well in a feeling?

MR. O. Yes, but first you must get a clear idea of this first principle. Then sometimes you can understand it emotionally, sometimes practically, sometimes by mind; because there are many different ways.

MR. L. Is there a general principle of thinking of new things in a different way?

MR. O. There are no general principles. This is the only general principle that exists.

MRS. S. If one experiments against a habit, does it make one remember oneself? ·

MR. O. Depends on length of experiment and intensity of effort. But yes, certainly it can.

MISS F. You said discovery sometimes could be false. In what way? In result, in process, or what?

MR. O. Difficult to answer. Suppose a discovery is made and after 20, 40, 60 years people begin to see it was not discovery, it was a mistake. At the time it was made it was a discovery. It may be like that. It does not mean it was a mistake in the beginning. At one moment it was right, then it became wrong. Because it was just relative, made with relative thinking, referring to relative truth. Relative truth can be right one day and wrong another.

MISS S. We cannot think in any other way but relatively?

MR. O. We must become conscious. We learn here to think in a right way, but it takes a long time, because it is necessary to be conscious.

[To Mr. A.] This is what I meant about microscope. Without this, at present, we cannot expect to see bacteria, small cells, even big cells. Very simple to try. Take some dirty water and try to see bacteria. Perhaps you will say you can. But I shall not believe you. Some people think they can; they will describe them, write about them—dictate about them. They have no time to write themselves!

MRS. P. Is to be serious to try to make an effort to find out what really matters?

MR. O. No, this is too special definition. We will make this a special task for next time. Everybody write what to be serious means. Then we will see whether we. . . .

We do not understand even such small things. What means to be sincere, to be serious—many things like that. At the same time we use these words and think we understand.

MR. A. How can I start to make myself a magnifying glass?

MR. O. Ask yourself this—can you tell me sincerely are there any people in the moon or not?

MR. A. I do not know.

MR. O. Yes, but how many people on how many occasions know they do not know? They think they can tell whether there are people on the moon or not.

MR. A. The probability is that there are not. . . .

MR. O. There, you see, already!

*   *   *

Thursday. January 27th 1938. (Warwick Gardens.)

[Written questions read.]

MRS. M. To be serious, it seems to me necessary to have achieved unity. But, as we are now, I suppose to be serious is to remember our aim and to judge and value other things in relation to it.

MR. R. To be serious is to think, in relation to what one thinks or feels to be important, about those things which one considers relevant to that.

MR. H. To be serious about a thing means, for me, to consider it in relation to my own ultimate profit; to try to eliminate things which are mechanical, but to make use of things which lead to greater awareness.

MISS J. Is to be serious to be able to see things on their right scale?

MR. B. Is seriousness to do only those things which are important from, as far as possible, absolute standards?

MR. O. And what is important? That is just replacing one word by another.

MR. A. Seriousness in my opinion is not grimness nor the opposite of joyousness nor the absence of gaiety. I think that joyousness and gaiety are greatly enhanced if tempered by a measure of seriousness. From this I incline to the deduction that seriousness and self-remembering are identical.

MR. O. No, you cannot replace one word by another. That would be too easy.

MISS S. It seems that it must be impossible to be truly serious without having a permanent 'I'. I think that to be serious one would have to have a very large scale view of everything so as to know all the time which things are of permanent, lasting importance.

MR. O. If we wait until we have permanent 'I', we will never have it. We must be serious before that.

MR. S. To be serious is to seek for a way of life which will give meaning and purpose to existence.

MR. H. If I enquire of myself whether or not I am serious about this work, the answer is best revealed when I consider the extent and quality of my actions. I shall expect to find my actions consistent with my profession of seriousness. The reverse and yet not quite the reverse is the case. I find I am not serious but that I have times of seriousness.

I do not think men 1, 2 and 3 can be said to be serious about anything they do, for while they profess to be serious their actions contradict them. . . .

MR. O. Yes, but they have to be serious if they want to get something.

MR. H. . . . Seriousness is, I think, an attribute of waking and conscious man, is somehow connected with will and cannot be mechanical.

MR. O. No, the question was not to be like that—what it means to be serious now, as we are, to-day, not to-morrow.

MR. S. On thinking about what seriousness means, it appears impossible to know when one has no permanent 'I' or a sufficiently strong aim so that in all circumstances one can relate one's thoughts and motives to that aim.

MR. T. Unless an aim is determined, there is no possibility of being serious. The direction of the will towards doing only those things which would help one's aim should produce a state of mind which could be described as serious. Until one has a permanent will and a defined aim one could not be said to be capable of real seriousness.

MR. O. But aim may be not serious. No, no, that is wrong.

MRS. S. To be serious is to want to have understanding.

MISS R. It seems to me that to be serious means an understanding of the scale of values and treating important things with care and attention.

MR. F. Seriousness implies unity for a certain time.

It implies the weight of at least two centres working together.

It implies the use of intelligent parts of centres or the effort to use them.

It implies the clear separation of the positive and negative parts of centres.

MR. O. No, no, no. This does not apply at all.

MRS. S. To be serious is to have singleness of purpose, to which all minor things are subsidiary.

MISS R. Does to be serious mean to try to face facts?

MR. O. You have to face facts, serious or not, just the same.

MRS. S. To be serious is to try and avoid, by seeking a true objective, aimless drifting through life. It is to desire to attain fuller consciousness (or conscience) and not to allow lesser things to divert one from those which one comes to believe are the important ones.

MISS F. Being serious seems to require more than one centre, it seems to involve both intellectual and emotional centres.

Imagination seems to spoil sincerity.

For instance, when I am trying to resolve to be less negative, I find that what was for a moment a sincere resolve has turned into an imaginative picture where the fault is already cured.

To be serious in one's attitude towards other people means, I think, trying to understand them without letting any false personalities come between you and them.

Being serious, to me, seems connected with being practical, trying to see situations objectively and wanting to understand.

MRS. L. Is to be serious to take things on their right level—that is, to give importance to what is important?

MR. D. To be serious is to remember the relative scale of things.

MR. A. I think there are three qualifications for seriousness:

1. Permanent aim, knowledge of the result to be achieved;
2. necessity to avoid distractions from this aim;
3. knowledge of objective values.

One can only be really serious when one keeps all the three qualifications constantly in mind. Speaking for myself I cannot do so. Not only is it obvious that I cannot in my present [state] have any objective values, not even any values apart from my subjective interpretations, but I cannot have a permanent aim or know what I really want. Whilst as regards distractions—I find that this continuous change of 'I's in me, with their attendant conflicting desires, predilections, ready-made likes and dislikes, makes it quite impossible to really concentrate or for any length of time attempt to do work both with effort and attention.

I am sure that seriousness implies both effort and attention, and feel somehow that it means working in the higher parts of centres than the ones normally in use. I would like to know whether we can be serious in our present state—I mean, at our present level?

MR. F. To be serious is to be prepared to make an effort, either mental or physical. The system teaches the necessity of constant effort and thus encourages seriousness. Greatest effort is required in the higher or less mechanical parts of centres and, since consciousness urges one to live in these higher parts, consciousness and seriousness are similar terms. It is, however, possible to be serious without being conscious, but not possible to be conscious without being serious.

MR. O. No, no, no. They are not similar terms. You lose the idea.

MISS L. For me, seriousness consists in a realization of the urgency of the moment. The only time I can make an effort is now; if I do not make the effort now, I shall never escape.

MR. J. Is an understanding of the task we have to tackle in our attempts to become conscious—the realization of the constant effort that is necessary; but in so far as we can be led away from that constant effort by the smallest external influence at any time we cannot be serious? We have not enough 'I's interested in the work of self-development.

The importance of creating the serious atmosphere to others in the system that can help us.

The importance of appearing normal. (Sly man.)

MR. O. Is that all? You see, most of these remarks include too many things—work, self-remembering, higher parts of centres. This is not sufficient. Necessary to look how we can be serious now. For instance, one says it is remembering aim. Quite good, but as I say, aim may be wrong. 'Want to understand.' Also good, but not sufficient. So subjective. Being serious is something simpler, if you like. Necessary to divide two things. To be serious and to take things seriously. You speak all without exception only about how to take things seriously and which things, and not one thing about what it means to be serious. I will tell you what it means. To be serious means to take nothing seriously—with the exception of the things you know you want, that they are important and so on. Not to guess, not to try to justify things because you take them seriously. To be serious it is necessary to take nothing seriously unless you know it has to be taken seriously, and only the things you know for certain must be taken seriously. It looks too small, but when you apply it to things you will see this is the only solution and this is what is necessary.

MISS H. Does to be serious mean not wasting energy on things that are unimportant?

With regard to the six forms of action, do a combination of centres enter into each of these? Or can one centre predominate in any of the actions?

MR. O. Centres do not enter into it.

[End of written questions.]

MISS H. Do these triads of actions exist in the whole Ray of Creation, or do they refer only to organic life?

MR. O. We speak about man's activity at present. Certainly we are in the Ray of Creation and they are in the Ray of Creation, but that is going away from the task. The idea is to find actions analogous to those given. Our actions, intentional actions, which fall in one or another of these six categories.

MISS H. I cannot remember what is the intellectual part of emotional centre. I know it is to do with magnetic centre, but that does not help me very much.

MR. O. Intellectual part of emotional centre is the intellectual part of emotional centre.

MISS H. But how can you describe it? What sort of example. . . .

MR. O. Description will not help. But again, take simple thing. Simple thing will help you to understand it. It is a kind of emotional activity, intentional and with controlled attention. That will be the work of higher part of emotional centre.

MR. A. I feel there must be a connection between action and doing an action. Action implies performance and the performance may be up to the standard of what I understood, so to speak, an action to mean and the usual kind of action made by us at our present level. Is there anything in the performing of an action? And does work in various centres, or rather in the higher parts of centres have anything to do with it?

MR. O. Centres have nothing to do with it and the rest of the question is unnecessary philosophy.

MR. A. How is it possible to avoid the kind of laziness one is unconscious of?

MR. O. Necessary to find cause. Reasons can be very different.

MR. A. How is it possible to avoid giving way to various weaknesses? Is it possible to increase in the right way one's will?

MR. O. Different in different cases. One weakness one remedy, another weakness another remedy.

MR. R. During physical sleep is energy wasted due to frequent dreaming?

MR. O. Yes, but a comparatively small amount. Necessary to have normal sleep, but you cannot lose much. Unless it is very bad. Then it is pathological and must be treated.

MR. R. If this is so, how can one prevent this wastage?

If one can control the negative emotion of day-dreaming, does this curtail one's dreams at night?

MR. O. What means curtail? It may increase, but then this does not matter at all. Energy cannot be wasted to a great extent, so it is not important.

MR. R. Would Mr. O. explain how different dreams occur and how it is that certain centres may be responsible for these dreams while one is physically asleep?

MR. O. This is not an important question. We have to speak about things we can improve or change or control. Dreams are not important.

MISS M. Last week Mr. O. said that being busy did not always mean not being lazy.

MR. O. It is a form of laziness to be always busy.

MISS M. In this case, would the activity of the person concerned be a buffer which prevents him seeing the side of himself which wants to be lazy?

MR. O. Quite. Yes.

MISS M. Would it be right to define seriousness as being willing to see ourselves as we are without attempting to justify what we see? Or would it be trying to see where our actions correspond or do not correspond to our aim?

MR. O. Yes, very good, but if you put it shorter. Long definition always needs interpretation of some kind.

MISS M. In the New Testament we are very often told to watch and pray. What is it in the system which corresponds to prayer?

MR. O. Difficult to say what is meant, you know. Because New Testament is written in one key, so to speak, and we speak in another key. This is first thing. Secondly, words in two thousand years change their meaning. This is a religious thing, that means there is recognized or admitted the possibility of addressing higher powers, God. It is based on that.

MRS. S. Can we regard other people as impressions from which we live?

MR. O. No, certainly not. People are people. Impressions are impressions.

MRS. S. If that is so, should we avoid if possible those that waste us?

MR. O. Certainly we should avoid it, but not because of that. It may be our fault that they waste us—we may identify, then accuse them that they affect us. If we stop identification, they stop annoying us.

MRS. S. Or should one accept them as necessary friction, which might help growth of being?

MR. O. Everything is friction, or may be. Can we deal with it is the question.

MRS. S. Does full knowledge of triads help us to understand this?

MR. O. Full knowledge will be when we are man No. 7. Even very small knowledge may help us.

MR. H. To be serious would seem to mean to try and avoid identification with the voices of different 'I's, seeing each for what it is worth and to make judgment without being influenced by these inner voices.

I find that deliberate muscular relaxation helps me to throw off identification better than most other efforts, but often I cannot even begin to relax. Is there any method or exercise to help me do this?

MR. O. Sometimes physical tiredness helps.

MR. H. I know the emotion caused by considering, such as stage fright or embarrassment, is negative and should be overcome by right thinking beforehand. Can Mr. O. indicate on what lines this may be thought of, as so far I meet with no success at all?

MR. O. That is not quite right, because there is very much which is physical in these emotions, so it cannot be destroyed just by right thinking or reasoning.

MISS L. Is a genius simply a man who repeats the 'paint a picture' action and the criminal one who repeats the 'steal a picture' action very often?

MR. O. No, no, you cannot use such language. It makes it quite impossible. You cannot make terminology like this. Examples cannot be transformed into terminology.

But genius is a little different; cannot be described just like that, it includes many other things besides.

MISS L. If so, is this essence or is it accident become habit?

MR. O. Too complicated. Not only essence. It cannot be brought to one definition. First each must be separate. The two put together makes it impossible to discuss this question.

MISS L. Is the feeling of disgust with myself and unhappiness in my present state negative?

MR. O. Probably.

MISS S. When you like or dislike a complete stranger, has that anything to do with type?

MR. O. No, only imagination. In most cases based on associations.

MISS S. But can we ever see type?

MR. O. We can sometimes, but that is quite a different question. For instance, you can have experience of certain types and when you meet them a second time or a third time, you may recognize them. That is the only way we can come to an understanding of types. Suppose you knew somebody and saw how they act in certain circumstances. Later you meet somebody you think is like them and then you find him in the same circumstances and you see he acts in the same way. That means you will have guessed right.

MRS. S. I don't understand the working of centres. Suppose I notice a draught and shut the window, is it instinctive centre which notices the draught, moving centre which shuts the window and intellectual centre which makes the connection between them?

MR. O. Instinctive centre told you it was cold. Intellectual centre told you, necessary to shut window. Moving centre went and shut window.

MR. B. My life seems to have become a series of more or less frequent jerks, of becoming suddenly aware how asleep or mechanical I have just been. Is this a helpful form of friction? If so, can it be usefully intensified?

MR. O. If it helps you to remember yourself. Then it is helpful. If you identify, it is wrong.

MRS. S. In a moment of realization of my mechanicalness, it seemed as though all my usual outlook was imagination. Now it seems to me as if my feelings at that moment were imagination. I want to know what is thought and what is imagination. Is it imagination to try to remember the thoughts and understanding of a previous moment?

MR. O. Begin with simpler things. Then there can be no mistake.

MR. T. Is it a feature of the different types of energy that a different centre predominates in each?

MR. O. No, you cannot bring in centres. It is more complicated.

MR. L. You said just now that considering might be purely physical. . . .

MR. O. I did not say considering. I said just reasoning cannot help because it may be partly physical. I did not say considering was physical. This is not only considering. It is more than considering that I spoke about.

MR. F. I am not quite clear about self-remembering. Is it correct to think it ought always to be started in the most difficult circumstances?

MR. O. It is desirable. If you learn to remember yourself in easy circumstances, you will forget in difficult ones. If you learn in difficult circumstances, you will always have it when you want.

MR. F. I am not clear either whether one should try the whole time?

MR. O. Even five minutes would be good! We have to begin with minutes—seconds.

MR. F. One should not wait until the critical situation arises?

MR. O. One must be prepared. But what is important is self-remembering in the critical situation.

MISS M. Is it not possible to self-remember without knowing how to deal with the situation?

MR. O. It has nothing to do with the situation. But if you remember yourself, whatever the situation is you will be on the level of the situation. We identify with changeable circumstances. If we remember ourselves, nothing can shake us.

MRS. N. If we were rid of identification, should we be rid of all mechanical troubles?

MR. O. Many, certainly. Most of our troubles come from identification, one kind or another kind.

MISS N. I do not understand clearly what 'being' is.

MR. O. You. What you are.

MISS N. Is it connected with essence?

MR. O. First try not to explain one word with help of another word. I said being is what you are. The more you know yourself, the more you know your being. If you do not know yourself, you do not know your being. If you have never learnt you have being, being of all people is the same to you. Someone who has never heard of self-remembering, if you ask him, he will say he can. This is one being. Another knows he does not remember himself. This is different being. A third begins to remember himself. This is third being. This is how it must be taken.

We understand differences of objects, but in ordinary thinking we do not understand difference of being. What do we learn? First that we are not one. That we are many 'I's. This fact that there are many 'I's in us on the same level; that one is not stronger than another; that there is no central 'I' in control. This the state of our being. When we begin to acquire permanent 'I' that will be another level of being. There are four states of consciousness. We are only in two. Relative consciousness, waking sleep, this is all we have. We have to start to work in this state. This is our being. If we begin to work, to acquire self-consciousness, we shall have a third state and that will be different being. All you heard about the possibility of development, it all refers to being.

MISS H. Is knowledge of what identification is [   ]? Do you gradually understand?

MR. O. Gradually, everything gradually. When first you hear about it, you do not understand. Second you find in yourself or in other people a very clear case of identification and then another case. You begin to compare. Then find in yourself cases of more identification or less identification, then you can compare the two states. You learn everything gradually, never anything at once.

MISS M. Isn't there an element of becoming in being?

MR. O. In school only. In ordinary life there is no becoming.

MISS M. But if one makes any progress, one changes.

MR. O. In life one does not. One can make progress in knowledge only; not in being. What we are, we remain. How can one change in life? Everything is balanced. If one acquires one thing, one loses another.

MRS. S. But surely people do get better—more unselfish, kinder?

MR. O. Better one side, worse another.

MRS. S. But you come across people who seem to grow.

MR. O. I never saw them. Maybe you are lucky, me unlucky.

MRS. S. But I have seen some wonderful people.

MR. O. Some kind of religious system, perhaps, but not in life. You see, very often that is why some misunderstanding happens. We do not realize for a long time the difference between man in ordinary life and man connected with some kind of system. Without any kind of system, some kind of way, man cannot progress, he remains what he is, generally going down. With the help of some system he can change. The system must suit him. System may be very good but not suit the particular man.

MRS. D. You said to be serious meant to take nothing seriously. . . .

MR. O. Unless you know you have to take it seriously.

MRS. D. I think that is going to be very difficult. One tries not to, but goes right on doing it.

MR. O. That does not mean to be serious.

MISS R. How can one start not to be identified with the result of something? Something you hope very much will happen—where there is apprehension.

MR. O. Facts must be described. Otherwise I do not know how to speak about it. But again, if we leave that and take only identification, you must understand that identification does not help. It only makes things more confused and more difficult. If you realized even that— that alone in some cases may help. Sometimes people think it helps them; they do not realize it makes it more difficult.

MISS J. If one is identified with getting somewhere in time, it is still there even if you get it out of your mind.

MR. O. Yes, difficult moment. Particularly if you are already late. But even then you can say 'If I miss train, I miss train. Train will not wait.'

MR. A. I suppose identified mind is imperfect mind?

MR. O. No. Mind is mind. It is the same. It can be identified or not identified. Sometimes even direction of attention is sufficient.

Suppose one never heard about identification and possibility of getting rid of it. One considers identification with best things. You meet people who sincerely think this is their best manifestation; you will find it very often.

MR. A. I suggest that a great many things would not be accomplished without identification.

MR. O. Quite possible, but they would be accomplished better without it and many wrong things would not happen. This is exactly our ordinary thinking. We think it is necessary when actually it only spoils things. It is not a thing which has useful energy in it at all, only destructive energy.

MR. A. Take an aviator concentrating on making a record. . . .

MR. O. If he identifies he will have an accident, nothing more. The whole chance of his getting this record is not identifying. He may call it concentration, control or something. The moment he identifies he is lost.

MISS F. Is identification mainly emotion?

MR. O. Yes—a kind of emotional disturbance.

MR. A. As soon as a man throws himself into his task in the ordinary sense, he is identified?

MR. O. Not if he can control it. He may control or not control his state. If he can control his state, this is not identification. If he cannot control it, this means identification and bad work. This is what it is necessary to understand. Identification always means worse work than without identification.

MISS A. Can one get to such a point that one does not identify with anything?

MR. O. One day we identify more, another day less. We can try.

MR. A. Is there a state between self-remembering and identification?

MR. O. Different sides of the same thing. Not remembering is identification. Not identified one must remember oneself to a certain extent, perhaps even without knowing it. There are many different degrees.

MR. A. I thought it was an essential part of self-remembering—to be aware of it?

MR. O. That is intentional self-remembering. In this case we speak about not intentional. Man in ordinary conditions who can control himself better than another man. It is already a certain degree of consciousness. By itself, without school, it cannot become consciousness. It will always remain half-consciousness, so to say.

MRS. N. Can you possibly do anything wrong while self-remembering?

MR. O. It depends on degree, you know. Self-remembering by itself does not prevent one from doing wrong. It depends what is connected with it, what degree. Only one thing you can be sure [of]. There is less chance of doing something wrong if you remember yourself, and more chance if you do not remember yourself. That is definite.

MR. A. Was self-remembering a feature of the old esoteric knowledge?

MR. O. Always, everywhere. Only sometimes, in religious schools, for instance, it is called by a different name. It is not arbitrary. It is a necessary stage in one's development, not an arbitrarily imposed task. One has to pass it and one can pass it only in one way.

MR. A. Did Christ at any time speak about it—in what words?

MR. O. Every page. Different words. For instance, 'Do not sleep', 'Watch'—all the time.

MR. H. If identification is an emotional disturbance, what causes this disturbance? Why is it so?

MR. O. Anything, anything in the world can cause it. Difficult to say why. It may be too many 'I's, lack of control, if you like. But 'why' is not so interesting. We do not study why. We study how. We cannot know why, or only sometimes. We have no control; do not know we have no control and many other things. That causes it. We are born surrounded by people who are always identified and by unconscious imitation we become just the same.

MISS R. You said Nature was against the development of man. The development of man is not unnatural, is it?

MR. O. Yes, on a certain level. Levels are different. Nature created man half-developed and, so to speak, left him there. That means Nature, the nearest Nature, so to speak, needs him as he is. At the same time, Nature created him with the possibility of development, which means it can use developed man for some purpose. Both things are natural—the fact that man is half-developed and the fact that he can develop.

MISS M. You said a long time ago that we lived under 48 laws. What are they?

MR. O. Earth is under 48 laws. Gravity, things like that. Many, many laws under which earth lives—movement, physical laws, chemical laws.

MISS M. You said as we progressed we should eliminate some of them.

MR. O. I said earth lives under 48 laws. Man lives under many, many more than 48. Some we know—physical, biological laws. Then coming to quite simple laws—ignorance, for instance. We do not know ourselves, this is a law. If we begin to know ourselves, we get rid of a law. We cannot learn 'this is one law, this is another law, this is a third law'. For many of them we have no names. All people live under the law of identification. This is a law. Those who begin to remember themselves can get rid of the law of identification. In that way we can know these laws.

MISS N. In our present state, can we judge what is a moral action?

MR. O. Certainly it is possible.

MISS N. I have noticed several things I thought I did from one motive, I really did from a completely different one. Therefore, what I thought was a moral action probably was not at all.

MR. O. Very easy to make mistakes, but at the same time we can. We are just beginning. The more control we have, the more consciousness, and consciousness in that sense includes will. If you have no control, in ordinary state, we cannot speak except about conventional morality. When we have control we become more responsible. The less consciousness we have, the more our actions may be contrary to morality. In any case, the first necessity for moral action is that it must be conscious.

MR. A. What about when you perform a moral action so often that it becomes a habit?

MR. O. What do you mean by a moral action?

MR. A. Any good habit.

MR. O. That is not a moral action. That is habit. You must first have a feeling of good and bad, right and wrong and some interpretation—this is right, this is wrong; this is right, this is wrong. Your feeling of right and wrong may be right. Definition may be wrong or just arbitrary. You may not know what is right and wrong in reference to decisions. You can say only conscious or unconscious. This is where we must begin. Then later you will come to right or wrong. We can begin with conscious and mechanical and sooner or later come to an understanding of right and wrong—it does not mean we know, but we can know what is conscious and what is mechanical. This is the starting point.

MR. B. Is it incorrect to think of identification as always existing when we are asleep?

MR. O. No, in ordinary conditions. But it is not necessary. Almost all the time. We pass from one identification into another identification.

MR. A. Is a bored man identified with nothing?

MR. O. Boredom is also identification—one of the biggest.

MR. A. With what?

MR. O. With oneself. With false personality. With something in oneself.

MISS S. When you speak about triads, do you mean crime in the ordinary sense—against criminal law and so on?

MR. O. No. I mean that crime is objective. Not only convention. Crime is some different action from action which is not crime.

MISS J. Are there a lot of our actions which are criminal and we do not realize it?

MR. O. Lying is criminal, for instance, and we do it all the time. What is lying in the system sense? You remember how it is spoken of as 'speaking about things we do not know as if we knew'. Pretending to know, but even pretending is not what it is, we are so accustomed that we do not notice when we begin. This is criminal action. Same triad.

Necessary to think about it. To get this principle about different actions. We know there is bread that we can eat, and things that are poison. But we do not understand that actions may be equally different. One action may correspond to bread, another action to poison, but we do not feel it. It does not enter into ordinary thinking.

MR. R. Can one know differences between actions without knowing the state of mind of the person who does it?

MR. O. I do not mean state of mind. I mean actions themselves quite apart from that. Bread or poison remain different apart from state of mind of man who analyses them.

MISS F. Are the consequences of the action part of the triad?

MR. O. You may take it like that. But leave triads for a time.

MISS F. Does the result of the action belong to the action?

MR. O. Yes, certainly—all included in the action itself. Same as the results are included in bread and poison. One result in bread, another result included in poison.

MISS M. Can we say that actions which take us away from our aim are criminal?

MR. O. No, we cannot start from this point. Definition itself must be based on other things. At present it is quite sufficient to understand criminal as definite fact. It does not mean it is simply called crime from one point of view and may be called not crime from another point of view. Definite action means crime, is crime.

MR. A. What does the word crime mean to you?

MR. O. Oh, that is dictionary question. Dictionary definition will not help to understand. It is some kind of special action, different from other actions, from work, for instance, different from adaptation, different from many other actions. It has its own specific gravity, its own specific meaning. It is very easy action, one of the easiest actions in the world, and that is why crime is so popular, in our time particularly.

MR. A. In our mechanical state, then, are we very often criminals?

MR. O. Why?

MR. A. We speak about things we do not know.

MR. O. That is lying. That is another thing. Same triad but not same thing.

MRS. S. Is crime always the result of identification?

MR. O. Not necessarily. Again that does not enter into it. This is much bigger scale, you know. We are not talking on psychological scale when we speak of this thing.

MRS. D. Do all results of criminal actions have something in common which we can recognize, or could if we knew what it was?

MR. O. Not only results—by actions themselves.

MISS N. I think you said people who belonged to Mr. G.'s system had to be able to make a certain amount of money . . .

MR. O. No, it was somebody else said that.

MISS N. . . . had to have a certain success in life, in material things.

MR. O. Why do you speak about it?

MISS N. It seems to me that in the making of money there are a great many negative and criminal actions necessary.

MR. O. Yes, I see now. But not necessarily, you see. In *Fragments* G. said people at that time had to have a certain amount of money. Later that was changed. He decided to have only a few people and with these people to do very complicated work. So they had to pay for themselves. The question of making money does not enter. They could have it from their grandmothers. Quite different idea. Also he said people must be able to earn money, but it does not mean by criminal practice. This is not included at all!

MISS N. It seems to me very difficult not to use lying, selfishness. . . .

MR. O. Not necessary. This is just an arbitrary connection. It does not mean it always happens. Take professional people. Not necessary for them to steal.

How can any work be done without money? Travels may be necessary, experiments, place, house and so on.

MR. A. You said earlier this evening that action had a moral value in itself independent of state of mind.

MR. O. I said we could judge only if action is conscious or unconscious; if we started from that, maybe later we would come to understanding of their moral value.

MISS R. In recognizing difference in actions, is it any good to approach it with intellectual centre, starting by thinking about it?

MR. O. Yes, certainly. You can do nothing else and in that way you can judge, 'is it conscious or not?'

MISS R. I mean, the difference between bread and poison—would one be able to recognize it intellectually?

MR. O. You must try. You must start with intellectual centre. Again with intellectual centre you can have more knowledge or less knowledge. You can know more, observe more. If you know more, result will be better.

MISS R. You once said criminal actions smell.

MR. O. Yes, there is some kind of definite feeling about it. Quite right, but you cannot base it on that.

* * * *

Thursday. February 3rd 1938. (Warwick Gardens.)

[Written questions read.]

MRS. D. Are optimists and pessimists examples of different types of people?

MR. O. No, I do not think so. I think these words have meaning more in literature than in actual life. I never met an optimist and never met a pessimist yet.

MRS. D. We were told at the last lecture that sometimes we might be able to recognize similar types of people by their reactions in similar situations. Does this mean only in critical or emotional situations?

MR. O. Any situation. I will read you next time one experiment with types from the book you heard something from before.

MISS F. Much of my behaviour, mental attitudes, mannerisms, etc. seem to originate and to be bound up with the fact that I belong to the female of the species. I can't believe that I shall ever be able to combine the qualities and outlook of the male with my own qualities and outlook.

Does this imply that none of us can ever be complete and can possess only one side of the emotional and intellectual qualities?

Does the idea of male and female persist with astral bodies?

MR. O. No.

MISS F. I have thought about this often and would find it helpful if Mr. O. would talk on this subject.

MR. O. It may be, but you see our words are not sufficient. Our idea of astral bodies is not sufficient. I have nothing to say really. I think it is an exaggerated idea. Actually man or woman in themselves are balanced. They must be different. It is quite all right to be a man or woman—nothing wrong with it.

MISS D. I am beginning to get an idea of the significance of action where before I had considered only motive and result were important. I can see that action, to be effective, must be deliberate, but I cannot connect different kinds of actions, such as burning and stealing, with different triads.

MR. O. This is the idea. Necessary to understand that actions by themselves are different, the same as things are different. They do not change with motive or depend on motive.

Leave triads alone for a time.

MISS M. When one is required to sympathize with other people's troubles, how can one determine at what point one becomes too identified? Or, on the other hand, if one hardens the heart too much in the attempt to avoid identification?

MR. O. Where imagination enters. If you learn to observe yourself, you can find the moment when identification begins—the moment when imagination starts. So long as you deal with facts, you may keep away from identification, but when imagination starts you are lost.

MR. B. If I try to do some customary action in a different way from usual, sometimes there is a small intellectual effort which adjusts the mechanical action of moving centre. Is this the intellectual part of moving centre?

MR. O. No, centres cannot come into it. Later possibly one can make deductions, but it sounds as if you observed which part of centre you use. This is analysis and you mix it with observation.

MR. B. If we anticipate some future event by day-dreaming about it, instead of waiting or working for it to occur, are we using action similar to that used in burning a house?

MR. O. No, it is accidental. No connection. Burning a house has nothing to do with it.

MR. R. Can two types of action manifest themselves at the same time or must they be consecutive?

MR. O. They may. They can all be manifested at the same time.

MR. R. Example: I take a photograph of a beautiful scene. Are there two actions involved (a) preparing the camera, analogous to building a house (b) seeking out the best position for a good artistic effect, analogous to painting a picture?

MR. O. No, no. It has no connection; from this point of view it is not action.

MR. R. When undertaking any kind of work or pursuit, should one purposely consider which of the six actions should be used?

MR. O. You cannot do that. What I said study you try to do. People always think how they can do on the basis of—what?—new words. New words are not sufficient for changing methods. You can study the problem, not change your action. You must first try to understand these six categories I gave you; you must try to put in these categories corresponding analogous actions. Then perhaps you will see how, why we act in one way or another way. Even that is far from change. Then perhaps we will be able to see what will be acting in a wrong way. You have a certain aim and then you start to work in such a way that you can never get this aim. You will learn that it is necessary to stop because you are acting in the wrong way. You cannot learn first to choose which action you will use.

MR. R. Following this, should one analyse the result, which may be good or bad? For instance, if I have to reprimand a man, I should consider:

a. my method of dealing with him;

b. the reaction upon the man due to the methods I employ;

c. the result accruing from the way the man has been dealt with.

Presumably this forms a triad, does it not?

MR. O. No. And in most cases you do nothing like that. You simply shout at the man and think afterwards. And sometimes it is much better.

MR. T. In trying to discriminate between actions, would it help if we considered them as we do emotions, classing as negative those from which we derive no profit?

MR. O. No, no, no. There are no negative or positive. Simply different.

MR. S. When the fact of sleep becomes such an emotional thing that one realizes for a moment one just does not exist, there occurs a longing to do something, anything that will keep me, at least, alive. This longing never gets any further. Can Mr. O. explain what is the best way to deal with these sudden states of urgency to stop oneself falling asleep again?

MR. O. First, in what sense 'sleep' and second, in what sense 'alive'? We will find something later perhaps; we may come to some answer.

MR. S. Is having an attitude to something only substituting another word for identification?

MR. O. No. Attitude means point of view. You can have a point of view on things without being identified.

MISS M. Is it better from the point of view of the system to agree when you actually think 'no', rather than be involved in an argument which might possibly develop into negative emotions?

MR. O. That depends when and how and with whom.

MRS. N. What is meant by attention? Can one control it only by working so intensively that there is no room for any imagination and is it impossible with identification?

MR. O. You see, you ask what is attention and then you introduce identification and imagination. If you limited yourself to one, it would be possible. But three in one, impossible to answer. I do not know what you mean by the words.

MR. F. Does work on oneself improve one's judgment of a situation? If so, how?

For instance, if one has to make a difficult decision, the less identified, the easier it makes it to see the various factors. Does self-remembering enable you to sum it up?

MR. O. Yes, theoretically. But we cannot approach these questions in that way. I mean from point of view of profit. Then we get nothing. We must want to remember ourselves because we realize what it means not to remember; not because of profit. If we want profit, we never get it. We must want it because of what we may escape—that means our present state.

MR. F. I was told by somebody that the capacity of the brain decreases after a certain age. Does work on oneself improve brain capacity in this sense—I mean, the actual grey matter? It means, I suppose, that the older one gets the more formatory one tends to become—the cumulative effect of sleep.

MR. O. Quite right. But not only this work. Any kind of persistent work keeps brain working quite all right for a long time. Because this work can be regarded only as intellectual. Certainly the intellect must work up to its possibilities. If it stops, then certainly all other work may stop.

MISS R. It seems to me there are several different ways of doing the same action. Does the way of doing it affect the type of activity?

MR. O. You cannot give an example? No, the fact remains that certain actions mean certain things and how you can do it in a different way I do not see.

MRS. S. Do all criminal actions belong to the stealing a picture class?

MR. O. No, please, do not repeat this stealing a picture business. It was simply a joke—painting a picture, stealing a picture. Just an example.

MRS. S. It would seem that burning a house could be criminal action.

Killing a man, does that belong to the burning a house class? I think it could result from a very small action.

MR. O. You come to it from the wrong end. Burning a house can be not criminal at all. There is a fire coming that way and to stop it going further you have to burn a house—simply using violence, using some kind of violent method. You cannot come like this to these problems, asking what is criminal. You must take different cases you <u>know</u> are criminal and then you may put them in a separate category, but you cannot ask what criminal means.

MR. R. Do I take it none of the six actions is good or bad in itself?

MR. O. Nothing is good or bad in itself without relation to causes and effects.

MR. F. Is understanding of scale a function of the higher part of intellectual centre?

MR. O. Yes, but not only understanding. It has also the capacity to operate with different scales at the same time. Formatory centre cannot work like this.

MRS. S. What is the best way to look for one's own chief feature?

MR. O. Simply see oneself. I do not know how to say it better. It is possible one may find something—chief feature of the moment. It is imaginary personality; this is chief feature for everybody.

MRS. S. What is evil from the point of view of the system? Is it mechanicalness?

MR. O. Mechanicalness in the case where action can be conscious. Evil can come only from such action.

MISS R. With regard to my question about doing things in different ways. It seems to me you can do a job hating it or. . . .

MR. O. You may do it as you like, but if you are building a house you will put bricks. This is your personal, subjective attitude and does not mean anything. It is only what you feel when doing a certain action. The action remains the same.

There are cases where it may change, but that is not what we speak about now. You want very complicated cases. In the simple cases it means nothing at all.

MR. F. In working on oneself, would you consider it a legitimate reason if one wants to eliminate accident and replace will?

MR. O. One can think like that, but that means one does not know what accident means. Accident is not always detrimental, it may be beneficial. For instance, in Paris, if you go in a taxi, you come home alive only by Law of Accident! Normally you would be killed.

MR. F. One cannot control it entirely, but I thought the more conscious one was the more one could eliminate. . . .

MR. O. If one becomes conscious one will know. As I say, it may be good or may be bad, equally.

MR. M. You have explained that it is impossible for a man of infra-sex to evolve to supra-sex. May one conclude it is impossible for a man of infra-sex to evolve at all?

MR. O. No, there are special methods. But that was in my book, so it is not in the system. The *New Model* was written before I met this system myself. It does not contradict the system, only I must make this remark.

MR. M. Do you draw a distinction between congenital infra-sex and acquired infra-sex?

MR. O. I do not know. I have not gone into it, but I do not think it can be acquired. It may be, but that is already modifying the question.

MR. M. Have you not told us that at birth the machine is perfectly balanced?

MR. O. In normal cases, if you like. But I never said that anyway. At birth it may have in itself possibilities of development in one way or another way. So how can we say at birth it is perfect?

But your first question, is it possible for any kind to develop. I say it may be, but only through special methods. From the point of view of the Fourth Way, we suppose only normal people. People with some kind of abnormality may look for a special way. Certainly through that they may find. With this kind of system, they can perhaps better find their way than without, but it does not mean that this system is adapted for them. This is a short cut, so to speak, so one must be able to use all capacities.

MR. M. Would you call infra-sex pathological?

MR. O. Yes, definitely. Under-development in one way or another. At the same time there are different forms. It is difficult to speak in general.

MR. M. Is it important?

MR. O. Some deviations are not important, some are very important. There are deviations which are reflected in all other functions. Or there may be some kind of under-development really, but simply incomplete development which does not affect other functions. It is necessary to go into each particular case.

MR. M. You do not really think a type like Othello was infra-sex, do you?

MR. O. Oh, that is acquired. That I do not call infra-sex from this point of view. That is identification and imagination, not sex itself. That is why I say we cannot speak about sex until we know about the other centres and until we know many things. Until then many things will be ascribed to sex which really belong to other functions.

MR. H. I do not understand what you said about evil arising from mechanicalness which could be conscious.

MR. O. When you can be conscious; if you do things mechanically—without thinking, without feeling—then, you can do something very evil. If you just wait at this moment, you may stop.

There is a principle that evil can enter in life only through our voluntary actions. Voluntary is not quite the right word, but there is no better word.

MR. H. You do not mean that only a person who knew what it was to be conscious could do evil?

MR. O. No, not necessarily. This is only an illustration. Separate cases must be studied separately. But it is a very definite fact that there can be no evil done consciously. This is definite fact. I said once to another group 'try to do something bad consciously', and I heard a very interesting result. Somebody explained that this system teaches people to do evil things consciously!

MRS. S. Might there not be action when you thought you were doing right and it turned out to be a mistake and you thought you were doing it consciously?

MR. O. It is difficult to speak like this. I do not think such a thing can happen if you really take everything into consideration.

MR. M. You have explained that it is impossible for man to start climbing the Ray of Creation until he has learnt the laws under which he lives?

MR. O. No. Laws is too much. Until he knows himself. This is the first step towards this climbing, if you like. Before one sees oneself one can do nothing. So this must be first aim. Laws ... this is very far and very difficult. One cannot know all laws. But one can study laws. This is very useful. It keeps the mind working in the right direction. Study—not knowledge of—laws.

MR. M. That is not an expression you would use—'climbing the Ray of Creation'?

MR. O. Too big expression for the beginning. It may be, only many things have to be changed here before one can change place, so to speak.

MR. M. But the Ray of Creation here is mechanical, is it not?

MR. O. Yes. Not the whole ray. When it comes to us, certainly all laws are mechanical on this plane.

MR. M. But how is it possible that a mechanical ray can create a machine which is capable of achieving a permanent will?

MR. O. You must remember that the Ray of Creation starts consciously, and in the starting point evidently there are plans of everything, or some plans may develop further. But in the 48 laws that work on the earth, there are three laws from World 3, which is under the direct Will of the Absolute. Take these 48 laws: three from World 3, six from World 6, twelve from World 12, twenty-four from World 24, and three of its own; so you see they are not equally mechanical. Some are more mechanical, some are less mechanical. If we take this octave, not starting from Absolute, but from the sun—the octave of organic life: the sun is much higher than the earth and it is evidently possible to create in this octave possibilities of development. Thus man, if he can be regarded as a seed, has in himself the possibility of growth. He is not only what he looks; there is something which cannot be seen in him—the possibility of development.

MR. M. Is all consciousness of the same essence, the same substance?

MR. O. That I am afraid we have not material to answer. Consciousness we can speak about only belonging to ourselves. Consciousness belonging to higher levels, Ray of Creation, sun and so on is really just metaphysical idea, nothing else. We cannot compare. Although we must know even from our own experience that consciousness can be measured—in duration, in many different qualities we can find in ourselves. If it can be measured in ourselves, it can be measured in other planes.

MR. M. Is there any conservation of consciousness? Is it the energy No. 4. . . .

MR. O. No, no. That classification is not according to any of these divisions of the system. I only said that ordinary observation shows four kinds of energy—but not No. 2, No. 3 etc. Ordinary observation, not principle. We can distinguish mechanical, life energy, psychic energy and conscious energy.

MR. M. And no amount of psychic energy would give conscious energy?

MR. O. No more than any amount of mechanical would give life energy. But in this system we have finer divisions according to hydrogens. You remember in the Table of Hydrogens each density of matter requires a special energy. So there are more divisions still. This is quite elementary, these four kinds.

MR. M. There is really only one element, is there not—hydrogen?

MR. O. No, this is not in the system; this is in some chemical systems. System is different, no parallel with chemistry.

MR. M. There is a distinction, is there not, between mind and matter?

MR. O. Yes, but what do you mean by that? Mind is material also, but we do not regard it from the point of view of materiality. There is nothing which is not material from the point of view of the system.

Hydrogen is matter taken without regard to which force works through it. The same matter, if active force works through it, is called carbon; if passive force works through it, is called oxygen, and if neutralizing force works through it, is called nitrogen. The same matter taken without relation to forces is called hydrogen—hydrogen 6, hydrogen 12, etc., showing its density.

MR. B. Is there any significance in the fact of the names being the same as those found in organic chemistry?

MR. O. That means organic chemistry is taken as physical chemistry. Opposite to the ordinary point of view. From the ordinary point of view they do not use the word organic chemistry; organic matter to them is just accidental fusion. From the point of view of the system it is the original state of matter, and inorganic matter is simply the result of the decomposition of organic matter.

MR. F. Does work on oneself gather momentum after a time, or remain equally difficult? Like pushing a cart uphill?

MR. O. I think it becomes more difficult, because it is coming to more and more ramifications. You start on one line, then after some time on three lines and each divides and divides and divides, and all the time requires attention and effort. There is no inertia in this action. That is a different triad.

On the other hand, one acquires more energy; becomes more

conscious, and that makes it easier in a sense. But work by itself can never become easier.

MRS. S. Does one ever learn to administer shocks to oneself?

MR. O. Not only one way. First one must learn about three lines of work. Then one line gives shocks to other lines. If you understand it from this point of view, then you will find out.

MRS. S. Then experiment will not help?

MR. O. Necessary to understand three lines of work and how one line helps another. Not theoretically, but from observation.

MR. S. Can you explain what you mean by 'seeing oneself'?

MR. O. How can I? How can I explain what means seeing yourself in a mirror? Just the same.

MR. S. Well, but one sees many selves.

MR. O. No. Certain combinations. More one can see them separately the better.

MR. M. You would never expect anything theatrical, would you, like what you quoted about the man who drove home in a hansom cab and was enveloped in a cloud of fire?

MR. O. Subjectively anything may happen. Some people do react in that way. It means really in our language a moment of connection with higher emotional centre, and some people in this connection react by many subjective visions. But it is not obligatory. It may be with visions, it may be without visions.

MR. M. Are there any signs one might look out for?

MR. O. Signs only in the sense of self-remembering, because it happens as a result of self-remembering for a certain period. How self-remembering comes, that is another thing. In this case it was described in this book (Bucke's book, I think, wasn't it?). That is one case; there may be many other methods. Always one or another kind of self-remembering which produces these connections with higher emotional centre. First it creates subjective visions. One begins to see things in allegories and symbols, sometimes in a very interesting way. Then one begins to see things which it is impossible to describe. Things we cannot see with our ordinary eyes, with higher emotional centre we can see them. I do not mean 'astral', but things which look quite ordinary. You are astonished you could not see it before. Things which we see without this, but at the same time we do not see them.

MISS M. What sort of things?

MR. O. How can I explain? Many things. For instance—only that is in higher degrees—you can see what one thinks. We do not see it, but we can through higher emotional centre. This is not the beginning, this is higher degree. In the beginning you see many things you do not see ordinarily.

MR. M. Will you explain one day the means you used in those experiments you wrote about?

MR. O. Not practical, you know. I did not use one, but many different methods. Many of them I would not use now for instance, even if I could not do it any other way. Necessary to be very young and strong for some of these methods.

MR. M. Drugs?

MR. O. I tried many interesting drugs, but you cannot control the results and do not know what you receive. But there are much more dangerous methods, like fasting and breathing. With these you can control the result to a certain extent.

MR. M. What truth is there in the thing about 'uncoiling linga'?

MR. O. Just terminology of different school which we do not use, so it means nothing for us. Words. In any case, I never found anything serious in all that, and although I did not know anything at that time about, for instance, higher centres, yet when I learnt about higher centres everything fitted. For example, I knew the difference between higher emotional and higher mental, before I knew of the existence of higher centres.

Higher emotional centre uses same forms, may give more knowledge on the same subjects we know now or present them in the form of allegories. But in higher mental centre there are no forms. It is quite different thinking—quite different ideas.

MR. M. This subject-object relationship I can never get away from! I do not know anything else.

MR. O. But I assure you just one step, <u>one step</u> from our ordinary state and all these values change.

You see, we base our intellectual construction on certain ideas, certain concepts, certain words, and if we make just one step from our ordinary state, all this changes. That is why it is so difficult to trust to words.

MISS R. You said higher emotional centre had forms and higher mental had no forms. I thought you once said they were all in one? It was in connection with seeing mathematics emotionally.

MR. O. Yes, but it is very difficult to put in words. One thing only can be understood. Intellectual and emotional are divided only in lower centres.

[About a page and a half missing.]

*   *   *

MR. M. When one's mind wanders over the past or one is making plans for the future, that need not necessarily be day-dreaming, need it?

MR. O. No. Day-dreaming is when you indulge in it, so to speak—repeat the same thing, same thing, over and over. Making plans is quite different. Practical way of thinking. Trying to remember, to reconstruct, trying to find something in the past again is not day-dreaming. Day-dreaming is lazy, just letting things come. But again it may be useful sometimes. I do not call all day-dreaming imagination. Imagination is generally ascribing to oneself some knowledge, some power, some quality one does not possess. This is dangerous imagination. Day-dreaming after all is harmless if it does not occupy twenty-four hours of the day.

MISS L. Have people of each type the possibility of changing?

MR. O. Yes, certainly. Type by itself is not an obstacle. Only necessary to understand differences. Some types create obstacles for themselves more easily, and some types perhaps not so easily.

MISS M. Ought one to avoid communication with people one feels an instinctive dislike for, or try to overcome it?

MR. O. I do not believe in this instinctive dislike. I think it is just imaginary. First, the word instinctive is wrong. Our instincts do not go so far. You mean imaginary.

MISS M. But there are people you do dislike as soon as you see them.

MR. O. I can say quite sincerely that there was only one man I really disliked in all my life. All the rest was imaginary. So it does not need a special rule for that if it happens only once.

MR. M. Has it ever occurred to you that you might have lived ten thousand years hence and come back, and this is the past?

MR. O. I certainly read about that, but never thought it was possible. I think that even if one lives longer than one life, one is adapted to a certain period. I do not think one can live in a different period. I think it would be absolutely impossible for us to adapt to some other period. We dislike the present, but at the same time we are accustomed to it, and periods differ so much that I do not think the same souls could live in different ones. (I mean souls in the ordinary sense.)

MR. S. Does self-remembering help one to remember oneself in the past? I mean, for instance, I have not the slightest idea what I have been from boy up.

MR. O. Yes, it certainly helps. That is the second degree of self-remembering. First degree, you must remember yourself as you are, and second degree, as you are all your life. Some people have more memory of the past, some less, but sooner or later it will develop with self-remembering. It is a very, very strong feeling. Sometimes you cannot believe it.

MRS. S. Could you remind us about the three lines of work?

MR. O. With the first line only, one can progress but very slowly, and one cannot be sure of this progress. The first is work for oneself—self-study, study of system and so on. The second is work with other people, for instance here: you ask questions, hear other people—this refers partly to second line, not all second line. Third line of work is work for the organization, not for yourselves at all.

In the first line the work is for yourself and in the second line for yourself and for other people. In the third line, it is work for the school, not for yourself at all. One line helps another. This is one of the secrets of school-work. Only in that way work can go straight. Otherwise it will deviate.

* * *

Thursday. February 10th 1938. (Warwick Gardens.)

[Written questions read.]

MISS L. Mr. O. said there must be something wrong with us if we do not ask questions. I find it very difficult to formulate them. Is it because the part of me which is interested in the system has not got enough energy?

MR. O. I cannot answer that. You can find out the causes. I can simply see the fact.

MRS. N. When trying to remember myself, it seems as though I am aware only of moving and instinctive centres and cannot include either intellectual or emotional centres. Is this possible?

MR. O. If you observe yourself observing yourself, that will be intellectual. Every time you are angry or irritated, like something or dislike something, this is emotional.

MR. T. In the activity termed 'invention', is one of the attributes a search by the intellect?

MR. O. Certainly, but what is the idea? I do not see what is the question.

MRS. D. Is one of the differences between the building and inventing actions that when building you have a definite knowledge of what the result will be, and when inventing the result cannot be known beforehand?

MR. O. No, quite wrong. Actually, building house needs these two actions. What is called invention here is as trade—some kind of professional knowledge—and the first is simply labour. Some kind of knowledge is necessary. Two triads. Characteristically, we put it under the form of labour, but at the same time the other thing is also necessary.

This is the first example of how different triads must combine. Our actions consist mostly of several triads at the same time.

MRS. D. If this is so (difference in relation to result), don't the actions start with a different kind of force?

Does a destructive action start with the active force?

MR. O. This does not enter here. If you do not see that, you must start without triads, just studying destructive action.

MRS. S. You said last week that evil doing was always the result of being mechanical. But did you not say in a very early lecture that a man _may_ achieve consciousness and use it for evil ends? Otherwise would not the temptation of Christ in the Wilderness lose its significance?

MR. O. I never said that and do not see which of my words gave the possibility of thinking it. And Christ does not enter into our conversation. I see no connection.

MRS. S. But he was tempted to do evil. . . .

MR. O. And he did not yield because he was conscious.

MR. D. We have been told that we are born with essence and acquire personality, and that essence should dominate personality.

Does heredity have any influence on essence?

MR. O. Heredity we know only in relation to body. We do not know it in relation to essence. We have no material to answer this. Only physical features are hereditary. Essence may be quite different. Observation shows this.

MR. D. Are knowledge and being both limited to an equal degree by essence and personality?

MR. O. No, this is wrong construction.

MISS M. Are considering and identification attributes of false personality?

MR. O. This has no practical meaning.

MRS. N. What is attention?

MR. O. That is a matter for observation. Lack of attention, bigger attention, smaller attention, and so on. Description won't help.

MR. A. Are states of higher consciousness essentially accompanied by physical alertness? I know, for instance, that one cannot self-remember when physically asleep or anywhere near it.

MR. O. In most cases, yes. One becomes more alert in all centres.

MR. A. Is inner awareness a matter of mind or emotion or both?

MR. O. Of more even than that. Instinctive feeling and moving feeling.

In relation to the first question, about physical alertness, it is very difficult to make a general statement about that, because in some cases higher states of consciousness can produce trance states. That happens in two cases. First when it is intentionally done like that, for the purpose of saving energy or something like that. Secondly, when wrong methods are used, wrong school. There are many schools which can produce higher states of consciousness only with a condition of physical half-paralysis, trance. Generally this is wrong, because it cannot be done otherwise. Sometimes this can be a quite right way when they can do it this way and in another way.

Sometimes to the casual observer it may look different from physical alertness.

MR. H. I find relaxing a help in breaking away from identification. But I heard that there was a wrong way and a right way to relax. Could Mr. O. tell me if there is a special technique?

MR. O. Yes, it is a science. You may know it is necessary to relax to lose identification, but just cannot relax. I would say there is one right way and ten thousand wrong ways! Like many other things. Yes, it has to be learnt specially.

MR. H. Last week Mr. O. said that when connected with higher centres we could see things with our ordinary eyes which we didn't ordinarily see. Is it also possible to hear things in these states?

MR. O. Probably.

MISS R. Is killing necessarily a criminal activity?

MR. O. No, you cannot put it like that. It would be wrong to say no and wrong to say yes. It depends in relation to what you take it.

MR. F. Mr. O. says we are incapable of 'doing'. Does he mean by this we are incapable of permanent, controlled action?

MR. O. Certainly we are incapable. Otherwise why come here?

MISS M. Can one find one's chief feature oneself?

MR. O. Sometimes one can, theoretically, but one never does. Even if one is told, one does not believe it at once, one cannot accept it. It looks quite absurd, impossible. That is why one never can find it.

MR. F. Mr. O. has said we have to observe our 'I's for a long time before we can do anything else. How can we know when it is time to take the next step? Is it not true that all we can do is to try to <u>stop</u> things?

MR. O. You will know. You go on and you will see more, you will know where to start other things. And I can judge by your questions.

MISS M. Mr. O. said it was not possible to make comparisons of things on different scales. I don't know what kind of scale he had in mind.

MR. O. We may talk about scales later.

[End of written questions.]

* * *

MRS. S. Ought one to be able to induce sleep whenever one wants?

MR. O. Yes, I think one must be able to do that.

MRS. S. How?

MR. O. That is the thing. There are very many different causes that may prevent sleep, and first one must know which and then perhaps one will be able to remove it.

MRS. S. How can one learn to stop thinking?

MR. O. By self-remembering. Thinking stops at once. Everything in yourself that you can stop must help self-remembering. Pain, physical or mental, thoughts—all can be useful for self-remembering.

MR. M. I think a man with higher consciousness must soon become far more acutely aware of his various organs, does he not?

MR. O. If he has control, he will be aware of what he needs to be aware of. What means control? He will not be aware of what he does not need to be aware of.

MRS. S. Can he cure himself of illnesses?

MR. O. First, there are different illnesses. Some are the result of imagination; some the result of disregarding the demands of instinctive centre. Or perhaps the cause happened long ago and he cannot change it. Or perhaps it comes from an external cause. You cannot speak of illness all together like that.

MR. M. There is one very curious fact he would perceive, is there not, namely that these organs, although they can think, are incapable of thinking beyond themselves? So they have no sense of teamwork, so to speak, of the human body as a whole.

MR. O. But there are centres. This is right in relation to organs, but suppose you take the organs controlled by instinctive centre. Each separately does not know, but instinctive centre looks after them and controls them, adjusts one to another. Instinctive centre looks after all organs if it can. If energy is taken by another centre or goes some way on useless work, then it cannot. Then one becomes ill. But in the normal organism it has many possibilities of controlling, repairing organs and so on. So certainly we can suppose that in higher states of consciousness this faculty can be increased and can be quite conscious. But this is only supposition. We must study our present state.

There are several centres, several mechanisms. Intellectual centre looks after one side; emotional centre looks after another side; instinctive centre looks after another, and moving centre helps, too, very well. There is nothing left to chance.

MR. M. Then what did you mean when you said that every organ knows all there is to know about itself?

MR. O. That is in *New Model*. That was written before I met the system, as a result of personal observation. For instance, I did not know about centres then, and when I spoke about consciousness of organs I meant this: that organs or inanimate objects do not have abstract thinking as we have. We can think about this system, but this table can only think about itself. It knows what it is, that is all. It is a very strange, self-centred knowledge. The organs of our body, even each finger, has its own self-consciousness, if you like.

MR. M. Is there anything that controls unruly organs or cells?

MR. O. Yes, instinctive centre.

MR. M. But an ordinary man would not know. . . .

MR. O. Intellectual is not connected. Instinctive knows these itself. Do you think we would be alive for half an hour if instinctive centre did not work? It knows right work of each organ and wrong work. It tries always to make them work right. We think organs work by themselves. That is imagination. They are controlled by instinctive centre. That is instinct in the real sense in relation to man.

MR. M. Is that true in practice?

MR. O. It can be verified very easily by observation. Sometimes even, if you observe it often, even intellectual centre begins to know many things. In ordinary life instinctive centre works by itself and is not connected with intellectual centre.

MR. T. I have had a little experience of the taste of non-identification and now find that this taste traps me into thinking I am not identified when I find I really am.

MR. O. Yes, imagination. Moment to struggle with imagination.

MISS R. Are those trance states you were speaking of useful for development?

MR. O. If they are produced by somebody who knows. Generally speaking, they are the most harmful things possible.

MRS. S. But the Indian Yogis one reads about. . . .

MR. O. Yogis? What do you know about Yogis? There are many people who call themselves Yogis—some just to get a rupee from you. Some who are described in books are not Yogis at all, but sort of superstitious people who have imagination in higher emotional centre—all they can produce without real school. And they are just absorbed in this imagination. That is all. Most undesirable. So you see, there are Yogis and Yogis.

MRS. D. I asked about whether destructive action starts with active force. But I suppose we ought to know this ourselves?

MR. O. I already said much better if you study it without reference to triads at first.

MR. M. I think Mr. G. was often asked about the source from which he derived his knowledge, and you said he gave many answers on different occasions?

MR. O. Yes, all different. When I noticed they were different, I did not pay much attention, I knew he did not want to say.

MR. M. But could they not be different yet not contradictory?

MR. O. One cannot be at the same time in different places, meet different people. . . .

MR. M. Were you not interested in that side of the thing?

MR. O. I saw that he answered as if he did not wish to answer. Some people said he could not answer. Why I do not know. But that is another question. We knew in which places he had been and I knew before I met him that there were strange schools. Then he knew various native languages—of Turkestan and Persia chiefly. So he could mix with natives and could easily have met schools of dervishes or something like that. So sources were known more or less, though not definitely—he did not say definite names, times and so on.

MR. M. Did you agree with some things he told you and reject others?

MR. O. That depends what. In the system? In the system I did not agree. I simply studied. Because from the beginning I saw great value in it, so I was interested in studying. It was not a question of agreeing or disagreeing. You know he studied himself, and he told us many things in a practical way and tried to give us practical examples. For instance, we had once a conversation about types, and I want to read you about this from *Fragments*—the book from which you read before the first three chapters. They referred to the spring and autumn of 1915, and this which we will read to-night, to the summer of 1917 when we were in the North Caucasus. We stayed there most of the time during the revolution. This was our first year there. In this chapter I describe how we lived and how we worked there. There were only twelve people there besides G. We often used to walk in the hills and we had many talks. This was one of these conversations.

[Reading.]

MISS M. That gives an example of how little the planets influence situations, but does he say more about how far they do influence them?

MR. O. They do not influence situations. Our type is the result of planetary influence. According to our type we will act in one way or another way in certain circumstances.

MR. R. Do the number of types correspond to the number of planets?

MR. O. No. There are considered to be twelve, or sometimes eighteen chief types and then combinations of these. Very seldom you meet a pure type.

Q. Does this have anything to do with the saying that one is born under a certain star?

MR. O. That is just language. Read description of these various types, and you will see each has everything. That is why our mind cannot study types. But different features play a different part in different types, though each has everything. Astrology is psychological language. Psychology expressed in astronomical terms.

MISS R. It has nothing to do with the moment of our birth?

MR. O. No, unfortunately.

MR. D. If you were born a certain type, could you ever change it?

MR. O. If it is very bad type and you work very hard you can change it. First you must know type. That means essence. If you find in essence something incompatible with work, then if you work very hard you can perhaps change it.

MRS. S. If astrology is only language, what are planetary influences?

MR. O. Combinations of influences produce combinations of types. We do not know what it is and it does not mean that by making a horoscope we can find out. That is something like mediaeval psycho-analysis!

Q. But the combinations do come from the planets, do they?

MR. O. Yes, originally. Take for instance all our emotions, all our ideas. They come from the planets originally. Not born here.

Q. According to the types in control of events will the planets' influences be felt?

MR. O. Certainly different types control different events. For instance, there were two brothers who went together to some big performance in St. Petersburg. One had his money and his watch stolen by a pickpocket; the other found four gold watches in his pocket. The pickpockets took him for their assistant. That is fate!

MISS J. Can you say there are certain types which are always more subject to accidents than other types?

MR. O. No, this is not types, if I understand what your question means. That comes from development very much, not type.

MR. M. Have the Signs of the Zodiac anything to do with it?

MR. O. Only language. They do not exist, you know, actually. If you look from the top of the house and see five chimneys and say they mean something, and one belongs to a house in the next street, one is several streets away, one is the other side of the river ... there is no connection between them, only from your window they look connected. Zodiac by itself does not exist.

MRS. S. Must one work harder to alter one's type than to alter acquired personality?

MR. O. If it is necessary. Perhaps it is quite all right. But personality in most cases must be changed. Uncontrolled personality cannot be right.

MRS. D. Did you not say certain types had certain types of memory?

MR. O. No, not exactly. But yes, certain types may have different kind of memory.

You see, about what we were saying just now, you forget that psychology has existed in many disguises—astrology, one disguise; alchemy, another disguise. Very many disguises. Some we can understand more or less; some—the secret is lost and we do not know really what they mean. There are many school systems of that kind.

MR. A. What do you yourself mean when referring to planetary influences?

MR. O. Where and when?

MR. A. At any time.

MR. O. Planetary influences determine many big events in the life of humanity—wars, revolutions and things like that. Essence or type of man is the result of planetary influences. Things in us, for instance emotions, have come from the planets originally. If you take the Ray of Creation, Table of Hydrogens, you see where these hydrogens come—from which level. So they are somehow connected with planets.

We must remember the interconnection of all these ideas, and keep working on them. Then later we may find fuller and fuller meaning in them.

MISS D. You said, I think, that the planets keep us in balance?

MR. O. No, I never said that. I said <u>moon</u>. Moon balances us. Planets make us what we are.

MISS L. Will you tell us what you did when G. dropped the stick?

MR. O. Oh, I had not seen it.

MR. A. When you say planets make us what we are, are you using terms of disguised psychology?

MR. O. Partly, yes and partly I mean that everything in the same system is connected. Many things in organic life depend on planets and things which happen in organic life.

MR. H. I did not quite understand. Do planets affect situations—wars and so forth?

MR. O. Yes, they may create wars.

MISS R. Do they affect different people?

MR. O. They create different people. Different combinations of planetary influences create different essence.

MISS R. Then some people are influenced by some planets?

MR. O. Combinations. Some people by some combinations, other people by other combinations.

MRS. N. Does life itself come from the planets too?

MR. O. According to the system yes. It starts from the sun and passes through the planets.

You remember this diagram of the Ray of Creation and the octave coming in as <u>do</u> at the sun, then <u>si</u> at the planets, then the earth's surface, the film round the earth, with the three notes of organic life—<u>la</u>, <u>sol</u>, <u>fa</u>—<u>mi</u> the earth itself, <u>re</u> the moon? This is the world in which we live. We live on the earth. Earth is one of the planets; planets are in Solar System; Solar System is one of the Solar Systems in the Milky Way; our galaxy is one of many galaxies and all these are part of the Absolute.

MR. H. Are notes a way of understanding these things or does it actually mean. . . .

MR. O. Actually in this case. Every kind of creative movement, evolution can all be traced as coming by this Law of Octaves if you find right scale. So it is not just language.

MR. M. This is a descending octave?

MR. O. In the sense of expanding, differentiating.

MR. M. We cannot quite escape the conclusion that the Absolute is limited somewhere in space.

MR. O. It is space, although space begins only in World 6. Absolute and World 3 are beyond space or out of space. Space is limitation and that begins only in World 6.

MR. M. Do you remember saying that man's time is his life?

MR. O. His time. Earth's time is earth's life. For sun it is sun's life.

MR. M. What is space for man, life?

MR. O. Space is limitation of his possibilities on the earth. For all it is only limitation in this case. Space and time are the same thing really. One way it looks like space, another way it looks like time.

MR. M. Then it is just subjective, really?

MR. O. There is objective limitation. One can have more time, one can have more space than one has.

MR. H. What is the average time for man?

MR. O. How long can man live? That is his time.

MR. H. How is that connected mathematically with the time of earth and sun?

MR. O. About that we will speak later. It is connected. Did you hear about time in different cosmoses? We may speak about that next time.

MISS L. What is the difference between type and essence?

MR. O. Different words for the same thing. Essence in one man. Types in different people.

Q. About space and limitation. Isn't space infinite?

MR. O. No. On each level there is its own space. You see we are not accustomed to take these things practically. For instance for the sun, its space is the Solar System. It cannot get out of it. This is limitation.

MR. M. I concluded from what you said the other day about three lines of work that there is a certain tie between us, a certain obligation towards each other.

MR. O. In school, yes. Those who are really in school. Those for whom school becomes more important than anything else—that is what being in school means. Otherwise they are just listeners and school has no demands on them. The more school demands from people, the more they can get from it.

MR. M. How best would you suggest one should try to help those who are far away who belong to this system?

MR. O. One must begin first with those who are here. Then if it is necessary find ways to help those who are away. This is very difficult to explain. School is always practical, first of all. This means nothing against those who are away, only we cannot begin with them. Suppose all are away, then where will be school? So whether we are limited or not we have to begin from those who are here.

MR. T. What happens to type if we can get away from the influence of the moon?

MR. O. Type has nothing to do with that. But what happens? You see you take it as if there were only one possibility. We can get sometimes in some cases very easily away from the influence of the moon and then it is not very pleasant situation. There are people who are naturally free from moon. But it is not an advantage if they have not will and have not moon in themselves. If they have, that is another thing. If not, they just bounce, cannot attach themselves—too light.

MR. A. Where lies the connection between the moon and man? What kind of a thing is it? I mean between the moon and a man with this bouncing quality you have just described.

MR. O. There is no connection. That man is free of it. Moon does not keep him down. It is like marionette on strings and here strings are cut; marionette cannot move, falls and dies or flies one way or the other with the wind.

Moon affects everybody. All movements are controlled by moon. We cannot have a single movement without it. It is like a clock with a weight; moon is the weight, moves all the wheels. Organic life is the mechanism.

MR. R. By moon you mean actually the thing we see in the sky?

MR. O. Its reflection, yes. That is what we see. Really it is much bigger.

Q. What do you mean by 'free from moon'?

MR. O. Some people, either accidentally, or by wrong work, may become free from moon. Moon does not control them. If they have will, they control themselves. If they have no will, they are driven along by the wind.

MRS. S. Can one recognize these people?

MR. O. Yes.

MISS F. Is that why you say we should 'create moon in ourselves'?

MR. O. We must create weight in ourselves. Struggle not to be blown along and around. Replace the word 'moon' by 'weight'.

MR. A. I have never detected any lunatory influences on myself. How can we?

MR. O. We do not notice it. We do not know it. If we study we can find what it is. But in ordinary life we do not know it because everybody is equally under the same influence. If one was more influenced, another less, then it would be easier to notice.

MISS M. Is there a difference in the moon's influence according to the time of the month—full moon, new moon?

MR. O. No.

MRS. S. When you refer to weight, are you referring to permanent centre of gravity?

MR. O. Yes, that is the beginning.

MR. M. Which is larger, earth or moon?

MR. O. Earth.

MISS R. It is very necessary to become free from the moon then?

MR. O. It is necessary at a certain time, certain period in the work. It is better to remain under moon's influence than to become free before time. Better bad government than no government!

MISS M. What happens when people go out of their mind?

MR. O. Many different ways. Generally something broken, like a leg, or something swells. I do not know. There is no evidence that it may be not physical. Sometimes physical cause can be found. It must be something difficult to find, but still physical. At any rate there is no evidence of anything else, so far as I know.

Q. If things are as you say, would it not be better instead of trying to get free from this influence to swing with the moon?

MR. O. Yes, humanity cannot go against moon. Only a small quantity of people, if they feel action of moon oppressive. You see everything is necessary in the economy of Nature. Everything has its place. If we do not like our present position we can change it, but we must take everything into consideration. First we must know where we are.

MRS. D. Do you know any good book on astrology?

MR. O. No, I know only bad books. They are all bad.

MR. M. Have you ever come across any evidence of the existence of consciousness without brain? Apart from brain?

MR. O. You see, it is very difficult to be sure about it. I think I had experience of consciousness without thinking, without feeling; consciousness separate from psychic functions—but where is the guarantee?

In any case I felt like that. That is all I can say. Or do you mean consciousness apart from man? You may have personal experience of that kind, but you can have no verification. So I think this, like many other problems, must wait until we become more clever.

*   *   *

MISS. L. Is there any news about the house?

MR. O. Yes and no. I cannot say yet. I think it is all finished from our side, but when we shall have it I do not know yet.

*   *   *

Tuesday. March 1st 1938. (Warwick Gardens.)

[Written questions.]

MRS. C. Is lopping off the bough of a tree with one stroke like burning a house? It is one small effort and the bough comes off and decays.

Is amputating a human limb successfully like inventing an electric bell?

MR. O. These are wrong form of questions. You must not ask me such things as this. At this time we cannot give much time to discussion of theoretical subjects, but I will just repeat that you must try to see what it all means. That actions are as different as things. We know the difference between an orange and a pencil. Actions are even more different. I gave six examples, six types of action. You must try to understand each separately and find what is analogous. But that is your work, not my work.

MRS. P. Is militarism a human activity that belongs to the category of crime?

MR. O. Militarism is not activity. It is a theory.

MR. H. Are the laws of accident and cause and effect less organic than those of fate and will?

Would change in being mean that a group of 'I's no longer expressed themselves, or would it mean that one was no longer negative and had no loss of energy through that group of 'I's?

MR. O. You must understand you cannot bring everything to one point. You must understand all the features of your present being and then you will see in what order they can change. That is the only way you can understand.

MR. H. Would Mr. O. explain in what way conscious music can act as magic? I was thinking of the influence of vibrations.

MR. O. Well, it will kill you, for instance.

MRS. C. What is wanting when I am reminded to remember myself by negative emotions and when the negative emotion fades away but I still cannot remember myself?

MR. O. That means you made the negative emotion fade by trying to remember yourself and that already is good. Incidentally, this is the way to make negative emotions disappear. They cannot stand before self-remembering.

MISS T. I do not find I have any real idea of what self-remembering is. I can become aware of myself at certain times, but there is nothing in those moments to fix them in my memory. Is there any scale or quality by which we can measure our understanding of self-remembering?

MR. O. By experience and understanding of the idea. What we lack when we do not remember ourselves and what we get when we do remember ourselves.

MR. H. I have not got any results from trying to think of different kinds of activity except the realization that the difference between them is not clear to me. I have a sort of hope that if I could keep my mind on the question for long enough I should understand something. Should it be possible to make a start with this in any state?

MR. O. It is necessary to go on thinking, but just keeping your mind on it cannot do much. Mind must bring material, but it is necessary to feel. Then we think we have only one state to start with, but we have better and worse moments, more concentrated and less concentrated, more awake and less awake.

MISS M. Can one think of money-making on a very large scale—the scale of the multi-millionaire—as a special kind of activity?

MR. O. This is an imaginary example. It will not help.

MISS M. Can one think of different parts of centres in connection with trying to classify different kinds of activities?

MR. O. Not different parts of centres, no. In connection with centres you can say this: that one kind of activity can be made with one centre. One centre, if it works right, is sufficient. Generally speaking, parts of centres mean only good work or bad work. Then there is another kind of activity for which more than one centre is necessary. This is the difference between two particular kinds of activity.

MISS M. Some time ago Mr. O. said that we should make a mental image of self-remembering. When I try to do this, I find it is all thinking and without emotion, so that nothing happens. How can I understand better how to make this mental image?

MR. O. I already answered this in connection with another question.

MISS P. The three shocks in the Octaves of Radiation are filled by three notes of a cosmic octave. What are the octaves of which this <u>la</u>, <u>sol</u> and <u>fa</u> become the <u>do's</u> at the level of hydrogens 6, 96 and 1536?

MR. O. That is not necessary at present. Just remember how it was given. That is quite sufficient.

MR. B. Do games fall into the same category of activities as burning a house?

MR. O. Not necessarily.

MR. S. As a result of studying the Cosmos Table, I first of all notice that the time relation of one cosmos to the next is the same as from one centre to the next in man, i.e. 30,000.

Next I notice that three seconds is the only time which we are aware of properly and over which we have any degree of control. So it seems that the breath of any particular cosmos is the indication of the time with which that cosmos works. If this is so, could there be any material in the following connections:

Man	and intellectual centre
Cell	and instinctive centre
Gene	and emotional centre

MR. O. That end part is invention. Up to this point it is right.

MR. L. Is objective art a means whereby C influences can be received by those able to receive them?

MR. O. Better not connect them. C influences can be received only through school.

MR. L. Is it the only means outside a school? And must one have come under the influence of a school before one is able to receive C influences from objective art?

MR. O. That I answered.

MR. L. Can one receive B influences from certain art in the world, such as the paintings of Picasso or the music of Bach?

MR. O. It depends how clever you are.

MR. L. Concerning the question what it means to be serious, is one serious about a thing when it is always with the same group of 'I's uppermost that one feels or thinks of it? If it is the system about which one is serious, is this a step in the direction of permanent aim, since one group of 'I's has got permanent aim attached to it?

MR. O. No, that is wrong. There are two things between [which] you must learn to distinguish in your thinking. To be serious and to take things seriously. When you understand this difference, then it will be clear to you.

MR. L. It has been said that it is necessary to sacrifice suffering. What is to sacrifice? Is it giving up something near at hand with the intention of obtaining something higher and more important? Does the meaning include the killing or the burning of an offering?

MR. O. No. Find right examples, several examples that people do not want to sacrifice their suffering. If you cannot, wait.

MRS. L. I have been trying to write the Ray of Creation and Octaves of Radiation round the enneagram . . .

MR. O. You cannot do that because it is not their place.

MRS. L. . . . Is it correct in the Ray of Creation to put the Absolute (do) at point 9 of the enneagram; all worlds, si, at 8; all suns, la, at 7; our sun, sol, at 5; planets, fa, at 4; 3 being organic life and providing the shock; earth, mi, at 2; and moon, re, at 1?

Then, fitting in the Octaves of Radiation: the first octave, Absolute-sun, would go from point 9 to point 5 and the fa-mi interval would get its shock from point 6; the octave from sun-earth would be from point 5 to 2; point 3, organic life, providing the fa-mi shock; and the octave from earth to moon would be from points 2 to 1. Point 3 would also be the la, sol, fa of organic life in the octave of our ray of existence. Are these right?

It seems that the moon must go beyond point 1 in order that that should provide the fa-mi shock in the radiation octave earth-moon. Would this shock be Man, as I think it is at point 1 that man would come in writing the cosmological octave?

It seems also that an octave proceeding in triads of 213, 321 or 231 would be ascending and octaves proceeding in triads of 123, 312 and 132 would be descending. Is this so?

MR. O. Leave triads now. It is too theoretical for the moment.

MRS. L. In the Food Table, the octaves ascend in triads of 213 sequence. Would this have to alter to triads of 321 sequence if the impressions octave is to continue? Would this make the first triad of the impressions octave neutralizing do 48, passive mi 96, active re 24? Is the ratio of densities of forces always the same?

MR. L. I have observed that when my eye is caught by something (for example, an advertisement) or I overhear a chance remark, a large number of unnecessary thoughts and emotions are started in me. A similar kind of unnecessary activity goes on when I am trying to think or to do something, particularly with my hands. On one scale these can be explained as results of identification, but, on another scale, are these unnecessary things examples of that movement which is referred to in the statement 'moon controls movement'? I find it difficult to understand that statement because I do not see the scale of the movement referred to and also I do not clearly see the distinction between 'movement' and 'mechanicalness of man'.

MR. O. It refers to every movement. And so you need not take examples about which you are not sure whether they are movements or not. Take simple examples.

MR. L. I have been trying to see some relation between man's capacity to have such high hydrogens in him as H_{12} and the laws shown in the Ray of Creation. Are these higher matters in man in some way connected with the expression in him of laws derived from higher bodies such as the sun and our galaxy?

MR. O. Maybe, but it does not mean very much. It is the same thing really.

MR. L. The Table of Cosmoses seems to be a measure of differences in scale, but I do not see how it can be used in many comparatively small differences in scale because I do not understand the meaning of the word cosmos. Will you please explain more about it?

MR. O. No, I cannot now.

MR. A. Can the Ray of Creation with its increasing number of forces and with each world derived from the one above it be considered as the activity of propagation? There seems to be a difference between this activity and the propagation of a species in its own world.

MR. O. Maybe you can consider it this way, but it will not help. And cosmic activities we must take separately.

MR. A. Is the following attempt at classifying the six main types of activity properly formulated?

1. Those which serve to maintain the existence of organic life on earth. Propagation.

2. Those which serve to sustain the life of the individual organism for its customary period (man, seventy years) by feeding, i.e. absorbing matters of certain density and transforming them into matters less dense suitable to sustain the machine. Transformism.

3. Those which require certain impressions which, when received and used by man, create in him less dense matters than he has normally, and permit his attaining a higher level of understanding. Psychotransformism.

4. Those which seem to be the antithesis of the previous activity and in which man seems to use his highest ability for the lowest aims. Crime.

MR. O. No, that is wrong. First of all you must understand that we speak about man's activity just in the ordinary sense of the word. If you read that to a person who has never been to these lectures he would not understand a single word. It should be so that every child could understand what you say.

We will speak later about cosmic activities, man's machine and man's activities, and in each of these lines we will take the simplest examples. This is all mixed.

[To Mr. M.] Now read the questions from last time.

MR. B. Is it suggested that people who know nothing about printing should begin to learn zincography?

MR. O. No, I never suggested that. I asked that those who know something about it should communicate with me, nothing more. But this is not an immediate question. When we have the house, if we arrange something about printing, then we will come to it.

MISS G. Are the activities connected with energies?

MR. O. Certainly. Every activity needs energy.

MISS T. I think Mr. O. mentioned six activities. Can examples of these activities be found in every individual person?

MR. O. In human activities.

MR. B. Can we be told what the sixth form of activity is?

MR. O. There is no secret about it, only in our present state when we use it we use it without even our ordinary [awareness]. Generally we use it when trying to do something else, and in a rather deficient form. It may be called magic. In ordinary life it is used in the form of suggestion, like advertising, for instance, propaganda.

MISS C. It seems that agriculture, growing things, does not fit into any of the kinds of activity we have had examples of. Could this be another kind of activity?

MR. O. Why does it not fit? You have to work.

MR. S. There is a certain kind of routine job which, when you know it, only requires initial effort to begin with and then seems to go by itself, the only difficulty, almost, being to <u>stop</u> doing it. What kind of activity could this be?

MR. O. This is subjective. Your subjective feeling about one particular piece of work. It depends what you are doing.

MR. A. Does the Food Table change the nature of its activity when self-remembering occurs. It was said, I think, that it was automatic until the impressions <u>do</u>, and that after that the nature of the activity altered. Does the Food Table in this way exemplify two different kinds of activity after a certain point?

MR. O. It is not automatic. It is arranged. Machine is prepared and spring is wound up. This is how it works. There are two intervals where one octave depends on another, touches another, does not work properly. Then a shock is necessary. This shock is given by another triad.

There are many forms of activity in this. Necessary to find them.

MISS T. Can one talk about 'group activity'? I do not mean these groups, but a group of people who are trying to follow out some plan in ordinary life?

MR. O. It will not help. Individual or group, activity remains the same.

MR. B. Can every ordinary activity be put into one of these six categories?

MR. O. Yes. That is the idea. Although you must understand that there are combinations of these in our ordinary activity. But we must not speak about combinations yet. We must try to find examples of pure triads.

MRS. D. What is the activity of exploring an unknown land?

MR. O. That depends by whom, for which purpose, how. You cannot take things without their constituent parts. For instance, the bolshevik voyage on the ice floe is simply advertising bolshevism, nothing else.

MR. A. Is it correct to say that in the activity of transformation there are no completed octaves without the activity of consciousness? I mean transformation in the sense of the Food Table. Even the first octave does not go beyond <u>si</u>.

MR. O. Which transformation? Of food in the human body? We are speaking about man's activity outside for the moment. So I will not answer that question. We will come to it later.

MR. S. It seems to me that each of these activities can take place at various intensities or various speeds. A house can burn or be demolished slowly. Can this be explained by different ratios of the densities of the three forces one to another? For instance, in the Food Table, first force is half of second force.

MR. O. No, that is quite wrong. These do not alter at all.

MR. H. Would the printing press be used for printing matter for private distribution or for sale to the public? I think this might make a difference to the question of the trade union feelings.

MR. O. There will be time to speak about that later.

MR. S. Did Mr. O. say that when one had proper attention it formed a centre of its own? It seems you can't see it unless it goes on in more than one centre.

MR. O. I do not understand. In any case, I never said that.

MRS. J. Is it possible to direct attention with any centre but emotional centre?

MR. O. Yes, certainly. You can direct intellectual, moving.

MR. H. I should like to understand how to keep attention on something that really needs attention all the time—I find I cannot keep my attention fixed for more than a second at a time. I can see it has gone and bring it back, but I should like to know how to keep it fixed.

MR. O. Then you have to do something. When you have to do something you have to keep your attention, otherwise you will do something different from what you intended.

MRS. S. I should like to know how to prevent identification when reading books—it is so difficult to see where attention in emotional part of intellectual centre slips into identification.

MR. O. Only experience can show you. Observation. There can be no description.

MR. B. Is trying to be conscious really trying to do things at once?

MR. O. Conscious means conscious. It does not mean to do anything.

MR. M. Is it advisable to look for the force which begins an activity, for example in painting a picture? Is it a right observation that the triad starts with third force, that is, the completed picture, in the same way the effort to remember oneself starts off with the result which you are aiming at?

MR. O. No, thinking in that way will not help.

MISS B. Painting a picture starts by knowing what you want to do, but how does the image get there?

MR. O. Ah, that is the secret.

MISS B. If you sit down and try to think about it you can't get it, but sometimes it happens. Has it something to do with memory?

MR. O. No.

MISS B. Can there be degrees of the activity of painting a picture?

MR. O. Yes, certainly, there are many degrees, from bad pictures to good pictures.

MISS M. Is scientific research the same activity as building a house, because it is bringing order out of chaos?

MR. O. No, it is not the same.

MR. S. Can one see the forces in a triad like scientific research in connection with the ideas of the system: first force, the person doing the research, second force, the subject of the research and third force, the system, because the idea is connected with the system?

MR. O. No, no, that is too complicated, unnecessarily complicated.

MR. H. Are activities octaves, because they take time? Or points in octaves?

MR. M. All my activities seem to be mixtures, one part like building a house and the other burning a house and so on. Is this possible?

MR. O. You must try to find pure standards. Then we will talk.

MR. H. Are all activities which end in second force bad?

MR. O. What does bad mean? ... You see? You cannot answer, so your question means nothing.

MISS B. Is the reason why we can't think about activities that we should feel them by an emotional process?

MR. O. I do not know. There is no evidence.

MR. B. Could a thing like reading the newspaper be two quite different activities? It nearly always leaves me in a lower state than when I started, but we have been told that there is a right way of reading the newspaper. Is it two different triads working?

MR. O. You can read differently. So you cannot take reading, when it is only the standard of something.

MR. S. Do we ever use the emotional parts of centres? Attention that goes by interest is said to belong to these, but if I read a detective novel, it keeps my attention, but it is a very flat interest which I can't feel is really emotional.

MR. O. This is only observation.

MRS. S. Can you connect work of various centres with activities? For instance, work of art must be work of higher centres?

MR. O. No, not higher. You cannot work with higher centres, you see. But it means as many centres as possible working together. As many as you can collect.

MRS. S. Does building a house correspond to routine work in which we don't invent?

MR. O. That is a question to be answered by observation. But returning to the previous question, about centres. Magic is another triad. If it is really intentional, magic means at least a little of higher centres. Without, it will be only accidental, as I said. Then there are things like scientific work, for instance, or ordinary life work, that can be done with only one centre.

MR. M. Is the principal feature of criminal activity careful planning?

MR. O. I do not know. That is not the way to come to it.

MRS. S. Is it right to say that no chance comes in at all in the activity of work of art?

MR. O. It is difficult to say what you mean by 'chance'. If you can give me some reasons for what you mean to say, then perhaps it will be possible to answer.

MR. H. What is the real use of formatory centre?

MR. O. Registering, recording.

MISS L. Are all activities starting with first force destructive?

MR. O. No.

MR. B. Can one think of the life of a person as an octave?

MR. O. Yes, but you cannot find the right scale. It is too difficult.

MR. D. Can it be explained how it is that the higher the hydrogen, the quicker the centres work, and yet the bigger the cosmos the slower the time of its mental impression?

MR. O. That is one of the questions that lack perspective. Slower or quicker, it is only from our point of view. In itself it is the same.

MR. L. Is it correct to say that if intellectual centre did not interfere the intellectual part of moving centre would work?

MR. O. No, this is not sufficient. Other things are necessary.

MR. L. Is the idea of centres given us as a framework?

MR. O. How do you mean?

MR. L. The idea that came to me was that centres are not watertight compartments. . . .

MR. O. They are not, but they should be.

MR. L. It seemed to me that centres might occupy the whole of us at the same time?

MR. O. At the same time, they are distinctly different.

MR. L. I have not seen it.

MR. O. You cannot study centres. You can only study functions. You will see they are like liquids of different kinds in one glass—but even that is not quite right, because each occupies the whole glass but they do not mix.

MISS H. Is the kind of government that admits freedom of thought a higher kind of activity than oppressive government?

MR. O. Where is this government? First we must have facts, then we will discuss it.

MRS. D. Is it correct to say that it is the kind of effort which determines the nature of the activity? By this it seems possible to distinguish between activities which externally seem the same.

MR. O. It is the same word. Kind of effort, kind of activity mean the same thing.

MR. A. Is psychotransformism the activity which begins after do of the third octave of the Food Diagram?

MR. O. No, you cannot put it like that.

MISS H. Did Mr. O. say self-remembering was the only thing belonging to that kind of activity which we could know?

MR. O. No, there are many others besides.

MR. D. Should one, when trying to relax, direct attention to various parts of one's body in order to stop the flow of thoughts? Can anything be said about the actual technique of relaxing?

MR. O. Yes, only that is a special conversation. It cannot be put in between other things.

MRS. J. Are all negative emotions activity of the kind of which burning a house is an example? You cannot stop the continued results and they are destructive.

MR. O. No, negative emotions are not activity.

MR. D. Is burning the house the same kind of activity as the Ray of Creation?

MR. O. No, thank God! No.

MISS H. If the Ray of Creation is bringing life to the moon, can it be called destructive?

MR. O. Why should it be called destructive?

MISS P. What means have we of recognizing types?

MR. O. I do not understand the question.

MISS H. Is the Table of Cosmoses contained in the Ray of Creation? How can I begin to think about the Table of Cosmoses?

MR. O. That I explained.

MR. P. On what scale would one look for these activities? One can take agriculture on a large scale or else sowing a field or running a farm, or again on a smaller scale, pushing a wheelbarrow.

MR. O. It is your business to find out if they change with change of scale or not.

MR. P. Crime seems on a much bigger scale than building a house—crime as opposed to a crime.

MR. O. I do not quite understand.

MR. B. It would be interesting to know the difference between crime and stealing a picture.

MR. O. Why this 'stealing a picture'? I have already told you, this is just wrong association.

MISS S. Do these six activities need the same amount of effort to start them? The effort to start a house burning could be very slight.

MR. O. This is the same thing. Activity is the same as effort.

MISS S. It seems there are three ways you could burn a house:

1. accidentally,
2. to make room for another,
3. as a crime.

It is difficult for me to understand the difference between the two first activities. In building a house, the activity goes on, whereas in burning a house the thing goes on by itself after the activity has stopped.

MISS. T. It seems, when one is looking for activities, it is difficult to divide them up. For example, we cannot call music one kind of activity, because there are many kinds of activity in music.

MR. O. Well?

MR. B. Is the motive important?

MR. O. Everything is important, only that does not enter into it. You can say there are six kinds of efforts, motives, activities. It is only changing the word.

MISS S. Would not music be like painting a picture?

MR. O. Maybe. Good music like good picture, bad music like bad picture.

MR. B. Is it useful, after distinguishing the different forms of activity in ourselves, to find out what leads to bad activities such as burning a house, and to learn, where we can, how to eliminate them?

MR. O. We do not speak about ourselves here. We are speaking about our activities.

MISS T. In trying to watch my efforts at attention, there seem to be two different kinds of attention—passive and active. For example, the attention when one tries to be passive, relaxed, controlled, where impressions can come in and the attention with concentration—as in studying or learning by heart. What is the difference between these two kinds of attention?

MR. O. If they are really different, they may belong to different triads.

MR. P. How can one try to let moving centre work without interference from other centres?

MR. O. I do not understand why it is necessary, for what purpose, desirable or undesirable. Generally speaking, it is necessary to have certain plans of work of centres, then each centre has its own work and they can help one another.

MR. S. From where does the shock come in the interval between fa and mi in the Ray of Creation?

MR. O. That does not matter. The interval is filled by organic life. This octave starts from the sun. This was explained.

MISS I. Is there any way in which we can see the diagram of the Food Table again, particularly in small groups, so that we can discuss it?

MR. O. Yes, it will be given again.

* * *

[Written questions, February 15th.]

MR. D. When one sees a negative thing in oneself which always leads to identification and sleep, can one do nothing more against it than struggle with identification and try and understand on what it is based and its connections?

MR. O. One can remember oneself exactly with this feeling. This negative feeling can be made the weapon of self-remembering, the instrument of self-remembering.

MISS C. How can I increase my aim? I feel that such a small number of my 'I's are interested in, or even sympathetic to the work, and that when I am not in the work 'I', I haven't any aim at all. Because of this lack of aim I seem to have come to a full stop. For a few moments perhaps, from the observations I have made I may dislike myself intensely and wish to change, but the wish does not last; it seems all-important that I should be in work 'I's as often as possible, but how to do this?

MR. O. There may be many answers, but the best possible way to understand it is this: suppose you do not have enough energy for self-remembering, or for work or for interest in work, then you must save this energy, keep this energy. And how can you accumulate it? Only by making efforts. There is no other way. By trying to struggle with habits, trying to observe yourself and so on.

MR. B. It seems that in order to have moving centre working well, one must try to stop interference from other centres and this entails observation of how other centres interfere. Is this a correct line of work?

MR. O. Not quite, because you see you cannot do anything by observation. You can only learn by observation. If the interfering is very bad, then perhaps special measures are necessary. It is impossible to speak in general.

MR. B. Can we hear more about the law of fate? Why, for instance, is it called fate?

MR. O. I will try to speak later about this.

MRS. W. In trying to study different kinds of activity, I find it is difficult to combine certain kinds of work. For instance, if I am doing a lot of riding and outdoor work, it is not easy to settle down to writing or painting, yet these seem to go well with housework or gardening. Is this subjective, or are there really certain kinds of activity that combine better than others?

MR. O. Both are right. It is subjective, but on the other hand maybe there are different kinds that combine better than others.

MR. B. Do actions performed with and without aim objectively differ from one another?

MR. O. Again, it is the same thing—effort, aim, motive, all enter into the word action and the idea of action.

MISS B. It seems to me that driving a car, housework and writing a letter are the same kind of activity and could be applied to building a house. Is this so?

MR. O. Maybe, but not absolutely.

MISS B. Are they the same kinds of activity if a car is driven dangerously or a harmful letter written?

MR. O. There you complicate it. That means you speak not about driving, but about driving dangerously.

MISS B. Is thinking in any form an activity, or only the action produced by thought? For example, if I am thinking about system ideas and things become a little clearer and I find questions I want to ask, would this be like building a house? If, on the other hand, I let my thoughts wander to other things, would this be like burning a house?

MR. O. Maybe not activity at all. It may be just sleep.

MISS B. It seems to me that reading, listening to music, looking at pictures may be the same kind of activity. Learning a language and training for a career seem to me similar and yet different from the last three. In the latter cases, the effort would seem to be more compulsory, and one would probably be under authority. What is the difference between these two groups?

MR. O. It is necessary to take unmistakeable cases of action, not cases where there is doubt.

MISS S. Is the planting of an acorn an activity on a large enough scale for us to consider? If so, is it like burning a house because its end is worse than its beginning, i.e., it dies?

MR. O. If it is only one acorn, it is not enough.

MISS M. Under what category of activity does sport come?

MR. O. It is not an activity.

MISS M. Is the process of collecting information about a certain subject, drawing conclusions from this information and then acting on these conclusions, the same kind of activity as building a house?

MR. O. It depends on the case.

MISS M. Does motive change the nature of an activity, such as doing physical work by necessity or as an effort?

MR. O. I already answered that. It is the same thing.

MR. L. I do not understand the position of organic life in the Ray of Creation. It appears to be the film round the earth and provides one force in the triad bridging the interval between fa and mi; this seems to imply that organic life is on a separate octave. Is this correct and what is that separate octave?

MR. O. I do not know what you mean by saying it is one force in the triad bridging the interval. Organic life is in a separate octave, not the Ray of Creation, but an octave beginning in the sun, as do, planets si, organic life, mi earth, re moon.

MR. L. We have heard that men's souls go to the moon when they die. If the souls of men and nothing else from organic life go to the moon at death, men seem to occupy a special place in organic life.

MR. O. Not only man, everything. Every living being sends something to the moon when it dies.

MR. L. I find it difficult to think about the Ray of Creation and organic life because it seems to me there may be separate octaves for each of the groups of laws which govern the earth—i.e. one octave for the three laws which come from all worlds, one for the six which come from the galaxy and so on.

MR. O. No, you are mixing things. Accept the different octaves and do not mix.

MR. L. This has led me to the question, what is a man's soul and where does it come from? The question might, I think, be put differently: how does the machine described in the Food Table <u>start</u> to work?

MR. O. Too much, too much. The first mistake is you speak about man. Organic life does not mean man alone.

MRS. D. If knowledge is material, does it follow that negative emotions are also material? Does this mean that as long as there is no room in us for knowledge, we cannot receive it?

MR. O. No, that has nothing to do with it.

MRS. D. There are tears which are caused by a strong emotion which do not seem negative. What are these tears and is it bad to try to stop them? The emotion seems to get less strong or goes altogether if I stop these tears.

MR. O. That is more complicated. We may come to that later when we speak about expressions.

MRS. L. We have been told that organic life provides the shock in the octave of the Ray of Creation and transmits influences from the planets to the earth, but nothing of how it was created. Would Mr. O. speak about this?

MR. O. All that is necessary for practical purposes was given and you must work on this. The rest would be purely theoretical.

MRS. L. In the octave of our ray of existence, is there any distinction in the <u>la</u>, <u>sol</u>, <u>fa</u> of organic life?

MR. O. I do not understand about this octave. We must use precise expressions. There may be something in your question. I do not know.

MRS. L. Is the hydrogen given in the accumulator diagram the hydrogen of <u>energy</u> used by each centre? Can one say the slower the working of a centre, the greater the density of the energy used by it?

MR. O. No, in this diagram the principle is given, but really the system of accumulation is very complicated and you cannot put it on a blackboard. So you must take this diagram as sufficient to help you understand the principle.

MRS. L. In the table of the various hydrogens used by man, men Nos. 1, 2, 3 and 4 have intellectual 48, emotional 96, moving and instinctive 192. Is 48 the density of the thoughts that intellectual centre works with, 96 the density of emotions and 192 the density of the air, digestive juices, etc. that instinctive centre works with?

MR. O. Who said that? It is not like that at all. Intellectual centre works with 48, moving and instinctive work with hydrogen 24, emotional centre practically speaking with the same, very seldom higher. Then higher emotional works with hydrogen 12 and higher mental with hydrogen 6.

MR. L. I should like to know if the expression 'self-remembering' can include such things as the following, or if it is something quite different:

1. To find I have been lost in some activity and to realize for a moment or two that I am here in this room.

2. To hear myself in a new way for a moment in the act of speaking, when in a state of considering.

3. To hold my attention on some object in front of me and try to feel myself here and now in my surroundings.

4. To become aware of beauty in surroundings as if blinkers had come off my eyes and cotton wool out of my ears, accompanied by an increased awareness of self.

MR. O. Yes, it may be described like that. But you see description will not help.

MR. L. Is it useful to distinguish activities by the effect upon material used, such as transforming clay into bricks, putting together bricks to make a building? Could scientific research be putting together facts to make knowledge as a material, or the way of fakir transforming material in man?

Alternatively, should I look for activities nearer to me and group them by their feeling?

MR. O. Look at them more simply. It is necessary to find simple examples. Feeling will come later.

MR. L. Would the following represent types of activity?

1. Clearing table after meals, or studying a report or writing up

accounts. These require to be pushed along by effort, although during the process something arises to help. Otherwise I very easily stop.

MR. O. Too simple.

MR. L. 2. To express my ideas in writing, or to design a building. These entail holding a picture of what I wish to express whilst I try out different arrangements and shift the material about until a form arrives. Emotion drives this activity along and I find it very difficult to stop, unless something else very important intervenes.

3. Tackling a difficult business situation; or repairing a motor car break-down on the road. This type consists of searching for a way out and the facts themselves make it imperative to continue the activity.

4. Posting a letter, the results of which are not yet known; giving financial help to a friend; or a chance remark which another takes to heart and his life is affected. This means a small action on my part and the rest continues outside. Results are often known by chance, often not at all.

5. Teaching or influencing intentionally another person with a false superiority. This type seems to me distinct from the others, because its main characteristic is that I don't know what material I am using to work with; yet I feel at the time that my knowledge is complete. The result must be different from intention.

MR. O. No, there are too many different scales and different actions mixed together.

*   *   *

MR. O. This is what I wanted to tell you. There is not much use in continuing such meetings, such questions. Each question separately is very good, with the exception of some based on wrong memory, but together they do not give anything. You cannot go on theoretically too long. It is necessary to find practical application of these ideas and practical form of work.

At present we cannot change anything because we have no place. Soon we shall have the house and I think it may be much better if we wait for these meetings until we can arrange things better. There there will be bigger meetings and smaller meetings. The smaller meetings will have definite tasks, definite work, talk perhaps about special subjects and so on. The larger meetings can ask questions, maybe try to answer one another. In any case we will not waste so much time on questions that can be answered before I come.

You must understand that I would like to come every week, but I cannot because there are too many people. Soon I want to start a new group and for this I must have time.

I do not say we will not meet at all. We will meet here when this place is free. But chiefly I wish more serious work to begin when we have the new house. We may have it in the middle of April. Then certainly time will be necessary to prepare it and arrange things, but soon after that we will begin to work. So you can think about it, tell me what you feel, what you want, what you wish to hear.

You will hear from Madame K. definitely how it will be arranged and when I shall be ready for the new groups. If anybody has people they want to bring to new groups, will they write to Madame K. about it?

MR. E. You mean there is not going to be this meeting?

MR. O. If we have time, but I think it is really better to wait. That depends what you think yourselves about it.

MR. E. I would rather not wait.

MR. O. Yes, but that is not enough. I must have some reason. You see, there is need for practical work in this system. It cannot go on far without work with new people, with other people. Those who go to Lyne may have this at Lyne, although it depends of course on their own work, their own difficulties and all that. But here I can arrange nothing of this kind. When we have new groups only a few people who have been before can go to them as things are at present, and those are mostly going because they are of use to me, for taking notes and so on. As it is, there is no possibility of changing this. We have no room. When we have a bigger place, maybe, I cannot promise for certain, but it may be possible for us to arrange for those who wish to meet with new people and work with them.

MR. E. I missed three lectures. . . .

MR. O. That is all right, you know. Everything will be repeated.

MR. E. I find work becomes more difficult when I do not have them. . . .

MR. O. Maybe because of that. But you see, there are definite steps. You cannot remain indefinitely on theoretical questions. You must come to practical work. Now it is too theoretical. That I already explained. You cannot change it.

MR. H. Do you mean by that that there must be organized work?

MR. O. It will be practical work. If you can do practical work. If you have to speak to somebody, first you must be able to. If you can, then this is practical work.

Whoever wants can write to me about it. If anybody wants to say anything about it, I shall be very glad to have suggestions, anything of this kind. Then when we have the possibility we will begin to work.

It is necessary to prepare ourselves for this move. In the sense, for instance, that when you talk in smaller groups here, it may be very useful to see how you can work with other people, what questions you would like to discuss. Only one thing. Do not think it is possible to remain theoretical only. These endless talks about self-remembering, for instance, are quite useless. You must be able to know what self-remembering is in practice, and many other things. This talk about activities is not an example. This is a very difficult subject and a new subject. We can leave it and return to it later. But I mean these others— self-remembering, non-identification, this sort of thing. It becomes transformed into words if you do not work enough.

I think we will be able to meet next Tuesday and discuss it and write questions if you like. Only generally do not expect much until we have the possibility of better arrangements.

MR. H. Does it mean this work must always increase in numbers?

*　　*　　*

Thursday. March 17th 1938. (Warwick Gardens.)

MR. O. First we will read the questions and the questions you wrote for me last week. Some of these questions I will try to answer, but some are of such a nature that it does not enter into my plans to answer them. In many cases the reason is that I gave you principles and it is for you to find proof when these can be found in the ordinary way, by reasoning. We will talk more about that later when we come to it.

MRS. F. Could Mr. O. explain the function, if any, of prayer in the system? I find, by observation, that all my prayer is either mechanical or imagining or identification, yet I feel certain there must be a right way to use prayer—even in spite of having no will.

MR. O. [to Mr. W.] Read on, please.

MISS G. What would be the best thing for us to do if England became involved in a European war?

MR. O. Read newspapers.

MISS G. Is it possible for us to get an understanding of time, beyond having a feeling about it, or what is perhaps a theoretical knowledge of it?

MR. O. Such as we are, it will be good even if we have some theoretical knowledge of it.

MISS S. Is it possible for us in our present state to experience a positive emotion for a few seconds? Or is such a feeling only imagination?

MR. O. Certainly, it is imagination.

MR. A. Can a householder, through the Law of Accident, meet with the fate of a tramp, or is this a wrong formulation?

MR. O. Yes, it is absolutely wrong. All wrong from beginning to end, every word.

MR. A. What is 'doing'?

MR. O. Which doing? . . . Well, self-remembering is doing.

MR. A. I cannot quite understand Mr. O.'s remark that by considering three cosmoses side by side we shall see all possible scales of different times.

MR. O. No, I did not say that. I said that by study [of] one cosmos one could not find all laws governing cosmoses, but that by considering three cosmoses one may find them. That is a different idea, there is no promise in it.

MRS. D. I find there are intervals when all emotion about the system vanishes, leaving one with an intellectual interest only. What is the right way to think about these intervals before they occur, and what is the best way of dealing with them when they have occurred?

MR. O. It is impossible to say. There are so many different levels, so many different attitudes, understanding can be so different.

MISS A. Would Mr. O. explain what is meant by Magnetic Centre?

MR. O. That you are supposed to know. It is described in the very beginning, I think in the third lecture.

MISS A. Then I must have heard it, as I was here for the third reading. So I suppose I must have forgotten it.

MR. O. It has been repeated since then. If I have time I will try to explain, but you can ask somebody else and perhaps they will be able to explain it to you.

MR. D. We have been told man has seven minds, or centres, four of which, namely intellectual, emotional, instinctive and moving, have been explained to us. May we now hear more about the sex centre and be told what are the other two as yet unnamed centres?

MR. O. About the other two centres, you have heard. They are higher emotional and higher mental centres. Higher emotional which works in connection with the third state of consciousness; when you become aware of yourself that makes higher emotional centre work. In a state of objective consciousness, higher mental centre is working. We have spoken about this recently.

About sex centre, if you have any definite questions we can discuss them, but you have not enough material yet for me to speak about it in general.

MR. D. Does apparent familiarity with a sequence of events, which may not have been personally experienced previously, necessarily denote the presence of recurrence?

MR. O. Can you tell me something concrete? You see, you know what you are talking about, but I do not know. If you can tell me which events, what sequence, begin with an example, then perhaps I can answer.

MR. J. Did Mr. O. say last time that man had only vague recollections of having lived before and that these moments were only apparent during early years? Do these recollections vary in clarity according to the state of the development of a man's essence?

MR. O. I will speak later about that.

MR. J. Did Mr. O. say that man's essence either develops after death or goes to the moon?

MR. O. No, that is wrong. It is soul which goes to the moon. Soul is material, a certain quantity of fine matter, energy if you like, which leaves the body at death.

MR. J. Is it possible to make more of my 'I's interested in the system, or is it a case of making the ones already interested stronger to fight the ones that are always taking me away from the work of self-development?

MR. O. That is a wrong question, wrong observation. You ask if it is possible. Many things are possible, but whether they are possible for you only you can tell, by effort and observation.

MR. J. Can any of the octaves in the Food Table be completed?

MR. O. Again this is theoretical. Ask definitely what you want to know. Which octave? And explain what you mean by 'completed'.

MR. S. From observation I find that some kind of double attention is necessary before one can control it without identification. By this, I mean attention on oneself and on what one is doing. If this is correct, will one attain better control of attention by making efforts in this direction although it may slow up what one is doing?

MR. O. This is purely material for your own observation. What can I answer?

MR. S. There is some kind of energy I get from making efforts in this work. Is this an emotion or is it energy that one hadn't experienced before?

MR. O. As you give no example, how can I say?

MR. F. The body as chemical factory refers to production of ascending grades of energy. Is there a set of descending octaves in a similar fashion dealing with burning of energy? I have visualized this process as impressions causing the food and air energies to combine in a burning operation.

MR. O. You have to study what is given, not to speak just by opposites. This is a most formatory thing. What is given in diagrams must be studied, not just by trying to find what is opposite.

MR. F. Is the life of man controlled by life of brain cells?

MR. O. No, not his life. His activity is controlled by them to a certain extent, unfortunately comparatively rarely, but it should be.

MR. F. Mr. O. indicates that the quantum and wave motion theories of light can be reconciled by the use of three time dimensions. Can the three phenomena—gravitation, ether and direct magnetic force—be explained in terms of multi-dimensional time?

MR. O. Gravitation and ether cannot, for they are only words with nothing behind them.

MR. F. When I take a meal I often notice an increase of energy during the meal, i.e. long before digestion is completed. Is this connected with shock to instinctive centre?

MR. O. This is just observation. Why the question? I have nothing to say about it. It is just good observation.

MR. F. Does recuperative power of sleep essentially refer to renewal of big cells? And what is sleep for small cells?

MR. O. Again, that is the same thing—you must just observe, that is all. No theory will help.

MR. P. It appears that each cosmos has certain properties, e.g. power to receive impressions, to breathe, to sleep and awake, and a limited period of life. These properties, however, do not seem to be peculiar to cosmoses. Will Mr. O. say what is the distinctive property or properties by which a cosmos is defined?

MR. O. I cannot enumerate these properties, but you can take it that all that refers to a human being belongs to cosmoses. You can look on cosmoses as more or less analogous to man.

MR. P. Is it possible to find in man himself some part or function which bears to the whole man a relation analogous to the situation between man himself and some higher cosmos, e.g. organic life or sun?

MR. O. I do not understand that question.

MR. P. Has any part of man 1, 2 and 3 got any kind of immortality other than recurrent life on earth?

MR. O. We will speak about that later.

MR. P. Does intelligence always imply power of cognition?

MR. O. It would need a very long talk to go into that. In us, intelligence and cognition are connected, and that is quite sufficient. It is possible that there are different forms of intelligence, different powers of cognition, but, as I say, that is a very long talk.

MR. P. Does not power to invent the means to attain a known aim differentiate intelligence from mechanical adaptability?

MR. O. It is the same thing really, only much depends on circumstances, organs in different beings and so on.

MR. A. Am I right in interpreting the octave-picture with the missing half-tone intervals denoting calls for shock as being a telling way of illustrating the continuous need for periodically introducing into one's life fresh life-giving forces, so as to ensure the consolidation of any progress attained by further advance, failing which the direction must inevitably decline in retrograde?

MR. O. Before we can dream about such things as that, we must understand how things actually happen. We start to do something and then come to an interval, without so much as realizing the existence of intervals or knowing about their possibilities. This is our situation. Before we come to the possibility of aiming and attaining, first we must learn that this is very far from us, and we must study intervals in the given examples, such as the Food Diagram. In this the place is shown and the necessity explained for two conscious shocks. By studying these, learning to produce them, we may come to the possibility of quite different kind of shocks, but not before that.

MR. A. Am I right in this connection in thinking that the choice of mi– fa and si–do as denoting these intervals is just part of that picture, the sole significance of which is to denote that such times do inevitably occur, when the even tenor of one's way must be disturbed, but that in fact such times are in no wise confined to those particular occasions which tally with the sub-division of life into seven, the critical periods being at stages $A^3/_7$, $A^4/_7$, $A^7/_7$ and $B^1/_7$?

MR. F. Is only man No. 5 able to alter his fate, or can man No. 4 already have a choice between two alternatives?

MR. O. That depends when and how. But I see we must stop a little more and go into some of these things. I noticed from your talk last time that some things were not clear.

MR. A. Are the distinctions between men Nos. 1, 2, 3, 4 and so on definite, or, like tramps, lunatics, householders, about which we heard last week, are we a bit of each?

MR. O. You know you absolutely spoil ideas for yourself when you take them like this, and mix them up. These ideas are very important. First you must take one, quite separately, and try to understand it.

Then take another and try to understand it. The idea about men Nos. 1, 2 and 3 is one thing and it was not given parallel to anything else. You must study this as it is—what is meant by man No. 1, by man No. 2, by man No. 3, what are combinations of these, how they are mixed and so on.

Then take this second idea. In order to understand what is meant by householder, tramp, lunatic and the further degradations, so to speak, each must be taken separately. You cannot take them all together and talk about them in one breath. Then, when you have questions, I can speak about each separately, but not about all at once.

MISS N. What ought one to do about bolsheviks? Leave them alone or make an active effort to get rid of them?

MR. O. What can you do about them?

MISS N. I know I can do nothing, but I want to know how to think about it.

MR. O. You say you <u>know</u> you can do nothing about it, so you see your position. What else can I tell you?

MISS N. But if I could change my attitude in thinking about it?

MR. O. What do you mean by change your attitude? I ask you what you can do and you say you know you can do nothing. Well, that is all. I do not see what else I can say.

MR. A. Does the system put forward any thesis about will-power other than that by using it it grows and by disuse it fades away.

MR. O. System explains how you have many 'I's and each has its own will. When you become one, then you may have one will. Will, even in normal 1, 2 and 3 men, is only the resultant of desires. Certain conflicting desires or combinations of desires make you act in a certain way. That is all.

MISS N. Is the division between men capable and not capable of developing determined by fate?

MR. O. No, one cannot put it quite like that, but it is so in some cases. Some people are put in such a position that there is really no chance for them and no possibility.

MRS. D. How should we think about our inability to 'do' in relation to responsibilities?

MR. O. You are given certain definite tasks, things to do. When you learn to remember yourself, even a little, you will find you are in a better position in relation to all other things.

*　　*　　*

MRS. D. It has been said that one cosmos is to another as zero to infinity. This is not so as regards their space or time. So in what sense is it so?

MR. O. How can you say just like that? You must think about it. I cannot accept that as final. Perhaps we can speak about it later.

MRS. N. What is the voice in one that very often makes capricious and impertinent comments that one is far from wishing to make or even to be associated with?

MR. O. It may be simply automatic. Maybe you are just repeating some kind of phrase you heard somewhere.

MR. A. When I try to observe myself, I notice two curious divisions:

   1. self and what I call 'not-self';

   2. that my attitude to sun, stars at night, rain, clouds, is fundamentally different from my attitude to other people, animals, trees, etc.

I thought the Table of Time in different cosmoses could give me an adequate explanation, but I can't see that myself. Is all this purely subjective?

MR. O. To begin from the end of your question, this Table of Time takes a long, long time to grasp. You cannot get anything out of it on casual acquaintance. You must give time to it.

Then, in answer to the first part of your question, about attitudes, this is too theoretical. You do not think naturally. What you say is so, but you do not really think in that way and when you observe yourself you do not notice these divisions. These divisions come from your mind, from thinking.

MR. A. I can best observe myself when I do something with my hands. Is this the purpose, or one of the purposes, of physical work done at Lyne?

MR. O. No, this is nothing to do with Lyne. This is simply your own habit.

MISS L. Does the system teach us anything about illness, as to what it is, what attitude we should adopt towards it and so forth?

MR. O. No, you cannot find any special answer to that at the present time. You must know much more before it will be possible to speak about it. For the moment you must just understand that illness makes things more difficult and that is all.

MISS L. I believe that pleasant emotions send me to sleep more than unpleasant emotions. Often I even lose energy through identifying with them.

MR. O. Yes, that is it. It is identification with emotions, not the emotions themselves which cause you to lose energy.

MISS L. How, apart from struggling with identification, can one use them for the work?

MR. O. There is no other way. It is necessary to struggle with identification.

MRS. D. Do man, organic life and large cell form a triad?

MR. O. No.

MRS. D. Can we be told more about this particular group of cells whose life is twenty-four hours?

MR. O. This illustrates exactly what I said at the beginning of this evening. These sorts of things are for you to find. To discover all those things which can, to a certain extent, be used in ordinary knowledge, that is your part of the work. You can read, ask other people, and perhaps you will be able to find something. If, after long search, you find nothing, then you can repeat your question and perhaps it will be possible to say something. This problem of the individual life of cells is not really known, but there are things you can find out. You must read bacteriology, histology and so on, and there you may find many interesting things.

MRS. D. It is said that soul goes to the moon. What is soul? Could it be sent on; and how?

MR. O. I do not understand what you mean by 'sent on'. Soul is a certain amount of energy and matter, that is all.

MR. H. As the life of some cells in a man's body is only three seconds and of some of the others twenty-four hours, is it the eternal recurrence of cells that prevents a man's body from disintegrating?

MR. O. Maybe it is, but we cannot have a definite answer to this question. There are many other possibilities, and it is necessary to use other explanations first before coming to the idea of recurrence.

MR. H. What part does the eternal recurrence of a man's life play in organic life?

MR. O. We cannot speak in that way. It will be very good if we can find some ways to determine our attitude towards recurrence for ourselves, not from the point of view of organic life.

MR. H. Does eternal recurrence occur in all cosmoses?

MR. O. It is too difficult to speak like that. Theoretically, this may be so, but on other planes perhaps it may have no meaning.

MR. H. Does the eternal recurrence of a man's life end at the expiration of organic life?

MR. O. Again, this is simply theory. Whether I answer yes or no, it will mean nothing.

MR. H. If organic life is also under the law of eternal recurrence, is man's recurrence maintained in each repetition of organic life?

MR. O. Again the same thing applies. You must understand that recurrence is a personal question and can be understood only as a personal question.

MR. H. Where is the law of eternal recurrence shown in the Table of Cosmoses?

MR. O. The Table of Times in Different Cosmoses shows the necessity and the possibility of it.

MR. H. Is the Buddhist idea of possibility of escape from the wheel of rebirth in any way connected with the idea of higher man's consciousness expanding into cosmoses above and below him?

MR. O. That I do not know. Escaping means escaping and this is just theoretical description.

MR. H. In which category of cells (i.e. a life of 24 hours or 3 seconds) do the following come? . . .

MR. O. I have already answered that question. This is material for work. There are some things you can find out about it.

MISS N. I think it was said some time ago that we only knew those things we had really experienced. We do not know, for instance, that the earth is round. I do not feel I really know, in that sense, the things Mr. O. told us about cosmoses; nor for example, that the moon feeds on organic life.

MR. O. One can persuade oneself one does not know the earth is round, but what is the use of it? First, we know it is not round. That is all superstition, really it is not round at all. It may look round from the moon's point of view, but that is all.

Then about moon feeding on organic life, what is important? The important thing is to realize that everything is connected, that nothing is separate from everything else. If you understand this idea of the connectedness of all things, you will understand this by analogy, but as a separate fact it is difficult to prove, just as it is difficult to prove the ideas about cosmoses in this way.

MISS N. When I try to think about these ideas, I get a sort of negative feeling of helplessness, as if nothing I can do will prove them to myself. Whereas the psychological things I can more or less prove to myself.

MR. O. You put yourself in a wrong position. Formatory thinking in relation to these ideas can give no results. But if you can think rightly about one thing, you can think rightly about another thing.

MISS S. I do not understand the distinction between theoretical and philosophical ideas. Can this be made more clear?

MR. O. We may come to that later. It is very important to understand the difference of language and the difference in attitude as regards these.

MR. T. Some little while ago we were given a diagram showing how the three notes of organic life filled the interval in the Ray of Creation. Could it be explained why there are three notes and the part each of these notes plays individually?

MR. O. These three notes have no separate meaning. As time goes on you will see how they can be understood. They sound all three together. We may come later to what that means, but not in the way you approach it.

MISS L. May I go back to the question of illness? In the chapter of *Fragments* in which we heard about the enneagram, we were shown symbols of man on the way to change. When all five centres were working properly, man was represented by a five-pointed star. After he grew a sixth principle, he was represented by a six-pointed star, the Seal of Solomon. Can I assume from that that if instinctive centre is not perfect, man has not the possibility of that change?

MR. O. No, that has nothing to do with it. Also, as regards difficulties of instinctive centre, it is necessary to know what kind of difficulties you mean. It is impossible to speak in general. You just say 'if instinctive centre is not perfect', as if this were something uniform, whereas it may have many different forms. So I cannot answer this question as it is.

MR. D. Is intelligence due to essence or personality, or both?

MR. O. It must be understood without connecting it with essence and personality.

MRS. P. Does this system think that ill-health can be avoided by self-knowledge?

MR. O. Here again, all I can say is that there are ten thousand forms of ill-health. How can we discuss it, so long as [you] speak as if ill-health was always the same thing?

MR. M. Is instinctive centre always a sure guide?

MR. O. In a perfectly normal man it can be.

MRS. D. What is the Indian word (referred to in the reading we had about Khas-namous) meaning inhabitant, householder?

MR. O. In the Laws of Manu it is Snataka. I think in Buddhist writings another word is used, but I cannot remember.

MISS N. I do not understand why Mr. O. draws this tremendous distinction, when talking about Khas-namous, between bolsheviks and any other political party, say, the fascists. I should have thought that the ideals from which the communists started were as good, if not better, than any other political ideals.

MR. O. First, I do not draw any distinction between bolsheviks and fascists. It is the same thing, the one produced by the other. Then I do not call either a political party. Both are just criminal parties.

As regards the second part of your question, I do not think very much of the ideals they started from, but you must understand we are not speaking about ideals. Suppose some of them did start with very high ideals, these ideals in any case were perfectly formatory, and if these people had been relatively alive they would have understood they could not make people accept them, and that if they did they would become criminals, because these ideals were impossible and unrealizable.

I remember a conversation I had before the revolution, in 1905, with one rather mad revolutionary (not a bolshevik). He told me some things and I said: 'But how can you make people agree with you?' He said they would, and I asked him: 'What about *Roussky Izvyestie?* (This was a newspaper run by professors.) I know they will not agree.' He was perfectly sure they could be persuaded. Actually, when the bolsheviks got into power, they had to destroy this paper and all the professors.

What you do not realize is that bolshevism is only one practical realization of ideals which philosophically may be very good, just the same as fascism is only one practical realization of what is called *étatisme*, or extreme power vested in the government. It is not political.

MR. F. We were told these criminal activities depended on a triad. Why should the continual use of formatory centre lead to a certain triad? Do certain triads act in certain parts of centres more particularly?

MR. O. That I have already explained. Faith in formatory centre produces a definite triad.

MR. A. If the men at the head of the bolsheviks had known where the interval would come in the octave, would they have been able to apply a shock, and in that case would it not have gone in the wrong direction?

MR. O. But you are speaking about them as if they were men No. 7 and they are minus 1, or minus 3. How could they know? They are just carried by the current. They cannot be supposed to be conscious men, so the question cannot be put in that way.

MR. A. I am asking this really because I want to know if conscious man would really be able to subdivide, whatever the question was, into octaves and find out where intervals were without knowing necessarily the whole length of the action.

MR. O. It is quite possible, but the question cannot be put in this connection.

MR. P. What was the bolshevik revolution at first? Was it the result of earlier revolutions, of the emancipation of serfs and so on, or something quite different?

MR. O. To answer that would mean I should have to go all through Russian history and that would be rather difficult. But taking it nearer to our time, the bolshevik party was not important before the revolution. Other people with much better imagination prepared the ground for them and then had to give way to them, simply because the bolsheviks were bigger scoundrels and the other people could not use the same methods. They got power because at the end of the war they offered peace. They began to cry and shout, and the Russian people really wanted peace, and so the bolsheviks got power that way.

MRS. D. I feel somehow that all our activities go wrong. Do we never use the right triad, or is this exaggerating?

MR. O. Accidentally, we do. Or rather we do not use it, but it may happen. Just as we may find money in the street—about the same probability.

MRS. D. Does this mean that if one knew better what one wanted one would be able to calculate results better?

MR. O. Yes, but many other things are necessary—to be able to calculate results and eliminate wrong activity and do exactly what is necessary to do and so on.

MRS. N. Is not being able to distinguish between telling the truth and lying the same as habitual lying?

MR. O. Certainly, it is not the same thing. You cannot compare what was said about the bolsheviks with ordinary levels. You think of them as if they were the same kind of people as you, on the same level. They are quite different people on a quite different level. Maybe you are asleep, but you are alive. They are more than dead—ten times dead.

MISS M. Are shocks of different kinds? I ask this by way of trying to understand just what shocks are in the system sense.

MR. O. In the system sense shocks are shown in the Food Diagram. When you study these you will have two very good examples.

MRS. D. Are shocks in this sense always caused by the entrance of another force?

MR. O. You cannot speak about shocks in this theoretical way. Two shocks are given for study and we must speak about them. Also you can think about three lines of work. That also was explained, and just by using what is usually called imagination you can see how one line of work can help another line of work.

MR. A. Are shocks necessarily unpleasant or may they be quite the opposite?

MR. O. They may necessitate effort, but they are not necessarily unpleasant. Quite the opposite, at the moment of this effort, with the entering of new energy, one may be very pleasantly surprised.

MRS. S. If there is no shock, the octave goes off in another direction, doesn't it?

MR. O. Yes, that is the general theory.

MRS. P. Did what was said in the reading mean that the bolsheviks would not realize they had lied if they thought about it afterwards?

MR. O. Exactly. They would only justify it and lie more. It is a peculiar mentality which you do not understand.

MRS. D. Does Mr. O. mean that these people who are confessing things just now are inventing them; that they never did them?

MR. O. Certainly they talked about these things and thought them. Evidently you do not know them very well nor the fact that in many big criminal trials people lie about themselves; they write letters, for instance, inventing things, and when the letters are read they have to say they lied or else to continue lying. You can find many examples if you read the history of trials. But even that does not explain this case. With people like those in the examples you can find, it just happened. In the case of the bolsheviks, they are just this sort of material, they cannot be different; in all circumstances they will be the same and lie in all circumstances.

MISS W. Is the first or the second shock the stronger?

MR. O. You cannot compare them.

MISS W. I am not clear whether I, or anyone like me, can make the shock now, as we are.

MR. O. Which shock? And in what octave, what action? You do not explain what you mean.

MISS W. If the first one comes accidentally, can one apply the second one? What can one do when one feels one is reaching the interval in some activity, or can one do nothing?

MR. O. One must study different forms of activity and intervals. This means very much time and energy. Then perhaps one will be able to find what one can do, provided one develops other things at the same time.

MR. F. I think it was said that there were two sorts of people who could not come to the system. Could you give definitions of these two types?

MR. O. They cannot be called types, and two definitions will not help. First you must understand that when it is said that such and such people can or cannot come it does not mean necessarily to this system. It means that people who have the possibility of development are rather exceptional. The great majority of people have no chance, at least not in one incarnation. Maybe, if they get a little being in one life it will grow and grow, but in most cases, if external circumstances do not prevent them, they need maybe several lives before they accumulate enough material for magnetic centre.

So it depends, as regards your question, whether you mean in one life or a sequence of lives. If you mean in one life, very few people can come, very few people have the possibility to develop. And then these are sorted out and sorted out. First they must be able to find a school suitable to their type, 1, 2, or 3. Then they must have enough time to be capable of sufficient effort. Then on the ways of Fakir, and religious ways, big self-sacrifice, or at all events quite difficult things are necessary.

Again, if you ask this question in relation to people who can develop, you must realize the enormous amount of people who, by the state of their being, are incapable of the appreciation of any ideas.

MISS L. Could a tramp ever be outwardly successful?

MR. O. I do not know what you mean. You use these words too freely. This word was used to describe just those people who in the ordinary way are often supposed to be very near to the possibility of development, though actually they are very far from this possibility—further than quite ordinary, live people. People can know many beautiful words, speak very easily and be very far from the possibility of development.

MR. H. Are not most of us a mixture of all three types, tramp, lunatic and householder?

MR. O. You must try to understand each of them separately, and only then will you be able to see. If you mix, then you will never see. Again, you cannot take them together because they are not on the same level. And they are only the answer to one question. These words can be used only in that connection.

MR. M. For which reason are these people in Moscow labelled criminals? Because they were revolutionaries, because they confessed to poisoning, or because they have poisoned people?

MR. O. First of all, do you think they can be leaders of the bolsheviks without being criminals? Then there is a long history of crime behind each of them. So all their confessions certainly can never equal the amount of things they actually committed.

MR. M. Could you not look on them as first and foremost doctors whose misfortune it is to live in Russia?

MR. O. You know, it is awfully naïve, what you say. Do you think ordinary doctors can become doctors in crime, and can you imagine they were not tested in crime before they were admitted to their posts? For instance, there was a man who in some way displeased Stalin, and he ordered that he should have an operation, from which he died. I do not know which of these doctors performed the operation.

Q. If we can do nothing about bolshevism, why do you tell us so much about it?

MR. O. Because you ask questions about it and also because if you understand one thing rightly, there is a chance you will understand others. If you understand one thing wrong, then you have no chance to understand other things right. You must have some right point of view about such things.

MISS V. In what way is Hitler different from the bolsheviks?

MR. O. There is no difference at all. Bolshevism and fascism are two sides of the same medal. Bolshevism produces fascism.

MISS V. Do you believe that eventually they will destroy themselves?

MR. O. We will see.

MR. M. I do not find there is anything in my sex experiences which I cannot explain by blind instinct and blind emotion. I cannot find a sex centre in myself.

MR. O. That is why our study is limited to four centres. When we know about them, then we will see what does not enter into these.

MR. M. There was a revolution in Ireland. The leader of that is now a respectable Prime Minister. Is he or is he not a criminal?

MR. O. That is theoretical talk and will not lead to anything. I do not know whether he is or not. There was very much that was criminal in Ireland also, and that is why they do not get much out of their revolution, except that some people became Prime Ministers. This is the only gain in most revolutions—people who would have been shoemakers or house-painters become Prime Ministers.

MRS. S. Is it our mental and emotional parts which feed the moon?

MR. O. It does not matter. It will happen anyway. And again, it is not only we who feed the moon, but all organic life—birds, worms, everything. You somehow manage to take it personally. Actually there is nothing personal in it, but there is a very interesting principle behind it. It shows the connection between the moon and organic life.

MR. F. [Question not recorded.]

MR. O. In an ideal state, maybe. But where is the ideal state? How can people vote when they have only names to vote for? They do not know what it means, nor what they want to do. Really in democracy or in autocracy, it is just the same, only men imagine that because they vote it is a different kind of state.

MR. A. How are we to apply the Law of Seven in our lives?

MR. O. We can only do this in one way at present, and that is by looking for intervals, nothing more.

MR. A. Should we be particularly careful in our twenty-first, twenty-eighth, thirty-fifth years and that kind of thing?

MR. O. No, no. I do not know where this idea comes from, but certainly I am not guilty!

We just want to look for intervals, changes of direction, in our activity. Then we are on the way to studying the Law of Seven. Nothing more can be done at present.

MR. A. But sevenths of <u>what</u> are we looking for?

MR. O. We know generally. Intervals show the position of the octave. That is all. . . . Then again we can study intervals in the examples given, particularly in the Food Diagram. From this we can understand much about the Law of Seven. This is material for our study.

MR. M. Is the genius of comedy and tragedy the same?

MR. O. I do not know really. Can they be separated?

MR. M. How would you distinguish between a man who bursts into laughter and a man who bursts into tears?

MR. O. There may be many reasons in both cases.

MR. M. What is laughter?

MR. O. That is another thing. When an impression is received in two parts of centres at the same time, this produces the reaction of laughing. It is quite mechanical. But in some cases, and in extreme forms, this kind of reaction produces something very similar to self-remembering on a small scale, so the capacity to laugh, on our level, can help the digestion of impressions, and, in our state, is rather a useful quality. We transform many impressions with it which otherwise would disappear. At the same time you must remember that in higher centres there is no laughter. So it is very limited.

Well, we will continue next time. Try to prepare questions and avoid asking things you can find out for yourselves. You cannot expect me to explain things which you can find out in other ways.

* * *

Thursday. March 24th 1938. (Warwick Gardens.)

MRS. D. Mr. O. said that accidents in our lives need not recur. What does recur besides our essence and our fate?

MR. O. I did not speak about accidents recurring or not recurring. I only said that the one thing we know for certain does not recur is a school, because it is under different laws. Even the most elementary school is under different laws from those governing things which happen.

MRS. D. Are the six kinds of actions, actions on a certain scale? For instance, if I get up and close a door, that is not an action, is it?

MR. O. Certainly closing a door is action on a certain scale, only it cannot be described, it can only be understood by trying.

MR. A. There obviously must be some analogy or relation between centres and cosmic times, as the rate is 30,000 in both, but I cannot see it clearly. Could Mr. O. be good enough to make that clearer?

MR. O. I do not know how I can make it clearer. It is quite right, what you say, but I do not know what you really want to have explained. If you want me to explain further, you must elaborate your question a little.

MR. H. I am told that the shape of the moon is conical. Is this so? I was discussing it with a friend (having in mind something you said about 'we didn't see the whole of it') and he told me this was quite a well known fact.

MR. O. I do not think there is any evidence for it. Why conical? What I meant was something quite different. I meant that the moon, this three-dimensional body which we see, has three dimensions for itself, but not in the shape we see. If we take the earth, for instance, we know the earth moves round the sun in one year. One year, in earth's time, is equivalent to three-eighteths of a second in our time. Or, if we take one breath of earth, its psychological present, that will be eighty years. In that time earth turns eighty times round the sun and moves with the sun in an unknown direction. So for itself it will have a quite different shape from what we think of as its shape.

MR. H. How much is known about the development of cells? For instance, I have not yet found anything to explain how from a simple cell division all the specialized cells in our body arise.

MR. O. That is a special science, embryology. The trouble is that there is not really a single textbook on embryology which refers to man. They have the most awful habit in scientific books of mixing man with different animals. You begin to read about some kind of tissue and you find they are speaking about the badger or the rhinoceros!

MR. H. Does thought destroy brain cells? I seem to have read somewhere that every time we think we burn up lots of them.

MR. O. It is not quite like that, but certainly every activity destroys something, needs some kind of energy.

MR. H. If this is so, how are they replenished?

MR. O. That is one of the enigmas of science. Nobody can answer that question. There is no evidence of the development of brain cells from other cells; they cannot be immortal and yet they are not born, so really they do not know what it is that happens.

MR. H. What is a large cell and what is a small cell?

MR. O. I will not answer that question, because that is one of the things you can find out for yourself.

MR. H. Is the similarity between the structure of the atom and the Solar System analogous in every way, analogous in some degree or not analogous at all?

MR. O. It is very hypothetical. There are certain analogies, but we will speak about that later.

MRS. D. Giving up suffering can only be attained by creating moon in ourselves. . . .

MR. O. No, there you are mixing up two different ideas. Giving up suffering is your own action. Creating moon is the result of continuous action.

MRS. D. Man's soul goes to the moon. Man's soul is connected with life energy. Can these two ideas be connected?

MR. O. No.

MRS. D. Can I be shown how to create moon in myself?

MR. O. First it is necessary to study all that is given—not identifying, remembering yourself, observing, keeping rules. For instance, I find that nobody knows rules and you want moon. First learn rules.

MRS. N. If everything in the universe is so closely interrelated, it is difficult to see that final death is possible. Would Mr. O. speak about this?

MR. O. There is nothing I can say. This is philosophy. Final death means something different from what we call death.

MISS D. Mr. O. told us last week that we must think for ourselves about the conscious shocks in the organic interval. I have been doing so and trying to find out what I can. It seems to me that one shock might be connected with the need of constant effort to use higher parts of centres so that energy otherwise wasted in negative emotions might be consciously used to stir up and make use of organs now dormant.

MR. O. How can you use higher centres? Shocks were more or less described psychologically; self-remembering will produce the first shock and the struggle with negative emotions is the beginning of the formation of the second shock. That is all you have to know. Any kind of contact with higher centres will be the result of work, not the work itself.

MR. R. I notice that whenever I make a successful effort to overcome some resistance I have more energy at my disposal for further efforts, if I can manage not to dissipate it in self-satisfaction. Does this energy arise because a certain amount of self-remembering is involved in any effort which overcomes a resistance?

MR. O. The question is too long. This is an observation. It may be quite good, but it is quite subjective. So to answer your question I would have to verify every small point.

Questions must be not longer than three lines. I cannot answer long questions.

MR. R. Is it only instinctive centre which has to receive impressions continuously in order that the organism may remain alive?

MR. O. That does not matter at all. Whether I say yes or no, it will change nothing.

MR. R. It seems possible to have both thoughts and emotions which have not been aroused by any external impression. Does this mean that emotional and intellectual centres do not need external impressions to set them working?

MR. O. I do not know such things. You take it for granted that I know what you are speaking about. It may be delayed emotion, but how can one expect to get such things when we are entirely in the power of external impressions?

MR. R. There are certain religious paintings which always produce in me very powerful and, I think, real emotions. How do impressions I get from these pictures change in the course of producing these effects?

MR. O. I do not understand what you mean by 'change'.

MR. R. It has always seemed to me that complete understanding of the Food Table could only come through knowing certain parts of it with instinctive centre.

MR. O. No, no, that is out of our possibility, you know. We can be expected to do only what we can.

MR. F. Is hard physical work necessary for the correct working of instinctive centre?

MR. O. In most cases it is, but we do not think only from that point of view. We must take everything from the point of view of the work in the larger sense.

MR. F. Can Mr. O. give the explanation of crying?

MR. O. It is a certain reaction.

MR. A. Is it possible to self-remember while engaged in an occupation which demands all one's attention without interrupting it? For instance, writing a difficult letter, or listening to these lectures?

MR. O. Yes, certainly it is possible, but not in the beginning. The capacity has to be created. We do not have it, but we can have it. We have all the necessary organs, so to speak, but we are not taught, not accustomed. There are many things we can do if we are taught, and self-remembering is one of them.

MR. F. When I discuss self-remembering with older people in the system, they invariably tell me that it is only thinking about self-remembering. How shall I know when I really do remember myself?

MR. O. You will know. It will be quite a new sensation.

MR. A. In endeavouring to obtain a facility for self-remembering, should one avoid too much effort, pressing oneself? I feel one can swamp the effect by too much effort.

MR. O. What you mean is not too much effort, but just wrong kind of effort. Muscular effort will not help you to remember yourself. This is just the same. It is necessary for each person to find for himself the moment to make this particular big effort, particularly moments when all tendencies, emotional, instinctive, go against it. This is the moment to make effort. If you manage to remember yourself at that time, then you will know how to do it.

MISS M. Could Mr. O. explain further what is meant by 'creating moon in oneself'?

MR. O. Everything is repeated after some time and then with more material. If I explain now, it will be simply repetition.

MISS M. Is there any foundation for the belief held by certain peasants that plants are influenced by the moon?

MR. O. There is no scientific evidence for it.

MR. P. Can Mr. O. say anything further about the nature of the influence of the planets apart from their causing big events, such as wars and that sort of thing?

MR. O. This is not quite right. I never really said that. About the action of planets, the problem is quite different. We were speaking about events involving masses of humanity—nations, races—and I said there were many phenomena we could observe in the life of nations of which the causes may be outside of earth, possibly in the planets. We see certain events and, depending on how we have been taught, we ascribe them to certain causes; if we are religious we say it is the will of God; if not, we look for the causes in history, or something like that. But there are many other causes we do not know. That is what I meant. We can study historical causes, change of climate, necessity for different food, change of standard of living, but there are many other causes. We must remember that, but we cannot start from these.

MR. B. Can it be said that any of the planets has a definite sphere of influence, individually, like the moon controls movement?

MR. O. I do not know.

MR. H. Do I understand rightly that it is man's essence which recurs?

MR. O. Quite right. About recurrence we know very little. Some day we may try to collect what can be taken as reliable in all that is said about recurrence and see which way we can think about it. But it is only theory.

[End of written questions.]

* * *

MR. M. Brahma has periods of sleep, has he not? And he is Protocosmos?

MR. O. It is difficult to know what people mean when they talk of Brahma. In the full meaning it will correspond to Protocosmos, but I cannot guarantee that all you read will correspond. It is always dangerous to apply words of one system to words of another system.

MR. M. But did not you yourself connect them?

MR. O. Only in one sentence. There is some analogy between the system and Indian philosophy, but it does not mean we can replace system words by Indian words.

MR. M. Is the period of the earth's sleep anything to do with the glacial periods? And what is meant by 'day and night of the earth'?

MR. O. We do not know. Science can say nothing about it. You see we take what is given in the system. If we want to know what it means, we must refer to science. In this case science does not know anything.

MR. M. But the Ice Age was about two and a quarter million years ago. . . .

MR. O. It cannot be taken definitely. These geological periods are so uncertain. I would not base any hypothesis on that.

MR. M. I am very troubled in my spirit because, having had my mind enlarged and illumined by your books, I find this theory of time very naïve.

MR. O. It may look like that at first.

MR. M. I feel I am now in a fit state to receive more knowledge. This Table deals with one line of time only, not time going in all directions.

MR. O. No, it does not deal only with one line. All dimensions are here in this Table of Cosmoses. If you understand our relation to the electron, for instance, then you will see how they come in. The electron as a unit exists for such a short period of time that these particles of matter would not exist for us if we were not in contact with their fifth and sixth dimensions. Different dimensions come into the Table nearer to us than that, but I took the electron because it is more obvious. Just now we were speaking about the earth and how it would see itself. If you think this system is naïve, that means you have not grasped it yet. You must be more patient with it. There is very much material.

MR. M. What do you mean when you say every cosmos comes to an end?

MR. O. Why should they not? Everything comes to an end. Everything has a definite time. Even modern physics accepts that.

You see, dimensions of time again are relative. Much depends on the scale, much depends on the observer. It is not absolute. This is what it is important to understand. This system teaches relativity. We take things too logically and we must get rid of logic first of all. We must be able to think of several logics at the same time which contradict one another.

MR. B. The transition from one cosmos to another means the addition of one dimension, so on passing from one cosmos to a higher cosmos you see ordinary movements as stationary or quite different. How does the movement we call light seem to higher cosmoses?

MR. O. Light is the most difficult thing to speak about. You see it is just a word, a label. Science does not know what it is.

MR. B. Are physicists right in thinking it is very fast movement?

MR. O. Yes, but movement of what? Science does not know of what. Leave out light for the time being and speak about something surer.

MR. H. Is it true that scientists can photograph the electron?

MR. O. No, do not believe it—it is imagination.

MR. B. Is it only that they see the effect produced by the movement of electrons?

MR. O. Some effects produced by something. That is what is photographed.

Q. Did you say we could associate instinctive centre with cell and organic life?

MR. O. No, that is too formatory. You can associate the speed of instinctive centre with the time of organic life, not with organic life. The analogy is not complete, and it is dangerous to continue analogies.

MR. F. On the scale of the electron, is there any difference between organic and inorganic life?

MR. O. From the ordinary point of view, yes; from the point of view of the system, no. Because from the point of view of the system there is no dead matter. Dead matter would not exist. Matter in which all movement ceased would disappear.

MR. C. It seems there must be some kind of life in decomposition.

MR. O. Decomposition is relative. It means a passing from one state to another. But matter remains alive.

At the same time, the ordinary distinction between organic and inorganic is quite good and must be accepted. We can take different states of matter. Protoplasmic structure, cellular structure is one thing. Then molecular structure we know. Electronic structure, like light, we know very little about, but it is definitely different from molecular and cellular structure.

MR. M. Do you remember saying that one microscopic cell has more power than a volcano?

MR. O. Yes. That was from the ordinary point of view of organic and inorganic. In a limited sense it is true.

MR. M. When a potato is baked, although it gains in intelligence on one scale, it loses on another, does it not?

MR. O. Everything has to be paid for, you know. The potato pays for one thing with another thing. The same applies to us. If we want one thing we have to pay for it by another thing.

MR. M. Could these two types of intelligence be compared?

MR. O. Which measure do you use? Yes, they are comparable, if you like. In the one case it is simply reproduction, growth. The potato can produce other potatoes. But the baked potato passes to another level of existence, it sacrifices itself.

There is a diagram relating to this problem, and I cannot really answer your questions about different intelligence until we have had it. It is rather too long to give it now, but we will try to come to it soon.

MRS. S. Surely a baked potato loses adaptability?

MR. O. Yes, it does, but it is food for man, and this, for a vegetable, is already a great step up.

MRS. S. Is adaptability the thing it sacrifices?

MR. O. It sacrifices its life. It shows you how everything must be paid for. Nothing can be had for nothing.

MRS. S. Can a school function as food in any way for men on a higher level?

MR. O. No. It is necessary first to know what is meant by food. Secondly, school has nothing to do with it.

MR. S. You said once that the origin of organic life was a series of experiments of which man was the last and most successful. Is it possible to have these experiments in order and see what was added each time? Would not that be a correct and useful study of evolution?

MR. O. That was my own description, not the system. There are too many experiments to try to do this. But if you begin to study natural science, you will see such a wonderful profusion, even absurdity, in these experiments; such strange insects, for instance, that you understand they were just experiments to see how a certain principle could work. But it cannot be put in simple formulas. What is generally called evolution does not exist; it cannot be observed and it could not produce all this variety of things. Evolution or experiment, they are both hypotheses.

MRS. S. Do all the experiments serve a purpose?

MR. O. We do not know, but we can suppose, taking what we know from the system, that the purpose was to build a self-developing being, which is man. Nature brings him to a certain point and then leaves him to develop by himself if he can. But what was the purpose of, say, this fly's eye, which is made up of a thousand eyes? Why this experiment was necessary for human evolution we do not know.

MRS. S. Could it not be another purpose, apart from man?

MR. O. There is no evidence. Quite the opposite. Everything points to the purpose having been to invent the different principles by which man is built. Man is a very complicated being, and it is evident that all this work was necessary in order to invent the principles of the human body. It is the only reasonable explanation.

MR. M. If man could understand the laws under which he lives, would he be concerned with conforming to them or avoiding them?

MR. O. When man begins to understand he finds many laws he can be free from. That is what happens. Then he begins to work to become free. Self-development is work towards freedom.

MR. M. But some he would strive to obey, would he not?

MR. O. I cannot answer yes or no to that. What do you mean by 'strive to obey'? It is difficult to answer without knowing what you are thinking of.

MR. M. Does one know any of these laws?

MR. O. Certainly one does. Physical laws, biological laws, laws in the legal sense, and so on.

MR. M. So he is always swimming against the current?

MR. O. He must have system. Without system he can do nothing. System, school shows the different relative value of laws and the relative necessity of laws. Certainly it means he has to swim against the current, but he cannot do this without school. With school he has a chance.

[To Mr. P.] You asked a question a little time ago which I did not answer because it interrupted another conversation. What was your question?

MR. P. I understood you to say that the one thing one could take it for certain could not recur was a school. I supposed it might mean a person could only meet a school in one life?

MR. O. No, that is introducing another idea. It is simpler than that. Recurrence, if it exists, is all mechanical, based on mechanicalness.

School cannot be mechanical, so it must be under different laws. It very often happens that when people first hear about recurrence they think everything recurs. But what would be the idea of school if it were like that? If a school exists once in one form, that means that next time it will not be in the same place, at the same time, in the same form. That must be understood. How it changes it is impossible to say in general, but it cannot be the same thing or it would be mechanical, and mechanical is not school.

MR. P. Then it means an individual who came across a school in one life might not find it in the next?

MR. O. He may find another, better one, or he may find nothing. It depends what he made of it. 'Came across' means nothing. He did not 'come across' anything.

MR. S. You said once that if man toyed with self-remembering and did not take it seriously he would suffer consciously on the moon. Could you explain what that meant?

MR. O. I remember what I said and I did not say 'toyed' with self-remembering. It is rather long to explain, but there is a possibility of that. Man can create a sort of half-consciousness which can pass to the soul, and then the soul going to the moon may be aware of what happens to it, but this occurs only in very rare cases when essence dies during life. Then the soul can get some material from essence in this way. Although there are many people, of course, who kill essence and are really dead in life, but that does not concern us.

*   *   *

Well, I will begin to speak about the new diagram. I must explain some things before I give it to you.

Very often questions are asked referring to animals. I always say that man is not an animal. He is quite different. It is necessary to understand that all living beings, all animals on the earth, including man, are divided, from the system point of view, into three categories: three-storied, two-storied and one-storied. Man has three stories, animals have two stories and more elementary animals, like earthworm, have only one story. So all living beings have three, two or one stories. These categories are different one from another and are under different laws.

Then you know the usual classifications in the scientific sense, grouping living beings by families, species, by what they eat—

carnivorous, herbivorous, omnivorous, etc.—or by the way they are born, whether alive or in the form of eggs and so on. There are many different divisions and all really are unsatisfactory because they mix many things and there is no one general principle for division. In the system there is one definite principle for classification. At first it looks too simple and people are inclined to think it means that many different beings can belong to the same category according to this division. Really, however, it is very definite and very strict in spite of being simple.

All living beings are divided by three principles:

> what they eat;
> what air they breathe;
> in what medium they live.

If you understand this right you will see that there are no two identical beings on earth. They are all different. There are no two different animals which eat the same things, breathe the same air and live in the same medium. In order to see it, it is necessary to think well and find many examples.

I remember a conversation I had a little while ago with a doctor who came down to see me at Lyne (he was not in the system). We were walking round and went to look at the pigs. He told me how near the pig is to man—perhaps the nearest animal—because of the length of its intestines and many other things; because it is omnivorous and so on. Really he was terribly mistaken; the pig is very far from man. It eats quite different things. Man will die if he eats what a pig can eat. The pig can easily live on pure ptomaines for a long time. So you see it is dangerous to accept ordinary scientific classifications.

Man is limited in what he can eat, to hydrogen 768. All other animals can eat something different from that or cannot eat all of that. Even animals as alike as the donkey and the horse are really quite different. They cannot live on exactly the same diet. The horse will probably die on the donkey's diet and the donkey will get too fat on the horse's diet.

MR. H. I do not understand what you mean by 'what air they breathe'.

MR. O. Just that. Take, for instance, the bee. The bee's food is higher than ours, but the bee can live in the hive where man could not live. He could not live in that air.

MR. S. Most birds can eat the same things, can't they? A lot of different birds eat worms.

MR. O. They eat different worms.

MRS. D. What do you mean by 'medium'?

MR. O. Man lives in the same air he breathes. A maggot, for instance, may live in a flower, in what he eats. That is his medium, our medium is air. Fish live in water, but breathe the same air as we do.

MISS R. Do animals feed on impressions?

MR. O. Impressions do not enter into this talk.

Well, for next time prepare questions again and we will start with questions. Then I will try, if there is time, to explain the new diagram. Only I must warn you that this diagram must be taken quite separately from all other diagrams. It is not parallel to any other, and the expressions used cannot be explained by words connected with other diagrams. It is on quite a different scale and is quite different. If you try to translate it into other language, you will get nothing from it.

* * *

Thursday. April 28th 1938. (Warwick Gardens.)

MR. A. I find as a result of contact with the system that I am really quite nervous about doing many intrinsically harmless things as being bound to involve leakage of energy. Am I right in thinking this tendency to be wrong and that any harmless outlet of energy is desirable since this energy has to be used up somehow?

MR. O. I cannot answer that without more facts.

MISS C. In trying to consider other people and give them what they expect, it seems possible when they expect a certain manner and kind of conversation—old jokes, well known phrases, etc.—but when they expect certain spontaneous feeling and sincerity external considering seems to mean control of emotional attitudes and their expression. Is this so?

MR. O. Quite right. And people can expect too much, in which case no external considering will help.

MISS C. What must be the inner state of a person before he can make the desired impression, for instance, leaving the room unnoticed by anyone?

MR. O. That is difficult to describe. Certainly it must be a state of not identifying, but at the same time it must be different in different cases.

MRS. N. I find it difficult not to get external and internal considering mixed up. I feel I do always try not to make people negative, but only because I want them to like me. How should I begin to distinguish between one and the other?

MR. O. By observation. You must try to find the difference once and then you will be able to see it afterwards. Try observing it, not in relation to yourself but in other people's relations one with another.

MRS. N. I do not see how it is possible to attain any degree of invisibility without will. Is this misunderstanding on my part?

MR. O. That is far, far, far. You cannot become invisible yet, so this is not a practical question.

MISS L. I find that even the most helpful things in me are mechanical and the result of outside stimuli, such as going to a lecture, seeing Mr. O. or reading the Gospels. I have no one in me on whom I can depend to make me look for these stimuli, and even if I decide to make some effort and it happens that I do, the original decision was just accident, a thought thrown up in my mind I do not know how. What can one do to keep oneself working before finding one's real self?

MR. O. At the same time you must find differences. We can talk only when you are able to distinguish between more mechanical and less mechanical. So long as you think everything is the same I cannot answer.

MISS L. I find that most of my identifications and distractions come from bodily sensations and cravings. So that in effect I am constantly saying, 'I want to change, but not until I have smoked this cigarette or looked into that shop window.' How can one use physical sensations as a help rather than let them be a hindrance to work?

MR. O. Everything can be used for self-remembering.

MISS M. I am told of the existence of five centres and that by observing I may note my possession of them. But this observation does not carry me on unless I can gain control of these centres, and I do not know how to do this. Will Mr. O. tell me if there is any immediate way by which I can cultivate this control or whether I must wait till the practice of self-remembering brings the promised new realizations.

MR. O. You cannot get control of centres before you know them. You must know much more than you do now. The first thing to learn about control is how not to identify. There are no special tricks or secrets. It is necessary to do all that has been said.

MR. S. While falling from a horse a short while ago I noticed an expansion of time between the period of leaving the saddle and meeting the ground. This happened in the space of approximately three seconds, but during those seconds I noticed very vividly more negativeness than I have in many hours previously. What is the difference between this time and the apparently much slower time in ordinary circumstances?

MR. O. I do not know. It is so subjective this kind of impression. I have never experienced it myself, this lengthening of time.

MR. S. Has this observation anything to do with speed of centres?

MR. O. No.

MR. S. After approximately twenty minutes of chaff-cutting and at the same time trying to prevent the machine from crushing someone else's fingers, I had a strange feeling of having done as much as I had in many years, and that those twenty minutes had expanded enormously. Has this feeling any significance as regards time?

MR. O. No. As I have already said, in general these feelings about time are subjective, unusual feelings compared with usual feelings.

MR. S. Would this possibly have been the result of the work I was previously doing, or do these states happen by accident?

MR. O. It is not a question of states, only of subjective feeling. From time to time, particularly in the work, we happen to have new sensations, sensations to which we are not accustomed, and these we interpret with our senses in a certain way, that is all.

MRS. T. How can one express a justifiable protest (for example, if people are stealing one's possessions) without expressing negative emotion, if one can't help feeling negative emotion?

MR. O. About that you must ask a lawyer! I do not know English law.

MRS. T. Can one hope to attain invisibility before becoming man No. 6?

MR. O. I do not know. Why man No. 6? That is too definite. Some people have special capacities for this producing the desired impression, and if they learn in the right way they may learn it quickly. Whereas for other people it may be very difficult. It depends on the kind of person apart from other things.

MRS. T. Has Mr. O. ever been invisible?

MR. O. I do not enter into this, you know. I cannot give myself as an example. I could tell you anything I liked and you would have to believe me, and the first principle is that you must not believe anything you have not verified.

MRS. D. What degree of understanding have men 1, 2 and 3?

MR. O. Relative understanding. They are in a state of relative consciousness. One understanding can be compared with another understanding, that is all.

MRS. D. Is it easier for man No. 1 to understand man No. 1 than man No. 2?

MR. O. Yes, certainly, though again relatively. In any case he will think he understands him better.

MRS. S. Some of the moments of my life which I can remember the most vividly have to do with fear. Fear in this case surely cannot have been a negative emotion, for how could a negative emotion have left such vivid memories?

MR. O. This means that at those times you were more awake and that is why you remember them vividly. It is not the fear which makes you remember, but violent emotions very often produce a moment of awakening, though you have no control over them.

MRS. S. If I am very tired or very negative and circumstances change my 'I', I find myself entirely refreshed. I do not understand why this is so, as I thought that all centres used the same reservoir of energy.

MR. O. It is difficult to say about that without a better description. It may happen.

MR. P. Does the Step Diagram represent a man as well as the universe?

MR. O. Yes, man as a whole—mankind.

MR. P. In the Step Diagram plants are represented by hydrogen value 192, that is the same as air for breathing. Does this mean that the purpose of plants from this point of view is to produce oxygen for man?

MR. O. No, no, nothing to do with that.

MR. P. Is the chief cosmic purpose of the processes of nature in man to produce higher hydrogens as food for higher categories?

MR. O. If you like to put it like that, but there are many other things we must know. We cannot put it only in that way.

MR. P. What is food for 6144?

MR. O. There may be something still lower, but again there may be a difference. Study what is given. If food for 6144 is not given, it is not given. Why it is not given is another question. You ask what it is.

MR. P. Does the Step Diagram indicate the cosmic purpose of school-work?

MR. O. No. This is a diagram of the universe, very compact, very simplified, from one definite point of view.

MR. P. Is the whole of mankind necessary for this purpose?

MR. O. I do not accept this about purpose, so I cannot answer that question.

MR. P. Does the Table of Hydrogens represent a reverse process to balance the Step Diagram?

MR. O. No. The Table of Hydrogens refers simply to matters and the Step Diagram is called the 'Scheme of all Living'. It is quite a different idea.

MR. H. I understood from the last lecture that external considering included trying to understand what other people expected of you. This seems to me to be very like internal considering. Can Mr. O. point out the difference?

MR. O. You must not mix them. You must find differences for yourself. If we just go on talking about it, the conversation can last for ever.

MISS N. Is there any virtue in keeping silent? I notice I talk a great deal in my most mechanical moods.

MR. O. If one is accustomed to talk and if one struggles with this and makes oneself silent, it can provide material for observation.

MR. H. How does the system explain hypnotic sleep and the peculiar suggestibility of people in such sleep?

MR. O. We have not come to that yet. But this suggestibility is not an accidental feature of hypnotic sleep. It is its only feature. Hypnotic sleep can be defined as the state of highest suggestibility. Sometimes the subject is really in deep sleep. This is more accidental than the suggestibility. Later perhaps we will be able to find which functions, which processes are involved in this case and why even deep sleep can happen like that. But we have not enough material yet.

MR. T. I find that one does not remember for long that a particular activity is profitless. What can one do to increase one's memory?

MR. O. Just observe more and try to remember yourself. There are no special ways for one or another thing like that in general. All methods have already been explained. If you remember yourself more, your memory will be better.

MISS M. In dealing with people who evoke different 'I's, is it desirable to try to achieve one 'I' and show this 'I' to everybody?

MR. O. But that is doing. You cannot do, you can only observe. You ask this question as though you could do what you describe. Suppose I answer that it is desirable, then you will ask me how to do it, and I say you cannot. You have to observe things as they are. We think we have much more control than we actually have. We think we do not do something because we do not know whether it is desirable or not or because we do not want to do it. We do not try and so we think we can do it.

*   *   *

I want to say something about people for new groups. I find that older people have not explained sufficiently the conditions about not talking about coming to lectures and what you hear here. It constantly happens that people in new groups start to talk, and they talk about lectures to people when they meet them outside and sometimes put them in a very awkward position, having to deny that they know them or something like that.

I find by just analysing two or three cases that really they were never seriously told about these conditions which have to be undertaken if they are allowed to come. From now on everyone who brings new people or recommends them must tell me about this. First he must understand clearly what people must not do and why. Then he must write and tell me what the person he wishes to bring says about the conditions, if possible in his own words. Later the conditions will be written for once and given to everyone.

Also from now on people who bring new people remain responsible for them, even if they leave, so please be careful and bring only people whom you know more or less well. You see this rule about not talking in front of other people is first of all a test. It shows the level of being of the person. People who cannot remember this, or make excuses for themselves, or think that after they have left they can talk (it does not matter for us much, but we have to study people) show one level of being. When people can remember it shows a better quality of being. Also if they remain and if they work, this rule will help them to remember themselves, but that cannot be explained in the beginning when they do not know what self-remembering is. When they learn, they realize that all rules are in their own interest and give the possibility to go against mechanical habits.

MISS N. How much is one allowed to tell a person?

MR. O. You can say that there are lectures, and if you remember the first lecture or the first two lectures you can talk within the limits of the first two lectures. That is if you know already that the person is interested. First you must begin by talking with the material from the *New Model*.

MR. S. Is it necessary for them to have read the *New Model*?

MR. O. I think it is useful for them to start with the book.

MR. S. If they make no comment when told the rules, should we try to make them?

MR. O. You must say it in such a way that they will make comments. It is your fault if they do not, and means you do not say it in the right way. You must know the person to whom you are explaining the conditions, and put it so that he will say 'but I hate beastly secret things like that . . .' or whatever it may be.

MR. M. Will you explain how it is possible for a man to live co-existent lives simultaneously in two time-places at the same time?

MR. O. There are many things that look impossible, but that is because our thinking apparatus is not good enough to think about such things. It simplifies things too much. These problems need mathematical thinking. For instance, we cannot think about time as a curve, but only as a straight line. If we could think of time as curve and all that that implies, this question of yours would not arise. In this case we are in exactly the same position as plane-beings trying to think of a three-dimensional world. Really there is no problem of this kind. The problem is the structure of our own mind. If one could think through higher centres (which means getting the third and fourth states of consciousness, which is the aim of all our work) problems of future life, absurdities like this time question and so on do not arise. As things are we can only make theories. We know more or less how we can approach them, but we can know nothing.

But about this question of former lives, I think some people can remember something, although only in very rare cases, since this implies already a certain definite degree of development. Ordinary man 1, 2 and 3 has no apparatus for such memory. Essence is mechanical. It does not live by itself; it has no special thinking apparatus, but has to think through personality, and personality has no experience.

MR. M. Can a man be No. 5 in one life and No. 3 in another simultaneously?

MR. O. I really do not know. One cannot become No. 5 at once; one has to approach slowly, and if a man develops into No. 5 outside school, then it is a very slow process, so I do not think the difference would be so big from one life to another. I can say only one thing about it. I think that if one knows consciously, fully, can more or less speak about this idea of recurrence and accepts it, then one cannot fully forget it next time. So if you accept it and know it in one life, there is a great chance of remembering much more next time. We have no experience, but if you think—in literature, history, philosophy—people return again and again to this idea. They never fully forget it. But to fit it into a three-dimensional world is very difficult. It needs a five-dimensional world, and the question of remembering really refers already to six dimensions. In the fifth dimension man returns and returns without knowing. Remembering means a certain growth in the sixth dimension.

Dimensions you must understand simply in this way. The fourth dimension is the realization of one possibility of each moment—what we call time. The fifth dimension is the repetition of this. The sixth dimension is the realization of different possibilities. But it is difficult to think about this so long as we think about time as a straight line. The problem is not a real thing. It is just our weakness, nothing more.

MR. S. I do not understand what you mean when you say the fourth dimension is the realization of one possibility.

MR. O. Life is the fourth dimension, a circle, the realization of one possibility. When this comes to an end, it meets its own beginning. The moment of death corresponds to the moment of birth, and then it begins again, maybe with slight deviations (but they do not mean anything, it always returns to the same line). Breaking a chief tendency, starting this life in a quite different way will be sixth dimension.

We cannot think of simultaneous moments; we have to think of them one following another, though actually they are simultaneous on another scale. But our own experience in relation to small particles, electrons, is that their eternity is in our time, so why can our repetition not be in earth's time, for instance?

MR. L. Are there very definite possibilities for one man at any given moment?

MR. O. People think there are many possibilities. At any rate it looks like that. But really there is only one possibility, or sometimes two. Man can only change in the sense of the sixth dimension. Things happen in a certain way, and one possibility out of many supposed possibilities is realized at each moment, and that makes the line of the fourth dimension. But conscious change for a definite purpose, which is the idea of work, the idea of development, when you seriously start in this system, that is already a start on the sixth dimension.

MR. F. You say there may be two possibilities at a given moment. Do you mean one mechanical and one not?

MR. O. No. There may be several mechanical possibilities, because small deviations are possible, but you always come back to the line. I remember, long ago, before I became interested in these things, I began to write a story about a man who tried to do everything in his own way. I remember I put him in an impossible position. He came up a staircase to get into his flat, and when he came to the door he realized that in order to get in he must unlock the door and open it, so he would not do that but went down again, and there realized that in order to get out he must ring for the porter to let him out, so he did not do that. And there he remained, and there he has been for over forty years already!

MR. M. Where do you place man in the scheme of things? Is he Lord of Creation or a worm, or what do you call him?

MR. O. I do not define. It depends on which scale we are talking about him. If it is on our own scale then we talk about possibility of development, self-study, study of the world we live in. On the scale of earth, for instance, man does not exist individually, only in the general mass of organic life.

MR. M. And what do you mean when you talk of the intelligence of earth?

MR. O. It is only a principle, the principle that every cosmos has intelligence. What degree of intelligence we have no way of knowing. Every cosmos that may be explained by the enneagram must have intelligence. This is its meaning. Degrees of intelligence we can compare only in ourselves. But if every cosmos is an enneagram, it means there are certain analogies between cosmoses.

MR. M. But man can create intelligent beings. A chair, for instance.

MR. O. Yes, or a picture—even Notre Dame—things more intelligent than himself, maybe. Only not living beings, of course. So man is limited in all ways.

MRS. F. If one brings a new person, what happens if they recognize people that they see?

MR. O. If they meet people amongst other outside people they must not speak about groups or lectures, but if they recognize them and do not show it and do not talk, why not recognize?

MR. A. Do you think I am right in regarding time as only arbitrary man-made distinctions of eternity?

MR. O. Not quite. Time is our life. Life is not our invention. Some people live longer than others. That means time has some sort of objective existence. You cannot call it simply an imaginary quality, but it has many features we do not recognize. We do not realize, for instance, its curvature, the three dimensions of time, but take it as a straight line.

MR. M. Is there any essential difference between time and space?

MR. O. Just as we feel it. In the beginning of this system, as you have probably realized, simple, empirical sensations must serve as guides, because after all it is better to trust in them than just in theories. We must start simply with a yard-measure for space and a watch and compass for time. Little by little we will not need them, but we have to begin with them.

MR. P. Is the length of a man's life always the same?

MR. O. We do not know. We cannot compare. We must try to avoid questions we cannot answer. I think it may be different. Why should it be the same? There is a quite possible theory that man's life is determined from the day of his birth, that for everybody there is a definite hour when he must die. Can this be changed or not? From the point of view of one theory it cannot, from another it can be changed up to a certain point, not much generally. These are simply different theories, and which is true we know only when we die ourselves. Perhaps we do not know then, probably we don't. There again there are different theories.

MR. L. I find, in trying to study myself, that I always want to avoid unpleasant emotions, and miss many opportunities of seeing myself.

MR. O. That is your business. You must judge what is best.

MR. L. How can one prepare for unpleasant emotions?

MR. O. I do not know which emotions you mean, so I cannot answer. Sometimes one has to face them, sometimes one is right to avoid them.

MR. R. I find it very difficult to avoid catching negative emotions from other people.

MR. O. Yes, it is difficult, but there is a good way to avoid it, which is not to talk about unpleasant things. Most people cannot resist the temptation to talk about unpleasant things and increase and increase their negative emotion.

* * *

Tuesday. June 28th 1938. (Warwick Gardens.)

[Written questions.]

MISS S. Just recently I have been able to observe myself a good many times during the day. However, for the last four or five days I have found it increasingly difficult and could think of no reason except that I have been rather tired physically. Can delicate people put as much energy into work as strong ones?

MR. O. It is always going up and down, you know. Better days, worse days.

MISS S. In connection with this, I find that when I get over-tired physically, which it is difficult for me to avoid, this often results at the same time in negative emotion, in the form of depression generally, which I do not find it easy to get rid of. I cannot understand why the emotions should have anything to do with a physical state, and would like to know if this is wrong work of centres and also how I can get rid of it.

MR. O. It may be wrong work of centres and also many other things. It is a fact that when one is really ill one is more mechanical than usual. Then, of course, one can imagine one is ill when one is not ill at all. Most of our illness is imaginary, at any rate in its effects.

MISS S. Did you say we could distinguish between 'I's and groups of 'I's?

MR. O. Yes, sometimes we can, only you must find examples for yourself and tell me, if you want me to say more.

MISS T. Mr. O. last week mentioned that complicated physical work will make us more aware of ourselves. How are we able to undertake this, as it seems very necessary for work?

MR. O. I will speak about it later.

MISS T. As the week advances I find myself more and more asleep; lectures once a week do not seem sufficient. Is there anything I can do to keep awake?

MR. O. Quite right, but you must begin somewhere. Too much at once will not be good either. There is nothing special to do. Try to remember. I will come back to that later.

MISS T. Are there any particular books on esoteric ideas which you can advise? The choice of books seems important.

MR. O. No. There are many books, but how can I advise? I must know what you have read before, what you are prepared for and so on. There are many books from which you can find something, but you must expect very little from books always.

MISS T. Making effort will sometimes cause tension, particularly of the head muscles. How can I avoid this?

MR. O. This is more imaginary than anything, you know. It is necessary to continue to make efforts.

MISS A. Does consciousness exclude the possibility of disliking a thing—for instance, deliberate cruelty? . . .

MR. O. Such things as cruelty (what we call 'deliberate' means that one can do it or not do it) can be only mechanical, it cannot be conscious. There are many reasons for that which you will understand later on. But the expression 'deliberate cruelty' is a wrong expression. This is one of our chief illusions, that we have choice. We always deceive ourselves. In mechanical manifestations, we have no choice. If it happens, it happens. We are machines, and if our machines work in a certain way, and if we let them work, then we have no power to do or not to do

MISS A. Can dislike exist without its emotional colouring, which, I take it, is always negative?

MR. O. No, like or dislike is a sign of emotion. If I look at this table, I neither like nor dislike it. Like or dislike may be instinctive emotion, but in this case it is just the same.

MISS A. Under what centre do you classify the desire to confide in people? I find it very hard to resist even when realizing it is against my own interests.

MR. O. It may be different in different cases, and I cannot give one answer to fit all cases. It may be weakness, habit, self-pity. Generally some kind of weakness.

MISS A. Are ascetic practices useful in that they strengthen the will, or do they only strengthen the illusion of will?

MR. O. Ascetic practices may be on very different levels, so it is difficult to answer that in general.

MISS A. Would the higher type of man feel the need to express himself in art forms?

MR. O. It depends on many other things.

MISS A. Would he preserve his instincts intact, or would they become sublimated or would they fall away?

MR. O. That depends what you call instincts. For a long time you have thought wrongly about this question of instincts. Will you explain what you mean by this word?

MISS A. Well, self-preservation, the sexual instinct. . . .

MR. O. That is too general. What else?

MISS A. Running away from danger, for instance.

MR. O. This is not instinct. That is why I wanted you to make it clear what you meant. We call instinctive only the inner work of the organism. Self-preservation as an instinct is more literature than actual fact. Particularly in man, there are many kinds of intellectual ideas which enter into it. About higher type of man we cannot say, as we are not higher type of man, but we know anyway that we do not use all instinctive centre as it can be used, so in higher development a man will have more instincts than we have, not less.

MISS A. I find it very hard to reconcile the existence of carnivora with 'plan'.

MR. O. In thinking about plan, we put too many of our own ideas into it. Why are carnivora worse than other beings? Why do you mention them particularly?

MISS A. I do not think they are worse, but I think the idea of creating carnivora is hard to understand. Why create one form of life if it is to be preyed on by another?

MR. O. But why do you mention this particular form?

MISS A. Because the point about life seems to be that it is living, not that it should be eaten.

MR. O. The whole principle is that one form eats another, that nothing exists without eating something else.

MISS A. But what about herbivora?

MR. O. They eat plants. There is no difference. All things passing into another without interruption or change of plan.

MISS A. But was it meant to be like that or is it a sort of distortion of the plan?

MR. O. We have no right to speak of distortion. We have to take it as it is and suppose they were made like that for some purpose. But the point is that there is no difference between one and the other. All organic life on the earth is based on this principle that one thing lives on another.

MISS A. Does it help one in the understanding of the ideas of time, set forth in your chapter on Eternal Recurrence, to think of the human race as a living organism and lives of people as cells constantly renewing themselves?

MR. O. Yes, it may help, but it is not exactly our subject. We may return to this when we have more material to speak about it.

MISS A. What discarded human trait does a cat embody?

MR. O. That is difficult to answer. It is an idea taken from the *New Model*. It may be useful, but at present we must look at things from another point of view. Discarded traits is only one idea which was suggested. More probably, from the point of view of plan, of Great Laboratory, all animals, insects, plants and so on are the results of experiments made in order to develop certain new possibilities; not discarded, but each complete in itself. But it is only one hypothesis, not necessarily true in all cases.

MISS A. You talk in your book of the existence in man of a principle from which barbarism develops. Is this something apart from the bad working of centres?

MR. O. It is mechanicalness. All centres can work mechanically, can work by themselves, so that things just happen. Barbarism, evil, if you like, all comes from this mechanicalness.

MISS A. Is missing a person a negative part of love? And if the person died and one felt sorrow, would this still be negative emotion?

MR. O. You must learn to distinguish. Negative emotions are generally based on imagination and identification, so you must not in your mind try to find causes for real grief, feeling of loss and so on. That will not explain it. You must try to look at things where there is no real emotion, because real emotions happen relatively seldom, whereas we can be negative twenty-four hours of the day.

MISS T. For school-work to be constructive, it is evident that constant attention is required on the part of the individual, which I am personally most anxious to apply. Progress to knowledge is, of necessity, slow; but there comes a time when desire for a more complete understanding of the teaching demands material which can only be supplied in lectures. For this reason I feel that it would be an advantage to attend lectures more frequently than once a week.

MR. O. I quite agree with you, but at present there are six groups and only four evenings, so that many people cannot come even once every week. We shall have a bigger house next year, and then it will be possible to come more often.

MR. B. I realize, however, that, apart from the difficulty of arranging this, the content of each lecture is too vast to be completely apprehended by those who attend, even during the period available between lectures. Possibly, therefore, it would be more advantageous for a beginner to be able to discuss the lectures as they occur with others who are also hearing them for the first time?

MR. O. Yes, quite true, but again we cannot offer you space for that. But it is on the way to being organized, and I will speak again later about this.

MISS T. We are not all in the same state and each of our minds is different, so that perception varies with the individual. For this reason some of us could probably help others to assimilate more completely what has been said at each lecture.

MR. O. Quite right and quite necessary, but generally discussion is a little later. All groups have to discuss things at a certain time.

MR. B. Is such discussion recommended? If so, would it be possible to arrange such discussion?

MR. O. Yes, as I have just said, you will be told about that. It will be arranged and organized.

MR. B. Is there any essential difference between imagining and associative thinking? Is associative thinking also a bad habit?

MR. O. Yes, there is associative thinking which goes quite by itself, and imagining in which you give at least the original shock to start it. Associative thinking you can be quite indifferent to.

MRS. L. Are what we term 'natural laws' false deductions arising out of our wrong conception of time and space?

MR. O. What do you mean by 'natural laws'?

MRS. L. I meant, really, the laws from which you said we could free ourselves. The law of cause and effect as we see it. . . . The law of gravity, the law of the changing seasons.

MR. O. Gravity depends on the point of view. It may not be a false deduction. Seasons are not a law, just pure observation. In a sense it may be, but it depends on which scale we are speaking. All that we call natural laws from ordinary deductions are not reliable because they are made with our eyes half shut, more than half shut—just through a slit. So we cannot see many things and do not have fundamental knowledge. Esoteric knowledge begins with the study of fundamental laws, and with this knowledge what we call natural laws, the result of scientific and philosophic deduction, verified by means of the fundamental laws, can be more reliable.

MRS. L. How can we begin to understand the true nature of time and space?

MR. O. We do not begin with that in this way. I will speak about it later.

MR. D. Once, after having decided to put off some work to the next day, I suddenly found myself in the middle of doing it. Would you give me an explanation of what is working in me there?

MR. O. Different centres. Different 'I's, personalities. We are so different, you know. Yet we always say 'I decided' and again 'I found . . .', 'I did . . .' and really you are at least twenty people. One 'I' decides to put it off, another begins to do it and so on.

MISS L. Is the deciding the property of intellectual centre?

MR. O. There is no means of judging from what was said. One does one thing, another does another. That happens at every moment of our life. When you begin to observe yourself you begin to notice it. That is all the difference.

MISS Y. Is being the result of the way in which knowledge is used?

MR. O. No. Being is what you are at a given moment. All these different twenty personalities, groups of 'I's, many of them do not even know one another, and all say 'I' thinking they speak for the whole, which is quite wrong.

MISS Y. Is physical fear the identification of oneself with one's body?

MR. O. Not necessarily. It may be identification with something else—imagination, some fantasy, dreams.

MISS Y. Am I right in thinking that when one feels a strong response to the truth of ideas such as those in the teaching of the Bible, or in the ideas of the system, one is using emotional part of intellectual centre, and when this immediate feeling passes and one thinks further of how these ideas affect oneself, one is using the intellectual part of emotional centre?

MR. O. No, not intellectual part of emotional centre. In any case, this observation of centres is a little too much from thought. You just think about this problem, whereas the study of centres and parts of centres must come from many practical observations and comparison of these.

MR. H. In the Vedânta philosophy, the expressions 'the self' and 'the essence' appear to be used to describe the same thing. Is the unified 'I' a part of essence according to the present system?

MR. O. I cannot be responsible for the terminology of other systems. They may occasionally coincide or they may not. Particularly in Indian philosophy, it is difficult to be sure about the terms because of translation. In many cases the meaning cannot be found; in others the meaning has changed through the years. So we cannot compare terminology.

MR. H. When a man dies, the different parts of him go to different places. Of how many separate parts does a conscious man consist, and what are their names?

MR. O. We can speak about this only theoretically. We cannot know about conscious man. About ourselves we can speak theoretically, but not about degrees of men different from us.

MR. H. What is the meaning of the word 'soul' according to this system?

MR. O. That I mentioned last time. It means simply life principle. Some kind of higher matters which make the body alive, and disappear from the body after death.

MR. H. Buffers were mentioned the week before last. What are they?

MR. O. That will come a little later. In the meantime, I can just say this: buffers are connected with conscience. Conscience is a word we use generally in a conventional sense, to mean a sort of educated emotional habit. Really conscience is a special capacity which everybody possesses but which nobody can use in the state of sleep. Even if we feel conscience for a moment, accidentally, it will be a very painful experience, so painful that immediately we want to get rid of it. People who have glimpses occasionally invent all kinds of methods to get rid of this feeling. It is the capacity to feel at the same time all that we feel at different times. Try to understand that all these different 'I's have different feelings. One 'I' feels that he likes something, while another hates it and a third 'I' is indifferent. But we never feel them at the same time because between them are things called buffers. Because of these we cannot use conscience, cannot feel at the same time two contradictory things which we feel at different times. If a man does happen to feel it, he suffers. So buffers in our present state are even necessary things, without which a man will go mad. If he understands about them and prepares himself, then after some time he may start to destroy the contradictions, and break the buffers down.

MR. H. A child born with a minor internal malformation may therefore be subject to chronic ill-health. Is this in essence?

MR. O. Yes. But there are many different possibilities. It is impossible to speak about this in general.

MISS G. If, as I understand Mr. O. to say, the planets may influence the world, that is, cause wars, and so on, how is it that they have no influence on men personally?

MR. O. We will speak about that later.

MISS G. May we hear again what was said about telepathy? A question was asked about whether there was such a thing.

MR. O. And I said no. Not for us, in any case. For higher man, but not for us.

I must repeat first what I spoke about in the Tuesday group at the previous meeting. At the same time those who heard should try to listen, as I shall add to what I said then.

I spoke about the necessity, in the study of man, of studying the world in which he lives; first, in order to find the place of man in the universe, and secondly with the idea of trying to find why man is such as he is, why he cannot be different, why he cannot do differently. We cannot find the answer to these questions through the study of man apart from the universe. Man in a certain sense is analogous to the universe and he lives under certain laws. Some of these laws we can understand better from the study of man himself, some we can only understand from the study of the universe.

In relation to the study of the universe you must first try to understand and remember that we use one particular method. We will study the universe on the principle of scale. To take a very simple instance of what I mean by scale: you know your own house on a scale proportionate to your own body; the town you live in you do not know on the same scale—you cannot know the whole of London, and even the parts you do know you do not know in the same way as your own house. England you know on a still smaller scale. It is the same principle which you know from geography, maps and we apply it all the time to the study of the universe.

The earth is on one scale for us, because we live on it. We take the other planets separately from the earth and all together; they have a certain effect on our life, but only all together and only those in our own Solar System. Those in other solar systems we do not consider as planets, but take just suns with all that is included in them. Later you will find for yourselves examples of the difference between this method and the ordinary scientific point of view.

So in studying man and the world in which he lives, we begin by the earth. The earth is one of the planets in the Solar System and is in the sphere of influence of the sun. The planets, the earth and the moon depend on the sun in many ways. The sun is one of the stars in the Milky Way. This galaxy is one of many, one of an unknown number of similar galaxies, with the possibility of many different ones which we do not know at all. So you see we have all worlds, all suns, sun, planets, earth, moon. We can put them in this form:

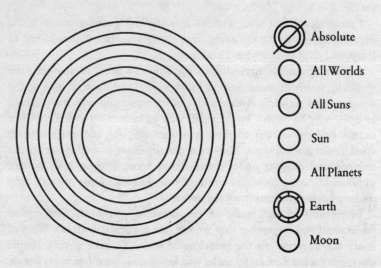

This is called the Ray of Creation. You see man is part of organic life on the earth. Organic life is a kind of sensitive film which covers the earth and serves a certain definite purpose. It serves as a connection. The sun, the planets and the moon may connect with the earth to a certain extent, but not sufficiently; many vibrations will be lost. Organic life catches these vibrations and transfers them to the earth. In that sense, mankind, plants and animals all play the same rôle. Plants catch a certain kind of vibrations, animals and man catch others, and all serve the same purpose of connecting different parts of the Solar System with the earth.

Then there is another interesting thing. We are here on the earth, in this film, under the influence of the moon, under certain influences of the planets, under the influence of the sun, under the influence of all suns and possibly under the influence of all worlds. Certainly the influence of all suns and all worlds on individual man is very small. About the influence of the moon we do not know much, but it plays a very important part. So you see everything is connected. Without understanding how everything is connected with the moon, with the planets and with the sun, we cannot understand the position of man and the possibility of development and life as it is. When all this is taken into consideration we understand, for instance, one expression which it is impossible to explain without understanding this diagram: that man 'lives in a very bad place in the universe'. Many things which we regard as removable and possible to change and against which we fight are really the result of this position of organic life on the earth. If we were on the moon, the position would be still worse. On the earth there is still the possibility of development. Development means that we can develop certain parts of us. Suppose planetary influences are supposed to be responsible for wars and revolutions, but individual man is very little under planetary influences. This part of him that can be affected is not developed. On the other hand, man physically is under the influence of the sun, but he can be under a much bigger influence if he becomes connected with higher centres. Development comes from passing from one kind of influence to another. We can become free from moon's influence and can be under the influence of planets, sun, stars.

MISS T. Will you explain why higher parts of man are under the influence of the sun?

MR. O. Remember only one thing: higher and lower means conscious and mechanical. Moon's influence is only mechanical, and only mechanical parts can respond. Other influences become more and more conscious and we have to become more and more conscious to respond.

You will see later that there is nothing new in it. It is a different classification of well known facts.

MISS C. Wars and revolutions are caused by the influence of the planets; what is the effect of the moon?

MR. O. The moon is in control of movements. If I move my arm, this is moon's influence. The moon is like the weight on old-fashioned clocks. All the mechanism works because of this weight. The weight drags and the mechanism revolves.

MISS C. Why is it that the planets can affect man in masses and not individually?

MR. O. That part of man which can be affected by the planets—essence —is either small, undeveloped or mixed with personality. Personality is not affected, it reflects these influences. Because of this, man lives under the Law of Accident. If man lived in his essence, he would be under the law of planetary influences, under the law of fate. Whether this would be an advantage or not, that is a question.

Essence is hidden in personality. The rays of planetary influence cannot penetrate because personality is accidental, it may be in one state or in another. In masses, people are affected only in certain parts of themselves, parts which are always there. So planetary influences can affect masses of people but in normal cases seldom affect individuals.

MISS C. Does a crowd have essence and personality?

MR. O. A crowd is rather a different thing. The majority of people are No. 1, men with instinctive and moving centre predominating, and their chief motive powers are imagination and imitation. Being in the power of imagination and imitation they very easily accept some kind of mechanical influence, which is immediately exaggerated by imagination, and begin to copy one another.

MR. S. If more people were conscious would there be no wars and revolutions?

MR. O. We must speak about things as they are.

MRS. C. If our aim is to develop ourselves, shall we come individually under the influence of the planets? Isn't that a bad thing?

MR. O. Bad can only be mechanical. We must forget these words, good and bad. They can mean only one thing.

Individually, the influence will be different according to type, not uniform. Individual man will be influenced according to essence, whereas the influence on masses of people is uniform and always disastrous.

MRS. H. Would the relation of earth to sun have any relationship to one's 'I's, for instance?

MR. O. No. The difference is too big. We cannot find psychological influences. We have to wait and speak now about general principles.

MISS C. You say we have a great many 'I's. Does each 'I' have a separate centre?

MR. O. No. You remember the divisions? We have thousands of 'I's; they are divided first by centres, then by personalities, and these divisions run into one another, are not parallel.

MISS A. What is the difference between personalities and 'I's?

MR. O. A personality is a permanent group of 'I's. An 'I' is just one desire, one wish. But this distinction is only for convenience. You may forget it if you like, although it is like that. Just take it that 'I's are small, and personalities already more complicated desires.

MR. M. Do planetary influences differ for man 1, 2 and 3?

MR. O. They are different in their effect on man individually. But in order to be affected individually, man has to develop essence. Man No. 1 can develop essence, and so can man No. 2 and man No. 3. So men 1, 2 and 3 are in that way practically on the same level. The majority of men are No. 1, but that refers to another idea.

MRS. C. Can you tell us more of the nature of the influence of the sun?

MR. O. In the ordinary sense, you can find a lot about it in books. Conscious influence, that is another thing. That will come later, but we must come to it from another side, the possibility of consciousness.

MISS A. Do you mean from books we can read how the sun gives warmth and light? That sort of influence?

MR. O. Physical, chemical—how the rays bring all necessary elements.

MR. M. I do not understand what you mean by conscious influence of the sun.

MR. O. I cannot give simple examples of that. We have not enough material to talk about it now.

Now we must review all that from another point of view. There are two fundamental laws of nature which we must understand. The first is called the Law of Three; the second the Law of Seven.

The Law of Three means that there are three original forces in the world and that every event, every phenomenon is the result of three

313

forces meeting together. When three forces do not meet there is no event, nothing happens. The three forces are called positive, negative and neutralizing. Positive and negative we can observe in many different manifestations. Neutralizing force we are not accustomed to see, although its presence is very clear in physiological and psychological phenomena. If we know about the necessary existence of this force, after observation we begin to notice it, but when we do not know we do not realize that this third element is there. It is a very big subject, so it is quite sufficient if you remember this and try to find three forces in every action. Sometimes you may succeed. Then much later we will come to another aspect of this study, and in this way we meet Indian philosophy really, only it is so mixed with commentaries that it is difficult to find its original form.

The Law of Seven (I will explain later why it is called the Law of Seven), we will take first like this: we imagine the world as a world of vibrations going in different directions, different energies, all vibrations going either up or down. Suppose we take this line here as vibrations growing from five hundred to one thousand:

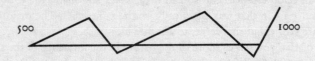

Then in the distance between we can observe two very interesting phenomena. While the vibrations grow and increase in frequency, they do not increase regularly. They increase for a time, then go down; then increase again and go down again. So there are two places where they slow down. This is the Law of Seven. At a certain period there was created a formula of this law which is a representation of a cosmic law. It was shown as a musical scale in which two missing semitones show exactly this slowing down at two intervals between the seven notes.

It is easiest to observe this Law of Seven in human actions. You can see how when people begin to do something—study, work—after some time, without any visible reason, their efforts diminish, work slows down, and if there is not some special effort at a given moment it changes its direction. There is a small but real change in inner strength. Then after some time again there is a slackening and again, if there is not special effort, a change in direction. It can change completely and go in an absolutely different direction, still appearing to be the same thing. There are many phases of human activity which exactly answer to this description. They start one way and without noticing go in exactly the opposite direction.

In cosmic arrangements we can take it like this:

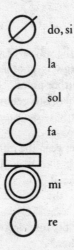

do, si

la

sol

fa

mi

re

This is a descending octave. The interval between <u>do</u> and <u>si</u> is covered in a special way which it is not necessary to go into in this plan. Organic life, the part in which we live, fills the second interval.

So you see that if these intervals are known, and if a method of creating some special effort or arrangement is used in these places, it is possible to avoid these breaks in the octave. Everything goes by octaves. No vibration, movement, activity goes otherwise. Scales vary so we cannot follow them, but we can see the result of them, the result of this Law of Octaves. Even the inner physical work of the organism is under this law.

With certain kinds of effort we can produce these missing semitones and in that way change the work of our machine.

For instance, you remember we spoke about self-remembering, the effort to be conscious, to remember oneself? Later I will explain to you how this effort to remember oneself changes many things in the chemical work of the organism.

MISS S. How can one start to observe this Law of Seven in something?

MR. O. Find how one thing starts and then becomes another thing.

MISS W. If you discover an interval in a certain action and when you start missing, is it likely to go on repeating in that way or will the range of the octave change?

MR. O. If you find examples it will be easier to talk. To answer generally, if nothing is done, the interval will increase with each octave, at the same place.

*   *   *

[Written questions.]

MISS L. Is creation of energy the way over an interval?

MR. O. No, creation of energy is another conversation. How it is created and from what, is a further point.

MISS L. I meant the kind of energy to get over the interval.

MR. O. The origin of all energy is the same, but it can be directed in one way or in another way.

MISS L. Do the intervals lie between the different levels of waking up?

MR. O. No, you cannot put it like that. That anyway is a particular case, and we are talking in general.

MISS L. As you proceed up the octave, do you gather increased energy?

MR. O. It is impossible to say because octave is a general word. It may be one kind of octave or another.

MISS L. Isn't there one octave right up to self-consciousness?

MR. O. It depends on the octave of your efforts.

MISS L. Is the potential energy the same in any octave?

MR. O. No, there are different kinds. You will have more material about this later, but even now we can divide it roughly. There is mechanical energy, life energy, psychic energy and conscious energy. They are not the same, and in our organism all these are produced.

MISS L. How can I use the observation that the Ray of Creation is a descending octave and the attainment of higher consciousness ascending?

MR. O. Ray of Creation is growing that way. Take it as a growing branch. Moon is the growing point. We are on the earth. If we develop, we climb up this. We are not going with creation, but against creation. Development is against Nature and against God. God in Nature is growing, the way of Nature and the way of God.

MISS L. Does emotional centre take over at a definite point?

MR. O. That we cannot specify. It must work all the time. Without emotional centre it is impossible to work.

MISS L. In going against anything mechanical, is energy created through impressions?

MR. O. Partly, yes, but not only.

MISS L. Is there any power outside centres which can be compelled to serve one's aim?

MR. O. Consciousness cannot really be connected with centres. It is outside centres.

MISS L. Can I have awareness in a centre which is not working?

Does awareness in instinctive centre consist also in awareness in all other centres?

MR. O. I do not know what you mean by awareness. Better observe more. Such things cannot be explained except on the basis of concrete examples.

MISS L. What is awareness of a centre?

MR. O. You see, you ask me questions about awareness as though I must know what you mean, and then you ask me what is awareness. You can see that in order for me to judge I must have concrete examples of what you call awareness.

MISS L. Does awareness in the moving part of moving centre always bring in the emotional part?

MR. O. Not necessarily.

MISS L. Can instinctive centre know one is asleep physically?

MR. O. Not instinctive. Either intellectual or emotional.

MISS L. Memories that were clear-cut are now faint. For instance a very clear memory I had of something which happened some time ago was clear until I came into the system. Now if I recall it it is just a memory of a memory. Is this due to being a little more awake?

MR. O. It was probably connected with strong identification. When you look without identification it becomes fainter and may disappear.

MISS L. Is complete non-identification self-consciousness?

MR. O. They are two different sides of the same thing.

* * *

MRS. S. Could you tell me, as regards the seven phases of vibrations going up from five hundred to one thousand, how do the other five semitones of the musical scale come in?

MR. O. Later we can take other figures referring to it, but at present I want you to understand only this principle. We are speaking only about the missing semitones between _fa_ and _mi_ and between _si_ and _do_ which indicate the places of these intervals in the cosmic octave. This is a symbolic representation of a cosmic law.

MRS. S. What is an example of neutralizing force?

MR. O. This is a most important question. In this state, as we are, men Nos. 1, 2 and 3, with slow intellectual centre, insufficient emotional, we are really third force blind. We do not see it. If we know about its existence we begin to notice it. After some time, if you make yourself think, you will begin to notice it.

Q. You spoke about octaves of remembering. . . .

MR. O. Not exactly. I said that if you work, your work may form itself into octaves and will have intervals. If you do not know where the intervals come, then your work will change.

Q. In attaining one's aim, self-remembering would be the octave. Up that octave, do you gather increasing energy?

MR. O. This is the most difficult octave. Because, such as we are, we cannot make octaves in self-remembering. It will only start and disappear. If we make two notes or three notes it will be very good. We have not enough initial energy. But we must start and start and start until we make an octave.

Q. But coming from the beginning there is one main octave?

MR. O. Theoretically, yes, but not in actual work. Such as we are it will be interrupted. We have to start every day afresh. _Do_, _re_; _do_, _re_, _mi_. . . . For a long time no further than _mi_.

Q. And when you get to the interval?

MR. O. Then you stop. You do not know what to do. But you must not be tired. If you go on, some time you will learn to pass this interval.

MR. D. Are there many people who do not go on at all?

MR. O. Certainly. People who think they already remember themselves.

MISS C. If you get a _do_, _re_, _mi_, then what happens?

MR. O. Then you go back. For a long time you will not pass the interval.

MISS C. And when you have passed the interval?

MR. O. When you have, then we will talk about it! It is different, doing and talking.

MISS C. Is it possible to recognize going from _do_ to _re_?

MR. O. It depends on the octave again. Some octaves are mechanical, descending. All ascending octaves have to be conscious, with effort every moment.

MISS C. Is the missing <u>do</u> below the moon the same as the one above all worlds?

MR. O. We will speak about it when we come to it. But I will put it in if you like. It does not mean any special thing, but just that all the rest is one thing. Take an apple: you have seeds, skin, juice, cells. You can study all these. Then you have the apple as a whole, the universe as a whole.

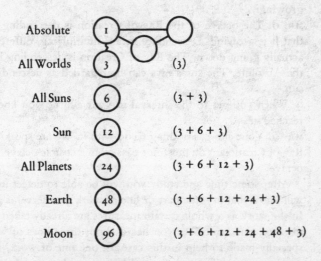

Absolute	1	
All Worlds	3	(3)
All Suns	6	(3 + 3)
Sun	12	(3 + 6 + 3)
All Planets	24	(3 + 6 + 12 + 3)
Earth	48	(3 + 6 + 12 + 24 + 3)
Moon	96	(3 + 6 + 12 + 24 + 48 + 3)

Here we have Absolute; then all worlds and here there may be many other similar or different Rays of Creation. The three forces in the Absolute are one, three, but one. Each can be another, positive can be negative, negative neutralizing and so on, according to the need of the moment and the Will of the Absolute. The Absolute is supposed to have absolute will, so it is called World 1. In the next, all worlds, the forces are already separated. Three forces, World 3. The next is all suns, where there are three forces from World 3 and three of its own, World 6. And so on, down to moon, where there are ninety-six forces. There are two interesting things you must know. First, the Will of the Absolute expressed in World 1 reaches only World 3 and cannot reach further. From here, in World 6, begin mechanical laws. The forces from World 1 do not reach our world, but the energies of all worlds reach the earth. These figures mean the quantity of orders of laws. In the Absolute there is only one law, the Will of the Absolute. Then there are already three laws in World 3, and so on. Earth exists under forty-eight laws, moon under ninety-six. We will learn many details about this later. So you see, since we live on the earth, we live under forty-eight laws apart from our own laws.

Q. You said the Ray of Creation was a growing branch and a descending octave. Is not man trying to attain consciousness also growing?

MR. O. The octave of the Ray of Creation is descending in the sense that it is growing. Descending means multiplying, differentiating, not actually going down. The Ray of Creation is descending in relation to the Absolute. The sun's rays can be regarded as descending from the sun.

Q. When you get to the interval in your aim do you know you have reached it?

MR. O. Your aim has nothing to do with it. We are speaking about the Ray of Creation. You must not pass from a cosmic octave to a personal octave.

After some time and study you will be able to detect intervals. You will know that in some part or line of work an interval is approaching. In the work as a whole certain measures are already taken for this. For instance, you remember you heard about three lines of work. That is specially made to help in this case. In one line of work, say first line, you come to an interval. Second line of work may come in there and help you over it. You will see the application of the same principle to many things, even in our organism. School work uses many cosmic ideas. Suppose your work begins (not self-remembering, that is special); this refers to all your first line of work. Then you come to an interval, after do, re, mi.

Do Re Mi -		first line
	Do Re Mi -	second line
		Do Re Mi · third line

The second do represents here second line of work. Then this also reaches the interval. Then begins third line. In that way one line of work will help another. You have octaves in everything—personal work, group work, third line.

I just want to tell you about one other thing to do with these intervals. Maybe some of you have heard that we have a house in the country where people can come and work if they feel the need of it. It is almost full now with people from other groups, but at the same time there is a possibility for some more people to come and try to work.

I will just give you a short history to explain. In 1917, when the revolution began in Petersburg, a certain number of people went to the North Caucasus. At first there were very few people and then more people came, and in the spring of 1918 we numbered about forty, I think. Unfortunately, we had to move about from place to place all the time, but all the same we had to work together. In the country we cut down trees and sawed wood. When we lived in towns we had to work in the house, go to the bazaars and so on. From the beginning we realized what an enormous difference it made, that it was one thing to talk and another to work together. Later, when some of us came to Europe, we tried several times to organize something of that kind. There were several attempts, but they failed. Here in England, ten years ago, we began on a very small scale, with just a few people. From 1931 we had a permanent place at Sevenoaks, quite small, but with a garden and so on, and about twenty people could come at week-ends and work there. Then we got a bigger place. Then, two years ago, we got a much bigger place still, where we are now. It is called Lyne Place, two miles from Virginia Water. About twenty people generally live there, some people come down on week-days and on Sundays there are usually more than a hundred people. They work in the fields, with animals—all kinds of things. At present I cannot promise for certain that even those who wish can join the work there. You must ask and then you will have an answer. But I want to arrange small groups there, every Friday at 3 o'clock, of fifteen to twenty people. Those who would like to come on Fridays should give their names to Madame K. and when it is possible you will be invited there. If one particular Friday you cannot come, just mention it or write later. In this way you can see the place at any rate, and later perhaps you may like to come and work. In any case it will be interesting, and in some cases very useful.

MISS C. Must it be 3 o'clock? Not later?

MR. O. We will start to talk at 3 o'clock. Perhaps later it may be arranged for another day or something.

Q. Will this be in addition to these Tuesday meetings?

MR. O. Yes, for those who have time. Later when we have this big house in London everything will be much easier. At the same time it is a chance for you to see this place. You may be interested in it.

MRS. H. Is one directed what work to do?

MR. O. Oh yes, certainly. It is real work there. Some people have some profession, know some kind of work. There are many things.

Q. Is that psychological work?

MR. O. Yes, very! Try it and you will see.

Q. Is there any chance of going in the evenings?

MR. O. Not just at present.

MISS S. How long will it last for? About two hours?

MR. O. Yes, about that. But if it is difficult, do not increase difficulties for yourself. There will be another time. Later perhaps it will be possible to come on Sundays. At present there are too many people already coming there for more to come.

Q. What about Saturday afternoon?

MR. O. Please, do not bargain! Friday afternoon.

Q. Is everything we do done in octaves?

MR. O. Unfortunately not yet. We work on just one note most of the time—do, do, do, do—that is our music.

Q. I am not very sure what self-remembering is.

MR. O. That is why I say that we must become clear about these things before we come to observations about intricate things, so you had better concentrate on self-remembering. It is more important than observations. You cannot understand by definitions. You must try, and the more you try the clearer your understanding will become.

MRS. S. Will you say again what are the three forces?

MR. O. All events, phenomena, are the result of three forces meeting together—positive, negative and neutralizing. Or they are sometimes called active, passive and neutralizing.

Q. Will you later be able to tell us where the low do comes in the Ray of Creation?

MR. O. Yes and no. It is here below the moon. It is nothing. It is also absolute.

Q. Are vitamins an example of neutralizing force?

MR. O. In asking a question like that you must say: 'If this is active force and this is passive, is this neutralizing force?' Otherwise it cannot be answered.

Q. Last week somebody spoke about neutralizing force being a catalyst. . . .

MR. O. You have two matters, only they do not produce an effect. A small trace of a third matter is added and they produce the desired effect.

Q. Is the latent heat in the evaporation of water an example of third force?

MR. O. I think that is a little dangerous. In experimenting we cannot take all circumstances, cosmic circumstances into consideration. In every phenomenon of that kind there are present psychic circumstances and cosmic circumstances which we do not know and cannot take into account . . . for instance, psychic conditions connected with the intelligence of matter it is out of our possibility to know at present. In some cases I think it is easier to find such things in purely chemical and physiological manifestations. Hormones and vitamins, for instance, definitely play the part of third force.

*   *   *

Monday. July 4th 1938.

[End of meeting only.]

MR. H. If one sees a feature in oneself, such as a mechanical habit, does it become weaker the moment one sees it?

MR. O. No, seeing does not diminish it.

MR. H. What does?

MR. O. Working against it.

MR. H. What to put it in its place?

MR. O. Nothing. Why put anything?

MR. H. How to check it?

MR. O. It depends on the feature. First one should try to check it by direct struggle. Suppose one finds that one argues too much; then one must not argue, that is all. Why put anything in its place? No need to put anything in its place—just silence.

MR. H. Is the idea to save energy?

MR. O. No, don't call it saving energy or anything else; just call it arguing. Otherwise it will be justifying, or arguing again, or bargaining.

MRS. H. There are some things one believes in very strongly; could one only fight them with intellectual centre?

MR. O. When you say 'believe' it may be an inner conviction based on unconscious observation. One may 'believe' something in oneself because by experience one knows that one can believe in it. Do you mean that, or something different?

MRS. H. I think it is more a useless personality which I enjoy although I know it is useless. And I cannot cope with it by saying it is useless.

MR. O. In such a case you can struggle with this personality by strengthening other personalities opposed to it. Suppose you have a certain feature you want to struggle with, then try to find some other feature incompatible with it and which may be useful. If in your present equipment you find nothing sufficiently strong to put against it, look in your memory. Suppose you find some feature that is incompatible with the one you want to get rid of, and that can be useful, then just replace one by the other. But it can also happen that even then they can both live happily together: one can be in the evening and another in the morning, and never meet.

MRS. H. What then?

MR. O. It is necessary to think in every case. In each particular case sometimes it is possible to find something. There is only one real danger: if for a long time one goes on without making sufficient efforts, or without doing anything seriously, then, instead of becoming one, one becomes divided into two, and all features and personalities are divided into two groups, one part useful to the work and helping work, and another part either indifferent or even unfriendly. This is the real danger, because if two parts begin to form like this, indifference of one spoils the result of work of the other. So it is necessary to struggle very quickly and very strongly against that, otherwise it may lead to double crystallization.

MISS C. What do you mean by crystallizing?

MR. O. We use this word in a particular sense—any feature may become crystallized, like buffers crystallize. This term came from the theosophical terminology, it is sometimes a useful term. I think everybody has heard about higher bodies, astral, mental and causal? This terminology is useful because it explains things that other terminology does not explain clearly. The idea is that one has one physical body only, and development consists in the development of higher bodies. So man No. 5 corresponds to crystallization of the astral body, man No. 6 to crystallization of the mental body, and man No. 7 to crystallization of the causal body.

MR. H. Would one know of those two groups forming in one?

MR. O. Yes. If one learnt to observe oneself one can find when it begins to happen, and one cannot leave it going on for a long time, because if one leaves it for a long time it becomes every day more and more difficult to struggle with it. So one has to struggle with it very quickly. But it manifests itself differently in different cases: in one personality it manifests itself in one way and in another in another way.

MRS. S. Are you speaking of something different from identification?

MR. O. Yes, I don't speak about identification. I am speaking of the danger when, instead of becoming more and more one, one becomes divided into two parts.

MR. H. Is that characteristic of most people's work at one point or another?

MR. O. If they wait too long without making serious efforts or serious decisions in their work, they may have the beginning of this double crystallization.

MISS H. One side would be for the work and another against it?

MR. O. Not necessarily consciously against, but simply through slackness or something like that.

MRS. J. Then the important thing is to make them meet?

MR. O. But you cannot make them meet; they are so well divided that they do not meet—each has its own part.

MRS. H. They sort of acknowledge one another so that you get no resistance?

MR. O. Yes, you get no results in your work, and after a time you may even get wrong results.

MR. C. Is that a case of acquiring a lot of knowledge without understanding?

MR. O. No. Even understanding is possible in such a case, only without action. You see, even knowledge and understanding cannot help if one does not work on being. If will does not grow at the same time, one can understand and not be able to do anything.

MR. C. You mean one has theoretical understanding, but one does not do anything about it?

MR. O. Yes.

MRS. R. Could Stevenson have it in such an idea as Dr. Jekyll and Mr. Hyde?

MR. O. No, that is extremes; it is too visible. It is much more clever than that; they disguise themselves all right.

MR. H. You say in this state it is possible to understand and not be able to do anything about it?

MR. O. Yes, if from the beginning one did not start making serious efforts to develop will. If will remains undeveloped then development of understanding will not help much. One can understand very much, but at the same time not be able to do anything about it.

MRS. N. Is will part of being?

MR. O. Yes, the same as consciousness or understanding. Only if you work too much on understanding and disregard will, then instead of growing stronger your will will become weaker, or will remain the same as it was. With our will, the will of men Nos. 1, 2 and 3, we may only control one centre, with all the concentration possible for us. We can never control two or three centres, and yet centres are dependent on one another. Suppose we decide to control one centre and, meanwhile, other centres go on by themselves, then they will immediately corrupt the centre that we want to control, and bring it again to mechanical reaction. We will speak more about it later.

MR. H. How can one attain this kind of will?

MR. O. This was explained in relation to stop exercise. Those who heard the lecture about stop exercise may remember it. This is at the basis of stop exercise. It was explained, in relation to stop exercise, that it can be done only if you put yourself under some other will, because your own will cannot do that. Sometimes it may be necessary to control four centres, and the maximum of your energy of will can only control one centre. So another will is necessary. This is why school discipline is necessary, and school exercises.

MR. H. Can we have them?

MR. O. First it is necessary to know about it. It will be the subject of the first lecture in the new house, so just wait a little.

MR. H. Is it never of any use to replace one bad identification of a long standing by a lesser one as a means to try and break the first one?

MR. O. No, this is self-deception. If it is identification, it will be the same; one identification cannot be better or worse than another.

MR. H. I thought it would take less energy and less time.

MR. O. First you cannot control it or destroy it, so why replace one with another? It is simply self-deception.

* * *

Tuesday. July 1938. (Warwick Gardens.)

MISS L. Last week you said three forces couldn't work without three elements. Could we hear more about that?

MR. O. Yes, in the course of the lecture. If you have a definite question I will answer it.

MR. R. Does the normal life of a man represent an octave? I thought from birth to the reproductive period might be the first stage, the reproductive period the second stage and the period of senility the last stage.

MR. O. No, it will be artificial. People are different in this case; and there are many people whose lives consist only of beginnings of octaves.

MR. B. Does the energizing quality of certain impressions not depend to a certain extent on identification?

MR. O. It is quite opposite to identification. Identification destroys it.

MR. L. Are the hydrogens that are at present classified under the one heading 'impressions' divided into categories?

MR. O. Yes, they are. As I said, four hydrogens constitute what we call impressions; impressions are divided into four classes—48, 24, 12 and 6.

MR. B. Why is hydrogen taken as the basic substance? Has it anything to do with the hydrogen atom being the simplest?

MR. O. Yes, it is connected with this theory. Evidently, at the time when this language was accepted or formed, this was an important theory, and it was based on that. We will talk later about it.

MR. B. I do not understand why schools are necessary. Would it be possible to work without a group, as a chela working under a guru?

MR. O. Yes, why not? It is quite possible if you are rich enough. That is the question. In some cases some people—like some Indian emperors, such as Akbar and Shah Jehan—had their own guru. So it is a question of possibility—how much one can pay. At the same time it must be understood that one loses in any case in this way because a group helps—school helps.

MISS R. Is the desire to dress well necessarily a sign of considering or identification?

MR. O. No, it may be very different—it may be based on quite different considerations. It may be quite real and quite necessary.

MR. S. You stated that it is necessary to learn how to store up energy for advancement—that we now use up all our intake for living. How can we learn to accumulate such a reserve or store?

MR. O. About that we will speak later to-day or next time. But this is the second question. The first is how to stop waste, how to stop leaks. There are too many leaks in the machine.

MISS G. What exactly is meant by 'knowledge'?

MR. O. Well, it is just meant in the ordinary sense. Take what you ordinarily call knowledge. There is no need to try to formulate such ordinary ideas. What was necessary to understand was that knowledge is not all that we can want; that knowledge is different from being, and you have to work by two lines—on knowledge and on being. One cannot replace another.

MISS W. Is knowledge used up and replenished, or is it more in the nature of a store which can be borrowed from?

MR. O. I don't quite understand the question. Both probably.

MISS W. Can 'intention' be one of the three forces?

MR. O. In some cases it may.

MR. M. Are the earth, the sun and the planets different hydrogens? If so, what is the hydrogen of each?

MR. O. No, you see for celestial bodies like that there is a different term. They are called points—'points' in the scheme of creation. You remember the diagram of Three Octaves of Radiation? In this case, Absolute, sun, earth and moon are called points. It can be established which hydrogens pass through them—even which hydrogens they are themselves; but at present we don't need it; although in the Table of Hydrogens you can see where each hydrogen comes from.

MR. M. Does any of the forces 1, 2, 3, passing through a hydrogen cause it to become a different hydrogen?

MR. O. No. They cause it to become either carbon, oxygen or nitrogen. It depends which force passes through the hydrogen.

MR. H. Nature is to me a word that personifies the forces governing all that happens on our world and in the cosmos; God the spirit or single force that unifies all. Hence the system appears to me to be within God or nature. Can you please simplify your statement that the system is outside God and nature, so that I may understand it in your sense?

MR. O. I didn't say outside God and nature; I spoke about work—the individual work of each person—going against nature and God—and what is called God is the mind or general intelligence behind all creation; that must be accepted because things couldn't happen; and nature is all that is created. And in this things partly happen and are partly regulated by mechanical laws and so on. And work doesn't enter into the idea of creation, nor into the idea of mechanical continuation, mechanical happening—it is against both—it is a current against the current.

MR. H. In the sense that I understand the word 'nature', no happening can be unnatural, since all appears to me to happen within nature's framework. For example, it is commonly considered for it to be unnatural for a mother to be cruel to her child. The forces that actuate the mother are of nature. She is wrong but not unnatural. Does this viewpoint need correcting?

MR. O. No. That is pathological and negative—that doesn't enter into this. Nature created man and let him go in the world in a certain form. Nature doesn't produce further development of man; he must develop himself if he can, and if he wishes. This is what I mean. Nobody said unnatural; if it happens, it is natural. But this work doesn't happen; it must be done. It is not on the level of things that happen—it is incommensurable with things that happen, because it doesn't happen, but it can be done consciously, intentionally.

MR. B. We were told that impressions were food, imparting energy; does this imply some principle for selecting nutritive impressions—as surely some impressions are relatively poisonous?

MR. O. Yes, certainly—self-remembering, first of all; because impressions that come when you are asleep produce one effect, and impressions that come when you are awake produce quite a different effect—you are able to select and not take unnecessary impressions.

MRS. D. Last Friday I asked whether it was possible for people who collect money to collect knowledge at the same time. You said that you had never met a person like that.

MR. O. If one concentrates on collecting money, then generally one doesn't care for knowledge—in any case, that is my personal experience.

MRS. D. What about people who are born rich and need not collect money: could they collect knowledge? Or are they too busy in keeping and spending their money so that they have no time for anything else?

MR. O. That is quite another question—then they keep the money. It is not prohibited; it is their own business. And some people like Shah Jehan and Akbar managed to collect knowledge at the same time, although they were very rich.

MRS. D. Why is it that people are insincere? I have noticed insincerity specially in English people; is it due to upbringing?

MR. O. No, I don't think there is any national difference. I think all people are insincere. There are many reasons for that; first it is mechanical, and second, you cannot be sincere. You think it is a question of education or decision; it is a much bigger thing. One must be conscious in order to be sincere. If man is asleep how can he be sure he is sincere? Words just happen. He does not speak in the way he wishes—he has no control, and he doesn't know—both things are necessary—knowledge and being. It is a very serious thing to learn how to be sincere, even in small things.

MR. C. How can one try to escape from using formatory apparatus when trying to think of the Hydrogen Table?

MR. O. Not only about the Hydrogen Table. This is a very important question, because there is not a single question in the system, and not a single part of the system that can be understood by formatory apparatus. It diminishes everything and distorts everything. And what particularly helps not to think formatorily? Certainly it is necessary to think about the Hydrogen Table, the Ray of Creation, and all these things in a new way. That is what is meant by thinking in a new way, to use all machine, not only the formatory apparatus. The best way to begin is to think about the principles of the system and the rules of the work, school-work. There are many rules. Really all these rules come down to one when you understand them. You remember what rules are? First conditions—not to talk about the work to people who do not come here, not to start certain kinds of conversation, and things like that. And in this study of rules you can only understand them when you don't think formatorily. As long as you think formatorily you will never understand them; and on a bigger scale be able to separate principles, important things from less important things. To be able to control thinking, start with rules and you will find the way.

MISS A. When a man who has acquired knowledge dies, does the knowledge return to the amount generally available?

MR. O. That I cannot answer. There are many other things in that. It depends on many things which would be too complicated to mention in connection with that.

MISS A. Do you think there can be such things as ghosts? If so, what are they?

MR. O. I don't know what you call ghosts, and really I cannot answer that. In many cases they are simply hallucinations—dream figures in waking state. But there may be other things. I had two or three strange experiences in my life which I cannot explain—only it doesn't mean that dead people walk by night, or something like that.

MISS A. Do you think lines on the palm of one's hand are any indication at all of one's character or future? I ask this because you hinted that skin, being turned outermost, is important.

MR. O. Yes, but I meant that in quite another sense. But at the same time, not in connection with this idea of skin, these lines in the hand show something, if you know what they can show. I will give you just a few hints, because really I don't know much about it. It is interesting to see whether the two hands are equal. If they are equal, or almost equal, it shows there is no conflict between essence and personality. If they are different, it means essence and personality look at things from very different points, and there is a constant conflict. And there are certain lines, which I never met with in any book, which show a certain capacity for work of this kind; but absence of these lines does not show that one cannot work, but that one is just starting this work.

MR. C. Is there any inequality in the development of centres at birth?

MR. O. I don't quite understand the question. How can you verify? On which facts can you base it? Can you explain?

MR. C. If one could draw an analogy between that and the physical organs—a strong arm or a weak arm?

MR. O. I think, particularly in little children, it would be very difficult to establish the relative value of centres; so that is why I do not understand from what you came—from an idea, or from an observation of facts?

MR. C. From observation.

MR. O. I think we had better leave it for a time.

MR. C. Is such an inequality, if present, an important factor in causing wrong work of centres?

MR. O. No. You see, in the work we start with the normal person whose centres are normally developed, because if it is deeper really in essence, it is difficult—then it doesn't enter into our programme. It is generally the result of abnormal development of personality—bad habits of moving centre and instinctive centre, and so on.

MISS S. In the diagram of the Octave of the Ray of Creation, man does not appear separately, but is included under organic life?

MR. O. Scale! Scale!

MR. C. If man develops, that is to say, attains higher consciousness, does his position change, and can it be shown on the diagram?

MR. O. Yes, it can be shown, only we must talk later about that.

MR. C. It was stated at the last meeting that there were reasons for the naming of the three forces as carbon, oxygen and nitrogen.

MR. O. Not forces—matters through which force works.

MR. C. Could these reasons be given, and also for hydrogen?

MR. O. They can be; if nobody offers an explanation then I will say how I understand it.

MR. C. You said that it was of the utmost importance for us to attempt to identify the three forces, active, passive and neutralizing, in the events of everyday life. Would you please give the reasons why it should be so?

MR. O. Reasons I will not give. Because you must find these for yourselves. And how to start it? That will be in the next diagram. There will be some explanations and examples how these triads work. But you will have to find analogies for yourself, because it is a long process—you cannot be given them ready-made.

MISS C. You said that when an active force passed through a material it became carbon. Why is the active force associated with carbon in particular and not oxygen and nitrogen? Similarly, why is the passive force associated with oxygen and the neutralizing with nitrogen?

MR. O. I can answer you if you follow what I mean, with two words. It is organic chemistry. We will speak later about it.

MISS S. Can we be told what are the different impressions that range between 6 and 48 of the Hydrogen Table?

MR. O. Yes, we will speak about that. They belong to different centres—they are impressions of different centres.

MISS S. From the Table of Hydrogens I understand that certain even densities of active, passive and neutralizing forces create the various forms of hydrogen. But when they have created the hydrogen, do they permanently remain in it? I mean, would it dissolve if they were taken from it?

MR. O. They cannot be taken from it. If they are, then the hydrogen will disappear.

MISS S. How do the three forces obtain a greater or a lesser density?

MR. O. Density of forces—or density of vibrations—means speed, simply; and density refers to matter, in the sense of weight. And these are opposite to one another—the bigger the vibrations the lighter the matter, the heavier the matter the smaller the density of vibrations.

MISS S. In connection with the three forces in each action, I would like to be told if the following examples are correct.

Yesterday a bus did not take me as far as I expected, therefore, when I got out, first force said I must walk, second force raised the objection that it was a considerable distance and I was already tired; third force settled the question by pointing out that there was no alternative.

MR. O. Maybe.

MISS S. I wanted to know if it was more or less. . . .

MR. O. Not quite. Examples must be more material in the beginning.

MISS S. Going along the road I admired the scenery and wanted to sit down and look at it; this became first force; second force wanted to get home, but third force suggested that it would be good to complete an action that I could observe so clearly. So I sat down.

MR. O. Well—and the third?

MISS S. When I was approaching home, rather tired, I felt I would like to rest on the bed—this became first force; second force pointed out that I had a lot to do, but third force, in the shape of my physical self, settled the matter by just quietly lying down.

MR. O. Yes, it may be; only very soon you will see that it is better to find examples in a little different way. But it is useful to think in that way.

MISS S. Why is it that although one is quite friendlily disposed towards people, they pass like something unreal, and only one or two in a lifetime can come really close to one?

MR. O. It is very difficult to say. That is material for observation.

Perhaps it is possible to explain why—it is partly because—well, I will think about it. Maybe I will speak about it later.

MISS S. Someone struck me as rather pitiful the other day, and while thinking how to help them I tried to self-remember at the same time. The result was somewhat surprising in that I found I could give very little help, and then only materially. In such a case, when the person's outlook is obviously at fault, and yet they are quite unsuitable for system work, is there anything one can do to put them on the right path?

MR. O. What is the right path?

MISS S. To try and do what we are doing.

MR. O. Yes, but you say if they cannot.

MISS S. Yes, but couldn't they approach it slowly?

MR. O. There are many more answers than people.

MISS S. Can we be told soon how to find and bring new people to the system?

MR. O. Wait a little. It will come.

MISS S. In the middle of a lecture I often feel myself getting extremely tired and dull mentally. But if, on the other hand, some new thing that comes up interests me particularly, the tiredness disappears. Is this the interval in the octave, or is it genuine fatigue?

MR. O. This is third force.

MISS S. I think I asked before, only I do not remember the answer: can one make a whole octave by oneself in an ordinary state?

MR. O. It depends in what, how, and all that. We cannot speak in relation to practical things about abstracts. You must describe—in doing what?

MISS S. Is essence always good?

MR. O. No, not at all.

MISS L. Is the neutralizing force the circumstances surrounding the passive force which allow the active force to work?

MR. O. No, not only. It is a force by itself. They are equally forces, both active and passive.

MISS L. Is it connected with passive force?

MR. O. Everything is connected. Active is connected, passive is connected, neutralizing is connected. What is neutralizing in one triad, in another triad can be active, and in a third can be passive. Forces are not always active, passive or neutralizing; they become active, passive or neutralizing only in a triad—according to their function. It is more complicated. If they were always the same it would be easier to find them; but unfortunately they change all the time.

MISS L. The order of the three forces changes; is the change when the active becomes the passive force of the next triad and so on?

MR. O. No. You mix two things here. Perhaps later, when I finish, I can give just a little idea of how one triad comes out from another. And then there are different lines of triads.

MISS L. Does the passive force of one triad become the neutralizing force of the next?

MR. O. In some cases.

MISS L. What happens in the order of the three forces when there is a deflection from the course of an action?

MR. O. Many things may happen. It is impossible to say in general.

MISS L. Can there be a complete octave originating from a deflection?

MR. O. It depends from what. Maybe to-day or next time I will speak about some complete octaves; but this is arranged by nature. In some the intervals are filled up, but in some we have to put something there ourselves.

MISS L. A deflection can bring one back to <u>do</u>. Why doesn't the original impulse die completely?

MR. O. It dies; but we suppose the original impulse still works. But the action can change direction.

MR. W. We have been told that hard physical work results in the right working of centres.

MR. O. It may help; there is no law.

MR. W. Are we justified in inferring from this that it is the moving centre which is chiefly responsible for the wrong working of centres?

MR. O. No. It is different in different cases. But inactivity of moving centre is often responsible for it.

MR. W. We were told last week that the work at Virginia Water had been specially designed to prevent identification and to assist self-remembering.

MR. O. Not quite like that.

MR. W. Can you suggest any work based upon the same principle that might be done at home?

MR. O. This is a strange question because, you see, this work is specially organized for a definite purpose—so all the organization is necessary for that. If it could be arranged privately, there would be no need for all this organization. This formulation about not identifying is wrong. It helps in many ways—it helps your own work—and it is specially made for that.

MR. W. Should one consider one's thoughts, emotions and physical sensations as objective phenomena, in struggling against identification?

MR. O. Well, I don't know how you can do it. I really don't quite understand what you mean by objective. They are mostly subjective and change very quickly. One thing happens and you pass to another 'I' and everything changes.

MR. W. Will you please explain again the four states of matter?

MR. O. There was another question about the four states of matter. It is very simple. You must understand there are three forces. When they come together they come, one in the form of active force, another in the form of passive force, and the other in the form of neutralizing force; and they pass through certain matters. On the material side, three matters meet together; one of them becomes carbon, another oxygen and the third nitrogen.

MR. W. Which is which?

MR. O. When active force it is carbon, when passive force it is oxygen, and when neutralizing it is nitrogen. You see, what I just said, this is organic chemistry. When I first heard that, I had no question about it. It means that in this system organic chemistry is taken as the basis of this. Because organic chemistry is concerned with these four elements, and their relation is very near to that. For instance, carbon is always active, it brings the active element to life and everything.

MR. W. I am still not very clear about the Hydrogen Table, and should like it explained again.

MR. O. It will be explained.

MR. B. After doing some unusual muscular work I was reminded of it the next day by a sharp ache in the muscles. The thought which seemed to be simultaneous with this pain was an accusation to myself of identification, and seemed to be accompanied by a mental picture of the details of the work concerned. I was paying attention to the work I was doing at this moment. Could identification take place in so short a time?

MR. O. Yes. I don't quite understand the question. I think there is some wrong formulation. Identification doesn't need time. It works so quickly you can never catch it. But I don't think this is because of identification.

MR. B. Was the accompanying thought a matter of observation only, or could this be, in a small degree, self-remembering?

MR. O. That I don't know. Only you can say that. But thought cannot be self-remembering. Self-remembering is something different from thought.

MR. B. In the thought about identification there was an unusual sharpness and intensity. Would this be from the emotional centre?

MR. O. Again this is for you to decide. If there was an emotional element, it was from emotional centre.

MR. B. When a person in ill-health makes the effort to be more aware and to self-remember, does such effort tend to enable the instinctive centre to do its own work more efficiently, with a speedier return to good health?

MR. O. No. Man in ill-health cannot be taken as a general standard; there are ten thousand possibilities of ill-health, so I don't know which you take.

MR. B. Could one be told why nature is against the development of man?

MR. O. Nature is not against; and we cannot say why—that very seldom enters into our possibility. What we can say, by observation and study and what we can find in the work, is that nature doesn't do that.

MRS. D. Which people are normal?

MR. O. At present you must be satisfied with a very insufficient explanation—those who are capable of development. And if you ask me who is capable of development, I will say—normal people. But it is not wrong—it is right. Only you must think. These two things make one. If you ask what is a sound grain, it is that which can grow, can germinate. So, you see, it is a quite sufficient, quite right explanation. What is a normal egg? One which can become a chicken—only this is nature's work. All this is nature's work, and in relation to man, nature brings him to a certain point, and then leaves him and says—either live and die as you are, or go on, and you may do something, there are possibilities. Nature only creates possibilities, but does not help.

MRS. B. Coming along this evening, I saw a cyclist who had been knocked down. Previously I would have imagined all the horrible things that could have happened to him, the sorrow of his family, and so on. This evening I took it that he was hurt and did not think very much about it. Was this a question of identification?

MR. O. I don't know. In this case we can leave out identification. It was simply your imagination that didn't work. But certainly identification wouldn't be useful in any way.

MISS W. I should like to ask whether indirect thinking about a thing can sometimes be more help than thinking about a direct thing. For instance, when I come to these lectures, certain things I think I understand and take in, but there seems a lack of connection between my understanding and being able to give any idea of what has happened at the lecture when I meet the person who introduced me afterwards. It isn't that I have forgotten it but. . . .

MR. O. No, that is a little different. You must understand first of all that you mustn't say anything of what happens in these lectures. Why? Because you cannot. That is taken into account, and by this rule you are made free of useless attempts to say what you cannot say. It is one thing to understand for oneself, and another thing to explain. And this that you call understanding will change and grow. Different things will connect together. Now suppose you understand each thing separately; after some time you will understand them together. And then you will come to a certain moment when you will be able to speak about it. You will understand enough.

MISS C. Is it no help to discuss afterwards?

MR. O. Yes, it is very useful. Sometimes it is useful—sometimes it is even worse than no help.

MR. M. Are essence and personality different hydrogens?

MR. O. No, hydrogens don't enter here. You had better wait about that. It is quite a different idea. You cannot put it in the scale of hydrogens. Later you will see that you can, in a certain way. Not essence and personality, because essence can be different, but in a certain way it can be connected with hydrogens, only we haven't come to that yet.

MISS L. You said impressions vary according to centres. Would you say more about it?

MR. O. Yes, certainly; we will come to that.

You see, centres work with certain hydrogens. For instance, intellectual centre works with hydrogen 48, instinctive and moving with 24. Ordinary emotional centre doesn't differ greatly from instinctive and moving; but higher emotional centre works with hydrogen 12, and higher mental with hydrogen 6. That is four degrees of impressions.

Well now I will speak about one diagram. This Table of Hydrogens

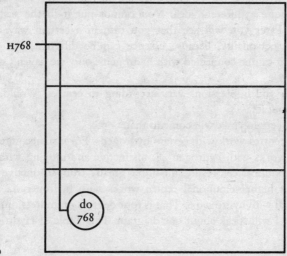

HEAD
MIDDLE BODY **and** **BACK**
LOWER BODY

we will have to repeat; so don't worry about it. It will not remain like that. We take the human machine—or this chemical factory. It is divided into three stories—roughly the head, the middle part of the body and the back, and the lower part of the body—but these are very rough divisions.

Then food enters first in the form of hydrogen 768, like that: [see diagram] and it passes into the lower part of the body. Really the process is a little more complicated, but this is a diagram, so we can take it like that. It enters as <u>do</u>, from the point of view of notes, and it enters as oxygen—that means that it comes as the conductor of the passive force. Then here, in the organism, beginning from the mouth,

H768

do
768

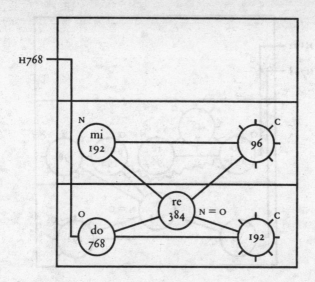

it meets all sorts of matters, which work on it and transform it into a different consistency or state. I put these rays to show these matters are in the body. This carbon 192, working on oxygen 768 produces nitrogen 384. Nitrogen 384 is re. [See diagram.]

This re 384 meets with another hydrogen—a carbon, really, which is in the body—carbon 96; and this carbon transforms this 384 into nitrogen 192. Nitrogen in the first triad becomes oxygen in the next triad, so, in the second triad 384 is oxygen, 96 is carbon, and 192 is nitrogen. If you study only these triads you will see how it works. What is nitrogen in one triad becomes oxygen in another triad.

Now here in this diagram, nitrogen 192 is mi. Do transforms with the help of this carbon 192; re transforms with the help of this carbon 96; then comes an interval at mi; it cannot be transformed in the same way. It couldn't be transformed, but here the additional shock comes in the form of the second food. It enters as do, oxygen 192, meets with some matter, carbon 48, and is transformed into re 96; and the formation of this triad gives a shock to that—mi 192, which also meets with carbon 48, and produces another triad. This mi 192 becomes fa 96. [See diagram.]

Then re 96, again meeting with some matter 24, gives mi 48; and fa 96, again meeting with this same 24 produces sol 48.

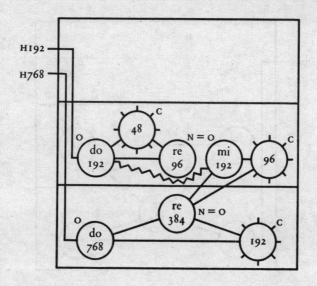

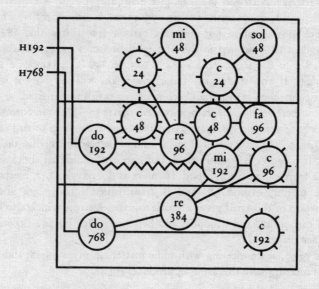

Then what happens at this moment? <u>Mi</u> 48 stops; it cannot go further because of the interval here. <u>Sol</u> transforms further and becomes <u>la</u> 24, and <u>la</u> 24 becomes <u>si</u> 12.

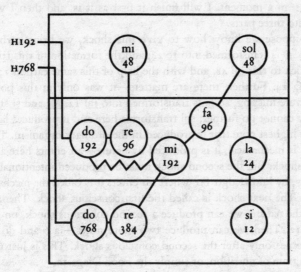

So we have seen two stages. One up to here (<u>mi</u> 192); but I continued it because nature took measures against that interval. In the second stage, the first octave continues up to <u>si</u> 12, and the second octave comes to 48 and stops there. At this moment impressions enter as hydrogen 48; but with impressions it is a different thing—they enter here and stop here. They cannot go further because there is not this matter here which helps to transform them. There are carbons 192, 96, 48 and 24, and here there should be a certain matter 12; but it is not here; nature did not provide it, or only in a very small quantity, not enough to have an effect. Sometimes it transforms a little, but not enough for serious results. So we have to bring this carbon 12. If you know how to do it, then you have to bring it here and this (<u>do</u> 48) begins to transform further and gives a shock to <u>mi</u> 48. If you don't, then it doesn't go further and stops at that; this is ordinary man 1, 2 and 3 without school and without work.

MR. M. Does self-remembering bring carbon 12?

MR. O. Just wait. I didn't say that.

MR. H. What is that mark between the two 192s?

MR. O. That shows shocks. One produces a shock on another. It not only makes its own triad, but it gives shock to the other triad.

MISS L. Could you go through it again?

MR. O. Yes, in a moment. I will finish it first as it is, and then I will divide it into three parts.

Now, suppose we know how to give this shock, we bring carbon 12, and _do_ 48 is transformed into _re_ 24; and the formation of this triad gives a shock to this _mi_ 48, and with the help of this same carbon 12 it produces _fa_ 24. Further, there are matters—it was only at this point that they were missing; so _fa_ is transformed into _mi_ 12. _Mi_ and _si_ stop here—they cannot go further; _sol_ transforms here and it produces _la_ 6. This is the highest note that is produced in the ordinary organism. The first shock is mechanical; it is produced by nature—air enters here and gives this shock. But the second shock must be produced intentionally, consciously, by knowledge. So, where air enters it is called the mechanical shock. The next shock is called the first conscious shock. Then, if we know the nature, we can produce a second conscious shock, on _mi_ 12 and _si_ 12. Then we can produce two more notes—_fa_ 6 and _do_ 6. But that comes only after the second conscious shock. This is just the general diagram of nutrition, or simply the Food Diagram.

MISS S. Does self-remembering produce the shock?

MR. O. Now we don't speak about the psychological side. We speak only about the diagram.

MISS T. Is it the carbon which always produces the shock?

MR. O. No, not carbon always. In the diagram certainly it does not produce the shock, it enters as active force. Otherwise, without carbon there is no active force; that means there is no triad.

So, in general, about this diagram—just think about it and then connect it with the conversation that we had before—that nature brings man to a certain state. Nature gives man possibilities but doesn't develop these possibilities by itself. Nature gives man the possibility to live, to exist. It gives air, when otherwise this first octave wouldn't go on. The machine is arranged like that, that air enters at the right moment, in the right consistency. But further development can only be if man understands and knows, works and makes efforts. This diagram is exactly the continuation of the idea we spoke about— to which state nature brings man and what nature doesn't do.

Now, if you have no more questions, I can do this diagram. We will

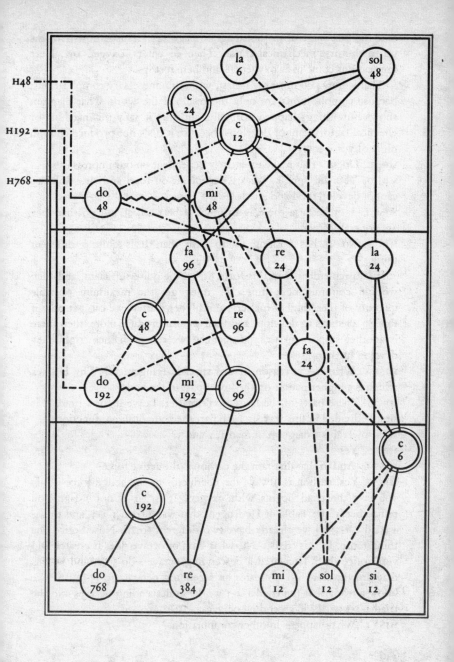

take the first stage of it. [See diagram page 345.] This is how it works up to the first mechanical shock. Then air enters, oxygen 192. Here impressions come in as oxygen 48 and here it stops.

That is how you must see it first, without unnecessary complications; because complications are only the result of the work. That diagram shows how things happen normally; and that is why this machine or chemical factory cannot develop—because it does not produce enough higher hydrogens.

MR. B. Doesn't that make us entirely dependent on our impressions?

MR. O. Yes, the same as we are dependent on food and air—only we cannot develop food and air.

MISS L. Is it because there is an interval between si and do that they are not connected?

MR. O. No. It has nothing to do with that. It is quite a different thing.

If you remember it in this form, it will be quite sufficient, and then we can continue next time. We must get the maximum possible quantity of these higher matters, and higher matters we can get only if this do 48 starts to develop, and then we can produce more, then there is another stop at mi 12, and again, if we can push them right they develop further.

MISS T. What is the reason of this special arrangement? Why is si 12 which is a higher matter on the lower part of the body?

MR. O. These parts of the body don't matter. Leave it for a time. It is simply divided in this way. In each part there are different functions.

MRS. D. Is this a diagram of man 1, 2 and 3?

MR. O. Yes.

MISS L. And in that diagram the carbon is the active force?

MR. O. Yes, carbon is always the conductor of the active force. Only you see, the triad begins with oxygen. It is 2-1-3, not 1-2-3. You remember in the Table of Hydrogens that was a triad 1-2-3, and this is a triad 2-1-3; so we already have two different triads. Now notice one thing more. In this triad 1-2-3, what kind of octave does it create? Did you notice that? It created a descending octave—do-si-la; and in this diagram the triad 2-1-3 creates an ascending octave, do-re-mi. So we know already that the triad 1-2-3 works in descending octaves and the triad 2-1-3 works in ascending octaves.

MISS L. What happens in other combinations?

MR. O. I will say when we come to them.

MISS T. How is it you obtain these different numbers—oxygen 768 and then carbon 192, and so on?

MR. O. 192 is there, in the body. Oxygen 768 meets with it and they mix together and produce 384.

MISS T. How do they produce 384? Is it a matter of calculation?

MR. O. Yes, you can take it like that.

MR. S. Are the three carbons constantly present?

MR. O. You mean 192, 96 and 48? Yes, they are always present—and 24.

MR. S. And each one is from the previous one?

MR. O. Yes, carbons are there. Dr. R., explain what carbons are.

DR. R. When food enters the mouth it meets with several different sorts of saliva. This is part of 192. This transforms starch and other parts of the food; and this digestion goes on in the stomach, where further enzymes, peptic juices and so on, transform it further, breaking down sugars, proteins, and fats. From there it comes into the small intestine and meets with bile, pancreatic and intestinal juices, which transform it into the smallest elements. These go through the wall of the bowel into the venous blood, which is taken to the liver, where it meets with other enzymes, which change it chemically, and so to the heart which pumps the venous blood to the lungs. Here is it oxygenated by the entry of air, and returned to the heart as arterial blood. After that it is difficult to follow.

MR. O. After that science cannot follow further. Science brings us only to 96. 96 is arterial blood. 48 can also be taken as blood, only it is blood with the addition of something. Science cannot say what the difference is between 48 and 96. So, up to 96 we can go by the way of chemistry and physics, but further we can only go psychologically. We cannot distinguish one matter from another, but when we come to sensations, we can know sensations 48, sensations 24, sensations 12. So really we can follow through the whole diagram. It is a scheme only. Science doesn't lead us far—up to 96. But these carbons up to 96 we know are many different matters in the body, such as saliva, and so on. They bring the food to such a state that it can be absorbed into the venous blood, and the venous blood by way of the heart is then oxygenated.

Q. Do the figures indicate anything but identity?

MR. O. They show the place in the Table of Hydrogens where these hydrogens come from.

MR. H. You said fire was 96.

MR. O. Yes, that is a parallel meaning. If you take it in the form of air, 192 is atmosphere that we can inhale. If you take it in the form of gas, 96 will also be rarefied air, fire, incandescent gases; and in a physiological sense, it is also arterial blood. Hydrogens have different meanings. It depends on which line of their development you take them, because each kind of matter also passes through different stages of development. They can become lighter or they can become harder, in different processes. But there is a parallel in this—they come from the same plane. The same hydrogen can be quite different matters from the ordinary point of view, but there will be something in common—their place of origin.

MRS. D. How long does it take to understand a diagram like that?

MR. O. It takes some time. I remember in Petersburg, I heard it once, and then the second time there were new people. I was sitting in a corner and didn't listen, and they asked me, 'Why are you not listening?' I said that I had already heard it. Later I realized that I did not understand it. So, it takes time.

MR. S. In the Hydrogen Table, hydrogen 192 is sol, and here it is do.

MR. O. It doesn't matter. It is sol in that scale. Here it enters as do.

MR. S. In one or two instances they vary?

MR. O. Yes, but every note can become do.

I want to give you one more diagram that may help us to understand.

We take the Ray of Creation. Organic life is between the planets and the earth; really it is round the earth. But the origin of organic life is in the sun, sol. Just as in the case of food it becomes do. It produces si on the level of planets, and then three notes, la, sol, fa. Then mi enters into the other mi, and re into the other re—mi into the earth and re into the moon. So organic life—these notes la, sol, fa—belongs not to this octave, this main octave, but to this special octave, which begins in the sun.

MISS S. Organic life, in that case, comes exclusively from the sun?

MR. O. Entirely from the sun.

MISS C. It has always puzzled me why the moon isn't do working upwards—why necessarily it should work this way round.

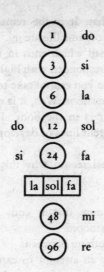

MR. O. I don't follow.

MISS C. It seems more natural to say <u>do</u>, <u>re</u>, <u>mi</u>, <u>fa</u>. There is always a missing <u>do</u>.

MR. O. No, the <u>do</u> is not missing. Don't worry about it. It is there. I didn't put it in.

MISS L. You say organic life came from the sun. Do you mean the heat and warmth of the sun feed it?

MR. O. That we don't know. We don't know what <u>do</u> and <u>si</u> mean. Out of all this octave we know <u>la</u>, <u>sol</u>, <u>fa</u> and <u>mi</u>. <u>Re</u> we don't know, even. We are told only that when man dies, or anything dies—man or cockroach, it is just the same—their souls go to the moon.

MISS L. When you say that we know what <u>mi</u> is, do you mean earth?

MR. O. No. All that goes into the earth—the physical body—all physical matter, when one dies, goes into the earth.

MISS S. Why do we have three notes?

MR. O. I don't know. That again I learnt by heart.

MISS T. What do we know about <u>la</u>, <u>sol</u>, <u>fa</u>?

MR. O. We are <u>la</u>, <u>sol</u>, <u>fa</u>—all organic life is <u>la</u>, <u>sol</u>, <u>fa</u>—all organic life is three notes of this octave.

MISS T. Didn't you say it was <u>mi</u>, too?

MR. O. No. We know that. It is the remains of organic life. Coal, chalk, oil—all remains of organic life are <u>mi</u>.

MR. B. In the physical triad which ends in 12—earlier in the evening you said hydrogen 12 corresponded with higher emotional centre.

MR. O. Yes, but that again you cannot take too literally, in an exclusive sense. I spoke about impressions. Well, it is quite right. And this is not impressions—this is matters in the body. It takes some time to get accustomed to these different lines of development of matters; but they are parallel.

MR. S. Is there any special reason why this new octave stops at the sun?

MR. O. It starts there.

MISS A. How do you know that it ends in the moon? Why not between the earth and the moon?

MR. O. Because there is nothing between.

MR. K. Is this cosmology an attempt to express the relation between the Absolute, sun and moon?

MR. O. That was in another diagram on which the Table of Hydrogens was based.

MR. K. Is it an attempt to express the relation between things in themselves?

MR. O. No. To explain the relation between matters in our body, in our food, in our world.

MR. K. Because our science cannot give us this relation at all?

MR. O. They can if they are trained, if they know; because I said we can distinguish between the lower hydrogens, but with the higher hydrogens we can understand their difference one from another only psychologically. Not this diagram showing the octave from the sun, but the Food Table, the Three Octaves of Radiation, the Table of Hydrogens—they deal with matters. They are not so much cosmology as the study of matters, and this shows that matters in our life have very different origins. It has a continuation—it is not the whole thing. But this is the beginning. In the ordinary way when we think without the idea of scale, relativity, we think matter is the same everywhere. But matter is different. In the Ray of Creation matter is different.

MR. M. Can we understand the difference between carbon and oxygen in a scientific sense?

MR. O. In some chemical relations and in biological also.

MR. M. Is there a chemical change when a substance changes from carbon to oxygen?

MR. O. In some cases it may be. But it is necessary to understand the principles now. Later we will be able to see what we can see and what we cannot see.

* * *

Thursday. July 21st 1938. (Warwick Gardens.)

MR. A. I conceive thinking subjectively and living subjectively fail in that they are based too much on one point of view.

In acquiring the opposite frame of mind of objectivity, is there not very considerable risk of coming to live and to think with what amounts to no point of view at all? This presents itself to me as a really grave danger in acquiring an attitude of non-attachment.

MR. O. I do not quite follow that. These expressions 'subjective' and 'objective' do not correspond to any real psychological fact, because we are subjective and can be objective only in very few things. We can say that it is our desire, perhaps, to enlarge our objective point of view, but we cannot change things suddenly. It is a question of very slow, laborious growth, so there is no question of any danger. One grows so slowly that there is time to adapt to new understanding. Your question would be possible only if sudden change were possible.

MRS. F. Can Mr. O. explain the difference between time and duration?

MR. O. Duration is only one feature of time. There are other qualities of time, speed and so on.

MISS D. You said we should try to hear the sound of our own voice. I so much dislike the sound of my own voice among a number of people that I have a habit of interrupting and talking at the same time, so that I shall not be left talking alone. Is this inner considering?

MR. O. We cannot be controlled only by our likes and dislikes. If I said that one must try to listen to one's own voice, I meant that one must do it to get certain observations. If it becomes a constant practice it may lead to self-remembering. If it is done in a negative way it gives no result.

MISS D. I also find that I have some powerful 'I's in me that make me become terribly negative when in the company of a number of people, so that I seem only to exist in a small circle surrounding me. Does that mean that I am the type that could not be helped by school, as I do not seem able to co-operate?

MR. O. No, it means simply some considering. First you must think right about it and realize that this is not a quality which will follow you for all eternity, but a small thing which will change if you observe yourself rightly.

MR. A. I have noticed that when I try to observe myself at all deeply I become dimly aware of certain feelings and moods in myself which I cannot fully account for as I have no words. Nor can I use properly system words to label these states of mind. How can one use words to make these feelings clearer to oneself?

MR. O. You must use ordinary words. You cannot describe things that happen once, but if you connect these feelings with another moment when you feel something the same and with another moment, then in some way you will find words.

MR. P. I am trying to understand what false personality is. Does it ever make efforts to self-remember? Is it ever interested in the work?

MR. O. False personality may pretend to take an interest, may take things for itself, may call some negative, mechanical action not identifying or something, but it cannot do any useful work. It can only spoil the work of personalities which can do some work and get some results.

MR. T. If someone in this room were to declare his willingness to work and to accept discipline, is there a school in existence which he could join?

MR. O. It is not enough to say that one is willing. One must know first what one can join and how. How can it be otherwise? Many people would declare and say they were ready and want everything made for them. That is not the right way. There is very much work already in connection with our work here. One can show how important it is, decide, make choice, many things.

MR. T. Can school exist before school is actually in existence?

MR. O. This is school work, making school. Schools are of different degrees, very different degrees. There can be schools where man No. 6 is preparing to become No. 7; schools where man No. 5 is preparing to become No. 6; where man No. 4 is working to become No. 5; where men 1, 2 and 3 are working to become No. 4. And of the last again there can be many different degrees, nearer to No. 4 and further from No. 4. Then schools can be on one level or on several levels at the same time, and so on.

MISS H. I have once or twice in my life experienced moments of intensified consciousness during times of strong emotion, and I have imagined that this is a taste of self-remembering. These moments all happened before I met the system, and I have never deliberately been able to get anywhere near them.

MR. O. It is quite possible that these moments gave you a taste of self-remembering, but this is the whole point about these moments of emotion which come by themselves—that we cannot produce them intentionally. That is why we have to go by this very slow, intellectual road.

MISS H. When I first tried to self-remember, by trying to remember exactly what I had been doing for the past few minutes, I found that I could remember very little and the realization gave me a slight shock which I fancied was a stage on the way to self-remembering. Lately, when I have tried I seem to be able to remember much more of what I have been doing so that I don't get any shock, and I don't know how to go on from that point. Do I choose the wrong moments to try to self-remember?

MR. O. From what you say I cannot tell which moments you choose to try to self-remember, but you must try at different moments. The method is as good as any other, but you must be aware of yourself and remember what it means to remember, and what it means not to remember.

MR. H. Apparently I have a 'work face' such as Mr. O. mentioned last week.

MR. O. You must try to make your questions self-dependent, and not refer to past weeks. I do not remember what I have said and perhaps nobody remembers.

MR. H. . . . From what people tell me about it I can only come to the conclusion that I look as grim and gloomy as thunder when I meet them, and especially am I told how fierce I look. I can't help laughing because it is just at those moments when I meet people that I imagine I look calm and gentle, with a sweet piety written all over me, my whole being impregnable in a quiet, rocklike strength.

In what manner are work faces produced? And how are they to be dealt with?

MR. O. There is only one thing I can say. You cannot believe what people say. Keep that in mind. They will all have different impressions, and if you believe them all you will find nothing.

MR. H. I have been arriving at my office anything from half an hour to an hour late for years now. Spasmodically I make some effort to get in on time, but even when I get up earlier and in good time I never seem to arrive any earlier. To what part of one is such a feature apportioned?

MR. O. It is impossible to say. If it is so persistent it may belong to several centres at once.

MR. H. Last week I asked a question in which I likened friction to a fire that could be made to burn brighter and brighter. I now see it is first necessary to light this fire. How is the fire kindled?

MR. O. By friction. Friction is a certain action or combination of actions which produces this fire.

MR. H. To be accepted into a school is it not first necessary to offer and to ask?

MR. O. It is first necessary to be ready for any level on which we can begin, not only from the point of view of knowledge, but from the point of view of being. You must realize your situation, know what you cannot do yourself, know that you need help and many other things. It is not a formal question but a question of being ready.

MR. H. If one finds something which one thinks would be useful for the work, does one take advice or say nothing, but act?

MR. O. It is difficult to know what you mean by 'finding something', but in any case it is always better to ask advice.

MR. F. I recently read a book, *Man, the Unknown*, by Alexis Carrel, which gives much information I have found useful in understanding system ideas, such as memory of cells and consciousness of organs. Do you approve of this book?

MR. O. Some of the scientific parts which he knows better can be read as a text book, but when he begins to philosophize, he is very childish. It is typically American—'the best art in America, the best science in America' and so on—a very childish book on the whole.

MR. F. You say the body cannot live without impressions. What are the impressions received in deep sleep?

MR. O. Suppose a man is asleep and the temperature changes. He will feel it immediately. He may dream he is at the North Pole or walking in the street with nothing on, or something like that. That means he reacts to the change of temperature.

MR. F. When I have been engaged in some very exacting work, I find I develop a state of muscular tension which interferes with the work of instinctive centre, such as digestion. Can you suggest a way of relaxing such tension in instinctive parts?

MR. O. First of all it is necessary to begin with simple things. This may be due to some kind of identification or considering, identifying with the success of the work, or lack of success, considering people who may be present or not present. Either of these two factors is quite sufficient to cause the tension, and these possibilities have to be eliminated before we can speak about it further. Perhaps if these are found the tension will stop.

MR. F. With the exception of the lungs, the work of the inner organism appears to be remote from our consciousness. Can you say why the lungs can be controlled consciously, and is the control by moving centre or intellectual part of instinctive centre? Can such control be extended to other organs?

MR. O. There are many other functions that can be controlled to a certain extent. There are what science calls voluntary muscles and involuntary muscles, muscles which work through moving or instinctive centre and muscles which can be moved by intellectual centre. First it is necessary to know that. As for the lungs, it is only the chest really which we feel. Intellectual control of the chest must never be encouraged. The chest must move by instinctive centre without our noticing it much. There are special exercises for extending control and you are always warned not to count the movement of the chest for a continuous period. You can count the heart without danger, but not the chest because that will interfere with it after a time.

MR. F. Then control can be extended to other organs?

MR. O. That I have just said, that there are things in us which can be controlled over which we have no control now. But at present I have nothing to say about this. First of all we must learn muscular control. Without being able to relax we can control nothing.

MR. F. Dieticians say that man must have a varied diet with carbohydrates for energy, protein for self-replacement and many minerals for odd purposes. Is this correct or can man synthesize all his food requirements from a simple prototype cell?

MR. O. What does this mean? I do not understand the alternative, but anyway I think different food is much better. I think one must learn by experience, maybe even by reason, what is the best food for him. It is quite personal; there are not two people for whom the same food is best. What is best for one is worst for another. I have lived all my life on hors-d'œuvres. Who else could live on this?

MR. F. Is the consciousness of cells superior to man's consciousness since cells know their future functions and destiny in an exact manner?

MR. O. There are different cells, you know. And you do not say which man you are comparing. There are men 1, 2, 3, 4, 5, 6 and 7 and there are also cells 1, 2, 3, 4, 5, 6 and 7—animal cells, vegetable cells, all sorts. So which cells are you taking?

MR. C. I have very little choice in my actions. Until my selective power has considerably widened and I am able to observe more clearly, certain theoretical concepts present themselves. Would you be good enough, meanwhile, to bring me to a nearer understanding of a triad by answering a hypothetical question? If, by accident, I chose a right triad to carry out an action, would all three forces of the triad be operating at the same time, at the beginning and for the duration of the action or might they be in some sort of sequence?

MR. O. The idea of different triads is based on the principle of time sequence. Really it is not like this, but we have to take it that way—the order in which the forces enter into the triad. 1-2-3 means one triad; 1-3-2 another triad, and so on. That is how we study them at present. Perhaps later we will not need to describe them in this way, but we have to start studying them as we are. How we learn to use different forms of action comes partly from experience, partly from the development of self-consciousness. The one will help the other. That is all I can say.

MR. P. Is a change of hydrogen value a characteristic of all activities? If so, is the kind of change always connected with the triad involved? I ask this because I am trying to see what is meant by activity.

MR. O. Take it in the ordinary sense, anything we may do. In order to limit the question, not to make it too rich at the beginning, we are considering only human activity. But here we come to a great difficulty. We have never thought of activity itself being different. We understand that motives can be different and results, but not the activity itself. When you begin to look at human activity from this point of view, remembering that there are different kinds, you will begin to see it. It is not the capacity to see which is lacking, but knowledge of this principle, which we never heard before. Some people have come near it in a philosophical way, but have not made the right deductions. Tolstoy, for instance, described it well and said that for certain results certain kinds of activity were necessary, but he could not follow it up.

MISS F. I find I am becoming negative over the things I observe in myself—as I see I am very trivial and inconsistent about everything. I feel doubtful that I shall ever change. How can I avoid becoming negative and what is the right attitude?

MR. O. The right attitude is to understand that you are not one, that you are many. What you describe is only one 'I' out of many. Try to see others.

MISS F. You said that with increasing consciousness one develops conscience. I don't know if I have developed one, but I find myself worrying over all sorts of details which I never thought about before. Since worrying is a form of negative emotion, I suppose this is not conscience working. How can one recognize real conscience and what is it?

MR. O. Try not to identify. Accept all this worrying and then perhaps you will see something more. That will be the next step.

MR. A. I believe that the understanding we are seeking is attainable only by some. Is it not very probable that many of us may get to a blank wall of eliminations and no further?

MR. O. Nothing can be guaranteed. I have now a comparatively long experience and in some cases I can say almost at once that it is not worth while for the person to try. I never try to keep anybody when I am sure it is no use. It happens sometimes. But if one wants something and tries to work and does not show some particular unpleasant feature which is very difficult to deal with, then one has a chance. That is all I can say. One has exactly the same chance as anybody else. You may see one side of people and not another. One person may have very good and very beautiful features, and yet behind this have one small feature which makes work very difficult for him, more difficult perhaps than it is for somebody else who does not have such brilliant features.

MR. D. Is some special school discipline necessary in order that a man may be able to struggle against self-will successfully?

MR. O. Yes, it is useful in some cases. It is one thing just to try and orientate and work on the principles one has learnt, and another thing to be told 'do this, do not do that!' If one is told, it produces many objections, many difficult moments, and sometimes this is useful.

MR. S. Is it the addition of the third force to the two others that makes an action happen, or are the three forces in equilibrium, the removal of one making the action happen?

MR. O. No, not the removal. There must be three forces meeting for an action to be produced.

MR. A. We are told that there are four ways to the attainment of unity. If, while we are learning here, we think we discover we belong to another way, that we are, for instance, of the religious type, should we abandon the Fourth Way?

MR. O. You see, this happens very, very seldom. Generally, if one comes to this, for instance, to group of the Fourth Way, and is able to understand and follow it, it means one can follow that. The other forms will be more difficult for him. In any case he may find there is not so much difference. I remember being told a story once by a man who said it had been his own experience. Some disciples of a school which was half Yogi, half religious, found the school difficult, so they came to another school. To their surprise they found they were immediately given the same tasks to do, but with some additional difficulty. One of them asked the man who gave them the task how he knew, whether it meant that schools communicated with each other when a man left. The teacher answered: 'It is not worth while communicating when a man runs away from one school and comes to another school. As soon as I saw you I saw what was the task you had been given, and could only give you the same but perhaps a little more difficult.' You see there is really no choice. Here everything is explained. You can ask any questions and have them answered. But the Yogi uses quite different methods. Some time before the war, a young man in Paris started to study Indian philosophy with some pundits in France. They gave him a certain symbol on which to meditate and told him to come back in six months' time, to write down what he had done and bring it with him. In six months he came back with heaps of papers. They said: 'Very good. Continue and come back again in six months.' At the end of six months he came again, and again they told him it was very good and to come back in six months' time. He became desperate and went off to Benares, where he met some learned man and asked him to help. The man asked what he had been doing in Paris. He repeated it all except that he did not say he was displeased but just that he thought perhaps there in Benares he could do more. The man answered: 'Very good. Continue. Come again in six months' time.'

MR. W. Can emotional centre be made to work better only by removing the causes which take its energy?

MR. O. Yes, but these causes may be in other centres, so we have to work on all centres at the same time.

MR. W. Is no other direct effort possible, such as we try to make on intellectual centre, like trying to think in a line, for instance?

MR. O. There are many things which have been said about work on emotional centre, such things as struggle with identification and considering, struggle with the expression of negative emotions and right thinking about negative emotions. Four practices. If you really used all that is given in that direction, then very soon you would acquire quite perceptible control over emotional centre. Again it needs other things, self-remembering, new state of consciousness for real control parallel with the control we can have over intellectual centre. Really control of emotional centre belongs to the third state of consciousness, so it is a long way off and we must use auxiliary methods. The most important is to have the right attitude towards negative emotions.

MISS F. Is there no relation between the system meaning of conscience and the everyday meaning?

MR. O. Yes, there is a relation, certainly, only in the everyday idea it is made very small. In the ordinary meaning, conscience is simply a kind of habit. One is told to do things in a certain way and if, by laziness, neglect or something, one does not do them, one has a panic of 'conscience', which in this case is really just a kind of negative feeling because one did something or did not do something against what one was told. This is not really conscience.

MR. D. Is chief feature a food for false personality?

MR. O. Chief feature is not food. Chief feature _is_ false personality. False personality in most cases is based on one feature which enters into everything. Some day we will take some examples of chief feature and you will see how it is really that which makes false personality.

MR. T. I do not know how to think about the word 'neutralizing'.

MR. O. Then do not think about it. The word means nothing. It is simply a label. Call it just third force.

MR. H. I can understand the idea that man plays a small part in a large plan, but cannot believe that he has any possibility of playing any other part.

MR. O. You think too much about man. He may play no rôle in any plan. I do not know what you mean by plan. If you mean the plan for all organic life, then certainly man plays his part, though, since it is quite mechanical, it can hardly be called a part. From my point of view plan begins when the part can be played consciously, with understanding. For this, he must be conscious man. Then it may be different, the question of how he can come into a plan, what part he plays and so on.

MISS R. I find it hard to make myself copy out questions to bring them to the meeting, although I write them down roughly with great enthusiasm when I first think them out.

MR. O. Then get somebody else to copy them out for you. That is the only solution if you cannot find some sufficiently neutral 'I' who will not say 'this is not interesting', 'this I know the answer already'.

MISS L. How can we strengthen and fix the moments when emotion is felt so that there is no doubt we want to work and use this at moments when there is no doubt we do not want to work?

MR. O. By just trying to connect them. When you are in this state, remember other moments in this state and make a mental link between them.

MR. D. I am not clear about the relationship between first and second conscious shock. Is a high level of self-remembering necessary before second conscious shock becomes a practical possibility?

MR. O. Yes, and not only self-remembering. Self-remembering must produce results, must produce a quite different quality of material in the body. Only then comes the possibility of second conscious shock. The transformation of mi 12 into fa 6 means producing positive emotions. This is only possible for man No. 5, so you see we are very far from it. At present our work consists in the struggle with identification. This leads towards it, but we cannot think at present of producing it in its full form.

MR. F. Does a buffer which separates two opposite personalities always consist of two ideas, one corresponding to each personality?

MR. O. Buffer is not ideas. It is just buffer. Something which cannot be described, a matter for your observation on yourself and on other people. It may have one sentence which makes it possible not to see from one personality to another, but it is not ideas.

MR. A. Why do we use the term 'buffer' and not, for instance, the word 'excuses'?

MR. O. Because it is not excuses. It is just buffer. There is a great difference between excuses and buffer. Excuses may be different every time. If the excuse is always the same, then it becomes buffer. You have to think about excuses, find them. Buffer is always there.

MR. D. Some of the things I see in myself are so mechanical that I accept them almost as being unalterable. Can this tolerant attitude towards one's chief mechanicalnesses lead to that sort of duality which was spoken of recently?

MR. O. No. Duality is not a danger. If it comes it comes only much later, not comparatively in the beginning. One must justify oneself for a long time before it becomes possible.

MR. K. In making junket, one is obliged to use rennet in order to make it set. Is it possible to say that the rennet is the third force when the milk and the heat are the passive and active forces?

MR. O. Quite possibly, but I do not quite know what you mean—this is English cooking. But it must be, I should think.

* * *

Monday. July 25th 1938. (Warwick Gardens.)

[Written questions handed in.]

MISS T. I have great difficulty in trying to realize that I have not got one central 'I' that is behind everything I say and do. I know that different impressions cause varied reactions and moods, but I always feel I have one 'I'. This is wrong, I know, but at present I can make no progress towards thinking about this.

MR. O. This is as if you looked at different things and people and thought they were the same things and people. Try to see contradictions, and you will see that it is not the same 'I'.

MISS B. I am trying to fight considering and feeling tense with other people by preparing myself beforehand, but although it may be better to begin with, I have not yet been successful. Directly I forget myself it is on me. Is this method of fighting it worth persevering with, and is there any other?

MR. O. No, that is the only method. You must understand what considering means and how absurd it is, and think right beforehand and not justify yourself.

MISS B. Is it possible to develop magnetic centre after one comes into the work?

MR. O. No, it is then too late. Magnetic centre collects influences B before you come to the work, and afterwards it ceases to be magnetic centre and becomes definite personality which is interested in the work.

MISS C. I have often observed intellectual centre interfering with moving centre, and emotional centre interfering with the others. In the case of intellectual interference, trying to work more quickly seems to help, and with emotional interference it seems better to try to go more slowly. But I do not know why this is so. I do not properly understand what I am trying to do or what principle to apply. Please can you explain more why this interference takes place and how one should work against it?

MR. O. You must collect more material. This may be quite right, or later you may find things that contradict it.

MR. L. How can one see the difference between energy and desire? I have not one single observation of having a strong desire to do a thing and yet, lacking the energy, I have always thought afterwards that if I had badly wanted to do it I should have been able to, and the reason for failing was lack of desire, not lack of energy.

MR. O. You can't compare energy and desire in that way, and also more observation is necessary.

MRS. M. I seem to waste so much energy in unnecessary fear over small things all the time. And I can see that I decide even important things by taking the alternative of which I am least afraid. I think probably it started from having an unhappy time as a child. I do try to stop it by seeing how stupid it is, and by making myself do things in spite of being afraid of them, but is there any better way to try to get over it? Does this state of mind cause adverse things to go on happening?

MR. O. The last is not right, and it is necessary to have right attitude and see how unreasonable it is. There is no need to invent things about childhood. It may even be connected with something of which we will speak later about breathing and tension. By a quite unconscious reaction breathing may stop or become irregular, and that may bring certain thoughts, produce fear, but it is not the thoughts themselves. It is necessary to observe from that point of view.

MR. H. You once said that, in the last century, there had been somewhere on the continent a school, similar to a Fourth Way school, in which painting was a regular part of the work; and that Rossetti was connected with it in 1855. But Rossetti seems never to have been out of England for more than a month at any time, and in 1855 only for ten days. Could you give us any other clues about this school, and tell us what evidence there is for connecting Rossetti with it? You also mentioned a Russian poet as belonging to it. Could you tell us his name?

MR. O. Name is in *New Model*—Tolstoy. About Rossetti, one of our people found by accident, not in looking for schools, that he was connected with a school in Düsseldorf—it was officially a school of painting, but there are reasons for thinking that there was an esoteric school behind it.

*　　*　　*

[Questions asked before the meeting.]

MR. I. I would like to ask what is meant by the expression 'the Law of

Accident'. I can see 'cause and effect', but I don't see how things can be accidental—they must have a cause.

MR. O. We don't call things that happen cause and effect, because they have a cause—that is too large. We call cause and effect something that happens to you because of your own actions, and then it is not accident. You can observe accident if you find two lines of events, when you have nothing to do with the cause, and where these two lines cross is accidental.

MISS B. Is it possible to develop emotional interest after one comes into the work? Is this magnetic centre?

MR. O. Certainly one can develop it, but it has nothing to do with magnetic centre. It may correspond to the line of the work, or it may be contradictory emotion, but there is not sufficient description here.

MISS B. Is it impossible to come into the work unless one has magnetic centre?

MR. O. Possible to come, but impossible to stay.

* * *

This is the last time this group meets till September. If anybody is not satisfied with answers to old questions, please ask again, but better if you speak of new things.

MR. L. Can we observe the connection you spoke of between fear and certain kinds of thoughts? Have we, as we are, the machinery to observe this?

MR. O. The theory of how emotions work can be found in ordinary literature. James and Lange described it in the nineties, and it was modified by Ribot. It means that sensations of fear or depression are really sensations or feelings of some inner physical change that happens when we see or hear something. It is not an emotion, as the feeling is not produced direct, but as the result of some functional change which is felt as an unpleasant emotion. If you understand the different manifestations, you can observe this, particularly in relation to fear.

* * *

Well, there are some strange questions that have been asked about the new house, and also what we have spoken of the Society is not quite clear to you, so you had better try to think of that and ask questions. As it is, you create wrong expectations, and because of that you may not see what actually there is.

MR. L. It seems to me we have a certain responsibility towards the Society which demands initiative from us.

MR. O. It is not a question of immediate responsibility, but many things were said before in relation to different question, and it would be interesting if you could connect these things with the new house and Society. Certainly there will be many new things, or not exactly new because we have come to them before, but they did not touch everybody, but now it is possible for them to touch more people.

MR. P. The constitution of the Society is part democratic—some of the officers are to be elected by the groups.

MR. O. It has not really any democratic idea. For some time, for two or three years, according to how work goes, certain definite principles are laid down, but as people don't know these principles they will just be told what to do. Later, when they begin to understand, that will be another thing. You speak of the organization of the council and groups of twenty people. In the beginning it has to be arranged, and will be more or less accidental, but later groups will be sorted so that they can work better. When they understand they will have certain freedom, but if you think work on school principles can be organized by people who don't know anything, that is a wrong idea. In any case, I will not use the word 'democratic' because it has no meaning. In general, it should mean freedom of parties, but in the Society there are no parties.

MRS. H. How can I decide what are the more important things in a life sense? So many duties come in and I never know what is duty and what is not.

MR. O. It is necessary to know duty first—what is necessary and what is excuse, and only work in connection with some kind of organization, and trying to understand different sides of this work will give discrimination between things which are more important and less important, and little by little one learns to understand for oneself. There is no other way.

MISS T. I suppose it is a great disadvantage if one is not able to bring other people to the work?

MR. O. Quite right, and also not quite right. You remember what we called the staircase, where, if you want to be raised to the next step, you must place someone on the step where you are. This does not mean individual persons, but groups. Here we have a group of people who started almost together, and we have three new groups, Tuesday, Wednesday and Thursday. They will only take part when a new group takes place. It is not only actual bringing of new people, because that very often depends on chance, on acquaintance, ability to speak. At present there is a chance that belongs to all to take part in placing of other groups, particularly in the new house we shall have new possibilities, and we may have four or five new groups, and after a time all groups will enter into other work and prepare new possibilities. When the house is opened, I think all who come now will come in the general meeting once a week—I am not sure about Tuesday, but Wednesday at any rate, and immediately after that we will start new groups, maybe two at once, but there will be now no new group until September or October. It will be simpler, the more it grows, to find people who want to come, but certainly a little later we will have to sort them out much more—I mean there will be bigger demands than now, but this is not so important. The preliminary study of the system is by itself, and those who are more prepared will stay, and those who are less interested will be sorted out. Certainly it will be interesting to have this large meeting, because you will see everybody and hear all sorts of questions and answers at once. Also there will be the possibility of coming to new groups, although I cannot promise. Only after some time it may be obligatory, even, for some people to come to new groups and talk to new people.

MR. H. In what way, what arrangements can be made to ensure that as the work gets bigger the ideas can be kept pure—when work was much smaller all could have personal contact with you.

MR. O. Well that is your work—big or small you must try to get personal contact with me or with other people, and work not to spoil ideas, because if people begin to distort them, they will have to leave. Ideas become distorted when people begin to invent their own explanations and theorize, but so long as they work sincerely and try to verify anything that comes into their minds, and work according to rules and principles, distortion is not at all necessary. In organization of school-work, all measures are taken against distortion, and if it happens it is only because people forget these precautionary measures. It is generally the influence of formatory centre, and when people begin to work with formatory centre and nobody corrects them, there is no idea in the world that cannot be distorted in less than twenty-four hours. I have met some extraordinary distortions of these ideas, only, happily, not in my own groups.

MR. L. Is that the sort of scale of distortion that you mean? I certainly distort the ideas for myself.

MR. O. For yourself it does not matter—you have chance to correct it. Everybody does it in the beginning until they have the whole range of ideas, but understanding one part corrects understanding of another. You cannot understand the whole thing and misunderstand parts, and if you can think rightly of the whole, you will understand every part. Then again, there are meetings, and questions show whether you think rightly, and if you think wrongly it is immediately corrected, so there is no chance of big distortions. It will all continue in this way, so there is no fear of distortion, although many people who don't understand the necessity of thinking in a new way let formatory centre think for them, and that will distort anything—even the multiplication table.

MISS H. You said once that we must try to think about the new Society as our pyramid.

MR. O. Not so much—not so big.

MISS H. What I was trying to see was that every individual must try to work and work a lot. Must we find out ourselves how we can be useful or shall we be told?

MR. O. Time will show. From time to time you can ask about it, but not in a formal way, using philosophical terms. Every esoteric society must have some kind of external work apart from itself. The right organization of the Society will be such objective work for us. One difficulty that I see will be to understand what belongs to the older work going on now, and what belongs to the Society. At the same time the Society will be a façade, although there will be no show. But if people ask what it is, we can say that it is the Historico-Psychological Society, but for us the Society will be the form in which we work. That is the only way to organize it. There will be some difficulty for new people, but older people must be able to explain to them how they should understand. We had a similar thing long ago—I think it began much earlier, but particularly after '27, when we read here chapters from *Fragments* and chapters from the *New Model*. At the beginning I did not divide them, but spoke of things not referring to the system in *New Model* and of things referring to the system, and made it a task for people to decide which references were to the special doctrine, and which to general ideas. Older people had to explain to newer ones what referred to the system and what to general ideas. In the same way, you will have to explain to new people what refers to the Society and what refers to school-work. So you must understand yourselves— I mean you must understand before, for when you have to explain, it will be too late, so you must think now.

MR. S. What, for example, is historical research in art and religion? Is this something that belongs to the Society?

MR. O. Yes, but how will you take it? You can formulate it in the ordinary way or from the point of view of the system. From our point of view we introduce many ideas—of relativity, of being, of schools, etc. It is not ordinary research in sculpture, architecture, etc.

MR. S. Would the work which is apart from special doctrine take a concrete form, such as a book?

MR. O. That would refer to a special moment.

MRS. L. Will there be any members of the Society who are not in the system?

MR. O. Not at present—maybe never. If you have people in the Society who do not understand these groups, it will create many difficulties and give no useful results.

MRS. J. Will it be necessary to be able to explain to any new people what the Society meant in the first place?

MR. O. There would be no need to explain to them or mention the Society until they understood more of the work. They might hear of the Society first, and then they would be told that there was no room for new members—only the possibility of coming to some lectures with the idea that they might be able to come to the Society in a few years' time.

MRS. J. I was thinking of that in connection with your saying that it will be necessary to know the difference.

MR. O. I did not mean quite new people, but people of different stages. Perhaps somebody who came only a few months might ask how to understand this or that. If you cannot explain, you must refer this person to someone who can explain.

MISS T. I do not quite understand, if the Society is not to have anybody in it who is not in the work, what difference there will be to explain.

MR. O. No difference. There are people on different levels; some have come five years, some ten months, so their understanding is different.

MRS. J. When one is not actually at meetings or going to Lyne, is it better to try to work in ordinary small social life, for instance, any kind of worldly activities, going to the theatre, parties, etc.?

MR. O. I can only answer questions referring to this work—not outside things. This is your own personal work and relationships. You must decide yourself and decide right. If you decide wrong, then you will be responsible.

MRS. J. I want the thing that keeps me awake.

MR. O. I cannot guarantee what will keep you awake. . . . Everything in ordinary mechanical life makes us more asleep.

MRS. L. May we have a copy of the objects of the Society?

MR. O. You will have it later.

MISS T. Do we understand correctly that that programme is actually going to take place, or is it written just as an explanation?

MR. O. It is all happening, with the exception of two or three things that are put in as possibilities. The possibility of publishing something and of giving public lectures was discussed many times.

MR. L. It seems to me that one of the objects of the programme is to publish information that may become B influence for other people?

MR. O. No, it does not enter into the present work. There are other things that must happen first. Somebody asked me when we should have public lectures, and I said, 'When we have lecturers.'

MISS O. Our division into groups will be in connection with the work and not the Society?

MR. O. No, it will be part of the organization of the Society, but it will be intermixed, and it will be necessary to understand which is which.

MRS. L. Is it wrong to think of the Society as a camouflage for the system?

MR. O. Quite wrong. We have nothing to camouflage. The programme includes in itself all that we are actually doing and all that we intend to do. Certainly the idea of school does not come into it, but it enters as the study of the normal development of humanity, and all that, and there are references to the study of esotericism. It is all there, but it is in such a form that it can be given to people who do not belong to it. It is very useful to think of it in that way. For a long time we have thought about which form is better and what name is better. Try to think what you would propose for organization, and the form in which you would put explanations. It is very interesting to see whether you can find a better form or not, without introducing anything new or wrong or not belonging to it, and without giving a wrong impression.

MISS T. Has the word 'psycho-transformism' been used in general language?

MR. O. No. That explains our view. Later on something will be written about it. At present you do not find it in ordinary language. The word 'transformism' has been used in regard to evolution. 'Psycho-transformism' is based on other ideas, opposite to mechanical evolution. It is the one new word we have used, and we must not make it popular before we explain it, or people will steal it and give it quite different meaning.

New copies of the programme will be ready in September. They will be numbered and must be returned after a certain time. Old copies must all be returned.

People who are not going away in August or September should leave their names with Madame K., and say which days they would be free, as there may be small meetings at Lyne, although I cannot promise anything for certain.

* * *

Thursday. September 15th 1938. (Warwick Gardens.)

MR. S. Last week Mr. O. compared the Society as a piece of objective work to a material object such as a bit of paper. Does this mean that a society can have a real objective material existence, or has it an objective existence only in a figurative sense?

MR. O. But it will exist quite objectively. Perhaps there is something I do not understand in the question, but all I can say is that it will be quite a real thing.

MR. N. Can one have a _real_ positive or negative attitude towards anything if one does not recognize different kinds of actions?

MR. O. I do not like the word 'real' in this question. Real is opposite to imaginary, and we do not speak about imaginary attitudes. But yes, certainly one can. Different kinds of action is quite a new line of thought, and it was in quite an ordinary way that I meant what I said about it being necessary, in order to understand certain things, to have a positive attitude towards them and that there were other things which one could not understand unless one had a sufficiently negative attitude.

MR. N. Is the objective work of the Society the same as third line of work?

MR. O. No. That is quite a different scale. First, second, third lines of work, these refer to _your_ work and the Society is not your work, it is the organization. If you begin to work there, then you will see, but at present it is quite different.

MR. C. It was said that for a school of this kind an objective work was often necessary, and that one idea of forming a society was to provide this work. If the Society will change nothing, how will its organization provide an objective work?

MR. O. Wait and see. How else can I answer? It will be like an exoteric circle, work being the same but divided into two circles, but it will be the same.

MR. C. Why is an objective work necessary?

MR. O. For many reasons. It is difficult to explain them, but in practical work you will see.

MR. C. Is the building of cathedrals by mediaeval masons a parallel example?

MR. O. No. Historical examples are never parallel—people are different, circumstances are different, the relation to other lines of work is different and so on.

MISS S. Unless I have misunderstood it seems that men are divided into two classes: those who wish, however feebly, to attain consciousness and those who do not. What determines this dividing line? Is it arbitrary and the result of the Law of Accident?

MR. O. No, it is not quite Law of Accident. You can understand it from the point of view of what was said about influences A and B— that it depends on the amount of absorption of influences B that creates the desire to awake, or something like that.

MISS S. Has the system anything to say about the theory of the progress of humanity through reincarnation?

MR. O. No, nothing.

MR. H. What does it mean when people say that in order to go up one step you must put somebody in your place on the ladder?

MR. O. It is in relation to this staircase idea. You can understand it from this point of view: take a group starting to come to lectures here. After some time, when they have learnt a little, when they know what they are doing, they arrange the possibility of another group. This group starts, and in that way take their own place as beginners, and the first group can do more, work with the new group and so on, and that gives them many advantages. But to put somebody in your place is not an individual demand. One person by himself cannot do that. It means school and school-work. The results are felt by the individual.

MR. H. What kind of people are fit for this work?

MR. O. That was explained in connection with influences B.

MR. H. Is it right to think of a school as an instrument upon which we can ascend?

MR. O. I think that is rather a complicated conception. School, in the sense in which you are using the word, begins when one not only acquires new information but starts to work on one's being with the help of school.

MR. H. What is the relationship between the work as it is now and the Society?

373

MR. O. If it was possible to put it into plain words, I would put it into plain words. But you see these are things you must understand. Take, for instance, the programme of the Society. We put into that everything it is possible to put on paper. It describes our work completely. It even looks ahead (like the possibilities of public lectures, publishing and so on) to things we cannot do at present. But how can one put in the programme the idea of its being a way or about the struggle with false personality and things like that? That enters into psychological study, but it cannot be explained in the programme. But the programme says what the work is and when necessary (this is not your worry, but that of the management, so to speak) the programme may be published and some people made acquainted with it. At present, even if it were necessary, there would be nothing to show.

MR. H. And what will be the relationship between the Society and the outside world of men and of events?

MR. O. No relationship.

MR. H. Will the Society provide more opportunities for working with other people?

MR. O. This is not only Society, but simply because we shall have a bigger house.

MR. H. When the suggested smaller groups are organized, will it mean that we shall, to some extent, lose the opportunity of asking you questions directly?

MR. O. No. Quite the opposite. There will be more chance.

MR. H. What are the kind of things to look for in oneself in trying to separate false personality from the rest of yourself?

MR. O. It is necessary to understand the features of false personality— what makes it. You may be able to see in your life glimpses of the age to which you can attribute the beginning of false personality. For any serious study of oneself it is necessary first to know it a little and remove it a little.

MR. H. Sometimes at meetings with other people I gradually become heavier and heavier. This is an extremely distasteful experience and appears to be infectious.

Is it right to say that at such times intellectual and emotional centres are . . . ?

MR. O. No, leave centres out of it, then it will be possible to speak about it. It means identification or mechanical attitude.

MR. H. What part does the negative side of instinctive centre play in the life of the body?

MR. O. A very important part. If we did not have it, we should eat poisons, drink poisons, die in a very short time.

MR. H. Is the following an example of emotional part of moving centre? . . .

MR. O. That cannot be answered. It is the wrong way to come to it.

MR. H. . . . I start to saw a log and for some time I have to push against my own inertia. Then quite suddenly it becomes effortless and I have slipped into an easy, rhythmical movement.

MR. O. You are not yet clear about parts of centres. You can observe them only by studying attention.

MR. H. There are moments when I want to laugh. For instance, whenever I suddenly understand something further, or when for a brief moment I come to myself and see all the mass of sleep and heaviness I cling to so dearly, the difference between that and being only slightly more awake is so ludicrous that I at once want to roar with laughter. Is it safe to trust this attitude?

MR. O. That would be all right except for the question. The observation is all right, but you do not see the difference between questions and observations. Questions must be short, and when you describe an observation you must just describe the observation, nothing more.

MRS. S. Sometimes I observe myself considering or identifying and find I do so because of a picture I have of myself. This picture has many aspects. Can I in this way come to know my false personality and by observing it, weaken it?

MR. O. Very good, yes. It is the only way, but only if you do not get tired. Because in the beginning many people start very eagerly, but soon get tired and begin to use 'I' indiscriminately without asking themselves 'Which "I"?' 'Which part of "I"?' Our chief enemy is the word 'I', because we have no right to use it really in ordinary conditions. Much later, after long work, we can begin to call 'I' one of the personalities (like what has been called 'deputy steward') which develops from magnetic centre. But in ordinary conditions, if people speak to you and say 'I do not like', you must say 'which of your "I"s" does not like?' With newer people you can do this, and in that way you remind them about this plurality in themselves, and also you must constantly remind yourself of this. If you forget it for a time, it will be easier to forget it next time. There are many good beginnings in the work, and then this is forgotten and they start to slide down, and in the end all that happens is that they become more mechanical than before.

MRS. S. Will the Society have a library from which we can borrow books?

MR. O. There will be a library, but how it will work I cannot say yet.

MRS. S. Will there be opportunities for practical work in the new house for people who can give one afternoon a week to it but who find it difficult to go to Lyne?

MR. O. Yes. It will be very good if people who have time and want to work give their names to Madame K. and say which days they are free and what time. At present it is too early, but in a week or maybe two weeks the contractors will have finished work there and work will begin which we can do ourselves. The contractors have only done one part of the house, and there will be much work in the other part.

MRS. S. You have said that we should try to avoid lying. Am I right in thinking that this applies to lying for our own escape or gain? I observed myself lying to a child to-day to give it reassurance, and I cannot feel that this was wrong.

MR. O. [Unrecorded.]

MISS L. Will research in connection with the Society be organized so that it will be possible to know what is being done, and to suggest other lines of research and find out if they would be useful?

MR. O. It is organized now. But certainly, if anybody suggests something, something may happen, and if they do not suggest then they just do not know what is happening.

MRS. D. When driving a car an apparently extremely dangerous situation occurs. I am frightened for less than a moment, then an extremely lucid state occurs—the accident does not happen and then I have time to be frightened again. There is no doubt about the lucidity of the state, and I feel that if it did not come the accident would. It is an experience which remains very vivid for some time.

The understanding of a system idea is practically the same experience. I feel that there is something in me which prevents me from reaching the lucid state on a larger scale, so that I only get as far as having a feeling of shame and fear at not having understood more of the system.

I am persuaded that there is something I should know which I do not, and that now I cannot get it without extra help. Or, that if I cannot understand this something which I should already have understood, I shall understand no more and even gradually forget what I have. Yet I do not <u>know</u> how to ask for help or how to find the way to it, nor whether this is all imagination and an excuse to myself for not working more, in spite of feeling strongly that it is not. But I have noticed that in the process of practical work in the system ideas have been made quite clear to me which I have known before but not understood.

Will the Society provide chances to do practical work . . . ?

MR. O. Society has nothing to do with this. Very often you spoil observations in this way. It is not the real object of the observation.

MRS. D. You said once that we have no emotions, but only identifications. Since then I have observed that this is true in almost all cases, but sometimes I feel an emotion which seems to have a different flavour. Is it quite impossible in our present state to have an emotion which is not an identification?

MR. O. Oh yes, it is possible, but only for a little time. Like all these things—moments of consciousness and so on—we measure them by time. How long [   ].

Q. [   ] are too strong for me. How can I get round this difficulty?

MR. O. I think in this case you are wrong to accuse mass suggestion. Facts are bad by themselves without any suggestion. <u>Why</u> they are so, <u>how</u>—that is another question.

MR. T. The relief caused by the news of the Premier's visit to Hitler has created an emotion which has been very helpful. I realize that this emotion is mechanical, but is it better to avoid such emotions or to make use of them?

MR. O. We cannot go into political questions really, but at the same time it is useful to think right about such things because you have to think about them, and if you understand rightly, it will help your work in general. About the Prime Minister going to see Hitler, it is a very brave action and a very interesting action. It may have no results because from Hitler's side everything may be decided already, and if people decide to steal you cannot persuade them not to steal. You have to let them steal or fight them. But what it is always necessary to think about these questions is this: in the ordinary way people always take the present situation as all, without thinking how the present situation was created. Even if we take the last twenty years, we see such mountains of imbecility. And people have to pay for this imbecility. Since 1914 it was realized that an armed Germany was dangerous. Then they let them arm and again they come to the same result but now in a worse position. Before there was Russia, for instance, and everything was more stable. Now everything is very shaky, and if Russia is our ally it is very dangerous. Russia will sell her alliance and then she will sell it to other allies and go on selling.

MR. T. Will the activities of the Society be organized for the associate members according to their needs as at Lyne?

MR. O. I cannot say anything about organization. So many things will come into existence when they are necessary, step by step.

MR. T. Can the objective work of the Society be seen as the guarding of esoteric knowledge by the present membership?

MR. O. I think those are too big words. We have no right to use them. These words can be used only in general descriptions of schools, not in descriptions of our own work. Our work must be described in psychological language.

MR. T. Will further readings of *Fragments* be withheld until they can be given to larger numbers at the same time in the new house?

MR. O. No. Simply there is nothing ready just at this moment. I am trying to work on it, but the chapters you have not heard and that were read are at present in a state of transformation.

MISS M. Is it possible for false personality to be interested in or attracted by system ideas?

MR. O. Yes, very much. Only then you will have system in the light of false personality and it will be a quite different system.

MISS M. If it is possible for this to be, what happens to this interest in the process of weakening false personality?

MR. O. It strengthens false personality and weakens the system for you. The moment it takes it to itself it adds one word here and another word there. You cannot imagine how extraordinary some of these ideas are when they are repeated back to me. One word omitted from some formulation makes a quite different idea and false personality is fully justified and can do what it likes and so on. This is where the danger lies.

MISS M. I ask these questions because I sometimes doubt the genuineness of my interest in the work—I may be lying to myself.

MR. O. But only you can answer that and there, again, only if you do not forget the fundamental principles and say 'I' about something when it is only one 'I'. You must get to know other 'I's and remember about this. If you forget this you forget everything. So long as you remember this you may remember everything. Forgetting this is the great danger. Then a tap, a slight change in something is sufficient to make everything wrong.

MR. P. Is the work carried out by groups to be the 'building' of the new Society?

MR. O. 'Building' means nothing in relation to this.

MR. P. In the event of world war, will the formation of the Society be carried through?

MR. O. That I would like to know very much. But we did not develop the capacity for fortune-telling, so we shall have to wait and see what will happen.

MR. A. Is self-remembering the sole and ultimate source upon which one who guides his life by the system may draw his strength when confronted with the probability of yielding to some weakness he would much prefer to be without? I do not find much practical moral strength necessarily emanating from introducing a pause wherein to contemplate oneself and one's ideals.

MR. O. Speaking for myself, I would not use these words. I think it can be said in simpler words, but that this is right. You can get strength from this idea that you do not remember yourself, that you can remember yourself and what it means to remember yourself.

MRS. S. My memory—or is it my imagination?—seems to be so much stronger than any efforts to be self-aware. When I try to self-remember I find it impossible really to see myself, though looking back on similar efforts I have a distinct picture of the moment which makes it more real and emotional, but whilst making the effort there seems to be a very strong 'I' which is stopping me from seeing myself. Is it that we cannot see ourselves properly and the person I remember is imaginary?

MR. O. It is not quite like that. You must continue observation and get better acquainted with 'I's and remember them consecutively. When you know some 'I's better, then you will see others better.

MR. L. I would like to know why it is that strong emotions cannot be held. It seems to be too much to hold, and I have found that the reaction is a strong urge either to laugh or to cry. I couldn't just <u>hold</u> the emotion, for example when I get a strong emotional feeling about the work.

MR. O. This is a very interesting observation. Taking it just as a statement, the observation is quite right, but if you ask why this is so, several answers are possible. I think it is best to say that there is inconsistency between centres. The degree of one centre does not correspond to the degree of another centre. That is all I can say at present without long explanations of things we are not speaking about yet. Centres, in our state, are too much connected, too much co-ordinated, and a mechanical state in one centre immediately brings all other centres to that state.

Speaking in different language, we can say that we cannot keep the right kind of emotions because we cannot put them in the right place in ourselves. They disappear and, exactly as you said, sometimes by laughter. What is laughter? Well, one definition of it is that it helps to throw out materials from emotions which we cannot use in the right way.

MRS. D. I am not quite clear about the law of fate. Is that the law that is determined by our essence?

MR. O. Yes. Essence, type, fate are practically the same, but facts connected with fate are very difficult to find except perhaps just almost physical facts, a certain kind of health or capacities and things like that. There are many other things, but they are hard to distinguish because in our state essence seldom works separately from personality. Many things we have the inclination to ascribe to fate really belong to personality, so it is dangerous to make conclusions. But there are some things we can see. For instance, certain types of people attract certain types of people. They have the same kind of friends, the same kind of troubles, the same kind of difficulties, but of course never without personality taking part, so you cannot call it pure fate—more cause and effect.

MR. F. Will much more objective work be done in the new house than is now done?

MR. O. I do not know what you mean by 'objective work'. There are no such terms as subjective and objective work. When we speak about work, we speak about doing work or doing nothing.

MR. D. Is there a danger of negative attitude having a negative emotion attached to it?

MR. O. Great danger yes, but if you do not identify with the negative attitude then the emotion cannot come.

MR. N. If man were less mechanical would influences from planets affect him in a different way? Not by making him make wars and that kind of thing?

MR. O. It is difficult to say. You take it as if it were known how one is affected, but even in the ordinary state one can be affected in different ways, so what do you really want to compare? Speaking in general, I think one can only look at it from one side—that of identification. If one is less identified one takes other things without identification.

MR. L. How does one learn to put emotions in the right place?

MR. O. There is only one universal key to all this—remember yourself. There are many methods used in different schools especially for this thing, but from the point of view of the system the strongest, surest and quickest method is become more conscious. When you are asleep emotions have the tendency to go to the wrong place. You can put them right by being more conscious, because in one who is more conscious of himself everything is different. One can be more conscious and less conscious, more asleep and less asleep and that is what determines this really.

MR. A. My question was put with the object of ascertaining whether higher states of consciousness can produce more thoroughly bad people or more thoroughly good people equally.

MR. O. No, that is wrong. Bad people can be produced only by increase of mechanicalness. Self-remembering cannot produce wrong results, though again it is necessary to keep the connection with everything else. If one omits one thing and takes another thing from the system, if one seriously works on self-remembering without knowing the idea of division of 'I's, takes oneself as one from the beginning, then it will give wrong results and can even produce wrong crystallization and make development impossible, as it happens in wrong schools, for instance, or even without relation to schools. You see, there is the possibility to work on this line or parallel lines (Yogi, religious) and, although it is not fully formulated by this, for work to be based on false personality and on struggle against conscience. Such work certainly will produce wrong results. First it will create a kind of strength, but it will make the development of higher consciousness an impossibility. There is even a special name for this, for people with pseudo-development. I will tell you this some time and explain it. It is a very difficult word, a combination of two Turkish words, a very beautiful description which cannot be translated properly into any other language.

Self-remembering is a thing which can only be based on right function. At the same time you must work on the elimination of false personality. Several lines of work are suggested and explained from the beginning and all must go together. You cannot just do one thing and not do another. All are necessary for creating this right combination, but first must come the understanding of and struggle with false personality. Suppose one tries to remember oneself and does not want to make efforts against it, all features of false personality will come into play in one: 'I dislike these people', 'I do not want this', 'I do not want that.' Then it will be, not work, but quite the opposite. If one does some kind of work in this way it can make one stronger than one was before, but in this case the stronger one becomes the less is the possibility of development. 'Fixing before development', that is the danger.

MISS P. Could the strength of Hitler and Mussolini be due to this wrong crystallization?

MR. O. They do not concern us. They do not belong to our groups.

MISS P. They seem somehow to be extra strong.

MR. O. I think that is illusion.

MR. F. Can system create false personality in one?

MR. O. Certainly system cannot create it. System means all that is said in the sense it is said. If one corrects it consciously or unconsciously, then it cannot be called system. Then it will be pseudo-system, falsification of system. So your question is wrong. System can be compared (if you remember that conversation) to objective art. Objective art differs from ordinary art in this way: a work of art created objectively, with all knowledge of methods, triads, octaves, will always produce the same effect, whereas in ordinary art the results are accidental, one day one thing, another day another. As with objective art, so with the system, but only so long as it remains correct. The moment it becomes incorrect or something is forgotten or falls out it will give wrong results at once.

MR. J. What did you mean by 'mechanical attitude' when you said this might be the cause of heaviness in a meeting?

MR. O. Mechanical attitude is not conscious, just ordinary—things as they happen. You talk either by imitation or simply without thinking. You cannot see things right through this mechanical attitude, everything becomes dull and that creates this feeling.

MRS. S. Is energy used in changing about from one 'I' to another? I notice myself not doing any particular work but constantly changing over, almost in thought, and find it very exhausting.

MR. O. I think I understand what you mean—the enormous waste of energy in changing from one side to another in oneself that enters into imagination and mechanical, associative thinking. Certainly you can spend a quite unnecessary amount of energy quite uselessly. There is only one thing, to replace it by conscious work and not give yourself free time. Do something you have decided to do, or try to remember yourself, to talk to somebody, or try to remember ideas of the system. This is the only way.

MR. T. I find a great desire sometimes to assess the progress I have made, and wonder if this is a wrong thing to do?

MR. O. No, quite right if you can take a photograph of yourself by memory as you were earlier, and compare yourself now. You may find very interesting things. But one must be very sincere.

MR. T. That is what I find difficult.

MR. O. Yes, it is difficult.

MR. A. Without giving the power of thought a free rein, surely you miss a great deal of intellectual exploration?

MR. O. Yes, thought must have a free rein, but that does not mean it must be blind. You must be aware of your thought. Awareness does not mean keeping it back. Quite the opposite, it helps it.

MR. D. Is false personality the main barrier to being aware?

MR. O. First of all, yes. But many mechanical habits besides, sometimes even mechanical habits in other centres. Mechanical habits in one centre. . . .

[Remainder missing.]

*   *   *

Thursday. October 13th 1938. (Warwick Gardens.)

[Written questions.]

MRS. S. Can other kinds of work besides the struggle against false personality, work against identification, for instance, be represented by a static triad?

MR. O. The static triad represents you, not work. It shows the state of your being, what you are at a given moment. One of the points, body and essence, is always the same, but the relation of the two points changes.

MRS. S. In this triad, the deciding factor seems to be the neutralizing element. If it has sufficient of one sort of energy the action goes towards the formation of 'I'; if there is less than normal of this energy, the result is to strengthen false personality.

MR. O. No, you cannot describe it only as energy. It is all together.

MRS. S. Is it right to think of the latter as a different class of activity from the former?

MR. O. All your actions depend on the kind of static triad. Certain kinds of action require a certain state of static triad. Other kinds of action require another state of static triad.

MR. L. In connection with this diagram, does false personality change from active force into passive force in the moment that one sees it?

MR. O. No, not at the moment one sees it. It cannot change into passive force without many efforts.

MR. A. Why is the word 'static' applied to this triad?

MR. O. Because of the permanent point, body and essence, which is always there.

MR. A. I had the impression until now that false personality was the collection of all the many 'I's. This diagram has made things a little obscure to me.

MR. O. Amongst these many 'I's there are many passive 'I's which may be the beginning of other personality. False personality cannot develop, it is all wrong. That is why I say that all work must be on false personality. If one fails it is because one did not give enough attention to false personality, did not study it and did not work against it.

MISS R. Has false personality different 'I's?

MR. O. It has many 'I's, only they are imaginary.

MISS M. I seem to possess any amount of physical energy first thing in the morning and feel ready to do anything but think or sit still and try to self-remember. Is it only through trying to self-remember that we can use this energy constructively?

MR. O. I do not know what you mean by 'self-remember'. Just trying to remember oneself is rather a useless thing. You must try when you are working, when something goes against the grain, so to speak, not just when you are sitting doing nothing. At the same time some kind of exercise of the memory of self-remembering can be useful. Trying to stop thoughts, for instance, at the same time trying to remember yourself. This is a very good exercise, because it is a more tangible thing. You can never be sure whether you are remembering or not, but you can be sure whether you are thinking.

MR. T. Can I usually trust the personality which welcomes friction?

MR. O. How can I tell? Which personality? Which friction? Most friction which can be useful we do not notice at all. So it is necessary to give an example.

MISS R. What happens to magnetic centre when false personality goes?

MR. O. Magnetic centre and false personality cannot be together. They are sun and moon from this point of view.

MISS C. In trying to find examples of other negative emotions besides irritation which could be changed to something useful by non-identification, I have wondered whether this is possible with a certain primitive kind of jealousy?

MR. O. No, you must not mix what I said about irritation with other negative emotions. I spoke of it as a very special emotion. Other negative emotions can be changed, but they need other efforts. Irritation is simply identification with a certain emotion you do not know. If you remove identification and imagination you will find it. You will be able to see through irritation comparatively soon, but with other emotions you can do nothing, so you must not think they are exactly the same.

MR. R. Are we to understand from the static triad that the existence of false personality is essential in order that man may work on himself?

MR. O. What does essential mean? If man is blind, is blindness essential?

MR. R. When permanent 'I' starts does it mean that false personality does not appear at the same time?

MR. O. That is so far away that we cannot speak about it. But false personality cannot appear even at the same time as magnetic centre. It will spoil it if it does.

MR. H. Is it necessary to work on false personality in order to eliminate the unnecessary 'I's which don't belong to 'I'?

MR. O. I do not understand the question, but, as I have said, all work has to be on false personality. If you do any other work and leave this, it is useless work and you will fail very soon.

[End of written questions.]

* * *

MISS R. How can one deal with the conceit of false personality?

MR. O. You must know all features first and then you must think right. When you think right you will find ways to deal with it. You must not justify it. It lives on justification, even glorification, of all its features. At any moment of our life, even in quiet moments, we are always justifying it, considering it legitimate and finding all possible excuses. This is what I call wrong thinking. So first you must know false personality and then you must think right about it.

MRS. S. What is it that changes passive force over to false personality?

MR. O. Use your own words.

MRS. S. What is it that makes 'I' develop and false personality fade?

MR. O. First it is a question of time. Say false personality in ordinary life is there twenty-three hours out of the twenty-four; then when work begins it will be twenty-two hours only and the other an hour longer. Then in time all false personality diminishes, becomes less important, becomes negative and the other becomes positive. You cannot diminish it in the sense of size, but you can diminish it in the sense of time.

MR. P. Did you say that if we did not identify we should find imagination something different?

MR. O. No. I spoke about irritation. I said that this was a very particular emotion which had the near possibility of being turned into another emotion if you removed identification and imagination. There are also many ordinary likes and dislikes which in our present state only make us more blind, but which, if we did not identify with them and connect imagination with them, would show us quite different things which we cannot see now. Since our likes and dislikes are all in false personality we cannot use them. We have many 'I's, but cannot use even these two.

MR. M. Would you explain why it is that an impression, however intense, cannot be a shock?

MR. O. I do not quite understand what you mean by 'shock'. In our language this word is used only in connection with something else, not just like that by itself.

MR. M. You said you would explain to-night what shocks were.

MR. O. They cannot be explained by themselves. You must take a definite octave, find intervals and then perhaps in some cases it can be explained what may serve as a shock. By itself shock means nothing. It is the same as when people ask what is meant by neutralizing force. I answer that first they must show me first and second force. I cannot explain a word. The word 'shock' is used in this sense, that when we find an octave cannot go on but at a certain place stops or changes direction, a shock is necessary to send it on or make it go straight. What the shock may be depends on the octave. In one octave one kind of shock is necessary, in another another. It means an additional force at a given place which helps the octave to go on in the same direction at the same strength.

MR. F. Can I get a clue to false personality by thinking of events in the past, outside the orbit of present influences, i.e. events which are dead and buried?

MR. O. Sometimes you may. Either in the past or, as I said, in your friends. Only you must understand that you also have false personality, not only your friends!

MR. F. In the past the events themselves seem of little significance, but the original emotions reappear and I feel I can see myself in caricature.

MR. O. Maybe.

MISS R. I do not quite understand what you mean by passive 'I's.

MR. O. Which are controlled by another 'I'. Good intentions, for instance, are controlled by laziness. Laziness is active, good intentions passive. The 'I' or combination of 'I's in control is active. The 'I's which are controlled or driven are passive. Understand it quite simply.

MR. M. Can a man provide his own shocks, or must these always be external?

MR. O. It depends what octave. For instance, in the Food Octave one shock is provided by nature. In the second place one must provide the shock for oneself. Generally one cannot, without special study, training and help. The same refers to the third shock, which is more difficult.

MRS. D. Did you say all our likes and dislikes are in false personality?

MR. O. Most of them are. And even those which did not belong to it originally, which have real roots, all pass through false personality.

MISS R. How can one deal with the negative things which would arise if one did see false personality?

MR. O. You have to bear it.

MRS. N. Does one have to know the whole of false personality in order to struggle against it?

MR. O. One must know it. It is like a special breed of dog. If you do not know it you cannot speak about it. If you have seen it you can speak about it.

MR. R. Is it possible to know the whole of it? It seems to me you could only know bits.

MR. O. That is quite enough. Every small part of it is the same colour. If you saw this dog once you would always know it. It barks in a special way, walks in a special way—everything is different.

MISS C. Is pity a negative emotion that has the possibility of being changed into something different?

MR. O. Leave possibilities. We are not speaking about the possibilities of negative emotions. That will only create imagination and nothing more.

*　*　*

Tuesday. October 18th 1938.

[Written questions were read through.]

MR. O. There are some interesting questions here, but first I want to speak about some general things which must be known to everyone.

If you remember, I said in the introduction to the first lecture that generally our work is divided into three parts: study of man, study of the universe and study of schools, school organization, school-work, etc. We spoke to a certain extent about man, not enough, but enough for practical purposes. We spoke a little about the universe, but I see, even from these questions, that the idea of school is very vague, and sometimes mixed with formatory conceptions which really do not lead anywhere: there is too much of 'superman' and cosmic ideas, and things like that. Schools must be taken simply: as I have said, school is a place where you learn something. And then there are different degrees of schools. When you have learnt what one school can give, you can go to another school and learn other things. But there is always a certain order of things and you cannot learn them without following this order. Speaking of schools connected with the Fourth Way, or connected with some kind of higher schools, because otherwise such schools have no meaning (you can call them esoteric, if you like, although it is a big word), in such schools knowledge without being is not sufficient. You have not only to acquire a certain knowledge but also to learn how to change your being; and you must work on your being at the same time as on your knowledge, because without that it will be quite useless knowledge; you will not be able to make use of it or derive any profit from it.

But I really wanted to speak of things referring to organization, because just now, not so much owing to the present moment in your particular group, but owing to the situation of the whole work which began some years ago, there will be some changes. And partly because of these changes, and partly because your group came to this moment, you must understand your position in relation to this organization.

You must understand (certainly it is quite obvious) that every kind of organization needs material means, needs money, needs people who look after it and so on. And at the same time you must understand that you have already been coming for some months and had all these lectures, and that nobody has asked anything from you. This is possible only because other people pay for you. And now the question comes—will you be able to pay for yourself? It is generally calculated like that: a certain group is taken together, and then I see how much this group can pay, and according to that the future is arranged. Because, suppose that group cannot pay, or can pay so little that it cannot exist independently, then the question arises: is there another group that will continue to pay to make its work possible or not? It has been going like that for a long time. We have tried to arrange or establish some kind of equal payment for everybody, but found that it was impossible, because, even with the minimum standard which would make it possible to go on, the majority of people cannot pay. This is very natural because there are many people who have to earn their living and earn only just enough, or even not enough, and there are young people who have no possibility to give anything, and so on. Until now, owing to the organization which I am explaining, we have never refused anybody because they could not pay. But it may not go on like that for much longer, because the number of people increases, and with it the number of people who cannot pay also increases. So perhaps we shall be obliged to limit the number of people who cannot pay, or who can pay only very little. It was impossible, as I have said, to arrange any equal payment, so it is really a matter which people have to decide for themselves, how much they can pay. And, as I have said, it is counted for the group (fifty, sixty or seventy people) and then all further arrangements are calculated on this basis.

I think now you better try to ask questions—I have given you the general idea. Now let me know which details you want to know and then later we can pass to other questions.

I only must add some other things to that: at present we have very many people, and it is really the fault of older people that they did not explain this situation well to newer people. As a result of this many people who have been coming for a long time do not pay any attention to the question of material means of the work, and that creates a strange atmosphere. And not only do they not do anything themselves, but they bring other people, and those who have arranged things before have to arrange things for them. Because of all this, at present, beginning with this moment of a new organization, everybody must think about it. I do not say that everybody must do something, as that depends on circumstances, but everybody must think about it. This work has already been seventeen years in London, and it had existed many years before that in other countries. And there have always been people who could not pay for themselves, but it was exactly those people who did most for this work. There is not only one, but many ways to help the work, and one must find these ways for oneself. At present this organization can exist because for a long time certain people have helped it. Some people gave even much more than they should, so at present there must be a new basis for this. I have already told some people that they must not pay any more. Now all groups must think what they can do in relation to all these questions. Otherwise a certain reduction of the number of people in groups is inevitable.

Now I must explain one principle (it is not a rule but a principle)—nobody has the right to pay ahead, in advance; people only pay for what they have received. If they realize that they must pay for what they receive, they pay; if they think they cannot pay, or if they think it is not worth paying for, then, quite naturally, they don't pay. New groups are only possible because old groups pay for themselves: and for the new groups, until the new groups begin to pay for themselves. In any case there is no question of paying in advance, one pays only for what one has received.

Now ask questions and perhaps I can explain better.

Q. One should really have some idea as to the amount.

MR. O. No, one must have an idea about one's own means and one's own valuation.

Q. May we have a gauge, say a percentage of salary?

MR. O. No, this is a personal thing. You see, if you think in the right way you will see your position in relation to this thing. There is nothing difficult or obligatory about it.

Q. To whom do we pay?

MR. O. That you can ask Madame K.

Q. As a group?

MR. O. No, everybody pays individually.

Q. Do I understand that contributions, say from a group, will finance a second group?

MR. O. No accounts are given. Only one thing can be said in relation to this—people pay for what they have received, that means one pays after some time. As to how the money is used—afterwards you may come to that, even take part in the distribution of money between different branches of the work. Now other people do this.

Q. In certain cases it might be difficult to keep to the same contribution as circumstances might alter.

MR. O. If they alter, they alter; certainly it is possible. What I want you to understand is not only the question of contribution, because that depends on circumstances. But there is something else that does not depend on circumstances, and that is _understanding_—understanding of the necessity of an organization and the need of material means for this organization. That is what is obligatory. One can easily find oneself in such circumstances that one can give nothing—but not a single word will be said about it, particularly because one can do many other things, not only give money. And this is where the centre of attention must be.

Q. If we could be told about the new basis of organization, I think it would be easier to see how we could help.

MR. O. No. But what do you mean by a new basis of organization? I said we might have to limit the number of people who cannot pay: that is the only new basis—because we have too many people who cannot pay.

Q. How can we find out in what other ways we can help?

MR. O. This is _your_ work, i.e. quite an individual question, to find your way to help. It could not be explained in a general way. If you find, you find; if you don't find you don't find. This is your own work to find it if you can find.

Q. Has the paying got anything to do with belonging to the Society?

MR. O. No. As a matter of fact we have decided that there will be no payments in the Society, at least in the first year. Those who will enter the Society will not pay any fees. Only one organization will remain. The Society will exist on the money coming from one central organization. So the Society will have no financial side. Later on it may perhaps be organized in the way it was intended with some kind of definite subscription, but not at present.

Q. Should contributions be made at stated intervals or whenever there is a new group?

MR. O. Just individually.

Q. I mean at any time?

MR. O. There is no limitation of time—even twice a day if convenient!

MR. M. Could we be told how much money is needed?

MR. O. No, because too much is needed: you would be afraid of it if you hear.

Q. Will the Society provide possibilities for practical work for those who cannot pay?

MR. O. The Society has nothing to do with that. The Society, you must understand, changes nothing. The Society is only a name, work remains the same. But work grew to a certain size and it was found that it was necessary to find a name. Society by itself will not change work in any way.

Q. May we help in getting this new house ready?

MR. O. Yes, that is quite separate work.

MR. M. You say that we pay for what we get; I find it very difficult to strike a balance between. . . .

MR. O. Why, what is difficult? Pay more, if you have it.

MR. M. I mean it is difficult to translate what one has got into terms of money.

MR. O. Very easy—count more until you can be sure; what can be simpler?

*   *   *

Incomplete, undated record begins here. (1938)

MR. W. Recently I had to go a whole day without food. I found I did not much mind the hunger but that, in spite of all I did to pass the time, the day seemed very <u>long and dull</u>. This surprised me, as I never thought I took much interest in food. Does this mean that we attach too much importance to eating without realizing it, or has eating a special function in providing impressions?

MR. O. Try for several days and you will see what you think about it and whether you can think about something else.

MR. H. When it is said that animals can be classified by their medium, food eaten and air breathed, does air breathed mean actual air taken into the lungs or that part of the air which is used by the animal after inspiration?

MR. O. No. It is meant in the sense in which it is generally taken.

MR. H. In parasitic living can the tissue of the animal lived upon be regarded as a medium in itself?

MR. O. Probably, yes.

MISS S. Mr. O. said that certain negative emotions make serious work impossible. Does that mean they must be absolutely exterminated before one begins, and what is serious work?

MR. O. By serious work I meant not only study but change. But even serious study enters into that, because generally first you must study certain things, then you work to change them. But as even study cannot go without certain change, because these two processes of study and change are not fully divided, so serious work can be called more serious study than just at the beginning. And with certain negative emotions it is practically impossible, because they will spoil all results; one side of you will work and another side will spoil it. And after some time, if you start work without destroying negative emotions, you may find yourself in a worse state than you were before, and it happened several times in our work that people made continuation of work impossible, because they wished to keep negative emotions—

there were certain moments when they knew it, and they didn't make sufficient effort at that time, and later the negative emotions were more strong.

You must connect it with this principle that in the work demands increase. The more you do the more is asked from you. So if you don't want demands to be made on you, you must not try to show that you are working. If you show you are working, immediately more is asked of you—first more time. Demands grow according to time and according to efforts. The more efforts you make, the more you have to give. So it is necessary to be careful about that!

MISS S. I have found recently that when I am negative, if I go on persistently questioning myself until I find out the cause, and then suggest a new attitude in its place, the negativeness has really seemed to disappear in every case.

MR. O. Not serious negativeness. Serious negativeness will not disappear.

MISS S. . . . But I notice that for every similar recurrence, I have to go over the same process, although perhaps more easily. Is this because I have not got down to the real cause of the emotion, or would I be right in thinking that with persistent resistance it will gradually die away?

MR. O. It is impossible to speak in that way. Keep this question for small groups and ask it then, calling everything by its name, saying what emotions and so on.

MISS M. If I am doing some kind of physical work, such as walking or driving a car, and at the same time trying to think about the work, I have a feeling of relaxation, but if something occurs which forces my attention back to the process of walking or car-driving, I immediately become more tense, and in this tense state identification may occur. Is this a correct observation?

MR. O. Quite possibly.

MISS M. When alone it is easier to try and think while performing some other kind of routine work. Is this because centres are then doing their own work and not interfering with each other?

MR. O. No. It is simply because then you have to do one thing; otherwise you have to do two things at the same time. And you must try to do three or four things at the same time; only that will give an approach to super-effort. Otherwise it will be simply effort, easy effort.

MRS. B. Never having been rich, I have no feeling about travelling on buses without paying my fare, etc. As I have to be more awake to do my swindling, it does not go against my aim. Would it be necessary or useful to try and acquire ordinary standards of right and wrong, and from what point of view?

MR. O. It doesn't enter into the programme.

MRS. B. Is it possible to know eventually what is objective right and wrong, if one has no ordinary feelings about subjective right and wrong?

MR. O. It is all relative. There is right and wrong for this table, right and wrong for the stage, right and wrong for the room. You must understand the relativity of it first; then you will understand. And if you want to understand objective right and wrong, that means right and wrong generally, for the whole universe, then it will have no meaning for this stage.

MISS M. At what point in our progress may one expect to be able to make our centres work more fully? Mr. O. has said that now we can only use ten per cent of their capacity.

MR. O. Much less than that. Ten per cent will be almost all that you can get, but we don't have one-millionth per cent.

MISS M. What are those higher centres that we do not often contact with?

MR. O. Never. It would be very good if we could contact even not very often. They are machines in us that can work only in different states of consciousness. If you have some observations and material, we can describe the difference between higher emotional and higher mental. Higher emotional is supposed to work with the third state of consciousness, and higher mental with the fourth state of consciousness. That is all we can say about it; but there are so many descriptions of these manifestations, and these descriptions are so similar that there is nothing wrong in accepting them, because we can compare them, and see the inventions. There are many false descriptions, but by comparing many of these descriptions we can easily see what is right and what is wrong, what is real and what invented. In religious experiences, philosophical writings, there are many descriptions of that. Some time I can speak about it, and particularly about how to distinguish the real and false.

MR. W. If, as Mr. O. says in *New Model*, 'We have every right to consider that our thoughts move along the fourth dimension' . . .

MR. O. That is only a metaphor.

MR. W. . . . will the development of higher centres enable us to make more use of this and control it?

MR. O. Yes, but I wouldn't use this description or speak about the fourth dimension. That was in the first preliminary description of the fourth dimension.

MR. W. Why is it much more difficult to work and formulate questions at some times than others; it seems to go in waves. Is this due to the Law of Octaves, or to the quality of the impressions one may have received?

MR. O. No. Quite simply, we are not always the same. One moment we are in one 'I', another moment in another 'I'. That is the difference between different 'I's. It is necessary to remember you are not <u>you</u>, you are many; and one moment there is one group of 'I's, another moment another group of 'I's. You have no control.

MR. W. Are there any relaxation or other exercises to help right functioning of centres and assist in self-remembering that one can do during one's ordinary work?

MR. O. Yes. I already said that there are. You will come to that soon. Only you must not hope that your work begins from that. It will just be a certain side line. With some people it may help them to understand, but you cannot do these exercises twenty-four hours a day, and you live twenty-four hours; so the question is not what you do when you do the exercises, even if you do them, but what you do at other times.

MR. W. Is not the Fourth Way actually very much the most difficult, owing to the continual choice entailed under conditions of maximum outside distractions?

MR. O. It depends what you call most difficult. The way of Monk or the way of Fakir needs a very big decision in the very beginning, when you really know nothing. You have to renounce everything, give up everything absolutely, without leaving anything. If you can do that, and if you have other qualities, you can go by the way of Monk, or the way of Yogi, if you find a Monk school or a Yogi school. But if you don't know a Monk school or a Yogi school, and if you do not want and find you cannot give up even small things, certainly this is the only possible way for you. It is not a question of more or less difficult; it is a question of which is most possible, and then you will find there is only one possible.

I told you the story about one Yogi in some school in India who worked for many years, and there was always one thing that he couldn't do. At last he became disappointed, dispirited, left the school and went away. Again, several years later, he found another school, and when he came there the first task they gave was exactly what he couldn't do in the other school. He asked: 'How did you know?' and they said: 'That is written on your face.'

MR. W. If one was able to do so, and it was permitted, would it be valuable to give up one's ordinary work and spend one's whole time working at Lyne, etc. for the system?

MR. O. If they accept you at Lyne. It is not my business.

MISS M. In answer to a recent question, Mr. O. said time has different speeds. If we could get into higher centres, would we find the speed of time greater and on going back to lower centres would we be unable to understand what we had experienced on the higher level?

MR. O. In answer to the last part of the question, yes, that is a definite fact. You come in contact with many things which you think you understand quite well at that time, and when you come to your ordinary mind you don't understand it at all, because it is very quick, and even in the elementary levels of higher emotional centre you already come to some things you cannot explain later, and when you come again to the higher emotional, you are astonished why you couldn't remember; it looks so simple. When you come to normal state again, you don't remember.

MR. C. What forces are responsible for tropisms?

MR. O. It is necessary to define; we cannot just take a word because there are many different associations, and in every term, a scientific term, or something like that, there are many affirmations and many negations, so we cannot take the word without counting how many negations and how many affirmations there are in this word.

MR. C. Is there any mechanism in the body for integrating the memories present in individual organs and structures? I was thinking of a physical activity, like swimming or skating.

MR. O. Moving centre, if that's what you mean.

MR. P. Has the system any direct methods by which, under guidance, one could be put in touch with higher centres?

MR. O. There is no difficulty at all to be put in contact with higher centres. The difficulty is to remember something or use it, and to do it by your own self. But there is no difficulty in making contact with higher centres. The difficulty is to be conscious in higher centres, and there is no quick method for that; it has to be attained by the slow method of self-remembering, non-identification and so on. And other schools and other methods, in different words, do exactly the same thing; because too quick methods all come to this empty room.

MRS. C. I have noticed that when I don't like a person or a work of art, I find it very difficult to appreciate their good points intellectually. Is this an example of unnecessary co-ordination of centres?

MR. O. In a certain sense, yes.

MRS. C. Is unnecessary co-ordination sometimes caused by tension, as when anger or fear upset the digestion, make it impossible to think, and one is tense all over physically, or does the co-ordination cause the tension?

MR. O. Both. The one increases the other.

MISS W. Last week I had occasion to be with someone for a long period while they were in a very negative state. At last my energy seemed to give way and I found myself rapidly becoming identified against all reason. I could not prevent myself from feeling violently negative. The only thing left seemed to be to run out of the room to avoid at any rate an explosion. I was conscious of having within me an enormous amount of energy. To try and remember myself seemed quite impossible in such an uncollected state, though I felt how urgently I needed to try something, if only I knew how. The only thing I seemed capable of was something physical, and I held out my arms, which helped me stop feeling negative. Can one make use of that sort of energy in such a state, and what is the right way?

MR. O. If it helped, that means it is right. That is all I can say. And the rest is slow work and preparation. In order to swim in a difficult place, difficult water, you have to swim first in more quiet water.

MISS S. I have been unwell recently and I found on the first day in bed although I felt seedy I had a great deal of physical energy and was very restless and quite unable to concentrate my thoughts. But on the second and subsequent days I was considerably more tired and very glad to be able to rest, and then it was that I found I could both think and feel much more intensely and be in a better state generally. I do not understand why this is, but I have noticed before that when I am tired physically I often seem to be in a better, or at least quieter state.

MR. O. That means it is useful for you to be tired. Try to be tired more—but don't overdo it.

*   *   *

[Questions written down while Mr. O. was out of the room.]

MISS T. What is meant by third state of consciousness? Is trying to remember ourselves third state of consciousness?

MR. O. No. It is only the approach, the way to it. Third state of consciousness can be described as self-consciousness, self-awareness.

MISS W. Can we make super-efforts with our own will? Is it a case of somebody else's help?

MR. O. It is very difficult to make by your own will. You always find some excuse. I will describe to you later some cases of super-effort.

MISS S. What are the special negative emotions that make serious work impossible? Do we have to find what our special negative emotions are?

MR. O. No, don't use that as a term—special negative emotions. What is special for you will not be special for another person. And there are some which make it impossible for everybody. But first observe, and then we can talk about it.

MISS S. I personally dislike a particular person rather intensely and although I seem to be a little better the dislike is still there. Is that one of the emotions Mr. O. meant?

MR. O. No, I don't think so. It depends who this person is. If you always live with this person and continue to dislike them, then it may become difficult.

MR. S. Mr. O. said it was necessary to do several things at once in order to make a super-effort. Does that mean effort of several centres simultaneously? For example, struggling with a negative emotion like irritation needs emotional effort; it might also require some physical effort and change in mental attitude.

MR. O. But when you make super-effort, that means in all centres, because one centre cannot make super-effort.

MRS. S. Is super-effort something different from the most intense effort we are capable of at the moment, some different thing altogether?

MR. T. Does super-effort imply sticking at something for a very long time?

MRS. B. To go back to the question of right and wrong, did Mr. O.

mean that from the point of view of the system it didn't matter about cheating bus conductors?

MR. O. I don't know. Bus conductors don't enter in the system.

MISS N. Is it possible to stop thoughts when listening to the answers to other people's questions, or are there only certain occasions when one can try to stop thoughts?

MR. O. How can I say? Try, and then you will see whether you can stop thoughts or not.

MR. W. Before one could make any kind of super-effort would one not have to strengthen one's effort and get a few more 'I's together to work on this? I understand super-effort as greater attention on one definite aim.

MR. P. Mr. O. said something I didn't understand—that it was quite easy to make contact with higher centres but the difficulty was to be conscious at such moments. I had always supposed from what was said before, that you could not make contact except in a higher state of consciousness.

MR. O. That's it. But there are many ways. In any case it is not a question of difficulty in centres; the difficulty is in consciousness.

MRS. S. If we make contact with higher centres without being more conscious, would we know it? I was connecting it with what was said in the first lectures, that centres work but we are not in contact with them.

MR. O. Then you gain nothing by that. It will be just the same. You will fall asleep; you will become unconscious.

MRS. W. Is the taste of super-effort the same as that of effort only stronger? Or is it different?

MR. O. It is a very unpleasant taste, in any case.

MRS. W. Could Mr. O. say more about super-effort, because one can't ask concrete questions until we have experienced it.

MR. O. Well, I will describe to you one super-effort. It was at the end of 1917. We were a small company living on the shore of the Black Sea in the Caucasus, about twenty-three miles from the nearest town. We generally went there by horse once a week. It happened once that for some reason, because there was no horse, or I was late or something, I walked these twenty-three miles, and it was raining all the time, and it was a high road like the Corniche, and I was all wet and very cold and had heavy boots on. At last I came to where we were living, and then

Gurdjieff, who was there at that time, said: 'How about making a super-effort?' I asked: 'What kind?' I saw that it was warm inside, and supper was prepared, and so on. Gurdjieff said: 'I want to post a letter.' It was two miles' journey to the post office. Then I decided, and I noticed exactly then how legs did not wish to go, and although my mind wanted it, legs didn't wish it. So I had to use all centres to make myself go. You cannot go with one centre in such a case. Particularly from the house to the road it was uphill and very slippery; and it was more unpleasant when I came back, because they had finished supper and it was dark and cold.

This is an example of super-effort.

MRS. P. Did Mr. O. not say super-effort was doing several things at the same time more consciously?

MR. O. That's it. Moving your legs, and trying not to fall, and swearing and all that—all at the same time.

MRS. C. Did Mr. O. mean physical things or not considering and not identifying and things like that, when he spoke about doing several things at the same time?

MR. O. And not considering, and not identifying, at the same time.

MISS M. I remember once Mr. O. said we should try to do more than we think we can do. Has this anything to do with super-effort?

MR. O. Yes.

Well, I will have some more material next time, but in any case prepare questions, as many as you can.

*   *   *

Incomplete record. [?] End of January 1939.

not repeat now, first, because I have no blackboard. I will explain: it is a kind of permanent triad in man. It changes only in a certain direction. By study of the static triad, you can determine the being of a man at a given moment—I mean the gradual development of being.

MR. H. What is necessary in order to understand more about the octave starting from the sun?

MR. O. But I just said that we cannot understand. If you have some material, if you think you heard something, or connect it with something, then think about it and perhaps you will find something. But we cannot begin from the lecture. If we had material, we could start from the lecture. If you have some idea, then perhaps it is possible to find more. If you take this octave starting from the sun, you will find we know three notes in it—la, sol, fa—which is described as organic life on earth. We know what mi is—remains of organic life on earth. The system mentions what re means—matters which go to feed moon, which are liberated by the dying of individuals of organic life. But what si and do are, the system does not say. If you think you heard something, or if you connect it with something, then we can discuss it. But you must find yourself first what we can connect it with. I can give you a hint, if you like to think about it, but you must understand it must be your own thinking. It doesn't mean I will help you. This is what in the *New Model* I wrote about the Big Laboratory. That is all that I can say.

MRS. D. I find I can sometimes get out of a feeling of negative emotion by allowing myself to get identified with something pleasant.

MR. O. You use the word 'identified' in the wrong sense. If you allow yourself to be interested . . .

MRS. D. That's what I mean.

MR. O. . . . then you mustn't use 'identified'—you cannot say, 'if I allow myself to be identified'—it is wrong. If you allow yourself to be interested in something, it may work for some time. If you allow yourself to be identified, practically it is just the same, only in a pleasant thing you can be interested without being identified; in an unpleasant thing you cannot be interested without being identified.

MISS S. I want to ask about desire to get on in the system. With me it seems too much. I always want to do and I can't, and it makes me irritated.

MR. O. Well, try not to want to do too much. What else can I say? Try not to want to do more than you can.

MISS T. I always seem to have more energy when I get up in the morning.

MR. O. You are not an exception; I think all people have.

MISS T. Also I have least in the afternoon. Do we always start a new octave in the afternoon?

MR. O. No, you cannot speak about an octave just like that, because you like to think there is an octave. There must be some material for that.

MR. C. Did you say in the study of personalities one should concentrate only on the personality that was magnetic centre?

MR. O. No. If you already started and know some other personalities then go on. I said, in the very beginning. Although, again, you can know other personalities before you know what is magnetic centre or what is connected with magnetic centre. So start from what you know.

MR. M. What is the relationship between man and organic life?

MR. O. No relation. Man is part of organic life. Organic life includes all living things on earth.

MR. M. I thought in the chain of cosmoses organic life was above man?

MR. O. No, it is all the same, not above. It is simply bigger in relation to individual man, not humanity. Mankind is part of organic life, but individual man is a lower cosmos, the same as individual dog would be.

MR. M. Is that the reason why there is not a possibility for a great many people to escape?

MR. O. Partly that, but I think there are simpler reasons, easier to understand.

MISS F. I believe quite a lot of very vivid memories are about things where I have made an exhibition of myself, and it seems that if I had done this, I must be considering.

MR. O. Yes, maybe, but maybe it is not considering, but just right thinking. Considering is a useless kind of emotion, you know. It doesn't bring any useful result.

MISS F. But if you feel foolish, it must be considering.

MR. O. No, it isn't considering; it is just, you feel foolish. Why should it be considering?

MR. M. Can we learn anything useful from the study of what you call half-dream states?

MR. O. I don't think so. It was a long time before I discovered that, and then I found that they cannot be useful.

MISS W. Are some of the things that happen to us and that we cannot remember, completely absent from our rolls of memory?

MR. O. You mean things which happened but which we forgot? There are different theories about it. I don't know. Probably, there are different kinds, again; some that can be reconstructed and some that cannot—like from the ordinary point of view.

MISS W. I think I can remember back a very long way, when I was very small. Is that quite common?

MR. O. Not quite, but it happens. It makes no difference. Some people recollect themselves earlier, some later.

MRS. H. Is magic the same sort of action. . . .

MR. O. What does magic mean?

MRS. H. I don't know.

MR. O. Well, if you cannot explain it, don't use it. That is one of the principles of the work.

MRS. H. Will you tell me what you mean by magic?

MR. O. No. I didn't say anything. I didn't mention magic. If I did, then you have a right to ask, you see. No. That is a wrong start, you know. If you start from the other end, then some time we can speak about it.

MRS. S. When one is in a bad state and against the work, should one try to shock oneself into better effort or just observe?

MR. O. Yes, if you can. Why not? Self-remembering is the only one real shock—but that doesn't refer to five minutes. If you try to remember yourself for a day or two, it will pass probably.

MRS. L. Can an imagination be thought of as an incomplete action, lacking one of the forces of the triad?

MR. O. Why such a complicated explanation? Such a thing as imagination we can study psychologically. We can understand it just turns round and round and we cannot control it, so very soon we see it is quite useless and takes energy and causes a very great tendency to sleep and become negative and so on.

MISS S. Is it wrong to think of Lyne as the only place where one has the opportunity to self-remember?

MR. O. You must try to remember yourself when you can. You cannot decide to remember yourself in connection with some special place, special time, special weather and so on.

MRS. H. When it was said, man has to die before being born again, does it mean false personality has to die?

MR. O. No. Everything has to die, not only false personality. Why false personality? Again, this is rather a complicated terminology, so wait until we come back to it. You don't remember it quite right like that. It was said that if man dies before he awakes, then he cannot be born again. Man first must awake. Then he can die. And then he can be born again. But these expressions 'die', 'born', they have different meanings, so you had better leave it. But first it is necessary to try to awake.

[Mr. O. left the room and questions were written down.]

* * *

MISS. S. I still do not understand about self-remembering in connection with Lyne. I mean hard or at least intense work seems to be necessary to help one to stop thoughts, and as Lyne is where I get most chance of doing this, then surely it must be a more important place to be at. Or otherwise have I misunderstood about self-remembering?

MR. O. No. Quite right. If you feel like that, then it is quite all right, but it doesn't mean you must neglect to remember yourself in other places.

MR. M. What is 'instinct' in insects and animals?

MR. O. The same as in man. The word instinct is generally used in the wrong sense. Instinct, in man and in animals also, is chiefly inner work of the organism; and all the strange manifestations of animals which we know may sometimes be called instinct and may sometimes not be called instinct, because ordinary science does not know about the independent function of moving centre. Really many of these things called instincts are moving functions. We may continue some time. It is a word that needs speaking about.

MR. M. Mr. O. has referred to reservoirs of higher hydrogens in nature. Could we hear more about this?

MR. O. We will come to that some time, but not yet.

MR. M. Am I right in thinking that the work of the system is that of transforming dense matter into higher matter?

MR. O. No. Work in the system cannot be described in that way. It must simply be understood in a psychological sense, not like that.

MR. H. In the study of the octave from the sun, has anything more been done about translating *Biosphere*? Would it be helpful to read it in that connection?

MR. O. I think we had some of the translation, but we didn't finish it. I don't think that this book is really necessary. There must be English books written since then or about that time. I will look. In any case, all new ideas in geology are very useful.

MISS T. I am often emotionally moved by music or I remember I liked certain books when I was young. I can't remember very well, but only a certain taste. Other people remember so much better than I, I can't help envying them and thinking they must be more awake than I am.

MR. O. It is difficult to compare, you know. Maybe you remember what they don't remember. Memory is such a strange thing. Everybody has his own combination of capacities for memory. One person remembers some things more, another remembers better other things. You cannot say what is better, one or another.

MR. R. I am not quite satisfied with the answer to my question. I asked whether it is not better for a humble student to limit himself to the basic things. I quite understand some people can think easier about octaves and some about triads. But there are certain basic things like not expressing negative emotions, not considering, and so on, and I don't seem to need these, so to speak, more intellectual things.

MR. O. Quite right. Everybody must choose what speaks to him at a given moment.

MRS. D. Mr. O. speaks about a quiet place in oneself. Is it the state you get to when you self-remember, because everything seems peaceful and quiet then and one really seems to be aware of oneself?

MR. O. Yes, you can take it like that.

MR. B. Is criticism of a thing you can do yourself quite well, negative emotion?

MR. O. It may be in some cases.

MR. B. For instance, I am very critical on dancing. Is it false personality coming up and thinking you can do it better?

MR. O. Maybe. It is difficult to say. You must observe yourself, and again, in different conditions, different circumstances.

MRS. L. The thing that worries me most is Mr. O.'s statement that things happen to us. I had to make a decision in a hurry and then afterwards heard of other facts and said to someone, if I had known these things I wouldn't have made that decision.

MR. O. But you didn't know, so you couldn't take that into consideration, so there is nothing to worry about.

MRS. L. They said I would have made the identical decision because I was I. How much choice have we?

MR. O. No, not always, because you didn't know. If you knew, perhaps you could make a different decision, but again, it would not be you who made this decision. The decision would be altered by your knowledge of the circumstances.

MR. K. Isn't sincere criticism a way to understanding? I mean criticism of things, weighing one thing with another. One has to have come to some decision about first principles of the thing one is criticizing.

MR. O. Yes certainly, but criticism mustn't become criticism of people, their attitudes, their being and so on.

MR. K. Is this different from criticizing actions of one's own?

MR. O. Yes. To one's own one has one attitude, to other people's another attitude. Again, people may be in the work or not in the work, older or younger than you. There are very many different possibilities.

MR. B. If I try to relax my muscles and stop my thoughts, I very soon become conscious of my breathing and this seems to interfere with relaxation. Can anything be done about this?

MR. O. If you feel it, you feel it, only you mustn't try to change your breathing in this way. But I think that with better methods it will disappear.

MRS. D. When I am interested in some question at the lecture but don't understand much about it, I begin thinking about it and so miss many other questions. What can I do about that?

MR. O. It cannot be helped. All questions are repeated from time to time.

MISS F. I am puzzled because when I am in a bad state of considering, I am very aware of my body as a large awkward mass, and when I try to self-remember I try to do this same thing, to be aware of my body.

MR. O. No, there is nothing to worry about. These subjective feelings mean nothing.

MRS. N. Would it be true to say what other people dislike in us are our worst mechanicalnesses, because if so any criticism of ourselves by other people would be useful, even if we only heard it in a roundabout way?

MR. O. No. You cannot say that necessarily they see only our worst mechanicalnesses. They may see other features—they also can make mistakes.

MR. H. Criticism in me is bound up with negative emotion.

MR. O. In most cases, in most people.

* * *

Well, next week we will have large meetings upstairs, so you will be two groups together, and you will hear definitely from Madame K. which day you will come. There will be two days, Wednesday and Thursday.

* * *

Wednesday. February 8th 1939. (Colet Gardens.)

MR. C. Is it of practical use to think of the events of one's past life when trying to self-remember, with a view to fixing them for any future recurrence?

MR. O. No, this is not practical. First, as I said, it is necessary to be sure about future recurrence; and second, it is necessary to be sure of remembering yourself. If you put too much like that, it transforms into imagination, nothing else. But if we first try to remember ourselves without adding anything to it, and then, when we can, also about our past life—you remember I spoke about trying to find cross-roads— then in combination it will be very useful. Only don't think you can do it; you cannot do it yet.

MR. C. I see the Oxford dictionary gives two meanings' for the word 'transformism': (1) Any doctrine of the evolution of the species. (2) Gradual evolution of morals and social relations.

MR. O. Yes, but morals and social relations don't enter into this. We speak only about change of beings. Certainly transformation is used in many senses—in the sense of evolution, metamorphosis (as in the case of the butterfly), metamorphosis in the fairy tale sense—so there are many meanings.

MISS S. I did not understand well enough what we were to look for about transformism.

MR. O. All that you can find. First of all it is necessary to establish gradation—in which sense the idea is used first; then how the meaning of the word went through a certain transformation; how it became connected with certain scientific theories which took a certain definite shape during the nineteenth century. So it is necessary to know transformism in that sense. Other meanings we must know only to put them aside. Only this idea of evolution, of the origin of species, the transformation of species interests us. We must not insist on any particular theory; that is not our business. We must know the existing theories. Then only when we come to man we can begin to speak about what we can accept and what we cannot accept.

MR. M. Last week Mr. O. said this was the first time we had come in contact with the system. Does it follow that this is the first time one has met the people one met through coming into the system?

MR. O. I am sure of it.

MR. M. Do we come under less laws in our activities in connection with the system, for instance at meetings or working at Lyne?

MR. O. I don't understand what you mean by laws in this case. You must understand that if we realize we are under many mechanical laws, then we can get rid eventually of some of these laws, by becoming subject to other laws. There is no other way. To get out of the power of one law, you must put yourself under other laws. This is the general idea. So there is not a single moment of your life when

[Intermediate pages missing.]

When will this group come to the discussion of our place in the world?

MR. O. We can come to it to-day even. We have some time yet. You see we don't realize one thing about our place in the world—we don't realize we live in a very bad place in the universe. Many things which happen in our life, for instance this extreme mechanicalness, this point which interests people, why only few people can get out of this mechanicalness. For many people it is impossible to get out of this state—it is not their fault, but simply that we live in a very bad place in the universe. For instance, if one lives very near the North Pole, one cannot expect to have a warm climate. One has to come to England for that!

MISS M. By that, do you suggest that we might have lived somewhere else in the universe?

MR. O. Not such as we are.

MISS M. Do you suggest that life exists elsewhere?

MR. O. No, that's too simple. We can begin like this: We know we live on the earth.

We know that in the sphere of influence of the earth is the moon.

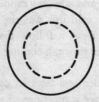

We know that the earth is one of the planets of the Solar System, so it is under the influence of other planets.

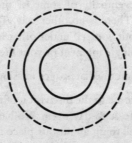

The planets are in the sphere of influence of the sun.

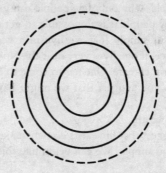

The sun is one of the suns of the Milky Way.

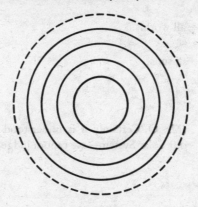

And the Milky Way—this agglomeration of stars, quite simply astronomically, is one of similar galaxies.

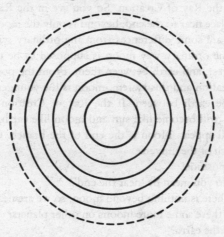

If we put it simply like this:

All galaxies—all worlds.

Our galaxy—all suns.

Sun.

All planets.   (Mr. O. Certainly it is understood to be planets of
our Solar System—we cannot judge other planets.)

Earth.

Moon.

This is called the Ray of Creation. So you see in the Ray of Creation
we occupy a place near to the end; beyond is only the moon.

Then there are some differences from the ordinary scientific understanding. In the ordinary way moon is supposed to be the oldest, the
sun the youngest, and earth between them. From the point of view of
the Ray of Creation and this system, moon is the youngest and sun the
oldest, and the earth between. If the Ray of Creation continues to
develop, earth will become like sun and moon like earth, and maybe a
new moon will appear. Moon is the end of the branch. Certainly, it is
only one branch of the universe.

This is our position.

MR. S. What do you mean by 'near the end'?

MR. O. Well, there is nothing beyond moon, so we are near the end.

MR. C. Aren't there some more moons on other planets?

MR. O. Round the earth?

MR. C. No, Jupiter.

MR. O. That doesn't enter into this. All those other things are taken
together. When we speak about planets, we speak about planets of the
Solar System.

MISS M. Does that mean that in the next stage of life one would be
living on all the planets at once?

MR. O. No. We are under the influence of all the planets. They are not all on the same level, but they must be taken into consideration between the earth and the sun.

We will continue only in one way at present, and later from different angles. The position and meaning of organic life is interesting—organic life, which covers the earth as a sensitive film. This is its real destination—it catches certain radiations which earth cannot catch, and transfers them to earth—radiations from the sun and from planets and maybe even from further stars in a small way.

MISS L. The moon is a case of degeneration?

MR. O. No. The moon is very important for organic life. Organic life depends on moon. All movements—not only ours—movements of trees, seeds, plants, branches, animals—all movements depend on moon; and at the same time moon feeds on organic life. Organic life, when it is alive, has one kind of function, that of transferring radiations to earth. Everything that dies, from bacteria to man, then divides in two. One part of its organism remains on earth and enters in earth and produces many different effects on the surface of earth; and the other part is attracted by moon and feeds moon. So part of us, when we die, feeds moon—but not only man—all organic life also. In that way moon grows and can become earth.

MISS C. How?

MR. O. If it feeds well and grows big and becomes warmer—like that it becomes like earth.

MISS C. Moon is older than earth?

MR. O. This is an astronomical fantasy, not based on anything.

MISS L. Suppose you take the evolution of moon—in its true sense . . .

MR. O. What does evolution mean?

MISS L. . . . in the system sense.

MR. O. We don't know—such a thing doesn't exist—neither in a true or wrong sense.

MISS L. But if you speak of evolution . . .

MR. O. There is no evolution.

MISS L. . . . if I reach higher consciousness. . . .

MR. O. That is another thing. This is the result of your own work. Human beings are in a different position. They are in a different state. Nature brings them to a certain state, but they are self-evolving. But other things are not self-evolving—they come to a certain state and remain there.

MR. S. If moon feeds on things from earth, is it not self-evolving?

MR. O. No. We cannot say. Quite possibly after a certain point it may become self-evolving. At present moon depends on us.

MR. C. Are we the only inhabited world?

MR. O. That doesn't enter into our problem.

MISS W. If human beings develop themselves as much as they can, does that mean they help to develop earth?

MR. O. That is too big a hypothesis. It means they themselves can develop and pass to level of planets and sun—part of their being.

MISS M. Does it mean they will be open to influences from sun?

MR. O. Quite right.

MR. M. Do you mean moon is growing materially larger?

MR. O. I don't know.

MR. M. We have evidence of the sun growing smaller.

MR. O. Yes, but that is not sure.

We are 1, 2 and 3, under a certain number of laws. Some are necessary—we cannot exist without these laws—and some are unnecessary—they keep us in a certain state, but we can get rid of them, and then we pass under other laws, which will be much more profitable for us. This is the reason for our development. So at present we must not think what will happen to the Ray of Creation or something like that. We must think only of our personal profit.

MR. S. When you said we are in a bad place in the universe, like living near the North Pole, what did you mean?

MR. O. Earth is the coldest place, with the exception of moon—it is further from bigger influences.

MR. S. Does the Eskimo have less chance of evolving?

MR. O. Maybe, but even Eskimos can travel.

MR. M. You said in an earlier lecture that man was immortal within the limits of the Solar System. . . .

MR. O. Quite sufficient—they are very big limits. Even man No. 7 cannot expect more. It means as long as the Solar System exists.

* * *

Sunday. October 15th 1939. (Lyne.)

MR. O. Well, what shall we talk about to-day? All questions are about war now, so start with war questions.

MR. R. To what extent can one alter the conditions in which one finds oneself?

MR. O. It is individual—first; and then general. But it is not a question of conditions; it is a question of understanding that really nothing changed. These are conditions in which we live. War is permanent really—the permanent state of humanity, with very short intervals of peace. That must be understood first of all.

So one must try to do what is possible. Certainly conditions may become such that it will become completely impossible to do anything. But as long as possible we must go on as much as possible.

I had many letters. People asked: 'Is war inevitable?' 'Can it be prevented?' 'What can be done?' It is not a question of what we can do. We can do nothing. Certainly at a time like this it is very useful to understand the situation, why it happened exactly in this way, how it could be prevented, and so on. Then you could see the situation better and perhaps it might help you to see your own place in all this—not how it can affect you (that is individual)—but just from the point of view of understanding. All that we can try to do is to try to understand.

MR. H. The great difficulty I have is that all the time I think of this as a war of right against wrong, and can't get it out of my head.

MR. O. Yes, but what is wrong?

MR. H. The other side.

MR. O. It is not enough. There is no question there about that, but this is not all the truth. It is one-tenth of the truth.

You see there are many causes for wars. First we must speak a little about cosmic causes. Cosmic causes are in the organization of organic life. Organic life is based on the principle of killing. One species feeds on another. But man really can be out of this law, at least partly, if

417

only man will be a little more clever. But men are what they are, so this is inevitable.

Leaving cosmic ideas and taking just historical causes, it is difficult to speak, because very few people know history. I don't mean history of ancient times, but present modern history. Many people don't know the history of the last twenty years—I mean history of the facts. If we want to understand the present situation, we must go to just after the Napoleonic Wars, to the Vienna Congress. The Vienna Congress, with all the faults that were made there, still kept Europe for a hundred years. It is necessary to understand in general the period from the Vienna Congress to the Crimean War; another period from the Crimean War to 1914, or better up to the Versailles Conference. Certainly the last years before 1914, say from 1900, one must study with more details. Then another period from the Versailles Conference up to the beginning of this war. So we must study these periods, and unless you know as well as possible these three periods it is very difficult to speak about causes, reasons, faults of this war.

MR. B. You have said that some wars are good or may be necessary. Is this one of those?

MR. O. Not necessary. I never said that. You see, if we start from the other end, many people speak and write books saying that wars are not necessary because all differences of opinion between people can be decided with the help of conferences, mutual talks and so on. This is right in principle, but not from the point of view of facts, because it is possible not at every moment. Up to 1914, if we take the end of the nineteenth century and the beginning of this century, it was possible. Now, before this war, it was impossible. Quite the opposite, all attempts of conferences and so on only created this war. To understand this you must begin from the Versailles Conference. Good or bad, the war was finished. Good or bad, something was decided. Many wrong things were done there, but in any case England and France were in a very good position and had all the trumps in their hands. But they let them out one after another. First they helped the bolsheviks instead of the White Army; then they recognized them; then they allowed Germany to arm—never openly, but they let them. Then they paid for that.

The chief cause was recognition of the bolsheviks. Hitler is the result of it; he is not the cause. If you understand that you will understand the situation. You can do nothing about it, but you will understand. I speak only from the point of view of understanding.

If you go further back, as I said, from the Vienna Congress to the Crimean War you can take in general; things that happened then affect us in general. But the first big sin was the Crimean War. Then the second was the Franco-Prussian War; after that at the beginning of this century, and again in 1914. This is what we have to think about. All that brought this situation. So we cannot regard it as simply the whole fault of Hitler. It is childish.

And for us, if we study psychology from the historical point of view, and history from the psychological point of view, we must understand. It is part of the work. It will help us, I suppose, in some cases to find our way.

I don't want you to limit questions to that, but I know I had many letters and you all had similar questions, so I spoke about it. But you can speak about anything you like.

MR. R. Why does this war seem so very unemotional?

MR. O. I don't know. That is your own subjective view. Also, it is interesting to know in details the history of the last war, because then you will understand what may happen. I remember at the beginning of the war I came to Russia and every conversation began with the phrase: 'When war ends . . .' and when war ended we found ourselves in quite a different world. And there was a kind of sense of false security after the war, but now it shows it was quite false. The war never ended really.

MRS. C. Are we to regard a man like Hitler as an inevitable result of the causes of the war? You say it is impossible to blame Hitler for everything, but what should our attitude be to a man who on the surface does appear to have brought things to a climax?

MR. O. Yes, it only looks like that. It was brought about by English and French politicians, who recognized bolshevism and didn't keep the Versailles Treaty and let Germany arm. If the clauses about Germany having no right to arm were kept, there would be no war. So who are our enemies? Just where they are fighting now, in the Saar, only three years ago they took the last troops out of there—because Hitler demanded it and they obeyed him.

MR. A. Is there any change in the nature of bolshevism in the Stalin régime now?

MR. O. It cannot change; it is a definite thing. If it changes it ceases to be bolshevism. But it cannot happen by itself. It can only be destroyed or left to grow. This is again one of the illusions created about Russia—that the bolsheviks are changing, that they have become nice and soft. Hitler was in the beginning accepted by many Germans because of the fear of bolshevism. The problem was: either communism or Hitler, and they said, Hitler is better.

About people like Hitler, psychologically, we can speak another time. It is a very interesting problem, because they belong to a quite particular type of men. There is even a name for these men. But it is better to have a special conversation about this, because it must begin from quite a different side.

The Germans were very much deceived about Hitler. I didn't speak with or meet many Germans during these last years, but a few years ago I met Keyserling. He was half Russian and had been in a Russian school and university. He said the only difference between bolshevism and Hitler is that everything under the bolsheviks can become only worse, and in Germany it can become better. Now we see that become better!

MRS. C. There is no possibility at the end of this war of the position being different?

MR. O. That depends how it goes, what happens, how long it will be.

MRS. C. You think the position might be different to that after the last war?

MR. O. It could be better, it could be worse. It depends how long it lasts, how many countries are involved in it and so on.

MR. R. From the point of view of the individual's recurrence, to be born in catastrophic times. . . .

MR. O. But all times are catastrophic. It is only that we have the illusion, because people of my age, for instance, had a long period of peace, younger people a shorter period of peace, but young people had no feeling of peace, those who have lived only between the last war and this war. And if you take a longer period of history you see that people never get out. Only certainly with the improvement of technical appliances, war machines, and so on, it becomes more and more dangerous, more and more deadly.

MR. B. Surely it affects the individual more nowadays?

MR. O. Certainly—it affects larger spaces, bigger countries. War destroyed schools in Greece. War always destroys attempts of esoteric work, school-work. Certainly it was impossible after this last war in Russia, Germany, Italy and Turkey. Here there are still possibilities, but how long, in this war, we don't know.

MRS. P. But is there not a spot in the world that one could go to?

MR. O. This is individual, you know. This is not a general question. Everybody must decide for himself. Then if they decide right they meet at some place; if they decide wrong they meet in a different place.

MRS. P. I meant school.

MR. O. It is difficult to say. School can only disappear and appear in another place. It will be different.

MR. R. For the mass of humanity, can we take this war as a turning point of growth?

MR. O. There is no reason to believe in it. If things go right and if people do right things, then it may be, but it may make things only worse. We don't know what will be better or worse after this.

MR. R. It appears our present civilization is about 3,000 years, whereas other civilizations had even less.

MR. O. Certainly. But again conditions change. You cannot speak like that.

MR. W. Do you think there is any significance in the present hesitation on both sides to begin anything on a really serious scale, or is it just fear?

MR. O. No. I think it depends on many things. It is impossible to say now. If we survive, we will know later. And again, if you compare with 1914, certainly there was bigger fighting, bigger events in the beginning, but then it came to the same position very quickly. This is only six weeks, and things began to be seen fully only about a year after the beginning—real conditions and real relation of forces.

MISS C. Do you think it is likely the United States might become involved?

MR. O. That I don't know.

MISS S. Do we come under new laws when a war is declared?

MR. O. Yes certainly. We were more free; now we are less free. The blackout—that is a new law—there wasn't a blackout. Rationing of petrol is another law.

MR. R. You once said knowledge is only for the few and in times like this there is no more knowledge to be had.

MR. O. Yes if you like you can put it in a similar way, but not exactly like that. I said that at times when people throw away and don't want to take even their normal amount of knowledge, that material of knowledge can be collected. Also, conditions are necessary for that.

MR. R. And it is more possible through a school than by the individual?

MR. O. That depends. If one hasn't been connected with a school then it is impossible; but if one already knows something, then it is possible—just by trying to understand and keeping this understanding of how things happen, how nobody can do anything.

MRS. P. Then is there more energy about for those who understand?

MR. O. No. We must not deceive ourselves about that. Although, again, we must remember that our work, which we are continuing, began really during the war. There was a small beginning before, quite private, but during the war it began to develop.

MR. R. Can the individual, as such, escape in these times, other than through a school?

MR. O. What can I say? Everything is possible.

Generally speaking, the continuation of the war and the end of the war depend largely on the actions of governments that remain sane—comparatively sane, because neither is quite sane. If they do right things, being only comparatively sane, then there could be good results and things can be better. If they do wrong things, everything will be worse.

The definite fact is that as long as bolshevism remains in Europe there will be no peace in Europe—and they fight with Hitler and leave the bolsheviks alone. Certainly the bolsheviks help Hitler. Sooner or later they will betray him. There is no question about that, but probably later.

And if they don't start war against the bolsheviks, and if they don't change the government in Russia and arrange a more or less normal government there, this war will go on twenty years, and what will happen in twenty years it is impossible to foresee.

We mustn't give all our attention to these questions. It is useful to think about it from right points of view in order to understand the situation, but the chief questions must be your own individual questions, school questions and so on.

MR. F. Does one understand the same laws with regard to the conflict of things by studying questions like that and studying conflict inside oneself?

MR. O. Quite, yes. Because after all, apart from political causes, the causes are in state of being, very low state of being. They don't want to know anything, can be easily persuaded, can be made to do things, can be too easily deceived. That is a sign of very low state of being. Right questions, right problems are to think about being and how to change being, how to find weak sides of our being and how to find ways to fight against them.

MR. A. I have found certain of the ideas which I thought I understood a bit and used to help me have disappeared in the back of my mind.

MR. O. You must try to drag them out. That is your own work. You must not let them disappear.

MR. R. I have a terrible fear that communism is gaining ground in India and that it will destroy what knowledge there is.

MR. O. Very easily.

MR. R. It seems to me the British politicians are very short-sighted.

MR. O. Quite blind, not only short-sighted.

MISS S. About the system, although I know what I want from it—I want to escape—I feel I don't understand what it would want from me, what my position is in it, how I should behave, in a big sense.

MR. O. There are too many questions in one, and these last questions cannot be answered in general. It is too individual.

MISS S. How do I start to try and see?

MR. O. You must try to study yourself. See yourself. See what is reliable in yourself and what is unreliable, what can help those 'I's that want to work and what is always against them.

MR. R. I know most people have not the right attitude towards fear of physical death.

MR. O. Yes, I think they have too much imagination or have no imagination.

MRS. C. How would you explain too much imagination towards death?

MR. O. It means simply identification with fear—unreasonable.

MRS. C. Unreasonable fear or unreasonable hopes of the future?

MR. O. No. Hopes of the future don't enter that. Mr. R. said simply one side of it. As I said, either there is identification or just indifference, generally artificial indifference.

No, what is interesting, what I would like to speak about, is the division of men from the point of view of the possibility of changing their being. There is such a division. Only your questions don't lead to that, so I will just wait a little. Perhaps some question will bring it nearer. Because there are people for whom there is the possibility of changing their being; there are many people for whom it is practically impossible, because they brought their being into such a state that there is no starting-point in them. And there are people who already, by different means, different methods, destroyed the possibility of change of their being. And in times like this, these people very often play a leading part. We can speak about it now or another time, only you must come nearer to that. I don't want to make it simply theoretical. It must start with some practical approach, for understanding.

MR. A. I feel if I only had to be told what to do I could do it.

MR. O. No, this is not a question of doing. It is a question of understanding—understanding of different types of men from the point of view of changing their being. The question of being told what to do doesn't touch it at all. You can be told what to do only in school, in school-work. Now we speak in general.

MRS. P. Then the people that really lead, whose being is destroyed, are lunatics, are they?

MR. O. May be even worse than lunatics. Even lunatics can recover sometimes.

MR. F. Does this bad state depend on extreme division in themselves?

MR. O. No. It is worse than that. But we cannot begin from this angle. We must begin from ourselves and see in what condition we are.

MR. L. I feel that my desire to change would be greater if I could feel the danger of my situation. The danger seems always very remote.

MR. O. Again this is individual. Either you feel it or don't feel it. Either you realize and understand or you don't.

MR. B. Does the destruction of possibilities depend on constant suppression of conscience?

MR. O. I said we cannot begin from this end. We must begin from possibilities, not impossibilities.

MR. R. As the greater mass of humanity are absolute recurrences or going down, only very few are going up or growing.

MR. O. It is difficult to introduce the idea of recurrence. But after all, it is possible. Yes, certainly the larger part is unconscious, repeating the same errors, the same states, quite mechanical. But again, very much depends on their mechanical life. Their mechanical life can be one kind, another kind, a third kind. In one they have more possibilities, in another less, in a third still less, in the fourth none; and these empty places, as they can be called, create many disturbances—like vacuums in the air. Suppose that in this room there were several vacuums, there would be hurricanes; and that is what produces hurricanes in politics.

MR. P. Does it make work on being more difficult if one is very actively engaged in some organization?

MR. O. It depends how actively. But if one still continues to work on oneself, practically there are no conditions in which one cannot work, if one already learned.

MRS. C. Is it more a matter of habit? If one is here for eight hours working one doesn't forget oneself so much as if one is away.

MR. O. Yes, that helps.

MRS. C. I mean, it is possible to work on oneself and yet work all day long. There is no necessity to give any work up.

MR. O. Yes, certainly one can work in all conditions, unless they are very bad, very difficult, very abnormal.

MRS. C. The difficulty is that one can watch oneself very much more now than formerly, but beyond watching oneself one doesn't seem to be able to do anything more.

MR. O. Yes, but one has to begin somehow, and watching is quite good, quite useful.

MR. W. It seems to me that this question of the possibility of change of being, as I feel it in myself, has a lot to do with whether one doubts sufficiently one's own capacities, and that it is only the possession of that doubt that creates any possibility. Without that I should have nothing. Is that connected with this at all?

MR. O. It is connected, but not sufficiently. In Indian and Buddhist literature there is a very well defined type of man and type of life that can bring one to change of being. Unfortunately it is very difficult to translate these words. The Russian word that was used was better, because it was very general, without any associations, or with associations that helped to understand it. It is the word 'snataka'—householder—householder means simply man who leads ordinary life, but the word householder is not very good. The Russian word translated means simply inhabitant, nothing more, with a slightly ironical meaning in ordinary life. But at the same time one must first of all be an inhabitant or householder. Then this man can have doubts about ordinary things, he can have dreams about possibilities of development, he can come to school, after some time, after a long life or at the beginning of life, he can find himself in a school and can work in a school. And the two other classes of people are either called tramps or lunatics. But tramps doesn't mean necessarily poor people. They may be rich, but still they are tramps in their attitude towards life. And lunatics doesn't mean deprived of ordinary mind; they may be statesmen, professors and so on. These two classes will not go to school, will not be interested in it. Tramps because they don't value anything; lunatics because they have false values. They will never go to school.

First it is necessary to understand these three classes from the point of view of the possibility of development of being. When you understand these three classes and find them in your own experience, among your acquaintances, in life, in literature and so on, when you find examples and understand these, then we can understand what I call vacuums—the fourth class of people, who destroyed in themselves the possibility of development in different ways. In ordinary conditions, in ordinary life, in ordinary times, they are just criminals, nothing more, or actual lunatics. But in particular periods of history they may acquire power and become very important people, this fourth kind of people. We must leave them for a time and concentrate on the first three.

MR. R. Is this possibility of growth of being connected with willingness to obey certain laws and principles?

MR. O. Not necessarily. This is on the Monk's way, for instance. You have to begin with obeying. But there are other ways that don't begin with obeying, but with studying and understanding. And general laws you cannot disobey, because they make you obey. You can escape some of them only through growth of being, not in any other way.

MISS H. Those people who have connection with a school, however slight, does it follow that they belong to those who can change their being?

MR. O. Certainly, if they are interested in school and are sincere in their attitude towards school, it shows they belong to those who can. But you see, in each of us there are features of tramp and lunatic. It doesn't mean that if we are connected with school we are already free from these features. They play a certain part in us, and in studying being we must detect them and know in which way they prevent our work, and we must struggle with them. This is impossible without school. As I said, tramps can be not only rich, but they can be very well established in life and still they remain tramps. And lunatics can be very learned people and occupy a very big position in life, and still they are lunatics. If you take tramp and lunatic only literally, then it is not sufficient.

MR. A. Is one of the features of a lunatic that he wants certain things very much out of proportion to other things in such a way that they will be bad for him as a whole?

MR. O. Generally false values. Lunatics cannot have right discrimination of values. A lunatic always runs after false values. He is always formatory. Formatory thinking is always defective, and lunatics are particularly devoted to formatory thinking; that is their chief affection, in one, another or a third way. There are many different ways to be formatory. For instance, I gave an example of formatory thinking half an hour ago. I said people say war is not necessary because all disputes and difficulties can be decided by conferences, negotiations and things like that. If you formulate it like that and don't add that it is possible only at certain periods, not always, if you think it is always possible, then it is formatory and quite wrong. Because it is not always possible. You cannot make treaties with bolsheviks. So that is wrong. That is how a right principle can be made quite wrong by making it absolute, and formatory thinking makes everything absolute.

MR. R. About negative emotions, it seems very easy to find results of negative emotions, but not the causes. The causes seem very far removed.

MR. O. Quite right. And sometimes the causes are so far that you cannot find them and have to deal only with results.

MR. R. How can one go back to causes?

MR. O. We must do what we can. If we cannot find causes, we must deal with results and in that way we may find causes.

MR. W. I never thought before of this trying to find tramp and lunatic in oneself. Is the tramp side sort of curious irresponsibility that is prepared to throw everything overboard?

MR. O. Quite right. Sometimes it can take very poetical forms. 'There are no values in the world', 'Nothing is worth anything', 'Everything is relative' are favourite phrases.

MR. R. It seems to me then that the rules which we have in this work would give us special opportunity of seeing the tramp.

MR. O. Some of them, yes. But really tramp is not so dangerous. Lunatic is more dangerous—false values and formatory thinking.

And this fourth—again, I will just give you a few definitions from which we can start later. We connect that with the question about Hitler, because in this system they have a definite name, consisting of two Turkish words. But until now I couldn't find whether it was ordinarily used in literature or not. I tried to study Turkish, so I know what they mean and what their combination means. It is: 'has namus'. And one of the first things about 'has namus' is that he never hesitates to sacrifice people or create an enormous quantity of suffering, just for his own personal ambitions. And how 'has namus' is created, that is another question. It begins with formatory thinking, with being tramp and lunatic at the same time in general.

MRS. C. Any change of being in the fourth type would be impossible?

MR. O. No, he became already a vacuum. Another definition is that he is crystallized in the wrong hydrogens.

MR. P. These people seem to be possessed of a great deal of energy.

MR. O. It may create it. They have nothing to lose, you see.

MR. R. What is it which determines which class a man belongs to?

MR. O. The first, a certain attitude to life, a certain attitude to people and certain possibilities that one has. In the second again the same things—a certain form of life, a certain attitude to life, and that's all, in all three cases. The fourth case is separate.

MR. F. This 'has namus' seems in myself the kind of caring for nothing and spending everything on something quite worthless.

MR. O. No, 'has namus' is quite different. You begin to speak about the second, by your definitions. 'Has namus' cannot interest you practically, because you have nothing to do with them, but you meet with the results of their existence and so on. But this is a special thing. There will be some special conversations. But this second and third are very important to understand, because we can find in ourselves features of the second and third, particularly the third. For struggle against the second, certainly school discipline and generally inner discipline; one must acquire discipline. Because there is no discipline in the tramp. And in the third there can be very much discipline, only in the wrong way—all formatory. So struggle against formatory thinking is struggle against

428

lunacy in ourselves, and the creation of discipline and self-discipline is struggle against the tramp in us. And about the characteristics of the first class—first he is a practical man; he is not formatory; and he must have discipline, otherwise he cannot be what he is—so a certain amount of self-discipline, and a certain amount of practical thinking. That is the characteristic of the first man. He has enough for life, but not enough for work, so in work these two characteristics must grow.

MRS. C. You said he had enough. . . .

MR. O. He may have enough for life, but not for work. In the work exactly this capacity, if he has the capacity for practical work, must increase, must grow.

MRS. C. Is there the possibility of the first man in everybody?

MR. O. Not everybody. I said some already lost the capacity for practical thinking or the capacity for development. Then they are full No. 2 or 3, according to what they lost.

MRS. C. You mean from birth?

MR. O. That we don't know. We cannot speak about that. We speak only about results. We know that in the work one must have the capacity for practical thinking and practical attitude and one must have sufficient discipline to accept school discipline.

MR. R. What do you mean by practical thinking?

MR. O. Just what is called practical thinking in ordinary language. The capacity to calculate things in different circumstances, nothing more. And the same capacity he can apply to ideas of the work, school principles, rules, everything.

MISS H. Can the tramp and lunatic be a complete personality or is it an 'I' or a feature?

MR. O. It is not necessary to think in that way. It is sufficient to understand the general chief characteristics. Details are not important.

* * *

always possible. It is really a longer way but it brings you to the same point. Always remember that realization of not-remembering is the beginning—if you want to remember yourself you must begin with that.

MISS T. I wish I could begin to understand more about diagrams.

MR. O. Diagrams are not coming in the present discussion. When we speak about them you can put your attention on them, but now we try to put practical attitude to everyday work.

MR. H. Is there any difference between what is ordinarily called concentration and the system term identification?

MR. O. I cannot explain ordinary terms in this ordinary loose language; it can mean anything, to one person it means one thing, to another another, and to a third a third. Ask yourself what concentration means; it may mean anything. You must begin from system terminology, because the aim of this terminology is that we have definite terms for definite facts.

MR. R. Can that part which has a right to be called 'I' have unpleasant features?

MR. O. If you speak about divisions, you must speak about both parts, 'I' and false personality. Quite possibly it can, but in any case it is question of observation, it is not a grammatical rule; you cannot make grammatical rules for that.

MISS A. I seem to realize more and more how little real effort I make in the work, and this realization produces a very strong feeling of fear. How can I try to overcome this negative attitude?

MR. O. By making efforts, it is the only one practical way, otherwise try to create such attitude that you don't make efforts (that means increase sleep) if you don't want to work, but if you want to work you must make efforts.

MR. B. One of the effects of my efforts to self-remember is that I become aware of the pulse in various parts of my body, or of the heart itself. It also seems that I am more intensely aware of it, in more parts of my body, as my effort to self-remember improves. Is this at all a reliable criterion of progress in self-remembering?

MR. O. It may be but this is not important; you must be aware of yourself as a whole, not as parts; it is subjective. These realizations happen sometimes but they don't mean much.

MR. B. When I am trying to stop a circle of thought, a mechanically repeated phrase or a tune, I often succeed in putting it out of my mind for a time, and find that sooner or later it will return unaltered, as if it had been kept alive all the time in another 'I' or personality. It seems that I have stopped it only by restricting my attention. How can I start to really break such a circle of thought?

MR. O. It is a very good method for self-remembering; the moment it appears try to remember yourself; if you attach self-remembering to it you will forget both; no persistent thought can stand that.

MR. B. I thought I understood Mr. O. to say that Finland was right to be at war, only since she was fighting bolshevism. Does he mean that Finland should really be a part of Russia and would be wrong to fight merely for independence?

MR. O. That would be impossible really. Finland was independent, but it was found before the last war that Finland was very dangerous in that state, it was a land of revolutionists; Lenin, Stalin and all those people always took refuge there and brought arms, and when the war began it was the centre of German spies, and all German spies came there. Finland was so near to Petersburg that they could not be independent and inimical country. If Finland behaved better they were almost independent, but they did not have their own ambassadors, but this independence was absurd because they showed themselves unprepared. They had all the privileges of part of a big country, but they were working against this country. Poland is just the same, it cannot be independent because they are not grown-up enough. And fighting against bolshevism, that is quite a different thing, it is only the beginning. I am sure that things are turning; as a matter of fact it is a very interesting time now, because for a long time things were going very wrong—for twenty-five years since the last war—and this last year before the beginning of new war, was a dangerous point; war was inevitable, but nobody understood the right cause of the war, and nobody understood the real possibilities of this war, and that the cause was the existence of bolshevik state because that by imitation produced all these dictators, Mussolini, Kemal and Hitler. It was all imitation of bolshevism because they thought, if it goes right with bolshevism why don't we try for ourselves. It is quite clear, and war was inevitable; the danger was wrong distribution of forces, and up till last August bolsheviks (what was called Soviet Russia) were supposed theoretically to be on the side of France, and England as they were allies of France, they made alliance with England, but this was broken because they were forced to show their cards and openly declare their alliance with Germany, and sooner or later England and France will have to declare war on Russia, and if they don't it is impossible to say what will happen to this war, and if they do, everything will finish in a year's time and very happily; that is how the situation stands now. But again, the danger is—why it doesn't happen is that bolsheviks have many friends. During these twenty years, partly by their propaganda and money, they made many friends, and these friends will fight against the possibility of war with them.

MR. B. The weight of all colloid particles associated with organic matter (in the ordinary chemical sense) is about 34,000 hydrogen atoms or a simple multiple of that. Can they be regarded as a cosmos intermediate between that of molecules and that of cells?

MR. O. I don't think we need that; only principles are in that. Between different cosmoses there are many other units, agglomeration of people, races (only this is not real), so between each cosmos there is at least an octave, or may be many octaves, but we don't know it now. If we think about cosmoses we need only to understand the principle and not details. Details we cannot go into, there is no time, and nothing can be found from it. If it becomes necessary, again it will be explained.

MR. B. Astronomers have observed, since 1900, four Novae stars which have suddenly flared up and expanded enormously in size and brightness. Can they be examples of beings evolving to a higher state?

MR. O. No, it is astronomical observation, it has nothing to do with psychology; we cannot connect it, it would be too arbitrary. Too little is known; you must remember that astronomy still remains a science for calculation of movement of celestial bodies, and nothing more. And about structure or happenings, it is all hypothesis, nothing more.

MR. T. Except for a few moments where someone is explaining them, I never seem to have enough material to keep myself thinking about cosmological ideas. Is this because subjects on which I can keep myself thinking are those with which I identify?

MR. O. No, why? Nobody can answer but you. But again, it may be that time hasn't come yet, or I have not spoken enough yet—future will show. Sometimes they are necessary because laws can be seen easier in them.

MR. T. Certain mechanical thoughts always lead to negativeness in me—for example, the thought of the position occupied by certain people in the office, or the thought of income tax. Are these thoughts pointers as to what T. is like.

MR. O. No, it is necessary to find the right attitude to these thoughts; you must understand that nothing can be different from what it is. We always think that things could be different, but they can be different only in the future. In the future you could say it could be that, but what has already happened could not be different, because if it could be different it would have happened differently. It is very difficult to get accustomed to that; we always like to think that things could be different.

MR. T. I saw somebody standing at a tube station and then found thoughts comparing myself with this person, saying, 'Well they have no central core provided by an all-engrossing job.' Is this just one 'I' speaking or am I all like that?

MR. O. Unfortunately I do not quite understand what this 'I' said.

MR. T. I say that I am a person who has an important central part because a great deal of me has an important job, and he hasn't.

MR. O. How did you know that he hasn't.

MR. T. I didn't.

MR. H. The world to-day is full of evil mainly caused by men who have killed conscience. Is there any hope of deliverance until a number of conscious men appear?

MR. O. No, these historical events are not decided in this case, as far as we know, with the exception of very short and small scale periods; it didn't happen in our memory of the life on the surface of the earth, but at the same time things change, and things can have one tendency or another tendency, so things can change mechanically. You must remember like all octaves that things can go too wrong in a certain direction. Because of intervals they can never reach certain degree of intensity.

Before reaching this highest possible degree of intensity they change their direction, they fall down. For instance, during last summer, things came to the worst possible situation in Europe, then suddenly they turned and became better because the danger was an alliance with bolshevism, and this danger nobody avoided, everybody tried to make this alliance and strengthen it, but something broke and things didn't happen. This is an example of Law of Octaves, and we will see in the future whether things turn in the wrong way; we don't know, but in any case this war with Finland spells necessity of war with bolshevism more and more. Again I say they have too many friends.

MR. E. I have a certain more or less permanent identification, the features and dangers of which I am fairly familiar with. In my present state I am fairly sure that if I tried to fight the effects of this identification it would be replaced by others which might have even more unsettling effects. Could one say in such a case that a known evil is preferable to unknown evils, if it can be held to prevent them or take their place?

MR. O. It is difficult to say; it is necessary to know all of both possibilities. It is very dangerous to make a general statement on general principles of that kind.

MR. E. Is the idea of 'cheating' to illustrate the working of the law of cause and effect?

MR. O. I don't understand. Cheating of whom and of what?

MR. E. In the programme. You said we mustn't try to do the exercise if one has missed it.

MR. O. It has no general meaning. It means if one has missed the exercise one must not do it, nothing else.

MISS A. Is there still a possibility of introducing new people into the system?

MR. O. Not just at this moment. We have no group for new people; when this will be possible it will be made known. If you have somebody in view you can write to me. It may be in the spring we can start a new group, but I can speak only about individual cases, not in general.

MRS. H. Mr. O. asked us to write our own programme. I have tried and failed. I feel it is an impossibility in my present state. How can I improve the carefully prepared balanced programme which I have been given? I do not know how to begin.

MR. O. Well, try; if you have something we can speak about it, or perhaps somebody else can write a programme and then we can read it.

MRS. H. Having written this I am wondering if this is the 'I' that enjoys being comfortable and does not wish to make a real effort to think.

MR. O. Quite possibly.

MRS. P. I want to find what it is that makes the difference between a bad state and a slightly better one. I have noticed that I can be more awake when I am feeling tired, or even ill, and that after a good night's sleep it is more difficult to be aware of myself. In both states I am identified and negative and lose energy, but in the better state I feel more alive. In the bad state my thoughts are more difficult to stop, and effort to work on myself does not last and has very little feeling.

MR. O. It is matter for observation; you must have much longer time to observe and then perhaps you will be able to make some deduction. Generally speaking it is wrong deduction; there may be something wrong with the observations themselves, or something is missing, because normally the better you are the more you would be able to remember yourself.

MR. T. I have been trying to observe the moment of waking from physical sleep for the reason that I thought the dreams of the night were carried on in the day-time as turning thoughts. But I find that dreams are of a quite different order from turning thoughts.

MR. O. Quite right.

MR. T. The necessity still remains for thoughts to be arrested at the moment of waking, but I find this very difficult. What is the right type of effort to make?

MR. O. I don't know; that is individual. You must try one thing and then another thing.

MR. T. The necessity for continual guard against identification is becoming very apparent.

MR. O. Very good.

MR. T. I feel the need of a drastic physical alarm clock, such as pressing something sharp into the palm of the hand. Nothing I have tried has any effect over any length of time, but the problem of identification remains. Can Mr. O. help me?

MR. O. You have many things but you must understand them and use them, like this example that somebody gave of music being a help for self-remembering; everybody has something, some kind of unpleasant thoughts come, or recurring unpleasant feelings—that is all help for self-remembering. Every kind of negativeness can be made help for self-remembering.

MR. T. I have a very strong habit of classifying something under headings. For example, I divided my negative emotions into three types; crying over spilt milk, offended self-importance, and depressions. Is this formatory?

MR. O. No, it may be quite right. I cannot verify your observations at the present moment, but this is the right way to do it.

MR. T. The other day I was very much identified with an experiment I had been doing for three hours, and every thought led to this subject. Then I tried stopping thoughts, and found that I kept off this subject but still had difficulty with other thoughts associated with impressions. How can I become able to keep my mind off a subject in which I am intensely interested, when it is the wrong time to think about it?

MR. O. Self-remembering generally speaking, but at the same time it may not be necessary; it must not be taken too literally. It depends— something happens somewhere sometimes, and turns and turns one thought without any result, and sometimes it may be useful thinking; you may get some results from that.

MR. T. I find that the obstacle that prevents me from self-remembering is the persistent chain of thoughts arising from physical impressions— how can thinking about system ideas prevent this form of identification?

MR. O. It is difficult to say; you cannot bring <u>one</u>, there are many different causes; that is the first weak spot in that.

MR. E. Self-remembering is much more difficult in some life circumstances than in others, in fact it is sometimes impossible even to remember to try and self-remember.

MR. O. You see before you go further I must say that mistake is in thinking that life circumstances, that means external circumstances, can change anything or affect it—this is an illusion.

MR. E. Should I try to avoid circumstances in which I become very identified, or should I simply accept this condition as part of my present state?

MR. O. Try to avoid, or try to take it as part. If you can avoid it try to avoid it and you will see exactly the same, or there may be such things that would be exceptional, but balance remains the same.

MR. E. I can only see the significance of conscience as it affects emotions I feel about myself. Emotions felt for other things are usually too habitual for much possibility of contrast.

MR. O. Don't mix—take one line and think on that line in relation to yourself. Don't think immediately about other things; continue this line long enough.

MR. E. It seems that conscience could only be really felt with regard to emotions I feel about myself. By using our memory and an intellectual approach can we get any nearer to feeling conscience?

MR. O. Quite true; it is individual; do that and then we will talk, but don't mix with other things.

MR. E. In order not to go round in circles ordinary effort is insufficient. My complacency in the past and then the spasmodic nature of my efforts have found justification in the general atmosphere of most meetings, but I have found that when a sense of urgency has been expressed at meetings, I have seen my need more clearly, and have made much more effort. Cannot I be told to work harder more often?

MR. O. I don't understand. You are told, but you want somebody to argue with you, to prove to you, to persuade you, that you can do it yourself.

MR. E. I work on myself. But work with others is still only an extension of work on myself. I feel no sort of collaborative spirit; even less am I in a condition to carry out duties for the work. Until I am able to do these things I shall probably not know what I am missing. But it might be an incentive if I were told how I could profit by these other activities.

MR. O. It doesn't go in that way—you mean about organized work? But you must be prepared for that, and you can be prepared only by remembering rules, studying rules, understanding rules, and study of rules is the introduction to what you want to speak about.

MR. E. Three lines of work have for part of their reason the purpose of bridging the gaps in the octaves of individual work.

MR. O. Not quite like that.

MR. E. Is the fact that I have so far only done work on myself part of the reason why I have found myself going round in circles?

MR. O. Possibly, but again only possibly. The first definition is wrong, but the second is possible, because lack of understanding of other sides of the work may keep one back, but one must go on making efforts, that is all.

MR. E. I have found interest in a subject is almost synonymous with identification—the more interested I become the more identified I become. This is clearly undesirable yet in a way it appears that this very identification gives me the energy and incentive to pursue the subject or work on it. It is very hard to see what 'interest' can mean without identification. Does real interest correspond to some quality of essence, if so, I can see that it must be possible to have interest without identification?

MR. O. No, it is not the same thing; we will speak about it when you find this out, only now there is nothing to speak about if you think they are the same thing, but when you find out then there will be material for discussion.

MR. E. The outer cause of anger or annoyance is usually something which opposes something I want to do. Being identified with my wish, I am unable to resolve these two opposed forces into a third. The result of this is an insoluble problem which sets up friction making me negative. . . .

MR. O. No, 'insoluble problem' was used as term; it was something of quite a different nature, you cannot use it as just imaginary quantity.

MR. H. There are two ways in which I think about the idea of unity, of permanent 'I'. Either I think, 'If ever I am to approach nearer to some kind of unity, <u>this</u> part of me will have to be got rid of, <u>that</u> part of me is harmless, <u>another</u> part of me is useful and will have to be retained.' At other times I think, 'All these different sides of my nature will remain, but they will be harmonized and subordinated before any kind of unity can be reached.' In point of fact I don't know how to think of the idea of permanent 'I' at all. My question is how to do so?

MR. O. By realizing your present state first—divided and impermanent; the more you realize the present situation the more you can understand what could be opposite to that. We ascribe to ourselves, we are accustomed to think of ourselves as something united and permanent, and these illusions must be broken in us.

MR. H. The following incident constantly occurs—I leave the house lost in thought; I shut the front door and am half way down the street when I suddenly think, 'Have I switched off the light?' I go back and I almost always find that I <u>have</u> turned off the light. Is it not one of the proper uses of formatory apparatus to notice that the lights are switched off, and is it not an incident of this kind that shows that it is too busy doing my thinking to attend to its own work?

MR. O. What is the percentage of times when you leave it on? If you know this you can decide for the future that if fifty per cent you have to return, if twenty-five per cent you might return, but if it is only ten per cent you could leave it. And in reply to the last part of your question, yes, but there are many other things connected.

MR. D. Is the following example of a triad right? Man's behaviour can be thought of as the result of (1) the circumstances, the stimulus (2) the given man with his peculiar make-up, conditioning etc. (3) his state of consciousness?

MR. O. Yes, but I don't quite understand what you want to know, and I think that these three classes are the same thing, they are just different aspects of the same thing, so it is not quite right.

MR. D. Would the stimulus here be active force, the given man passive force, and his state of consciousness neutralizing force?

MR. O. But it may be also different—what is active, passive or neutralizing is difficult to say, so at present, with the exception of given examples of triads, we had better wait until we have more. The right way to come to the study of triads, as I said some time ago, is trying to understand different kinds of activities. What does it mean? We must try to understand that activities (we only take man's activities, nothing else, not things that happen, not cosmic happenings, not inner happenings, but what man can do or what he thinks he can do); these activities of man can be very different, different by themselves, the same as matter is different. We know that wood is different from metal, but activities, doings, are all the same for us, we don't see the difference, but we must try to understand these differences, like examples I gave you of building a house or burning a house. When we understand the difference in these activities then we have sufficient material to study triads. This is not orthodox manner because it runs ahead, but I think it is the only way we can begin to think about triads.

MRS. P. When we have finished our programme are we to try it?

MR. O. It is better to read it and talk about it. You can try it certainly but it is better to speak about it here.

MR. L. Mr. O. spoke about negative emotions, and the expression of negative emotions as quite a separate subject; I want to know more about that.

MR. O. Because different knowledge is necessary for that. The idea of not expressing negative emotions belongs to the first lecture. At the very first moment of self-observation one is told to observe and try not to express negative emotions, and for a long time one has to work on that, self-observation with certain demands not to express negative emotions, then many other things come, explanations and practices, and after a very long time you come to the study of emotions themselves and study of methods of changing emotions, so you cannot put them together, they are quite different things. But you must understand that after some time coming to these talks, lectures and so on, you begin to forget chronology of the ideas, and it is very useful to remember the order in which ideas came.

MR. E. I have been thinking about negative emotions and I find a lot of mine spring from imagination. When thinking which is my chief difficulty, under which heading should I class this?

MR. O. I don't know. Facts are necessary first.

MISS L. Is laughter connected with moving centre because I seem to laugh all through some dreams?

MR. O. Maybe, but maybe not; it may be different.

MR. E. During the last few weeks I questioned the sincerity of an emotion which I have enjoyed for some time. I did not altogether like this questioning. In having to give up an emotion I felt a sense of martyrdom; is this a form of negative emotion, and is this what I am to understand by giving up suffering? Even if it is based on identification I should not have described it as a negative emotion.

MR. O. No, giving up suffering is quite different. It may be giving up imagination, but again that is for you to decide—illusions you know. We have very much imagination and sometimes giving up certain imagination looks difficult.

MR. M. Is it possible to have certain kinds of negative emotion without knowing it? I mean I have a picture of myself as a person who does not indulge in self-pity and is never envious, but I am beginning to think that I may really suffer from self-pity, and I wondered if it was possible for there to be such a complete barrier that one cannot see a big thing like that?

MR. O. Oh yes, it happens very often.

MR. E. It is possible, isn't it, to have an emotion which can both give and take energy in some cases?

MR. O. It is possible, but it is difficult to speak without facts.

MR. M. I find the most difficult forms of negative emotion not to justify, or even to see, are the ones masquerading as virtues, and when I do see them there is something in me that is absolutely scandalized that I should try not to feel when I should feel that they are wrong.

MR. O. It may be true, but there may be many other things, you cannot bring it under the heading of one thing, it is a complicated process.

MISS T. How can one learn to imagine less in one's thinking, because I am afraid my thinking is always so bound up with imaginary pictures that I cannot really think a thought without imagination?

MR. O. Perhaps by remembering this thing when it comes first time, and then second time; you cannot take just one thing.

MISS U. When I try to self-remember I find my efforts are always accompanied by as much muscular relaxation as I am capable of, and the more I manage to relax the more I realize that I cannot relax at all, I am still tight inside; how can I increase my ability to relax?

MR. O. When I spoke about self-remembering I did not connect it with any physical efforts, so it is not connected. You must just try to remember yourself and nothing more, because when you think it is connected it may not be connected at all, but with some kind of imagination. It may be subjective feeling which may increase. You must try to remember yourself without connecting any physical feelings.

MR. E. I am not quite clear whether it is actually desirable to be tense; I always find that in making an effort to stop thought, and if I try hard, I always get tense; it seems to just go with it naturally.

MR. O. That is your business; we did not speak about it specially, so it can be left now.

MRS. P. How much energy does one get in sleep at night?

MR. O. It depends how one sleeps, but in any case it is different. It is enough to know that all processes of the body go somehow differently, and energy may be distributed or accumulated, but this is only theory. Practically we can know only one thing, if we sleep well we feel one thing, or if we sleep badly we feel another thing, and quality of sleep can be different again.

MR. M. I find it very difficult to understand what being interested in things without being identified means.

MR. O. Find examples; find one case when you could be interested without identification, and other things when you are interested and identified at the same time. Until you find these two different things we cannot begin talking about them.

MR. E. I have asked a question also on these lines but I am not quite clear; when one is interested in a subject and very identified with it, is one actually wasting energy? I don't quite see what the waste of energy consists of if you are enjoying it.

MR. O. Again, I said we have already talked so much about this that I can only speak about examples of both identifying and not identifying.

MR. M. Another question I want to ask about identification, and this is not really a question of substituting one word for another, but is it the same thing as when one says 'dispersed'?

MR. O. That is one thing, and this is another thing—two different things.

MISS T. I think Mr. O. said last time that it was purely imagination and subjective to think that the pace of one's breathing altered when trying to self-remember or trying to stop thought. Well, I thought I had observed this over such a very long period of time that when he gave that very definite answer last week I wondered whether it could just be that when you are trying to self-remember you are more aware of the sound of your breathing.

MR. O. It may be, but it happens not because of self-remembering. It gives you quite unnecessary muscular tension, but it has nothing to do with self-remembering.

MR. H. How can I begin to feel the sense of interconnection between me and other people; I don't only mean people in the system, but all my thinking is in the form of 'I' and 'they' as though nothing whatever connected us?

MR. O. You will find interconnection in yourself between different functions and different states, different 'I's and so on; then perhaps you will find it.

MR. R. I find my attitude to other people is usually one of criticism, and comparing them with myself, but I wanted to know how to get rid of that attitude.

MR. O. Simply by realizing that you don't know them. Of yourself you can know more; think about yourself chiefly.

Next time I will try and come at the beginning of the meeting and we will try and read the programmes, so if anybody else wants to write a programme we can discuss them and perhaps we can come to some new programme. Just see if you have any questions now on what I said to-day.

MR. E. I spoke of an emotion being negative and making me happy. . . .

MR. O. No, I said all that I can say. Find an example.

MR. T. What is the purpose of teaching cosmological ideas?

MR. O. Many analogies. Later you will understand that many laws we can understand only thinking on the scale of cosmoses and then adapt to ourselves. Other laws we can understand only thinking on our own scale and perhaps later apply to cosmoses. We have to study man and the world, and some laws we can understand better by studying man and some laws we can understand better by studying the world.

MR. T. You spoke of trying to learn to remember ourselves irrespective of physical feeling; did you mean ordinarily during the day, also in the programme?

MR. O. I did not mean in the programme, I meant in general.

MRS. D. Why do we always believe that things will happen differently?

MR. O. Because we believe first that people can '<u>do</u>'; that is the basis of all wrong beliefs. We don't fully understand or fully believe even when we hear about it that things happen. If we realize that things happen we realize that if they happen in that form it means they could not happen differently; if they could have happened differently they would have happened differently. It is very difficult to realize that.

MRS. D. How can we think about it to understand it better?

MR. O. Just think. If you begin to see, if you take certain combination of events, and when you catch yourself thinking that they could be different and persuade yourself and really begin to see that they could not happen differently, then you begin to understand it; it is the only way. Only sometimes it is easier to think on a bigger scale before you think on smaller scale.

MR. M. Sometimes I try to think about circumstances in the way you have just said, and then I think that if I had been different the circumstances would have been different.

MR. O. It depends on what scale you take circumstances. If it is your own quite personal scale and limited to your friends, it might be true, but people exaggerate this idea, and think that if they were different circumstances would be different on a bigger scale, so if you take circumstances depending on you it would be right, but if you take circumstances quite independent from you then certainly it is wrong. There are many imaginary theories on this problem, but of that we will speak some time later.

MR. E. Can octaves be completed by accident?

MR. O. Which octave, and which accident, and what means completed, and why? You see how many questions there are in that.

MRS. D. Should one try to live according to one's emotions or should one always try to find a good reason for what one is doing?

MR. O. It is very difficult to say. Emotions may be different and one's capacity to control one's life may be different. Very often it is imaginary. Very often all questions, should I do this, or should I do that, are quite artificial because one can do only in one way; you see what I mean? Very often one thinks one can do this way or that way, but really one can only do in one way, one has no control, but coming to the question itself, I think it is useful to start from this point of view, to see what kind of emotions you mean, emotions belonging to essence or emotions belonging to personality, and very often (again I don't say always, but very often) you can trust emotions belonging to essence and mistrust emotions belonging to personality, but this is not a general rule; it only shows lines of study in connection with your question. Question itself shows by which line your thinking must go; you must think about essence and personality; you must think about things which you can control in yourself and so on. It is not a question for answer, it is a question for investigation.

* * *

Tuesday. June 10th 1941. (New York.)

MRS. P. Would you explain if triads that end with 2 become worse and worse, why the triad 1-2-3, corresponds to 'Invention and Discovery'? How can these become worse and worse? Is it because a point is reached where they become destructive?

MR. O. I never said anything like that. I am not guilty. I never said that one triad meant one thing and a second meant a second and a third, a third.

MRS. P. Why is it that the laws of the Absolute do not reach us?

MR. O. We cannot say 'why'. Why is too much. The point is that they don't reach the earth. The laws of the Absolute reach to 3 but not to 6.

MRS. P. If the Absolute is the Absolute why is it absent from our lives?

MR. O. That's exactly because it is the Absolute.

MRS. P. Do each of the 48 earth laws represent a phase of life or a material sphere that must be outgrown in order to come within range of the Absolute?

MR. O. Not quite, they are just mechanical laws under which the earth lives.

MRS. P. Is the belief in death, old age, illness, pain, discord, etc. included in the 48 laws?

MR. O. No, not in the 48. 48 are only for the earth. If we calculate in the same way we can see that organic life has 96 laws and man 192.

MRS. D. Will it be possible for one who has a heavy full-time job to work to good advantage in your school? That is, is much time needed daily?

MR. O. It is very difficult to answer because there are limits to everything. It cannot be described by a general description. Generally speaking one can. It does not need special time.

MRS. N. Does self-remembering release energy from the great accumulator?

MR. O. No, you only begin. It cannot give results so quick.

MRS. N. Where is the great accumulator? Inside or outside the body?

MR. O. In us. It is all physical.

MRS. N. How can we release energy from the great accumulator?

MR. O. We must stop waste of energy first. Like lying, talking, identification, etc.

MRS. N. What is considering?

MR. O. Considering is the same as identification only it refers to people. When people think what other people think about them.

MISS B. You said that one has to be normal to develop, and I was wondering what normal is?

MR. O. If we begin to study what is normal man we would have no time for anything else. Only results can show. Results show very much—valuation—when one recognizes the difference between these and other ideas. So the first sign that one is prepared is valuation.

MRS. N. Is it an advantage to remember oneself while doing concentrated work?

MR. O. You must try yourself.

MR. H. Can't you use formatory apparatus too much?

MR. O. Formatory apparatus uses itself. And you cannot use it too much. It has its own place, but it mustn't be used in the place of better parts of centres.

MRS. N. Is illness caused from not remembering oneself?

MR. O. No, no, no, it's too much to expect. It may be. It may be.

MRS. N. Is consciousness anything to do with higher vibrations?

MR. O. One is connected with the other. But we don't know about higher vibrations.

MISS H. Man being mechanical, what makes the machine go? Is it chemical or physical?

MR. O. No, no, we cannot define it like that. It is a machine created by cosmic laws. And it is well defined. It can have only certain temperature, certain air, certain food, etc.

MISS H. Then it is a chemical process?

MR. O. Chemical, yes, and physical and all that. But we don't enter into a description yet.

MISS H. There is no centralized mechanical process?

MR. O. It doesn't matter, you can call it what you like.

MR. N. By a cosmic shock you mean air?

MR. O. Yes, air.

MRS. N. Is man No. 7 mechanical relatively?

MR. O. No, we cannot speak of man No. 7. Only man Nos. 1, 2 and 3.

MRS. D. Is that 48 in the brain? [Ref. to Food Factory.]

MR. O. Yes, you can put it in the brain. It is in the head so it must be in the brain.

MRS. C. What effect would rhythmic breathing have on it?

MR. O. You cannot play any tricks with it. It cannot go any better.

MISS B. Then how you breathe isn't important?

MR. O. There's nothing mechanical. If so—one would only have to sit and breathe and so become superman.

MRS. N. I got a different sensation the other day—I was wondering if it was right?

MR. O. Maybe—if it wasn't imagination.

MISS S. Can you explain valuation a little more?

MR. O. In relation to work it doesn't need elaborate explanation. From the point of view of work it is connecting things with work.

MRS. N. Is it absolutely possible for one to shut out all thoughts?

MR. O. Absolute things happen only on the Absolute. Say you have a thousand thoughts in the moment—if you make an effort and have only nine hundred that is something.

MRS. N. Why does one remember oneself one day and not another?

MR. O. Everything happens like that. We are never the same. In a simple way—it is different states of consciousness.

MISS B. Suppose that one does not want to go back and live in the past, does one have to?

MR. O. This recurrence into the past is such a difficult thing that we cannot bring it in here.

MISS B. Does one have to keep repeating the same mistakes?

MR. O. First it is necessary to know that they are mistakes. Oh, if you know, you have a criterion—more mechanical, less mechanical.

MRS. N. Is it possible to remember oneself wrong?

MR. O. No, only imaginary self-remembering.

MRS. D. Do you see yourself as if someone was at the side of you?

MR. O. No, that's already from the Evil One—that's imagination, seeing one's self.

MR. C. The faculty to self-remember doesn't have its seat only in the mind?

MR. O. It begins in the mind, or it may begin in emotions.

MR. H. If one remembers oneself in connection with the world and the universe. . . .

MR. O. Any kind of connection spoils it. Instead of self-remembering you think and that's mechanical.

MR. H. Does that automatically control personality?

MR. O. Don't put more words.

MRS. N. Did you say that one ought to remember themselves nine times a day?

MR. O. Three times—five minutes each time. And I didn't say 'remember', I said 'try to'.

MRS. N. You said that energy was released when you self-remembered; where does the energy come from?

MR. O. All the energy that you have. And you don't waste it if you self-remember.

MR. Y. Where does one place those of whom one says: 'They are self-conscious; or self-centred'? Do they remember themselves permanently?

MR. O. This word exists only in English. It means a kind of embarrassment. And they permanently don't remember themselves.

MR. Y. Those people that think they are conscious are not self-remembering?

MR. O. That means a certain state of mind.

MISS H. Do you place a hypochondriac in that category?

MR. O. I don't speak of pathological cases. Only normal.

MR. N. If one remembers someone's name from many years ago, is that self-remembering?

MR. O. Simply an accident. I remember some telephone numbers I knew in Moscow forty years ago.

MR. N. Has it ever been possible for someone to get rid of imagination?

MR. O. What's that to you?

MRS. P. Suppose that you have a bad temper and you want to stop it?

MR. O. Yes, suppose that you struggle with bad temper you create two or three other worse things.

MR. M. Is there danger in self-remembering?

MR. O. No, self-remembering is so difficult there is no danger.

MR. M. And development is a physical process?

MR. O. I say 'physical' because there is nothing not physical. But efforts—one must make efforts.

MR. M. Isn't self-remembering in its essence a form of thinking?

MR. O. In the beginning, yes, but then it ceases to be.

MRS. D. What do you mean by a school? Is it a group that is wanted to start a school?

MR. O. Yes, but this is not the description of a school. A school cannot begin out of nothing. One comes from another.

MRS. N. What would contradict school-work?

MR. O. Development of imagination.

MRS. C. Could you explain something about school rules?

MR. O. It's too quick. You must ask something concrete. Principles are one thing, and rules another.

MR. M. Then there is always a school somewhere?

MR. O. Ah, that I don't know.

MR. M. Has there ever been one in the U.S.A.?

MR. O. We can't speak about this.

MRS. C. Can you continue with your other life while on the staircase?

MR. O. That's again impossible to make a rule out of. Take photography, one can say, 'I am interested in photography more than school-work or less than school-work.'

MR. B. Why is one man interested in school-work and another in photography?

MR. O. One accumulates certain material, and this makes interest.

MISS H. How does a group start on the first step?

MR. O. One meets something that exists.

MISS H. How do we meet it?

MR. O. I don't know, that's for you to decide.

MRS. N. Is there anything <u>above</u> the path?

MR. O. Yes, air.

MRS. N. Along the path are there many efforts too?

MR. O. You try. Then you will tell us.

MRS. N. Up to now there have been no breaks with schools?

MR. O. There could be breaks but we don't know about that.

MR. N. How was the first school created?

MR. O. It's the question about the first shoemaker.

MRS. N. Then those mysteries couldn't be brought back in a book or anything?

MR. O. No, first nobody knows about that, and second, it's a question of being.

MRS. N. Isn't the higher mental mixed up with the emotional?

449

MR. O. Yes, the difference between intellect and emotions exists only on our level.

* * *

Wednesday. June 11th 1941. (New York.)

MISS R. Regarding your theory of Eternal Recurrence whereby the end of a man's life corresponds with the beginning, would this also apply to the universe, i.e. that the universe is perpetually returning to, and emerging from the Absolute?

MR. O. What is the universe?

Yes, but they are all different. You cannot take them all together. This is the meaning of the Ray of Creation. The whole thing cannot be taken together. Take wheels—if the small wheel turns, all wheels must turn.

MR. F. Is a man on the steps, No. 4?

MR. O. No, no, no.

MISS B. Are we attempting to become No. 5?

MR. O. We cannot become No. 5 without becoming No. 4.

MRS. C. How are we to know when we become complete No. 4?

MR. O. When you become it you perhaps will know.

MR. H. If you go down some steps will you reach some path?

MR. O. If you go down you cannot go up. We live below our level.

MISS B. What is our normal line? [of existence]

MR. O. Self-remembering—the third state of consciousness. Man is made for the third state and he can reach that without physical change.

MRS. C. Would man No. 4 remember himself all the time?

MR. O. This is a formatory question. He remembers himself when he needs it.

MR. Z. Is it possible to have will without being conscious?

MR. O. Who will have will, if he is not conscious? Somebody else!

MR. Z. If I decided on a certain action, would I have will?

MR. O. It depends on who decides. Who in you decides and on what action.

MR. F. Do I understand that a man doesn't become conscious until he is No. 5?

MR. O. Certainly he can become conscious, but only sporadically. A real state of consciousness begins only when a man can control it.

MRS. R. Is it higher emotional centre that begins with No. 5?

MR. O. Higher emotional centre. Quite right. Third state of consciousness—self-consciousness.

MRS. W. Was the Christ man No. 5, or was he higher?

MR. O. We cannot speak about Christ. There is no evidence of the historical existence of Christ.

MISS B. How about Buddha?

MR. O. Buddha is more historical.

MISS B. What was he?

MR. O. I don't know. I never met him.

MRS. C. Can we know about people in the past?

MR. O. We don't know. Again, that's formatory.

MISS H. In self-remembering should one remember one's actions and thoughts? What is self-remembering?

MR. O. Being aware of oneself.

MR. Z. Man No. 4 has two bodies; is that right?

MR. O. If you want to use this term, but I see no use for it.

MRS. N. How do you know that a cat _has_ an astral body?

MR. O. By the quickness of his movements. It's all connection of centres.

MR. H. Regarding the Yogis—they go into a state of complete oblivion. Is that right?

MR. O. I don't know what you know about Yoga. Almost all that is written is wrong. Yoga cannot exist without a school. It has no value without school.

MR. H. But Yoga does mean 'awakening', doesn't it?

MR. O. Yes, it means awakening—that is one of the meanings. Yoga really means 'control'.

MR. Z. Do you mean by that the reading of Oriental philosophy is no use?

MR. O. Depends what you want. If you want many words—very good.

MISS B. Is the Fourth Way this system?

MR. O. No, not 'the Fourth Way is this system' but 'the system is part of the Fourth Way'.

MISS H. How can you put someone else on the steps?

MR. O. This is group work. One group makes possible another. But who made this group possible? You don't know it, but the London groups.

MRS. C. Must a man be partly awake if he is attracted to the group?

MR. O. Certainly, yes.

MRS. C. What is the purpose of new groups?

MR. O. They are in your interests. You can get some things only from new groups.

MRS. C. Then I suppose that when you get frightened enough you begin to work?

MR. O. Ah, yes, yes. Until you become frightened you will never work well.

MRS. B. How long is it before one can work?

MR. O. You haven't heard the answer to that? Three hundred years. So we have to hurry.

MISS B. Conflict is needed?

MR. O. Absolutely yes. I mean conflict for oneself—not other people.

MRS. C. What happens if one does not get afraid?

MR. O. Oh, one will be very happy but remain in the same place. Nothing can be acquired without effort.

MRS. C. I don't see why one should have fear with pain.

MR. O. Oh, fear is rather a painful thing.

MRS. S. Can individuals help others in the group?

MR. O. Yes, certainly, some people can help one type, others, another. But it's my business to arrange that.

MR. R. What is the difference between attention, will and self-remembering?

MR. O. Try to understand each separately, and don't ask what is the difference.

MR. R. I mean in life when we want to do something we think that it is our will.

MR. O. Our will is only the resultant of desires. In most cases it is simply the will of one small 'I'.

MR. R. But they always seem the same to me.

MR. O. Again I say you cannot understand three things at the same time.

MR. R. Where do I get the will to self-remember?

MR. O. But you speak about will—then speak about will, don't bring in self-remembering.

MISS H. If one is reading the Upanishads should one give it up because one hasn't understood them?

MR. O. One can understand something. But it does not mean that one can have anything practical.

MRS. W. Do you feel that the Yoga of Love and Bhakti are practical?

MR. O. Individually, maybe, but not in school-work. Bhakti Yoga in school is used in connection with Monk with Yogi.

MRS. W. In this school if we want to help others we are then using the Yoga of Love?

MR. O. I don't know, I can only speak about what I am doing.

MRS. C. What do you think love is?

MR. O. Depends who loves. Remember man No. 1 and man No. 2 and man No. 3. There is the man who believes in A influences—there is the man who has magnetic centre.

MRS. S. If man No. 4 has only one life, is self-consciousness the difference between him and men Nos. 1, 2 and 3?

MR. O. No, no, no. No. 4 differs from 1, 2 and 3 first because he has certain knowledge, then he has certain balance and a permanent centre of gravity.

MRS. S. And he is free from the Law of Accident?

MR. O. No, no one is free from the Law of Accident. But a man in school is free in one point—knowledge.

MRS. M. Do you mind repeating about knowledge? In this case No. 4.

MR. O. Centres are more balanced—and he is doing something.

MR. H. In your centres of man, is moving and instinctive the same or different?

MR. O. Quite different. But they have almost the same speed.

MR. H. What is moving centre? What constitutes it?

MR. O. All external movements—walking, sitting. Instinctive is all internal movement—circulation of the blood.

MRS. N. Would you tell us about man No. 5?

MR. O. It's really gossiping, because we know nothing about man No. 5.

MRS. N. But I think that you must know something.

MR. O. I may lie. You cannot verify it.

MISS B. Is there conflict in man No. 4?

MR. O. Conflict, yes, certainly. Why not?

MRS. C. Is there conflict in man No. 5?

MR. O. Ask him.

MISS R. Do you think that the plasma of the blood can affect consciousness? Alexis Carrel says so.

MR. O. But he doesn't know what consciousness is.

MISS R. Well he is searching for truth!

MR. O. Yes, but one cannot find truth by writing about things that one does not know about.

MISS R. Have you any idea of the symbolism that is given to the word 'water' in the New Testament?

MR. O. No, there are different ideas described at different times.

MRS. S. Isn't it possible that we can deceive ourselves?

MR. O. Very easily. We can deceive ourselves about everything.

MRS. S. Is it hard to know if it is real consciousness?

MR. O. No, if you work on it you will see the difference.

MRS. N. At a moment of consciousness, wouldn't you know that it was real?

MR. O. One cannot be conscious unconsciously.

MRS. N. You wouldn't have a moment when you think that you deceive yourself?

MR. O. Perhaps you lie so much it is a habit.

MISS B. Is there any relationship between the thousands of 'I's and centres?

MR. O. Certainly, they are divided. There are 'I's belonging to emotional centre, 'I's belonging to moving and some to instinctive.

MISS K. Is the exercise of self-remembering, remembering the past?

MR. O. First, self-remembering is not an exercise and secondly, it has no subject. Simply—try to be aware of yourself.

MISS R. Why did you pick carbon, oxygen and nitrogen out of the ninety-three elements?

MR. O. Because it shows that at the basis of chemistry in this system is put <u>organic</u> chemistry. You will see that organic chemistry consists chiefly of oxygen, nitrogen and carbon. At the same time it has meanings in connection with other language in other systems.

MR. Z. If I make an effort to self-remember will it become easier next time?

MR. O. No, more difficult. Because you become more and more tired with the effort. Self-remembering <u>may</u> be easier.

MRS. S. Is self-remembering possible without control of the centres?

MR. O. How can we get self-control without self-remembering?

MRS. R. What corresponds to air and earth? [Comparison of chemical terms of this system to terms of others.]

MR. O. H192. Yes, but that won't help. It's only words.

[Here were asked short questions pertaining to the Food Diagram, illustrated on board.]

MRS. C. Ordinary breathing, is that a mechanical process?

MR. O. Partly mechanical—nature arranged it, and we can't improve it.

MR. H. Do those correspond to fire, earth, air and water?

MR. O. I don't know about other, better to call them first, second and third forces.

MRS. W. In this system does one rely on instinctive centre?

MR. O. Absolutely. In the Samkhya philosophy, gunas remain permanent, but in this system they do not remain permanent.

MISS R. When man No. 7 has developed would he have to depend on this [Food Factory] or would he depend on the cosmic rays?

MR. O. The same thing again—we don't know the physiology of man No. 7.

MRS. K. Do the moving and instinctive centres have the same speeds in everyone or are they different?

MR. O. More or less the same.

MRS. K. We work all that change by self-remembering?

MR. O. By self-remembering. We have proved this function.

* * *

Wednesday. June 18th 1941. (New York.)

MRS. R. What is nitrogen in the Food Diagram?

MR. O. There are many, not one.

MRS. R. 48, is it oxygen?

MR. O. It comes as oxygen. All foods enter as oxygen. Food, air and impressions.

MR. H. If we study the system do we have our own will?

MR. O. We have no will at all. But it is necessary to know the system first.

MR. H. But what is the purpose?

MR. O. To become conscious. And every step will show you larger horizons.

MISS R. Why should there be 96 laws for the moon and only 3 for the whole universe?

MR. O. Why, we cannot speak of; we come to that later.

MR. L. Why does this scale go in the opposite direction? [Ref. to the Ray of Creation.]

MR. O. Because creation begins from the Absolute.

MR. Z. Is there supposed to be a shock between 1 and 3? According to the Law of Seven there should be.

MR. O. It is filled by the Will of the Absolute.

MISS R. What is No. 3? The universe?

MR. O. Astronomically we can call it 'All galaxies'.

MISS R. Why can't the Will of the Absolute go beyond No. 3?

MR. O. Because the laws are divided there. In World 3 they are divided there, and when they come to 6 they are different.

MISS H. How does organic life help to connect the earth with the rest?

MR. O. It is a certain sensitive film and conveys certain influences from the sun, stars, etc.

MISS R. Would you accept the definition of matter as being made of electrical waves?

MR. O. In a certain sense, yes, in certain conditions.

MR. C. That H3072, what's that?

457

MR. O. Food—hay.

MR. L. Would emotional centre work with H12?

MR. O. Higher emotional.

MISS C. H48 works with which centre?

MR. O. Intellectual.

MR. F. How can we possibly remember all this? Can we make charts?

MR. O. Oh, yes. We can make them later.

MR. Z. How do we produce carbon in order to bring it to 48?

MR. O. It was already said—not to express negative emotions, not to identify, not to consider, not because it is bad in itself but because it wastes energy.

MRS. C. When that carbon 12 does arrive, what will it be?

MR. O. Carbon doesn't enter with notes. They are in the body.

MISS R. Why do all these foods become intellectual in man and not in animals?

MR. O. Animals are a quite different machine. Man is not an animal. That is the great mistake of science.

MISS R. Where did consciousness enter in those seven worlds?

MR. O. We speak about consciousness only in relation to man. We try to be scientific, so to speak.

MISS R. You have no explanation of where consciousness begins then?

MR. O. Only in ourselves. We must take ourselves.

MR. Z. Would you consider the earth to be more important than any other planet?

MR. O. For us. We cannot live without it.

MR. H. Do we see the universe as it is in relation to the universe?

MR. O. We see nothing generally. And what you mean is the universe in relation to the earth.

MR. K. Is it necessary for man to get the higher activities for the earth?

MR. O. No, we must think about ourselves. We cannot work for the earth—we must work for ourselves.

MRS. C. Does that carbon 12 arrive anywhere else in the body?

MR. O. No, we speak only about this place. In the natural order of things it is not there.

*   *   *

Thursday. June 19th 1941. (New York.)

MRS. M. When you say self-remembering, is the difference something physical?

MR. O. Very simple, you begin in that way but you cannot do that all your life. But you observe all the manifestations of all the four centres. You begin with moving and instinctive and later come to intellectual and emotional.

MRS. M. We try to remember all our gestures and so on, but what do you mean by self-remembering at three particular times a day?

MR. O. You can observe your gestures for one month—not for six. But the chief point is to remember that you don't remember yourself. And try to stop thoughts, three times a day for five minutes. But this must not be called an exercise.

MRS. H. Do you say physical observations for one month then emotions etc. after?

MR. O. No, it is very useful to observe _how_ to observe oneself. Observe gestures etc. But after some lectures then it is possible to observe lying, manifestations of negative emotions, talking, etc.

MR. W. How do you stop thoughts?

MR. O. Just pure effort. If thoughts come, just throw them out.

MISS R. Would you explain more about considering?

MR. O. Considering is a sort of identification with people. But there are two forms; one is identification and the second is external considering.

MRS. M. You could observe your tendencies?

MR. O. No, that would be philosophy. The less philosophy the better.

MRS. M. With me I feel that I change my breathing and I fall asleep.

MR. O. No, breathing must remain the same. It means you are making a physical effort. And that is unnecessary.

MR. R. That means that you do it under special conditions?

MR. O. No, more or less under any conditions. Sitting, standing, walking, or anything.

MRS. W. Do you think that you could do it while working?

MR. O. Not think—just see. No, certainly after some time.

MRS. R. I try to think of darkness but when I relax a whole flood of thoughts come.

MR. O. Probably, yes, but better not to have any points, darkness, etc.

MRS. W. I have tried to keep out all thoughts and get darkness, but I don't know if that's the right exercise.

MR. O. No, it's not an exercise, exercise is doing the same thing.

MRS. M. Isn't the card the same thing? [Ref. to Tarot Cards.]

MR. O. No, this is doing a different thing.

MR. W. I found the other night that I was doing it for forty-five minutes.

MR. O. No, you mustn't, you lose energy to try again.

MRS. M. What do you mean when you use the term essence?

MR. O. Man is divided into four parts. Body, soul, essence and personality. Personality and essence don't appear separate, but we can study what belongs to essence and what belongs to personality.

MRS. M. Essence, is it hereditary?

MR. O. Only physical features and pathological.

MRS. M. Where does essence come from?

MR. O. Mr. G. insisted that we speak only of things that we can verify.

MR. W. How do we create that 12?

MR. O. First, by self-remembering; second, by struggle with negative emotions.

MR. W. If you make the effort to self-remember do you create 12?

MR. O. It's not created, it's already there but in the wrong place. Using old-fashioned words C12 is in the heart and we must bring it to the mind.

MR. N. The final result of effort gets into essence?

MR. O. Oh, the final results, yes. But first it must go through personality.

MRS. M. What relation has 'chief feature' to essence?

MR. O. Chief feature is not obligatory. In some people you can see it—in others, no. But false personality is a chief feature—better—chief fault.

MR. N. Early Christian writers used essence and divine essence.

MR. O. Oh, no. They speak different words. Don't think that if there is a similarity in words that there is a similarity in meaning.

MR. N. You can't relate it to the outside?

MR. O. No, sometimes there are slight differences, but they are very big.

MRS. M. In the effort to remember oneself do we work on essence?

MR. O. No, one tries to be conscious.

MRS. W. You mean physically?

MR. O. No, of oneself.

MR. N. If you accept the theory of recurrence there is very little one can do except remember oneself.

MR. O. But that's very much. It's not little. It's a big thing.

MR. N. But the main events of one's life are still there.

MR. O. It may change—if it is necessary. If it stops one's progress—something like that.

MISS A. In stopping one's thoughts I have found that my breathing changes and the blood seems to change.

MR. O. Well, if it doesn't produce tension and change the breathing it doesn't matter.

MR. W. I also found that my vision changed.

MR. O. I don't think it is good for the eyes! No, it means that you make some unnecessary physical effort.

MRS. M. Do you find it easier at one time of the day than another?

MR. O. That depends on the arrangements of the day.

MR. N. Does considering come from fear?

MR. O. Not fear—they may be some time.

MRS. N. I should think that it was the opposite.

MR. O. It may. But it is material for observation.

MR. W. How can we stop it?

MR. O. First you must study it.

MRS. W. Is there any identification when you self-remember?

MR. O. Self-remembering is one thing, identification is another. It's one or another. It's opposite things. Self-remembering itself is struggle with identification.

MRS. M. That is very severe. What hope can we have to achieve illumination?

MR. O. Illumination is very far from us. But if you work seriously there is some difference.

MR. R. The trouble is that you go to sleep.

MR. O. Sometimes you cannot go on for long. But we must try to do something when we can.

MISS A. I have had an experience—a feeling of extreme well-being.

MR. O. It could be. It may have different meaning and you don't know how you produced it. You must repeat all efforts.

MR. W. Are there any books that you can suggest if available?

MR. O. It is impossible to say in general. It depends on what one has read—in what direction the reading went, and so on.

*　　*　　*

Tuesday. June 24th 1941. (New York.)

MRS. N. Will the Russian Revolution, the Great War and this war be the same next time?

MR. O. Oh, yes, you can be sure. The worse things are, the more chance for them to be repeated.

MRS N. Are these big events accidental?

MR. O. What is happening now really was created, say twenty-five years ago, so theoretically it might have been prevented then.

MISS B. Can we make the past occur in a different way?

MR. O. Our own personal past. But it's when we change the present.

MISS B. Do we have to become self-conscious to change that?

MR. O. Yes, we cannot change anything if we are not self-conscious.

MR. Y. We speak of one day—is it the same for us as for the Chinese? And infinity—where do you place it?

MR. O. Twenty-four hours is for everybody. And infinity can be understood in many different ways. Mathematically it means the limits of possible calculation.

MR. M. Time dies with the individual?

MR. O. Yes, but there is the time of organic life, time of the sun.

MISS B. What is your interpretation of the Buddhist 'Nirvana'?

MR. O. Nobody knows what it means. So we can make only a hypothesis.

MRS. C. When you find yourself in the same situation, how can you stop it recurring again?

MR. O. The situation may be very different. So what do you mean by the same situation?

MRS. N. Why can one die before the time to die comes?

MR. O. Why not? We are under the Law of Accident.

MR. M. Why is the beginning so certain?

MR. O. Because it can't be changed.

MR. M. When you die you step into another time?

MR. O. Probably, yes.

MRS. N. Why did you say that a suicide dies earlier?

MR. O. Oh, because they destroy their resistance. And they are not suicides until they kill themselves.

MISS H. Could one end life entirely in this way?

MR. O. Oh, yes, certainly. Then one ceases to be born.

MR. M. You really discard it then?

MR. O. Discard, yes, but it may happen in many different ways.

MR. M. Is that deterioration deliberate then?

MR. O. 'Deliberately' is very rare. Laziness—not doing what one knows one ought to do.

MISS B. What happens if one stops recurring?

MR. O. Nothing, he just disappears. Then something remains and may even suffer. But that's in the moon.

MRS. N. How could one become dangerous?

MR. O. By lying. One continues to think, but one does not wish to know right things—so one invents.

MISS B. If one becomes conscious, does that mean eternity?

MR. O. Some things go on for ever. But it's relative. Even man No. 7 is immortal only in the limits of the Solar System.

MRS. N. Then the soul has separate existence on the moon?

MR. O. In normal man it has no consciousness. It's just mechanical, so it doesn't suffer.

MRS. C. Can one ever reach a point where one can control the Law of Accident?

MR. O. You see it is a very strange thing, the Law of Accident.

MRS. N. What do you mean by knowledge?

MR. O. Well, first, self-knowledge. We don't know who we are, etc. And when you begin to learn yourself you begin to learn other people.

MRS. N. Then a person with no book knowledge can have knowledge?

MR. O. Certainly, but it's difficult to begin.

MISS B. How would you explain a man like Jacob Boehme?

MR. O. Oh, I don't explain this. It is so far away.

MR. N. A man feels that he should develop himself.

MR. O. Man cannot.

MR. N. What happens to a man who wants to develop and doesn't?

MR. O. I don't know. Who looks <u>may</u> find. Who doesn't, won't.

MR. N. Suppose that a man thinks that he ought to enter this system and doesn't, what happens?

MR. O. I don't know. I can speak only of positive facts, not negative.

MR. N. I mean does it mean that he doesn't understand it?

MR. O. It may mean anything.

MRS. N. Well, if you teach each person differently, how do we all reach the same point?

MR. O. That comes later. In the beginning all the people who come have to learn the language, and they have to learn to speak it.

MRS. N. How can one make more effort?

MR. O. That is a personal question to find for oneself.

MR. M. The human race increases numerically and deteriorates mentally.

MR. O. Unfortunately, and decidedly mentally.

MR. M. Where do they come from?

MR. O. Oh, I don't know. We have only one hint on that. <u>Do</u>, <u>si</u>, inside the planets.

MRS. N. What do you mean by big cells and little cells?

MR. O. Cells differ very much.

MRS. N. And they also recur?

MR. O. Yes, otherwise there wouldn't be any continuation of life.

MRS. N. Are the smaller ones in the brain?

MR. O. No, they are the larger ones.

MRS. S. Do animals recur?

MR. O. Yes, those that are connected with man's life.

MRS. S. In your book you said that people who went back in the past became conscious. Did they go back to help others?

MR. O. No, they didn't get consciousness by going back. But went back because they became conscious.

MRS. S. Would you say then that a great philosopher or teacher came to teach for the future?

MR. O. I didn't mean philosophers.

MR. M. If a man is to be sent, who sends him?

MR. O. School.

MRS. C. Could we be in the past now?

MR. O. No such chance.

MRS. N. You don't think that there is any progress at all?

MR. O. How? Now there are baths!

MRS. N. I mean in consciousness during some period.

MR. O. Perhaps more. Perhaps less.

MR. M. The human race is growing bigger and stupider every day?

MR. O. That again shows that the amount of knowledge is limited. The race grows and the mind does not.

MRS. N. Was there life on the sun sometimes?

MR. O. That we don't know. Only it is said in this system, and it is said in mysticism, that organic life begins on the sun.

MRS. C. Could we have ever looked in the past for a school?

MR. O. No, you must do it first in the present.

MRS. C. We could not have begun this before?

MR. O. I see no signs unfortunately.

MISS B. What is the purpose of becoming conscious? Not to suffer?

MR. O. Suppose you are in an aeroplane high over the earth, and you are asleep. Then what is the purpose to awake?

MRS. N. Why do you say in your book that people who have terrible experiences deteriorate?

MR. O. No, that's too complicated. It's a description of types of people that were not admitted to the Eleusinian Mysteries.

MRS. N. What would cause that bad fate?

MR. O. They had their own explanation about that.

MR. M. Have you ever met any other persons except teachers who showed signs of schools?

MR. O. I don't know what you mean by teacher. I have never liked this word.

MRS. C. Were the disciples of Christ on a higher level?

MR. O. Christ is literature, so let's leave him alone.

MRS. N. What are the signs of school-work?

MR. O. The first signs of school-work are that nothing is forgiven.

MRS. N. What kind of things are not forgotten?

MR. O. Anything—nothing is forgotten. And nothing is indifferent to the school. Every effort is known and each effort left out is known.

MR. M. Paul was a school man.

MR. O. Exactly not. He was a mystic, yes.

MR. M. There is not much doubt about Luke.

MR. O. Yes, but you see the man who wrote the third Gospel was not Luke. Maybe he was a disciple of the real Luke.

MRS. N. Where did schools originate?

MR. O. Either on the sun or on the planets.

MR. M. Were the cathedrals of Europe the result of school-work?

MR. O. Yes, no question about that. For definitely they knew mathematical laws that were not known to science at that time.

MR. M. Were the Pyramids constructed by laws that are not known?

MR. O. No, by themselves they are not difficult to construct. But how the stones were lifted?

MR. C. Is all pioneering thought that is ahead school-work?

MR. O. No, it's quite different lines.

MISS B. Was the Taj Mahal the product of school-work?

MR. O. The Taj Mahal? Yes.

MISS D. Take a new country like America—doesn't it develop?

MR. O. Yes, but that develops in the ordinary way. It has nothing to do with esoteric ideas. And new countries are usually bad for schools.

MRS. N. Well, the artist who conceived the Sphinx must have been in a school.

MR. O. Most probably. I don't think that there could be a mistake there.

MRS. N. Is it only in architecture that one can see school-work?

MR. O. Literature of the Gospels again. Certain Indian poems and Persian.

MISS B. What about Shakespeare?

MR. O. I am no judge.

MISS B. You don't think that was a product of school?

MR. O. Simply, I don't know enough.

MRS. N. Do we have to find a way to make efforts by ourselves?

MR. O. Through connection with school-work.

MRS. N. But the school won't tell us.

MR. O. All that it is possible to say is said. Nothing else can be said. If the time comes, more will be said.

MR. M. Was Zanoni a product of school-work?

MR. O. No.

MRS. N. What kind of sentence (written) would show that a man was remembering himself?

MR. O. No, it cannot be found anywhere. So many people write about schools and it is all nonsense.

MRS. C. Then you couldn't tell from reading a book whether it is school-work?

MR. O. Sometimes you can.

MRS. C. How can you know that it is?

MR. O. I don't know—what you can't invent yourself.

* * *

Wednesday. June 25th 1941. (New York.)

[Written questions.]

MR. B. In the intellectual centre of the Food Factory diagram we see that carbon 24 is changed into <u>mi</u> 48, but then in order to proceed further it requires a shock which may be given by emotions which come from impressions through <u>do</u> 48 to oxygen.

Further, if we look at the Ray of Creation diagram we again see that the earth is placed on the scale as <u>mi</u> 48 and in order to ascend to the next step it is necessary to have the help of organic life.

So it would seem to me that there is a certain analogy between the microcosmos and the macrocosmos and that organic life gives the necessary help like the shock which is required in the intellectual centre.

MR. O. There are no centres in the Food Diagram. This question cannot be answered. You mix two things. The Ray of Creation and the Food Diagram. Try to take everything separately.

MISS Q. According to the system, is there a universal morality or is there a distinct morality for each individual based on his emotional and intellectual development?

MR. O. Neither—you see, morality is always relative. It's different in different countries. But consciousness is always the same.

MRS. R. Which word can be used for the designation of 'controlled imagination', because the word imagination is used for the uncontrolled only?

MR. O. There is no such word. It is necessary to understand that words won't help. Don't invent new words.

MRS. R. Influences   A   Three forces   Passive
                   B   Active
                   C   Neutralizing

Any connection?

MR. O. No, no relation.

MRS. R. I do not understand what is the state of matter 'hydrogen'. 'No force working'—how can it exist?

MR. O. It doesn't mean that it doesn't work. It means that it is taken by itself without connection with any triad.

MRS. R. What should be the state of 'interior peace'—state of nitrogen or state of hydrogen?

MR. O. No, it cannot be defined in that way.

MRS. R. I do not understand the musical scale in relation to the scheme of the Ray of Creation. Is every musical note triple?

MR. O. Well, it can be applied to any kind of orderly development. And what means triple?

* * *

[Oral questions.]

MRS. F. Does that mean that impressions go on coming?

MR. O. Certainly, certainly, certainly.

MRS. F. How are they registered and how are they transformed?

MR. O. Observe. This is material for observation.

MR. H. Do you consider that man has a soul?

MR. O. Soul in this system means simply—life principle. It is not a psychic principle.

MRS. R. The soul, is it matter?

MR. O. It is matter, yes.

MRS. R. Where to find the matter if it isn't hydrogen?

MR. O. When it will be necessary, we'll study it. It doesn't enter now.

MISS H. What is the difference between essence and spirit?

MR. O. We don't use the word spirit.

MRS. F. Does the life of the sun feed us?

MR. O. No, it is quite a wrong analogy.

MRS. F. The soul doesn't come from the moon?

MR. O. The sun is the sun. If you speak about the moon, then speak about the moon.

MISS R. In the Table of Hydrogens, No. 3072 is the highest. If it's densest does it mean that souls are densest?

MR. O. Soul certainly is higher.

MISS Q. Can you give us some example of how to use energy?

MR. O. We cannot use it exactly, that is the same half pound of energy that we would lose through waste.

MR. L. How can we know when we really remember ourselves?

MR. O. Oh, when we remember ourselves we know the difference. But it doesn't happen all at once. After some time you will see that it begins to change.

MISS Q. Is it something emotional or something intellectual that limits our understanding?

MR. O. Quite right. Understanding is not a function of one centre. It is a function of at least two centres, maybe three, and perhaps four.

MISS R. Does higher mental energy come from the Absolute?

MR. O. Nothing comes from the Absolute to us. What comes from the Absolute comes only to World 3.

MRS. F. What do you mean by themselves they are three-dimensional?

MR. O. Like earth—man. Man by himself may be three-dimensional.

MRS. F. Do we have connection with the fourth dimension?

MR. O. Time. Time is the fourth dimension.

MISS B. Is eternity the fifth dimension?

MR. O. We may call it that.

MRS. N. Are these ideas fifth-dimensional?

MR. O. No, no, we cannot bring that. How can we measure ideas by dimensions?

MISS H. Is evil negative—just lack of good?

MR. O. No, we cannot speak like that. That puts evil and good on the same level.

MRS. B. Does it come from people who have killed conscience?

MR. O. No, that is a rare case.

MISS B. Does it have anything to do with the triad of destruction?

MR. O. No, it's much more simple. Take just mechanicalness.

MRS. N. Is it a force?

MR. O. No, it's just a description just at present.

MISS B. Suppose that one has power and misuses it?

MR. O. It depends what power.

MRS. F. But you said that evil could be conscious.

MR. O. If you like.

MISS H. Is evil ignorance?

MR. O. Very often.

MISS B. Suppose that one acquires power and develops it in the wrong way?

MR. O. You know we cannot really discuss development in the wrong way. It's too rare. But if consciousness develops, possibility of evil diminishes.

MRS. C. How is it possible to destroy consciousness?

MR. O. You know, this is not a school principle. It is not taught in schools.

MRS. F. You said that negative emotions are in ourselves yet that we must also avoid making other people negative. How is this?

MR. O. They are not ourselves.

MRS. C. Are dead people evil?

MR. O. Not evil intentionally.

MRS. F. Is evil, matter?

MR. O. If you like, but it's not necessary.

MR. Z. Does irritation and impatience matter?

MR. O. Certainly. Lack of control.

MRS. F. Is there tremendous value attached to the soul of the individual?

MR. O. Depends which soul and which individual. But there is no value in that—you take an idea that does not touch the system and ask me to explain it.

MR. L. Would you mind explaining being?

MR. O. Being is very difficult to define. Everything that is one's own, is one's being.

MR. H. Then is knowledge important?

MR. O. Knowledge is separate. We divide two lines of man. But it is very important. If there were no growth of knowledge it would be very difficult to develop being.

MRS. N. How can I understand what is to suffer without negative emotion?

MR. O. One has to risk it. There is too much habit in negative emotion.

MISS Q. Do you think that self-sacrifice helps to develop?

MR. O. You see—self-sacrifice is a rather big word. It doesn't enter in the beginning. But if one makes big efforts one gains so much that it can hardly be called self-sacrifice.

MR. Z. If one self-remembers in this life will it change the next one?

MR. O. No, if you only begin it doesn't mean anything. But if one attains something that is another thing. But one must get pretty much—not just a little.

MRS. C. When can we begin to think how the different triads operate?

MR. O. We can see some, and some not. But don't worry about it. You will see more than you like.

MISS Q. Is the power of mental telepathy acquired or born?

MR. O. Mental telepathy—that may refer to only man No. 5. Otherwise it is either self-deception or imagination. But it is not really mental, it is emotional.

MRS. C. How about a definite experiment that people have made?

MR. O. Don't believe in that. It is either guessing or bad observation.

MRS. C. No, but I mean the experiments at Duke University.

MR. O. No, scientifically, experiments are not possible. For experiments are only possible in an emotional state, and who can produce that?

MRS. F. Why is it necessary to be in an emotional state?

MR. O. Because the power of these things is only in emotional centre. And what is true of this refers only to higher emotional centre.

MRS. N. Is it useful to be in an emotional state?

MR. O. Oh, that you have to decide for yourself.

MRS. S. Don't you think that it is important to think of nothing?

MR. O. As an exercise. I said three times a day for five minutes.

MRS. S. Is it better to work that way than to try and be self-conscious?

MR. O. It's the same thing.

*　　*　　*

Wednesday. July 9th 1941. (New York.)

[Written questions.]

MR. Z. Why is carbon 6, being of such high character, placed down in the lower part of the diagram [Food Factory]?

MR. O. First, it is carbon 12. And secondly we cannot define one thing by itself—one particular detail of the structure of an organism.

MR. Z. Any orderly development proceeds to develop according to the Law of Seven. Could the development of an organism, say a frog from its egg, be considered an orderly development and subjected to the Law of Seven?

MR. O. It may be.

MR. Z. Do minerals possess soul? If so, how is it possible for a mineral to die?

MR. O. Man possesses a soul and he dies.

*   *   *

[Oral questions.]

MR. H. Can negative emotions in men Nos. 1, 2 and 3, cause disease?

MR. O. If it is sufficiently strong, perhaps.

MRS. F. You said that one remembers the moments when one is more awake. Which moment is that?

MR. O. No, it's not 'which is which'. Generally speaking, one remembers moments when one is awake. But it cannot be described as you wish.

MRS. F. Does the kind of memory depend on the type of person?

MR. O. No, some have one sort. Simply—they are different.

MISS R. Is your description of six dimensions the same as in your book?

MR. O. No, you begin with three dimensions—then come to six. You cannot begin with six.

MR. L. I don't understand those three laws that come from each world. Where do you get those three forces?

MR. O. Each new world develops three new combinations of its own.

MRS. F. Does the energy that comes from food and energy from impressions mean the same thing? Is it the same?

MR. O. No, we don't enter into that. That again would be speculating on the ideas of science. It's not the same; it comes from a different part of the Ray of Creation. For us energy and matter are not divided, so the presence of one means the presence of the other.

MRS. S. Does the cosmic ray that Prof. Milliken discovered have anything to do with this?

MR. O. No, it is just a word. It may mean something, but what he really means and on which scale—that is another thing.

MISS R. Where is the atomic world? [Table of Cosmoses.]

MR. O. Farther down on the scale.

MISS R. Where do you start to measure time?

MR. O. I haven't finished it yet.

MR. L. What is meant by big cells and small cells?

MR. O. Oh, this is quite definite. Twenty years ago it was only known in bacteriology.

MR. L. For instance, in botany you must deal with the large cell.

MR. O. Yes, in all possible manifestations you can find this difference.

MR. Z. Are bacteria small cells?

MR. O. No, large. Small cells are virus.

MR. Z. What is the difference between megalo- and meso-cosmos?

MR. O. Megalocosmos is World 3 in the Ray of Creation. It means simply big cosmos.

MISS R. Can you take any three to compare them or a particular three?

MR. O. I think it is better to try it later. Sometimes you may find something that way, sometimes not.

MR. Z. The life of the earth—what is the figure?

MR. O. Twelve.

MRS. S. Is three seconds supposed to represent the present?

MR. O. Not supposed. But in ordinary moments the present is three seconds.

MRS. F. Is it possible to have time in all the cosmoses?

MR. O. If you like. I don't know what sense in which it can be useful.

MR. Z. If the protocosmos represents the Absolute, then we can figure out the life of the Absolute.

MR. O. Yes, yes.

MRS. M. If one can figure out the life of the Absolute then it means that it must end. Then what?

MR. O. And then repetition.

MR. Z. The life of man is not exactly eighty years, so this would make the other figures wrong.

MR. O. Well, more or less. There are no exact figures. One figure more or one figure less makes no difference. It's only the principle that's important.

MISS R. I read the other day where two scientists found that there were two principles in everything. The 'growth' principle and the 'inhibitory' principle. And that the reason a man died was because these became unbalanced. Isn't that like your three principles?

MR. O. Yes, but they begin without a plan. It cannot go without a plan. Each science is quite separate. There is no plan for all. Even chemistry and physics do not agree. And biology stands quite alone.

MRS. N. Do you think it likely that our lives recur?

MR. O. Well, it doesn't matter what I think at all. If you are asleep it will make no difference. There is no advantage at all.

MR. Z. If a man is asleep one life and doesn't wake up, and the same for the next, how much time does he have?

MR. O. Unlimited quantity.

* * *

Thursday. July 10th 1941. (New York.)

MRS. B. I would like to hear more about the activities.

MR. O. Yes, I gave you an example of six categories. But now you must find analogies. But that doesn't cover the whole ground, and the whole conversation can only begin when you find analogies. Take the triad of school-work and higher art—the same triad is genuine religious feeling, also altruistic activity, provided that it is genuine.

MRS. K. What do you mean by educated people?

MR. O. Oh, in the Vienna Conference they were mostly hereditary statesmen—they had tradition. At the Versailles Conference they had neither.

MR. R. Do we understand the system suggests the study of history chiefly for the understanding of people?

MR. O. No, events. Certainly you must understand the mechanicalness.

MR. R. In the system there are no economics and politics?

MR. O. Economics, yes, and politics, yes—but economics doesn't enter so much. They are always a background. But events change things very much, and population changes things very much.

MRS. W. Did I understand you to say that self-will was used in this situation? [Situation of Germany attacking Russia.]

MR. O. Yes, that can be compared only with self-will. The Germans can't win anything in that way. They had all they wanted. [From Russia.] But I think that the Russians began to bargain. And in the end refused to give.

MRS. B. How do you suggest going about the study of modern history?

MR. O. As I said—it is necessary to have certain preparation. In the last hundred years you must know more or less what happened. And then certainly follow the present—current events.

MRS. K. Is it possible for someone who is not a German to understand a German?

MR. O. But why not? I'm sure that some Germans understand things very differently. Not all understand them in the same way.

477

MRS. W. What are the conditions that bring communism and fascism about?

MR. O. Oh, certainly not economics. It is agitation and lies, lies, lies. And people who could not play an ordinary part in the government.

MRS. W. Don't people think that economics can make it change?

MR. O. They make it worse, first, and secondly economic ideas don't change—or slowly, but political ideas change. Certain ideas appear in the wrong place and produce an explosion.

MRS. R. Why is it that all the wrong people have influence and the right ones, like people in school, cease to have it?

MR. O. Yes, that's a sign of the time.

MRS. R. Teachers and Christ never seem to have anything to do with politics.

MR. O. No, Christ is a legend; we can't take Christ. No, certainly it's important—a school can work only with people who want to learn.

MRS. R. Isn't it possible for someone like that to have power?

MR. O. But how can they get active power? Active power comes from force. No, it's important only to understand that we cannot change anything. And if we understand things we may foresee what may happen.

MRS. R. In your book you said only people who studied Raja Yoga could have power.

MR. O. No, in this book I tried to make contact with life when I spoke of castes. Castes are not artificial.

Another thing—in relation to your group it will be very difficult for you to come to any real work. Because you have not heard many important things.

MR. W. What are some of these school rules?

MR. O. But you see, that's the most difficult thing—you cannot describe them like that. One of the chief rules is not to write about rules.

MR. W. When you speak of self-will, do you mean people who follow automatic desires?

MR. O. No, in this case it means only 'initiative'. In the second line of work initiative is always wrong. One is told to do something in a certain way and one does it in their own way.

MRS. K. Why are there three lines of work in school?

MR. O. Because one line helps another. If you take it from the point of view of the octave, three lines must go.

MRS. B. Do you do all three at the same time?

MR. O. No, it is not necessarily the same as a cosmic process.

MR. B. What do you mean when you refer to the solar plexus?

MR. O. The solar plexus is anatomical knowledge. But I mean several other machines that work with carbon 12.

MR. W. What do the dotted lines represent? [Enneagram.]

MR. O. The Law of Three.

MR. W. Do the sides represent specifically any forces?

MR. O. It may—but that is for the future.

MRS. B. What do you mean by accumulator?

MR. O. Oh, we didn't speak of accumulators.

MRS. W. When we say that we have our second wind. . . .

MR. O. Yes, second wind very often means passing to second accumulator.

MRS. B. Is it possible for one accumulator to get from a second accumulator?

MR. O. Yes, it always happens.

MRS. R. In the state of rest or sleep do the accumulators fill automatically?

MR. O. Yes, all energy that accumulates from food, air and impressions accumulates in the big accumulator.

MRS. R. But in conscious effort nothing is lost?

MR. O. In conscious effort nothing is lost. It comes back.

MRS. R. Does this diagram represent all kinds of food or just ordinary food?

MR. O. Three kinds of food—768, ordinary food; 192, air; 48, impressions.

MRS. K. Is that 0·1428571, circulation?

MR. O. Yes, but it's not only circulation. It's more complicated.

MRS. R. What is the technique for resisting negative emotions?

MR. O. Technique? No. First of all there are many different steps. The first is not to express negative emotions.

MR. W. Did you say the first step is not to express negative emotions?

MR. O. Yes, not to express negative emotions. Then to understand negative emotions in oneself—then in life. Next—struggle with identification and imagination.

MR. W. When you do observe imagination and identification you stop it?

MR. O. Yes, when you observe it, after a long time. You know when it begins and you have the energy to stop it. You are not fully identified.

* * *

Friday. July 11th 1941. (New York.)

[Written questions.]

MRS. S. On page 477 of the *New Model*, it is said, 'Death is really a return to the beginning.

'This means that if a man was born in 1877 and died in 1912, then having died, he finds himself again in 1877 and must live the same life all over again. . . . He is born again in the same town, in the same street, of <u>the same parents,</u> in the same year and on the same day.'

How can this be if his parents are alive on the day of his death and are old people?

MR. O. Logically it looks absurd, and you can't find a way to rectify it. At any rate, in order to think about it, take longer periods of time.

* * *

[Further questions: Are we dealing here with parallel lines of time? In what kind of time are our mistakes rectified?]

* * *

MRS. P. When is a person in a more positive state of mind: when entirely relaxed and at ease? When highly elated and joyful through emotional or religious fervour?

MR. O. I think both cases are the same. One is laziness, the other identification. Subjective feelings don't change anything.

MRS. P. In proportion as our consciousness expands and we begin to acquire power over ourselves, must we bear in mind that the soul may develop at the expense of our spirit, or should we forget it altogether?

MR. O. You have to wait until we mention them. They weren't mentioned in lectures.

MRS. P. One reads frequently about semi-intelligent forces called 'elementals', which are said to be dangerous. Why are they dangerous? Are these forces felt as sensations or seen as images? Will you please tell me just what they are supposed to be?

MR. O. Again, quite a new idea for me. I can speak only in the language I know.

MR. D. You explained how knowledge of the three forces helped in school-work. Will you please tell us how can we know which are the three forces in any private undertaking and how can we apply them?

Since in application of the three forces we have to work with other people, doesn't it make altruism a scientific necessity?

MR. O. Again I must say some things about language—try and specialize in the language that you have learned. Altruism—it is a foreign word.

*   *   *

[Oral questions.]

MISS B. Do we lead this life over and over again, or do we lead multiple lives?

MR. O. What do you mean by multiple lives?

No, certainly not, we live in <u>this</u> time, until one gets out of it.

MR. M. There is still the intellectual phrase, 'born of the same parents'—that I don't understand.

MR. O. It means that. One word cannot be guaranteed—'immediately'.

MRS. N. What do you mean by the second line of work?

MR. O. You cannot work alone in the second line—you work in a group.

MRS. D. Would you say something about not remembering ourselves?

MR. O. No, that must be a matter for self-observation.

MRS. S. What are negative emotions?

MR. O. Again, matter for observation. At least half of them will disappear if imagination and negative emotions go.

MRS. D. Can there not be creative imagination?

MR. O. Man is a machine; he cannot create anything. At best he may imitate.

MISS B. How can one tell the difference between imagination and a real experience?

MR. O. First you see imagination has the particular power of turning like a wheel.

MR. D. What is the mental state of a composer, inventor, painter, when he thinks about his work before?

MR. O. Exactly the same as a carpenter, who makes benches.

MRS. P. You wish us to establish with our consciousness the difference between the creative and the imagination?

MR. O. Not only they don't go together, but there is great self-deception in imagination. Many lazy people avoid making effort through imagination.

MRS. N. Well, if thoughts are not negative, what are they?

MR. O. Thoughts? Or not thoughts? I specially speak about negative emotions.

MRS. N. Well, if they don't make you unhappy?

MR. O. Again this is a private situation. But to have positive attitudes to wrong things is quite wrong.

MRS. N. You mean we don't see reality?

MR. O. We don't see anything.

MISS B. If a person tries to choke out all these ideas is he escaping?

MR. O. First, he deceives himself, because he can't shut anything out, and second, he tries to escape.

MRS. N. Is there anything outside of ourselves?

MR. O. Certainly, the table, the chair and New York, unfortunately.

MRS. N. You mean that we don't see the outside?

MR. O. Yes, almost, but I would say it is because we don't see ourselves.

MRS. Z. You say self-remembering; what is the self?

MR. O. Me, me.

MISS B. Where were we ten thousand years ago?

MR. O. I don't think that we existed ten thousand years ago.

MISS H. Is creative power controlled imagination?

MR. O. I already said you cannot control imagination. Try and find a case.

MISS H. Where do you place the ability to work without imagination?

MR. O. It's different in different cases. In some people who really can write, it's <u>work</u>. Only people who write badly write without effort.

MRS. C. How would you define a real emotional experience?

MR. O. You cannot define it. You will know perfectly well if you have the experience once.

* * *

Tuesday. July 15th 1941. (New Group. New York.)

MR. Z. What is the purpose of human life?

MR. O. It depends whose. This is not a question. And in a certain sense—who speaks. In connection with this it is interesting to think that everything in nature has not a <u>single</u> purpose, but several, maybe three, and on different scales.

MR. B. What, if any, is the object of the universe?

MR. O. You see—what is meant by the universe? We will come to that later.

MRS. N. What is meant by three different scales?

MR. O. No, you must ask your own questions. If you continue in that way you will never get out of it.

MISS S. How many different levels of consciousness are there?

MR. O. That will be in the lecture to-day in more complete form. But first I would like you to think what 'levels' of consciousness means. And in this sense we must try to make it practical.

MR. B. Are there not some Tibetans who have acquired higher degrees of consciousness?

MR. O. I haven't met any Tibetans in my life, so I couldn't say.

MR. M. Have you ever met any men No. 5?

MR. O. Three. Maybe less, it doesn't matter.

MR. B. When you refer to seven different categories of men you must refer to dead men.

MR. O. I refer only to living people.

MR. B. What is your evidence for making that division?

MR. O. Psychological evidence.

MR. M. You say that the state of sleep is the lowest form of consciousness. Isn't that the negation of consciousness?

MR. O. No, it <u>is</u> a state of consciousness. There are glimpses.

MRS. N. Is memory possible without consciousness?

MR. O. Oh, yes, memory is mechanical.

MR. F. But didn't you say, sir, that the only moments that we remember are conscious moments?

MR. O. Yes, but we don't remember consciously. I may remember something because I was conscious, but when it comes back I may not be.

MRS. N. Is it a degree of awareness if one enjoys the theatre?

MR. O. No, it may be quite mechanical.

MR. M. You referred to Yoga as one of the six philosophies.

MR. O. Yes, it is generally called like that. I can't guarantee it.

MISS S. Since what time has our psychology been in such a low state?

MR. O. I think chiefly from the beginning of psychoanalysis and all that followed.

MRS. M. You said that it was long work to attain consciousness, so when and where can we attain it?

MR. O. Nobody can say that. And I didn't say full consciousness. When we realize that we don't have consciousness then we try to become just a little conscious.

MRS. N. What do you mean by functions?

MR. O. Oh, reading something and not understanding it.

MR. B. If one has what one believes is self-consciousness and then examines it and finds it false, and then goes on to what one imagines is self-consciousness. . . .

MR. O. Not so quickly—there are many ups and downs. No, the first step is to realize that you are not conscious. When you make the effort to be conscious you realize how rarely it happens and how difficult it is.

MR. M. Are flashes of objective consciousness possible without self-consciousness?

MR. O. I don't know. I don't think that one can remember in this case.

MRS. N. What do you mean by objective consciousness?

MR. O. Objective consciousness is a state that we do not have. In the state of sleep you see a wall and walk through it. In waking state you know the difference between the wall and the door. In self-consciousness you know something about yourself that you could not know in waking state. In objective consciousness you know all about things that you cannot know now.

MR. M. You could not be in a state of self-consciousness in sleep?

MR. O. Oh, glimpses are possible. But these are usually purely physiological.

* * *

Wednesday. July 16th 1941. (New York.)

MRS. H. In walking I use the moving centre. What else is used?

MR. O. No, no, you observe one thing. You can't observe all things. But if you walk slower or quicker, or take longer steps and so on, then you can observe. If you change things a little you begin to see something.

MISS D. You said last week that by observation alone one cannot do anything. What can you do then?

MR. O. It changes something but not enough. And that depends on the observation. But some things are quite definite that we must change, like expression of negative emotions, imagination, etc.

MRS. F. Could anger appear as a dream in sleep?

MR. O. Yes, but it's harmless there. Sleep is a dustbin where we throw what we don't want.

MISS D. If we want to increase energy we have to learn how?

MR. O. Before we try to increase anything we have to study how we waste. Then we must stop this waste. And then we can increase this energy only by self-remembering.

MRS. B. Are leaks mostly negative emotions?

MR. O. Negative emotions, mechanicalness of many kinds—talking, for example.

MRS. B. I know that one can work better with other people, but I was wondering if one could work by oneself?

MR. O. Try—no, you ask me; that means that you don't want to do it by yourself.

MRS. B. But then you mustn't be identified?

MR. O. One mustn't identify. In any case one must notice the forms of identification.

MRS. S. Does a person ever remember themselves in sleep?

MR. O. Only in a dream. Normally, in sleep, if one remembers or pronounces one's name, one awakes.

MRS. D. Why does self-remembering act on metabolism?

MR. O. Oh, many other things. First it means increase of self-awareness.

MRS. S. If a person has a dream and it comes true, how would you explain that?

MR. O. Necessary to study details. How many similar dreams has one had and what percentage came true? This is what usually spoils the whole theory.

MISS D. What about pleasant dreams that one has that one doesn't experience in life?

MR. O. One very good explanation is compensation.

MISS H. Is it possible to write or paint without becoming identified?

MR. O. That depends how—to write well, or paint well, it is necessary to be without identification. To paint badly, identification is all right. To produce good things it must be without identification.

MRS. V. Does identification belong to emotional centre?

MR. O. It's complicated really. You cannot say it belongs to one centre. It may affect all centres.

MR. F. If one is really doing something the best one can, is that identification?

MR. O. But one can do that only without identification. If one tries to do that and identifies, the work stays and we put it in our dreams.

MR. H. Is it possible to concentrate on something and not be identified with it?

MR. O. Try, that is material for observation. And if you observe several times, you may see. And you may see that if one concentrates it is very liable to become identification.

MRS. H. You said that if one could remember during an emotion—I remembered once and it went away.

MR. O. I said if you had negative emotions that you cannot conquer, you can remember yourself by the help of the negative emotions.

MR. L. Are the results identical for self-remembering and five minutes per day of putting out thoughts?

MR. O. Yes, yes, what results mean is that self-remembering will come of itself. And it will come at the moments of important decisions.

MR. F. Even when one is attempting without thinking?

MR. O. What do you mean by not thinking? But that means intense thinking. You must think—I must not think.

MR. L. Is it practically having your mind blank?

MR. O. Yes, if you can. But the effort must be constant. The moment that the effort stops you begin to think about some quite useless thing.

MR. H. By controlling negative emotions do they disappear or do they recur?

MR. O. I didn't speak about the control of negative emotions. I spoke about the control of the <u>expression</u> of negative emotions.

MRS. S. Being not identified means not to be attached?

MR. O. Yes, but not to be identified means to remember yourself.

MR. H. If a train goes by and you think that you wish it would stop, is that identification?

MR. O. No, it's only the beginning, if it's for a moment, but if it continues it becomes identification. Say you think how you would like to put a bomb under it.

MRS. S. To have a positive emotion we would have to remember ourselves?

MR. O. Oh, positive emotion is far from us. Yes, one must almost have full control. But that is quite interesting because before we can think to have positive emotions, we must become more emotional.

MRS. B. Then the education that the English receive is bad—self-control?

MR. O. Oh, why accuse the English? No, self-control is always good. But <u>how</u>—that is the question.

MRS. M. Thank you for saying that, Mr. Ouspensky. Because all the other teachers teach the opposite.

MR. O. Yes, I would like to know about anybody who teaches anything. They teach either the cultivation of imagination, or negative emotions or identification.

MR. H. What is a positive emotion?

MR. O. Something that we don't have. In the New Testament it says that if you have enough faith that you can move mountains, also love your enemies. But who can do that? We cannot even love our friends.

MRS. W. Why are we afraid of emotions and of being emotional?

MR. O. Because our emotions turn into negative emotions so we prefer to have none.

MRS. R. One way to work on positive emotions is to work on negative emotions?

MR. O. Yes, work against negative emotions is one thing. But you must realize that you have not enough emotion. And emotional centre is like another brain and quick—very quick. Also the limits of intellectual centre are well known.

How is another thing—but we must learn not to stop them.

MRS. W. The only way to stop them is to remember at the time?

MR. O. Oh, there are many things. Buffers—they stop them automatically.

MRS. W. It is difficult to find a buffer by oneself.

MR. O. Oh, you can find them in somebody else. If you can't find something in yourself, look for it in somebody else.

MRS. R. When we stop emotions do we stop them consciously?

MR. O. No, we are not conscious. So how can we do anything consciously? We don't like emotions and all that taken together stops them. Emotions are necessary for many things.

MR. H. What stops our emotions from existing?

MR. O. They are destroyed. If we destroy them they disappear.

MRS. S. How can one stimulate them?

MR. O. No, it's not a question of stimulation. One must simply stop attempts to destroy them.

MRS. H. How can we tell which emotions are which?

MR. O. Oh, everyone has some particular favourite negative emotion. And if you are sincere with yourself you can recognize them even when they disguise themselves.

MRS. S. If there is not laughter in higher centres then there is no sorrow?

MR. O. Oh, that I don't know. Laughter is one thing and sorrow is another. Why opposite? Who said that they were opposite?

MRS. S. Do you think that telepathy exists?

MR. O. For No. 5. Even then he has to learn it. Telepathy is a function of higher emotional centre. It is not in ordinary centres.

MRS. V. Has everyone higher emotional centre and the possibility of using?

MR. O. Yes, everybody has it. But not the possibility . . . you have to be aware.

MR. H. Can't you use it by accident?

MR. O. Oh, accident may happen. But you cannot use accident.

MRS. S. Does clairvoyance exist and in the higher emotional centre?

MR. O. Yes, only no ordinary centre can see anything at a distance and so on. They may be accidental. You know I investigated this question very much and I never met a single case, except a case definitely connected with the work and higher emotional centre.

MRS. M. Some people say that they know something, but isn't it a bad thing to use when you don't know how?

MR. O. But nobody has it.

MRS. M. But it must be dangerous?

MR. O. No, not in connection with school-work.

MRS. B. What about black magic?

MR. O. Oh, school doesn't teach black magic, so there is no danger. It is not in our programme.

MR. L. Does the word 'adept' mean man No. 5?

MR. O. I don't know. It depends who says it. That's why we have words, because if we use word we at least know what it means. The fewer words the better.

MRS. S. Would you say a little more about understanding?

MR. O. No, I mentioned only one side to-day. If we suppress our emotions we cannot increase our understanding. And understanding is the function of two, three or all centres.

MRS. R. Has emotion a number in the Table of Hydrogens?

MR. O. No, no, but you can say generally that emotion can be either 24, 12, 6 or—very big—3.

MR. R. What is satisfaction and contentment?

MR. O. Yes, it is simply 24. Instinctive, not more.

MR. R. That means that satisfaction should be used and dissatisfaction not?

MR. O. Yes, but you cannot do. You can only observe.

*   *   *

Thursday. July 17th 1941. (New York.)

MRS. R. In saying the Lord's Prayer over and over I hear other thoughts behind.

MR. O. You can't help it.

MRS. W. Sometimes in saying the prayer I seem to hear the numbers in my chest and the sayings in my head, is that imagination?

MR. O. Yes, but it doesn't matter again. It is imperative only to do it. Later—much later, you can do something with it.

MRS. K. Is this [enneagram] a very ancient symbol?

MR. O. They say so. I couldn't find it in any books. Ennea is like penta—so it means nine.

MRS. K. In the *New Model* you mentioned the dervishes. Did they make a figure of the Ray of Creation?

MR. O. No, no. They didn't make definite figures. They turned round themselves and round the man in the middle.

MR. W. What are we supposed to do with the diagram?

MR. O. Oh, nothing at present. If something comes to your mind we can discuss it.

MR. W. I would like it if you said something about self-remembering and self-observation.

MR. O. I can say nothing about it, because I already said all that can be said. Self-observation is simply a method of self-study. And it's only when you want to know yourself and want to study yourself that it becomes serious.

MRS. K. Do individuality, will and consciousness operate through the higher centres?

MR. O. Those are not centres—will is not a centre. Individuality is not a centre. Centre is a machine. Those are manifestations.

MRS. K. This is very different from what we were taught.

MR. O. I can't help it, you know. This is what we learned from the very beginning.

MR. W. You can't really say that individuality is a function?

491

MR. O. Individuality is not a function. Individuality means when the small 'I's come under control of the central 'I'.

MRS. K. We were taught that individuality was consciousness of will.

MR. O. It's only words. It's not Mr. G. It's Orage. I don't like to say this, but he forgot many things and had to invent.

MISS A. What would be the function of higher centres?

MR. O. You see, higher centres are only names. Higher centres are not divided into two parts. Certain functions which exist in ordinary centres do not exist in higher centres. And intellect and emotion are not divided. Intellect and emotion are only different in ordinary centres. Then a difference can be described—in higher centres we can see things and thinking is often symbolic. And higher intellectual centre is so quick that we can't catch it. And some of the experiences that I describe in the *New Model* are some of higher emotional and some of higher intellectual. It is not very hard to connect to higher centres but it has no value. Only control is valuable.

MRS. R. I heard a long time ago that each observation deposited something for higher centres.

MR. O. It cannot touch higher centres. Higher centres can be connected only through self-remembering. It's the only way. Observation is useful by what one observes.

MRS. W. Do these centres have existence after the body is dead?

MR. O. Yes, certainly. But what they are in the body we don't know.

MRS. K. There seems to be connection between will and consciousness.

MR. O. No, we must not mix terminologies.

MRS. K. What would represent higher instinctive? What is that which is sex?

MR. O. No, instinctive is one. And sex is by itself. We don't bring it in because you study all the laws through the four centres.

MR. R. These hydrogens—why can't you connect them into triangles like the Food Diagram?

MR. O. Yes, but they are not connected. Centres are too little connected for that. I don't know, perhaps you can take it as a triad, but I don't see how it will help.

MR. W. Do you mean that no centre works with the correct hydrogen?

MR. O. They all steal from other centres. When we see 24, 48 and 12, it means the hydrogen they <u>should</u> work with.

MR. W. How can you collect data on that?

MR. O. There are two forms of wrong work of centres.

(1) They may use wrong energy. (2) They may work with the lower parts of centres.

MISS S. Do you mean by suppressing imagination, imagination that is used by someone writing music or painting a picture?

MR. O. Mr. G. always strongly insisted that it was not imagination. There are notes for that period. He insisted that imagination cannot be controlled. If you control what you think is imagination, it is something else.

MISS A. If the centres should work properly what would it be like?

MR. O. What it should be. Brain would think, heart would feel, stomach would digest.

MRS. K. In what centre does imagination take place?

MR. O. Imagination takes from all centres. It may begin in intellectual, it may begin in moving, it may begin in emotional. But it's only the beginning.

MR. W. What do you mean by imagination? Day-dreams and fantasy?

MR. O. Day-dreams are only part of imagination. Imagination can be imagining existing features, powers and qualities in oneself. This is a much worse form. This is a matter for observation and you will see several categories.

MRS. W. How can you discriminate when you think that you have some feature and you find that you have not?

MR. O. Well, you see, I have met certain Theosophical people who read many books and they believe all that they read.

MRS. K. A buffer is imagination, isn't it?

MR. O. No, a buffer is something—like wood. And it is something that can be permanent in man.

MRS. R. Does imagination begin to work early in children?

MR. O. Oh, yes, probably before they are born.

MR. W. We were told that fairy stories were very useful.

MR. O. Some, yes.

MISS A. When you speak of higher centres do you mean lower centres that function properly or something quite different from them?

MR. O. No, you see, as long as lower centres function improperly there is no possibility to think of higher centres. And it is only when centres use higher parts that this connection becomes real. And these higher parts can be developed through <u>attention</u>. So certainly balance of centres is necessary.

[Unrecorded question.]

MR. O. Yes, for a long time. It is intellectual centre. Then by different methods you transfer it to moving centre. When it is firmly established in moving centre you change it to instinctive centre. Then the last stage—you transfer to emotional centre.

MRS. W. Since we have heard so much about them I think that we would like to know some of the rules.

MR. O. At every opportunity I will try to point them out to you. But it's no use to speak of them academically.

MR. W. In this connection is it useful for us not to show negative emotions?

MR. O. Always useful. This is the first thing.

MR. W. What about talking?

MR. O. Ordinarily it's nothing. But in certain moments one must not.

MISS S. Must not the student wait for the teacher to give permission to speak to new people?

MR. O. Oh, yes, certainly. It is necessary to know certain things. But we found in London that it was possible to speak about the books.

MR. W. Should we attempt to discover other people that we know, to bring to lectures?

MR. O. It cannot be done just like that, you know. There must be place for them; one must know what to say, like that.

*   *   *

Tuesday. July 22nd 1941. (New York.)

Q. How are we to associate the moral law of determinism of the physical world and the freedom of free will?

MR. O. This is a difficult question in the present state. But first it must be divided. We must speak separately about moral laws and then about determinism.

About moral laws—they cannot be taken like that—they are different in one country at one time and in another country at another time, and not in another, and so on. There is no general law. One cannot define it. The only one <u>objective</u> definition of 'good' and 'evil' is that good cannot be unconscious, and evil can only be unconscious. Try and understand that consciousness will destroy the possibility of evil.

About determinism we must speak from a different side. You see, it is a question of scale. Many things happen around us on different scales. And what is determined on one scale is not determined on another.

And freedom of will is a psychological problem, not philosophical, because our will, the will of man Nos. 1, 2 and 3, is the resultant of desires. And further, each 'I' has a separate will.

MRS. N. What do you mean by permanent ego?

MR. O. I mean that when you say 'I' you can be sure that it is the same 'I' each time. Now, you say 'I want this', and half an hour later you say 'I want that'. The 'I' is quite different.

MRS. N. What relation has it [ego] to the essence?

MR. O. You asked one question. Be satisfied with that. And ask without reference to permanent ego.

MRS. N. Did you say that the personality was all lies?

MR. O. No, I said that personality was almost all artificial. The same as essence is almost all real.

MR. F. Does self-remembering help to get rid of excess of personality?

MR. O. Yes, but I would prefer to wait about self-remembering until we come to that.

MRS. D. Why is it that personality is artificial?

MR. O. It was mentioned in lecture, 'Artificial likes and dislikes'. Say that one dislikes music but some friends like it. Then one begins to speak about it and so on—artificial.

MR. B. Are you using artificial in a derogatory meaning?

MR. O. Not derogatory—just, not yours.

MR. B. But perhaps it can be useful?

MR. O. It can't be useful because you can't use it.

MRS. H. Would you explain what you mean by creating obstacles to negative emotions?

MR. O. First we should learn not to express negative emotions. Many negative emotions just disappear if you do not express them.

MRS. F. Isn't identification the same as attachment?

MR. O. These words mean 'degree of absorption'.

MRS. S. Does that apply to friendship or is it just abstract?

MR. O. It refers to everything—again it _may_ be without. It spoils the best friendships, the best love, and so on, because it immediately brings negative emotions.

MRS. N. Are there activities in consciousness that are not identification?

MR. O. No, this is only the second lecture and you have already used several words that nobody has heard.

* * *

Wednesday. July 23rd 1941. (New York.)

MR. Z. Suppose I knew a man for a long time and I met him and forgot his name, does that mean I am not conscious?

MR. O. That's your business to decide. From ordinary point of view you forgot his name. Were you conscious or not I can't say.

MR. Z. But as I remember, one can only remember when they are conscious?

MR. O. No, that's all formatory. You want rules where there are none.

MRS. H. Is it important to know which is essence and personality?

MR. O. We cannot. Later on you may begin to notice that. It's more a theoretical division.

MR. F. In order to understand lying, identification and negative emotions, is it possible for us to do anything besides self-remembering?

MR. O. This is only one thing in general. We may do it in many ways. Also about negative emotions, we may try to understand them, the place they occupy in life, etc., but really only self-remembering produces results.

MISS S. How do we know when the weak spot is coming into our lives?

MR. O. There is no answer to that. Even if I give you an explanation it will not help. It is necessary to know results.

MISS B. Is it a cyclic rise and fall?

MR. O. Yes, to a certain extent. But what do you mean by that?

MISS B. If life goes in certain rhythm.

MR. O. Yes, but I don't believe much in that.

MRS. B. Will Nazism stop?

MR. O. But it's stopped already. Hitler fights with himself. Even speaking theoretically, if he had any chance to end war with something remaining, it was when he was friends with the bolsheviks.

MRS. B. What has made him make that mistake?

MR. O. The Law of Octaves. One Russian author said about the last war: in thirty years we will know about it.

MISS S. Is it a different rhythm for everybody? For instance, you can measure a musical octave.

MR. O. Rhythm—there is no rhythm. But this is cosmic law, not music.

MR. L. Does it happen by all the triads?

MR. O. Triads in everything. But triads follow one another by Law of Octaves.

MR. Z. Suppose a man went a certain direction and he keeps on doing it, does that mean he continues to do this?

MR. O. Oh, I don't know, again different people.

MRS. B. If one finds oneself slacking can one give themselves a shock?

MR. O. If one knows how. But generally shocks must be arranged beforehand.

MR. Z. Can the Law of Octaves be studied by observation?

MR. O. In certain cases, yes. If you find where to begin and how to look.

MR. T. What sort of shock did Hitler have that made him go back?

MR. O. That's what I say we read in thirty years' time. We had to deal with results only. How can we know causes?

MR. T. Then everyday things are capable of giving one a shock?

MR. O. You can't expect to obtain a shock before you discover the gap. We must know how to obtain the interval. And it's not shock—it's absence of shock.

MISS B. After the first interval is it possible to go back?

MR. O. That I don't know. That depends on the facts. It depends on the importance of the octave and the scale of the octave.

MISS S. Can one change direction two or three times a day?

MR. O. Depends in what.

MR. F. Why is it called the Law of Octaves?

MR. O. Because there is an octave between 500 and 1,000.

MR. Z. Suppose I try to solve a problem, does my intensity of thinking obey the Law of Octaves?

MR. O. You see—you want to 'do' already. You cannot do. All we can do is to study and observe. You cannot begin by changing things. But you must try to find explanations and analogies.

MRS. R. Are our emotions under the Law of Octaves?

MR. O. Everything is. But in different ways. You can't find exact analogies maybe. Again one octave may produce one kind of effect and another, another. But it is better to see it in our work.

MRS. R. What do you mean by change of direction?

MR. O. I merely based it on the example of Hitler starting the war against Europe for the sake of Germany, but now he fights against the interests of Germany. There will be more yet—there are many stages. But it has already turned. You can find many examples in history of something that started in one direction and turned.

MR. H. Are the shocks that come at the interval accidental?

MR. O. There may be accidental shocks. But one cannot live on the money that one finds in the street.

MRS. R. If you pass successfully through the first interval, is the second easier?

MR. O. No, harder.

MRS. R. Is the interval remembering ourselves?

MR. O. No, what it is has nothing to do with self-remembering. It has simply to do with the change of movement.

MR. T. Do most people end up in the opposite direction from which they start?

MR. O. Yes, if you could see that—like higher intellectual centre can see it, you could see that people go back.

MR. L. There is no way of controlling it?

MR. O. Yes, you can. But one can do nothing yet.

MR. F. Can one learn in advance what direction this is likely to take?

MR. O. Oh, yes, if we take facts.

MR. H. Is not the octave of the individual at the mercy of the octave of the State or society?

MR. O. Yes, there are many octaves. Some things can be taken into consideration. But you should take more normal examples.

MR. Z. Does this preliminary work on different occasions prevent this change?

MR. O. Not prevent. If we can foresee we can provide against certain circumstances.

MRS. R. You have two intervals on the straight line and four on the broken line.

MR. O. No, no, you take it too literally. But for the sake of understanding laws and principles we take it that way. Many things just begin and fall down, begin and fall down like that. But take it practically, not theoretically.

MR. H. If a person is prepared for an interval and he knows that it is coming and does not understand it, is that just his bad luck?

MR. O. No, it is a normal state. It's just how things are. But it is possible, with the things that we are given, to catch this.

MISS S. Can that be by oneself or is a school necessary?

MR. O. Oh, no, without school it is impossible. Again one may accidentally foresee and prevent, but one can miss ten other things at the same time.

MRS. M. People want things on a silver platter and they don't care enough to make the effort.

MR. O. But these efforts make certain demands that are extremely difficult—like sincerity. So many people are quite insincere with themselves. And some people need to be brave.

MRS. B. Is that what they mean in the Bible when they say, 'Unto everyone that hath shall be given . . . but from him that hath not, shall be taken away even that which he hath'?

MR. O. Oh, yes, in a way. It may have many meanings.

MRS. R. In a state of identification with negative emotions, is that already the first stage? [Impact.]

MR. O. We cannot speak about stages yet. I spoke about it from the *Philokalia*.

MR. T. Which are strongest in us—centres or 'I's?

MR. O. What is the difference between centres and 'I's?

MR. T. Is it the centres that divide us, or the 'I's?

MR. O. Well, if you take the diagram of 'I's we can see that some belong to intellectual centre, some to emotional, and so on.

MR. T. If something says to me that I want to listen to some music, is this an 'I' or a centre?

MR. O. No, it's different. It may be one part of a centre; it may be another. It may be habit, and it may be imitation.

MR. Z. Do you mean that 'I's communicate with one another?

MR. O. Yes, certainly, they always communicate with one another. But they communicate in the wrong way.

* * *

Thursday. July 24th 1941. (New York.)

MR. W. Is it meant by imagination, imagining oneself talking to someone, and so on?

MR. O. Yes, that's one form of imagination. But there are many other forms.

MR. W. Imagining qualities in oneself and in others?

MR. O. In oneself, first of all.

MR. W. How can you test this in yourself?

MR. O. One must verify it. One must be sincere. One must be brave, and one must not be afraid if they find unpleasant qualities in oneself.

MISS S. With Hitler going against himself does that mean that he goes contrary to the Law of Octaves?

MR. O. Turn, turn. The Law of Octaves can go in one direction and turn.

MRS. R. Does that change occur at _fa_?

MR. O. Oh, any place. There are many intervals. If we don't know the scale we can't say.

MRS. W. Then this was just a lucky accident?

MR. O. Like everything else, it is an accident.

MRS. W. How can we know the intervals in our lives?

MR. O. By studying the past. It's useful to look through your life, and look for what you think were your cross-roads. You think that there was a choice, but really there was none.

MR. R. Then if you knew all the octaves you could know all about your life?

MR. O. But you cannot know that. You would have to be, well, say man No. 7 to see all the octaves.

MISS. S. Would an analysis of psychology help us to understand the Law of Octaves?

MR. O. It may be, but in certain cases we may be able to see and study it without any particular analysis.

MISS. S. Is it desirable to achieve this emotional state?

MR. O. But it's impossible.

MISS. S. Would you see colours one after another?

MR. O. No, no, no, that is fantasy. The fact is—stop thoughts for one half hour and you will see things that you don't see now.

MRS. H. If you hear sounds, it means that you don't stop thoughts.

MR. O. Yes, but those we always hear. Of course it would be good <u>not</u> to hear, but our aim is always control.

MRS. W. One ought to try to stop thoughts so that one does not hear noises?

MR. O. There is no should. The question is—if one can.

MRS. W. It was not the results that I wanted to know. I wanted to know if that was right.

MR. O. But we can't try for that—like not hearing noises or feeling cold. If we do, we lose everything.

MISS S. Why is it that ordinary intellectual centre is slower than emotional centre, while higher intellectual centre is faster than higher emotional centre?

MR. O. That's only the fault of names. There is no division in higher centres. There is no difference between thought and feeling in higher centres.

MRS. H. Why do you give to higher mental centre 6, and to higher emotional centre 12?

MR. O. Because it's quicker.

MISS S. You say that there is a difference but that there is also a great similarity?

MR. O. Similarity when we look from here, but there, there is no difference.

MISS S. Is that like Samadhi?

MR. O. No, that's different.

* * *

Tuesday. July 29th 1941. (New York.)

MISS B. I didn't understand the word 'rolls'—impressions on rolls.

MR. O. Rolls—phonographic rolls. And our memory is simply reading these rolls.

MRS. D. Do these centres bear any relation to the endocrine glands?

MR. O. No, please don't try to interpret this language with another. And this idea is not fully scientific yet.

MRS. S. What about the memory of dreams?

MR. O. Dreams also leave an impression. I have met some people who thought something had happened, but really it was only a dream.

MRS. N. What is it in a man that dies?

MR. O. Everything. How can something remain from a sleeping man?

MRS. D. Is not a man who is awake automatic in his actions?

MR. O. We cannot speak about man who is awake. We have never met him. We must awake first.

MRS. D. Wouldn't the moving and instinctive centres remain automatic if man was awake?

MR. O. It is a wrong question, you see. We can't say 'if' man was awake.

MRS. D. But should we not try to awake the mechanical parts?

MR. O. There is no should. If we realize that we are asleep, we may try to make some efforts to awake. There can only be observation in all this. In all these ideas we must think only of what we can do, not what we should do. There are many things that we should do, but we cannot.

MRS. N. Why does identifying and considering make centre take from centre?

MR. O. Because you are lost in it. You are immersed and things just happen.

MR. S. Could you say what the energy of these centres is? Is it different energy?

MR. O. Energy? That will be explained later. It may be answered in both ways. Better to say different energy.

MRS. N. Are there two different kinds of memory? One mechanical and one conscious?

MR. O. No, not two kinds. Many kinds—each centre has its own memory. And there are different kinds in each centre.

MR. F. Do all those inscriptions [on rolls] come in this life, or are we born with some?

MR. O. They come in this life. No, in instinctive centre it is born with us; there:—a very few things in emotional, and everything has to be learned in moving and intellectual centres.

MR. S. Then each centre has its own way of feeling?

MR. O. Feeling? Intellectual centre thinks not feels, and instinctive feels.

MR. S. Then there is no feeling in the intellectual centre?

MR. O. No, there isn't. And we don't observe it as moving. It is all thought process. And emotions are all pleasant or unpleasant.

MR. S. Then there can't be change without movement?

MR. O. No, we can speak about movement only when we see something.

MRS. W. Would an intellectual process stimulate the emotions?

MR. O. It may sometimes. At other times they may be separate.

MRS. S. Should intellectual centre control the emotional centre?

MR. O. We have no control of emotions at all. We have some control of intellectual centre.

MRS. S. But we can control anger.

MR. O. You cannot.

MISS B. What about counting one hundred before getting angry? Isn't that a form of control?

MR. O. Count how many times that it will help you—then we can speak.

MR. H. Doesn't the quality of our intellectual state have an effect on what is pleasant or unpleasant for us?

MR. O. Unfortunately, in our intellectual state, very little.

MISS S. How can the intellectual centre take the part of moving and emotional centre?

MR. O. No, not in that way. It's too complicated. You see, each centre is divided again into three parts—emotional, moving and intellectual.

MRS. D. In man that has become conscious does each centre work independently?

MR. O. Yes, only in the right way. Centres begin to interfere with one another as we are now.

MR. B. Why do centres interfere with each other's work?

MR. O. To ensure the possibility of uninterrupted work. But it takes too much time. Actually we live below our level. You see, centres are designed to work best in the third state of consciousness.

MRS. D. When one centre steals from another, does it mean that the vibration has changed?

MR. O. We don't need 'vibration' in this case. It's too indefinite. Results—results will show.

MR. S. Are all functions necessary?

MR. O. Yes, originally, they are all necessary. But many functions are quite unnecessary, like imagination.

MR. S. In normal man are all the functions normal?

MR. O. Normal is a very difficult word, you know. Asleep—normally we should not be asleep. Normal man can be defined only by the possibility of development.

MR. S. Supposing that one loses one of the functions?

MR. O. We don't take pathological cases. Life is not long enough.

MR. S. Normality is true, then, only for the individual?

MR. O. We speak always of the individual.

MRS. N. How can one distinguish from the past a memory that comes from a moment of consciousness?

MR. O. By observation. Only if you observe yourself for long enough will it show.

MISS S. Why is imagination a bad thing?

MR. O. Because we cannot control it.

MISS S. I always thought imagination a valuable thing.

MR. O. Yes, we always think of it in that way.

MISS S. What stimulation in creative work should be used besides imagination?

MR. O. Oh, work itself. Hard work. Imagination is not work. It is escape from work.

MR. S. Then by imagination you mean day-dreaming?

MR. O. Not only. That is only one form of imagination.

MR. S. Then to work without imagination you have to expect things as they are?

MR. O. Quite right. Imagination cannot be connected with reality.

MR. S. But to plan you have to use visualization?

MR. O. Why should I? Why spend time visualizing dinner?

MISS B. If someone did not visualize dinner who would get it?

MR. O. I don't know. I am not a cook.

MR. S. What is the part of imagination that is not day-dreaming?

MR. O. That depends which line of thinking.

MR. S. There seems to be some wrong thinking about imagination and 'creative thinking'?

MR. O. It's the same word.

MR. S. Then imagination is anticipating in the mind?

MR. O. We don't speak about things that happen every thousand years. We speak about things that happen every day.

MISS S. You said that you would give us an example of the six different kinds of activity.

MR. O. I can only touch upon it. It is based upon a fundamental law of Nature—the Law of Three.

MRS. F. Would glandular secretions have anything to do with it?

MR. O. No, glandular secretions, no. Science knows too little about it.

*   *   *

Tuesday. August 5th 1941. (New York.)

MRS. S. I don't understand about each centre.

MR. O. That can't be explained in plainer words. But when you begin to think about it you will see that the body will respond according to the point of view of different centres.

MR. F. Does the emotional centre not function at all in man 1, 2 and 3?

MR. O. Functions, but not sufficiently. That's the difference. When it functions, one identifies. And this is so uncomfortable that most people prefer not to have emotion. And without emotion there are many things we can't understand.

MR. S. Are things learned from the intellectual centre?

MR. O. The limit of the intellectual centre is known. Intellectual centre can have a certain number of ideas. At the same time, there are too many problems it can't understand.

MR. S. Has that anything to do with conditional reflexes?

MR. O. All reflexes are conditional. There are no unconditioned reflexes.

MRS. N. How can we learn to use the emotional centre?

MR. O. By trying not to identify—that means developing consciousness. So the whole problem is to become more conscious. And this is just what ordinary psychology missed. We are not on the right level of consciousness. There are many insoluble problems. And as long as we remain on the same level of consciousness they will remain insoluble.

MR. S. Then you become more conscious through higher centres?

MR. O. No, you cannot use higher centres. Higher centres only begin to function or become connected when you become more conscious.

MR. S. What do you become more conscious of?

MR. O. Of yourself. You are not conscious of yourself. You are asleep. There are only occasionally very rare glimpses.

MR. S. Can we become conscious of anything but ourselves?

MR. O. That's a useless question.

MR. S. You seem to imply that man can become conscious of something else besides himself?

MR. O. If one is not aware of oneself, how can one be aware of anything else?

MRS. D. In what way does that change the chemistry?

MR. O. About chemistry, we begin to speak very soon. At the present state the organism produces certain fine matters or energy, and in that sense this organism is considered a certain kind of chemical factory. And it produces all energy necessary for life, but not enough to develop. This factory receives three kinds of food—food, air, impressions.

We can only improve impressions.

MR. S. I am not sure what you mean. What is the difference between consciousness and identification?

MR. O. Identification means absence of consciousness.

MR. S. Then you are conscious of things you are not?

MR. O. Consciousness means to be self-aware. And no word explanation can help at all.

MR. S. Has the state of wonder anything to do with intellectual curiosity?

MR. O. Curiosity is needed. If you don't know something, it is necessary in order to know.

MR. S. What actually makes you more conscious?

MR. O. When you realize that you are not conscious and realize what it means to be unconscious.

MRS. M. How do you measure when one is conscious or not?

MR. O. Only he can know.

MRS. M. Then it would really be awareness of emotional reaction?

MR. O. No, no, simply without other things.

MRS. M. But can you be aware of yourself?

MR. O. You can, but you have no command of emotions.

MRS. S. Is stopping thought useful?

MR. O. As an exercise, yes, two or three times a day.

MRS. S. Is that being self-aware?

MR. O. No, no, it is only as a preparation.

MRS. F. If you keep on stopping thoughts, will the picture one sees stop?

MR. O. Anything may happen. What happens you cannot help.

MR. S. What generates thought?

MR. O. Thought—it's function of intellectual centre. It's going and going and you never notice it.

MR. S. Trying to think of yourself, how can you know you are not imagining?

MR. O. I speak of not thinking. No, imagination doesn't enter.

MRS. N. Shall we always be third force blind?

MR. O. No, for instance in chemistry, if one studies seriously—not superficially—one can see three forces are necessary.

MR. S. Then the only thing that can help you is consciousness?

MR. O. All we can do is to try to realize that we are asleep.

MR. S. How can we feel the lack of something we never had?

MR. O. That's a fact. First and last, truth, and that we must learn we are not conscious.

MRS. D. Are we nearer to sleep when we are mechanical?

MR. O. Certainly, yes. We are aware that it is very cold, but not that we are asleep.

MRS. S. What about the deeper sleep, like anaesthetic?

MR. O. Oh, it's the same thing. Quite opposite, under anaesthesia we may be more aware.

MR. S. Anaesthesia implies there is no memory?

MR. O. Yes, it is all very vague and not established.

MR. S. There is no consciousness without memory, is there?

MR. O. Yes, certainly, but it is local consciousness.

MRS. M. You can't avoid thinking you are trying to stop thoughts.

MR. O. Well, what you cannot avoid, remains.

MRS. Z. You spoke in the lecture about movies and theatre producing negative emotions?

MR. O. No, no, we only put them anywhere.

MRS. S. Is fear negative emotions?

MR. O. Yes, they are negative emotions, but there are about 40,000.

MR. S. Is the memory of one centre better than another?

MR. O. Not better, different. And in each centre there are many different kinds of memory.

MR. S. How can one deal with that long term of emotional states?

MR. O. One can use them for self-remembering. They can create a very good energy for being aware of yourself.

* * *

Wednesday. August 6th 1941. (New York.)

MR. H. What actions in myself can I justify when I am aware that previous actions in my life have always been dictated by imaginative thinking, and I desire to correct this? Or is observation of myself in my present situation of life sufficient at this time?

MR. O. There are two questions here, both very vague. Even the observation that most actions are based on imagination is sometimes more imaginary and sometimes less. When you realize that you are sometimes more asleep and sometimes less, you will not ask such general questions.

MISS R. In connection with the Law of Three, are the forces equal or unequal?

MR. O. What means equal or unequal? In this sense, they are analogous.

MISS R. Are the three forces energy?

MR. O. If you like, it doesn't matter really. We're not interested in words, you know.

MISS R. I assume that they cannot be the same, otherwise they would be one. So, if they are different, wherein does the difference lie?

MR. O. They are not the same, but in one triad one force may be active and in another, passive.

MISS R. If they can substitute for one another, why are they not the same?

MR. O. They cannot be taken separately. It's very difficult. They are so similar that our mind cannot understand it.

MISS R. Do they attract one another, or do they repel?

MR. O. That we cannot say.

MISS R. Were they created, or are they self-existent?

Since the cosmoses created by the three forces tend, in the lower end of the scale, to extreme diffusion, one would expect to find, ultimately, nothing left of the universe except chaos. If this is not so, then how are the forces renewed and stabilized?

MR. O. Try to look at it from the point of view not of cosmoses but from the Ray of Creation.

MISS R. In studying the Table of Cosmoses, it appears to me that each cosmos is a part of the ones above it on the scale. However, the small cell, for instance, could not possibly know that it is part of a man, because its whole lifetime is only three seconds, which is the length of the breath of a man. Similarly, I assume that it would not be possible for man to recognize his relationship with a planet, much less the universe. If this is so, what hope is there that man, even if he becomes self-conscious and has will, can ever use his will in life for a purpose that will bring him into harmony with the rest of creation?

MR. O. Again, the Ray of Creation.

MISS R. As a man attains a higher state of consciousness, such as self-consciousness and objective consciousness, does the time of his functions change? In other words, can he ever hope that an impression for him will be longer than one ten-thousandth of a second, a breath longer than three seconds, etc.?

MR. O. But it is possible. So it is not similar. And useless to find dissimilarity. And they are longer now. We speak only of the impression of intellectual centre. There are others.

MISS R. If a cell could become conscious of its function as part of a man, would it forget that it is a cell? Similarly, if a man became conscious of the way that he contributes to the life of a star, for instance, would he lose the memory of his life as a man, and disappear from the cycle of endlessly recurring lifetimes?

MR. O. Quite the opposite process. It would remember that it is a cell. Same for man—he would remember that he was a man. It would be the same as self-remembering. He would not lose memory, he would get memory.

MISS S. If the Law of Octaves stops, how is the shock produced?

MR. O. No, when I say that, I mean when Nature wants something to continue it creates a certain shock.

MISS R. I can't understand three forces. Has one force three attributes?

MR. O. You must be brave and realize that our mind is very weak. And there are many ideas that escape from our mind.

MISS R. Well, if this is not a theory, why can't someone point out what are these three forces?

MR. O. That's exactly what we are learning. You hear, for instance, that you cannot understand the meaning of forces. But there are many meanings that you cannot understand. If we can change our state of consciousness we can understand things better.

MRS. H. What is the relation of the triads and the Law of Seven?

MR. O. This is one of the most difficult of the insoluble problems. There is a diagram to formulate this problem.

MISS R. You said that a cell being part man, and man being part of the universe. . . .

MR. O. You see, man is a special cosmos. Each cosmos is not necessarily analogous in all respects. Man is capable of development due to his own efforts.

MISS R. A life consists of memories from one moment to another?

MR. O. No, it's too complicated. You know that there are many different sorts. And memory is passive—you don't use it. Life can be said to be a process.

MR. Z. Does the whole of society depend on octaves or the Law of Seven?

MR. O. We don't know that. But it is necessary to understand one principle—octaves within octaves.

MRS. H. And there is no limit to the octaves?

MR. O. Yes, there is a limit. There is an end. And it may not reach the end.

MR. H. Does the inner octave depend on the outer octave?

MR. O. Certainly, it depends on it. And somehow it must conform to this in a certain way.

MRS. H. Is it connected with creation of the Laws of Creation?

MR. O. Yes, if you like—creation. But creation from World 1 does not reach World 6. It is another creation.

MRS. F. Is it the Law of Seven that makes man live and die?

MR. O. No, not the Law of Seven that makes him die. He is built like that.

MR. Z. If we understand the Law of Seven, is it possible to avoid our misfortunes?

MR. O. Some misfortunes, yes.

MR. Z. How can you keep that do?

MR. O. But do cannot be kept.

MRS. H. If we understood parallel time, would we understand it?

MR. O. No, that won't help.

MRS. F. How can one send help ahead?

MR. O. We cannot discuss life problems. But we can discuss school-work. In school-work we learn to work in three lines, and that means to send help ahead.

*   *   *

Wednesday. July 28th 1943. (New York.)

MRS. B. From the standpoint of the player of a musical instrument, may not musical memory be located in the intellectual and moving parts of the moving centre, such as the muscles of the hands and arms?

MR. O. We may come to that later.

MRS. E. If you control yourself from reproaching someone who, in your opinion, has done something wrong, is that controlling a negative emotion?

MR. O. Very often. It may be not—but often it is controlling the expression of negative emotion.

MRS. S. Does living in the fourth dimension involve the possibility of development?

MR. O. I don't know what living in the fourth dimension means. I think we all live in the fourth dimension.

MRS. S. Can one become conscious of the fourth dimension momentarily in a certain kind of very vivid dream?

MR. O. [Unrecorded.]

MISS R. Would the desire to awaken conscience create the necessary means in one's experience?

MR. O. I don't know what desire can do, and what kind of desire is necessary.

MISS R. Would the means to awaken conscience be buffers—if so, of what kind?

MR. O. No, this is a formatory twist. Buffers help to keep conscience asleep—so they cannot be regarded as help.

MISS R. What did you mean when you said many unpleasant things may happen if conscience is not ready to awaken?

MR. O. That's what I meant. The rest—when it happens you will know.

MISS R. Is grief over a death an example of a useful negative emotion?

MR. O. Why useful? I never spoke about useful negative emotions.

MISS R. Would being desperate about something before discovering the cause and reason for it through past actions, be a useful negative emotion?

MR. O. First, there are no useful negative emotions. Second, when you know the cause we will discuss the question.

Q. Would the recent events in Italy be an example of an octave, as far as Mussolini is concerned?

MR. O. What would I know about Mussolini?

MRS. B. If one stops thoughts while walking, does one stop thought only in the intellectual and emotional centres, since the intellectual part of the moving centre would have to continue directing the walking movement?

MR. O. This is material for observation. But I never spoke about stopping thoughts—I spoke about trying to stop thoughts.

MISS S. Is finding a school equivalent to finding an accumulator?

MR. O. Accumulators are in you.

MISS S. Is it a rule not to speak about what we are studying here to people who are not able to control their speech?

MR. O. To nobody. Where did you get this qualification?

MRS. S. Should we assume that schools are in great danger of destruction by outside forces?

MR. O. Which school?

MRS. S. This school.

MR. O. We are not a school—we have no right to call ourselves a school.

MISS S. The beginning of forming an accumulator in oneself is carrying out the rules of a school, isn't it?

MR. O. Accumulators belong to essence. In a moment I will repeat what I said about accumulators.

MRS. B. What is a god?

MR. O. Did I ever speak about a god?

MRS. P. Are there centres of gravity in different parts of the body, or is it just in one point?

MR. O. It depends on how you understand it. You use this word before you understand what it means. Better wait till you understand.

* * *

[Diagram of man in life, subject to A, B and C influences.]

MR. O. Well, here is the general circle of life. And man in life under many influences—A and B. B influences originally came from schools.

People who live exclusively under A influences, and who take B influences, if they meet them, on the same level, usually die in this life.

Although men are asleep, influences B may keep them alive. But getting out of this state in which we are born depends on influences C. Here schools enter. So people are divided into three classes. Dead people, asleep people, and people coming towards C influences—coming towards help.

In thinking about life, we forget that many people are dead. A fourth category is of people who are already beginning to work. These four levels are important—dead people, asleep people, people with possibility of waking, and people beginning to awake. In life, sleeping people easily fall under the influence of dead people.

MRS. H. What are the characteristics by which I can recognize the dead?

MR. O. At a certain moment you can see them. Just as, at a certain moment, you can see that people are asleep.

MR. H. Can dead people be brought to life?

MR. O. No, dead people are dead—not even spiritualists can do that!

MRS. B. What became of their essence?

MR. O. They may be physically alive, but it does not mean that essence can develop.

MISS R. Are people who are asleep helped through recurrence?

MR. O. No guarantee. What means 'helped'?

MISS R. Are they able to repeat life and have more opportunity?

MR. O. One of the theories of the principles of recurrence is that all tendencies—even acquired tendencies—increase. So a man who showed a real love for sleep from childhood may fall asleep even earlier.

MR. H. Do dead people recur?

MR. O. We don't know.

MR. B. Is there any analogy between these three states and the three categories of man 1, 2, 3?

MR. O. Numbers 1, 2, 3 mean nothing in this case.

MRS. W. What makes people go dead?

MR. O. Either fate, or accident, or will, or cause and effect.

MRS. H. Would too much sleep cause it?

MR. O. Yes, or not enough.

MRS. S. Are most people dead?

MR. O. This was much discussed in our group in Petersburg. Some thought most people were dead, but I was always against this. Everybody is asleep, but even in life you find pleasant people who may not work through laziness, lack of opportunity, or something. But they are not dead.

MRS. S. Could you give us an example of a dead person?

MR. O. When you meet sufficient quantity of dead people you will not want examples. You will not want to think about it.

MISS S. How can dead people influence sleeping people?

MR. O. In comparison with sleeping people they are very strong, because they have no conscience and no shame. And what makes ordinary people weak? Conscience and shame.

MRS. S. Do dead people influence races of people?

MR. O. I don't know. If people sleep well they can be stolen out of their beds.

MISS R. What value is there in understanding recurrence?

MR. O. At the present moment it is just a question of trying to understand. No visible profit. But, if later it is connected with the development of consciousness, it may be useful.

MRS. S. Are there many ways of recognizing dead people?

MR. O. Yes—smell, touch, sight.

MISS S. Is that what you mean by crime—dead people influencing sleeping people?

MR. O. We did not speak about crime to-day. Crime means guilt. How can the dead be guilty?

MRS. S. Do dead people look like everyone else? Do they live as we live?

MR. O. Quite, yes. Because they have soul, and the remains of essence. They can insure themselves.

MR. S. Is art an influence to keep people awake?

MR. O. Not specially. It may have different aims. But if people are open to influence B, it helps to keep them from dying.

MISS O. Does one's essence determine whether one will be influenced by A or B?

MR. O. It doesn't determine. Is one interested only in influences A—money, fashions, pleasure? Influences B are then just annoying things that prevent one from enjoying life.

MR. H. Are there cases of a person becoming awake, and then becoming dead?

MR. O. Nobody awakes by accident.

MR. B. Are there different degrees of death? What is the difference between the way a dead person functions and man No. 3 functions?

MR. O. No. 3 can be dead or alive. So there is no direct difference. But No. 3 is normal; he can become No. 4.

MR. B. What is the change, as far as being dead is concerned, in man No. 3 who begins to wake up?

MR. O. There may be a little change. Many parts of his essence may disintegrate. Some, which are necessary for physical life, may remain.

MISS R. Could a person who was only interested in gambling, and to whom something overwhelming happens, change to a person of greater development?

MR. O. It depends on the degree of gambling.

MISS R. But does this not indicate that the person was of higher development before?

MR. O. I don't know. It is a question of degree. If one cannot accept B influences at all, there is nothing to keep man from dying. B influences are sent to keep men from dying, even though they are asleep. But if they reject them, there is nothing to prevent them dying.

MRS. W. Since dead people are predominant, is that the cause of our slow development?

MR. O. That is too easy to say. We cannot develop without schools, and there are no schools. I was looking for schools, knowing what I was looking for. After some years I met others who were also looking for a school. But if you ask for the address of another school, I cannot give it to you.

MRS. P. What is one to do who wants to awake?

MR. O. If one has met some kind of instruction, one knows what to do. If one has not, one must stick to influences B, because influences B may bring him to influence C.

MRS. H. I wonder why you put the circle which represents schools entirely outside life?

MR. O. Because it is under different laws.

MRS. H. You mean they are entirely free of life?

MR. O. This is formatory. Sufficiently free to be put outside.

MRS. P. Are schools sufficient unto themselves, or do they need people?

MR. O. What means sufficient unto themselves?

MRS. P. Are they complete?

MR. O. We speak about schools which need new people. That is their life-blood. Schools are for teaching, and if there is no one to teach they must shut up shop.

MRS. P. I thought there might be some schools that were independent.

MR. O. Ah, schools of man No. 7. We speak of schools where man No. 1, 2 and 3 can learn to be man No. 4. Very rarely we may meet man No. 5.

MR. H. In the diagram, the lower small circle represents what?

MR. O. It is in some way connected with schools.

MRS. S. Is religion one of the B influences?

MR. O. It may be. B influences come through philosophy, art, religion. But at a certain point religion may become cut off from schools. Particularly divisions of religion—first Christianity, second Christianity, third Christianity, tenth Christianity, and so on. Which has connection with school?

MISS R. Does one strengthen influence B if one obeys the rules of school?

MR. O. No, when one comes to C influence, there is nothing more to say about B influences. B influences are important before one met C influence.

MRS. B. Do B influences become superfluous when one comes into direct contact with influence C?

MR. O. No, not superfluous. I did not say that. Sometimes you change the whole meaning of an idea by wrong use of a word. I said we do not speak about it. There is not time enough.

MRS. P. Do teachers in schools go to schools themselves, or do they have something permanent?

MR. O. Which teacher, which school?

MRS. P. You said teachers like to have new pupils . . .

MR. O. Not teachers. The schools cannot exist without new pupils.

MRS. P. . . . I wondered if teachers had to go to another school? What keeps them enlightened?

MR. O. That is complicated. They started somewhere. They may keep contact with this school. They may find a new school.

MRS. S. Does a school remain a school if it loses its teacher?

MR. O. It may find another. It may not.

MISS R. Are we under influence C with ideas of this system?

MR. O. This is not a school, first. And second, that depends on you. C influence cannot be advertised, you must find it.

MRS. A. If we are not permitted to talk to people outside the school or system, how is it possible to get new pupils?

MR. O. It depends how you speak. There is no need to speak about what you hear here. How can it help you to speak to people who have not heard the language, who understand nothing?

MRS. H. In your opinion, is the proportion of dead people greater now than in ancient times?

MR. O. How can I know? I did not live in ancient times.

MRS. P. What is the relationship of moon to dead people?

MR. O. No relationship. What was said about souls going to the moon refers to the physically dead.

MRS. H. Would khas-na-mus be dead people?

MR. O. That is why they can be so strong and brave. Because they have no conscience and no shame.

MR. A. When you said that 'school depends on you', did you mean individual persons at the meeting?

MR. O. This is not a school. Maybe it is a possibility, a beginning. But a school is more.

MR. A. What does a school need more that we can understand?

MR. O. This is what you are learning. But it cannot be put in one phrase.

MRS. B. Does a person have to be awake to create more B influences?

MR. O. Real B influence comes from school. But it may reach us in a very disguised form.

MRS. H. Is there any objection to saying to people who are interested in your books, that you are giving lectures by invitation?

MR. O. It is quite useless to say it to dead people.

MRS. S. Does it take any particular number of people to form a school? Is it a great number?

MR. O. Yes. It depends on circumstances. In some circumstances, very few can form a school. In other conditions, many more.

MRS. S. In the conditions in which we live, would it take many people?

MR. O. You have to learn that, understand that.

MR. H. I understood you to say that the Gothic cathedrals came into being through C influence. Is that correct?

MR. O. No, I didn't say C influence. I said they were built by schools.

MR. H. I would like to know more about them.

MR. O. That is a question of finding. Much can be found.

MRS. P. Have we the right to assume that we are not dead people too? Most people seem to be the same.

MR. O. No, they are different. That you must find yourself.

MISS H. The effort that we must expend to understand what is taught here—does that come from being?

MR. O. And from essence and personality.

MRS. B. Are 'I's part of personality or essence?

MR. O. Both. There are 'I's belonging to essence, and 'I's belonging to personality.

MRS. B. Are 'I's connected with different centres?

MR. O. Certainly there are intellectual 'I's, moving 'I's, instinctive 'I's.

MRS. B. What should people who are awake do with a talent? If they wish to become awake, they cannot simply acquire more A influences.

MR. O. That is their business. There can be no prescription. But if they want to awake, they must first understand. And they cannot understand without at least a little school influence—bigger than B.

MRS. S. If we are within reach of a school, is it up to us to determine whether we will become a member of the school, or is it a matter of circumstance?

MR. O. Different. In some things it depends on you. Sometimes it depends on circumstances.

MR. S. Is it possible for people under influence B to make people stay under influence A?

MR. O. I don't think so. Because people who are asleep cannot do anything. Only about themselves. If they have sufficient interest in influence B they can receive more.

MRS. B. Could finding one's centre of gravity be defined as. . . .

MR. O. What do you mean by centre of gravity? You begin as though you know. We cannot continue. This is a wrong beginning.

MRS. B. There seems to be something very familiar about certain emotions recurring, and the way perceptions recur.

MR. O. Better leave perceptions for a time. I think you put too many things in here.

MR. B. Is the compound of emotions the same as the compound of perceptions, or is there any similarity? I am thinking of the chapter in *Tertium Organum* about perceptions. I thought I understood you to say that emotions have a correlation. . . .

MR. O. We had better not mix that. But what about emotions? Ask your own question. We always lose ourselves in several questions.

MR. S. Is the mere fact that one realizes that one may be dead, an indication that one is not dead?

MR. O. No, sleeping people may have many ideas. Imagination of sleeping people does not enter into this.

MRS. B. In the diagram, what is the difference between the circle with magnetic centre, and the circle lower down in touch with the circle outside life?

MR. O. This man is directly connected with school, in some way or another.

MRS. S. Would a great period in art be when a school existed?

MR. O. I don't know. It is a general idea.

MISS R. Do sleeping people have memory?

MR. O. Sometimes.

MISS R. Dead people have none?

MR. O. I don't know. Psychology of dead people will come later.

MISS R. Memory is most important, isn't it?

MR. O. Yes, for certain practical purposes.

MRS. B. Does man with centre of gravity or magnetic centre. . . .

MR. O. I did not speak about centre of gravity. I spoke about magnetic centre.

MRS. B. Does that man have magnetic centre because he came under influence A and B?

MR. O. No, because he accumulated enough influence B to leave certain traces.

MRS. W. People with magnetic centre do not need schools?

MR. O. Only these people can use something from school.

MRS. S. Are dead people born dead?

MR. O. Some are born dead; some die later.

MRS. S. Does death at birth have anything to do with the death of parents?

MR. O. In this case, no. Parents may be alive—or dead in a natural way—and the children may die.

MRS. S. Why are dead people born?

MR. O. Many different reasons. Perhaps people who die in one life may be born dead in the next. But these are differences which do not concern us. Questions must be limited by ourselves.

MR. H. Is it possible for a very young child to come under influence B?

MR. O. Maybe, in a small way. But it is not a question of coming under B influence once or twice. It is a question of living under it.

MRS. P. How can moving centre be controlled?

MR. O. We always control moving centre, or we would never arrive where we want to go. We would start to write a letter to one person, and write to another.

MRS. P. When we attain consciousness, will we be able to serve a much higher purpose in life than in our individual lives?

MR. O. We cannot talk about it. We must attain first.

MRS. B. Does the Ray of Creation emanate from the Absolute?

MR. O. Well, we can say that.

MRS. B. Is there anything of the Ray of Creation in us?

MR. O. I don't understand. We live in the Ray of Creation. What does it mean, the Ray of Creation in us?

MR. W. You said last week that there were many things in the Food Diagram that we do not understand.

MR. O. Many, but that will be repeated. We cannot go straight to that.

MRS. W. If dead people do farm work will they become awake?

MR. O. How can dead people come awake? Dead people are dead, and must be buried. The sooner they die physically, the better for them, and others.

MR. B. What is it that makes people dead—failure to respond to irritation?

MR. O. Irritation can be used in an emotional or physiological sense. But that is not the point. Dead people cannot awake. Sleeping people have at least a theoretical chance, a possibility of waking in favourable circumstances.

MISS H. Christ used 'dead' in this sense in the parable of the prodigal son? 'He was dead, and is alive again.' Does that mean spiritually dead?

MR. O. I don't remember this sentence. But it could mean he looked like dead, but he was not.

MRS. S. Are there different ways of being dead? Could people be dead physically and alive otherwise, as well as vice versa?

MR. O. We speak of people physically alive and mentally dead.

MRS. S. What about the things people call spirits?

MR. O. We don't use that word. It means nothing.

MRS. S. Are there people who are dead physically, and still have a form of existence?

MR. O. We speak of people who walk in the streets, and do everything—and yet are dead.

MRS. B. I still don't understand what happened to their essence. If it was absorbed somewhere, it doesn't seem fair.

MR. O. There is nothing fair in the world.

MRS. B. They had not free will in the first place . . .

MR. O. Nobody has free will.

MRS. B. . . . and they started with influence A.

MR. O. That doesn't matter.

MRS. B. If they had essence it must go somewhere . . .

MR. O. Why?

MRS. B. . . . it is not fair for people to have only influence A and therefore be dead.

MR. O. It is essence and personality together. They like B influences or they do not like them.

MRS. B. Then it must be a quality in essence which makes them like influences A.

MR. O. If they are not interested, B influences for them are like A influences. They do not profit by them.

MRS. B. I don't know what makes people start choosing one or the other influence.

MR. O. We deal with results. People live under two kinds of influences, one from life, the other originating in schools. If one is interested in these they accumulate, and in time produce certain effects.

MR. B. You said once that a psychology which did not include man and the infinite was no psychology.

MR. O. I never spoke like that. I said psychology which does not study possible evolution cannot affect us. But people are not equal in relation to evolution. Either they lost the possibility of evolution, or did nothing to deserve it.

The relation of man to the universe comes in school teaching. We only just began this.

MISS R. Does man who is under B influence . . .

MR. O. What does it mean, man under B influence?

MISS R. . . . that is, man asleep—is he subject to the law of cause and effect, and accident?

MR. O. Certainly, in relation to these big laws, all people are the same.

Only when one comes under school influence, one becomes little by little free from the Law of Accident.

MRS. H. Is school itself subject to the Law of Accident?

MR. O. I did not speak of that—so it is a distortion of the idea. Repeat what I said to yourself and you will see that the question is impossible.

MR. S. Has every man who is dead no conscience and no shame?

MR. O. What do you mean by this question?

MR. S. Well, there are a great many people whom we consider dead because they are under A influence only.

MR. O. I did not say that. That is a deduction, and not quite right. I said, if people do not use influence B they die—in time. But maybe they are not dead yet.

MRS. S. Are there some people who are dead physically, but who have. . . .

MR. O. People who are dead physically are buried. We do not speak of them; it is not our business.

MRS. B. Sleeping people then should forget dead people, so that they will not come under their influence?

MR. O. But they do not know about dead people. If they knew they were dead they would be worried, and perhaps afraid of them. But they learn about dead people only in school-work.

MR. H. Does that large circle represent organic life or life in the sense of human affairs?

MR. O. In the sense of human life.

MRS. P. Did I understand you to say that unless we were in contact with school, we would not recognize dead people?

MR. O. I did not say exactly that. This is a school idea. If you do not come in contact with school ideas, how do you learn about it?

MRS. A. By dead people do you mean those who are incapable of any further development?

MR. O. What can dead people develop into? Dead No. 5?

MR. S. Have we the right to assume that anyone is dead?

MR. O. Yes, we have the right. With certain awakening, you can see dead people—and sleeping people.

MRS. S. Did you say one can be dead No. 5 man?

MR. O. [Unrecorded.]

MISS O. Are all dead people negative, that is, lacking in power to influence?

MR. O. No, they are harmful certainly.

MISS S. I can't reconcile the thoughts that a dead person cannot really do anything, and that he can influence sleeping man.

MR. O. I don't know. Think. Perhaps you will find how to reconcile them. First, they will never agree that they are dead, just as sleeping people will never agree that they are asleep.

* * *

Wednesday. August 4th 1943. (New York.)

MR. B. It is difficult to recognize states of 'mingling' apart from its place in 'identification', yet so much of one's life consists of mingling.

MR. O. What does mingling mean?

MR. B. I can see that stopping general identification in the order and change of concept given thus far is necessary for change of being, but what of identification on a different level?

MR. O. I don't understand what 'identification on a different level' means, because identification is a state in which we cannot observe. We have to start such as we are; we cannot wait for a change.

MR. B. For example, the distinction between identifying with a news-item pertaining to an alleged Nazi sex-atrocity, and with a Beethoven chord progression seems infinite. One feeds undesirable emotional growths, and the other can lead to a mingling with the inner substance of life.

MR. O. Yes, that may be quite true. But if we want to observe, we must exactly get rid of this identification. Or we see only ourselves in the centre of things.

MR. B. The different speeds and strengths of impact-association-mingling vary with different subjects. Can this be studied successfully now?

MR. O. Yes. We must first try to follow the examples given, and also use as few words as possible.

MR. B. What sort of influence was Swedenborg under?

MR. O. That is his business. Maybe religious, maybe mystical. The historical approach is not this way. Nobody can prove anything. But there are things on which we can be on surer ground—in particular referring to schools and school systems.

MR. B. In self-remembering one can observe a certain tendency of the physical body to change position, instinctively desiring to avoid any cramped position and sit or stand balanced and unencumbered.

MR. O. It has no relation to self-remembering. One must keep attention only to one point—that one does not remember oneself. Do not mix with other observations.

MR. B. Is this work of instinctive intelligence the same that creates change in one's face, etc.?

MR. O. I do not understand what instinctive means. Instinctive can only be used safely in a physiological sense. We talk about 'instinct of truth', desire for truth, but this is not really instinct.

MR. B. What is seeing oneself in a dream state as a geometrical figure with lines and angles along which power flows, and, at certain junctions, more power is generated than at others? If it is imagination, is it not a valuable kind of imagination?

MR. O. I don't know. That is subjective—it cannot have a general interpretation. Imagination can become valuable only as much as one can control it. But I don't call this imagination. It may be a kind of interpretation.

MISS R. Please explain how Fakirs, Monks, Yogis and four-centred people fit in relation to dead, alive and awakened people?

MR. O. I don't think it can be put in this way. People who can go by way of Fakir and of Monk—these are different. Who can be a good Fakir cannot be a good Monk. We may come to that. But it is dangerous to mix one line with another.

MISS R. How can dead people influence sleeping people if they are dead and have no will?

MR. O. That is material for study, because it can be observed.

MISS R. How can dead people commit a crime if they are not conscious of what they are doing?

MR. O. Nobody is conscious. At the same time crime exists. Crime does not mean consciousness, it is a kind of activity.

MRS. H. Some people seem naturally attracted by B influences, as though they were born like that.

MR. O. That means they don't feel the difference between A and B influences.

MRS. H. Is it only C influences that affect essence?

MR. O. This is a useless question, because if I say 'yes' or 'no' it doesn't change anything. But with a certain amount of B influence absorbed, then, when one meets C influence, one feels that it is new. And this is very rare. People who have a chance do not always see that it is new.

MR. H. Is it possible to make a living in the sphere of A influences, and yet be deeply interested in B influences?

MR. O. Necessary to try.

MR. A. How do A influences have the effect they do have?

MR. O. People like things, are attracted by them, sell their souls for them. This can be observed.

MR. A. Why do they produce this constant diminishing of being?

MR. O. This 'constant diminishing of being' seems too definite, and yet it is almost true. If one's whole attention is attracted by accidental influences of life, there is no time to understand.

MRS. S. Is it possible for a person to be dead and come occasionally under B influences?

MR. O. That means the condition is not clear. What do you mean? Give an example.

MRS. S. People interested in art, for example.

MR. O. Yes, but they take it as ordinary influence, as A. This question does not exist for them. They are interested only in ordinary things.

MISS R. Can some fakirs be under B influence—also monks?

MR. O. That has nothing to do with what we speak about.

MRS. B. Would not ignorance be an example of crime?

MR. O. Ignorance is ignorance. Crime is crime. Must not mix them. Ignorance is a certain state; crime is an action.

MRS. B. Can someone who has truth commit crime?

MR. O. There is certain particular emotion—desire to know truth. A kind of curiosity to understand the foundation of things, how they began, and so on. This helps B influences to be absorbed. Nothing else.

But don't enlarge before we come to that. It can be said that if one's interest in truth is sufficiently big, it will exclude the possibility of crime. One will have no time for that.

MRS. B. Are there some people who belong to the world?

MR. O. Everybody belongs to the world. What does that mean?

MRS. B. Why do some people accept just world influence?

MR. O. Why? Because B influences do not attract them. You can ask them why. That is material for study.

MRS. S. Do people who are dead sometimes have a physical sign unconsciously—something in their face?

MR. O. Try to find. Collect a certain number of dead people, and see— can you notice anything or not.

MR. H. Do dead people recur?

MR. O. Material for observation. I think there can be no general principles. When you begin to study, you begin to see. But why begin with the most difficult thing? We must begin to study ourselves, and use all the time we are alive to do it.

MR. H. I always prefer the most difficult things. When I was a child learning arithmetic, I started to multiply by seven before two.

MRS. S. Would there be a certain amount of dead person in each one of us?

MR. O. This is philosophy.

MRS. S. Well, how can we see. . . .

MR. O. That is another thing. Observe.

MRS. S. If sometimes, on a first encounter with a person, one has a feeling of horror. . . .

MR. O. That depends on how much you can trust yourself, and your feelings. How much you studied your imagination. Why do you feel this? There must be a reason.

MRS. S. I am thinking of one particular person.

MISS H. How can we learn to control imagination?

MR. O. First by studying. If you give a certain time every day to studying imagination, you will learn about it. How some kinds one can struggle against, others not.

MRS. S. Can we get rid of a dead person by practising self-remembering?

MR. O. It is a question of imagination. Some kinds of dead people are much stronger than you. They will control your life whether you will or not. This is your study. Try to think of yourself as dealing with facts not words.

MISS S. If you try to stop the influence of the dead person. . . .

MR. O. Then you will see—can you see or not? But facts, facts. Suppose dead people start a war or a revolution and you have to run away, and live miles from where you could work. How can you resist? You cannot destroy all dead people.

MRS. S. Is that fate?

MR. O. That is one word instead of another word.

MISS D. Then you really resist A influences by going away from them?

MR. O. If you find some A influences are too oppressive, you can struggle with them, as much as you remember yourself, and resist imagination and identification.

MRS. T. In the example you described, dead people control your external life. . . .

MR. O. I said dead people have an extraordinary influence over sleeping people. Sleeping people cannot resist. They admire them so much, they want to be like that.

MRS. T. But regarding resisting dead people. . . .

MR. O. Well, sleeping people cannot resist anything. If people realize they are asleep, they may begin to resist. Good absorption of B influences may produce this realization. But awakening means school.

MISS O. Are all A influences harmful?

MR. O. No. We must eat, and we can be more interested in one kind of food than another. But even this can become dangerous. Supposing one finds a very interesting food called chocolate, and begins to eat chocolate from morning till night. . . .

A influence becomes harmful through too much identification; because we are asleep. But if we realize we are asleep, then we can begin to resist. Even B influences can be taken wrongly. They produce right effect on the right people. But other people must not be too identified with them, or pay too much attention to them. I understood that well when I was looking for school. One must find the right school for one's type, for one's interests.

MRS. W. Who is the judge of right school for one?

MR. O. One must try, and see results, or one can feel right. Here we come to an interesting point. There is one function in us, to know the difference between right and wrong—conscience. This is emotional understanding of one's own actions. But if one develops this, one can understand many analogous things. This is why, at a certain moment in work on consciousness, one must study what is right and wrong.

MRS. W. Is our conscience influence B?

MR. O. No, influence B is outside. Conscience is in us, like our sense of smell. When we begin with this question—looking for truth—we see how many things are connected. We will see that our work is looking for truth. Then there are some things we can know, and other things we cannot know. So if we want to know more, we must try to raise the level of our consciousness. Questions about recurrence, future life—we cannot know about them. Our consciousness is not sufficient. But if we can raise it higher, perhaps we can know.

MRS. S. You said, sometimes influence B is not right for certain types of people. Could you explain that?

MR. O. It is not that influences B are not right. They may not be right for them; for some B influences are made for one type, some for another. Suppose that one wants to use B influences that are made for a different type.

MRS. S. Do you mean that it could be a lower type of person, or a person who could be doing something else?

MR. O. No, simply a different type. Remember—No. 1, No. 2, No. 3.

MR. H. Is there any real relationship between conscience and remorse?

MR. O. I never used that word. Conscience is a definite psychological fact; remorse may be imagination.

Try to think, beginning from this: supposing we come to the decision that we want to know truth. We must begin where we are. There is a definite law. First one must learn the truth about oneself, and one meets many unpleasant things.

MRS. W. There is so much inaction in action; does that belong to the category of triads?

MR. O. Better think first.

MISS R. Then one must find the particular right method for finding the truth in oneself?

MR. O. It is not a method; it is sincerity with oneself. I remember one man in Petersburg. He got several encyclopaedias—German, French, Latin—to find the meaning of sincerity, and he could not find it.

MRS. S. Is man No. 1 ever exempt from art?

MR. O. This cannot be explained theoretically. This must refer to one person. Enough material was given to study this. Predominance of physical or emotional or theoretical. Remember moments of decisions, and you can find what decided.

MR. C. What distinguishes B influences from C influences?

MR. O. B influences are just thrown into the general turnover of life, in theories, legends, fairy tales, anything, but C influences must be passed by a man. Not any man—somebody must give you something.

MISS O. You said conscience distinguishes between right and wrong. It seems to me that sometimes it is very difficult to know right from wrong.

MR. O. Yes, without conscience. But with conscience you can't make a mistake in relation to your own actions. If conscience is not quite asleep, you know if you do something wrong. We have this power in us, but we don't use it.

MISS O. It has no relation to what other people think?

MR. O. No, no relation to what other people think. Nobody can make you change your opinion, if you have it.

MRS. B. Does 1, 2 and 3 man ever use conscience?

MR. O. Oh yes, there is no difference between 1, 2 and 3 man in this sense.

MRS. E. Is conscience a part of personality?

MR. O. No, it is in the essence.

MISS R. Doesn't one have to be developed to a certain degree to have conscience?

MR. O. No. Normal man is asleep, yes, but conscience can awake, for a short time, though only No. 5 can keep it awake. The difference between 1, 2 and 3 is that if man No. 1 can develop his emotional and intellectual side he is all right; if man No. 2 can develop his intellectual and physical, he is all right, and so on.

MRS. B. What does magnetic centre build on?

MR. O. Magnetic centre is in personality, not essence. It is acquired in this life. It is in intellectual part of emotional centre, though perhaps also in intellectual part of intellectual centre, and it is built on B influences.

MRS. B. What I meant was, I wondered if sleeping people ever use conscience?

MR. O. Yes, they may, only if they remain very fast asleep it does not help them very much, because they forget.

MISS S. Is conscience always the same, or does it differ with different people?

MR. O. Each person has his own conscience. At the same time, comparing results, consciences do not contradict one another. In this way conscience is different from morality, because one man's morality may say that a thing is right, another man's that a thing is wrong.

MR. B. Did you say that connection with conscience can be maintained through school-work?

MR. O. I didn't say maintained. By certain kinds of B influence one can awake conscience. How long I don't know; it may be seconds, it may be minutes, it may be days, but in that case one may go mad. It is very dangerous, so it is put in the lowest drawer, covered with all unnecessary newspapers.

MISS R. Don't we need conscience awakened to find truth in ourselves?

MR. O. It would be very good if one could. Becoming conscious is a fully conscious process all the time; one cannot become conscious unconsciously. But conscience can awake simply by a strong impact coming from B influences, or from C influences, only one cannot keep it awake.

At the same time there are many things in one's personality that try to stop conscience, try to put it out. This is why so few people are interested in the attempt to find truth. Because one has to find the truth about oneself first.

MR. A. Is it possible for conscience to grow in a person?

MR. O. I don't know how to answer that. I think it is better to speak about conscience keeping awake, and this is difficult, because there are many appliances for keeping it down, keeping it asleep.

MR. H. Does effort at self-remembering help to keep conscience awake?

MR. O. It is already awake. Effort of self-remembering is for consciousness. Conscience needs a shock, and one cannot keep such a shock. One is too sympathetic to oneself; one does not want to hurt oneself. One sees so many unpleasant things in life; why be unpleasant with oneself?

MISS O. Some of us are influenced a great deal by being sympathetic, and by being afraid to hurt other people. How do you connect this with conscience?

MR. O. Why hurt other people? I spoke of hurting yourself. You cannot do anything to other people—it is all imagination. Try only not to express negative emotions, and so on. One can do nothing to others unless one is in school, and one has enough knowledge, and they also are in school. We have to change many of our views as to what we can do and what we cannot do.

MISS S. Does it necessarily follow that a person who has frequent attacks of conscience knows himself better than others?

MR. O. Very doubtful. I never met such a person. In any case, frequent attacks of conscience are very dangerous. One must go to a doctor, and he will cure it quickly.

MISS R. Did I understand you to say that a shock from conscience will help us awake?

MR. O. No, I did not say that. It cannot happen. I said conscience can awake, and the shock can be given by B influences. In another case we can get it from C influences, but that is another thing.

MR. C. Is it possible to stimulate conscience by exposing it to the B influence which brought it to life?

MR. O. If you like you can put it in those words. If we are interested in B influences, and put time and energy into that, we may find something which will produce a shock. But this is dangerous, because, if one tries to do something about it, one may choose unsuitable B influences.

But in relation to what was said before about schools, and why they are destroyed so easily—this also is because people do not want to find truth. They say: Who is looking for truth? Why do these people pretend?

MR. B. Do schools all agree with each other?

MR. O. I cannot guarantee that. They work on different methods, but at a certain point they must agree, though if you do not belong to a school you may not see this.

MISS R. Is the one point that they all agree on that you have to know the truth about yourself?

MR. O. Yes, I don't think any school would contradict this, except those schools which say you must first know the truth about your friends.

MISS O. Is intelligence part of essence?

MR. O. Generally speaking, yes, but I would like to know what you mean by intelligence. If I say 'yes', you cannot apply it; it will remain dead capital.

MISS O. Can intelligence grow or increase by certain treatment?

MR. O. That is what I said. If we speak about ourselves, we will see that intelligence belongs to essence and personality in a very mixed way, though, in a cosmic way, a certain amount of intelligence is given to every essence.

MRS. W. What is the difference between essence and substance?

MR. O. I did not use the word 'substance'. Wood is substance, not essence. We use the word 'matter' rather than 'substance'.

MISS R. I am beginning to see how terribly difficult this is. I want to know how to put it in order.

MR. O. What is difficult? It is difficult, but try to formulate.

MISS R. I try to put it into practice; to try to observe how I am identified, how I imagine—this is difficult. I want to know the order of things.

MR. O. But after all there are not many things, and one cannot practise without trying them. Certainly one will make mistakes, but better to make mistakes than do nothing. If you think, you will see that it is not only an individual difficulty. How difficult to organize something, to give something. Plans may be right, but a certain number of people are necessary, and constant arrival of new people is necessary. By their arguing, their ideas, remarks, you get many things you missed before. This is school-work. If people want to go on, they must help to teach new people.

Our work in London, for example, reached a very interesting stage, but the war came, and now they cannot have new people, so they move in the same circle they were in before. It is always like this. This is not our special misfortune.

MRS. S. Is there any reason for school-work to end in that way?

MR. O. I gave many reasons. What would you call sufficient reason?

MRS. S. I was thinking of the story of the caterpillar becoming a butterfly by disappearing to another plane.

MR. O. It needs a long time for the caterpillar to fly away. It will continue to crawl for years and years.

No, we must never disregard facts. Many things depend on the conditions of life. In certain conditions, school-work is possible. Conditions change for the worse and school becomes impossible. There are very definite limits, and there is nothing you can do about it. We met in Russia. Then came the revolution. Some people got away to Europe, some stayed there.

MISS R. The continuation of school depends on new people?

MR. O. Yes, among other things. A certain number of old people are also necessary.

MRS. T. In considering people for a new group, should we not find people with right qualifications?

MR. O. Certainly, if you bring wrong people you will get no profit from it.

There is a very definite principle that was explained. You remember it was explained about the staircase. The path does not begin at the level of life. When you are on the staircase, if you want to take a step, you must put somebody in your place. This is part of organization. It will be explained how to do it, and so on. But it is very difficult to put people on your step, if sleeping people under the guidance of dead people produce disturbance all round you.

MISS O. In the Food Diagram, there are two places where conscious shock is necessary for further refinement. Do they have any relation to B influence?

MR. O. No. Even for the first conscious shock, all material comes from C influence—and your own desire. Second conscious shock is very far. C influence means school teaching.

MISS H. Is it effort to self-remember which produces first conscious shock?

MR. O. Yes, but only if it is well made. It must be a good effort.

MISS H. Do we produce energy that way? Is that impression la 24?

MR. O. No, that theoretical terminology will not help. Self-remembering, if it is successful—that is, if one continues regularly—may produce second conscious shock. But this is not a question of accidental effort. It must be permanent effort.

*   *   *

Wednesday. August 11th 1943. (New York.)

MRS. W. If we grasped that our 'I' is the centre of consciousness and independent of our body, is that becoming aware of oneself?

MR. O. That's thinking, and not quite right thinking. In our present state we only have glimpses of consciousness. 'I's belong to manifestations of functions: they are not independent.

MR. B. Is there a relationship between centre of gravity and permanent 'I'?

MR. O. Yes, how can one have permanent 'I' without centre of gravity? Though even permanent 'I' is not very permanent.

Q. Does permanent 'I' transcend the Law of Three?

MR. O. Everything depends on the Law of Three.

MR. B. What is the relation of centre of gravity to desire?

MR. O. There is no such thing as desire. There are desires.

MRS. K. What is the origin of the Law of Three?

MR. O. What do you mean by the Law of Three and its origin? In the system?

MRS. K. On what is the Law of Three based in the system? How did it come into the system?

MR. O. The best explanation of the Law of Three is in Indian philosophy—in the teaching of the three gunas. These correspond to the three forces. Where they are wrong is that they say active force is always active, whereas it changes.

MR. B. It is possible to observe thoughts after their creation. But simultaneous observation of thoughts in process of creation seems impossible. How can this be made possible? Through somehow distributing attention to enlarge one's focus?

MR. O. I don't understand what you mean by creation of thought. Can you give me an example?

MR. B. It is possible to observe hands playing the piano. But with attention on this, it is impossible to understand the music simultaneously.

MR. O. Maybe. Maybe not.

MR. B. It is possible to observe an emotional feeling that occupies the machine. But as soon as one observes it, the feeling gradually diminishes and one is left with his state of observation.

MR. O. Not always. It is a great mistake to think that observation prevents emotion. Observation does not interrupt thinking or feeling.

MR. B. Is that why students of the system at a certain point need others to observe, why man No. 5 must have men No. 4 before he can become man No. 6?

MR. O. I did not expect that—about man No. 5 finding it necessary to observe man No. 6.

MR. B. In the fifth lecture, intellectual part of intellectual centre is said to contain the power of discovery, invention and creation. Intellectual part of emotional centre has the power of artistic creation. How do you distinguish the two processes of creation?

MR. O. Oh, ordinary psychology. But like all emotional experience, artistic creation starts from the end or whole. But this will come in connection with another thing I wish to speak about.

MR. B. Is it correct to understand 'possibilities' and 'impossibilities' as referring to different states of being? Possibilities seem to increase for man in proportion to his awakening, and impossibilities increase with sleep.

MR. O. Sometimes, yes.

MR. B. Yet the possibility of man No. 7 becoming a dead man in two days exists as an impossibility, and the possibility of a dead man becoming man No. 7 in two days exists as an impossibility too.

MR. O. No. No number 7!

I don't understand—in speaking of dead people, we speak only of ourselves—man No. 1, 2, 3.

MR. B. Before working with the system, a certain amount of self-observation comes naturally through realizing the inner principle within self and all things . . .

MR. O. I would not say it is principles. It is natural observation.

MR. B. . . . although the maintenance of observation was dependent on depth of mood. From this basis, is not observation the result of B or religious influence?

MR. O. Maybe, maybe not. If you speak about horse-racing, it is not religious.

MR. B. What are the relationships between A, B and C influences in respect to their inner contents?

MR. O. We will come to influences again. Read the whole question once more.

MR. B. Before working with the system, a certain amount of self-observation comes naturally through realizing the inner principle within self and all things—although the maintenance of observation was dependent upon the depth of mood. From this basis, is not observation the result of B or religious influence?

MR. O. What means 'maintenance of observation'? What means 'mood'? That is why we must learn the language, in order to understand one another. You observe—but observation needs the separation of the four functions.

MR. B. In the machine, is the manifestation of the active principle the will, the passive principle the essence, and the neutralizing principle the conscience?

MR. O. No, no. It does not work that way with the three forces.

MISS H. I asked the other night if this were not the same sense in which Christ referred to the prodigal son. When he says, 'This my son was dead, and is alive again'—does it not imply that those spiritually dead may come to themselves again?

MR. O. This has nothing to do with what we said about dead people.

MRS. B. Jesus said, 'Let the dead bury their dead.'

MR. O. No, it has nothing to do with it.

MISS H. I would like to ask about the meaning of the transmigration of souls.

MR. O. We did not touch transmigration of souls. I think it is a distortion of certain ideas.

* * *

MR. O. It is very important for us to understand the difference between emotional and intellectual experiences on a higher plane. Someone at Mendham asked Madame a question about realizing one's smallness. Everything that was said was right. But one thing especially must be understood. One must _feel_ this—then it penetrates. In higher centres it is necessary to feel. This is the difference between higher and lower centres. In higher centres there is no thinking without feeling. Of course, without self-consciousness these experiences cannot be sustained or realized to any extent. But this shows the importance of realizing that feeling is necessary for man to be conscious of his smallness.

This brings us to influences. Influence A is just influence of the world. Influence B is that which comes from schools. These ideas are generally distorted, but what one really gets of value from influence B is the realization that there must be schools. C influence begins the moment one meets schools. With C influence there can be no distortion, or it would not be C influence. B influence does not come direct, but C influence always comes direct. If you want to know more, find examples and ask questions. Often C influence may be mixed with B influence.

MR. B. I spoke of the inner content of these influences. If a person is receiving A influence and observes A influence, as we learn it in this system, examining it in the business of life. . . .

MR. O. Under influence A may be anything which attracts you in the world. If there is only influence A in one's life there is no school.

MR. B. I wondered if possibility and impossibility were words referring to degrees of being?

MR. O. I don't see the way to come to possibility or no possibility. Man lives under influence A, but may come under influence B. Influence C can only come to somebody who has acquired or absorbed as much influence B as he could.

Many things can be got from influence B in a religious and philosophical way. It may contain big ideas which we miss, and which may be influence C. In this way we get an idea of what truth may be.

MRS. B. Is it impossible for a dead person to receive influence B?

MR. O. We don't speak about the psychology of dead people.

MR. B. Are possibilities and impossibilities related to being?

MR. O. Don't bring impossibility into discussion. It is only a word, and can just confuse the issue. We must understand that we are only living under A and B influences, and the possibility of touching C influence depends on contact with B influence. B influence prepares us with ideas and emotions which originally came from schools. We meet many people in the world, who are intelligent people, but who simply cannot do this work. They entirely miss the idea of self-remembering. They do not realize that it is the one thing European psychology and philosophy entirely missed. They always refuse to accept it as a new idea which they never heard before.

MRS. K. Does self-remembering during a negative emotion help to diminish it?

MR. O. Leave that for a while. Now I speak of principles.

MR. H. Is the permanent 'I' built up by a selection of superior 'I's or developed from one 'I'?

MR. O. It may be very different. You may not see the process, but after a certain time you may feel it in yourself. You will feel after some time that there is someone in yourself that you can trust. Permanent is really a relative term. But at least you can find that for a time you can trust some part of yourself.

MR. B. What is the distinction between the emotion one feels in realizing how small one is, and a feeling of pantheism?

MR. O. It may be very similar.

But it is extraordinary how many experiences we can have in life without emotion—people can write books, and do everything without really having feeling.

MRS. S. How can we get it in emotional centre?

MR. O. We can do nothing about emotion, except work towards the development of consciousness. All we can do is try to become more conscious.

MRS. W. If emotional centre is really in action, I find that all thoughts stop.

MR. O. It may be sometimes, but again it may be quite different.

MRS. S. Also by overcoming negative emotion. . . .

MR. O. Only by remembering oneself. One may continue to enjoy negative emotions.

MRS. B. Why is it that one can succeed in stopping thoughts for whole parts of several minutes, and yet one cannot remember oneself?

MR. O. Don't ask questions. Do more. More questions will be only talk.

MRS. T. What did you mean to imply, that we must accept intellectually and emotionally how small we are in relation to the universe?

MR. O. We must think that only by emotion can we get real realization of an idea. We don't get the real meaning without emotion. The same thing applies to B influence. People can read many books about philosophy and religion. But they can mean nothing because they do not feel.

MISS R. Does the awakening of conscience help us to reach the higher emotional centre?

MR. O. Conscience, yes, very good. The development of conscience brings the development of consciousness. It is the same thing in different words.

MR. B. Is there much that one can observe about instinctive identification—identification with instinctive centre?

MR. O. What do you mean by identification of instinctive centre? Certainly people do this all their lives in eating.

MR. B. I mean identification where mingling occurs with instinctive centre, where one mingles with that which one is observing.

MR. O. What does mingling mean?

MR. B. Trying to check identification is sometimes impossible because it all occurs so quickly. Intellectually it takes more time, but emotionally it is so quick.

MR. O. Yes, it may be. But what about instinctive centre?

MR. B. I can understand where it occurs intellectually and emotionally, but I can't understand where it occurs instinctively.

MR. O. Sometimes it is difficult to distinguish emotional from instinctive. But instinctive is always physical, so use the word physical instead.

MR. B. To protect oneself against physical identifying, one can see just the moral thing—and that doesn't seem quite right. For instance, one looks at a person and thinks of their face instead of identifying. Is this right?

MR. O. It may work all right, but like all other things of that kind, it needs a certain amount of self-remembering and control. Just thinking about it is not enough.

MRS. T. What are some of the ways in which one can determine whether this system is for one?

MR. O. It is much easier to say when it is impossible for one.

MRS. T. The reason I ask is that you said that some people come under B influence, and come to this school, and it is not for them.

MR. O. Only by trying can one really know. But sometimes one can know and then be mistaken. If you really think about the system, you will begin by hating it. I always suspect people who begin by liking everything at once.

MRS. K. Suspect them of what?

MR. O. This kind of liking often turns into identification. C influence is so different from anything else in life that one must acquire a taste for it.

MISS R. Does the philosophy of Bhakti Yoga help to develop higher emotional centre?

MR. O. There are many forms of Bhakti Yoga. But often they begin with function instead of consciousness. There are many schools which may be right in one sense, but wrong in another.

MISS R. Would the philosophy of not having a will of one's own help?

MR. O. What does it mean—having no will of one's own? Explain.

MISS R. Trying to carry out the philosophy of Ramakrishna. . . .

MR. O. I don't know. You see, when I speak about Yogi schools I speak about Gnana, which means study of mind, and Raja, which means development of consciousness. Bhakti is the best way to bring Fakir to higher levels. Karma Yoga is necessary in all ways. In some rare cases, people can get something through Karma Yoga without anything else.

MISS D. You don't include Gnana Yoga as essential then?

MR. O. Gnana Yoga and Raja Yoga mean Yoga schools. Bhakti and Hatha are auxiliary. For some people they may be good.

MISS R. Does Bhakti Yoga help one rid oneself of self-will?

MR. O. For some people it can be good.

MRS. K. How can you tell when you reach higher emotional centre?

MR. O. Oh, you cannot be mistaken about higher emotion, about the real thing, that is. Of course one can always imagine.

MR. B. Is self-remembering the only way by which the development of emotional centre comes?

MR. O. Self-remembering is the only right way. There are schools which begin with functions. But it is dangerous, and it may produce wrong results to start with higher emotions.

I will give you an example. I think I wrote about it, but I will tell you. When I made some experiments in Moscow in 1910, I went to St. Petersburg for a few days. We were going on a tram, and passed another tram. And, although I am very near-sighted, I saw the faces of people on the other tram, at a distance that ordinarily would have been quite impossible. When we reached a gendarme sitting on a horse I got off to see his face close to. It was the same face I had seen.

MRS. K. How long had you been self-remembering?

MR. O. It is not a question of how long.

MISS R. Can you also catch what a person, a total stranger, is like by this higher emotional centre? His habits by something he says?

MR. O. I don't know. There are different degrees. So that if one unusual thing happens, you may feel that others will grow with consciousness.

MISS R. You consciously experimented with that; it didn't just happen?

MR. O. It was the result of experiment. Things don't happen. They happen only in the ordinary way. Things like that do not happen.

MRS. W. If things don't happen, how do you explain cause and effect?

MR. O. I see no connection. Cause and effect are ordinary terms. It means something happens to you as a result of your own actions. It is only a term.

MRS. W. The Law of Accident?

MR. O. I say ordinary things always happen. We live under the Law of Accident.

MRS. W. I don't understand why we have accidents, as long as you tell us things don't happen.

MR. O. It is quite opposite. Everything happens.

MR. B. I think the difficulty is a misunderstanding. I think she didn't hear you.

MR. O. Yes, yes, these things just don't happen.

MRS. W. You said before that nothing happens. . . .

MR. B. When you said you saw those faces at a distance, it just didn't happen. I think the question arose because she didn't hear.

MISS R. Can one experiment while self-remembering?

MR. O. It was an experiment before I heard of self-remembering—years before.

MR. A. Was it given as an example of wrong connection of centres?

MR. O. It was given as an example of how you will not doubt actual experience of higher emotion. But I would not advise experiments, even if you know how. For they can be quite wrong. But you don't need to experiment in order to try to remember yourself.

MISS R. Can't it also be called clairvoyance?

MR. O. If clairvoyance exists, it exists as a function of higher emotional centre. One cannot have higher emotional centre functioning if one is not self-conscious. Long, long ago in France, someone offered a large sum of money to anyone who had clairvoyance enough to see through a sealed envelope. Nobody claimed the money.

MISS R. Maybe if one had higher emotional centre developed, one wouldn't be interested in the money or the experiment.

MR. O. I don't know.

MR. H. Did people come and try to read it?

MR. O. I don't know. I think I found it in some encyclopaedia that in some place in France was a purse of money for any man who could read a letter in a closed envelope.

MISS R. Is it true that the more you self-remember, the more you can see the truth about yourself?

MR. O. Yes, if you put it like that. Only it would be better to say, the more you become conscious, the more you know about yourself.

MRS. T. You spoke last week of the tremendous power of A influence. For example the Russian revolution broke up a school. How can a school dealing with higher influences be broken up by a political system?

MR. O. Events that happen can make it impossible to work. Certainly the bolsheviks made it impossible after the second revolution. Just as it became impossible to do anything in Europe because of fascism.

MRS. T. I don't know why these ideas would be considered anti-social in Russia.

MR. O. That means you don't know what happened in Russia, or what happens now in Germany, France, Italy or even England.

All schools in the past were broken up by external events, especially by wars and revolutions. Read about the mysteries. In the *New Model* I quoted the Laws of Manu, which state the conditions which make it impossible to do school-work. [Quotation read.]

This refers to influence B not C. It is an old book and somewhat distorted. But something remains.

MISS D. Is the whole theme of the Laws of Manu about influences A, B and C?

MR. O. No, it is not only about that. This means that a man who has B influences, that is, who may come to school, must not live in Russia, Germany, Italy, and so on.

MRS. K. What can he do about it?

MR. O. Nothing at all. That is what we did without thinking about the Laws of Manu.

MRS. B. What does 'sudra' mean in our language?

MR. O. 'Sudra' means lower caste. They cannot govern a country. If they do, they make a mess.

MRS. K. What is the ideal form of government according to the system?

MR. O. The system has nothing to do with politics. If we think, we think about the possibility of awakening. But even for efforts to wake up, certain conditions are necessary. So we have to think about the external conditions a little.

MRS. K. When enough people are awakening, can't there be an influence in changing conditions?

MR. O. It was said, two hundred conscious men can change conditions. We thought about it in St. Petersburg. This must mean two hundred men No. 5, and each man No. 5 can teach a hundred men No. 4. That means 20,000 schools, which would be sufficient to change conditions. But before this is possible there is bolshevik Russia.

MRS. T. Has there ever been a time in history when schools dominated civic life?

MR. O. You don't know enough. But in the sixth and fifth centuries B.C. in Greece there is evidence to think so. In Egypt also.

MISS D. Would you associate Plato with a school?

MR. O. Who spoke about Plato? Plato wrote very much about school. But also much nonsense.

MRS. H. How about Pythagoras?

MR. O. And what do we know about Pythagoras?

MR. H. Some of us are trying to find out.

MR. O. When you find, we will talk.

MR. H. Not 'when' but 'if'.

MISS D. Is Socrates associated with a school?

MR. O. I don't know. Did Socrates exist?

MR. B. There are things in Hesiod. A section called 'Work and Days', which the editor says is about agriculture, seems to refer to school-work.

MR. O. On the whole there are many traces of school. But right now we are interested in the present. And in the present, things disappear so quickly, we must study in which form they can exist.

MR. H. Would you care to tell us of any theories about how the first schools originated?

MR. O. I don't know. Who can know about the first school?

MR. H. As I remember, that was touched on in the *New Model*, and I would be glad to know more about it.

MR. O. I forget. That was written so long ago.

MRS. A. Would it be possible to have the Food Chart again on the blackboard?

MR. O. Yes, we will have all charts again.

MISS R. How would clairaudience fit into higher centres?

MR. O. Same place as clairvoyance. That means it belongs to man No. 5.

MISS R. Do the senses become one for him—seeing and hearing?

MR. O. Why? No, senses don't become one. Eyes don't become ears. In some way higher emotional centre gives another kind of manifestation.

MRS. W. If we become more aware of ourselves, is it not necessary to sharpen our senses?

MR. O. There is no way. If we sharpen them, we may sharpen too much.

MR. B. You spoke of 'when the way is open to higher centres'. Is it possible to think anything in addition to feeling?

MR. O. Why?

MR. B. You said that one could not think without feeling.

MR. O. Yes, in higher centres thinking and feeling are not separated. Thinking means feeling and vice versa.

MR. B. I was thinking of the connection of that with conscience. If, as you say, conscience is the emotional perception of truth. . . .

MR. O. We must not try to mix. I spoke about higher emotional and higher intellectual centres. We must not try to bring the idea of conscience to our level.

* * *

MR. A. If this were the last meeting, the last week of lecture, how could we as individuals carry on this work—assuming it could be carried on?

MR. O. You cannot. Thank God you realize at last that you cannot. Every lecture is the last. In the dictionary we had, there was a word 'examination'. This is a permanent examination. So every lecture must be taken as the last, and every day as a final examination.

MRS. N. Some time ago we had a dictionary of words. Was 'action' included in it? Are action and effort the same thing?

MR. O. No, there is no such word.

MR. A. What was the principle about the rule in the Eleusinian Mysteries, not to divulge anything that went on in the mystery itself?

MR. O. They were so good at not divulging it, that now we know nothing. That was one thing that was successful.

MRS. N. Can better impressions come if one tries to be more silent? I think I have an observation on this. The mind seems less confused.

MR. O. Sometimes. Talking may kill impressions. But not only talking.

MR. W. How can one increase one's sincerity with oneself?

MR. O. By being sincere. It is not a question of decision, but of long study.

MR. P. What is the source of knowledge possessed by schools?

MR. O. First, knowledge comes to one school from another. Second, it is a question of being. If someone writes all school knowledge in a book, someone else may read it and understand nothing. But school knowledge is knowledge of man No. 4, 5 and 6.

MRS. V. If tension impedes effort, doesn't relaxation correct tension, thereby making effort more effective?

MR. O. I don't think I ever used the word relaxation technically. What relaxation? Relaxation, which we have not studied yet, means muscular relaxation only. I don't know what you know about it. It is sometimes dangerous, particularly with stopping thoughts. You will hypnotize yourself, and who will dehypnotize you?

MRS. S. In discussing recurrence you said we meet the system now for the first time. Is this accident or the effect of some cause?

MR. O. Certainly, accident. What else can it be? Do you think you deserve it? It is pure accident. For some, lucky accident; for most, unlucky accident.

MR. S. After we have overcome identification, lying and talking too much, what is the next step?

MR. O. We cannot discuss that. We can only discuss the beginning of these things. If we start we will see the next step.

MISS O. When you speak of the 'higher hydrogens' do you mean the hydrogens that are higher in the vertical scale, or the hydrogens with higher numbers?

MR. O. Relatively, H6 is higher than H12, and H12 is higher than H24.

MISS O. Did you say that intelligence of matter varied with its density?

MR. O. Yes, density is one of the qualities of matter, from an alchemical point of view. Another is intelligence.

MRS. G. In trying to determine which centre predominates in ourselves we are told to observe which centre influences our decisions. But how can I tell whether I am acting under compulsion of emotional centre, or emotional part of instinctive centre?

MR. O. I did not speak of parts of centres. This will confuse the brain with too many details. About centres, if you have good observation, you can see. You will see that with functions decisions are connected. For some people—No. 1—decisions are connected with sensations. For others—No. 2—with emotions. For others—No. 3—with theories.

MRS. G. We have been warned against self-analysis. How is it possible to avoid analysis in trying to discover the motives of our decisions?

MR. O. Analysis needs knowledge of laws. There is a good word in French, German and Russian for what we want—'constater', 'constatieren'. This is sufficient. Analysis is difficult.

MRS. P. Just what do you mean by the word 'examination'?

MR. O. What is final examination in school? When you have to explain all you have learned. Take these words in their first meaning, then you will see at once.

MISS R. Does being a vegetarian help one to develop higher impressions?

MR. O. You see, there are many talks about it. Some think it important, others not. I don't know. I am on the side of the vegetarians because I like it. Only I can't keep it up too long.

MISS R. But if one could, would it help to find higher hydrogens?

MR. O. No, don't believe that. Who was it said, 'Not what goes into the mouth befouleth man, but what comes out'?

MRS. N. I think you said we did not know how to be sincere.

MR. O. We are learning. First we must learn about simple things, then more complicated things. It needs long study. We may be quite sure we are sincere, and not be at all.

MISS R. Are there different kinds of energies that produce different effects in the body?

MR. O. It may be said like that. But I don't think it is a useful explanation. You must know what you want.

MISS O. If some people seem to make us exhausted and tired, does this mean that they are A influence?

MR. O. That's complicated. There cannot be a general description of that. It may depend on many different causes. It may be imagination, or may be identification of the person exhausted.

MISS O. Would it be better to avoid people like that, or try and control it?

MR. O. It is first necessary to find why, and whose fault. If I say someone exhausts me, it may be my fault. I may identify or consider. There are a hundred different possibilities.

* * *

Well, some people asked me about a new edition of my book which appeared recently in New York. I heard about this from Mr. B. So I write a letter to him about new editions. It is very interesting esoteric knowledge!

[Letter is read.]

MRS. S. If people ask us about this, are we to say anything?

MR. O. It is all nonsense.

MR. S. Where does re 48 come into the Food Factory?

MR. O. I don't think there is a re 48. It doesn't matter. Soon we will come to that.

MR. S. Can we discuss solid time at this point?

MR. O. No, I don't think so. We are far from that. I don't like the name. But we may come to what is meant by it later.

MR. S. Does eternal recurrence suggest that nature is unwilling to carry her experiment further than man?

MR. O. We cannot say anything about that. What is difficult about eternal recurrence, is that we try to explain too much by it. If we have the theory, we may understand something about human life—but not further.

MRS. P. Is not that serpent on the cover of the book used as a sign of eternal recurrence?

MR. O. Yes, but quite imaginary. In any case, it's not mine.

MRS. B. Did you approve of those geometric designs beginning each chapter in *Tertium Organum*?

MR. O. There are no geometrical designs on my book. This is not important. What is important is that I don't know how long we can continue. What has happened is very far from the original idea. It is nobody's fault. It is the war. Wars always and everywhere have destroyed everything. But the question is, can we continue to attract new people and start new groups till the end of the war. I don't know if I can come. I cannot promise every week. So the room may be open but I may not be there. You can talk, and invent questions. In London, when we were translating the book, I was away in Paris quite a lot. People continued though.

When I came here before the American war, I thought of something like the Historico-Psychological Society in England. But this needs many people who understand what is being done. And we are further from that now than in 1941.

If there are any questions, I will answer them. But not about some special diagram. That will all be published in a book. Here we have the glossary we spoke of before. I said we had learned many words. Let us read it. If any is not clear, you can ask. [Glossary is read.]

'Accumulator' for instance. I would say that it is necessary to add 'Small Accumulator' and 'Big Accumulator'. And someone told me that this word is not used in the same sense in America as in England. Well, you must think about it.

MR. S. What does 'First Threshold' mean?

MR. O. The word 'Threshold' is connected with the idea of the path. Path means a way that leads somewhere. It doesn't begin on the same level as ordinary things. First Threshold is the moment when one meets with influence C. From this moment begins a staircase with a definite number of steps. Second Threshold begins at the end of the steps.

MRS. W. How is 'grain' used?

MR. O. We may come to that.

MISS H. I never thought of 'considering' as 'internal' or 'external'.

MR. O. External is very good, internal very bad. External is almost self-remembering.

MRS. G. What is external considering? Would it have anything to do with observation?

MR. O. You must already have enough observation.

MRS. P. Are the inner octaves the food, air and impression octaves?

MR. O. It was never explained. Many words refer to things that were not explained—like 'vertebrates', and 'inner octaves'.

MRS. G. Have we had 'external considering' explained?

MR. O. If you meet some time, you may ask who knows about external considering.

MRS. P. What are 'postures between postures'?

MR. O. This is very far away. It is connected with the idea of co-ordination. You see, our actions, our manifestations of centres are too co-ordinated. After a time, in working against this, one may come to postures between postures.

MRS. P. Does the word 'prayer' have a definite specific meaning in the system?

MR. O. [Unrecorded.]

MISS D. What is meant by 'pseudo-centres' in this system?

MR. O. There are many.

MRS. B. What would be the matter with a person's intellectual centre who was normal, and then suddenly had hallucinations?

MR. O. Hallucinations cannot be normal. They are a symptom of something not normal.

MISS R. Why is not 'health' included?

MR. O. Maybe it is included. Maybe it does not concern us. Or maybe I forgot about it, since I'm always very healthy.

MR. W. What is 'crystallization'?

MR. O. Just talk.

MRS. N. Would you explain 'rôles' and 'rolls'?

MR. O. 'Rôles' we can leave. 'Rolls' are all our life, our thinking, feeling, understanding.

MR. S. What is the nature of these steps leading to the path? Are they recognizable, clear?

MR. O. Yes. It was said, for instance, that one must put someone on the step on which one is, in order to go higher.

MRS. P. How does one do that?

MR. O. One cannot. And when one realizes that one cannot, then one may learn how. This refers to school-work, where you cannot work by yourself.

Well, you see you know some words. Later you may learn to put them into groups.

MRS. V. What is the 'realization of nothingness'?

MR. O. It may come from realization of how small one is, how little time one has. Or in the connection with the realization of false personality.

MRS. G. What is 'locum tenens'?

MR. O. This is in connection with this story of the house, servants, steward.

MRS. P. What are 'mental powers'?

MR. O. This is a special parable. We don't use it much.

MISS D. How does external considering resemble self-remembering?

MR. O. Self-remembering is necessary for external considering.

MR. W. What is 'poison'?

MR. O. Poison is not a special thing. It is any hydrogen in the wrong place. There are combinations of substances which do not occur in large quantities on the earth's surface.

MRS. N. How is repetition used?

MR. O. There are methods in Monk's way, and similar methods in Yogi schools. It can be used in the Fourth Way also, but it is very complicated.

Q. Why is not 'permanent I' included?

MR. O. 'Permanent I' is included in imagination—for us.

* * *

Wednesday. November 17th 1943. (New York.)

MISS R. Do shocks of awakening conscience help one toward the development of consciousness?

MR. O. Yes, certainly—very much. One cannot avoid it. One must pass through many shocks.

MISS R. Why was recurrence omitted from vocabulary words? Is it because it is only a theory?

MR. O. Partly because it is a theory. But it is too much to speak about in one word.

MISS R. Please give meaning of your vocabulary word 'fusion'.

MR. O. That will come. It is in connection with one particular example.

MRS. N. If, as you say, there is no civilization except in the inner circle, would you say then that civilization sprang solely from the idea of the possibility of individual self-development?

MR. O. No, you cannot say one idea. There are many ideas which create civilization. And unfortunately in ordinary life they are not known.

MR. N. Although B influences exist in the outer circle, can they not be considered as a civilizing influence?

MR. O. Yes. But first they are distorted. Though some people manage to get something from them. But they are not civilization.

MR. N. Would you say that the relative economic and political security of a particular territory, as far as schools are concerned, is the result of the indirect civilizing influence of the inner circle or of just pure accident?

MR. O. What do you mean by relative state? But not because of their economic or political security. At certain periods in certain countries, schools exist between wars.

MR. B. How can right thinking be developed?

MR. O. That is all explained. First, struggle with imagination and so on. One day it will be repeated. But it is necessary to remember everything. And you will have more concrete questions.

MR. H. I have been trying to observe which 'I's are connected with self-remembering. It seems to me that 'I's which are connected with the use of the intellectual part of the emotional centre make one self-remember. Is this observation correct?

MR. O. They must. But you cannot notice it. You must do that, not think which 'I's. Efforts are necessary.

MR. H. Did you once say that in order to awaken consciousness one had to awaken conscience?

MR. O. Conscience awakes on the way.

MR. H. To awaken conscience does not one have to eliminate buffers?

MR. O. When buffers are only shaken, conscience awakes.

MR. H. How can one discover what one's own buffers are?

MR. O. Sometimes it is possible. If one has the right idea of buffers, one may find one's own.

MRS. P. What is the meaning of 'discipline'?

MR. O. Many kinds of discipline.

MRS. P. How does one find the method of discipline that is most beneficial to one?

MR. O. One cannot find method of discipline, it is wrong word.

MRS. P. All discipline, ordinary or school discipline, must have originated in schools, mustn't it?

MR. O. Not all. There may be discipline which has nothing to do with schools. In old languages, every system of thought was called discipline.

MRS. P. As I see it, discipline is a training for a certain desired action.

MR. O. No.

MR. S. In order for discipline to do us good, it must be a discipline imposed by the outside and not ourselves.

MR. O. Quite right. For us it is useful to think only about discipline of work, or discipline of school.

MISS D. Suppose a person has a negative emotion—about something that is done the wrong way, and another negative emotion steps in to try to prevent the expression of the first negative emotion, wouldn't it be better to express the first negative emotion in this case?

MR. O. That's a question of taste.

MRS. G. When I remember myself, the scene in front of my eyes suddenly appears very strange to me. My surroundings appear unreal as a moving picture. Is this imagination?

MR. O. When you try to remember yourself—probably.

* * *

MR. O. I want to speak on two questions I received in letters. Someone asks: If one feels something is wrong in oneself, should one regard it as physical, mental or what? Well, everything is physical. We are physical and only physical things can happen to us. All the rest is imaginary. So the principle is, first try to eliminate all physical causes. Connected with that are strange experiments I described in the *New Model* long ago. I asked myself all the time: Could I invent this? If I decided I could invent it, then I did not take it very seriously.

The second thing is connected with a question which I always refuse to answer. That is: What is intuition? The mistake is to think that if you call something intuition, it is intuition. There is no proof. But as we know how to come to that, I can answer—that if it is not imagination and so on, if it is really intuition, then it is the work of the intellectual part of emotional centre.

MRS. B. Are Brahmin and the Absolute the same?

MR. O. Brahmin is a high caste priest. Brahma is cosmic. They are quite different.

MRS. B. Is Brahma as used in the cosmic sense the same as the Absolute?

MR. O. I don't know, because everybody can use it in his own sense. But sometimes, in older Hindu teaching, it may correspond. I even spoke of it in connection with the Table of Time in Different Cosmoses.

MRS. B. Where is the Absolute with relation to that table?

MR. O. It is impossible to try to answer such a question. What is the Atlantic Ocean in relation to this table? The Atlantic Ocean is much smaller than the Absolute, but this table does not exist in relation to it.

MRS. P. If it is not possible for one to find a system of discipline for oneself, how can one develop?

MR. O. What do you mean by a system of discipline for oneself?

MRS. P. You said there were many systems of discipline. . . .

MR. O. This word is used in many senses. But we speak only of schools. Or discipline of certain work. If one decides to do something, this immediately creates the necessity of certain discipline.

MRS. S. I don't understand your answer to Mr. S.'s question on discipline. You agreed with him that the discipline should be external. I thought the only valuable kind was internal. Do you mean that you need help?

MR. O. Yes. One cannot invent discipline. You need outside help, suggestion, explanation that makes discipline comprehensible, otherwise it will be invented. Discipline must be part of a certain task. But by ourselves we can do nothing. We must accept certain ideas, certain methods, and in this way we meet with discipline.

MISS R. You mentioned about all being physical. Then each centre can affect other centres and the results?

MR. O. Even the Absolute is physical. Centres are physical.

MISS R. Then if all is physical, what other causes could there be?

MR. O. Why did you bring centres into it? The question was about causes. I said you must first exhaust physical causes. Physical causes must be understood simply. They may be psychic causes—they are also physical of a different materiality. But still we must make a difference. Well, it is clear.

Thank God, it is not quite clear to me.

MR. S. The other day I was in a situation of great excitement and emotion. It seemed altogether unreal. How is this explained?

MR. O. Probably it was not unreal. Emotions are always real, that is our misfortune. But without facts I cannot say.

MR. S. When I am lost in an emotion, is it because emotional centre predominates?

MR. O. No, it means identification, if you are lost in it.

MR. S. The cause of the emotion seemed very real.

MRS. S. Coming back to discipline. What is the weakness in self-imposed discipline?

MR. O. No aim. Why discipline? Why not live quietly and pleasantly without discipline, if there is no aim? Discipline is only justified by aim.

MRS. P. Is not the desire to be a better person an aim?

MR. O. Who knows what is a better person? Do you know? At the same time it is necessary to know that one can be better or worse. It can be explained from aim.

MRS. P. I have read frequently that when the pupil is ready, the teacher appears. . . .

MR. O. Theosophical imagination. It is written in some theosophical book and people repeat it without knowing what is 'ready' and what is 'teacher'.

MRS. P. What is the meaning of 'teacher'?

MR. O. One who teaches. But necessary to know first what you want to know.

MISS R. How can you know if you are asleep?

MR. O. You must wake enough to know what you want. Suppose you want to learn how to wake and I begin to teach you Russian.

MISS R. How to awaken?

MRS. A. Is the process of self-remembering designed to effect a tie-up, or a bridge between the thalamus and the fore-brain?

MR. O. First of all, self-remembering is not a process. It is a state.

What is that? I think I never saw such a word.

Who knows? Don't believe the person who tells you he knows. No, we cannot explain self-remembering anatomically. But psychologically one can know. It is to be aware of oneself. That is not connected with any part of the brain.

MRS. N. Is all emotion identification?

MR. O. No, normal emotions can exist without identification. All negative emotions must have identification. But some emotions can only exist without identification. If identification enters, it spoils them.

MRS. N. There can be higher emotions that aren't identification?

MRS. A. I have never understood how you would define the term 'emotion'.

MR. O. You must feel emotions. They are all pleasant or unpleasant. In older psychology books you find quite good explanations of divisions.

MRS. V. I think I understood you to say that the Absolute was physical? Does that mean it is only physical or psychic is included?

MR. O. I think you had better not mix two different things. First speak about our own experience. We can decide between physical and psychic causes. If I have a headache because I hit my head on the door, this is physical cause. If I have a headache as a result of too much negative imagining, this is psychic cause.

MRS. P. Did I understand you to say that pain is a negative imagination of the instinctive centre?

MR. O. Never. Pain is pain. ... It may be. How can I say? It may be imaginary pain.

MISS H. When one would reach the state where one could use the intellectual part of the intellectual centre or the intellectual part of emotional centre, does that mean that we would be influenced by anything we have been taught, and really think for ourselves?

MR. O. It will mean only that you can use the brain better than before. You can think better, learn better, remember better. But what is produced cannot be promised. You must try.

MISS R. Psychic causes arise only from negative emotions or imagination?

MR. O. Maybe from quite pleasant imagination. Not only imagination. But you must find yourself. This was an example. From it you can find other things.

MR. S. What can you introduce into your thinking to stop negative imagination? Doing anything that takes the mind off imagination helps? I find most of the time my mind is not occupied.

MR. O. You cannot do that. Well, you can occupy your mind with learning, even Russian language. But if the mind is unoccupied, the easiest pleasure is negative emotion.

Well, find some occupation for it. This is a dangerous state.

MR. S. In what direction would I try to put my mind to?

MR. O. Well, there are many things to study in the system. I said, you try to teach this system to imaginary people.

MR. S. Is it all right to teach it to imaginary people, but not real?

MR. O. Better to real people.

MRS. S. Isn't there a rule against teaching real people?

MR. O. There was never such a rule. But it depends who.

MRS. D. Suppose you are a person who keeps the mind busy all the time, studying Tibetan and Russian, can't you still be given to negative emotions?

MR. O. Quite right. Negative emotions can hide themselves so cleverly. You may learn Tibetan and everything and still live in negative emotions.

MRS. D. Wouldn't you suspect a person like that?

MISS R. If you control them at the point of expression, how could you find out what they were? Wouldn't the solution be to find out the cause of them?

MR. O. Put it all together—what do you ask me?

MISS R. What is the point of controlling negative emotions at the point of expression?

MR. O. Because you cannot go on without that. You must achieve a certain proficiency in the control of expression of negative emotions. You must get that first.

MRS. P. What is possible to do after that?

MR. O. When we come to that you will be told. No imagination. I will know that you came to this point by your questions. They will be quite different.

MR. S. What is there in negative emotion that makes it so pleasant?

MR. O. That I don't know. Different tastes. That you can find yourself.

MRS. V. Is all attachment negative emotion?

MR. O. What do you mean by attachment?

MRS. V. Isn't there always a negative feeling connected with identification?

MR. O. You speak of identification. This is not negative emotion by itself. But it is a necessary element in negative emotion.

What you call negative emotions need imagination. Without it they become something different. Good negative emotions need good identification.

MRS. S. Is it possible to distinguish between a real pleasant emotion and an imaginary one?

MR. O. There is no such distinction. It is not only words. Facts are no different.

MRS. N. If I am able to watch myself at work and be aware of myself at work and watch myself at work—suppose I think I am—I'm a little bit confused. For instance, as I work I try to be aware that I am doing.

MR. O. About work I don't guarantee. We begin only with being aware of oneself.

That is another thing. I did not speak about it. I spoke only about self-remembering. You can work asleep, and I want you to awake. This is a certain state that we can have now only in flashes. We can prolong those flashes by self-remembering.

MRS. N. If the next day I remember something I said or did and didn't repeat it, would that be it?

MR. O. Something may be very different. Impossible to give an answer that will fit all 'somethings'.

MRS. N. Then that wouldn't be a slight bit of self-remembering?

MR. O. Not enough material. You say 'something' and I try to explain that 'something' may be different.

MR. S. Is it a good practice to try to apply intelligence and reason to an emotion?

MR. O. Yes, but sometimes you cannot. Emotions are so much quicker than reason. You think of applying reason to an emotion and it has already disappeared.

MR. S. The emotion comes quickly, but if I apply reason to it it may not become negative emotion.

MR. O. Many people have tried this method and it does not work. Emotion can appear and do much harm before you start thinking about it.

MR. S. Then you either have the emotion or you don't. . . .

MR. O. How can you not have emotion? You have no control. Any change, even small change, needs long work. We cannot speak of elimination of emotions. We must start as we are.

MR. S. I try to work on it by self-remembering.

MR. O. Self-remembering is only for developing itself. If one gets a certain length of self-remembering it can be used. But just thinking about it will not help.

MRS. V. A person's house burns down and the person feels regret; the feeling would be negative emotion?

MR. O. Not quite. Negative emotion needs identification. One may suffer—it may have been beautiful and there may be memories attached to it. But if one is not identified, it will not be right negative emotion.

MRS. V. I'm afraid that I don't understand identification then.

MR. O. Identification is a certain kind of attitude. One is personally offended. One is offended with house, God, anything.

MRS. B. Is the beginning of self-remembering a thought process?

MR. O. Not quite. If you like, thought only to eliminate thinking. Thought process is only first preparation. One must understand what one is doing, why one is doing it. This is definition. Important only to try to do it. It is dangerous—because people take only words. But one must begin with the idea—'I am here' and exclude all the rest.

MRS. P. I thought you said once a long time ago that we did not have the right to say 'I am'?

MR. O. Quite, because we are not. Well, try to deceive yourself that you are. Even that is better than nothing. Only don't believe it.

MRS. U. Is it essence that makes one man have more negative emotions than another?

MR. O. I think everyone can have as much as he likes.

MRS. U. I think even without study some people seem to express more negative emotion than others.

MR. O. Quite right. Different talents. One has more capacity for expressing negative emotion, another less.

MRS. U. Does that have to do with development of false personality?

MR. O. It can be put like that—but I see no necessity. Why bring false personality in here?

MRS. U. Only I wondered why it was that I express negative emotion more than other people.

MR. O. More identification. That is the real answer. False personality is a different question, a different problem.

MR. S. When I find I have negative imagination developing I apply stopping thoughts as a brake to stop it.

MR. O. If it works, all right. It is not really for that, but sometimes it may help. Though really it is for another purpose.

MRS. A. In the system, is the emotional centre thought of as localized in any particular part of the body?

MR. O. Yes, only with certain reservations. You see, each centre occupies all body, though long ago it was said intellectual centre was connected with brain, emotional with solar plexus, instinctive and moving with spinal cord. But these are only centres of gravity. Because centres are not organs.

MRS. B. Is that why we can work asleep, because intellectual centre is in our hands and we can work asleep?

MR. O. Much better awake. Safer.

It's all good. You ask good questions. But I would like you to ask more. For instance, in connection with accumulators, it was said that each organ, each part of the body had several functions. Eyes, for example, have their own function, and at the same time they are accumulators for some other function. We don't realize how many things an organ can do. Only when we begin to realize the enormous variety do we understand something about accumulators.

MRS. A. If the three centres are not to be thought of as organs or localized functions, how can we think of them as being different from one another?

MR. O. Different by functions. Intellectual centre thinks. Emotional centre feels. For instance, you cannot count with emotional centre. But if you want to like or dislike, you cannot calculate it. But each centre

563

sends rays, so to speak, to every part of the body. Though they are different for instinctive, emotional, etc.

When we become more conscious we will be able to be in contact with intellectual parts of centres. Now we cannot even control moving parts. That shows how little we know about ourselves.

MRS. B. Are the accumulators connected with every little part of the body too?

MR. O. We may better take them as connected with centres. Each centre has two small accumulators. You remember how a man exhausts one accumulator. Then he changes over, by yawning perhaps, and the other accumulator fills up.

Here you can see eight accumulators. Actually we can count twelve. If, on the enneagram we take the intersection of the lines and of the triangle and draw circles around them, you have twelve of the most important accumulators. There are a thousand others. It is very interesting to study ordinary things, like eyes, ears, from this point of view. Ears are for listening, at the same time the inner ear gives sense of balance.

MRS. A. What form of energies do the accumulators work on?

MR. O. [Unrecorded.]

MRS. N. What are the accumulators filled with?

MR. O. Energy produced in the chemical factory.

MRS. S. Imagination and identification use energy, do they not?

MR. O. It is not indicated. Suppose you imagine on an empty accumulator. Then you smoke a cigarette and imagine some more.

MRS. P. Does the sex centre use energy from the same source?

MR. O. That's another thing. It doesn't enter at meetings.

MISS R. Is effort an accumulator?

MR. O. By effort we pump energy into accumulators.

MRS. W. Can we increase or decrease the amount of energy in our accumulators?

MR. O. No, it is difficult. But from the big accumulator the right energy is sent to each centre. Each centre receives energy as it needs.

MRS. W. Does everyone have the same amount of energy?

MR. O. By effort we make it flow quicker. . . .

No, that was explained in relation to the Food Diagram. How to create more energy.

MR. S. Is it a good idea to conserve energy? Not to waste it?

MR. O. But what does waste mean? We take these words for granted. But we do not know what they mean.

MR. B. Giving vent to negative emotion would be wasting energy.

MRS. S. What is meant when you say that the enneagram is an accumulator?

MR. O. No, I never said that. The enneagram is a chart that can be applied to each cosmos, and to man because he is also a cosmos.

MRS. W. Does this energy—in the big accumulator—come from different sources?

MR. O. It is created by three-story chemical factory. Only you remember that it is different in different states. It works so far in ordinary man. Then it is known how it works, after man works on himself.

MRS. S. Would impression 6 put more energy into accumulator than 48? Impression 12?

MR. O. Nobody has impression 6. This is not our subject. It was explained in the Food Diagram—if you have enough H6 in yourself, you can have impression 6. But we don't have much higher energies.

MRS. P. You say that when one yawns one is depleted of energy—but is it also done by imitation? I have noticed that when people yawn. . . .

MR. O. Yawning is mechanical pumping.

Yes, it is quite mechanical. Yawning and laughter are very important. Only we will speak some other time about laughter.

MRS. W. Is physical tension a possible source of wasting energy?

MR. O. Oh yes, you can become more tired than walking or carrying big logs.

MRS. H. What function does weeping perform?

MR. O. I think it something similar to laughing. Redistribution of energy in some cases.

MISS C. If one comes upon a beautiful object suddenly and it makes one cry, is that negative emotion?

MR. O. But another will laugh. Why? Different people. And it may be the same thing. They got too many impressions.

MRS. S. Since laughter is very good for an individual, does it make any difference how it is produced?

MR. O. Sometimes there are different kinds of laughter. We are not ready to talk of it yet.

MISS H. This chart—is it mechanical or can we control it and regulate the energy?

MR. O. No, we cannot. Man cannot control it. But if a man feels tired—that means instinctive centre feels lack of energy—one may rest.

MR. B. How do we know there are only two small accumulators, and not three or five?

MR. O. Maybe more. This is only to understand the principle, that they are not all used at the same time.

MRS. B. Would you explain—if a person has more of H_{12} in him. . . .

MR. O. That doesn't enter into our discussion. But for each centre there is a feeling of being tired, which shows us that accumulators are low.

MRS. H. If we live partly by impressions, are all impressions accumulators?

MR. O. No, impressions are energy.

MRS. H. Could we discuss impressions? Influences B are impressions, aren't they?

MR. O. Impressions we receive without efforts. Influence C needs effort to accumulate it. Effort of both sides. Who gives and who receives. Quite opposite. It can be said influence C gives many new impressions, if you get it. But it is not an impression in itself.

MRS. H. I don't believe I understood that. . . .

MR. B. In Food Chart, impressions are in conjunction with air and food?

MR. O. Impressions are called food. Food of impressions. But we speak only of H_{48}.

MRS. N. Are there any constant impressions?

MR. O. Yes, but we do not feel constant impressions. We only feel changes in impressions. And there can be no constant change.

MISS R. Can we receive impressions from self-remembering?

MR. O. Very much. Only necessary to get self-remembering first.

MISS H. Is H_{24} as shown here the same as in the Food Chart?

MR. O. Yes, yes, certainly the same. We use always the same for the designation of centres.

MISS H. Then the instinctive centre produces finer energy than intellectual?

MR. O. Not produces—uses finer energy than intellectual. Instinctive centre is not allowed to make mistakes, for instance, otherwise one would fall ill.

MRS. B. Is the instinctive centre closely connected with one's essence?

MR. O. Yes, it controls the necessities of essence.

MRS. G. Why is it that moving and instinctive centres have no connection with big accumulator?

MR. O. No, it is only that I did not connect them.

* * *

MR. O. Devil is very important. Some people think he is symbolic. I always thought he is very concrete. And I was very glad to hear it was accepted so by the system. . . . He works through considering, negative emotions, imagination. But if you fight against these dangers, you are safe. You are taught to fight against dangers, before you are taught where they come from.

Q. Is the devil in back of the moon?

MR. O. No, you make a very easy devil. He is much cleverer.

Q. Devil must mean embodiment of evil?

MR. O. Quite right. But with purpose. Before you think about purpose, you cannot say anything about the devil. No devil can keep you from self-remembering, if you work. If you don't, anyone can prevent you. The devil has so many faces, there are so many legends about him. If you study tales, it would help.

Q. He wanted to be as great as God?

MR. O. No, the devil has many different ambitions, not only to be God. It is—I don't know—too small. . . . He is real, quite real. It is not the system; it is my opinion.

[Here followed Kriloff's fable of the Monk and the Egg which is briefly as follows: There was a monk who lived in a very strict monastery. He did not like it, and one day during Lent managed to get an egg. Very pleased, he took the egg to his cell, and when night came thought he would cheat the abbot and have a nice meal. He lit a candle and began to cook the egg over the flame. Suddenly the door opened and the abbot stood there looking at him. Terrified, the monk cried, 'Forgive me, I do not know how I could have done such a thing; the devil tempted me.' But the devil jumped out from behind the stove, shouting indignantly, 'This is quite unfair, I have only this minute learned from you how to cook eggs by candle flame; I did not know it could be done.']

Q. Why is he so powerful?

MR. O. Because we don't know enough about him.

Q. What is the rôle of the devil?

MR. O. That's the question. If you think about it, you may learn more. . . . Try to ask yourselves, in which cosmos can the devil exist?

Q. Does he live in the moon?

MR. O. Maybe he has something to do with moon. But he is only connected with man.

Q. Devil's object is man's soul. Moon also feeds on souls?

MR. O. Moon feeds on souls only in the sense of life energy. The devil has better ideas.

Q. A man might think he is religious, whereas he is the opposite. . . .

MR. O. That is the best way to be caught by him. You cannot catch him unless you remember yourself.

Q. Is the devil man himself?

MR. O. Yes and no. In what cosmos does devil exist? You remember the lateral octave. The devil cannot belong to <u>do</u> in the sun. But maybe the devil can have his roots in <u>si</u>. <u>Si</u> is bigger than <u>la</u>, <u>sol</u>, <u>fa</u>. Not all <u>si</u>. But maybe when man was invented, the devil was invented also.

Q. Why should the devil want to stop school-work?

MR. O. That is his profession. And some people say he is a little afraid of those glass tubes in which he can be put. . . . In no period can he have more power than in this. Now he is in full bloom.

[Here followed the story about the Devil and the Sly Man, which is briefly as follows: Once the sly man met the devil in a Paris café where the devil came to sell carpets. The devil was very thin and miserable and looked starved. The sly man asked what was the matter, and the devil answered that all the devils in hell had fallen on evil times. They fed on souls, and in the past many people had fat souls, but now people were mostly born without souls at all, and all the devils were hungry. The sly man asked the devil if he knew how to make souls, and the devil said he did. So the sly man suggested that the devil should teach him to make souls and he would undertake to produce men with souls for the devil's benefit. The devil agreed. The sly man became very busy, organized schools and began to teach men self-remembering. But although men grew souls they still fell into the hands of the devil when they died, which was not what the sly man had intended.

One day when a man with a fat soul died, he was met at the gates of heaven by St. Peter on one side and the devil on the other. St. Peter asked 'Did you remember yourself?' And the man answered 'I did.' Thereupon the devil cried 'Mine!' and led the soul away to hell.

When the sly man heard this he said to his pupils 'Have I not warned you not to talk? What business has any of you to tell St. Peter that you remembered yourselves? Have you seen St. Peter in our groups?']

Q. To me angel and devil are opposites—one good, the other bad.

MR. O. Profession quite different—not only good and bad.

The first step is asking right questions about the devil. You don't put him in a bottle without asking right questions about him.

It was said most definitely—there can be no conscious evil. In relation to devil, it changes. In relation to devil, or with the help of devil, there is possibility of conscious evil. With devil, or his help, there may be some mind in it. . . . You can think like this: 'Can devil have any function in organic life apart from man?' No. Animals, insects, fishes, bacteria? No. Devil can manifest only through help of man. Man has possibility of evolution. Devil can stop him; create conditions against it.

Then, in connection with schools and inner circle—things like that you can think about. If you wish to speak of other things—if you speak about recurrence, you must understand the theory. Something is possible, something is impossible in speaking about devil. Devil much too big in ordinary understanding. He is not big.

Q. Is devil conscious?

MR. O. Conscious? Dangerous word. Intelligent he must be.

Q. The life-span of the devil must be more than that of an individual man?

MR. O. More than that of individual man, maybe, but not more than that of organic life.

* * *

Memory (*From New York Meetings 1944–7*)

20.9.44.

Q. In what centre is memory situated? Does each centre have its own memory?

MR. O. Not only each centre. There are many kinds of memory, and about some of them we can say whether they belong to essence or personality.

* * *

4.10.44.

MR. O. I advise you to think chiefly about consciousness. How to approach, how to start to understand what consciousness is. We can know in the past examples of consciousness.

Q. Is this a Vedantic scheme of thought?

MR. O. Some people may think like that, but it is not a system of thought. It is what I know. Moment of consciousness produces very strong memory. If we can find in the past moments of clear and very vivid memory, we can know this is the result of being conscious. At the same time, in the system, we can decide to remember ourselves to-morrow at a certain time in certain circumstances. I often described how, before the war, when people went to Paris, I told them to remember themselves at the Gare du Nord. Nobody could.

Q. I remembered myself arriving in Paris only because of an accident.

MR. O. This is not self-remembering. Something happened. This is Law of Accident.

* * *

11.10.44.

Q. How can one increase one's memory? How can one work on memory?

MR. O. Being more conscious. In no other system is there a method for improving memory. In this it is definite; remember yourself.

Q. Is it possible that memory is developed to a different degree in different centres? Would it be possible to have a very good memory in emotional centre and not in another?

MR. O. It is in all centres. Naturally, it may be more in one. But only one method of making memory strong—by becoming more conscious.

* * *

18.10.44.

Q. Is immortality impossible for man Nos. 1, 2, 3?

MR. O. Yes, he has to become No. 5. That is one answer. But there may be other answers. For instance, from the point of view of recurrence, man Nos. 1, 2, 3 may live again, may turn again, but they do not remember. But to remember they must become No. 5.

Q. What is it that becomes immortal, essence or physical body and soul?

MR. O. Only memory. Body is born again; essence is born again; personality is created again. So it is not question of immortality but memory. We may live ten thousand times without any advantage if we do not remember.

Q. Do you [mean] remember events or remember ourselves?

MR. O. Both. The more the better. Fact of mechanical immortality—if such a thing is possible—is no advantage.

Q. It would be terrible if we didn't have a chance to recur.

MR. O. I said, 'We don't remember.' All normal people have chance to recur.

Q. Does memory belong to essence?

MR. A.W. I should say there must be memory of every part of oneself, more or less.

* * *

29.12.44.

Q. If we remember our motives of our actions, then we will remember our actions. It that remembering oneself?

MR. O. No. It is just ordinary memory. Again I remind you: what is useful and necessary to remember is that we don't remember, never remember and we didn't know about it.

Q. Isn't there a difference between remembering the fact that you were going to remember at twelve, and actually to remember oneself?

MR. O. Quite different. In relation to self-remembering, it is necessary to distinguish what is self-remembering and what is not. Necessary to learn to think. We have much material for right thinking, but necessary not to forget it.

Q. How can we prove to ourselves that we don't remember ourselves?

MR. O. I spoke so many times about it that I have forgotten now. My friend who came to meet me at the Gare du Nord in Paris, I asked him to remember himself there. But he only came with a very worried face, saying, 'I've forgotten something you asked me to do. Was it something I had to buy?'

Q. I find in the morning I'll say I'll remember at twelve. Something happens and then I remember at one o'clock.

MR. O. Yes, it happens like that, but if you continue it may produce very unexpected results. The whole thing is to create this continuity. Glimpses may happen, but continuity. ... At the same time you mustn't be very dejected, because it works and grows.

Q. We must self-remember in order to get out of the prison?

MR. O. I forgot the prison. Yes, I think so. I think this is the chief part of the prison—that we don't remember ourselves. But you must frighten people. One lady in London said, 'Why do you speak about awakening if Christ didn't speak about it?' I said, 'But Christ spoke all the time about awakening.' And she was quite sincere.

* * *

25.1.45.

Q. Did you say that magnetic centre is a group of permanent interests? Would you explain?

MR. O. Yes. If one remembers what he liked last week, last month, last year—if he remembers it makes permanent centre of gravity. We forget. If we remember and continue to like, that will make centre of gravity.

Q. Wouldn't the nature of what we liked determine the centre of gravity?

MR. O. Nature isn't sufficient. We can still forget it. May have beautiful nature but we still forget it.

Q. Is it desirable to formulate a centre of gravity such as you outlined?

MR. O. It is simply that you have to call it something. Either it is there or not there. Certain things can be answered only in that way. One can say 'lack of centre of gravity'.

Q. It seems that a man with permanent centre of gravity would be happy if he could remember everything he likes.

MR. O. It doesn't mean—because memory doesn't guarantee. Good memory, bad memory. Yes, I think it is better to remember what he likes and even dislikes, than not to remember.

Q. Can the Law of Seven be observed in the way things happen or appear?

MR. O. Law of Seven you can speak about when you find two intervals in an octave.

Q. Can one only see it in operation over a period of many years or at once?

MR. O. You can use memory. Doesn't mean that you observe actual facts. But you must see two intervals in an octave.

* * *

7.3.45.

Q. How can we train our memories to remember everything that's said?

MR. O. Being more conscious. There is no other way.

Q. There are people with photographic memory. Are they more conscious?

MR. O. There are many different kinds of memory. You have a certain kind of memory. But you can use it better or worse by being more conscious or less conscious.

Q. What are some of the forms the first conscious effort takes?

MR. O. Be aware of yourself. 'I am here.' But not words. Feeling. Who you are and where you are.

Q. And what are some of the forms of work?

MR. O. This is work. There are many kinds. Suppose you are told not to talk in a certain way. This is work.

* * *

14.3.45.

Q. If you have a flash of self-remembering or consciousness, are you able to identify it always?

MR. O. Sometimes. With this flash of consciousness you have very clear memory—place, time of day, day of week, and so on.

Q. You don't speak of self-remembering in terms of memory only, but in terms of understanding.

MR. O. Quite right; at the same time these moments give very bright memory.

Q. In a moment of self-remembering would it be possible to hear something you don't ordinarily hear?

MR. O. Quite. But it depends what. You cannot expect to hear angels singing.

Q. Receiving impressions is a mechanical process, isn't it?

MR. O. They are used in different ways. Take knowledge—one may learn Chinese with enough Chinese words. If one collects enough musical impressions one learns music. Moving energy collects memories of a road or place.

Q. How does one become stronger in the system?

MR. O. Slowly. You must accumulate knowledge and being. Being is connected with memory of what we promised ourselves. In this way we can strengthen our being.

Q. Does the memory of our failures strengthen our being?

MR. O. Sometimes very useful. Sometimes quite useless. If you remember your failures and sit crying, or accuse somebody else, it will not help.

Q. Is memory a function of the body?

MR. O. Yes, if you like.

Q. Can it be compared to movement?

MR. O. But one thing is not like another. Memory is something in us— maybe in essence, maybe in personality. One recollects in personality. But one has memory of taste or smell, another doesn't. This is essence. But actually one remembers in personality.

Q. Is it possible to work on memory to improve it?

MR. O. We have to begin with ourselves. Self-remember.

Q. You spoke of 'Being' as being the promises you made to yourself and others. Could you explain that a little more?

MR. O. No, no. If one promises something to oneself or others and doesn't do it, that's a measure of being.

Q. I was told of another form of work that could be done. May I tell you later?

MR. O. There are older people who know about this work. They should not speak of it before me. I must speak at my own time. This brings us to rules. Rules are a measure of being.

* * *

25.7.45.

Q. What prevents man from having memory?

MR. O. Many things. As a matter of fact, I am preparing a book about memory, but it will be difficult. We will learn how we lose memory, spoil memory.

Q. How can we tell right or wrong activity?

MR. O. By result, very simple. If we want good memory and our memory fails, wrong result. We think it is mysterious. It is not mysterious, if we turn in the right way.

575

Q. Does memory depend on attention?

MR. O. There are many different kinds of memory. Ordinary memory—memory of what we hear—memory of this system—memory of smell—memory of roads. But we speak of memory that we know. It is very easy to spoil this memory.

Q. There is a popular saying, 'A liar must have a good memory.'

MR. O. Unfortunately for liars, it is quite different. But some day there will be material.

Q. I find it difficult to remember not to express negative emotions.

MR. O. Quite right. First necessary to remember.

Q. How can I strengthen that memory?

MR. O. Try to use what you can. Every day or every week you can do something. Do it. Do what you can. You cannot say nothing is possible.

* * *

1.8.45.

Q. What is the way towards developing memory in recurrence?

MR. O. This is very interesting and very important. Necessary to develop memory, as it is also possible to destroy memory. This refers to what used to be called psychological memory or intellectual memory. I observed—though from a distance—an extraordinarily interesting case in which memory was spoiled. Well, according to theory of recurrence, self-remembering is the only way of developing memory. If one remembers oneself in this life, one will remember next time.

Q. On what is the theory based?

MR. O. Imagination.

Q. How can memory survive death?

MR. O. Death is nothing.

Q. When you speak of self-remembering as you did in answering my question it sounded like a complete sort of thing. It doesn't sound like something that has degrees.

MR. O. Always degree. But if one remembers previous life, that means he remembered himself the previous time.

Q. What do you mean by 'death is nothing' in that tone of voice you used?

MR. O. You may not notice it.

Q. You said 'if one is born again'. Doesn't everybody get a chance to be born again?

MR. O. They may not notice it again. If they do not notice they die, they may not notice that they are born.

Q. Is there a way of trying to make memory connect?

MR. O. Study the system. The system is difficult and develops memory. All you heard in the system from the beginning.

Q. Say six months ago you could remember some things in detail; six months later, how can you bring them closer?

[No answer.]

Q. I've never been able to understand how eternal recurrence is compatible with our present time-sense.

MR. O. It is not compatible. The whole thing is in that. So you have to get rid of time-sense. It refers to eternity not time.

Q. Is it in self-remembering we could get rid of our time-sense?

MR. O. Different.

Q. Then how?

MR. O. Different effort.

Q. Would memory of a previous recurrence make it possible to change one's actions?

MR. O. That I don't know. That you will see when you have it.

Q. Would it be right to say that the only claim for recurrence is that in this life some people remember they lived before?

MR. O. No, it is very weak. Very few people, and you can always say they lie. Find other reasons.

Q. Does time exist for ordinary man?

MR. O. In certain conditions. If one has sense of sight, smell, hearing, then there is time.

Q. In recurrence from one life to another, do we retain same level of being?

MR. O. There are different theories about it. One theory is that if one acquires something in one life it is bound to grow. There are many other theories.

Q. How could we understand the word 'eternity'?

MR. O. Think about eternity. Very useful.

Q. A recurring life is not lived exactly as before, is it?

MR. O. Beginning is always the same.

Q. Can we keep the pattern from repeating or is it outside circumstances?

MR. O. If you have good memory, you can.

Q. I was under the impression you said that if anything survives it is memory.

MR. O. Probably not, quite. Because memory usually disappears first, if anything survives. Memory is very unstable.

Q. Some people seem to be born with some recollection that they are slaves to circumstance or life.

MR. O. Is this Freud or Adler? What is it? You must know these words.

Q. Will you explain connection between self-remembering and self-consciousness?

MR. O. Degrees of time. A long time, half an hour, may be self-consciousness. Two minutes, self-remembering.

Q. Why does man's time become shorter as soon as he knows about eternal recurrence?

MR. O. He knows too much.

Q. Can it be that during period of sleep man has no responsibility, but when he hears about it, then he has more responsibility?

MR. O. Very good. That is one answer.

Q. How can we have memory that's our own?

MR. O. We always have our own, not somebody else's.

Q. But it disappears?

MR. O. Disappears means ceases to be our own.

Q. Is psychological memory in essence?

MR. O. Better to say it is connected with 'I's, which are personality.

Q. Does false personality destroy memory?

MR. O. Yes, one can say false personality either destroys or distorts memory.

MR. A.W. Without idea of recurrence most things in life seem purposeless?

MR. O. Quite. And they are.

Q. What can one do to understand the illusion of time?

MR. O. One can understand that there is no such thing as time and why. Because there are facts which show non-existence of time.

Q. Is there one degree of memory that comes from higher intellectual centre, and one from higher emotional?

MR. O. A little too much in one question.

Q. It seems that in reincarnation if you are born in different circumstances you can develop more.

MR. O. I want to know what you mean. You cannot speak of difference (i.e. between recurrence and reincarnation) until you know one thing.

By reincarnation you mean in time—by calendar and clock. But with a little more knowledge this does not work. You have got to get rid of calendar and watch. Man dies and time is going. It is impossible. One means time, another means different attitude to time.

Q. What is the substitute for calendar and clock, if any?

MR. O. No substitute.

Q. Is it possible to have emotional feeling in idea of recurrence?

MR. O. Yes, it is possible. Particularly if one has even some recollection. I don't mean everything. But even slight memory can give interesting emotional understanding.

Q. How dependable is that emotional feeling?

MR. O. Different for different people. For one person it can be dependable, for another it means nothing.

Q. A person who remembered everything would feel that everybody around him was dead. That would be an uncomfortable feeling.

MR. O. Dead and buried and question is finished.

Q. When you throw calendar and watch out, do you mean that every moment is permanent?

MR. O. No, I don't mean that. That would be theory, philosophy.

Q. Wouldn't there have to be some change in order to throw time out?

MR. O. I don't know. You make deduction. I spoke of calendar and watch and you want to throw time out.

Q. Can one prepare oneself for recurrence?

MR. O. Why? Theoretically speaking. But how? This is a good question. First question that can be answered. How? Suppose in a certain life you want to do something and you find you cannot do it. This needs help. If you cannot physically get this help, you begin to think about it. And you realize you have to prepare for this help the life before. This life is too late. This is the situation.

Q. Do you mean feel what one can do in next life?

MR. O. Next life is too late. Life before is only chance. Think about it. Perhaps you missed some opportunity.

Q. Can we only think of past life in relation to mistakes made in this life?

MR. O. If one finds one cannot do something, he thinks of previous time when perhaps he could do it. Or perhaps he couldn't. Think what this implies.

Q. He would have had to have some memory to make that possible, wouldn't he? To realize mistakes in past life or lack of preparation?

MR. O. There may be no mistake. Simply lack of preparation, quite right.

Q. Does that mean that for some things that happen in this life we look back to some cause or symptom?

MR. O. Too many things implied. One needs preparation. One says one is not prepared. Perhaps one could have been prepared before. Can you do anything about it? It is difficult, I know. One may think one is not prepared for a certain thing.

Q. If man is working to overcome five obstacles to waking, is that not first step to prepare for recurrence?

MR. O. Very good. But he may think about something quite different.

Q. What must we do to avoid spoiling our memory?

MR. O. Imagination first, lying second; two things destroy our memory. When we first spoke of lying people took it as funny. They did not realize that one can destroy one's memory completely. Struggle with imagination also. Not just for sport or exercise. Well, try to find something. Occasionally we find some point from which we can start and then lose it again.

Q. When you say memory is spoiled by lying and imagination, do you speak of intellectual memory?

MR. O. I speak of intellectual memory.

Q. Man is born with limited capacity to remember—even this is spoiled?

MR. O. Quite right.

Q. What do you mean by psychological memory?

MR. O. Intellectual centre memory.

MR. A.W. Does this spoiling of memory result in physiological change?

MR. O. Oh, yes; it may bring complete lunacy. Old psychologists knew about that. They spoke about hysterics and so on, but they did not realize that just by our ordinary psychological play we can spoil memory. Lying about ideas, imagining about ideas and so on.

Q. How can we recognize in ourselves the degree to which memory has been spoiled?

MR. O. We cannot. We can only fight against spoiling it. Struggle against lying, struggle against imagination.

Q. How can we recognize characteristics of imagination?

MR. O. That we can study. We spoke five years about it. One must find one's favourite imagination. Classify. One prefers imagination, another prefers lying—question of taste.

Q. Wouldn't belief in recurrence result in a great urgency to make effort?

MR. O. Belief will not help. Belief is deadening. It has not sufficient power, but realization may.

MR. A.W. What can help us to recognize lying in ourselves?

MR. O. There are many different things. First, analysis of facts, words, theories. Recognition of other people's lying is very useful. And then one bright morning one can come to oneself.

Q. Is false personality a form of lying?

MR. O. Leave false personality. It is not a form of lying. It is a defence. Avoiding unpleasant results behind false personality, one can feel oneself in a certain way.

Q. How would we come to a realization of recurrence if we have no facts on which to base it?

MR. O. Perhaps some think they have facts. But they are not sure, so they say theories not facts.

Q. When one has a strong feeling of event having happened before, can one use that to develop memory?

MR. O. Oh, it can happen in many different ways. Only after very long and very serious investigation can one come to the conclusion that there may be facts.

Q. If man understood about recurrence would he change his activities?

MR. O. I don't know. It depends on man. And how long.

Q. In a lifetime?

MR. O. What do you know that lasted a lifetime?

* * *

8.8.45.

Q. Did I understand you to say that psychological memory was memory of the intellectual centre?

MR. O. That expression 'psychological memory' was used in French psychology about fifty years ago. It means intellectual memory.

Q. Does self-remembering belong to this memory?

MR. O. No. Self-remembering belongs to unexisting things—dreams, imagination.

Q. I understood you to say last week that in order to prepare ourselves for recurrence we should try to think when in a previous existence we had missed an opportunity to prepare ourselves.

MR. O. As good as anything else, if it gives results. How can one prepare? There are many ways, we speak about it a little from many sides.

Q. It seems to me that in order to realize where we had missed an opportunity in a past life, we would first have to reach a moment of awakening in this life.

MR. O. Very good. Only do that first.

Q. When I look back at the opportunities missed in this life, I have the feeling that only by being a different kind of person could I have acted differently. From this it seems to me that the only way to affect recurrence is to change one's essence.

MR. O. Again very useful. But how to do it?

Many of the questions last time and some of these refer to most important things. We can understand something by thinking. For example: Question whether all people are affected in the same way by recurrence. Impossible to say simple yes or no. But what can be applied to one man cannot be applied to another. For one man—same way, same house, same cats. But for other people it may be different. Great poets, great writers—they may not need to walk by the same streets. They may walk by different streets and do same thing.

Q. To what is the difference due—to efforts?

MR. O. No, I think to capacities, to achievement, to scope of thinking, feeling.

Q. Would the type of recurrence depend on the rôle one played in life?

MR. O. Very dangerous to answer 'yes', though it is very near to 'yes'. I must answer 'no', though it is nearer to 'yes'.

Q. You spoke about a great poet or writer and said he didn't need to walk the same streets.

MR. O. Or write same verses.

Q. Do you mean he extracted all he could or produced all he could with his environment?

MR. O. Maybe not all, but sufficient. He may try something else that he didn't try last time.

Q. Were the capacities and scope given at birth or did they increase with effort?

MR. O. We don't know. How can you be sure? It is there. We spoke of six triads. In one triad you can do one thing; in another, another thing.

582

But this changes all ideas of recurrence. What could be right for one man would not be right for another. For instance, I said even theoretical knowledge of recurrence changes one's whole relation to recurrence. And how deep he knows. There are many degrees. Well, try to ask something interesting.

Q. Is recurrence changed according to ability of person to use higher parts of centres?

MR. O. We cannot speak so definitely. Exactly this kind of question becomes too definite to serve as material.

Q. There seems to be an infinite number of possible recurrences for different people. What law operates then so that everyone fits in the right place?

MR. O. What will answer you? I don't know. I should say, for instance, different capacities of understanding. Some people already came to some understanding, others did not come. Some already understood so much that repetition would be useless.

Think about some of these ideas, but don't think you know. There are many variations, many possibilities. Think, because there is nothing more important for you.

Q. Man is subject to so many laws he can't escape.

MR. O. That's one of the laws. Quite right.

Q. Do you mean that recurrence is a law?

MR. O. Must be. Many laws refer to recurrence, not one.

Q. After reading of lectures people always ask if great poets have being of man 1, 2, 3. Now you say poet needn't do same thing.

MR. O. No. He may be great poet and yet not belong to objective art. Others less great may produce objective art.

Q. Do you intimate that eternal recurrence doesn't apply to all organic life but just man?

MR. O. We never spoke about cockroaches even in relation to recurrence. I think we can leave them alone.

Q. I was wondering if we could do something about what we are doing before death, it might help in next recurrence.

MR. O. Yes. What happens before may determine what happens afterwards in many different ways. This is not recurrence.

Q. What effect would hard work on stopping thoughts have on recurrence?

MR. O. Right or wrong, there is promise behind it.

Q. You say if one really accepted theory of recurrence it would make a difference.

MR. O. If one studies. If one works. There is material for understanding. We use understanding and lack of understanding. If we think enough we may understand something, and we actually change recurrence.

* * *

Monday. February 24th 1947. (Colet Gardens.)

MR. O. Well. Any questions? Anything?

MR. A.W. [to audience] Are there any questions you can ask?

MR. O. No, it is not moment or day for questions. [Pause.] Well, what you have?

Q. What do you expect from us, Mr. Ouspensky?

MR. O. At present I expect some work.

Q. Is that the question? Are you asking what we expect from you?

MR. O. No, I am sorry, I cannot answer this question. You already must expect something. Otherwise there is nothing to come here.

Q. From observations I have made in the past, I have come to the conclusion my present state of being is very unsatisfactory and inharmonious, and I would like to know how I can learn to pay more attention to my inner organism and develop in myself some permanent form of unity and harmony.

MR. O. Yes, I understand. It comes to that.

MRS. R. How can I make the ordinary help the extraordinary?

MR. O. We speak about ordinary and about extraordinary. But first we must decide how we can begin.

Q. Do you wish us to continue with the programme you gave us in 1940?

MR. O. Programme? I don't know programme. Which programme?

MR. A.W. [to Mr. O.] Programme which you gave in 1940.

MR. O. No, I don't remember.

Q. I want to know how to find wisdom.

MR. O. Where [? to find wisdom]? So far that I don't know where to begin.

Q. At certain moments I become aware that greater happenings are going on somewhere behind my ordinary life, and that I am meant to be playing some part in them; but I cannot keep these feelings. My life is passing, and I do not know what part I am meant to play. Is there any method of increasing these experiences and my understanding of them?

MR. O. Well, maybe . . . [words not heard]. So I can't say anything. But question is . . . [words not heard].

Q. How can I learn to become useful to the work?

MR. O. It would be very good if we find example and start with that.

Q. Can I learn to control my mind?

MR. O. Maybe far, but in any case it is possible.

Q. Can we hear some more about the enneagram?

MR. O. No.

Q. We have for years been trying to make our own efforts, and have met in groups to keep together and keep the work alive. We have been waiting for guidance from you.

MR. O. Without method it is useless. To begin without method is quite useless, so it is useless to [speak] about that. No way to begin. There were many things explained. Some . . . [words not heard]. There was no method to begin. Well, if you would tell me what you want it would be possible to come somewhere.

Q. We have been trying to follow out the teaching you gave us years ago.

MR. O. I gave no teaching.

Q. You told us certain things to help us.

MR. O. You misunderstand.

Q. Where can we begin to work now?

MR. O. I will see what you want to know and where you want to begin, and then we will see first step, and perhaps we will find second step. We don't know first step, that is the question. That you must remember.

MRS. L. I feel that life is so uncertain that I want something in myself that can be independent of anything that may happen.

MR. O. There is no such thing. Please give more material.

Q. You always stressed that what you gave us before the war was ideas and a system, but you said in order to work there are three lines of work necessary and school necessary. Can we hear more about that?

MR. O. Yes, time will come when we will have to speak about it.

Q. Can we have your replies repeated? It is very difficult to hear.

MR. O. Some time, maybe. [Here Miss Q. repeated question.] Well, some day I will be able to say something. Well, at present I cannot say anything.

MR. M. Are you willing to learn from me? I have a message for you. Are you willing to accept it?

MR. O. No.

Q. Why are we here?

MR. O. That you must ask yourself first of all.

Q. You represent to us reality. How can we become more real?

MR. O. You must find what is not real in you. What can be more real.

MISS W. Is it possible through teaching to learn to discriminate what is real and what is not?

MR. O. I don't know for whom. First question you . . . [words not heard].

Q. How is it possible to feel aim as a driving force in one's life?

MR. O. Depends whose aim. And why, and how, and where one begins: where one wants to begin.

Q. You told us how to begin, and now you say you gave us no teaching. I do not understand that.

MR. O. I don't know. I generally forget things that have no immediate connection with present, so I don't know where to turn, where to look for beginning.

Q. Can you tell us how to escape? I have a constant feeling that life is a trap and I want to get out of it.

MR. O. That needs explanation. Why a trap? What is opposite to trap? That must be understood.

Q. We are trapped in our limitations.

MR. O. Yes, but one must know where to begin. Even if it is one's own limitations.

Q. Is there a reason for our helplessness to help ourselves?

MR. O. I beg your pardon? I don't understand it.

Q. What is the aim and purpose of esoteric schools?

MR. O. Oh, that is very big thing . . . [words not heard]. Maybe not.

Q. The ideas given to us by working on them have produced in me a certain change of attitude. How can I increase this change of being?

MR. O. I don't know. Not like that. [? Plain] words. Necessary more material, to know what you speak about.

MISS W. I want to know how to get nearer these moments of inner quiet and clearness.

MR. O. No, too big. I can't do that. There is no way to that.

Q. How am I able to use, co-ordinate, and control my many and diverse natures?

MR. O. Necessary to prove them . . . [words not heard] . . . your own measure. Well?

587

Q. The only thing in my life which is wholly different is an occasional very strong emotional feeling. Is it of value?

MR. O. May be different. More valuable. Less valuable.

MRS. F. I have noticed that certain things, such as love for another person, or certain forms of exercise, can make one feel more intensely, live more intensely, and in between these moments one drifts, or is bored. I would like to be able to live intensely all the time.

MR. O. Very good if you can. But if you cannot measure this you cannot—how to say that—make it bigger, or longer—I don't know—then you don't know where to begin.

Q. I find it extremely difficult to formulate what I want. Is there any way in which I can be helped to formulate that?

MR. O. Yes, certainly. But sometimes things can be determined, defined. One must begin from known.

Q. What did you say?

MR. O. You listen. Perhaps you can catch.

Q. I should like to be more conscious, but I find this continual turning of thought prevents me. The moments I have been able to quieten the continuation of thought, I have definitely had an emotional feeling and a feeling of life around me, but I can only stop it for a second. Can you help me towards that?

MR. O. That may be seen.

MR. A. Why is it so hard to begin?

MR. O. What? Hard? About what? To begin what?

MR. A. To lead a different life?

MR. O. Why different life?

MR. A. To change oneself.

MR. O. I don't understand.

MR. A. To understand this life.

MR. O. That depends what. And if you ask me I may be able to answer it.

Q. I am very anxious to work, and I want the tools. Are those tools to be given to me, or am I to find them myself?

MR. O. It depends what you want.

MR. M. Are you going to publish *Fragments*, or are you going to be content to go down to those yet unborn as having broken your promise and worked against esotericism?

MR. O. I don't understand.

MR. M. May I explain?

MR. O. [to Miss Q.] Do you understand?

MISS Q. No.

MR. O. Well, leave it.

MRS. J. I am aware that there are times when I can feel and think and know things more clearly than at others, and I wish to know the very first step to enable me to help myself in the times when I am less clear.

MR. O. I don't understand. [Miss Q. repeated.] That is [? most]. So it is difficult to find the . . . [words not heard].

MISS N. How can we know ourselves better, and be more honest?

MR. O. That is the whole thing. We always want some special moment. Understand that any moment is good.

Q. What is the thing that we can do at any moment?

MR. O. That you must find for yourself. If you speak about yourself you must think . . . [words not heard].

Q. When you went away you left us a message to stop thought as often as we could.

MR. O. Why? For what purpose?

Q. As work.

MR. O. Must be some reason. No, it is rather complicated. What is the reason to stop thought? Well?

Q. I still find it very difficult to do so.

MR. O. Very good. Very good that you find it difficult. Other people find it easy.

Q. Have you any plans for the future of the work?

MR. O. Which work?

Q. This work that you have told us about.

MR. O. I don't speak in general about work.

Q. You have given us steps—man No. 4, and so on. You told us to make efforts, and these efforts are only one line of work. How can I get nearer?

MR. O. Which was one line of work? Which is second line? What it is?

MR. M. Are you going to publish *Fragments*?

MR. O. No.

Q. Is it possible to change being without discipline, or is discipline necessary?

MR. O. Probably necessary.

MR. L. Whenever things are comparatively difficult in life, and one encounters adversities, I find one is a bit more aware of facts, what is going on in ourselves or around ourselves. When things are easy one goes to sleep so comfortably. Isn't there such a thing as an alarm clock?

MR. O. I don't know. Please?

Q. When I am with people who know more about the work than I do, I can stop certain things happening to me for a short time. Can I do anything on my own?

MR. O. I don't know.

Q. We have been working on first line of work only all this time. Will it be possible to have the second and third now that you are back?

MR. O. Which is first?

Q. Work on oneself, I thought.

MR. O. May be last.

Q. Can you tell us again the way in which to change ourselves, to be less mechanical?

MR. O. No, I can't. I can't speak. That would be mechanical. Just talk, without any reason.

Q. If the reason is: one wants to change, to be different?

MR. O. Talk. Talk.

Q. What is wrong with us?

MR. O. I didn't say that anything is wrong. May be quite right. But necessary to start, to begin.

Q. If we say anything is wrong, will you believe us?

MR. O. Why should I believe or not believe?

Q. I meant, will you help us to get started?

MR. O. I don't know what you mean by 'started'.

Q. How can I empty my mind of trivial thoughts?

MR. O. I don't know. Maybe you have . . . [words not heard].

Q. Would a good place to begin be to assume that one knows nothing and does not know what one wants whatsoever?

MR. O. No, one cannot begin . . . no, you can finish with that.

Q. I would like to stop being the victim of circumstances. Can Mr. Ouspensky suggest anything to help?

MR. O. Why? You can help me? Or I can help? Please explain. I don't understand this situation.

MISS Q. I don't understand it either.

Q. You said just now that we must try to start from something known.

Do you mean what we feel that we know about ourselves? Because that is perhaps all I feel that is known: what we feel sure of about ourselves, that we are a certain sort of person to whom certain sorts of things seem to happen. Is this a useful way to try to look at how we are as a starting point?

MR. O. I don't see how there can be a general answer to that.

MISS N. How can we learn to use each moment?

MR. O. Why?

MISS N. To be here. Because one is not alive if one is not here.

MR. O. How can one prove that one is alive, even if one is here?

Q. Have you come back to help us to continue the work we had started before, or must we begin all over again?

MR. O. I don't know. Very difficult to explain, because first question is what you want. Only on the basis of that, something can be done.

Q. We do want something, or we should not be here to-night.

MR. O. This is not so. Many people come without any particular wish.

Q. I see more clearly what I do not want than what I do want.

MR. O. This is very good step. It may be, if you can explain better, then it may be that you can find what you want.

Q. You call this system the Fourth Way. I have chosen this way. How can I get on?

MR. O. I don't know.

Q. I want religious faith. Can you give it to me?

MR. O. No. Absolutely no.

Q. How does one begin to get to know oneself?

MR. O. Oh, that is another question. May be for many people different. It is possible to find out to begin with some reasons and causes—I don't know. Well, but it is possible to speak.

Q. To be more tolerant with other people.

MR. O. Sometimes more tolerant, sometimes less tolerant. I cannot make general rule. Maybe tolerant in one case becomes something different in another condition.

Q. I have been struggling all these years not to express negative emotion, and I do not express it nearly so often as I did; but I find that I have an inner layer of negative emotion which goes very, very deep, and although I do not express outwardly, my thoughts and my emotions are still inwardly negative. If I keep on trying on these lines, will it penetrate deeper?

MR. O. How can I know?

Q. May I ask a question about the Law of Accident and the law of fate?

MR. O. I am sorry, I cannot answer that question. Well?

Q. What shall we do to be saved?

MR. O. Saved from what?

Q. Being creatures of circumstance.

MR. O. Much to think about. There is much to think of, but where to begin, that is another question.

Q. Can you help us to understand self-remembering more? The more I try to understand it, the less I seem to.

MR. O. No.

Q. I want to be helped to know myself and to develop myself. That is why I am here.

MR. O. Well, very good. Well?

Q. Your ideas have shown me that there is nothing permanent within me. I want to know where to start from.

MR. O. To start? In what sense? I don't understand this idea of starting.

MR. H. I know what I want from the contrast of mechanicalness, but find it impossible to express it in words.

[Mr. O. nodded.]

Q. Is it possible to change a feeling of ill-will towards somebody into a feeling of kindness?

MR. O. I don't know.

Q. Mr. Ouspensky, I know that the ideas you gave me before the war have been of the greatest value to me. I do not want to ask you for any more information at the moment, because you gave me so much that I have not been able to see the tenth part of it. I would like to know, though, if conditions will be created for us now in which we can continue working in the same circumstances as we worked before the war?

MR. O. First I must learn teaching and then I will see what result of it will be, and so on, and so on. I must have more material. You must give more material. Otherwise I cannot say anything.

MISS W. If I make the necessary effort, can you teach me how to begin to understand myself?

MR. O. I don't . . . [words not heard]. May come to something. May come to nothing.

Q. I find that the answers are even more interesting than the questions, so may we have them repeated in the same way so that we can hear them?

MR. O. I will try. I am trying to do what I can. Well?

Q. Sometimes I seem to know what I want, but it so quickly fades away. How can I make it more permanent?

MR. O. Well, I can't explain better.

MR. R. How can I deal with the enormous identification with everyday work?

MR. O. Necessary to understand words. Must not use words without explanation. What means identification? So different in different cases.

Q. I believe you said that we should have to give you more material. How shall we go about endeavouring to give you this material?

[No answer.]

Q. In your opinion, has this meeting so far been a success?

MR. O. No, not yet. We may come to success.

MRS. A. How can I learn to use emotion so that it really changes my inner state, instead of disappearing without leaving any trace?

MR. O. What emotion?

MRS. A. Understanding; and compassion; or understanding and sympathy for people.

MR. O. Needs time.

Q. How can my pride, which seems to produce bad results, be of value in growth?

MR. O. I don't know.

Q. I want the power of great understanding.

MR. O. Very little you want!

Q. If I do not know what to work from, can you tell me what to work towards?

MR. O. Yes. I don't know. I can't continue. [Miss Q. asked if she should repeat question.]

Q. Will you please help us a little by giving a clue?

MR. O. Which clue?

Q. What you want us to talk about.

MR. O. I would like you to continue to talk in the same way. Then perhaps I will get something out of it.

Q. Would you like to know what we have been trying to do while you have been away?

MR. O. Yes, certainly. Only one real thing.

Q. I for one have made quite a lot of observations and found out what you told me is true for me. I know now that practically the whole of my day I am not aware of myself. I did not know that before until you told me to make observations about it, and I have made observations.

MR. O. Can you continue?

Q. Having come to that conclusion, what to do next?

MR. O. Well, very good. In any case one cannot prove this conclusion.

MRS. L. You said it was not possible to have something in oneself that was independent of the vicissitudes of life. But is it possible somehow not to be so attached to them, not to be completely dragged down?

[No answer.]

Q. Do you think that if everybody in this room had self-remembered since the moment they came in, there would not have been a single question at all?

MR. O. Maybe different.

MRS. J. I want to know the first step I can take towards the understanding of truth.

MR. O. Truth of what kind?

MRS. J. Truth which one feels with one's inner self.

[No answer.]

MR. J. I have been trying to ask myself what I am working for. In a narrow sense, so far as I myself am concerned, I think I know. In a larger sense I do not.

[No answer.]

Q. Is it possible to find the next step for oneself through observation?

MR. O. Very difficult to say. Is it possible . . . I don't know. I will try to come next week, and then we will see what we can do.

Q. What does it mean, to self-remember?

MR. O. That will be explained later, if I am able to explain.

Q. You have asked us, 'What do you want?', and I feel we can never get anything we want without paying for it. I feel I do not understand the currency of this, and this is the understanding that I want to grow.

MR. O. It may be if we speak another time we can come to that.

Q. In the present chaotic state of the world, is it really possible for enough people to be conscious to have any effect on it?

MR. O. No. Not mechanically.

Q. Do you want us to go on trying?

594

MR. O. Yes. Why not? You may ... [words not heard] ... enough energy and enough material.

Q. You said you would come again if possible next week. What can we do in the meantime?

MR. O. Well, prepare in the same way. Think about some questions, and see how we can apply better to them.

Q. What do you mean by material?

MR. O. Everything.

Q. Are these questions too personal?

MR. O. No. Quite right. They are necessary.

MR. W. I want to know my purpose in life. Is there any way or method I can get to know it?

MR. O. It is impossible to begin like that. Later we may come to that. In any case, if we have more time we can speak about. ...

Q. May we hope that you will be with us for some time?

MR. O. I may hope.

Q. I want to have a sense of detachment so that I see the world and everything that happens in it as one whole.

MR. O. Too far for me. But if we have time we may come to this sort of question. Well?

Q. So much of me resists the desire to change. How can I work against that?

MR. O. That I must understand a little more.

MISS B. I have certain bad characteristics which I wish to change. Can I get practical help towards this?

MR. O. Maybe.

MISS T. I feel I myself have failed so very badly while you have been away—I meant to do so much, and I have done so pitifully little.

MR. O. Not necessary. [?]

MR. P. I find that I notice weaknesses in myself quite frequently, but I do not really feel them with enough strength, so that I do not feel convinced the whole time that they are real weaknesses.

MR. O. Quite right. Quite right. You may look for weaknesses and may find weaknesses.

MR. H. Can we make up our mind by our own efforts as to what we want?

MR. O. You may try.

MR. H. I find I cannot successfully.

MR. O. Success nobody can know. Not once, not three times, but needs more time.

Q. Can you have a true self-critical mind of your own thoughts and actions?

MR. O. I don't understand. Who asks that? Well, we may come to such things.

Q. When one has a very difficult problem to try to settle, to try to think about, and one tries, one realizes that one cannot think about it properly. You are pulled first one way, then another, by stray thoughts coming in and out of your mind. Is it possible within a reasonable space of time to improve the thinking apparatus which we try to use to settle our various problems?

MR. O. Well?

Q. I feel we have dropped a very long way behind all these years, and it is very hard to bridge the gap.

MR. O. After some time.

Q. That is what makes me feel rather desperate: it is after some time, and it has been such a long time already.

MR. O. Oh.

Q. We are told that we should try and formulate what it is we want, but it seems to me that in my state it must be impossible for me to imagine the thing I want; but it is very possible to know what it is I want to get away from, because the information I have been given has shown me the state I am in.

MR. O. Sometimes it is good formulation. Must begin in this way. Well, I will try to come here next week. I hope to be here next week.

*　　*　　*

Wednesday. March 5th 1947. (Colet Gardens.)

MR. O. Some time we were meeting in New York; it was interesting because somehow it happened many people came that I knew before, but you know I was only six weeks in New York. People that I met in Petersburg, and they all happened to collect this day in New York. [Turning to Miss Q.] You remember this day? You have been there? I think so. Well. . . .

MRS. M. You said last week that it was useless to try and work without method.

MR. O. I beg your pardon? Please, who says that? I am sorry, I am speaking about different thing now. Not what I was saying last time. What began now? I don't know what I wanted to say. I was saying quite different thing, so it was not connected with what I was saying last time. Well, if you want to say something, please go on.

MR. J. I find at certain times between sleeping and waking and after working before I get home I hear or I see answers to problems I did not see before by hard thinking. How can I harness that?

MR. O. [to Miss Q.] Well, anything to say?

MISS Q. No.

MR. R. You have given me glimpses that the world and I are quite different from all I have ever believed, and I feel I need your help to extend these glimpses.

MR. O. What kind of glimpses?

MR. R. Glimpses that the world is not as I had believed it.

MR. O. Necessary to begin with that. How you can know?

I thought of what I was going to say. It was very interesting. I met many people I didn't expect. Several people quite unexpectedly without knowing one another, and they met. Most of them I met in Petersburg. All sorts. Or two or three. Well, I wanted to begin in that way. If you have anything, continue. I will try to continue myself.

MRS. B. Can I be told how to get rid of some of my own thought activity? Can I be taught how not to think?

MR. O. I don't know what you think. So it doesn't interest my speciality. If we find what we can talk about, perhaps we can find the way to [? it ? work]. But not straight away.

MR. W. I want a method by which I may know more about myself, in order that I may be able to change myself.

MR. O. I don't know such method. Aim. First of all, necessary to know your aim.

MR. L. How is it that one can change so little?

MR. O. [to Miss Q.] Well, is it finished?

MRS. M. There seems to be a very small part in me which occasionally can see my mechanicalness, and I feel it is only this part that has any possibility of change. How can I make it see that mechanicalness more often and feel it more deeply?

MR. O. Why do you want to see it? Why more often?

MRS. M. Because I feel unless I see I do not make efforts to change.

MR. O. I don't understand. If you don't like mechanicalness, then why you should see it? Really [or ? already] you should try not to see it. Anything else anybody wants? Doesn't mean that I can answer, but I will be able to know what kind of question interests you.

MRS. T. I want to learn to know myself, but when I try and see myself as others see me I only see what <u>part</u> of me wants me to see.

MR. O. Necessary to begin with that, and not to think about anything else. Begin with this. Then we can come to something else and can speak about it.

MR. H. Would it be true to say that the first thing I have to learn is the meaning of the word 'I will', with the 'I' and the 'will' both equally important?

MR. O. It will be lying to yourself. In order to avoid lying it is necessary to speak truth to yourself, and you know that you don't. . . .

MISS W. I have come to the conclusion that I simply do not know how a human being works.

MR. O. It is already arranged without your interference.

MISS W. Would it not be much more profitable to know how one works?

MR. O. Very long and very complicated.

MR. F. In moments of strong emotion I feel I have a place in the scheme of things or in nature. I should like to know if I have this place in the scheme.

MR. O. Well, who could say that?

MISS R. I want to live on the level of the great teachers of the world. I do not know how to get there.

MR. O. Very good. Very small thing you want!

MR. E. I do not presume to ask you to teach me or to give me one little bit of this precious thing which you hold, but what I would. . . .

MR. O. I don't own—I don't have—anything.

MR. E. But what I would ask of you is to give me enlightenment, so that I can adjust myself. I stand before a model. This model has been unveiled. When I go close to it, it is out of focus. When I draw away it is still out of focus. Sometimes it is between me and the light. When I walk round in a circle to get to the other side and I have the light behind me, the model again is obscured by my own shadow. I continue to get another angle, but the angle is again wrong. The adjustment in me is wrong.

MR. O. I don't understand what you say.

MR. E. I am asking for enlightenment. How I can adjust.

MR. O. I cannot do that. Needs long work. Long work, and very difficult work.

MR. E. How can I work at or work from. . . .

MR. O. I don't know. I cannot say that. I don't know.

MR. E. Bear with me one moment longer. I ask this for myself, and maybe for others, and I say this with humility. Will you let your light so shine before men that they may see your good works?

MR. O. I don't know. Well?

MRS. C. We have been told man changes his direction without knowing it. Is it right we have changed the direction of our work in the system without realizing it?

MR. O. I don't understand it.

MRS. M. How can we begin to understand a little of what is necessary to change ourselves?

MR. O. I don't know. Some people may know. They can ask questions. Maybe that I will be able to answer them. But they must know something they want.

MRS. L. Can one find what one wants when you try to observe your thoughts? I find if I try to think about some particular subject there are such a stream of thoughts.

MR. O. No, not that way. Please, let other people speak better. Perhaps they will say better what they want. I must understand; if you want to ask me about anything, I must understand you.

MR. C. I find that my efforts to change seem to be directed towards removing parts of my personality which complicate and distort. I feel if I could see my personality as it is and see it with disgust, then I might be able to change something fundamental. But I do not know how to do that. I cannot get beyond that.

MR. O. Well, may be quite right.

MRS. M. I have no will power at all. I cannot tell what I want.

MR. O. Necessary to create some kind of will.

MR. N. Sometimes I feel my actions are violating the intended pattern of things, but I cannot help myself. How can actions be made to obey such a relation?

MR. O. I don't know. There is no such simple method.

MR. A. Sometimes I understand things logically, and other times, very rarely, I understand them more deeply.

MR. O. How do you know that it is more deeply?

MR. A. I feel more strongly at the time.

MR. O. It doesn't prove anything.

MR. R. Is our mistake in always running away from reality into illusion?

MR. O. I don't know. Probably, yes.

MR. R. I mean, for instance, if I am bereaved, instead of facing the sorrow I run away to some illusion, some -ism, something that will cause me to believe for the time being in the survival of the one I have lost.

MR. O. I don't know.

MR. R. Death seems reality, whereas the thing I try to believe I really do not know and do not understand.

MR. O. Well, we never understand anything. [? Might be better, then, that way.]

MRS. P. I want to understand the real meaning of Christ's teaching. Is it possible that in getting to know myself better. . . .

MR. O. No, it is quite impossible. Don't think about it. Nobody ever understood, and nobody will understand.

MRS. E. I want to drop, like dead leaves off a tree, those parts of me which can never exist, so that they may no longer distort that person in me which wants to exist.

MR. O. [Either] Probably it will happen later. [Or] Probably it will happen like that.

MR. H. Is a realization of where we go wrong a first step towards improving oneself?

MR. O. I don't know. Why we start with certain suppositions which we cannot verify, and we cannot base anything on them?

MR. J. Is the [?] the first step towards getting knowledge beyond what I already know?

MR. O. I don't know. How can I say?

MRS. S. I often try and solve my emotional problems with logical thinking. My emotions do not understand logic. Can one become more united so that the different parts understand each other better?

MR. O. Why are you so sure that it is not understanding? Why they don't understand one another? Perhaps they understand perfectly well. [Another shorthand note has, 'Why are you sure that the different parts do not understand each other? Perhaps they understand perfectly well.']

MISS H. I believe one should start by finding what is real in oneself. So far I have found one thing. That is a kind of conscience, in that I am never satisfied with what I am.

MR. O. 'Kind of conscience' is a very big thing. Well?

MR. K. I should like to learn to bring my thoughts and emotions under control.

MR. O. They are different. Different things. They don't go together.

MRS. F. Is there a limit to what we can do through ourselves if we are not in a school?

MR. O. I don't know what you mean by school.

MRS. F. Esoteric school.

MR. O. What means esoteric school? Only word.

MRS. F. I do not know of one.

MR. O. Then you are happy, because then you cannot find it.

MR. S. I think there is a part of me which at times seems to know something about an activity which lies behind and is different from the ordinary activity of my life. I want to know whether it is possible to increase that part of me which seems to know different [or ? this], and to enable it to become more active in that direction.

MR. O. I don't know.

MR. D. What can I do to become better, even although I do not understand anything?

MR. O. I would be quite satisfied to become worse. I don't know how to do this.

MR. T. Some of the 'I's want to develop. How can they be stimulated at the expense of the 'I's which do not? [Miss Q. repeats question.]

MR. O. [to Miss Q.] You say one thing, and he says another. Please repeat. [Miss Q. repeats.] What does it mean? Do you understand it or not? [Miss Q. does not answer.] Do you, I ask you, understand it or not? [Still no answer.] Well, you also don't understand. I don't understand if you don't.

MR. T. Can one encourage the desire to change?

MR. O. Why change? First, idea of change. Why necessary to change?

MR. R. I see many things in myself which do not work properly, and very few things which do.

MR. O. Well, why not be satisfied with what you have?

MR. R. When life seems like a vicious circle of things which go on repeating themselves in spite of all efforts, is it not natural that one should want to change?

MR. O. Well, you must first of all decide yourself what you want to change or not to change, and can we change or not.

MR. R. I cannot. I have tried too long.

MR. O. Well if you can't, you can't. But you don't want.

MR. Z. I want to feel really the confused state in which I exist, so that I can make greater efforts to get out of it.

MR. O. I don't know. Who spoke, and who, or what? Well?

MR. L. When I look back at my life I find that nearly everything happens to me without any doing of my own. Isn't it a possibility that I can do a bit more myself?

MR. O. I don't know.

MISS W. I want to change because I am dissatisfied with myself as I am, and I believe there is something better which one could become.

MR. O. Why become better?

MISS W. I have an accumulation of bad thinking, automatic habits. I want to get rid of these and start again.

MR. O. In order to get rid of it, it is necessary to get, to acquire more and more things. [The other shorthand note adds something here about 'worth while'.]

MR. C. Could you repeat these last words?

MR. O. I cannot repeat. Otherwise it would be same things repeated and repeated. I cannot repeat. This is the third one, and it must stop.

MR. B. I ask this. Where and how may I find guidance to the threshold of my own knowledge?

MR. O. [to Miss Q.] Well, do you understand it or not?

MISS Q. No.

MR. O. But you must be able to repeat it.

MRS. R. I spend all my days doing jobs with only half my mind, and doing them badly. It would be a beginning if I could pay attention to what I was doing at one moment at a time.

MR. O. Don't do anything. With attention. You understand?

Q. What is the first practical step for self-realization?

MR. O. Learn first step. Then we can talk about it.

MISS U. I am being continually reminded that life is very short here. I should like to learn to use my life in a way which would bring more satisfaction to myself.

MR. O. Quite wrong. Very long. Quite enough time.

MR. CO. When it is possible for one moment to stop thinking, and it is very seldom possible. . . .

MR. O. No, it is impossible.

MR. F. Is life long enough to know really what one wants?

MR. O. If one wants real things one has quite enough. Well, anything else?

MRS. M. Can I learn to avoid waste?

MR. O. I didn't hear. Could you follow? [Miss Q. repeats.] I didn't speak about that. What they said before. Please, go on. I will try to answer.

MISS N. I want to see my position.

MR. O. Nobody knows. Nobody understands. This is most difficult thing.

MR. V. I know I am a machine and that I cannot work by myself.

MR. O. Who told you that? Don't believe anybody who tells you that. Somebody else can believe it or not. I don't understand. But that is a question of faith—believing.

MR. F. Why do we constantly presuppose a thing before we formulate a question?

MR. O. Well, why?

MR. Y. I have occasionally realized deeply that I am a victim of circumstances, and not really as a result of my own volition. I should like to realize this more clearly so that my desire and control could grow.

MR. O. I don't know.

MR. H. Is effort the key to our difficulties?

MR. O. Sometimes, but not always.

MISS A. Is there any time when one should not make efforts?

MR. O. Plenty of time, but it depends on people. Cannot speak in general. One case, one better; in another case, another.

MRS. J. Can one learn in one's own case?

MR. O. Yes, certainly. Only in your own case. You can learn only for yourself.

MR. A. How can one learn?

MR. O. Different. That is what I say. How can I say? Impossible to describe.

MRS. D. I feel method and discipline are necessary.

MR. O. There is no method, and no discipline.

MR. CO. Is our chief trouble ignorance?

MR. O. Some people think different. They don't think at all.

MR. V. How is it possible to start work?

MR. O. One must know what one wants.

MR. M. If one starts with 'Thy will be done' and the Lord's Prayer, what effort can one make to make that more real?

MR. O. I don't know. I never quote New Testament, and cannot repeat it.

MISS P. When trying to self-remember, do you use the intellectual part of emotional centre?

MR. O. Who said I am trying to remember myself? I never said that.

MR. F. Have we a common basis, a common want?

MR. O. No, no—all different.

MR. F. How can one become more conscious?

MR. O. We don't know. We don't have even this small point from which it could come.

MISS T. Why is it so difficult to realize what one wants? I know what I want to get away from but my aim is not good enough, I know.

MR. O. Then there is nothing to speak about.

MR. H. Must one start by thinking, and if so what is thinking?

MR. O. [Gesture of 'I don't know'.] We have ... too long to explain. Cannot spend time like that. How people can spend time on anything like that! Well?

Q. I want to learn how to think properly all the time.

MR. O. [to Miss Q.] Do you understand the question?

MISS Q. No.

MR. O. Then you remember it for another time.

MISS D. I never remember intensely enough, or long enough at a time, what my thoughts are, so that I do not have a great deal of will. If I remembered a lot, would more power come?

MR. O. Maybe. Maybe not. There is no proof.

MR. I. What do you mean by, 'All our wants are different'?

MR. O. Well—several people—one says one thing, and another says another. But this is quite good example of certain situation.

MR. I. Everybody's want is more or less the same colour. People seem to imitate each other.

MR. O. Well—or even don't imitate. Well?

Q. I find I can watch myself on and off for one or two days, and after that the part which watches goes to sleep.

MR. O. Well?

MISS N. I want to be able to distinguish fact from not-fact.

MR. O. What is a fact?

MISS N. I don't know.

MR. O. Then what you don't want?

MR. C. In the first moment after I have been very deeply asleep, I feel a little more aware of myself. Is it possible to prolong that moment?

MR. O. I don't understand. What means asleep? Why do you use this term?

MR. C. I meant asleep when I am not aware of what is going on through me. Sometimes I realize what is happening, and sometimes I do not.

MR. O. [to Miss Q.] Could you follow it?

MISS Q. I don't understand what you mean by 'the moment after being deeply asleep'.

MISS Y. I want to be able to control what I have got.

MR. O. Nobody can.

MISS Y. I mean, one has energy and wastes it.

MR. O. I don't know about that. That is your opinion, and another person probably has a different opinion.

MR. A. Is it dangerous to look closely into one's own thoughts?

MR. O. No danger.

MRS. M. One of the things which makes me want to change is that I have a very deep feeling of lack of unity in myself.

MR. O. Then you forget about it. Forget about everything.

MISS A. I want to know what prevents me from making effort.

MR. O. No need.

MISS L. I want to be able to think on a higher level.

MR. O. What means 'higher level'? Why do you like higher level? Is higher level better than other level?

MISS L. May I say better level?

MR. O. Who can know? Better level, or higher level, it is all words. [To Miss Q.] Well, can you follow?

MISS Q. I don't understand what the lady means by 'level' either.

MR. I. One of the difficulties seems to be that we do not understand one another. I have never understood anybody else and no one has ever understood me. Therefore we cannot help each other. Can we try and find someone who understands us like a doctor?

MR. O. Doctor? That is your business. Who is [? or 'Whose'] doctor you want? [To Miss Q.] Well, do you understand? I don't understand.

MR. U. Is the starting-point to learn to know oneself better?

MR. O. Yes, it may be.

MR. U. How can one do that?

MR. O. That you must ask yourself. [To Miss Q.] Can you follow? [Miss Q. repeats question.] I asked, could you follow it?

MR. R. Has the desire to change any value?

MR. O. Depends for which purpose. Not in general. Not as a general value.

MISS T. I feel I should have so many questions to ask, and then I realize that if I worked better many of those questions would answer themselves.

MR. O. Maybe. [To Miss Q.] Can you follow?

MISS Q. 'Work better'—what does that mean?

MRS H. Is learning to control your thoughts merely a matter of trying hard enough?

MR. O. Most cases probably. Maybe not.

MRS. D. Must one find one's own starting-point?

MR. O. Yes, certainly. First of all.

Q. How can I tell if my efforts are in the right way?

MR. O. Nobody can know. Necessary to try and try—and many times. Long time try. Without that, one can do nothing.

MR. R. By trying and trying, one can find the right way?

MR. O. One can listen.

MISS D. Can one learn anything about oneself by observing other people?

MR. O. Probably.

MRS. I. Sometimes I notice that things I dislike in other people are reflections of things in myself. I should like help to be able to notice it more often.

MR. O. I don't know. Necessary to know exactly that you dislike _this_ thing, first of all.

MR. U. What prevents one from knowing oneself?

MR. O. Either to be too clever, or. . . .

MRS. E. Apart from a few accidental moments, as far as I can tell I do not exist at all, but though I sometimes realize I do not exist, I do not [? act upon it], and I feel some practical work upon myself is necessary.

MR. O. I don't know.

MRS. J. I find great difficulty in thinking steadily. Is concentration the best thing to help me with this?

MR. O. I don't know that this is the right word. I don't know that I will use this word with the same meaning. [To Miss Q.] Do you follow?

MISS Q. [to Mrs. J.] Concentration: difficult word.

MRS. J. Can I say effort instead?

MR. O. I don't know. Not concentration in any case.

MR. N. Every time I formulate my aim it seems to be different.

MR. O. Very difficult to formulate.

MR. N. It seems to be a different aim every time I think about it.

MR. O. Also possible.

Have you any more questions that we can discuss?

MR. RU. The power is in me to develop my understanding and my awareness. How can I best use this power?

MR. O. How do you know power is in you?

MR. AD. Sometimes I realize that my life will not last for ever, and I want a process different from the gradual process of death.

MR. O. [to Miss Q.] Could you follow? [Miss Q. repeats question.] Well, could you follow it?

MISS Q. I don't know what you mean by process.

MR. AD. Life instead of death. Process means dying.

MR. O. [to Miss Q.] Well, have you got it?

MISS Q. Life instead of death is wanted.

MR. P. I think nothing will ever be possible for me until I can learn to live in the present moment. How can one train oneself to do this?

[No answer.]

MRS. A. I struggle hardest against something which I dislike in myself. This way I feel I might just try to live a more comfortable life, and if it is not related to something bigger than myself I get nowhere.

MR. O. [to Miss Q.] Well, could you follow?

MISS Q. I don't know how a comfortable life follows from going against what one dislikes.

MR. I. What sort of question do you want from us?

MR. O. When I hear similar question I will say, 'That is a question.'

Q. Is it possible to know what one wants until one has found it?

MR. O. Some people can.

MISS B. How can one find harmony? [Miss Q. repeats question.]

MR. O. [to Miss Q.] This is your question? [No reply.] This is my question now, and I have no answer.

MISS Q. What is meant by 'harmony'?

MR. O. It is musical term, nothing more. Well?

MISS D. People often ask me what I want to do and I never have an answer. Is it just because I am young, or will it always be that way? With more experience will I automatically find what I want?

MR. O. Maybe, maybe not.

MR. F. I feel that this very occasional strong emotional feeling which I get which seems to enter me is of value. Can you help me to increase that emotional experience? I want to do that. I do not know how to make the effort.

MR. O. What is the effort, and what prevents you from doing it?

MR. F. Because it does not seem to be part of my psychic make-up.

MR. O. Ugh, but this 'psychic make-up'! No, forget this word. You use wrong words, that is all, and you repeat them. Do not repeat other people.

MR. F. Is it possible to make effort by oneself?

MR. O. Yes, certainly. Only by yourself. Only possible. No other way possible.

MISS H. But you must have someone to help you.

MR. O. No, no, one cannot be helped.

MISS C. I do not belong to myself. How can I find mental independence?

MR. O. That is only in this case that you will have independence. If you say 'I', 'I', 'I'—believe only in yourself or something, it is all words, all words.

MR. U. What is effort? [Or possibly, 'What should we say instead?']

MR. O. I don't know.

MR. U. You said it was useless to say 'I'.

MR. O. I didn't say anything similar to that.

MR. R. I feel that seems to be the inherent mistake that you meant when I said I want to change.

MR. O. [to Miss Q.] Can you repeat it?

MR. R. I thought you implied that I have no significance.

MR. O. I or you have no significance?

MISS Q. I think the questioner is simply agreeing.

MR. O. I do not like to be agreed with.

MR. R. I was not presuming to agree, I was trying to find the source of my mistake.

MR. O. I don't know who finds it. Who can find in this way his mistake?

MR. N. How will I know when my aim is a useful one?

MR. O. For whom?

MR. N. For me.

MR. O. Ask yourself. You will know . . . probably—because I cannot guarantee.

MR. CA. Must I find out myself what type of effort to make in order to know myself, or can I be told?

MR. O. You may be told. It depends on different types too. Some people must [? be told, or, believe]. Some people must take things as they are.

MISS D. How is it possible to get physical energy out of listening to music or seeing a painting?

MR. O. I cannot answer this question. I have never understood music. That is why I cannot. Cannot answer exactly this question, about music. But there are things that have to be discussed before we can come to anything else.

MRS. C. I do not understand how much we can do by ourselves, because a man cannot do anything by himself. Is it only our efforts at self-remembering?

MR. O. I never heard about this self-remembering. Strange expression!

MR. RU. What is the nature of the universe around us?

MR. O. Ask somebody who understands it.

If we continue in that way we may find some method—not method—way—to come to certain conclusions, that we can speak about this, and not about that. Well, I may come another time.

*   *   *

Wednesday. March 12th 1947. (Colet Gardens.)

MR. O. Well, have you any questions—anything? We must avoid. . . .

MRS. R. I find that all the words I use are inexact and alter my meaning. Can I have any help in the translation of thoughts into a language which will not be misunderstood?

MR. O. Try Russian. Perhaps it helps.

Not last week, but seven years ago, when we met here. . . .

MRS. V. Has individual man any significance in the universe?

MR. O. Special question. We may come to many, many.

MR. C. Before you went away, I felt very strongly the possibility of increasing the degree of my awareness. I have a similar feeling again. Because of the interim period and my not having been at meetings, I feel that nothing can be done alone.

MR. O. Oh, yes. Only. Only necessary to start alone and come to something. Six or seven years ago we came to definite conclusion. We tried to avoid all usual questions, and we had some kind of system that we talked about, and then we came to the conclusion system would not help. So that is how we began at that time, and I think we came to something now.

So that we come to questions, please, speak, anything that you like, and either we can begin like that, or we don't begin [?] any time in any way.

MISS R. What is it can change man?

MR. O. This is a big question. If we knew what will change man and how to do it, then we would begin at once, without any difficulty.

MISS R. You have told us some of the things towards it.

MR. O. I don't think I have. What it was? Who was that speaking?

MISS R. You told us to try and do certain things.

MR. O. Certain things? Which certain things?

MISS R. For one, to try not to express negative emotion.

MR. O. I never said that. Did you do it?

MISS R. Sometimes. Not very often.

MR. O. How often? I think we stop at the. . . .

MRS. Y. Can you tell us the first step we can take to escape from man's mechanical descent?

MR. O. No, I don't know about such things at all. We tried to speak about it, but nothing came out of it. Six or seven years ago.

MISS W. Is there a part in us which can change?

MR. O. I don't know.

MISS J. If we know our aim, can you tell us how to start towards it?

MR. O. If I know your aim, perhaps I will be able to say something.

MRS. K. How can I find a permanent aim?

MR. O. Find an impermanent aim first. Why you begin with permanent aim? It is very difficult and very long. How can you find it?

MR. EA. Can one find a permanent aim by seeing one's situation, seeing what one is?

MR. O. I don't know. Depends what means permanent aim.

MR. EA. An aim stronger than those which we ordinarily know in life.

MR. O. Why these aims are bad? Why they cannot be used? If you cannot find permanent aim, why not to begin on impermanent?

MR. C. My aim is to increase my awareness.

MR. O. Why increase awareness? Enormous thing.

MR. C. In order that I may find the first step.

MR. O. I don't know.

MR. V. The more I try and think, the more it becomes apparent that I don't think at all, and do not know anything.

MR. O. Well, you have to begin with anything.

MR. FA. How can I become useful?

MR. O. Useful to whom?

MR. FA. To you.

MR. O. Oh, I don't know. I want many things. How can you begin to be useful to me? I don't know.

MRS. C. I have learnt that knowledge is useless for me without understanding. How can I learn to understand?

MR. O. I don't know.

MR. NA. When the system existed, I felt that I had a technique and a discipline which might help me to become something. Now that seems to be gone. How can that be replaced?

MR. O. I don't know.

MRS. U. Is fear a natural instinct?

MR. O. For some people.

MRS. U. Is it the root of many negative qualities?

MR. O. I don't know.

MRS. D. Is there a danger of your teaching. . . .

MR. O. Which teaching? I don't know. I advise you not to take any teaching just like that.

MRS. J. I have been trying to think only of what I know, and while I find that ordinary knowledge comes through my senses and logical thinking. . . .

MR. O. Very good. Sooner or later you may come to something.

Well, Dr. R., you had some questions. What kind of questions?

DR. R. There were some questions starting from your book.

MR. O. Oh, it is old story. Stories from books can be repeated and repeated, and nothing comes out of it.

DR. R. There was another question, that 'I think there is something lacking in me'. This man said, 'I feel an unreal person. No character. No solidity. Is there a way to arrive at this?'

MR. O. Please, you start with nothing?

DR. R. But I have to discover things before I can have something.

MR. O. I don't know. In this case question is what you want, and what you may want must be something permanent. Anything.

MRS. Y. I want to escape.

MR. O. Escape where, and why?

MRS. Y. I want to escape from mechanicalness and sleep.

MR. O. Probably impossible.

MR. WO. Is it possible in one lifetime to gain some freedom from the conditions that fix me in my present state?

MR. O. How can I know? Everybody has only one life, or one can speak only about one life.

MR. X. The basic facts of self-control and self-denial are more [?] pleasant and more [?] rewarding than self-indulgence. That surely is a paradox in terms. Doesn't that imply the existence of laws of which we know very little?

MR. O. I don't know.

MR. I. How can I learn to know the right part of myself and to listen to it?

MR. O. The thing is I don't know what you want—even first step.

MRS. L. I can see now everything about me is false, and the part of myself that I can rely upon is so small that it is very difficult to hold on to it, and I hardly ever can keep my centre of gravity there.

MR. O. Too many things at once.

MISS S. I feel a need of being able to find a way of beginning again with what understanding I have, but I don't seem to know how to think about this.

MR. O. So it is the same thing. [?] repetition.

MR. U. I should like to know the result of my decisions and actions prior to making them.

MR. O. You want something! You must ask me something I can answer.

MR. U. But I find I am quite incapable of making any right decision or any real thought.

MR. O. And what else?

MRS. Y. How can we start now to change?

MR. O. About change, it is another thing. Almost . . . if I have . . . you have nothing to change.

MR. F. How can I learn to help myself to keep a certain want permanently before me, to the exclusion of other wants?

MR. O. How can you do that? Nobody can.

MR. M. Is it ever possible to collaborate in this?

MR. O. No, no two people. One person. I spoke about one person.

MR. W. If I feel my existence to be unstable, is it sufficient aim to wish it to become stable?

MR. O. May be stable just the same.

MR. T. Is there a reason or purpose behind my existence in this world, and if so what is that reason and purpose?

MR. O. That is your question, and you must answer it.

MISS I. Are we asking you the wrong sort of questions?

MR. O. Quite, quite wrong. Begin with any simple question.

MRS. H. Is it a waste of energy when one is doing a job to allow one's thoughts to be concerned with something else, or should one think about the job?

MR. O. If they continue to keep you at your job, then you can be very successful.

MISS S. How can I become simple enough to be able to see more clearly and be able to ask real questions?

MR. O. Try. Try. Only they must be real.

MISS I. Have there been any real questions?

MR. O. Oh, that is your question.

MRS. WO. What is the proper function of humanity?

MR. O. [turning to Miss Q.] Can you know? Do you know? [Turning back to people in hall.] What can I say about it?

MR. AN. I want the most immediate thing. I don't want to drift on the past or dreams of the future. I want to live well and fully in the present.

MR. O. Well, continue in the same way. If you ask this, it is interesting, and then there is material to begin with.

MRS. I. I want to be real.

MR. O. What means real?

MRS. I. I don't want to live . . . [?] . . . myself and other people.

MR. O. I don't know.

MR. NA. How can I learn to tell what is right for me and what is wrong for me?

MR. O. I don't know. These are no kind of questions that I can answer. [To Miss Q.] Can you follow?

Well, Dr. R., are these questions that you asked, ones you heard before? I cannot answer them.

DR. R. Yes.

MISS F. I want co-ordination of brain and energy. Is there any way to achieve this?

MR. O. No, I don't know any way.

MRS. D. In the present world chaos, is there any danger of losing all that hidden knowledge can give us?

MR. O. I don't know. How can we lose what we don't have?

Q. I want to feel more, and be able to have control over impressions.

MR. O. I don't know how to reach it.

MRS. J. As well as ordinary knowledge, I feel aware of another knowledge in me, which goes against my ordinary feelings and thoughts, and which seems to come from another source.

MR. O. I don't know about that. Comes to the same thing, the system that we spoke about. And nothing came out of it.

MR. AS. I seem to be missing most of my life. Can I find a way of living more of it?

MR. O. Why don't you continue to live as you lived before?

MISS R. Can one start afresh?

MR. O. Probably, nobody. . . .

MISS R. One seems so tied up with everything that has gone before. Even the things one has heard before seem to prevent one asking questions.

MR. O. I don't know about it. One must know oneself what one can know and what one cannot know. But you must know something to begin with. One cannot begin without beginning.

MR. N. How can I know what is right and wrong in myself?

MR. O. Nothing is right: nothing is wrong. But if you talk about it—right and wrong—it is always wrong, always wrong.

MISS R. I do know one thing, and that is that I am very tired of being as I am, and I should like to know more how to become something.

MR. O. That means change.

MISS R. That is what the original question was that I started with to-night.

MR. O. I cannot say anything about it. I don't believe in change.

MR. A. Will you help me to become more conscious?

MR. O. Conscious? Such enormous thing! You must know a little to become even a little more conscious.

MR. D. Are you saying that you have abandoned the system you used to try and teach us?

MR. O. I never taught system.

MR. D. What are you going to try and teach us now?

MR. O. That we may see.

MRS. Y. Is the first step towards being conscious to have self-observation?

MR. O. I don't know.

MR. WO. What is it that prevents us from becoming even a little more conscious?

MR. O. Again I don't know. That is your business to find.

MISS I. What is will?

MR. O. What is will? I don't know that. I am too short . . . [words not heard].

MRS. Y. Is our approach wrong that we ask the wrong questions?

MR. O. Probably.

MRS. Y. What should be our first aim?

MR. O. To have a good question that I can understand.

MISS J. If we understood more, we should ask the right questions.

MR. O. Maybe, maybe not. I don't see the reason for that.

Q. How is it possible to learn what is reality and what is illusion?

MR. O. If I knew I would tell you. I assure you I don't know.

MR. J. I seek a knowledge beyond the ordinary. . . .

MR. O. What means beyond the ordinary?

MR. J. Beyond what I can feel with my ordinary mind, my logical mind.

MR. O. Why not to keep your ordinary mind?

MISS J. Is logical thinking valuable?

MR. O. I don't understand question. [Miss Q. repeats.] I said I don't know. It doesn't show anything. I am sorry to disappoint you, but I don't know, so. . . .

MR. D. What did you mean when you said you do not believe in change?

MR. O. That's all: I don't believe in change. One man is one and another man is another; I don't see it.

MRS. Z. Do you mean we cannot change ourselves into anything different?

MR. O. I don't know all worlds we live in, so how can I say? [Or perhaps it was, 'I don't know all worlds, all lives, so how can I say?']

MR. B. When I try to think of what I want, the only aim which really means something to me is an aim which I can understand. If I say I want to overcome certain weaknesses which I know, that is a real aim for me.

MR. O. I don't know. That means I don't understand.

MR. CO. People do change.

MR. O. Very lucky people.

MR. CO. So why shouldn't we?

MR. Z. The only permanent thing I know is something which makes me come here, to meetings. Is this a real thing?

MR. O. For you it is real, but for me it is not real. I cannot follow. I cannot understand. But we may come to understanding.

MR. L. How can one prove it, that it is real?

MR. O. It is impossible.

MR. NA. A long time ago you said that there were four possible ways to develop and that there was a fourth way in life. Is this still possible?

MR. O. When I said that?

MR. NA. Many years ago. Before the war.

MR. O. Oh, it was long ago. We went very far since that time.

MRS. D. If we could rid ourselves of some of the emotions and thoughts that spring from self-importance, then we could help others to rid themselves of these thoughts and emotions.

MR. O. No. . . .

MRS. H. Is the first step to try to know oneself?

MR. O. This is the first step. How can one say anything without knowing oneself? [To Miss Q.] Do you follow? Well?

MR. JA. All I really want seems to be entirely emotional. How can I express it or formulate it with my intellect?

MR. O. I don't know. Well, continue. Anything.

MRS. L. Can I learn to wear down and starve that big false part of myself?

MR. O. I don't know. There are people who teach this. What is the use of it, I don't know.

MR. C. For self-knowledge, is it important to try and remember and try and study what one has been in the past?

MR. O. No. One cannot remember what one has been. You don't go further.

MR. L. How can one stop lying? Even if I say I want something, it somehow does not seem really true.

MR. O. It may happen.

MR. MA. Because my observations have shown me how unsatisfactory my machine is, even for the ordinary things of life, I find I am stimulated to make efforts to remember myself if I know I have some particularly difficult piece of work to do.

MR. O. Well, necessary to find difficult pieces of work to do.

MR. MA. It seems to me this might be using work for the purposes of life, instead of life for the purposes of work.

MR. O. Purposes of life, or purposes of death, or anything. Use for anything—only use for something. [To Miss Q.] Well, can you follow?

MISS T. How can we understand better how to begin again?

MR. O. Nobody can. Nobody knows.

MISS A. You say you do not believe in change. You have never seen it. But some. . . .

MR. O. No, I never said that. If anybody says. . . .

MISS A. I want to ask a question about it.

MR. O. It may not be true. I don't know anything about change.

MISS Q. The lady wants to ask a question about change.

MR. O. I already said I can say nothing about change.

MISS I. Are our questions too theoretical?

MR. O. Simply don't refer to me.

MISS T. How can we understand better what you want from us?

MR. O. Simple things. Any simple thing.

MR. WO. How can we begin to know ourselves?

MR. O. This is very difficult question. Well, I answered.

MRS. C. Can I get anything from you?

MR. O. No, question if you like. Simple question.

MRS. I. I feel I am not in touch.

MR. O. I don't know what it means.

MR. S. If I ask myself honestly what I want, I find I get answers such as 'physical comfort', 'a good dinner', etc. Is this a useful observation?

MR. O. If you find it useful, for you. It depends how good judge you are. [To Miss Q.] Well, could you follow?

MR. K. You said that the beginning is difficult. Therefore there is a beginning.

MR. O. [shakes his head] It is not easy beginning.

MR. NA. What possibilities has individual man?

MR. O. Everything. He must know himself.

Q. Have you got some new knowledge to give us?

MR. O. No, no new knowledge; old knowledge.

MR. V. Is a sense of humour a wasteful or valuable asset?

MR. O. I don't know.

MR. V. Can you teach me to be more simple, less complicated?

MR. O. I don't teach simple. It does not work.

Q. How can one learn to become simple?

MR. O. I don't know. Words simply.

MRS. S. I want to become nothing, because I can only feel and understand things outside myself when I am not anything myself.

MR. O. I don't understand it.

MISS B. I want to know how, when my thoughts are still, how so often it seems as though there is blackness around me and I cannot get through that blackness.

MR. O. [to Dr. R.] Have you got some questions which you had?

DR. R. There was a question: Can we ourselves know what we have to discard, or what we can get without being told by you or someone who knows?

MR. O. How can I say for anybody else? What can I answer? Necessary to know what people want, and then you can say, can you answer it?

MISS H. I am so ignorant, I want to know things. To understand things.

MR. O. I don't know. Simple school. I don't know if it was a question for a simple school.

MRS. N. I think I know and feel my negative emotions. Is to try and stop justifying them the only first step I can take against them?

MR. O. They say so. I don't know about it.

MRS. W. I want to be able to find and keep the only small part of myself which is capable of understanding what is true and false.

MR. O. This is not small. This is very big.

MRS. W. Can you tell me how to make room for this?

MR. O. No, sorry. I can't do that.

MRS. U. If one could get rid of fear and obsession with the future, could one then live in the present?

MR. O. I don't know. Depends who he is. One man or woman can live, another cannot. But I have nothing to do with that.

MR. Z. Could you get help from people who have never heard of the system ideas at all?

MR. O. I always prefer people who have not heard about any system. It is possible to speak with them. Otherwise it is too complicated. They have not learnt so much.

MRS. X. What is reality?

MR. O. Nothing, probably.

MRS. Z. Are you telling us to forget all you have told us in the past?

MR. O. I am sorry, but I never told you.

MRS. H. How would you describe one who is living?

MR. O. I don't know. Many millions of people living.

MISS Y. I find the aims I formulate do not outlive difficult circumstances. Is it possible to find something I can put into practice?

MR. O. I don't understand what you mean by it?

MISS Y. For example, I find I want to be more free. But in practice, I cannot even control my voice.

MR. O. Then you must control your voice. First of all.

MR. Z. Can you give us a subject to ask questions about?

MR. O. You must know.

MISS W. Is what I call my conscience a real thing?

MR. O. You must try.

MRS. F. How can I save energy for what I think is important?

MR. O. Don't say what is not important. It will be important.

Q. Why have we to forget about the past?

MR. O. I don't know.

MR. E. Can you impart knowledge only in answer to questions?

MR. O. More or less.

MRS. M. Can one learn control? Or is it purely obtainable by one's own efforts.

MR. O. First of all.

MR. HI. Should one seek things beyond the ordinary things of everyday life?

MR. O. I don't know what other things.

MR. K. Is control of oneself the beginning, or a beginning?

MR. O. I don't know. This is your business. I cannot speak about another man.

MR. NA. Is it possible for man as he is to work on himself without a teacher, without school, without knowledge?

MR. O. He cannot, because he cannot begin. [To Miss Q.] Can you follow?

MRS. B. How can I increase the tiny part of me which wants to change?

MR. O. I don't know. How can one know which part of you would like to change?

MRS. U. Is enjoyment of life under all adverse circumstances a possibility?

MR. O. No, that is all words.

MR. NA. How can I begin to look for a standard of values?

MR. O. Find your own. Begin with that. With that we may start.

MRS. T. I want to be more peaceful inside and not so easily upset.

MR. O. Necessary to find cause of upsetting.

MRS. Y. If I try to observe myself when talking to people in ordinary life, I find I cannot do it long enough to be of value. Can you help me?

MR. O. You can speak long enough here.

MR. HI. Should I seek to understand things beyond what I understand now?

MR. O. That is your business.

MISS N. I know there is nothing permanent in me at all. Can I start from that?

MR. O. I don't understand. [To Miss Q.] Can you follow?

MISS Q. No.

MR. V. Can we receive help to understand ourselves?

MR. O. Not from me.

MR. NA. From whom, then?

MR. O. I don't know. I cannot say anything about such things.

MRS. U. Is sincerity of mind a measure to clarity of thought?

MR. O. No, no. No such question.

MISS K. At the first meeting, in answer to a question, you said there was no time—that time is limited. What did you mean by that?

MR. O. Well, two different things. One time said [or ? is] one thing, and another, another. That is all I can say about it.

MISS J. Are we listening to your answers properly?

MR. O. I don't know.

MR. RU. I want to discard selfishness. To know this, is that a step in achieving this?

MR. O. Try. You may try, and then you will know: can you, or can you not.

MR. NA. I feel now that without guidance there is a danger of making the wrong sort of efforts, trying to work on oneself in the wrong way. How can I find guidance?

MR. O. I don't know. There is no guidance for such things. I cannot follow.

MR. Z. Is anything likely to come of our asking questions in this way?

MR. O. I dare say. . . .

MISS T. If I say that my aim is to try and become more conscious, is that a simple and definite enough formulation?

MR. O. Very simple, and very definite. But impossible.

MRS. Y. What is possible?

MR. O. Ordinary things.

MRS. Y. What is the first thing that is possible?

MR. O. I don't know. I never knew.

MRS. Y. Is it different for each person?

MR. O. Certainly different.

Please, please. You answer only questions. My questions. Please, what was the question? Well, anything you have?

MR. JA. I feel there is one part in myself which I want to develop and preserve beyond this life and to use life to do it. How can I?

MR. O. Too complicated. Use life? I don't know. Well, what you can say about it? [To Dr. R.]

DR. R. I can only go on repeating questions asked me. Another one: Lady said she felt we were all living in complete chaos, and she felt that when she came here and saw this room and you came, that you could tell her what she wanted to know.

MR. O. How can I say anything?

DR. R. And she wanted to know what she had to do to be told.

MR. O. Very bad way.

MR. AN. I want direction that will be of benefit to my immediate energy.

MR. O. Please, can you repeat? Well, when I hear it I will see what I can say. At present I can say nothing.

MISS R. When you said the questions do not refer to you, what does that mean?

MR. O. Certainly they don't refer to me. Might refer to somebody else.

MRS. U. If one faces up to observing emotions, such as pride. . . .

MR. O. Cannot say anything. . . . Well?

MR. P. What form do you wish this work to take?

MR. O. Big, big words. [Or ? misheard as 'Big works'. v. inf.]

MR. DA. One of the reasons why I cannot be sincere with myself is because I make life too easy. But I don't see how to avoid this.

MR. O. I don't know. I cannot say life too easy or. . . .

MRS. P. I have never before felt such a need, that I cannot remember myself. That I am forgetting all day.

MR. O. I cannot help.

Q. Is there a possibility of bringing one's emotions under control?

MR. O. Everything is possible. We don't speak about impossible things, so it doesn't enter into it. . . .

MR. K. How and where can we meet these big works that you mentioned?

MR. O. Everywhere.

MRS. X. Why cannot Mr. Ouspensky give us direct help? Why is it so important for us to make the first step?

MR. O. I don't <u>have</u> help. Can't give help.

MRS. X. Is it that we have to help ourselves first?

MR. O. Yes, yes, evidently.

MISS J. We seem to be a very mixed group. If we tried and sorted ourselves out a little, could we get on better?

MR. O. I am afraid you will only create more mixture.

MISS N. Can we learn to be more humble?

MR. O. I never was humble myself, and don't know how I can.

MRS. J. Every day and everywhere I see things around me which I cannot understand by thinking in a logical way. Is there another way of thinking which I can learn?

MR. O. I don't know. I don't know.

Q. Do you yourself gain any knowledge from the assorted questions which are put to you, on the workings of the human mind?

MR. O. You can try.

MRS. Y. Is life apparently longer, if we live in the moment?

MR. O. May be.

MRS. Y. Is that where we start?

MR. O. You may start from that.

Well, Dr. R., I think I can say nothing now, because there are no simple questions, no ordinary, normal questions. There were some attempts at system questions—or supposed-to-be system, and there was nothing more. I would like first and secondly. . . .

MRS. E. I want to drop off those parts of myself which do not exist, so that part of myself. . . .

MR. O. No. I cannot give it to you or to anybody else.

MR. Z. What can you give us now?

MR. O. I can answer simple questions. Why you came? I was supposed to know how to answer simple questions.

MR. L. I don't like effort.

MR. O. Why? Why you don't like effort? How do you know? Well, necessary to begin, to start to like effort.

MRS. H. Is any sustained effort useful as a start?

MR. O. I don't know.

MR. H. The whole of me is always being enslaved by the different parts of me. How can I escape this slavery?

MR. O. How can I answer you?

Q. Am I right in believing that the possibility lies in every man or woman, or in every single soul, to understand what is true?

MR. O. I can only envy this man or woman, that is all.

MR. ST. I find that all my thoughts and understanding are coloured with system teaching from the past. How can I get away from this?

MR. O. I don't know.

MRS. A. I want understanding, and I feel that the way to this is to constantly bring my attention back to the present moment, but this alone is not enough. What else is necessary?

MR. O. That is all. All that you can say. All that you can repeat. And I can say nothing.

MR. AN. I want to become more cohesive. Natural mischief prevents it.

MR. O. I don't understand it.

MR. NA. How can I keep alive in myself a sense of the miraculous?

MR. O. I don't know.

MR. X. If one gives way to anger or emotion, and you feel ashamed of yourself afterwards, is that because you have gone against the teaching of your parents, and upbringing, or is it because you have gone against something else?

MR. O. Probably one or another.

MR. V. What should I learn about myself in order to enable me to ask a simple question?

MR. O. I don't know what it can be.

MRS. W. Why is it so hard to find the only part of oneself which is real at all?

MR. O. I don't know.

MISS M. What is it that controls me, as I so obviously do not?

MR. O. I don't. And I can deal only with simple questions. If we come to simple questions, then perhaps I will be able to answer them. I will be pleased to give Dr. R. all his answers, answer all questions, but I cannot begin like that, with difficult questions. Possible questions. Well, Dr. R., I go now.

Q. How are we going to find out what we want?

MR. O. I have already answered all questions that I could find words.

MRS. U. Why do we fear criticism?

MR. O. People always fear criticism. If anybody dares to speak. . . .

MR. Y. I want to like the people I now dislike.

MR. O. Well, I cannot help.

MR. CA. I don't know what you mean by a simple question.

MR. O. I cannot explain in two words or three words. But really it is very simple.

MR. AN. I have a need for something I have not heard before.

MR. O. Well, Dr. R. spoke.

Q. How can I get the courage to throw away worthless things?

MR. O. I don't know. Perhaps better keep them.

MRS. J. Should one first try to get rid of things one knows are not good in oneself?

MR. O. Do you know them?

MRS. J. I think so: I believe so.

MR. O. Well, you may try with them.

MRS. J. But sometimes I am not quite sure if they are wrong, and I have no means of knowing.

MR. X. What is courage?

MR. O. Different in different people.

MR. J. Is continual awareness of one's aim a means of gaining it?

MR. O. May be. Some people say that. Other people don't.

MR. JA. I want to establish contact with a school. Is that possible?

MR. O. No.

MRS. U. Would life be possible in this competitive world without our armoury of defensive emotions?

MR. O. Too complicated. This is not simple question. Very complicated.

MR. AN. Are simple words a key to simple questions?

MR. O. Sometimes. Not always.

MR. AS. When one is sure that there is something wrong in oneself, what can one do about it?

MR. O. One must think what one can do oneself first of all, and then continue.

Q. Can one work with more than one aim?

MR. O. Probably we can work only in several ways.

MISS R. I thought I had asked a simple question, but it was not so. How can one test one's own questions to oneself before asking them?

MR. O. You must ask yourself first. Well, I think I had better go. I am going now. If you have any questions I still may come. Dr. R. may persuade. He has capacity of persuasion.

DR. R. I cannot persuade you, Mr. Ouspensky.

MR. O. You persuaded me to come to answer questions. I said once I will try, that is all. But now I must go. Because it happened like that,

that I have no questions. I tried to persuade them, but they don't ask questions. [Here he was on his feet, and the next words may have been addressed to the whole room, or to someone in the front.] I hope to see you, if you want to see me.

MANY VOICES. Please do come. We want you to come.

* * *

Wednesday. May 7th 1947. (Colet Gardens.)

MR. L. I want strength to make more efforts.

MR. O. For what purpose? You have to begin with that.

MISS R. I have observed that when I break down my self-will something definitely happens. What is it?

MR. O. No. Please explain situation and perhaps we can start.

MR. M. I want a better understanding of myself and my position in the world. Can you help me to find out how I can get this?

MR. O. If there is aim, probably you will come to better understanding. More meaning, please give your words more <u>meaning</u>. What have you more you can get? More meaning, meaning.

MRS. S. May I ask how one can judge right from wrong?

MR. O. First of all judge for yourself—your own observation. Well, we tried to speak about it and then nothing came out of it, so therefore I came to the conclusion that as we are, in this condition it will not do.

MR. T. The question you asked us—what we want, is a very big question.

MR. O. Before I decide I must know what you want.

MR. T. By what means and work can one achieve the inner development and co-ordination necessary in order that one should not be one's own worst enemy and achieve peace and understanding?

MR. O. First of all discussion. It is quite right, but you have to begin somewhere.

MRS. S. You said we have to begin. Where is the beginning?

MR. O. Well, you have to begin from the beginning. Try to explain situation.

MR. A. You said that many of our questions do not refer to you.

MR. O. Yes, quite right.

MR. A. Is it because there is no understanding of a purpose other than one's own small purpose?

MR. O. I don't even see small purpose.

MR. A. I mean that the questions are based on the inevitable point of view—the personal one—and is it that they lack any idea of a larger purpose? Your purpose, or a possible purpose for everyone here?

MR. O. Well? Further.

MRS. J. I really want to know about how one can stop thoughts.

MR. O. Why stop thoughts? Why stop without reason?

MRS. J. Have wrong thoughts.

MR. O. And many other things. How can one know what is wrong and how to stop it?

MRS. F. Life is unsatisfying for me unless I can grow spiritually.

MR. O. What does it mean? What means spiritually?

MR. F. I want a standard of values which I can use to guide my actions so that they may be harmonious both to myself and others they affect.

MR. O. Could you repeat some of these occasions?

MR. R. How is it possible to improve memory?

MR. O. Oh, certainly, there are many ways. First of all, first question is why necessary to improve? How we can be improved—may be difficult—this is not first step. It will come after some time.

MRS. L. I want to learn to get my own knowledge.

MR. O. Must get it first.

MRS. L. I began by seeing how much I depend on other people's opinions.

MR. O. Necessary to remember, find cases where you stand.

MISS T. I know I want to change from what I am, but I have not got the right clear idea where I want to go.

MR. O. First necessary to realize more where to begin. Where the point is at which you can begin.

MR. B. I want to get free of the things in myself which spoil work and enjoyment and experience. How can I begin to do this?

MR. O. What spoils it? First of all it must be from that; which work?

MR. B. Work which I have to do—enjoyment of ordinary work.

MR. O. First of all, then, you must think about this work—why you don't do it.

MISS S. How can I get rid of real selfishness in myself?

MR. O. Perhaps it is a real thing. Why should you get rid of selfishness?

MR. J. I have knowledge of certain moments when I seem to understand a category of thought quite different from my normal thought, and I feel my difficulty is that I try to approach many things I really want from my ordinary thought.

629

MR. O. Well, that is the whole thing. Continue in the same way. Perhaps you can come somewhere.

MRS. A. Is one way to get what one wants to act as one would if one already had it?

MR. O. That is one way, but there are many other ways.

MR. E. I want separation or freedom from all that is me. I believe that exists at the same time.

MR. O. Try to find it, and then we can speak about it.

MR. E. I have glimpses of what I believe to be this separation.

MR. O. If you can speak with more details perhaps we can find it.

MR. E. I see clearly that I am tied all the time by habit and myself playing a rôle, and whatever new situation I am in, this 'me' adapts itself and destroys any possible new experience.

MR. O. Probably.

MR. W. Many of us have reason to believe that you have knowledge that would be very valuable to us.

MR. O. Necessary to find out what is wrong. What is here or there.

MR. N. Have we to break something before we can begin?

MR. O. Better, certainly, if you can begin in that way.

MISS R. Why cannot we think of two opposites at the same time?

MR. O. One can. Perhaps one can. Or one does not try.

MISS R. Is that the beginning? Trying to think about a thing differently?

MR. O. I cannot say for certain. But it must be tried in this way and in that way. In different ways.

MISS R. There is something in the middle all the time that is so difficult to get hold of.

MR. O. It doesn't mean anything. Explain it better—when it comes and in which cases.

MR. D. I want to get rid of fear.

MR. O. In most cases it is most difficult to struggle with that. But first of all it is necessary to see it—to understand what is fear. You cannot begin if you don't begin with purpose.

MISS R. I want to get out of the prison in which I live.

MR. O. May be easy, may be difficult. First of all it is necessary to see what is the situation.

MR. S. I want to destroy self-pity in myself.

MR. O. That can be easy if you really have intention.

MRS. E. How can I [?] my desire to be [?] without changing?

MR. O. Well, you have to do something about it.

MR. L. I want to be able to control my thoughts, but I have not the strength to make continuous effort to do so.

MR. A. What does it mean if a person knows what to do but does not do it enough?

MR. O. Well? Why does he not do it? That is the question to study.

MR. T. I feel one does an enormous amount of unnecessary things. One's thoughts buzz round everywhere the whole time, and I feel that one functions very badly. How can one start to co-ordinate this mess and make it work better?

MR. O. Begin with that and try to change it—insist on that.

MR. T. Try to see where one is most obviously wandering?

MR. O. Find examples.

MR. R. How is it possible to avoid repeating mistakes?

MR. O. Well, necessary to find one and another example and then it will be easy.

MISS D. How can I get inner peace?

MR. O. Maybe some things repeat. It will be easier to see. Aim. Aim. Must be some aim. [Referring to Mr. R.'s question.]

MR. T. With all the contrariness there is inside us and all the acting we do for ourselves and others, it is very difficult, even if one tries, to think about it, to realize which is the real 'me'.

MR. O. Quite. Yes, but can you begin?

MR. T. That is what I am wondering. We can judge a certain amount ourselves.

MR. O. Yes, quite right. After some time one can come to certain decisions. It may be useful to write it down—everyone for himself.

It may be useful if we meet again, suppose you write down what you have to say—what other people have to say. That may help. I don't say it helps for a long time, but it may help for a short time.

MR. P. I believe that when I want something I only want it because I am selfish and possessive. I need an aim which is outside myself.

MR. O. Right. Very good.

MR. H. How can I make my will come into action as quickly as my desire?

MR. O. Very good—we may see something from that.

MR. C. There are very rare moments when there is no past, no future. Can one increase them?

MR. O. May use them. That is all.

MR. T. It seems that one of the results of the various questions put is that we are beginning to feel that we have very little control over ourselves. From what point can we start to develop this control over ourselves?

MR. O. Quite. You can begin this way. Try something! Try.

MR. C. The only thing I have ever tried is trying to be still. Is that any good?

MR. O. Very useful.

* * *

Wednesday. May 21st 1947. (Colet Gardens.)

DR. R. [Reading.] I want an aim that has a permanent value. Part of that is to acquire a different kind of knowledge. I have had a taste of something different, and I want to continue to work in that way.

MR. O. Well, I would like to hear something like that, but not the same thing. It can be repeated, or what?

DR. R. [Reading.] How can I reinforce memory of my aim to be free?

MR. O. I think it is easy if one is serious about it. [Pause.] Come to something.

MR. H. Where does the urge come from that makes us all discontented with ourselves?

MR. O. That you must find. It is not my business to show.

MR. A. What is missing from the many wants that have been expressed?

MR. O. Everything is missing.

MR. U. If I say my aim is wisdom, knowledge, is that not concrete enough?

MR. O. Very concrete, but not for me. It does not refer to me.

DR. R. I feel that time is short. Will you show us a line of work that will help us to intensify our efforts?

MR. O. It is impossible. I cannot do that. Some reason necessary for that. I said there is none. I see no beginning. I see many [?] and so on. Cannot start with that.

MISS N. If one can learn to live in the present and there is no past and no future, is experience of any use?

MR. O. Useless experience, first of all.

MR. E. Some moments of experience have extension where opposites cease. I believe in those moments there is real knowledge. Is it possible to extend them longer?

MR. O. Maybe one find it, or one can choose. Perhaps. Well, maybe we will have continuation. No continuation of that?

MR. N. Everyone here seems to have an urge to [?] more about themselves. Does this urge come from a common source? It refers to you, since you would be amongst the people under the common source.

MR. O. [In middle.] Yes, yes, go on. [At end.] Probably. [Then.] I never can put myself in extraordinary position or anything like that. It would be greatest mistake.

DR. R. People who have been trying to do things tell me that they simply don't remember to go on with it. They forget every minute. They do it once a day. Is it possible to start by trying to improve memory in some way?

MR. O. Yes, if it is what I call memory. There are many misunderstandings about this.

MR. P. I was told that by changing my position while sitting I should remember myself more and be more aware of myself. I found this worked, but not enough.

MR. O. Quite right; quite right.

MR. P. Can you give us more methods of remembering ourselves?

MR. O. I just begin to say 'Quite right', because really it is necessary to start from that 'to remember'.

DR. R. If one tries to remember one finds that certain things stop it. One just thinks about it instead of doing it.

MR. O. Quite right. One remembers if one tries to make oneself remember.

MR. L. Does that mean we can remember ourselves if we really want to?

MR. O. In some cases.

MISS Q. Would it be necessary to distinguish the kind of memory of which you speak from ordinary memory, Mr. O.?

MR. O. No, no, there is no question about memory.

MISS Q. The important thing is, why does one forget, why does one not remember?

MR. O. You begin quite well, but please, there is no continuation.

MR. C. When we remember we make up little stories about what happened, and the real memory is gone.

MR. O. Gone or not? Maybe. Speak to Dr. R.

MRS. A. It seems to me the only time you can remember is when you are not caught up with other things. If you can keep yourself separate you can remember, but if you are caught up with other things the memory goes. I want to know how to keep that separateness.

MR. O. When you remember? Quite right.

MR. J. I know from experience that to-morrow after this meeting it will be easier for me to remember a bit, but after that almost any excuse will be good enough not to go on with it—as if something would drag me into just forgetting.

MR. O. There must be reason for that. Otherwise how do you take it?

MRS. V. What is this remembering people are talking about?

MR. O. If you use it, it must be that you remember. You use it in a certain sense. Have you heard it more?

MISS Q. We are speaking of remembering ourselves experiencing life, instead of forgetting as we usually do.

MR. O. Sometimes you have to come to that.

MR. B. Are our questions too personal?

MR. O. Cannot be too personal. You came here because you want to ask something. You must ask something that means something to you. When I was told about things that have no meaning for me, I could not answer them, so now they brought certain examples of memory, and I say I will take that. Dr. R. you came to something that you could explain, or in any case came here to. . . . Without that I could not say anything.

MISS D. I find it very hard to remember what has been said at the meetings. Is that because I am not remembering?

MR. O. I don't know that. But is fact—something is missed.

MISS S. Would it help our memory to have an exercise for it?

MR. O. There are no exercises. In any case I never heard about anything like that for memory.

MR. L. Is it fact that unless we remember we can do nothing?

MR. O. Certain cases. It is only one way.

MR. S. Is remembering a feeling or a thought?

MR. O. That you must ask policeman.

MR. S. If it is a thought, it seems to me one has to be thinking of two things at once. Is it possible to remember oneself and be doing ordinary things at the same time?

MR. O. No. Even policeman—nobody can do two things at once.

MRS. P. Is it lack of desire that stops us from remembering?

MR. O. Sometimes it is lack of desire, sometimes a lack of something else—lack of something. I am not prepared fully for any kind of question. [Pause.]

Have you got questions and I will listen. Otherwise I don't know how I can continue.

MR. F. Why does remembrance appear to be unconnected with our time?

MR. O. We tried several times, and on the whole we can say that it becomes a little better; we have more material each week.

MR. M. How can we understand more about the obstacles which prevent us from remembering ourselves?

MR. O. I don't know. Some things we understand; some things we don't understand. In general we make it a little more difficult. You must continue.

MR. C. Why do we say 'remember ourselves'? Surely it is other things. . . .

MR. O. I have such a strange idea of calling it that. Maybe whoever doesn't like won't follow, or maybe who follows must understand what I mean by that.

MISS R. Everything seems so accidental. I can't be certain that the personality in me who wants to remember will be there when I want to remember.

MR. O. I don't know again. I can't guarantee it. Everything may be quite wrong, or maybe I will see what is right. Or it may be necessary to ask a policeman.

DR. R. What is the beginning of understanding—what this means? Is it not to try to remember, to make the effort to do it?

MR. O. I don't know. Different. There are no easy trials. Try one thing, try another, then a third.

MR. A. You said we must proceed from what we know. That seems exactly what we know, about remembering. If we know to what extent we know what that is, that is our starting-point.

MR. O. Question for Dr. R., not for me—and you address it to me. Address it to him. I have many other answers if I have written questions.

MISS S. You said that one way to remember is to have a position. Can we also help remembrance by listening?

MR. O. No, neither position nor anything.

MISS Q. We cannot reduce it to anything so simple, can we?

MR. O. Well, what you have? In any case only one thing I can say. We can have more material just now. We can come to distinguish more material.

MRS. V. This remembering myself you just told me about seems to get upset in contact with other people.

MR. O. No, no, it is not a question of complicated words; it is just as simple as it can be.

MRS. V. If they are not particularly nice one gets upset and involved, and if they are nice one gets frightfully pleased, whereas it really does not matter at all.

MR. O. You must try in different ways, until we come to some decision or solution. But we are always helpless at the beginning. Too many questions and answers and other things.

MR. D. I have known moments of eminent accord within my being. I cannot remember what led up to that state, and I cannot remember what led away from it to my present position. How can I remember to achieve this connecting link? I am entirely cut off.

MR. O. I think it is all quite clear. It may need some time to establish relation of one to another.

MRS. T. It is so much easier to remember oneself in new circumstances of any sort. As soon as one gets used to a thing one forgets.

MR. O. Please try to remember next time what you want by this combination of words. It may be next time we begin to come nearer to it.

MR. W. Can you give us something to think about in the interval between now and next meeting?

MR. O. I don't promise anything. I can continue only without promises.

MRS. V. How can I learn to remember myself?

MR. O. Find what is missing. Maybe it will be sufficient.

MRS. C. Is it good to try to recapture what goes with a better state?

MR. O. Probably. This is what I have said last time—that if you try to recover—how I said this?—try to remember, it may help.

And when I come next time. . . . I don't know—I cannot promise a day for it, but I may come.

*　　*　　*

Wednesday. June 18th 1947. (Colet Gardens.)

DR. R. [Reading.] One question is: The reason I forget and fail most of the time is because my will is too weak. How can I make it stronger?

MR. O. That is all we [? are]—weakness, weakness.

DR. R. [Reading.] How can we sharpen the memory of the mistakes we made in the past so that we do not repeat them?

MR. O. We may come to it.

MR. D. In the past we used to be subject to certain rules in connection with your teaching. Do these rules still exist?

MR. O. No, nothing exists. They could not be used.

MR. D. Do I understand rightly that the rules do not exist any more?

MR. O. I don't know what means rules. In any case all that could be called rules never [? could or did] exist for a long time.

Question is what you want.

MR. L. I want to know myself.

MR. O. Well, that is one. Everybody will want it.

MISS D. Life and the laws of life interfere with inner development. Is it possible in one short span to get free of them?

MR. O. Nothing can be in a short time. [To Miss Q.] Have you got material?

MISS Q. People don't seem to know how to approach this matter of remembering which is so apart from their usual way of living.

MR. O. We have to begin. If it is more difficult to begin, how can it be easier?

DR. R. I wonder whether a number of people who wanted the same thing could achieve something that one person alone cannot.

MR. O. More material. I mean it is necessary to have more material.

MR. R. Is there anything one can do at any given moment now to make sure that one will remember that moment later?

MR. O. No, we have nothing of that kind—no help in that way. Each one must find chief thing for himself—why one cannot remember. [To Miss Q.] Can you understand it?

MISS Q. Yes.

MRS. A. I find that a state of excitement and tension stops me from remembering what I really want. If I try to relax it does bring a better state, but it does not bring the inner feeling.

MR. O. What is the difficulty?

MRS. A. Am I trying in the right way to self-remember?

MR. O. Probably not. Too much effort.

MR. I. Is it now an advantage or not to have attended these meetings before the war?

MR. O. It happened like that so it cannot happen otherwise. We had to stop it some time ago . . . or we can try to attempt again.

MISS Q. Would you say it is necessary, Mr. O., to know what it is one wants to remember more than anything else?

MR. O. Yes. Why want, what wants, and so on.

MRS. C. I have been noticing what goes on in myself and that I go on in a state of unconsciousness, and I cannot come out of it except by stilling my mind, relaxing myself. . . .

MR. O. You must know how to get out of it.

MRS. C. But then I go back by some thought coming into my head; something I notice starts me thinking, and then I am lost. . . . One cannot live without thoughts—cannot live in a state of not thinking.

MR. O. Quite right. But necessary to think more, and more definite. What you want.

MR. S. I feel I don't remember because I don't see myself in sufficient detail. I think I have a general picture of myself but that does not seem to give sufficient stimulus. Is this the right way to think about it?

MR. O. Well? Where you stop?

MR. S. I think it necessary that I must try to see myself at every moment of the day—a general picture is not sufficient. It is a very difficult thing.

MR. O. Do not try to think too much.

MR. M. To remember myself seems to me something different at different times, and yet how can one make something whole out of it? I don't really know what it means to remember oneself.

MR. O. Don't make it too difficult. Necessary to put all this material together. [To Miss Q.] Have you got something?

MISS Q. I feel that the only approach is that you have to try to remember yourself only in relation to a particular thing—something that interests one more than anything else. You cannot remember yourself in regard to everything in your life.

MR. O. Quite right. You have to remember. [Little laugh.]

MRS. T. I find it very difficult to see myself. I have tried to be aware of what I am doing. Is that a beginning?

MR. O. Well, begin in that way.

DR. R. When you say we must have more material, we don't seem to connect at all what we want with those words you gave us about the necessity for memory.

MR. O. Words mean nothing at all. We can replace one kind of words with another, and so on. You must find what you want and not forget it.

MRS. C. I don't want to live in a state where everything goes on by itself.

MR. O. Not same thing.

MR. J. I think if I am asked to reduce what I want to the simplest form, it is I want something in myself which is reliable, to which I can relate everything. . . .

MR. O. Everybody can formulate it in the same—in similar—words. Make use of that; but necessary to explain it more, to give more material.

MISS Q. Would it help if people tried to find out what it is they regret forgetting more than anything else?

MR. O. Yes, yes. Well, ask everything; what you want answered; how you formulate your question?

MRS. C. Is it necessary to see very definitely what happens within oneself?

MR. O. Chiefly nothing.

MRS. C. It seems to me I do see certain habits; when they happen again they wake me up.

MISS Q. I don't see how that is possible.

MRS. C. I have a habit of counting up useful things I have done. Little habits.

MR. O. Or something too big.

MRS. R. Why do you make it harder for us to get help from you now than you used to in the old days?

MR. O. _Now_ you accuse me of being hard. I don't know how I can make it hard. We can _try_ to make it more hard.

MRS. R. You say we must bring more material to you. What is material? Is it observations how our minds work?

MR. O. All together. What you want. I must be able to answer to understand what you want. Dr. R., how do you think about it? What do you want?

DR. R. I want to be able to think connectedly. What I ordinarily call thinking isn't thinking at all.

MR. O. That is the difficulty.

MISS R. I want to learn to be more present. Now I realize that I am not present nearly all the day.

MR. O. Well, try and avoid all sorts of difficulties. Go on. Perhaps we may come to something.

MR. H. Is it possible for me to acquire something that will not end with my death?

MR. O. No. We don't speak about such things.

MR. B. . . . I want to know whether finding what one wants is looking for the part of one that wants.

MR. O. Yes, that may be. I don't know, but we may try.

MR. B. Is this trying to find what we want more simple than I am trying to make it, because I have been trying to ask this question for eleven years, and I don't seem to have got anywhere?

MR. O. Probably more difficult.

MR. A. You were talking about consecutive thinking. In everyday work I find it very easy to think for quite a long period, but when I try to think about what I want in life I cannot do it for more than a minute. This seems rather odd. Why is it?

MR. O. Longer. Longer time necessary.

MR. N. Even in complete solitude when trying to remember, after a short time my mind wanders. Are there any physical aids that will keep my mind on what I want and what I am trying to remember?

MR. O. Yes, it is necessary to insist, to do something definite.

MR. N. I know of no physical aids. Can you help me?

MR. O. I don't understand. I don't think I can help. When you tell me what you do I can try, but not without.

MR. E. Is one reason that our efforts are too weak that in order to get something new we must give up a great deal of what we are at present, and we are not always ready to make that initial step?

MR. O. Maybe. Necessary to wait, continue and so on. [Referring probably to Mr. E.'s question.] There are many difficulties like that, but I cannot say anything [? without more material.]

MR. C. I think that what I have learned from these meetings is that I know less even than I thought I did. Is that a desirable result?

MR. O. Sometimes it may be.

MRS. S. I have often thought that many years of preparation were necessary in order to come to some understanding. Through this understanding one is able to formulate for oneself what one wants. Knowing what one wants makes certain conditions. Through these conditions, lots of things are demanded more. Have you the right to demand what you want?

MR. O. One has right to everything. One does not spend time wondering about has one the right or not. One has right to everything.

MR. F. I do recognize good states and bad states, ups and downs, and I get a sort of idea what to avoid in order to avoid bad states. Sometimes I can do it. This is no way near saying what I want, but are these states things to observe, and can one start with that?

MR. O. We can begin with that and we can go further, and so on.

MRS. W. Can one make good states more frequent and get from them to better states?

MR. O. I never could say it is good or anything. I never could say that.

MR. C. Have we to realize that we are powerless before we can begin at all?

MR. O. Who is?

MRS. R. Is it possible to find out what you want just by thinking about it?

MR. O. When you know one thing you must realize what you want.

MR. N. When I try to remember I find that I am completely calm because I am not worried by the events that are going on around me. I find even I don't want the things I wanted before. I try to remember but cannot keep it up very long.

MR. O. You came evidently with the idea that you don't. But you must try to find more and more what you want.

MISS R. Is it a good idea to set oneself a limited task and then give that up and try something else?

MR. O. Well, continue in the same way.

MISS R. I have tried on several things, and I find that very helpful, but it is difficult to set oneself a task.

MR. O. Yes. Try to observe. Try this way, that way—variation.

There are many things that you want. Necessary to try one, another and so on. Pass from one to another. Sometimes you don't know, sometimes you know more definitely what you want.

I will let you know; if I stay here I may have time. I may come another time, but I can't promise. We will see what material.

MR. A. I want to know, at a more conscious moment, what to make of that moment, how to connect it with some aim.

MR. O. Necessary to be able to say clearly what you want—what direction. Try to remember it—this moment—that moment.

MR. A. It changes because that moment is reliable; one feels quite different; false things stop for the moment. I can discriminate between the opposite times, but at that time I cannot get further.

MR. O. Well, you may continue. Sometimes it needs a longer time. We can go, and then if you can find something I may come again. I may still. I still may have some time.

MR. P. What is it that one must try to remember?

MR. O. You can try. Anybody can try to remember. What was said about that?

MR. A. You asked us to formulate our wishes. I want to notice things, more things which are beautiful and interesting. Other people do, and point them out to me, but I cannot do it myself. How can I learn to do it myself?

MR. O. Well, if you can. Time, occasions. [? patience.]

* * *

Index

Absolute, The (or World 1), 19, 21, 26, 28, 60, 87–8, 104, 109, 165, 184, 224, 239, 319–20, 323, 329, 445, 457, 471, 476, 512, 523, 557, 558

Accident, Law of, 72, 105, 112, 144, 168, 186, 221–2, 312, 364–5, 373, 454, 463–4, 516, 525, 545, 571
  as triad in World, 6 112–13

Accumulators, in three-storied factory, 144, 258, 445–6, 479, 515, 552, 563–7
  of knowledge, 75

Active Force (see Forces, Law of three)

Activities (actions of man), 20, 160–68, 171, 174–88, 190–98, 203–5, 207, 213–22, 225, 230, 232, 235, 243–5, 246–57, 259–60, 261–2, 274, 280, 334–5, 357–8, 358–9, 384, 439, 477, 506, 528

Adaptability (as measure of intelligence), 121–2, 267, 287

Aim, Personal, 50, 85, 92–3, 100, 137, 180, 189, 196, 201, 203, 219, 223, 256, 298, 502, 558
  of a historical period, 98
  of man's existence, 121
  of the system, of the work, 46, 128, 151, 159
  objective aim of schools, 36

Air, as food of man, 31, 33, 170, 290, 341, 344, 346, 347, 348, 457, 479, 508
  place in Hydrogen Table, 113
  breathed by different beings, 290–91, 394
  liquid, 114

Akbar, 328, 331

Alarms (alarm-clocks), 142, 435

Alchemy, 22, 237, 550

Alcohol, use of, 75

Alertness, 231–2

All Galaxies (see Worlds, All Worlds, World 3)

All Planets (see Planets)

All Suns (World 6) (see Sun)

All Worlds (World 3) (see Worlds, All Worlds, World 3)

Anaethesia, 509

Analogy, method of, 61, 64, 106, 175, 181, 184, 186, 443, 477, 528

Analysis, 12, 193, 550

Animals, 289–91, 305, 311, 406, 458, 465

Aphorisms, Book of, 24, 117

Arguing, 7, 11–15, 17–18, 47, 180–81, 324

Art, 174, 245, 382, 517, 519, 529, 583
  in relation to activities, 112, 160, 177, 185, 251, 477, 539
  objective, 174, 382, 583

Asleep (see Sleep)

Associations (associative thinking), 15, 196, 207, 306, 383

Astral (astral body), 217, 226, 325, 452

Astrology, 68, 124, 135, 236, 237, 241

Astronomy, 432

Attention, 70, 81, 94, 101, 133, 162, 204, 210, 225, 231, 250, 255, 283, 375, 494

Attitudes, 4, 13, 20, 72, 74, 85, 104, 142, 219, 272, 358, 360, 364, 372, 374, 381, 382, 408, 423, 428, 430, 433, 443, 483
  negative, 104, 372, 381, 430
  positive, 104, 372, 483
  towards negativeness, 104, 142, 360, 364, 433

Awake (awakening), 45, 53–4, 60, 83, 94, 104, 106, 115, 128, 170, 279, 295, 330, 370, 406, 452–3, 474,

Wrong work of, 99, 233, 302, 305, 333, 336, 396, 492–4, 503
and different 'I's, 188, 307, 313, 455, 500, 521
and 'rolls', 3, 504
and attention, 101, 204, 250, 375
and memory, 190, 398, 504, 509, 571, 581
and habits, 104, 333, 383
and hydrogens, energy, 33, 110, 114–15, 116, 259, 490, 492–3, 502, 566
and accumulators, 564, 566
and man No. 1, 2 and 3, 108, 107, 312, 318, 327, 550
and the four ways, 102–3
in relation to cosmoses, 61, 64, 245, 252
in relation to six activities, 107, 174, 177–8, 193, 203–5, 244, 251–2
impressions of different, 190, 333, 339
in children, 332
Each centre occupies all body, 63, 253, 563
We cannot study centres, only functions, 85, 253
Necessary to work on all, 101, 360, 459
Super-effort must be in all, 401
Balance or connection between, 452, 454, 494
Understanding a function of more than one, 471, 490
Imagination may begin in any, 493
Identification may affect all, 517
One centre may awake while others sleep, 74
Chemistry, 225, 333, 337, 455, 557
Chief Feature (see Features)
Children, Effect of other people on, 54
Centres in, 332
Choice, Illusion of, 303, 531
Christ, 152, 155, 211, 231, 452, 466, 478, 523, 573
Christian Religion, 155–6, 519
Circles, of humanity, 107, 515–26, 555
Diagram, 107
Inner Circle, 51, 64, 107, 548, 570
Civilization, 555
Clairvoyance (clairaudience), 489, 545–6, 578

Comfort, Desire for, 51, 132
Compassion (see also Sympathy), 122
Compensation, in dreams, 487
Concentration, 70, 430, 487
Conduct, 140, 151, 158–9
Connectedness, of everything, 271, 310–11
Connection, of moments of understanding, 143, 361
Conscience, 94, 99, 105, 151–7, 308, 358, 360, 381, 437, 514, 517, 520, 531–5, 542–3, 548, 555–6
Consciousness (conscious), 20, 45, 53, 61, 86, 100, 101, 103–5, 122, 189, 198, 211, 224–6, 299, 315, 331, 377, 381–2, 457, 461, 479, 485, 489, 507–9, 512, 528, 534, 538, 542, 543–6
States of, Levels of, 3, 45–6, 75, 88, 105–6, 152, 163, 209, 211, 231–2, 264, 294, 298, 360, 396, 443, 447, 451, 484–5, 507, 512, 531
Self-, 53, 83, 86–8, 105–6, 209, 264, 298, 317, 357, 360, 381, 396, 400, 451–2, 463, 473, 485, 535, 507, 540, 546, 578
Objective, 3, 52, 53, 83–4, 86, 105–6, 152, 154, 158, 264, 298, 396, 485
Degrees of, 74, 83–6, 105, 211, 381–2
Our lack of, 45, 53, 103, 198, 485, 489, 507–9, 528
Higher, 100, 231–4, 333, 381–2, 401
Conscious shocks, 21, 33, 34, 161, 169–70, 170, 267, 282, 344, 361, 388, 536–7, 574
Conscious evil impossible, 92–100, 221, 223, 231, 303, 471–2, 495, 570
and conscience, 105, 151, 166, 357, 531, 542–3, 555–6
and will, 144, 169–70, 212–13, 326
and memory, 484, 505, 509, 571, 574
and functions, 241, 317, 538, 544, 563
and higher centres, 399, 401, 507
and recurrence, 298, 517, 531
and soul, 289, 464
and activities, 112, 162, 528

Consciousness (conscious) – *contd.*
  and morality, 153, 166, 159, 174,
    212–13, 215, 469
  and ascending octaves, 319
  of other worlds, 59, 74, 224
  of organs of the body, 233–4
  in Ray of Creation, 25, 109, 184,
    224
  Attitude of modern psychology to,
    44, 171, 507
  impossible without effort and
    school, 20, 100, 101, 122, 211,
    225–6, 533–4
  measured by time, 86, 377
  Conscious energy, 225, 316
  Conscious influences, 311–12, 333
  Conscious music, 243
  Conscious men, 231, 361, 465, 547
Considering, 25, 178, 208, 292, 296,
  353, 356, 360, 363, 402, 405, 446,
  458–9, 461, 503, 551, 553, 568
  External, 135–6, 292, 296, 459, 553
'Constater', 550
Contradictions, Absence of, in system
  teaching, 19, 53, 89, 119
  Inner, 105, 151–2, 155, 309, 363
Control, 34, 70–71, 76, 85, 98, 113,
  165, 177, 194, 211–13, 233, 293,
  296, 331, 356, 360, 397, 444, 451–
  2, 455, 472, 502, 514–15
Cosmoses, 58–66, 71, 74, 110, 113, 115,
  173, 239, 245, 252, 253–4, 266,
  269–71, 280, 285–6, 299–300, 432,
  463, 475–6, 511–2, 557, 565
  Diagram of Times in Different, 62
  in relation to laws, 110, 113
Creation, Ray of (see Ray of Creation)
Crime (criminal), 152–3, 159–62, 166,
  176–7, 185–6, 213–16, 220–21,
  232, 252, 254–5, 276–8, 426, 517,
  528–9
Crimean War, 418, 419
Criticism, 7–8, 33, 442–3
Cross-roads, 72, 137, 410, 501
Crystallization, of higher man, 57, 325
  Wrong or double, 325–6, 381, 428

'Dead' People, 57, 121, 181, 289, 472,
  516–26, 528, 529–31, 536
Death, 20, 265, 299, 301, 308, 423, 463,
  576, 583

Survival after, 52–3, 87
(or time) as triad in World 6, 112
of essence, 289, 464, 516–26
Deception, self-, 455, 473
Decisions, 136, 144, 213, 326, 408, 487,
  532, 550
Demands, 143, 395, 500
Demonology, Mediaeval, 46
Density, of matter, 27, 225, 334, 550
Deputy-steward, 1, 2, 375
Dervishes, 235, 521
Determinism, 495
Deuterocosmos, 63
Development, 21, 33, 53, 63, 101, 121–
  2, 153, 197, 211–12, 222, 224, 236,
  276–7, 288, 289–301, 304, 311,
  316, 325, 330, 333, 338, 344, 382,
  384, 403, 415–16, 425–6, 429, 505,
  513, 516, 518
  Wrong, 171, 325, 381–2
Devil, 94, 568–70
Dictionary, of system words, 549, 552,
  555
Die, Necessary to, in order to be born,
  406
Diet, 174, 179, 180, 356–7, 550–51
Different, Things could not have been,
  433, 443–4
  Doing things in a different way, 196,
    486
Dimensions, 59–60, 64, 71, 280, 285,
  298–301, 396–7, 471, 474
Discipline, 118, 124–5, 146, 327, 358,
  428–9, 556, 557–8
Discrimination, 366
Distortion, of ideas, 77, 367
Division, of oneself (see Separation)
Doctrine, New or special, 137, 368
Doing, 3, 6, 20, 24, 41–5, 73, 103–4,
  136, 139, 146, 168, 229
  Man cannot 'do', 24, 41–5, 76, 104,
    232, 268, 296, 443, 490, 498, 558
Dreams, 73, 83, 204–5, 435, 487, 503
  Day-, 45, 74, 167–8, 228, 307, 493,
    505
  Half-dream states, 405
Drugs, 227
Duality, Inner, 325–6, 362

Earth, 20–21, 25, 27, 87, 110, 113–15,
  117, 119–24, 212, 224, 239, 241,

257, 271, 280, 285, 299–300, 310–12, 316, 320, 329, 348–9, 411–12, 414–16, 445, 457–8, 475

Earthworm, 289

Effort, 7, 50–51, 55–6, 72, 73, 83, 96, 145, 188, 194, 198, 225, 265, 277, 283, 303, 314, 316, 325–6, 395, 430, 459, 460, 462, 466, 472, 479, 500, 564, 566, 581

Awakening, consciousness impossible without, 20, 45, 53, 100, 453

Man can only develop by his own, 121, 122, 344, 512

to be conscious, to awake, 21, 34, 315, 503, 546

to self-remember, 58, 70, 112, 144, 185, 192, 283, 315, 448, 455, 461, 537, 556

to stop thought, 459, 488

in connection with conscious shocks, 21, 31, 33, 34, 275, 344, 537, 574

in relation to activities, 160, 162, 166, 178, 180, 184–5, 193, 197, 253–4, 256

Super-, 396, 400–402

Egypt, Schools in, 547

Eight, Man No., 152, 155

Electron, 61, 65, 285–6, 299

Elements, Four, 35

Emotions (emotional), 53, 56, 58, 67, 81, 116, 123, 169, 174, 206, 210, 270, 294–5, 303, 305, 354, 365, 377, 379–81, 385, 386–7, 440, 444, 473, 483, 489–90, 492, 504, 507–8, 531, 539, 540, 545, 550, 558, 562, 579

Negative, 33, 34, 50, 54–6, 58, 97, 97, 100, 104, 114–16, 134, 142, 145–6, 169, 173–5, 178, 187, 194, 253, 255, 282, 294, 301, 305, 360, 381, 385, 394–5, 400, 406, 407, 427, 436, 439–40, 460, 472, 474, 479, 482, 486–9, 494, 496, 509, 514–15, 534, 545, 559–63, 568, 576

Positive, 54–5, 170, 174, 263, 361, 488

Instinctive, 206, 303

Need to be more emotional, 473, 488–90, 540–43

Emotional understanding of activities, 177, 180, 198

and Man No. 2, 102–3, 550

and intellect not divided in higher centres, 492, 540

Emotional centre (see Centre)

Energy, 8, 20, 22, 31, 34, 54–5, 144–6, 167, 169, 173, 174–6, 190, 204–5, 210, 224–6, 233–4, 275, 281, 316, 319–20, 470, 479, 480, 493, 503, 508, 551, 564–6

Life-, 22, 225, 316, 508, 569

Waste of, Leaks of, 34, 54–5, 145, 190, 204–5, 233–4, 270, 329, 383, 406, 446, 448, 458, 470, 486

Saving, 8, 232, 256, 329, 448, 486

for self-remembering, 145–6, 256, 318, 509

Four kinds of, 225, 316

in relation to activities, 167, 174, 177–8, 180, 185, 187, 248

and matter, 475

Enneagram, 246, 300, 479, 491, 512, 565

Essence, 2, 3, 64, 74, 78, 82, 98, 100, 101, 124, 139, 144, 206–7, 231, 236, 239, 284, 289, 298, 312–13, 332, 335, 339, 380, 384, 444, 460, 495, 497, 515, 521, 524, 533, 535, 566–7, 571–2, 575, 578, 582

Esotericism (esoteric), 15, 16–17, 46, 53, 101, 156, 192, 211, 307, 370, 389, 467

Esoteric circle, 51, 64, 107

Eternal Recurrence (see Recurrence)

Eternity, 299, 464, 471, 577–8

Ether, 266

Evil, 92–100, 221, 223, 231, 305, 471–2, 495, 568, 570

Evolution, 19, 287, 371, 410, 415, 524, 570

Examination, 549, 550

Exercises, 3, 72, 128, 143, 327, 385, 397, 459, 460, 508

of repetition, 3–4, 491, 554

'Stop' exercise, 143, 327

Breathing, 227, 356

of stopping thoughts (see Thoughts)

Exoteric Circle, 51, 107, 372

Expansion, of organization, 126, 129, 135, 137, 149

Scale – *contd.*

in relation to growth of
organization, 135, 137–8
and higher part of intellectual centre,
221

School(s), -work, 35, 39, 45–6, 75, 101,
107, 127, 229, 320, 331, 353, 368–
70, 373, 389, 420, 424, 449, 466–
8, 477, 490, 513, 525, 536, 546,
554, 569

organization, 24, 107, 123, 366, 389
methods, 103, 327, 381, 399
discipline, 118, 124–5, 327, 358,
428–9, 556, 558
knowledge, 77–8, 192, 549
principles, 118, 229, 373, 466, 479,
536
Different levels of, 35, 107, 124–5,
136–8, 156, 353, 519
Different degrees in, 134, 135–6,
141, 156, 353, 389
of Fourth Way, 103, 389
of other ways, 103, 211, 277, 359,
381, 397–8, 531, 535, 544,
554
in history, 45–6, 101, 108, 237, 364,
520
Philosophical, theoretical and
practical, 50–51
origin of, 466
Objective work of, 45–6, 467
and B and C influences, 156, 245,
515–19, 520–22, 537, 540–41
and recurrence, 280, 289
and Law of Accident, 69, 454, 525
Change, development impossible
without, 23, 56–7, 100, 101, 138–
9, 168, 177, 209, 211, 288, 343,
373, 422
Preparation necessary for, 118, 122,
124–5, 134, 355
Wrong methods in, 145, 232, 381,
399, 544
'This work is not school', 39, 515,
519–20
'Our aim is to create school', 128
Work for, 127, 145, 239
Easy to lose, 119
destroyed by wars, etc., 93, 420, 535,
536, 546, 555
dependence on new people, 519, 536

dependence on those who went
before, 123, 449
Science, and system, 87–8, 117, 225,
285, 289–90, 310, 347, 414, 476
Secrecy, 90
Seed, Man as a, 224
Seeing oneself, 48–9, 105, 152, 156–7,
169, 221, 223, 226, 423, 447, 448,
483
Self-remembering, 7, 11, 12, 43–4, 70,
104, 269, 281, 283, 320, 352, 381–
2, 406, 407, 452, 455, 471, 531
'We don't remember ourselves', 43,
45, 58, 70, 171, 195, 208, 318, 379,
430, 459, 527, 572–3
not known in all psychology, 171, 541
as state of consciousness, 3, 79, 136,
168, 451, 559
as first step towards consciousness,
84, 156, 171, 211, 226, 400, 534,
561, 578
Degrees of, 211, 229, 576
different from thought, 136, 167–8,
338, 448–9, 562
opposite to identification, 208, 211–
12, 461, 488
important in difficult circumstances,
165, 189, 208, 283, 385
means control, action, doing, 165,
167–8, 169, 263
What we lose by not, what it would
mean, 220, 244, 354, 379
Importance of continuity of, 573
Descriptions, talk about, do not
help, 259, 262, 322
Everything can be used for, 293,
436, 487, 509
part of all esoteric knowledge, 211–
12, 573
in relation to rules, 5, 7, 9, 10, 118,
124, 125, 297
in relation to emotions and higher
centres, 226, 360, 381, 399, 492,
544
in relation to first conscious shock,
21, 33, 161, 169–70, 282, 315, 361,
405, 460
and stopping thoughts, 233, 385,
431, 487
and negative emotions, 243–4, 255,
381, 436, 487, 497, 509, 541–2

and memory, 296, 410, 511, 571–6
and recurrence, 410, 467, 472–3,
    572
    and impressions, 169, 330, 566
    and energy, 145–6, 169, 256, 383,
        486
    and triads or activities, 112, 161–
        2, 193–4, 253
    and external considering, 553
    and physical sensation, 431, 441–2
    and laughter, 279
    and division of 'I's, 136, 143, 173,
        382
    and meditation, 168
    and decisions, 136, 144
    Unintentional, 168, 211, 354
Sensations, 99, 347, 365, 550
Separation, between 'I' and 'Brown',
    'Smith' etc. (see also 'I'), 5–10, 13,
    48, 86, 89, 430
    between system ideas and others,
        138, 140–44
Serious, what it means to be, 10–11,
    14, 191, 195, 200–206, 210, 245–6
Seven, Law of (see also Octaves), 20–
    21, 51, 278–9, 313–17, 512, 573–
    4
Sevenoaks, 321
Sex, 217
    centre (see Centres)
    Abnormal, 44, 222–3
Shah Jehan, 328, 331
Shakespeare, 467
Shame, People without, 517, 550
Shocks, 21, 169–70, 171, 180, 226, 275,
    387–8, 405, 457, 498–9, 511
    in relation to Food Factory, 21, 31,
        33, 170, 249, 267, 275–6, 282,
        342–6, 361, 388, 405
    in relation to conscience, 534–5, 555
Sincerity (being sincere), 113, 178, 199,
    331, 383, 500, 501, 532, 532, 549,
    551
Sledge, Russian proverb about, 91
Sleep (asleep), 3, 45, 49, 53–4, 73, 74–
    5, 83, 100, 104–5, 115, 117, 128,
    146, 171, 219, 275, 308, 330–31,
    370, 381, 406, 430, 503, 505, 507,
    509, 510, 516–7, 531, 533, 539,
    559, 561, 578
    Physical, 73, 97, 173, 190, 204–5,

233, 317, 355, 434, 441, 484–6
Hypnotic, 296
    and waking, as cosmic measure of
        time, 59, 60–61
Sleeping people, 53–4, 146, 516–26,
    528, 531, 533, 536
Sly man, 569–70
Smallness, Realizing one's, 540–43,
    554
Snataka (see Householder)
Society, The, 126–33, 149, 365–71, 372,
    373–4, 376–9, 392
Solar System (see also Sun), 22, 60, 87,
    120, 239, 281, 310, 311, 411–12,
    414, 416, 464
Soul, 64, 82, 265, 270, 281, 289, 308,
    349, 460, 464, 470, 517, 520, 569
    of things, 22
    Different uses of word in literature,
        82
Special Doctrine, 138, 368
Speed of centres (see Centres)
Sphinx, The, 467
'Staircase', 366, 373, 536, 552
Stalin, 277, 431
Starting-point, 90
Static triad, 384, 385, 403
Stealing, 138, 140, 145
'Step' diagram, 287, 289–91, 295
Steward, 2, 554
'Stop' exercise, 143, 327
Stories, Three-, 289, 339–40
    diagram, 340
Study, Self-, 24, 129, 229, 300, 374,
    423, 491, 530
    as opposed to change, 394, 498
Subjective, We are, 337, 352
    thinking, 168
    visions, 226
Sudras, 546
Suffering, Sacrifice of, 246, 281, 440
Suggestion (suggestibility), 248, 296
Sun (World) (see also Solar System),
    22, 25, 27, 61, 65, 72, 110, 113,
    120–22, 224, 238, 255, 257, 280,
    310–12, 313, 320, 329, 348–51,
    411–16, 457, 463, 466, 569
    All Suns (World 6), 25, 60, 87, 98,
        109–10, 112–13, 120, 163, 184,
        224, 239, 310, 311, 413–14, 445,
        457, 512

The index contains no references to the meetings held at Colet Gardens in 1947 (pp. 585–643). The principal subjects referred to are mentioned in the Summary of Contents at the beginning of the book.